**Working with Adults:
Individual, Family,
and Career Development**

Working with Adults: Individual, Family, and Career Development

BARBARA F. OKUN

Northeastern University

Brooks/Cole Publishing Company
Monterey, California

Brooks/Cole Publishing Company
A Division of Wadsworth, Inc.

Printed in the United States of America

10 9 8 7 6 5 4 3 2 1

Library of Congress Cataloging in Publication Data

Okun, Barbara F. [date]
  Working with adults.

  Bibliography: p.
  Includes index.
    1. Adulthood—Psychological aspects. 2. Personality
and occupation. 3. Married people—Employment.
4. Family. 5. Counseling. I. Title.
BF724.5.038 1984   155.6   83-45527
ISBN 0-534-02869-1

Subject Editor: *Claire Verduin*
Production Editor: *Candyce Cameron*
Manuscript Editor: *Suzanne Lipsett*
Interior Design: *Debbie Wunsch*
Cover Design: *Vicki Van Deventer*
Art Coordinator: *Rebecca Ann Tait*
Interior Illustration: *John Foster*
Typesetting: *TriStar Graphics, Minneapolis, Minnesota*
Printing and Binding: *Halliday Lithograph, West Hanover, Massachusetts*

To Sherman

PREFACE

The idea for this text came directly from my teaching a graduate seminar entitled "Counseling Adults Over the Life Span." In this course, I encourage students to study and integrate individual, family, and career development theory as a conceptual framework for assessing and counseling adult clients. There is a definite lack of integration in professional literature: journals are devoted to either career or family issues, and academic courses rarely give equal weight to individual, career, and family development. This deficiency is also reflected in professional practice: many counselors and therapists trained to work with families ignore the impact of career-related issues, and career counselors frequently downplay family issues. It has become increasingly clear to me that these three areas are interdependent.

My point of view is that it is impossible to understand adult clients by separating them from their past and present career and family contexts. Whereas needs change throughout the life cycle, work, family, and individual factors continually interact. Whatever issues a person is dealing with in one area of life will have an effect in another area.

My objectives are threefold: 1) to provide a comprehensive overview of the most current research and theoretical formulations of adult development (male and female), family development, and career development, 2) to delineate the reciprocal influences of these three domains in early, middle, and late adulthood, and 3) to bridge the gap between theory and practice with the use of relevant case examples. The text is intended for human service trainees and experienced practitioners who wish to study the needs and tasks of adulthood from an integrated perspective.

I want to thank Claire Verduin and her staff at Brooks/Cole who have been encouraging and supportive. My graduate students and clients over the years have contributed enormously to my thinking and understanding and are as much a part of this book as am I.

My family has provided loving care and cooperation throughout this project. I have learned much from my husband Sherman and my children Marcia, Jeffrey, and Douglas as we individually and collaboratively struggle with our own transitions and stages of development. Other friends and relatives have also been inspirational. In particular, my mother-in-law Gerry Okun has modeled amazing adaptation in late adulthood and my dear friend and colleague Donna Raymer has lovingly and humorously pointed out the gains and pitfalls of middle adulthood.

I cannot adequately express my appreciation to the reviewers whose painstaking, sensitive, and creative comments have been invaluable to my final revision of the manuscript. They include: Donald Blocher, State University of New York at Albany; James Brine, Southern Connecticut State College; V. Lois Erickson, University of Minnesota; John R. Moreland, Ohio State University; and Fred Stickle, Western Kentucky University.

Barbara F. Okun

CONTENTS

PART TWO

EARLY ADULTHOOD   53

Working with Adults:
Individual, Family,
and Career Development

AN INTRODUCTION TO THEORY AND THE CONCEPTUAL MODEL

In the past decade, both adult development and the concept of life stages have received increasing attention. Articles and books have presented models of the family life cycle and discussion of career-development theory in light of life stages as well as changing societal and economic trends. And, as the population bulge moves into adulthood, demands on counselors and therapists to address adult concerns will increase. Under these circumstances, mental-health-care providers need to familiarize themselves with the interdependence of personal, family, and career concerns and the pertinence of these matters to critical adult issues. Concurrently, they will have to determine how counseling interventions can be most effective regarding adult development.

We know that more and more adults are showing stress symptoms as their concerns collide with changing societal expectations. Often it is true that while an acting-out child or adolescent is the identified patient brought into counseling or therapy, a systems perspective on the whole family, one that addresses the cybernetic effects of changing needs and personal, family, and career stages, can help counselors and therapists be most effective. Consider the following case as an example.

1

Mary Simmons, age 12, was referred to me by her school psychologist for a reevaluation. Mary had a history of learning disabilities, had experienced frustration in her academic studies, and had had poor peer relationships throughout elementary school. For the past seven months in junior high school, however, she had blossomed in a special program, making friends and showing remarkable academic improvement. Suddenly, without any obvious precipitating event, Mary's social and academic functioning began to slide.

In an intake session with Mary and her parents, I learned that Mr. Simmons, 49, had recently been terminated from an upper-management position after his firm was absorbed by a larger corporation. He was taken completely by surprise and was experiencing a great deal of anxiety about finding another position before his six-month termination pay ended. The family consisted of Mrs. Simmons, 45, Ben, 17, and Beth, 10, in addition to Mary and Mr. Simmons. The family had lived in this eastern city for fourteen years and had established roots here. The children liked their schools and the recreation programs. Mrs. Simmons had obtained a master's degree in library science and had recently received tenure in the local school district. The parents were very pleased with Mary's progress in school until now and viewed her school difficulties as the only problem in their family life.

At the time of Mary's referral, Mr. Simmons had been seeking another job for six weeks. He had four more months of pay coming to him, so the immediate pressures were not financial. But Mrs. Simmons was manifesting anxiety and depressive symptoms: she had lost weight, she was unable to sleep through the night, and she was increasingly irritable at home and with children in the school library. She told me that she was feeling despair at the possibility that her husband might not find another position in the same city and that the family might have to "give up everything" and move just when they had reached the "most settled, comfortable stage in their family life." Mrs. Simmons felt guilty about her resentment and reluctance to "follow her husband wherever his work took him." She kept reiterating that, aside from Mary's school difficulties, their lives had been relatively free of conflict and tension and that they had a "very happy marriage" and family life.

It turned out that Mr. Simmons was a finalist for an out-of-state position with enormous salary and management potential—far greater than he had ever aspired to. He was torn between the needs of his family, his feelings about turning down the greatest chance in his career life at an age where another similar choice might never occur, and finding economic, emotional, and social security. Further exploration clarified the historical aspects of the struggle between the family as a system and the individuals within it, the family's means of handling (or not handling) conflict and tension, and the fact that Mary's school difficulties fluctuated according to the tension level within the family.

Obviously, this case called for more than individual therapy for Mary, vocational counseling for Mr. Simmons, or individual therapy to reduce Mrs. Simmons' anxiety and depressive symptoms. I approached this case from a systems perspective of developmental theory. Therapy was intended to help the family understand and consider all possible options for individual, career and family survival development. It is my opinion that no one right answer or solution existed for this family. Rather, the therapeutic goal was to guide family members through a process of clearly communicating about their needs and expectations, negotiating conflicts and rules, and restructuring their personal, career, and family boundaries to arrive at a solution that seemed best for both the individuals and the family as a unit. Overall, the solution provided for growth and change. Once the therapy process began, Mary's school behavior improved dramatically, supporting my observation that her symptoms had been protecting the family from acknowledging and working through their other problems.

It is impossible to understand adult clients by separating them from their past and present careers and families or to understand child clients outside of their families and peer and school systems. Whatever the person's changing needs and roles throughout the life cycle may be, his or her work, family, and individual factors continually interact. As with other individual and family developments, career needs change with stages of individual and family development, and the issues one deals with in one area of life inevitably affect one's functioning in another area. Thus, we need to consider the role interactions of adults in three domains of life: individual, family, and career development.

This book is organized into four parts: (1) An Introduction to Theory and the Conceptual Model; (2) Early Adulthood; (3) Middle Adulthood; and (4) Late Adulthood. For our purposes, early adulthood here covers ages 20 to 40; middle adulthood, ages 40 to 60; and late adulthood, age 60 and older. This breakdown, while not necessarily the same as or as complex as other life/career schemes, is a convenient framework for loosely differentiating among the phases of adult life. Each section of this book contains chapters on individual development, family development, career development and their implications for treatment. The book's final chapter summarizes conclusions and identifies emerging trends and future research needs.

As we study the issues and tasks characteristic of early, middle, and late adulthood, it is important to remember that individual variation, social and cultural expectations, changes and chance opportunities as well as age cohorts influence our development. We use age cohorts as loose parameters in considering the biological factors involved in life-span development. At the same time, we must give equal attention to all the multiple influences on development and recognize that life stages are not identified with fixed age cohorts.

CHAPTER ONE

ADULTHOOD AND DEVELOPMENT

Although the paths of childhood and adolescence have been thoroughly charted, until recently adulthood (which might last five or six times as long as either childhood or adolescence) was considered to be a stable plateau preceding decline and death that comprised only gradual, if any, growth and change. Many students still believe that their college years are the "best years of life" and "that it's all downhill from here." Adulthood is popularly perceived to be a long endurance of responsibility, commitment, and hard work prior to the diminishing of faculties and freedoms—"the pits," in youthful jargon. No wonder many go to great lengths to cling to youth and acting out.

Fortunately for the multitude of people who live well into their seventies and eighties, research of the past several decades has led to the conclusion that historical, interpersonal, and biological changes continue throughout life and continuously affect one's self-concept and identity. The notion of adult development is recent. While it differs from concepts of child and adolescent development, which are more closely intertwined with normative age-related events, it nevertheless provides a framework for understanding change and growth and therefore

4

multipotentiality. The latter term refers to the notion that adults may consciously or unconsciously select from many different paths and options.

The purposes of this chapter are to define the concept of adulthood in relation to psychological theory and to provide a foundation for considering current adult-development theory by discussing the major tenets of basic general developmental theory. Covered in this chapter are the concepts of cycles and stages in development theory and the questions:

1. Who is an adult?
2. How is maturity equated with adulthood?
3. How do the major counseling theories conceptualize adulthood?
4. What gender issues influence our conceptualization of adulthood?

DEFINITION OF MAJOR TERMS

Before we begin our journey into adult development, let us define a few major terms. For convenience throughout this text, we use two sets of terms interchangeably: (1) *counseling* and *therapy* and (2) *stage* and *phase*. These terms are used in a general sense.

What Is an Adult?

Before we can pursue the study of adult development, we need to define precisely the term *adult*. We can base our definition on chronological age, the achievement of age-related developmental tasks, or psychological qualities such as maturity. Chronological age can only be used as a criterion if one keeps in mind the enormous variation of physiological and psychological functioning among same-age adults. Consider the furor that accompanied the move some years ago to lower the age of legal adulthood from 21 to 18 in some states. Youngsters felt that if they were old enough to take on such adult responsibilities as serving in the military, then they deserved such adult privileges as voting in presidential elections. And many states are currently grappling with the legal age for drinking and purchasing alcoholic beverages. Does one who attains a specific chronological age automatically become an adult?

Likewise, the notion of developmental tasks—for example, becoming financially independent or participating in a stable career and family—can serve as one of many criteria as long as we keep in mind that many adults choose *not* to achieve some of these tasks. Furthermore, who should decide (and how) what a stable career and family consist of? And if we use these criteria are we saying that a 40-year-old who chooses not to marry or to engage in a stable career is not to be considered an adult? Finally, can we define the term *adult* without defining the term *maturity?*

Maturity.   The term *maturity* has been defined by several psychologists. The psychoanalysts were the first to consider this concept. Freud (1949) considered maturity to be the ability to discipline the self in work and heterosexual relations;

the hallmark of maturity to him was the balance of the ego, id, and superego. This psychoanalytic view of human nature is negative and pessimistic, conceiving of a continuous warring between the self-centered id and the repressive, punitive superego. The ego, operating on the reality principle, mediates this conflict and attempts to organize the individual's life productively. Unconscious defense mechanisms help the ego protect the person from anxiety and threat. For Freud, maturation occurs as one passes through the psychosexual stages of development, each of which requires satisfaction of specific drives. If these satisfactions do not occur in sequence, the individual becomes fixated at a particular stage of development and is unable to progress to mature adulthood, when he or she is able to "work and love." For Freud, the concept of maturity implies that the individual passes successfully through the psychosexual stages of development after resolving old conflicts, thus becoming free to respond creatively to life's challenges.

Another psychoanalyst, Carl Jung (1933, 1971), believed that maturity could only occur in the second half of life, when one turned inward toward an introspection that initiates spirituality. Thus, for Jung, maturity included the discovery of a meaning and purpose in life, the gaining of a perspective on others, the choosing of values and activities in which one is willing to invest energy and creativity, and the preparing for the final stage of life, death. This spirituality is accompanied by a unification of opposite parts of the self, the *anima* and *animus,* which reflect the feminine as well as the masculine dimensions of personality.

Psychoanalyst Erik Erikson (1963) also believes that maturity is likely to occur in middle adulthood, after one has achieved a sense of identity, developed sustained intimate relationships, and begun to act out of generativity rather than egocentrism. We will consider Erikson's work in more depth in a later section, merely noting here that his concept of maturity involves a passage through sequenced stages of development.

Maslow (1971) was a major founder of the humanistic school. He identified six basic needs that must be satisfied in sequence. The lower level needs, physiological and safety, are present at birth. The needs for belongingness and love are middle-level needs that arise in infancy, and the need for esteem develops in childhood. Maslow characterized these low- and middle-level needs as *deficiency needs,* in that they can be fully satisfied and diminished when attended to. Higher level needs are those for self-actualization (the need to become the best and fullest possible personality) and aesthetic satisfaction, which arise as maturation proceeds. These needs Maslow termed *being needs* and he characterized them as growing as they are attended. For Maslow, the mature adult is one whose personality is free from the lower level deficiency problems of youth and from neurotic problems of adult life. Dacey (1982, p. 13) says that for Maslow, "mature persons are able to concentrate on the essential problems of life because they accept their inner selves. There is a high correlation between the way they present themselves to the world and the way they know who they really are."

Maslow's concept of self-actualization served as a foundation for Carl Rogers' (1961) humanistic approach to client-centered theory. Rogers also believes that people are capable of becoming fully functioning when they have sorted out their conscious values and attitudes and when they engage in a continuous process of self-actualization. This process of self-actualization is facilitated by receiving positive regard from significant others throughout the life span. For Rogers, maturity is characterized by honesty, openness to experience, self-trust, creativity, responsibility, and personal freedom. According to him, mature individuals are aware of their feelings and behavior and experience congruence among their self-concepts, their behaviors, and the feedback they receive from their environment. Such individuals are always in the process of growth, learning, and change.

Representing the Gestalt approach, Frederick Perls (1969, 1973) defined maturity as "wholeness [which] occurs when persons are able to be self-supportive rather than environment-supported, when they are able to mobilize and use their own resources rather than manipulate others and when they are able to accept responsibility for their own behaviors and experiences" (Okun, 1982, p. 120). For Perls, the mature person functions primarily in the here and now, rather than reminiscing about the past or daydreaming about the future. Further, such individuals reduce their avoidance behavior by facing and accepting previously denied parts of their being in order to become whole. Finally, mature people are able to take responsibility for all their sensations, fantasies, perceptions and dreams and can trust their intuitive senses rather than feeling compelled to adjust to society. For Perls, the mature person can do what he or she feels like doing without being controlled by family, society, or past learning.

For behaviorists, culture defines maturity and, through reinforcements, shapes the behaviors it considers mature. Because the concept of maturity is philosophical rather than scientific, behaviorists do not address it. Many humanists object to behaviorist theory because they fear an arbitrary definition of *maturity* that could be imposed unwillingly on subjects by the behavioral therapist.

Representing the cognitive approach, rational-emotive therapist Albert Ellis (1961, 1962) believes that mature people are able to think rationally rather than irrationally. Such people, according to Ellis, can take full responsibility for themselves and their fates. Because peoples' thoughts mediate between events and reactions, people are capable of controlling what they feel and do. Thus, a mature person can refute irrational beliefs and learn rational beliefs, thereby controlling his or her feelings and behaviors.

Another cognitive theorist, reality therapist William Glasser (1965), postulates that mature people can meet in themselves two basic psychological needs: the need to love and be loved and the need to feel worthwhile to oneself and to others without depriving other people of their ability to fulfill their own needs. Glasser sees mature people as capable of assuming responsibility for themselves and of engaging in rational thought and behavior. They have no excuse for failing to exercise these attributes.

Transactional analysis theory, as postulated by Eric Berne (1961, 1964, 1972) falls midway between the humanistic and cognitive approaches. Mature individuals are able to function appropriately in the parent, adult, and child ego states and are conscious of which ego state they are functioning in at any given time. They are aware of their interpersonal-relationship patterns and how they structure time, and they have learned how to achieve genuine intimacy. The mature person has achieved the "I'm okay, you're okay" lifestyle position, being able to feel confident about her- or himself and others and to feel capable without needing to control and manipulate others. These features characterize the adult position.

A working definition of adulthood.   A more eclectic definition, by Rappaport (1972), suggests that adult maturity involves the ability to take responsibility, make logical decisions, empathize with others, accept minor frustrations, and accept one's social roles. A problem with this type of definition, however, is determining how and by whom the terms are defined. In other words, who determines "appropriateness of social roles"? In an ever-changing society such as ours, social roles seem to change much faster than our notions of maturity.

This book considers Rappaport and the humanistic psychologists' definitions of a *mature adult* too idealistic to be useful. It is probable that adults achieve different aspects of maturity in varying degrees. For this writer, the concept of maturity has biological, psychological, and philosophical dimensions. Thus, the goals of maturity include:

1. The ability to be a self-differentiated individual with a meaning and purpose in life;
2. The ability to maintain intimate relationships and to care for oneself and for others—that is, to be connected and integrated;
3. The ability to take responsibility for one's choices and their consequences, to renounce unattainable choices, and to recognize that some variables influencing choices are out of one's control;
4. The ability to deal with the disappointments and frustrations of adult life;
5. The ability to balance continuously individual, work, and family roles.

Different adults will meet these goals at varying levels.

For adults, maturity consists of biological maturity, psychological maturity, a philosophical stance, and "perceived" maturity by oneself and by others. In addition, social milestones exist that mark the onset of development of these different aspects of maturity. For example, marriage is perceived to represent a certain level of biological and psychological maturity. Often the milestone precipitates the maturity just as the level of maturity may prepare one for the milestone. Kimmel points out that "age is a convenient index of a host of variables; and changes with age, differences between people of different ages, and the process of aging are of particular interest in the developmental study of adulthood" (1974, p. 10). Age, then, refers to more than merely chronological years; it includes as well the concepts of biological and psychological maturity and the opportunity for reaching specific related milestones.

Age also includes the development of a philosophical point of view regarding the meaning of one's experiences. For adults, a mediational process occurs between an actual event and one's reaction to it. It is in this philosophical mediational process that people differ the most. Three people of the same chronological age can have totally different qualitative and quantitative reactions to the same event owing to their differing perspectives and understandings of the event's meaning. Likewise, the philosophical mediational process and the maturation process reciprocally influence each other. The philosophical mediational process is also influenced by ethnic, gender, historical, intellectual, social, and experiential variables. Thus, aging affects one's philosophical views and vice versa.

CYCLES AND STAGES IN DEVELOPMENTAL THEORY

Although currently the concept of *life stages* is considered somewhat forced and mechanical, we use it in the way Kimmel (1974) suggests, as a convenient parameter within which to understand developmental tasks and issues. Thus, in this book the notion of life stages serves as a framework within which to understand role interactions and choice flexibility, the timing and sequencing of adult roles, and the transitions that occur throughout the life span.

Psychological-developmental theory began with Freud's explorations of the inner workings of human beings. Freud postulated a developmental theory of personality with his delineation of the psychosexual stages of childhood and adolescence. This theory, called the *psychoanalytic approach,* assumes that repression or fixation at an early stage of development can affect one's functioning in later life and that adulthood will be impaired until such early developmental impasses are worked through. Thus, the foundation for adult personality is laid during the early years of childhood. This Freudian view was largely responsible for the widespread belief that personality change and growth occurred only in childhood and adolescence and that adulthood was relatively stable. Further, Freud's theory led to our linear expectations about the nature of growth and development.

Sociological theory contributed the notion that social patterns regarding the timing, duration, spacing, and ordering of life events affect human development. These two perspectives, the psychoanalytical and the sociological, allow us to look at what we might call the pathways of the life cycle. Another way to say this is that we can identify age-differentiated phases or structures in the major role domains of life. Interfacing with these age-related pathways are physiological, developmental, personality, and social roles and variables.

The Life Cycle

Freud's work led to a myriad of research in child and adolescent development and later to explorations of adult development by Jung, Buhler, and Erikson. A major concept resulting from this pioneering work is that of the *life cycle.* The life cycle can be viewed as the entire span of human life, from birth until death, containing both age-related milestones and events unrelated to age. *Milestones* are major events, such as marriage, parenthood, divorce, and widowhood, that can occur any time throughout adulthood and that are experienced differently depending upon the life stage in which they occur. For example, one might marry at

20 or at 40, and while the event is normative at both ages, the impact on the individual will be different depending on his or her age and life stage.

Kimmel (1974) has likened the human life cycle to the seasons of the year:

> Spring is the time of growth and coming into bloom; summer is the time of maturity and greatest productivity; autumn is the time of harvest and culmination, when the seeds are sown for new generations; and winter is the time of decline and death. Each season is beautiful in its own right, yet each is unique; there is a definite progression from one season to the next; and one complete cycle prepares the way for the next [p. 15].

Development is a process characterized by continual change. That is, development is continuous and on-going from birth until death, and expected and unexpected stresses or transitions occur at both predictable and unpredictable points in time. Development is progressive and sequential, following the same pattern generation after generation. One cannot stop or turn back, although one can drift, stall, or stagnate. One can grow in one area, falter in another, and reach a plateau in still another. In other words, the life cycle goes on no matter how or when the various stages are passed.

Danish (1981, p. 40) summarizes the multiple influences on the adult life cycle as falling into three categories: (1) *normative age-graded influences,* which are the biological and environmental determinants that have a strong relationship with a particular age, that is, biological maturation and age-graded socialization events; (2) *normative history-graded (evolutionary) influences,* which are only normative if they occur to most members of a generation in similar ways, such as wars, epidemics, economic depressions; and (3) *non-normative life events,* which refer to biological and environmental determinants that do not occur in any normative age-graded or history-graded manner for most individuals. The impact of these latter events, such as the loss of a job or the death of a child, may depend on specific conditions of timing, patterning, and duration. Danish points out that age-graded influences seem to be most prominent during childhood, normative history-graded events most prominent during adolescence and early adulthood, and non-normative life events increase during the life span.

The concept of the life cycle, then, can be likened to that of life-span development as defined by Baltes, Reese, and Lipsitt (1980): "concerned with the description, explanation and modification (optimization) of the developmental processes in the human life course from conception to death. Like other developmental specialties [the life-span concept] is not a theory but an orientation" (p. 66).

Life Stages

Within the life cycle are loosely defined developmental *stages,* or phases, that emphasize some type of sequential development. Besides having age-related parameters, these stages are defined by the thesis that individuals must master certain tasks at each stage before progressing to the next and before dealing with the history-graded, nonnormative life events that could occur at any time. These developmental stages may be delineated in a number of different ways. Some theorists refer to decades—the twenties, thirties, forties, and so on—as life stages. Others consider early adulthood, say from 20 to 35 or 40, to be a stage; middle adulthood, from 35 or 40 to 60 or 65, to be the next; and later adulthood, from 60 or 65 on, to be the next.

In this book, the concept of life stage serves as a useful framework within which to consider normative developmental tasks and issues. The purpose of this framework is to provide some understanding for a lifespan perspective that rests on the following assumptions:

1. Developmental change is a continuous process not limited to any one stage in life.
2. Change occurs in various interrelated social, psychological, and biological domains of human development.
3. Change is sequential, and therefore it is necessary to view each stage of life in relation to the developmental changes that precede and follow it.
4. Changes in individuals must be considered in the context both of the prevailing norms of the day and of the historical time within which one lives (Danish, Smyer, & Nowak, 1980).

Developmental tasks.   Each life stage comprises developmental tasks resulting from both biological forces and age-related social or cultural expectations. These tasks prepare one to perceive the environment realistically and to cope and function effectively in a complex, ever-changing society. Successful mastery and resolution of developmental tasks at predictable periods or stages of the individual, career, and family life cycles allow one to progress on to the next set of tasks in the next stage. In other words, it is necessary to complete the developmental tasks in one life stage before successfully completing those in the next life stage. The tasks are sequential building blocks. For example, a male who fails to formulate a self-identity in late adolescence will have a most difficult time selecting an appropriate occupation in early adulthood and establishing intimate relationships with others. Though all developmental tasks can occur early or late within any phase and can take varying amounts of time to accomplish, the tasks themselves remain sequential.

The concept of developmental tasks within developmental stages provides us with an evolutionary map for understanding the processes of growth and change. The tasks are what one must perform to achieve health and satisfactory growth in our society. Havighurst (1980, p. 331) claims that "developmental tasks may arise from physical maturation, from the pressure of the surrounding society on the individual, and from the desires, aspirations and values of the emerging personality . . . [the developmental task] is a useful mental tool for the work of analyzing and evaluating progress through the human life span."

The two sources of developmental tasks are the following: (1) biological changes of the body that present an individual with new needs, opportunities, and problems of adjustment, and (2) expectations of society that lead to changing roles. Examples of the developmental tasks of early adulthood include selecting a mate, entering an occupation, and becoming financially independent. These tasks clearly originate in biological needs—for example, sex and intimacy—and from societal expectations such as independent living and achievement.

Family cycles.   Recently, family theorists have begun to look at the individual in the context of the family life cycle and to identify developmental issues regarding relationship systems. Furthermore, they have begun to view families in terms of age-graded normative influences, normative history-graded influences, and nonnormative life events. Using systems theory, the family theorists describe the family life cycle as circular, with the progress of one generation affecting that of the succeeding generation. The first steps toward delineating a family cycle were taken in the late 1940s by Duvall and Hill (1948). These observers wrote that developmental phases occur within the family life cycle, that these stages contain particular developmental tasks, and that family stress results when the family is unable to negotiate a particular task or a transition between two stages.

In the past decade, several family-therapy theorists have attempted to define these stages and tasks and to explore the interface of individual and family development. The family stages proposed are usually marked by the age of the oldest child and by such major milestones as the entering and leaving of the family system by the children.

Career cycles.   Although career-development theory began with the trait-and-factor theory (the assumption that individuals have unique patterns of abilities or traits that can be objectively measured and subsequently matched with job requirements), Ginzberg and associates (1951) were the first to formulate a theory of career choice from a developmental standpoint. They delineated three major stages of career development occurring between ages 6 and 17 or 18. Unfortunately, much of the theory of early career development posited a final stabilizing career choice in late adolescence or early adulthood and did not consider later adult processes and decisions in continuous development. However, this early work led to the development of other theories postulating career-developmental cycles based on the new assumption that career development was a continuous, progressive, sequential process, not one that ended with early adulthood occupational choice and entry.

As theories of adult development emerged, career-development theorists began to incorporate life-cycle and developmental-phase concepts into the notions of career-development growth and change. Thus, today the field of career counseling attempts to help the total person and integrates career counseling into family and individual life planning. Clearly, in this context, career planning must address changing individual and family needs as well as the situational circumstances that occur throughout the life cycle.

A career cycle is the life span of one's total vocational development. Throughout its stages, the cycle may consist of various career, avocational, and leisure paths as well as specific jobs. Moreover, different factors affect the career cycles of men and women. These sex differences will be explored in later chapters.

Overlapping Cycles

Whether we are talking about individual, family, or career life cycles, we must remember that we are not laying out a linear series of discrete stages or phases. Rather, we are looking at the overlapping cycles of individual, family, and career development with their concomitant phases and developmental tasks. These phases or stages do have age-related parameters, but we must be flexible in considering these parameters. When we look at childhood and adolescent stages, we notice that each stage may last a couple of years; in adulthood, a particular stage may last many years.

It is our purpose here to avoid rigidly applying the notion of a *normative life cycle,* since it is not clear that such a cycle exists. Therefore, the concept proposed in this book is that each phase of development within the family, individual, and career life cycles contains relatively smooth, easy stretches as well as relatively bumpy, difficult stretches, and that each cycle encompasses growth spurts, plateaus, and setbacks. Within each stage occur milestones that indicate what already has been accomplished, and choice points, that are like forks in the road at which the individual must choose a path.

To summarize, the three life cycles addressed in this text are the individual, family, and career life cycles. Within each of these cycles are stages: early adulthood, middle adulthood, and late adulthood. Roughly speaking, early adulthood encompasses ages 20 to 40, middle adulthood 40 to 60, and late adulthood 60 on. Each stage contains specific developmental tasks to be accomplished. One's individual, family, and career life cycle may not proceed at the same pace or in synchrony. Furthermore, slow development in one area may impede development in another area. For example, a young adult who has had difficulty in separating from his family of origin may succeed in the career-development area while failing to sustain intimate relationships, instead going from one relationship to another and never beginning a family life cycle. Perhaps not until midlife transition will this man, who has achieved a satisfactory career identity, begin to recognize and deal with relationship issues.

BRIEF HISTORY OF ADULT-DEVELOPMENT THEORY

The twentieth-century pioneers of adult-development theory were Jung, Buhler, and Erikson. They based their work on their inferences from clinical and empirical observations and suggested important dimensions and milestones of the adult life cycle. Table 1-1 is an overview of their work in this area. The following subsections examine their conclusions in more detail.

Carl Jung

The work of Carl Jung (1933, 1971) postulates two stages in the life cycle. The first lasts until the age of 40 and involves both the integration of various intrapsychic forces and a coming to terms with the outer world. The second stage involves the task of individuation, of self-realization and unification. Jung defines

TABLE 1-1.   An overview of the adult-development theories of Jung, Buhler, and Erikson

Theorist	Stage	Age Range	Developmental Tasks
Jung	Early adulthood	Thirties and forties	Individuation Expansion: family and career —Development of autonomy —Development of self-sufficiency
	Late adulthood	Fifties on	Contraction: self, family, career —Self-assessment —Acceptance of mortality
Buhler	Childhood	0–15	Tentative plans; exploration
	Youth	15–25	Preparatory expansion and self-determination of goals
	Early adulthood	25–45	Culmination—definite and specific self-determination of goals
	Middle adulthood	45–65	Self-assessment of results of striving for these goals
	Late adulthood	65 on	Retrospection; consideration of on-coming death, past life
Erikson	Adolescence and Youth (Stage 5)	13–22	Identity versus identity confusion
	Young Adult (Stage 6)	22–30	Intimacy versus isolation
	Adulthood (Stage 7)	30–50	Generativity versus stagnation and self-absorption
	Maturity (Stage 8)	50–death	Integrity versus despair

youth as the period extending from puberty into the thirties. He sees this period as a prelude to the real work of life, adulthood and the process of individuation. The period of youth is when one gives up one's childhood dreams, accepts and deals with sexual instincts and feelings of inferiority, and works through the conflicts of childhood.

Adulthood begins around the age of 40, a time of life providing a significant opportunity for psychological change and growth. The process of individuation is the major task of adulthood, involving the integration of the various intrapsychic forces within the individual. Jung's adult development is based on an expansion–contraction model. During the first part of adulthood, namely the late thirties and the forties, one expands one's life experiences by focusing on the establishment of family and career life styles. The developmental tasks of early adulthood include expansion (turning outward) and the development of autonomy and self-sufficiency (individuation). The second half of adulthood, the fifties and onward, involves contraction (turning inward), leading to a sense of meaningfulness and wholeness that allows one to accept death. During this later adulthood, Jung observed that one's values tend to change into their opposites—that is, women become more masculine and men more feminine in terms of their values and interests. This change is more noticeable in the psychological realm than in the physical, and is the first step in psychological theory toward a concept of androgyny. Jung points out that if an adult has not found satisfaction and meaning in early adulthood, later adulthood may be fraught with frustration and attempts to hang onto youth rather than "to discover in death a goal towards which one can strive, and that shrinking away from it is something unhealthy and abnormal which robs the second half of life of its purpose" (Jung, 1971, p. 20).

We see, then, that Jung adopted Freud's developmental concept of sequential change—that one must deal with the tasks of an earlier stage in order to deal with the tasks of the next stage. Jung saw development as continuous throughout the life cycle and expressed the idea that the serious problems of life are never fully solved. For him, the challenge of a problem rests not in its solution, but rather in one's working at it incessantly. Colarusso and Nemiroff (1981) comment that Jung believed adults to be wholly unprepared for the second half of life and wished that colleges existed for 40-year-olds to prepare them for the second half of life and its demands, just as ordinary colleges now introduce young people to the adult world.

Charlotte Buhler

Charlotte Buhler (1968) and her students examined the parallels between life stages and biological phases as reflected in 400 biographies and autobiographies collected in the 1930s in Vienna. She proposed five biological and developmental phases:

1. Progressive growth (up to age 15): the child is at home prior to the self-determination of goals.
2. Continued growth (ages 15–25): continued growth is augmented by the ability to reproduce sexually preparatory to expansion and experimental self-determination of goals.
3. Stability of growth (ages 25–45): the culmination of definite and specific self-determination of goals.
4. Loss of sexual reproductive ability (ages 45–65): self-assessment of the results of striving for goals.
5. Regressive growth and biological decline (age 65 and on): fulfillment or failure resulting in either continuance of previous activities or return to childhood's need satisfying orientations.

Like Jung's work, this model postulates expansion, culmination, and contraction in activities and accomplishments. In more recent work, Buhler has emphasized the process of goal setting within these various phases. The goals she identifies are personal, familial, and occupational, and are established during the first two phases, fulfilled during the third and fourth phases, and then reevaluated and reaffirmed, consolidated, or abandoned during the later years. Again, like Jung, Buhler considers an individual's sense of having realized goals and attained a sense of fulfillment more critical to adjustment in old age than biological decline and insecurity. Buhler was the first developmental theorist to consider biological variables.

Erik Erikson

Whereas Erik Erikson's (1963, 1968, 1973, & 1978) theory of individual development shares the general expansion–contraction format, his view is more heavily influenced by a Freudian orientation. Erikson's eight stages, or ages, of individual development are each critical transition points in a developmental scheme from birth through death. They are patterned sequences of stages encompassing appropriate physical, emotional, and cognitive tasks that the individual must master in the struggle to adjust to the demands of the social environment.

Each of Erikson's stages presents a different developmental challenge. He postulated a concept of positive growth versus unsuccessful resolution for each of the eight stages. The basic issue underlying each stage is that of defining and redefining one's personal identity. Erikson's first four stages follow the Freudian scheme of child development and are the building blocks upon which success or failure in the later stages depends. In other words, failure to negotiate successfully the developmental tasks in any early stage will affect one's development in a later stage.

The following is the scheme Erikson postulates. In stage 1, from birth until 1 year, occurs the development of basic trust or basic mistrust, focusing most significantly on the mother. Stage 2, early childhood, ranges from 1 to 3 years, and sees the development of autonomy versus shame and doubt, focusing on the parents. Stage 3, childhood, ranges from 3 to 6 years, and contains the development of initiative (ego ideal) versus guilt (conscience), focusing on the nuclear family. Stage 4, school age, ranges from 6 to 12 years, and encompasses the concept of industry versus inferiority, focusing on the neighborhood and school systems. Stage 5, adolescence, ranges from 13 to 22 years, and comprises identity versus identity (role) confusion and the relating to peers and to leaders and heroes as significant others.

The completion of stage 5 is critical to the successful transition into adulthood. Many important components of one's identity need to be resolved simultaneously, in the individual, career, and family realms. When one has achieved identity, the total personality is congruent with respect to self-image, beliefs, and values. The choice of identity means that the person repudiates previous or alternate identities in favor of a single identity. The repudiated aspects of identity form what Erikson (1973) calls a *negative identity*. Adolescents appear to need a negative identity against which to rebel in order to define themselves. If one does not take steps to begin to clarify one's identity in each of these domains, one may be confused and uncertain about one's roles in individual, career, and family cycles. Such confusion may in turn result in inappropriate choices and the inability to develop a stable pattern and resolve concomitant emotional issues. Conversely, the individual who successfully begins to form an identity in stage 5 progresses on to meet the challenges of the next stage.

Stage 6, young adult, ranges from 22 to 30 years and sees the development of intimacy versus isolation. This factor relates to partners in friendships, sex, competition, and cooperation. Erikson defines *intimacy* as including "mutuality of orgasm with a loved partner of the other sex with whom one is able and willing to share a mutual trust and with whom one is able and willing to regulate the cycles of work, procreation and recreation so as to secure the offspring, too, all the stages of a satisfactory development" (1963, p. 266). By intimacy, Erikson had in mind a deeper relationship than the sexual intimacy of which adolescents are capable. He refers to the capacity for a mature psychosocial relationship with another individual, for a full sharing of one's self and one's deepest hopes and fears with another.

Stage 7, adulthood, ranges from 30 to 50 years. The task here is generativity versus stagnation and self-absorption, and relates to care for a new generation and regeneration of society. Generativity refers to the contribution (through parenthood and/or in occupational achievements) that outlives the individual: to being helpful to others for the purpose of serving society rather than for obtaining recognition or material reward. In this stage, the person reaches the peak of productivity and contributes greatly to his or her sense of meaning and self-fulfillment in life. Stagnation, the negative resolution, can be manifest in boredom, overconcern with physical or psychological decline, and feelings of worthlessness and impoverishment.

Stage 8, maturity, ranges from age 50 until death and is characterized by the concept of integrity versus despair. As the culmination of the first seven stages, this stage is the time for final assessment and review, the time to determine whether one's life has made a meaningful contribution to humankind. This stage may be triggered by mandated retirement, serious illness, or impending death. It involves an acceptance of old age and death, and the avoidance of the hopelessness of despair, requiring that the individual come to terms with the future as well as the past.

Each of Erikson's eight stages is viewed as a psychosocial crisis. In each stage, one is particularly sensitive or vulnerable to certain developmental issues resulting from the interaction of biological, psychological, and social forces characteristic of the period in the life cycle. According to Erikson, adults define their self-identity through differentiation and integration. *Differentiation* is the process by which experiences are refined, clarified, and broken down into smaller, more specific subunits. *Integration,* on the other hand, is the process by which separate functions and experiences become organized, synthesized, and unified into large wholes or patterns.

Thus, Erikson defines an adult as follows:

> But now I have only one minute left to indicate what an adult is. . . . From the point of development, I would say: In youth you find out what you care to do and whom you care to be—even in changing roles. In young adulthood you learn whom you care to be with—at work and in private life, not only exchanging intimacies but sharing intimacy. In adulthood, however, you learn to know what and whom you can take care of. I have said all of this in basic American before; but I must add that as a principle it corresponds to what in Hinduism is called the maintenance of the world, that middle period of the life cycle when existence permits you and demands you to consider death as peripheral and to balance its certainty with the only happiness that is lasting: to increase, by whatever is yours to give, the good will and the higher order in your sector of the world. That to me, can be the only adult meaning of that strange word happiness as a political principle [1973, p. 124].

PERSPECTIVES ON SEX ROLES

The traditional concepts of mature adulthood presented in this chapter are sex-biased, for they are based on male norms and do not really consider gender differences. In other words, the distinctions resulting from sex-role differences are not accounted for in the overall theoretical formulations.

Freud was one of the first psychological thinkers to recognize that the major difficulties between males and females result from society's repression of sexuality. He encouraged his patients to become more aware of their sexuality by responding to the reasonable demands of their ids and resisting their overcontrolling superegos. However, many of his other concepts (such as penis envy and castration anxiety) served to maintain rigid differentiations between male and female normative behaviors, giving primacy to male norms. The adage "anatomy is destiny," attributed to Freud, stirs the wrath of contemporary feminists.

Jung's (1933) work laid the foundation for later concepts of androgyny, for he postulated the existence of male and female dimensions within any personality. During the first half of life, Jung contended, one's predominant dimension is developed with full cultural support. At midlife, the previously repressed dimension is allowed to emerge and to become integrated with the predominant dimension.

Erikson's (1963) work tended to support the biological determinism of male and female sex roles. Based on his studies of adolescence, which revealed sex-role differences in performance, Erikson argued that biological differences account for more aggressive behavior in males and for self-contained, nurturing behaviors of women. However, Erikson's stages of development do not reflect sex-role differences. They assume either that both men and women go through the same stages despite biological differences or that female development is not worth bothering about.

Likewise, none of these theorists posits sex-role differences regarding the concept of maturity. One can only assume that for these thinkers maturity is identical for both men and women. This assumption raises the question of how we are to explain the male/female differences in clinical diagnoses and evaluations that have been well-documented by research in the past twenty years (Broverman et al., 1970; Chesler, 1972; Hare-Mustin, 1978; Okun, 1983).

The psychoanalytic theorists believe that genital differences account for different behaviors. The humanists' views are too idealistic and general to permit easy recognition of the self-actualized adult. And neither the cognitive nor the behaviorist perspective acknowledges gender issues in its treatment of adult maturity. In discussing more contemporary adult-development theory in Chapter 2, we find that recent thinkers have begun paying attention to gender differences in human growth.

SUMMARY

This chapter covered three subjects: (1) the concept of adulthood, including the major psychological views of maturity; (2) the pioneering developmental theory pertaining to adulthood; and (3) the failure to treat gender issues in the foundational theory regarding adult development.

The major psychological views differ in terms of their emphases on determinism versus free will, conscious versus unconscious choice, and objectivity versus subjectivity. The psychoanalytic view posits that individual development is controlled by others, that immaturity results from fixation at some preadult psychosexual stage, and that maturity occurs when the adult achieves the stage of genitality and is able to fulfill basic adult sex drives. The humanistic view believes that mature adults have much control over their lives and that the life span is characterized by self-fluidity. This approach emphasizes growth, health, self-reliance, and progress. The behaviorist view does not acknowledge individual autonomy, but, rather, sees the actions of others in the environment as determining an individual's behavior and ultimate personality.

Although the pioneering developmentalists focused on adequate resolution of stage-related tasks, their concepts of adulthood are not as clearly delineated as their concepts of child and adolescent development. Since child and adolescent development are more closely related to chronological ages and biological parameters, the timing of the adulthood tasks postulated is less clear and therefore age cohorts, where adults are concerned, are more difficult to grasp.

Finally, sex role stereotypes have existed for many centuries and until very recently developmental theorists have ignored gender differences in building psychological theory. Therefore, the attitudes and criteria regarding adult behavior have been biased. This has resulted in confusion about the similarities and differences between male and female adult development.

REFERENCES

Baltes, P. B., Reese, H. W., & Lipsitt, L. P. Life span developmental psychology, *Annual Review of Psychology,* 1980, *31,* 65–110.

Berne, E. *Transactional analysis in psychotherapy.* New York: Grove Press, 1961.

Berne, E. *Games people play.* New York: Grove Press, 1964.

Berne, E. *What do you say after you say hello?* New York: Bantam Books, 1972.

Broverman, I. K., et al. Sex role stereotypes and clinical judgments of mental health, *Journal of Consulting and Clinical Psychology,* 1970, *34,* 1–7.

Buhler, C., & Massarek, F. (eds.). *The course of human life. A study of goals in the humanistic perspective.* New York: Springer, 1968.

Chesler, P. *Women and madness.* New York: Doubleday, 1972.

Colarusso, C. A., & Nemiroff, R. A., *The father at midlife: Crisis and the growth of paternal identity.* Unpublished manuscript, 1981.

Dacey, J. S. *Adult development.* Glenview, Ill.: Scott, Foresman, 1982.

Danish, S. J. Life span development and intervention: A necessary link. *The Counseling Psychologist,* 1981, *9,* 40–44.

Danish, S. J., Smyer, H. A., & Nowak, C. A. Developmental intervention: Enhancing life event processes. In Baltes, P. B., & Brim, O. G. (eds.), *Life span development and behavior* (vol. 3). New York: Academic Press, 1980.

Duvall, E., & Hill, R. Report of the committee for the dynamics of family interaction. Prepared at the request of the National Conference on Family Life. Mimeographed, 1948.

Ellis, A., & Harper, R. *A guide to rational living.* Englewood Cliffs, N.J.: Prentice-Hall, 1961.

Ellis, A. *Reason and emotion in psychotherapy.* New York: Lyle Stuart, 1962.

Erikson, E. *Childhood and society* (2nd ed.). New York: W. W. Norton, 1963.

Erikson, E. *Identity youth and crisis.* New York: W. W. Norton, 1968.

Erikson, E. *In search of common ground: Conversation with Erik Erikson and Huey P. Newton.* New York: W. W. Norton, 1973.

Erikson, E. (ed.). *Adulthood.* New York: W. W. Norton, 1978.

Freud, S. *An outline of psychoanalysis.* New York: W. W. Norton, 1949.

Ginzberg, E. et al. *Occupational choice.* New York: Columbia University Press, 1951.

Glasser, W. *Reality therapy.* New York: Harper & Row, 1965.

Hare-Mustin, R. A feminist approach to family therapy. *Family Process,* 1978, *17,* 181–194.

Havighurst, R. More thoughts on developmental tasks. *Personnel and Guidance Journal,* 1980, *58,* 330–335.

Jung, C. *Modern man in search of a soul.* New York: Harcourt Brace, 1933.

Jung, C. The stage of life. In Campbell, J. (ed.), *The Portable Jung.* New York: Viking Press, 1971.

Kimmel, D. *Adulthood and aging.* New York: Wiley, 1974.

Maslow, A. *The farther reaches of human nature.* New York: Viking, 1971.

Okun, B. F. *Effective helping* (2nd ed.). Monterey, Calif.: Brooks/Cole, 1982.

Okun, B. F. Gender issues of family systems therapists, *Issues in training marriage and family therapists.* Ann Arbor, Mich.: ERIC/CAPS, 1983.

Perls, F. *Gestalt therapy verbatim.* Lafayette, Ind.: Real People Press, 1969.

Perls, F. *The gestalt approach and eye witness to therapy.* Palo Alto, Calif.: Science and Behavior Books, 1973.

Rappaport, L. *Personality development: the chronology of experience.* Glenview, Ill.: Scott, Foresman, 1972.

Rogers, C. *On becoming a person.* Boston: Houghton Mifflin, 1961.

CHAPTER TWO

AN INTEGRATED MODEL OF DEVELOPMENTAL AND SYSTEMS THEORY

We turn now from the work of the pioneering developmentalists to that of the contemporary adult-developmental theorists, family-systems theorists, and career-development theorists. After reviewing their work, we will present the conceptual model upon which this text is based, one that illustrates the reciprocal influences of individual, family, and career development.

The major purposes of this chapter are: (1) to offer a synthesis of developmental and systems theory and (2) to present a model from a systems perspective integrating individual, family, and career development. In the process, the chapter will address the following questions:

1. Are there stages of development during adulthood?
2. Do all adults go through the same stages of development at the same age?
3. How do adult stages of development affect the family life cycle and career development?
4. How do we account for variance in the way adults approach major life events?

5. How is developmental theory affected by rapidly changing societal and cultural mores?

CONTEMPORARY ADULT-DEVELOPMENT THEORY

In the last few years, many researchers have begun to build upon the work of Jung, Buhler, and Erikson. The results have been some general but significant assumptions about development:

1. Although one has passed through childhood and adolescence, he or she does not simply and finally become an adult.
2. Adulthood is a continuous "becoming" in itself.
3. The movement from one stage or phase to the next is facilitated by the successful management of the critical challenges posed during each stage or phase.
4. Each stage differs from and is no less important than any other in the developmental cycle.
5. The stages of adulthood are separated by transition periods that are sometimes punctuated with crises.
6. These transitions provide opportunities for growth as one leaves a formerly comfortable way of relating to oneself and the world and seeks new ways to relate.

Schlossberg (1977, 1981) cites the contemporary theorists in adult development along a continuum in accordance with how they explain transitions and adaptive behavior: in terms of individual idiosyncrasy, life stage, or chronological age. At one end of the continuum she places the work of Levinson (1978), since he linked specific adult transitions with chronological age. Next comes the work of Gould (1978), who formulated a dynamic, sequenced pattern of adult development and transformations containing common themes associated with different age levels. Farther along the continuum comes the work of Lowenthal and colleagues (1975), which describes the balance of resources and deficits and focuses on adaptation to stresses at each stage of life. The life-span view, best expounded by Brim and Kagan (1980), Danish (1981), Holmes and Rahe (1967) and Dohrenwend and Dohrenwend (1978), is concerned not with life stages but with the impact on adult growth of such events and mediating variables as work, family life, physical development, and significant others. At the far end of the continuum is the work of Neugarten (1968) and Vaillant and McArthur (1972), which focuses on individual idiosyncrasies. Table 2-1 is a representation of this continuum.

Schlossberg (1981) herself offers a model based on transition, which she defines as an event or nonevent that alters the individual's perception of self and of the world, that demands a change in assumptions or behavior, and that may lead either to growth or to deterioration. In her model, development is a dynamic process, a movement through the various stages of a particular transition. She defines adaptation in terms of the individual's resources-deficits balance or in terms of the degree of similarity between the pre- and post-transition environment.

TABLE 2-1. A continuum of views

Individual	Neugarten: fanning out, social clock, psychology of timing
Life span	Brim and Kagan, Dohrenwend and Dohrenwend, Holmes and Rahe: perspective, not theory; opposed to life stages; study impact of events
Transition	Lowenthal and Chiriboga: stage not age; look at balance of resources and deficits; look at perceived stresses; sex differences
Stage	Erikson, Gould: mastery; release from childhood constraints; sequential resolution of internal crisis
Age	Levinson et al.: invariant sequence; life structure, dream, mentor, polarities

(*Source: From "A Model of Analyzing Human Adaptation to Transition" by N. Schlossberg, The Counseling Psychologist, 1981, 9, 3.*)

Troll (1981) points out that evidence can be marshaled to support the views of any of the developmental theorists, and that the continuum to consider is from total helplessness to total power over one's destiny, rather than stage versus individual idiosyncrasy. Troll's continuum is reminiscent of that along which the psychological theorists view maturity.

In the succeeding subsections we will review the crucial works of Levinson, Gould, Lowenthal, Neugarten, and Vaillant, along with Kegan and Gilligan. We will also discuss the recent research of Baruch, Barnett and Rivers. These works represent the most significant theoretical understanding of contemporary adult development. While these theories are considered in detail as they become relevant in later chapters, a basic overview will be presented here of these writers' research methodologies, major findings, limitations, and biases.

Daniel Levinson

The work of psychologist Daniel Levinson and associates (1978) is based on intensive interviews with forty men, ages 35 to 45. This sample consisted of blue-collar workers paid on an hourly basis, middle-level executives, academic biologists, and novelists. The twenty-hour individual interviews were conducted in the late 1960s and early 1970s in the northeastern part of the country. While this sample does not represent the average American male, it is diverse in terms of socioeconomic level, race, ethnic and religious background, education level, and marital status. Thus, it could be considered to represent today's typical American male society. The main focus of the interviews was on each man's life choices and how he coped with these choices in terms of his occupation, marriage, and family.

As a result of the study, Levinson postulates four seasons of a man's life: (1) childhood and adolescence, birth to age 22; (2) early adulthood, ages 17–45; (3) middle adulthood, ages 40–65; and (4) older adulthood, age 60 and on. These seasons overlap and are interspersed with developmental transitional periods. The purpose of these developmental transitional periods is to cause greater individuation—that is, to enable one to develop a separate personality based on one's own values and behaviors rather than on those of others.

Levinson formulated the notion of evolving *life structures*, the results of the meshing of one's social circumstances (work and family) and one's inner feelings and aspirations. These life structures need to be evaluated and reassessed during the transitions between life stages. Levinson's concepts of the dream and the mentor are elaborated in subsequent chapters.

The three phases that Levinson emphasizes in the course of life are: the novice phase, extending from ages 17 to 33; the settling-down phase, from ages 33 to 40; and the mid-life transition stage, from ages 38 to 43. The substages, tasks, and issues of these phases are presented in subsequent chapters.

Levinson's work is based on male norms and a small number of cases. Because his subjects were between ages 35 and 45, his study of adult development ends at the mid-life transition and does not include later adulthood. The concepts of growth and stable periods, and transitions and relative plateaus are Levinson's unique contribution to adult-development theory. Whether or not women's life stages parallel those of men remains to be researched.

Roger Gould

Psychoanalyst Roger Gould's (1978) work is based on questionnaires answered by 524 male and female adults and on group-therapy observations of a large number of out-patients in the California area. Gould's work is a theoretical discussion illustrated by selected case studies. He sees adult development as a struggle for freedom from the internal constraints of childhood and, like Erikson, he postulates a sequential resolution of internal crises dependent upon life stages. Thus, in each of four developmental periods of adult life, which are related to chronologically determined issues, adults must challenge and overcome false assumptions made in childhood. These four developmental periods are: stage 1, ages 17–22, "Leaving Our Parents' World"; stage 2, ages 22–28, "I'm Nobody's Baby Now"; stage 3, ages 28–34, "Opening Up to What's Inside"; and stage 4, ages 35–45, "Midlife Decade."

Gould defines adult development as "the act of transformation" (1978, p. 25). Reexamining one's childhood angers and hatred—what might be called childhood demons—is painful and difficult, and many adults avoid this struggle, never reaching true maturity. Gould suggests seven steps toward mastering these childhood demons: (1) recognizing one's tension and confusion; (2) understanding that people are faced with contradictory realities; (3) giving full intensity to the childhood reality, letting it be real; (4) realizing that contradictory realities still exist between childhood and adulthood; (5) testing reality by picking a risk that discriminates one view from another; (6) fighting off the strong urge to retreat on the verge of discovery; and (7) reaching an integrated, trustworthy view of reality unencumbered by the demonic past (1978, p. 34).

The specific phases and developmental tasks of Gould's work are discussed in subsequent chapters. Like Levinson's, Gould's work does not extend beyond middle age and is basically psychoanalytic in orientation. Also, while Gould includes females in his sample, he does not address gender differences in terms of developmental tasks.

Marjorie Lowenthal

Marjorie Lowenthal (1975) and her associates studied 200 men and women, ages 17–60, in a San Francisco longitudinal study. The sample consisted of high school seniors, newlyweds, middle-aged parents, and pre-retirement couples, and utilized interviews, questionnaires, and personality ratings. The four groups differed in their outlooks on life, indicating that life stage is more important than chronological age. Lowenthal's work looks at the balance of resources and deficits at these stages and focuses on adaptation to stresses at each one.

The study anticipated future role changes and their influence on the adaptation to major adult transitions. Semi-structured interviews assessed subjects' attitudes toward imminent transition. The transition implied role changes in status.

Responses were categorized into four areas: (1) how much planning subjects had done for the forthcoming role changes; (2) how much control subjects felt they had over the outcome of the transition; (3) whether subjects viewed the transition positively or negatively; and (4) how many problems associated with the transition subjects anticipated. The investigators found a sense of inner control to be the most important variable. Feelings of control and evaluation of forthcoming changes were more highly correlated with overall adjustment than either the number of problems foreseen or the amount of planning undertaken.

These researchers found that in transitions between later stages of life, involving decline and the loss of roles or power were more stressful than transitions between earlier stages involving growth and expansion. Middle-aged adults experienced both the most stress and the smallest sense of control, reflecting their perceived inability to prevent or delay the role changes expected with the aging process. Middle-aged women experienced the greatest maladjustment; the authors suggest that this group is improperly socialized for the "empty-nest syndrome."

The value of the Lowenthal studies lies in their emphasis on social and cognitive factors in development as opposed to the psychoanalytic variables suggested by the Levinson and Gould studies. According to Lowenthal and her co-workers, the greatest variables influencing adulthood transitions seem to be self-concept, role flexibility, a sense of control, and thought processes about the aging process and the meaning of changes. We will see, in the later study conducted by Baruch, Barnett and Rivers (1983), that Lowenthal's findings about middle-aged, "empty-nest" women are not supported.

Bernice Neugarten

Sociologist Bernice Neugarten's (1964, 1968, 1979) University of Chicago studies over a period of seven years in the late 1960s and early 1970s utilized a Kansas City sample of 159 males and females between the ages of 54 and 94. In these studies, the investigators focused on the psychology of timing of life events and analyzed age, sex, and social-class differences in their sample. Their instruments included in-depth interviews, the Thematic Apperception Test (TAT), and a general personality test.

Neugarten emphasizes the variability of the social rather than the biological clock. "As lives grow longer, as the successive choices and commitments accumulate, lives grow different from each other" (1979, p. 891). The network of age norms and expectations govern behavior and affect relationships among age groups. These norms and expectations are part of the elaborate and pervasive social attitudes toward middle and old age that greatly influence the course of adult development through phases of life.

Neugarten found that the personality traits identified in middle age tend to remain constant through old age. She acknowledges that aging has various effects on behavior, but suggests that it does not change personality traits. Thus, to her, the biological clock is less important than the social clock in the course of adult development.

While personality traits do not change with age, the processes by which people deal with their environments and their attitudes about these processes do change. Some such changes include: (1) a change in middle age of one's perception of time and death, resulting in more introspection, contemplation, and reflection; (2) the perception that one's ability to control the environment decreases with age; (3) the decline of psychic energy with age; (4) the reversal of sex roles with age; (5) the increase in rigidity regarding age-status expectations—that is, older people have stricter views than younger people about what are appropriate behaviors, both for their age mates and people of other ages.

Neugarten's sample is biased in that it is composed of white, middle-class, noninstitutionalized subjects. Moreover, a significant number of the sample dropped out during the course of the study. Also, the sample was better educated and of a higher socioeconomic level than is typical for this age group. However, the work is valuable as one of the most comprehensive male/female older-age samples ever studied longitudinally.

George Vaillant

The work of psychiatrist George Vaillant (& McArthur, 1972; 1977) was based on a 35-year study of 260 men who began their sophomore year at Harvard University between 1939 and 1944. These white males were selected because of their high success orientation and the superiority of their bodies, minds, and personalities. From the time of their college graduation until 1955, the subjects responded to questionnaires concerning their employment, family health, sports activities, vacations, drinking and smoking habits, and political views. Periodically, they were intensively interviewed about their lifestyles and their children's development.

Vaillant and McArthur learned that "the life cycle is more than an invariant sequence of stages with single predictable outcomes. The men's lives are full of surprises" (1972, p. 373).

Central to Vaillant's work is the thesis that if individuals are to master conflict and to harness instinct creatively, their ego-defense mechanisms must mature throughout the life cycle into adaptive styles. The changes he noted in ego-

defense patterns from adolescence to mid-life are evidence that intrapsychic structural change occurs throughout the adult years. Defense mechanisms are as significant in the development of life quality as are early childhood influences and
socioeconomic status. Vaillant developed a hierarchy of adaptive mechanisms
relative to their pathological import and to maturity. His major conclusions were:

1. Life is shaped more by relationship quality than by traumatic childhood
   events.
2. Given the constantly changing nature of human life, a particular behavior
   might be classified as pathological at one time and as adaptive at another.
3. Adults evolve higher level mechanisms as they mature, and these adaptive
   mechanisms help adults cope with crises.

Vaillant posits four developmental levels with specific defense mechanisms that
in part permit adaptation at each:

1. Level 1, psychotic mechanisms: denial, delusional projections, distortion;
2. Level 2, immature mechanisms: fantasy, projection, hypochondriasis, passive aggressive behavior, acting out;
3. Level 3, neurotic mechanisms: intellectualization, repression, displacement,
   reaction formation, dissociation;
4. Level 4, mature mechanisms: altruism, humor, suppression, anticipation,
   sublimation.

Level 4 is exhibited only by mature adults.
   Vaillant also posits four aspects of human behavior that people must contend
with and that often conflict with each other: (1) reality, (2) instincts, (3) conscience,
and (4) interpersonal relationships. The better integrated these conflicting aspects
of human behavior are, the more mature is the mechanism the individual selects
and uses.
   Certainly, Vaillant's sample is not typical. It is a white, upper-middle-class male
sample that could well be termed elite. Vaillant's study does offer support to
Erikson's eight sequential stages, although Vaillant suggests interposing a career-
consolidation stage between Erikson's intimacy and generativity stages and a
career-stabilization stage between ages 25 and 35. Unlike Gould and Levinson,
Vaillant finds no evidence for a "mid-life crisis" or for increased preoccupation
with one's mortality as a characteristic of middle age. His theory does not go
beyond middle age, and it too fails to consider female development.

Carol Gilligan and Robert Kegan

We have noted that most research to date on adult development has been
conducted with men born in the 1920s and 1930s. How these findings relate to
female development and to people born in other times, particularly those characterized by radical cultural change, needs to be researched. Carol Gilligan (1982)

and Robert Kegan (1982) of Harvard University have hypothesized a life-span-development approach that is based on the work of Piaget and Kohlberg and addresses sex-role differences.

Gilligan's work is based on the replication of Kohlberg's moral-development studies with nonrandom female populations. She was the first to question Kohlberg's hierarchical ordering of the affiliation/achievement dichotomy observed by McClelland (1975). From these studies, Gilligan concluded that sex differences arise in the social context, in which social status and power differentials along with differences in reproductive biology distinguish the experiences of men and women. These different experiences lead to sex-role differences and affect the relationships between the sexes. Gilligan notes that women are continually excluded from critical psychological theory and are assigned the roles in the life cycle of nurturer, caretaker, and helpmate to males. Whereas men's developmental theory focuses on their individuation and autonomy, Gilligan asserts, women's development occurs in terms of relationships, attachment, and nurturing. She criticizes the theories of Levinson, Vaillant, and Gould for giving relationships a subordinate role in adult development and she points out that men and women experience conflict in matters of integrity versus care, attachment versus separation, and helplessness versus power.

Kegan's work is based on clinical experience. He praises Gilligan's recognition of the male bias in adult-developmental theory and claims that society has wrongly supported and esteemed differentiation without due respect for attachment. For Kegan, the key to development is meaning, and the place of mediation between an event and reaction to it. Kegan takes a life-span-development approach to object relations, describing a sequence of emotional, motivational, and psychodynamic organizations as well as cognitive and sociomoral organizations. Meaning, Kegan suggests, results from a constructive evolutionary process of differentiation and integration. Development consists of a succession of qualitative differentiations of the self from the world. Each time the self differentiates from the world, the world becomes a qualitatively more extensive object with which the newly differentiated self interacts. Each hard-won qualitative change is a response to the complexity of the world and a further recognition of how the world and self are both distinct from one another and related.

This model pursues meaning and the experience of evolution and is intrinsically about differentiation and integration.

> Every developmental stage I said, is an evolutionary truce. It sets terms on the fundamental issue as to how differentiated the organism is from the world and how embedded . . . every evolutionary truce . . . is a temporary solution to the lifelong tension between the yearnings for inclusion and distinctness. Each balance resolves the tension in a different way . . . a continual moving back and forth between resolving the tension slightly in the favor of autonomy, at one stage, and in the favor of inclusion, at the next. We move from the overincluded, fantasy-embedded impulsive balance to the sealed-up self-sufficiency of the imperial balance. . . . [Kegan, 1982, p. 108].

Thus, for Kegan development consists of a process whereby one moves from embeddedness, where one remains in place, to a transition and separation. Next comes a transition leading to reintegration, with a separation occurring from the "old me" as much as the "not me." What we separate from, therefore, we find anew in reintegration. We lose not an object but some part of ourselves.

Referring to Piaget and Kohlberg, Kegan points out that each stage might be the consequence of a single underlying process of evolution that continually reconstructs the relationship of the organism to this bigger, newer environment. This notion of evolution consists of a lifetime activity of differentiating and integrating the self and others.

Kegan is the first developmental psychologist to superimpose the masculine instrumental/feminine expressive dichotomy onto the ladder of developmental tasks. (Instrumental qualities refer to achievement, competition, and logical, world-oriented ways. Expressive qualities pertain to affiliation, nurturing and emotional mediation.) He asserts that each stage is a process stage with three components: (1) confirmation, an expressive quality consisting of holding on and moving toward people; (2) contradiction, an instrumental quality consisting of letting go; and (3) continuity, a holding pattern that ensures at least a brief plateau in the movement across the expressive/instrumental schism. Males and females develop qualities in different sequences, at different rates, and in response to different cultural and biological stimuli.

Kegan's four stages are the following:

1. Stage I, impulsive, ages 2–7, favors inclusion or expressiveness;
2. Stage II, imperial, ages 7–12, favors independence or instrumentality;
3. Stage III, interpersonal, ages 13–19 (early and late adolescence), favors inclusion or expressiveness;
4. Stage IV, institutional, early adulthood, favors independence.

Kegan (1982, p. 87) believes that Erikson missed a stage between "industry" and "identity" "by failing to address the period of connection and inclusion and the highly invested mutuality between independence-oriented periods of latency and early adult identity formulation." For Kegan, late adolescence consists not merely in leaving home and parents, but in reconstructing relationships and the meaning of relationships between the self and others. Men have more difficulty acknowledging their need for inclusion since they are more oriented toward differentiation. Women have more difficulty acknowledging their need for distinctness, because they are oriented more toward inclusion. Since all developmental psychologists, from Freud to Rogers, relate the conception of growth to increasing autonomy or distinctness, they tend to demean the yearning for inclusion that Kegan postulates, implying that it is a kind of dependency or immature attachment. Further, Kegan argues, aside from women's inherent difficulty in emerging from interpersonal embeddedness and men's inherent difficulty in emerging from institutional embeddedness, the radically distinct nature of traditional societal and cultural supports for men and women has greatly impacted their development. "Cultural deprivations effect human development," (Kegan, 1982, p. 212). Modern American life has been characterized by offering less support for integration and more for differentiation. Kegan believes that one of the difficulties adults have today stems from the fact that more fundamental changes occur in adulthood than ever before and that once-available supports no longer exist to help adults deal with these basic changes.

The importance of Kegan's work lies in the doubt it raises regarding psychological autonomy as the hallmark of personal maturity. Kegan sees adult development as involving: (1) the emergence from embeddedness; (2) evolution of a new whole; and (3) the tense oscillation between distinctness and inclusion that characterizes male and female development. The work poses a new orientation to contradiction and paradox by suggesting that the poles of differentiation and integration are related rather than mutually exclusive and requiring a choice.

The methodology in Gilligan and Kegan's work is indeed tenuous but both of these investigators have focused on questions that need attention—namely, how women's development differs from men's and what the generational differences may be. Neither writer deals differentially with distinct periods of adulthood. Instead, the work of both is based on the overall process of development, not life stages and age-related tasks and issues of development. Nevertheless, this work posits many exciting possibilities for further research on adult development.

Recent Research

Supporting gender differences in patterns of adult development is the work of Baruch, Barnett and Rivers (1983), based on the study of 300 northeastern women born around 1935. The findings of this research highlight the importance of the role of work in women's lives. Adult American women find fulfilling, satisfying lives in various role patterns, none of which guarantees happiness and none of which is problem free. Women's well-being in adulthood is linked more to social changes than to internal psychological forces.

The subjects in this unique study reported more stress and displeasure with their lives in young adulthood than in their present state of middle adulthood. This contradicts Lowenthal's findings. Perhaps the dramatic changes in social attitudes over the past decade explain the differences in data collected.

The researchers in this study conclude that women's development is indeed different from men's, citing that the women researched did not have Levinson's "dream" or midlife crisis (which supports Vaillant's findings). However, they found that, like men, women's need for challenge and mastery is as important as their need for relationships. Because of societal attitudes, these women did not achieve identity formation as early in life as did men. This may account for the women's higher levels of displeasure in early adulthood.

Although the sample in this work is geographically skewed, it is important research that needs to be replicated and expanded to determine the generational and gender variables affecting adult development. It raises significant questions about the value of marriage and childbearing to women's well-being and it emphasizes the necessity of challenging, meaningful work for women's full development. It also shows the critical impact of social change on adult development.

A major implication of this work is the importance of the function of multiple roles in the lives of adult women. Married women, with children and challenging jobs, found that by "putting their investments in many stocks" they were better able to cope with the inevitable stresses associated with any one of these roles. As women take on work roles, they drop other low priority roles and feel more in control of their time and energy management.

AN OVERVIEW OF SYSTEMS THEORY

Systems theory underlies the conceptual model upon which this text is based. We will consider the main tenets of systems theory here as it relates in particular to family systems theory. The pioneering work of von Bertalanffy (1934, 1968) allowed social scientists to apply general principles of organization and operation to human systems—social groups such as families, classrooms, work units, communities, peer groups, and so on. Through the study of systems theory, we have learned to define any organizational structure—mechanical, biological, electrical, or human—as an entity with interacting components constrained by or dependent on other components. The two important systems tenets are: (1) that a change in one component part of a system will effect change in another part or other parts of the system; and (2) that the needs and goals of the whole system take precedence over those of a component part.

In von Bertalanffy's early formulations, based on his work in the biological sciences, he defined organizational structures as "composed of mutually dependent parts and processes standing in mutual interaction" (1968, p. 33). He saw this organizational system as having self-regulating capacities and as being intrinsically active. The primary motivation for the system's behavior, he asserted, was to maintain autonomous activity within its own organizations. Thus, in this view a system is a rule-governed organization devoted to its own survival. In terms of human systems, the development of individual members is also seen as a major goal, although this goal often conflicts with the system's overall goal of survival.

From this theory, we learn that the basic needs of a system are to adapt, survive, and maintain itself, and that to meet those needs a system takes action and behaves. When conflict arises between the needs of one or more component parts and the goals of the whole system (which is larger than the sum of its parts), the system attempts to regulate and control the behavior of its component parts to ensure its own survival. Control of the system is maintained by its structures and by its cybernetic principles of communication and feedback. When conflict among different or overlapping systems arises, the same principles apply.

System Properties

Systems theory posits five major properties characterizing human systems: subsystems, wholeness, feedback, homeostasis, and equifinality.

Subsystems. Each organizational system consists of special functional units called subsystems. A subsystem may be both a piece of a larger structure and a complete structure in itself. Thus, a life system would include an individual subsystem, a family subsystem, and a career subsystem. Within each of these subsystems would be smaller units, subsystems within subsystems. For example, within the family subsystem we can discern a spouse subsystem composed of husband and wife, a sibling subsystem composed of the children as brothers and sisters, a parent subsystem, a mother–daughter subsystem, and so on. All the subsystems together make up the total family system. And each subsystem interacts with the others as well as with the total family system. Likewise, the family system inter-acts with the individual and the career subsystems and with different whole social systems such as the school system and the community system. Moreover, an individual's roles within different subsystems may vary. One may be a "mover" at work, a "bystander" at home, and a "follower" with friends. The point is that a change in any one subsystem will effect change in other parts of the system and in other systems. Thus, a change in one's family system may effect change in one's individual and/or career systems. Figure 2-1 illustrates the myriad of possibilities of systems relations.

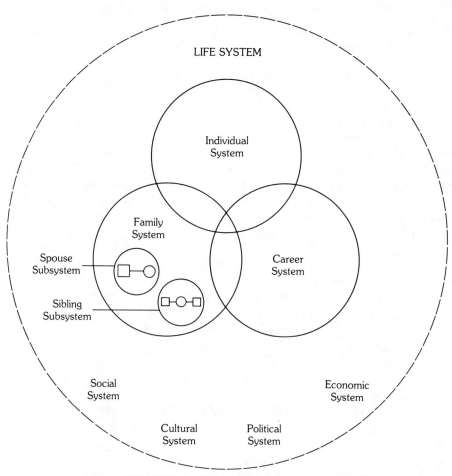

FIGURE 2-1.   Life system and subsystems.

Wholeness. The concept of wholeness refers to the relationship between the total system and its parts. The system is an integrated, coherent entity that is more than the mere composite of independent elements. An individual who does not have a career system still has a life system, since regardless of whether components of a subsystem are missing, the wholeness of the system transcends the sum of the component elements. As an example, a family system called the Greens consists of Mr. Green, Mrs. Green, Bob Green, Dan Green, and Jeff Green, but if Bob and Dan are away on a camping trip when you visit the Greens, you are still visiting the Greens, not the Greens minus Bob and Dan. Thus, one's life system is viewed as a totality that is greater than its components, the individual, career, and family systems.

Feedback. Feedback is the interactional process among the parts of the system. Feedback refers to how the component parts within a system relate to each other. This process of feedback keeps the system functioning. Feedback is circular rather than linear. One event influences a second event, which in turn influences a third event, which may impact upon either the second or first event, triggering off a new response cycle. With such circular feedback, a response to a stimulus becomes a stimulus to further responses, which may affect the initial stimulus either immediately or later. In human systems, we look at the communication process to determine the nature and functioning of feedback to learn about the rules and power structures of the system.

Circular feedback can alter communicative behavior at any point. This feedback can be sequential or spontaneous. Sequential feedback occurs when messages are communicated through a clear chain. For example, Mother may tell Daughter something that she knows Daughter will pass along to Older Brother, who in turn will pass the message along to Father. Mother knows that this is the path to delivering a message to Father in this family system. Spontaneous feedback occurs when each member of a system has communicational access to all members and messages are delivered via any combination of communicators or are even communicated directly.

Homeostasis. The automatic tendency of the system to maintain a dynamic equilibrium is called homeostasis.

> Homeostasis is the dynamic equilibrium that is established as the family evolves; it is continuously threatened by external stresses (for example, job loss, economic depression, war, geographical relocation, fire) and internal stresses (for example, birth of a new child, death or serious illness, developmental crisis of an individual family member) [Okun and Rappaport, 1980, p. 80].

Homeostatic mechanisms become activated when homeostasis is threatened. The system invokes rules and exerts considerable pressure to return the system to its known and customary balance. Whether or not the former homeostatic state is comfortable or painful is immaterial. A system would rather retain its familiar pain than subject itself to the vulnerability of change, even when the outcome of that change is likely to alleviate pain.

Equifinality.   The term *equifinality* means that the final results of the interaction within systems depend on the process of interaction, not on the number or characteristics of the individual members in the system. In other words, no matter where one begins, the same results are likely to occur. Therefore, interactions in a system are more significant than initial causal conditions. Let's return to the example above: the mother tells the daughter something that she knows the daughter will pass along to the older brother who will pass the message along to the father. If Father is the last one to receive messages in a family, regardless of their content or initiator, the pattern will be that the message always goes through everyone else before it ends up with him. To understand a system, one need not usually get a complex history of each member of the system, since the system pattern will be apparent from studying the current interactions of its members. It is the nature of the system's organization, the interactional process, that determines the results of the system.

System Structures and Communications

Two major characteristics of human systems are structures and communications. The structures and communication patterns within a human system are inseparable. In fact, they define each other in many ways, and it is often futile to attempt to assess which determined which.

Structures.   By *structures* we mean not only the relationship of the subsystems to each other and to the whole system, but also the rules and regulations for controlling and maintaining the total system. For example, in one's life system, an unwritten rule might demand that one's career take precedence over any other demands. If this had been so for the Simmons family described in the introduction, it would have become apparent that the structure would have compelled Mr. Simmons to go where the job took him despite the disruption to his family and despite his own personal preferences.

A key concept in the notion of system structures is that of boundaries—those existing within a system, between systems, and between systems and the environment. A boundary is defined as the rules and regulations that separate the system from other systems and the environment and that separate subsystems from each other and from the larger system. The characteristics of the boundary substantially determine how exchanges are carried out. Boundaries are the manifestation of the system's rules and regulations; they define the context in which communications occur. They can be external and internal, rigid or permeable. Boundaries, therefore, regulate the transaction of interactions between two subsystems. For example, the boundary between one's family and career systems determines how much work or how many career issues one brings home and vice versa.

A boundary can be highly permeable, permitting thoughts and feelings to be easily exchanged, or fairly impermeable, inhibiting thoughts and feelings from being exchanged at all or permitting such exchanges only with much difficulty. The degree of permeability of a boundary has no value in itself; rather, it is good or bad with respect to actual circumstances. With regard to the above example, a permeable boundary between family and career systems is functional if it allows one to spend more time with one's family by doing some office work at home, but may be dysfunctional if it allows the work done at home constantly to interfere with family relationships.

Much of the work on system boundaries emanates from the theoretical constructs on family-systems therapy of Murray Bowen (1966, 1975, 1978), David Kantor (1975), and Salvador Minuchin (1967, 1974, 1978, 1981). Their constructs can help us understand the creation, maintenance, and modification of boundaries within, between, and among various types of systems.

Communications.   By *communications* we mean the process and manner by which the rules and regulations of a system are transmitted. A particular structure provides the context for a particular communication style that implements a given system's rule or regulation. We can discern communication patterns by studying the human interactions within the system, the relationship of the members and subsystems, the rules that govern the members, and the next moves.

Theorists of family-systems therapy, such as Watzlawick, Jackson, Haley, and Satir, have helped us to understand that relationships can be studied by analyzing the communicational (verbal) and metacommunicational (nonverbal) aspects of interactions. As Okun and Rappaport (1980) have pointed out, common core concepts of systems communications can be summarized as follows:

1. The primary need of individuals within a relationship is to form and maintain the relationship itself.
2. Two major tasks are involved in this process: deciding on the rules of the relationship and negotiating who actually makes the decisions regarding the rules.
3. The tasks of setting rules and negotiating who has control over the rules are accomplished through the exchange of messages.
4. Messages form the substance of the communications between people in the relationship, and, as such, are the basic element of the interactional process.
5. Messages have two major aspects: the communicational, dealing with the content of the message itself; and the metacommunicational, dealing with the message about the message. The latter seeks to impose behavior or to define the self and the nature of the relationship.

As we observe communication styles and patterns within a system, it is important to remember that the metacommunicational message, the command aspect, defines the nature of the relationship and establishes the rules governing which behaviors are to be included or excluded in a relationship. The interaction of the sender's message and the receiver's acquiescence in accepting it is a process involving both members.

Again, consider the example of the Simmonses. As long as Mr. and Mrs. Simmons focus on the content of their messages (whether or not Mr. Simmons should take an out-of-state job), they are missing the real concern, the relationship issue. This relationship issue concerns a power struggle regarding whose needs take priority in this system; what the boundaries are between family, career, and individual development; and who the decision maker will be and how he or she will function.

Family-Systems Theory

Family-systems theory posits that the family functions as an organizational system in which each family member affects and is affected by the others. Family systems develop certain operating principles, or rules, that allow for constancy and predictability. These rules may have been passed down from generation to generation, and while they can be influenced by individual family members, they function largely implicitly rather than explicitly. These rules, along with family myths, reflect family members' needs to make predictions about their relationships, purposes, and environment. They become manifest in the establishment and maintenance of roles, beliefs, and values, which in turn influence the development and maintenance of family behavior patterns and traditions.

Systems theory allows us to view the individual as an organization of biological, psychological, and social components; the family as a system composed of members and subsystems; and career life as a system composed of individual needs, values, aptitudes, interests, and skills. These systems are interdependent, and a change in one system or subsystem will effect change in other subsystems or systems.

When conflict arises between the needs of the component parts and goals of the system(s), the system attempts to regulate and control the behavior of the component parts. Thus, if one's life system is composed of the personal system, the family system, and the career system, it follows that what happens in one of these systems will affect what happens in others.

AN OVERVIEW OF CAREER-DEVELOPMENT THEORY

To complete the foundational base of our conceptual model, we turn now to career-development theory. It is in the occupational realm that many adults learn their major social roles. The adult's work experiences have continuous and pervasive effects upon identity, lifestyle, and attitudes. Thus, the individual's identity affects and is in turn affected by work experiences. Moreover, one's self-esteem is inevitably related to one's occupational success.

Career-development theories attempt to explain why and how people choose careers. The major focus of career-development theory is on the individual, personality, and occupational characteristics that influence one's career decisions. Psychological approaches to the study of vocational development have traditionally focused on the person in relation to work, often attempting to show how personal characteristics affect job choice and job satisfaction. Recent psychological approaches emphasize cognitive-developmental processes. Sociological and economic analyses emphasize the work setting itself and the social context in which work is performed, minimizing the role of the individual in the process of vocational development. In the following subsections we, review those theories that have implications for adult development.

Psychological Approaches

Trait-and-factor theory.   The traditional approach to vocational development is to predict job choice and the subsequent adjustment of individuals to their jobs by assessing personality, motivation, aptitudes, interests, and previous experiences. The early trait-factor approaches assumed that vocational choice and satisfaction were determined by matching a person's traits with job requirements. This narrow view assumed that a person's motivational system was relatively stable and that everyone had a single career goal. Likewise, it assumed that one's unique patterns of abilities or traits could be measured objectively.

Holland's (1973) more recent modified trait-factor approach assumes that people's vocational interests represent an extension of their personalities. In this view, occupations are considered in terms of the interpersonal settings in which they are carried out and in terms of their associated lifestyles, rather than with regard to performance requirements alone. Thus, congruence between the person and the environment is the major determining factor in vocational choice, stability, and satisfaction. Six types of personalities and six corresponding models of environments have been identified: realistic, investigative, artistic, social, enterprising, and conventional. Figure 2-2 represents the degree of similarity between any two types (those closest together are the most similar to each other) along with typical attributes and occupations. Most people will have one predominant personality type with a second or third type contributing to their interaction with their occupational environment (Harrington, 1982). Thus, an individual can resemble different types in varying degrees. People are socialized toward this predominant personality type by their experience in their family system, school system, and neighborhood and community systems.

We can see in Figure 2-2 that a socially oriented individual would prefer to work in an environment that provided interaction with others, such as a school or hospital, whereas a conventionally oriented person might prefer to work in a bureaucratic organization that had clear rules and expectations about interactions. Holland developed inventories to measure the personality types, but his measurement of work environments is still embryonic. Holland's major premise is that people seek out and are satisfied in environments that match their major personality types, tending to leave or be dissatisfied in ones that are incongruent. He concentrates on the factors influencing career choice rather than the developmental process leading to career choice. Thus, his emphasis is on matching at the time of initial choice, an approach that fails to take into account changes resulting from the individual's development, varying job definitions, and changes in the social and economic environments.

The self-concept approach.   Super (1969) explains the importance of self-concept in initial job selection and throughout the adult's career. He says that one's vocational self-concept must be integrated with one's potential for imple-

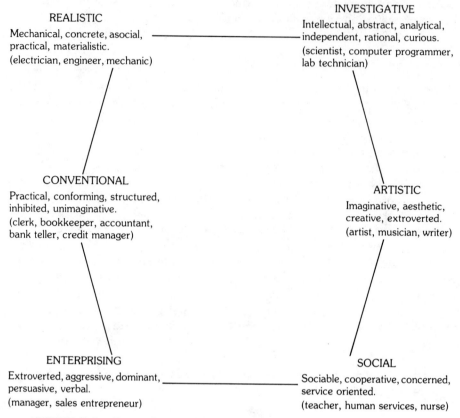

FIGURE 2-2. Types of personalities and models of environment in Holland's theory. *(Source: Adapted from Holland, 1973; and Harrington, 1982.)*

menting that self-concept and is influenced by the cultural, social, and economic conditions of the working world. Individuals choose occupations that allow them to function consistently with their self-concepts. He assumes that the vocational self-concept is formulated and implemented in late adolescence and early adulthood, and he posits that vocational development in later periods consists of further modification of one's self-concept and one's adaptation to an occupational role. Thus, he defines a career as "the sequence of occupations, jobs and positions occupied during the course of a person's working life" (1969, p. 3). One's self-concept, vocational preferences, competencies, and family and life situations change throughout one's career life, and one's career development reflects these changes. Super's developmental approach takes into account the evolutionary nature of adult development.

Using Buhler's concept of life stages, Super defines stages of vocational development as age-related periods in which developmental tasks lead to vocational maturity (see Table 2-2, page 41). An individual achieves maturity by completing the appropriate tasks at each level. Vocational maturity encompasses the following behaviors over the life span:

1. Selecting occupational preferences;
2. Obtaining occupational information and making the necessary preparations;
3. Planning short- and long-range objectives;
4. Formulating steps toward implementing the occupational plan;
5. Continuously reassessing and recycling throughout the life span.

Harrington (1982) points out that Super's career patterns contain "useful concepts" in relating career development to adult development. Super (1957) identifies four typical male career patterns:

1. A stable career pattern, whereby one goes directly from school into a job for the remainder of one's working life;
2. A conventional career pattern, whereby after school one has a few trial jobs and then enters stable employment;
3. An unstable career pattern, whereby after school one follows a cycle of trial jobs to a stable one and then returns to trial jobs again, thus never achieving permanent occupation;
4. A multiple-trial career pattern, whereby after school one takes many trial jobs, all of which are too short-lived to indicate a predominant type of work or the establishment of a career.

The seven female career patterns Super (1957) describes are these:

1. The stable homemaking career pattern, whereby almost directly upon leaving school, one marries without performing any significant paid work;
2. A conventional career pattern, whereby after school and working for a short time, one marries;
3. A stable working career pattern, whereby one goes directly from school into a job for the remainder of one's working life;
4. The double-track career pattern, whereby after school one maintains a double career of simultaneous homemaking and paid work;
5. An interrupted career pattern, whereby after school the individual works for a period, then marries and raises children, and later returns to the labor force;
6. An unstable career pattern, whereby after school one follows a random sequence of work, marriage, work, childrearing, and work, similar to the male's patterns;
7. A multiple-trial career pattern, similar to that for males.

These career patterns seem hopelessly dated and sexist in light of today's cultural norms. They assume that career development must follow a patterned progression in order to be considered "stable" and that career change and variety are abnormal. Though Super's theory addresses the interaction throughout the life span of one's job-related experiences with one's self-concept, it fails to take into account the social and economic forces that operate independently of one's personal development. Likewise, his theory assumes career stability to be the norm, and fails to account for occupational role shifts such as mid-career change and changes in needs, interests, and lifestyles. Further, the theory assumes that one has complete freedom to choose one's career. But in the practical world, social and economic conditions can limit or expand an individual's range of options at any given time regardless of one's preferences, interests, and experience. Super fails to consider that societal conditions at any given time can limit one's potential for synthesizing self and vocation.

Cognitive-development theories.   Tiedeman and O'Hara (1963) take another psychological approach. They conceptualize career development as a continuous process whereby one differentiates one's ego identity, processes developmental tasks, and resolves psychosocial crises. The career-development stages these writers propose are based on the eight stages Erikson discerns in his work on development. For example, in differentiating one's ego, one begins with the trust–mistrust crisis as it relates to the world of work. One reaches career decisions through a systematic problem-solving pattern that engages the individual's total cognitive abilities to match the unique qualities of the individual with a unique work situation.

Tiedeman and O'Hara identify four major stages of decision making:

1. Exploration, during which one attempts to define self and career identity and reflects upon and experiments with one's aspirations, abilities, and career-related interests;
2. Crystallization, during which one attempts to narrow down options and make tentative choices;
3. Choice, during which one integrates a focused goal and identifies with the career field;
4. The actual exhibiting of one's commitment to the choice as it relates to one's self-identity.

Jepson (1974) and Knefelkamp and Slepitza (1978) propose cognitive-development models of career development that combine the stage concept and the cognitive-developmental models of Perry (1970), Piaget (1952), and Kohlberg (1969), upon which Kegan bases his theoretical formulations. These works suggest a progression of cognitive processing; the stages they postulate are discussed in Chapter 5 in relation to career development in late adolescence and early adulthood.

Cognitive views of career development focus on the assumption that changes in career behavior are cognitively mediated and that thought processes, behavioral processes, and environmental processes mutually interact. The unique potential of these approaches lies in their attempt to view stage differences in intellectual and cognitive development as influences on career choice and behavior.

Sociological Approaches

Theories and research on vocational development from a sociological perspective address adult career patterns in terms of social-structure variables such as demographic characteristics and ethnicity, and political, economic, and historical

TABLE 2-2.   Super's vocational developmental stages and tasks

Stage	Age	Tasks	General Characteristics
Growth	Birth–14	Self-concept development; orientation to world of work and meaning of work	Developing capacity, attitudes, interests, and needs related to self-concepts through relationships with family, school, fantasy
Exploratory	15–24		
	14–18	Crystallization of vocational preferences through self-examination; role try-outs; school, leisure, and part-time work activities	Formulating general vocational goals through awareness of resources, values, interest; planning for preferred occupation
	18–21	Specification of work plans	Moving from tentative vocational preferences toward a specific vocational preference
	21–24	Implementation through first job	Entering employment of selected occupation
Establishment	25–44	Securing permanent place in chosen occupation	Trying and stabilizing through work experiences
	24–35	Stabilization	Confirming a preferred career by actual work experiences and use of talents to demonstrate career choice as appropriate choice
	35 onward	Consolidation	Advancing in career
Maintenance	45–64	Preservation of achieved status and gains	Continually adjusting to improve working position and situation
Decline	65 onward	Deceleration; disengagement; retirement	Retiring

(Source: Adapted from Super, 1969; and Harrington, 1982.)

conditions. In other words, a natural disaster, a change in government, or the rise or fall of a particular industry can create or eliminate career opportunities. In this decade, for example, many experienced teachers are being forced to consider new occupations as a result of declining school enrollments and diminishing teaching positions.

An early integrated approach to career development is that of Blau, Gustad, Jessor, Parnes, and Wilcox (1956). These authors present a synthesis of the effects of social institutions on career choice and development. They suggest that the individual characteristics responsible for occupational choice are biologically determined and socially conditioned through family influences, social position and relations, and the social-role characteristics. Eventually the individual creates a preference hierarchy from which he or she makes choices.

The process of selection evolves because of socially related influences and physical conditions such as resources, topography, and climate. The investigators consider these factors beyond the control of an individual but still determinants in the process of selection. Thus, they posit that career development is a continuous process affected by a social structure that encompasses patterns of activities, identification with models, aspirations of various social groups, and situational conditions.

The work of Miller and Form (1964) followed that of Blau and his colleagues. They recognized that sociological variables often influenced career patterns after the individual made an initial choice of an occupation. For example, occupational status and changes in the economy certainly affect the degree of stability a worker achieves.

An important interdisciplinary approach is that of Schein (1978), who examines the interaction of the individual and the organization over time. Schein has formulated the notion of "career anchor," which consists of a pattern of self-perceived talents, motives, and values developed over the life span that serve to guide, constrain, stabilize, and integrate a person's career.

Again, it is important to note that most theories and research on vocational development are based on samples composed of white, middle-class men. Currently, however, race and sex are considered to be highly significant variables, receiving increasing attention. While most researchers recognize that the influence of traditional sex-role distinctions on women's occupational patterns vary, most agree that all women are influenced by them either overtly or covertly. We discuss the findings on this topic in subsequent chapters.

It is clear to practitioners today that, to help adults cope with career pressures in the 1980s, they need integrated approaches to career development that take into account psychological, sociological, and economic variables. The meaning of work and career development today differs sharply from that of a decade ago; expectations, opportunities, and values have undergone changes that affect the continuous process of choice and change in people's work life. As we formulate an understanding of adult career development, it becomes important for us to consider these changes; what was considered stable and mature a decade ago may be irrelevant for the 1980s and 1990s.

Though the element of chance in career development has been considered by sociologists, no research has addressed it fully. Seligman (1981) points out how chance meetings and occurrences can influence one's career direction. It is probable, however, that to be influenced in this way one must be capable of perceiving the potential inherent in such chance happenings. This point demonstrates that theory is only of limited usefulness in explaining vocational development, since it is incapable of anticipating the many chance occurrences and situational events that affect one's occupational growth and development.

Another limitation of these theories of career development is that they recognize only indirectly the influence of one's family system on one's initial career choice, as Bratcher (1982) notes. He recommends that researchers focus on the hidden yet powerful family influences on people's ability to consider many career options.

Finally, it is important that career-development theorists consider the process throughout adulthood and develop a model that accommodates cultural trends and changes, particularly those involving gender differences and issues.

THE CONCEPTUAL MODEL

The model presented in this section is the conceptual foundation of this book. The model exhibits the reciprocal influences of individual, family, and career development. Figure 2-3 is a schematic representation of the mutual interaction of these three domains.

From systems theory we learn that systems resist change and attempt to maintain homeostasis. Also, in systems theory, systems are viewed as growing, fluid,

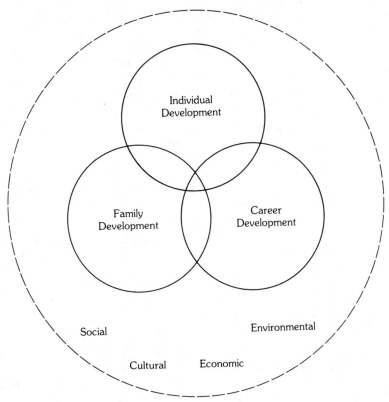

FIGURE 2-3.   The interaction of individual, family, and career development.

changing processes. People within systems develop problems when the system changes but they are unable to change. And from developmental theory we learn that challenge and change are necessary to growth, and that crisis, rather than being merely an illness or a catastrophe, is a turning point in an individual's or a family's life, a crucial period of both increased vulnerability and heightened potential. We can integrate these two perspectives by viewing a human system as being in constant struggle between change and homeostasis. Thus, we can expect no human system to remain continually in equilibrium, and we must realize that systems are sufficiently adaptable to move and change in complex ways within wide boundaries for survival. Another way of expressing this point is to say that change, as opposed to continual homeostasis, is necessary at predictable times in the individual and family life cycles. Admittedly, a homeostatic balance among the individual, career, and family systems is necessary, and as needs, interests, and situations change, the boundaries within and among these three systems will be reset. Again, our understanding of this process can rest in part on principles of systems theory—namely, that (1) a change in one system or in a part of a system will affect other systems and parts of the system, and (2) each system is rule-governed and kept balanced by homeostatic mechanisms.

The result of this perspective is a nonpathological view of human systems. In other words, this point of view is not concerned with "normality" or "abnormality"; rather, it seeks to elucidate effective human functioning. Optimally functioning systems have clear communication patterns, flexible boundaries, and the ability to view change as a challenge and to master the appropriate developmental tasks necessary to moving on. Less optimal functioning, from this point of view, might be the result of underdevelopment in some part of the system (individual, career, or family), or disruption by situational crisis, or of system overloading—that is, the addressing of too many complex tasks simultaneously. As an example of a poorly functioning system, consider a young person who has not yet successfully separated emotionally from his or her parents and who has also failed to fully establish his or her identity. The person moves on from jobs and relationships, never finding satisfaction for long in either realm of life.The person's occupational insecurity may well reflect the parents' expectations rather than the person's own values and interests; the person's work might also be suffering from his or her inability to form lasting relationships with peers. Further, this person's family of origin may be experiencing stress as the son or daughter goes from job to job and from relationship to relationship, returning home for comfort every time he or she is wounded in the work environment. This young person could well be viewed as suffering from a developmental crisis rather than as a "borderline" personality, and be treated accordingly.

The issue of adult personality change over time—whether or not personality changes in adulthood or is fully formed in childhood—remains controversial. At best, tension exists between change and stability. As Brim and Kagan (1980) write, "there is, on the one hand, a powerful drive to maintain the sense of one's identity; a sense of continuity that allays fears of changing too fast or of being changed against one's will by outside forces. . . . on the other hand, each person is, by nature, a purposeful striving organism with a desire to be more than he or she is now." This tension fits into our notion of adult development as based on the tension between change and stability.

Crisis

Crisis is the disruption an individual or system experiences when its homeostasis is disturbed. This disruption may be viewed as either a positive or negative change. In our conceptual model, crisis is important and is expected to occur periodically in life. We can view crisis as catapulting one into transition that in turn leads to a new stage of growth and change. Thus, in this view crisis is healthy, having the potential to engender growth as well as pain. The terms transition or turning point are synonymous with crisis used in this way.

The developmental perspective posits that each stage of life contains a set of appropriate psychological, social, and physiological tasks that are seen as challenges. As discussed elsewhere (Okun and Rappaport, 1980), most individuals and families experience crises emanating from these tasks within the context of their regular developmental life cycles. Such events are called developmental crises.

Many crises, however, that occur frequently in our society cannot be considered part of normal individual, career or family development. These nondevelopmental crises can be the result of voluntary behavior (for example, substance abuse and family violence) or involuntary conditions (physical or mental handicaps, for example). Though outside the realm of normal individual, career or family development, these crises may nevertheless affect those domains, for instance in the forced acceleration or deceleration of developmental processes. The way a human system handles a nondevelopmental crisis depends in large part on the particular developmental stages of those within the system. The systems perspective helps us to determine how family systems react to nondevelopmental crises—for example, by sustaining on-going disruption or by accepting the challenge and moving on.

Stress

Stress occurs when our biological or psychological needs are not fulfilled. It is the fight-or-flight reaction that causes changes in blood pressure, heart rate, respiratory capacity and muscle tone. Any change can be a source of stress. Stress can occur within an individual, a family, or a work system. Stress can result from internal or environmental variables, and it usually occurs when a biological or psychological need is frustrated and therefore unfulfilled.

Stress causes individuals and families to behave dysfunctionally, to develop a somatic symptom, or to feel some degree of pressure, conflict, or frustration. Selye (1956, 1974) describes stress as a general state of excitation but cautions us that not all states of excitation are stress. True stress involves a majority of the body- or family-system resources. "Stress is not necessarily bad for you; it is also the spice of life, for any emotion, any activity causes stress" (1956, p. vii).

From the developmental/systems perspective, we note that stress can accompany any of the transitions (changes) between stages and that it can occur between and within systems. For example, one might feel a high degree of stress in attempting to fulfill career and family needs simultaneously.

Stress can be experienced both negatively or positively. In this book, as we delineate typical developmental tasks and issues associated with stages of adulthood, we will identify likely areas of stress and their impact on development.

Life-Span Development

While we recognize that "normal" development does not exist, we can look at the longitudinal research on adult development to identify some common milestones along the way. Remember that most research has been conducted on white middle-class American males born in the first third of the century and on white middle-class American families. Figure 2-4 shows what might be considered a conventional developmental pattern for a typical white middle-class American male. Note that early adulthood requires a high degree of mastery of establishment tasks in the individual, career, and family systems. But whereas individual development has ups and downs throughout the life cycle, career development may typically reach a plateau in middle adulthood and then decline in late adulthood. Family development may peak again for a period during mid-life, and, if the mid-life tasks are successfully resolved, it may stabilize in late adulthood with a return to the original couple system.

Regarding our understanding of life-span development, we need much research on the effects of physical aging on personality, social role, time perspective, and

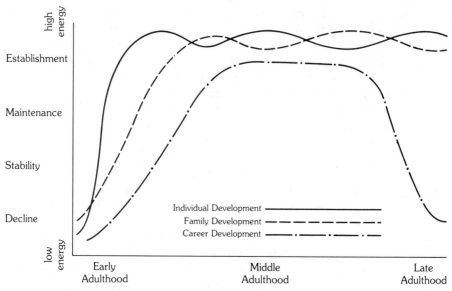

FIGURE 2-4.   The amount of psychological energy required for adult development.

subjective age identification as well as the effects of sex role. Also, we need to learn more about the effects of cultural changes, particularly when those changes are radical and compressed into short periods, as has been the case in the past twenty years. We know that these cultural changes have affected the structure and meaning of work in American society and that these effects in turn have influenced career choices and development. Until we have some definitive research findings, we must keep open minds in considering these variables and their effects on behavior and development. For example, as Rossi (1980) points out, it appears that a shift is occurring from the lockstep pattern linking schooling and job scheduling that characterizes a mature industrialism to one of greater flexibility, including the less rigid scheduling of school and work and the more subtle adaptation between work and family patterns that suggests a postindustrial pattern. We see that age at job entry is older, retirement comes earlier, mid-life career shifts occur more often, flex-time and part-time jobs are more common, adult-education courses are used more, and young workers are more discontented with lockstep career ladders than ever before. Do these variables impede, accelerate, or stabilize development? Research is necessary to answer such questions.

Our conceptual model favors growth periods interspersed with stability periods, permitting an increased vulnerability to stress during transition periods. The model is one of building blocks and process enhancement favoring lifelong evolution.

IMPLICATIONS FOR TREATMENT

The systems perspective allows us to regard problems and dysfunctions as emanating from the system rather than from the intrapsychic problems of any one individual. Regardless of the nature of presenting problems, we must consider them in relation to an individual's personal, career, and family—both current and original—systems. No longer do we treat symptoms as arising solely from unresolved intrapsychic conflicts. Thus, an individual's symptoms can be viewed both as a response to stress within a system and a factor necessary to maintaining the balance of the system. In this view, the unit of treatment—the individual, couple, or family—is less important than the contexts or systems in which that unit functions.

Using developmental theory, we have come to consider life as a series of growth stages, each of which the individual and family must successfully negotiate in order to avoid stagnation and chronic crisis. Most individuals and families go through the same sequences and stages, although not necessarily at the same ages or rates of speed. Developmental theory helps us to predict when changes must occur and allows us to view people with symptoms as "stuck" rather than "sick." Change is most necessary at predictable times—for example, at birth, marriage, and death in the family life cycle; at the onset of independent living for the individual; and at retirement in the career life cycle. Developmental theory serves as an optimistic orientation in that it considers adults as competent, experienced participants in their own treatment, clients requiring guidance in enhancing their inherent control over their destiny and in growing, changing, and coping with their environment. In such a context, interventions are directed at optimal development rather than at the prevention of crisis or a return to a precrisis state. Adaptation to crises is viewed more as actualization than as adjustment, and therapy is seen as helping adults to "become" rather than to react to the environment.

How a human system copes with crisis is influenced by that system's structures and communication styles. Likewise, the nature of the particular developmental stage the human system, or systems, is in affects the system's structures and communication styles. Transition from one stage to another inevitably transforms system structures and communications; conversely, transformations in system structures and communications are requisites for successful developmental-stage negotiation.

"The ability to conceptualize the interrelationship between the system's present structure-communication functions and its longitudinal developmental challenges is the key to choosing effective and appropriate intervention strategies" (Okun and Rappaport, 1980, p. 29). The conceptual value of integrating systems and developmental theories is that it enables us to differentiate between predictable developmental crises in an individual or a family and dysfunctional patterns that lead to stagnation and symptom formation.

Goal of Treatment

In this view, then, the goal of treatment becomes the disruption of the system's homeostasis to enable adaptation to change to occur, resulting in the creation of a new homeostatic balance. Note that we are striving not to return to the old homeostatic balance—that is, to the precrisis state—but to a new, higher level homeostasis. We attempt to help individuals and families reassess themselves and their relationships as role transformations occur, and to reframe the crisis or transition that precipitated the symptom or problem.

Intervention

We can use our understanding of some of the directive, active, verbal, and nonverbal strategies and techniques from the field of family-systems therapy, social-learning theory, and cognitive theory to disrupt and shake up the system, making the old homeostatic mechanisms ineffective and forcing the system to renegotiate boundaries and change its communication patterns. In this work we can focus on an individual's self-differentiation and emotional separation from the family of origin.

The strategies we use may include teaching clear, differentiated communication skills and problem-solving skills and restructuring boundaries within and among systems using paradoxical and straight directives, behavioral techniques, cognitive restructuring, and so forth. By being active and directive, a therapist encourages positive interactions among system members rather than using him- or herself as an expert who provides a corrective emotional experience. Therapists can effect this strategy by taking the following steps:

1. Escalating the level of stress to set the usual homeostatic mechanisms;
2. Blocking the use of these homeostatic mechanisms;
3. Relabeling the problem;
4. Restructuring system members' interactions;
5. Assigning homework tasks to transfer the relationship changes occurring in the session to outside life.

Another aspect of intervention is education—that is, teaching the individual and family about adult and family development to convey the concept of developmental crisis as opposed to the pathological view. Such a goal might involve reframing the presenting problem within a developmental perspective. Thus, treatment can become a form of consultation wherein the counselor or therapist arranges new learning experiences (augmented by bibliotherapy and homework assignments) to help clients achieve some cognitive restructuring and to reassess their thinking and values. The objective would be to clarify responsible values and teach effective problem solving.

The major purpose of treatment is to identify and support natural healing processes to help individuals cope with change, crisis, and development. This broad view includes helping individuals to improve and expand their repertoire of communication, coping, and problem-solving skills, which in turn entails helping them move toward self-actualization. The intermediate steps are to aid clients in individuation and responsible decision making, and help them to master appropriate developmental tasks and to work through transitional crises. The underlying assumption is that people within systems have the resources and abilities to do what they need to do except when they are stuck.

Thus, the developmental view of preventive treatment helps us to use whatever strategies and techniques work for us in teaching adult clients to strengthen their coping skills, continually to adapt to change, and to understand their experience from a normative, developmental point of view. In subsequent chapters, we identify specific techniques and strategies relevant to the specific cases presented.

Counselor Attributes

Recently, some investigators have focused on the special concerns of working with adults. Schlossberg and Entine (1977, p. 77) argue that "counselors need to understand the dynamics of the decision making process, they need to be aware of the salient issues of adulthood, and they need to confront their own age bias" in order to work effectively with adults. Others have noted the importance of the ability to work with individuals as well as families, and to develop programs and to strive for social change. Obviously, counselors' self-awareness and openness to personal adulthood issues and experiences will enhance their effectiveness. To this end, counselors who develop systems-assessment skills that include the simultaneous analysis of individual characteristics and external occurrences, and of patterns of interrelationships between individuals and systems, will be able to formulate their own operational goals and interventions.

As increasing attention is paid to adult counseling issues, more training programs and conferences are being developed that attempt to close the gap between the growing body of research on adult development and the implications for treatment interventions.

SUMMARY

This chapter is an overview of developmental and systems theory contributing to a model that integrates individual, family, and career development from a systems perspective. A fundamental premise is that stages of development occur throughout adulthood and that individuals continue to grow and change from birth until death. While we have reason to believe that all adults attempt to go through the same stages of development, we know that age, sex, and cultural differences exist, though their impact is only assumed, since they have not been identified and studied thoroughly. Adult development is subject to variations along a number of lines, including cultural, class, racial, ethnic and sex roles. In addition, nonnormative marker events can have a critical effect on adult development.

The systems perspective helps us to understand that individual development influences the rate and quality of family and career development. In other words, circular or reciprocal relationships exist among the three domains. It is impossible to describe these interactions linearly—that is, as one influencing the other, which in turn influences the next, and so forth. A more accurate, if confusing, description might be this: individual development influences family development, which again influences individual development, which perhaps influences family development, which influences career development, which influences family development, and so forth.

It makes sense that radical cultural and social change will affect all systems, although different individuals might feel the impact in different domains and to varying degrees. However, it is safe to say that the effects of change on one aspect of life will indeed affect the other aspects.

This perspective as applied to the treatment of an individual, a couple, or a family system can result in a preventive, developmental viewpoint as opposed to the pathological, medical one. Growth, change, and crisis are viewed as healthy in this context. Thus, the goal of treatment becomes to facilitate the constant struggle between the needs of systems and subsystems to maintain homeostasis and to set new levels of homeostasis as adaptations and responses to change. Strategies and interventions from all the modalities of theory can be applied in this treatment. Thus, the counselor serves as an educator, a consultant, and an agent of change, helping individuals to feel more competent, autonomous, and unafraid.

REFERENCES

Baruch, G., Barnett, R., & Rivers, C. *Life prints*. New York: McGraw-Hill, 1983.

Blau, P. M., Gustad, J. W., Jessor, R., Parnes, H. S., & Wilcox, R. S. Occupational choice: A conceptual framework. *Industrial Labor Relations Review*, 1956, *9*, 531-543.

Bowen, M. The use of family theory in clinical practice. *Comprehensive Psychiatry*, 1966, 7, 345-374.

Bowen, M. Family therapy and family group therapy. In H. Kaplan, and B. Sadock (eds.), *Comparative group therapies*. Baltimore, Md.: Williams and Wilkins, 1975.

Bowen, M. *Family therapy and clinical practice*. New York: Aronson, 1978.

Bratcher, W. The influence of the family on career selection: A family systems perspective. *Personnel and Guidance Journal*, 1982, *61*, 87-92.

Brim, O. G., & Kagan, J. (eds.). *Constancy and change in human development*. Cambridge, Mass.: Harvard University Press, 1980.

Buhler, C., & Massarek, F. (eds.). *The course of human life. A study of goals in the humanistic perspective*. New York: Springer, 1968.

Danish, S. J. Life span development and intervention: A necessary link. *The Counseling Psychologist*, 1981, *9*, 40-44.

Dohrenwend, B. S., & Dohrenwend, B. P. Exemplification of a method for scaling life events: The peri life events scale. *Journal of Health and Social Behavior*, 1978, *19*, 205-229.

Erikson, E. *Childhood and society* (2nd ed.). New York: W. W. Norton, 1963.

Erikson, E. *Identity youth and crisis*. New York: W. W. Norton, 1968.

Erikson, E. *In search of common ground: Conversation with Erik Erikson and Huey P. Newton*. New York: W. W. Norton, 1973.

Erikson, E. (ed.). *Adulthood*. New York: W. W. Norton, 1978.

Freud, S. *An outline of psychoanalysis*. New York: W. W. Norton, 1949.

Gilligan, C. *In a different voice*. Cambridge, Mass.: Harvard University Press, 1982.

Gould, R. *Transformations*. New York: Simon and Schuster, 1978.

Haley, J. *Strategies of psychotherapy*. New York: Grune and Stratton, 1963.

Haley, J. *Problem-solving therapy*. San Francisco: Jossey-Bass, 1976.

Harrington, T. F. *Handbook of career planning for special need students*. Rockville, Md.: Aspen, 1982.

Holland, J. L. *Making vocational choices: A theory of careers*. Englewood Cliffs, N.J.: Prentice-Hall, 1973.

Holmes, J., & Rahe, S. A social adjustment scale. *Journal of Psychosomatic Research*, 1967, *11*, 213-218.

Jepson, D. A. The stage construct in career development. *Counseling and Values*. 1974, *18* (2) 124-131.

Jung, C. *Modern man in search of a soul*. New York: Harcourt Brace, 1933.

Jung, C. The stage of life. In Campbell, J. (ed.), *The Portable Jung*. New York: Viking Press, 1971.

Kantor, D., & Lehr, W. *Inside the family*. San Francisco: Jossey-Bass, 1975.

Kegan, R. *The evolving self*. Cambridge, Mass.: Harvard University Press, 1982.

Knefelkamp, L., & Slepitza, R. A cognitive-developmental model of career development. An adaptation of the Perry scheme. In J. Whitely and A. Resnikoff (eds.), *Career counseling.* Monterey, Calif.: Brooks/Cole, 1978.

Kohlberg, L. Stage and sequence: the cognitive-developmental approach to socialization. In D. Gaslin (ed.), *Handbook of socialization theory and research.* New York: Rand McNally, 1969.

Levinson, D. *The seasons of a man's life.* New York: Knopf, 1978.

Lowenthal, M. F., Thurnher, M., & Chiriboga, D. *Four stages of life.* San Francisco: Jossey-Bass, 1975.

McClelland, D. *Power: The inner experience.* New York: Irvington, 1975.

Miller, D. C., and Form, W. H. *Industrial sociology* (2nd ed.). New York: Harper & Row, 1964.

Minuchin, S. *Families and family therapy.* Cambridge, Mass.: Harvard University Press, 1974.

Minuchin, S., Montalvo, B., Guerney, B. G., Jr., Rosman, B. L., & Schumer, F. *Families of the slums.* New York: Basic Books, 1967.

Minuchin, S., Rosman, B. L., & Baker, L. *Psychosomatic families.* Cambridge, Mass.: Harvard University Press, 1978.

Minuchin, S., & Fishman, H. C. *Family therapy techniques.* Cambridge, Mass.: Harvard University Press, 1981.

Neugarten, B. *Personality in middle and late life.* New York: Atherton, 1964.

Neugarten, B. (ed.). *Middle age and aging,* Chicago: University of Chicago Press, 1968.

Neugarten, B. Time, age and the life cycle. *American Journal of Psychiatry,* 1979, *36,* 887-898.

Okun, B. F., & Rappaport, L. J. *Working with families.* No. Scituate, Mass.: Duxbury Press, 1980.

Perry, W. Jr. *Intellectual and ethical development in the college years.* New York: Holt, Rinehart and Winston, 1970.

Piaget, J. *The language and thought of the child.* London: Routledge and Kegan Paul, 1952.

Rogers, C. *On becoming a person.* Boston: Houghton Mifflin, 1961.

Rossi, A. S. Life span theories and women's lives. *Signs, Journal of Women in Culture and Society,* 1980, *6,* 1-24.

Satir, V. *Conjoint family therapy* (rev. ed.). Palo Alto: Science and Behavior Books, 1967.

Schein, E. H. *Career dynamics.* Reading, Mass.: Addison-Wesley, 1978.

Schlossberg, N. A model for analyzing human adaptation to transition. *The Counseling Psychologist,* 1981, *9,* 2-19.

Schlossberg, N. K., & Entine, A. D. (eds.). Counseling adults. *The Counseling Psychologist,* 1977, *6,* 2-78.

Seligman, D. Luck and careers. *Fortune.* November 16, 1981, 60-75.

Selye, H. *The stress of life.* New York: McGraw-Hill, 1956.

Selye, H. "Stress," *Intellectual Digest,* 1974, *4,* 43-46.

Super, D. E. *The psychology of careers.* New York: Harper and Brothers, 1957.

Super, D. E. The natural history of a study of lives and vocations. *Perspectives on Education,* 1969, *2,* 13-22.

Tiedeman, D. V., & O'Hara, R. P. *Career development. Choice and adjustment.* New York: College Entrance Examination Board, 1963.

Troll, L. E. Comments. *The Counseling Psychologist,* 1981, *9,* 46-49.

Vaillant, G. *Adaptation to life,* Boston: Little, Brown, 1977.

Vaillant, G., & McArthur, C. Natural history of male psychological health. *Seminars in Psychiatry,* 1972, *4,* 415-427.

von Bertalanffy, L. *Modern theories of development: An introduction to theoretical biology,* London: Oxford University Press, 1934.

von Bertalanffy, L. *General systems theory.* New York: Braziller, 1968.

Watzlawick, P., Beavin, J. H., & Jackson, D. D. *Pragmatics of human communication: A study of interactional patterns, pathologics, and paradoxes.* New York: Norton, 1967.

PART TWO

EARLY ADULTHOOD

On the surface it appears that young people are growing up faster today than ever before. Yet they are taking a much longer time to become what we call adults. They seem to be engaging earlier than former generations in what have heretofore been considered adult activities (for example, sex, drug and alcohol use, independent travel, and political and social activism) but owing to social, economic and technological factors, they often continue their educations and their financial and domestic dependencies well into their twenties. Many of today's young adults deliberately postpone establishing independent living arrangements, selecting and committing themselves to an occupation, and marrying and having children. Moreover, these days young adults commonly "drop out" or "have a fling" for a period after completing high school or college.

What is really happening in this transition to adulthood? In this part, we will explore the years of early adulthood, those roughly between ages 20 and 40. We can divide early adulthood into three stages: (1) youth, about 20 to 25, which is the transition between adolescence and adulthood; (2) young adulthood, the period between the mid-twenties and mid-thirties; (3) the mid-thirties transition, the period from the mid-thirties into the early forties. It is important to remember that our use of age cohorts is as general parameters. For example, a 24-year-old graduate student experiences early adulthood differently from a 24-year-old laborer who has a spouse and two young children.

In early adulthood, the two major developmental tasks are: (1) the formation of an integrated adult identity that allows for career, family, and other interpersonal-role commitments; and (2) the formation and maintenance of intimate relationships. The second task is hard to accomplish if the first has not been successfully resolved.

To form and implement an adult identity, one must engage in realistic self-assessment regarding one's own interests, abilities, and needs, and develop consistent value and belief systems based on one's own internalized morality. The process of identity formation is ongoing throughout adult life, but the basic foundation to the process is built during adolescence and becomes stronger throughout early adulthood. Individuals must form their identity before they can sustain mature intimate relationships.

Chapter 3 covers the stages, tasks, and issues of individual development as they relate to the biological, social, and emotional aspects of the life cycle. Chapter 4 focuses on the early stages of the family life cycle, and Chapter 5 on the stages, tasks, and issues in the early part of the career-development cycle. Chapter 6 presents case studies and implications for treatment in early adulthood.

CHAPTER THREE

INDIVIDUAL DEVELOPMENT IN EARLY ADULTHOOD

The transition between adolescence and early adulthood is extremely complex and often fraught with turbulence. As a result, it is difficult to know exactly when adolescence ceases and adulthood begins. No physiological marker events, such as puberty for adolescence, signify the onset of adulthood. One moment a young person may appear to behave like an adult, and the next moment he or she will behave like a child. Much of the transition between adolescence and adulthood is uncharted, confusing, and widely variable among individuals. In fact, until recently the transition was expected to occur overnight and to be accomplished simply by passing into legal majority. Legal adulthood was 21 for many years and has only recently been lowered to 18. Clearly our expectations regarding adulthood are guided by chronological age, since today 18-year-olds are afforded the same legal and social privileges and responsibilities formerly denied them. Often, the expectations of parents, youngsters, and society conflict. In any case, chronological age cannot be the magic event that determines adulthood, and the distinction between adolescence and early adulthood is indeed vague.

This chapter explores the transition into early adulthood as well as the developmental stages, tasks, and issues of the first two decades of adulthood, the twenties and the thirties. Briefly, these include the process of identity formation; the influences of social, economic, and technological factors; and the crises, challenges, and potentials that characterize this part of the life cycle. By *identity* we mean one's self-concept—that is, the roles one chooses and the unique attributes one perceives in oneself. We also discuss the development of intimate relationships and the relation of this process to identity formation.

The chapter reflects two major themes: (1) that the phases of adolescence, youth, young adulthood and the mid-thirties transition involve coping with certain tasks; and (2) that these tasks are cumulative and are never completely resolved, but recycle throughout the life span.

Some specific questions covered in the chapter are these:

1. What kind of process is identity formation?
2. What variables influence adult identity formation?
3. What variables influence the development of intimate relationships?
4. What are the major needs and issues for young adults?
5. How do physiological and sex-role variables affect young adults?

Our discussion of early adulthood begins with a survey of the major developmental tasks and issues of late adolescence. For people who have not resolved these issues, emergence into early adulthood will be delayed regardless of the passage of chronological years.

LATE ADOLESCENCE

Late adolescence usually refers to the late teen years. However, like earlier adolescence, this period of development is characterized by contradictions and extremism, often manifested in shifts in the intensity of relationships and abrupt swings between over- and underfunctioning. The adolescent also has wide mood swings: for example, sudden inexplicable bursts of high energy followed by unhappiness, sluggish apathy, helplessness, hopelessness, and boredom. Adolescents typically vacillate between contempt for and idealization of their parents and other authority figures. Parents of college students often report receiving desperate, depressing phone calls from their youngsters, who say they are feeling helpless and hopeless, and are likely to flunk out at any time; those are followed twenty-four hours later, after the parents experience anxiety and concern, by phone calls expressing total unconcern on the part of the offspring. Two terms that characterize this entire period of development are *ambiguity* and *conflict*.

Clinicians commonly report high incidences of depression, suicide, and drug and alcohol abuse in this age range, rates that appear to increase as society becomes more complex. Values are in flux and youngsters are no longer confident that education or work have any real meaning. Families and other social institutions such as religious organizations, schools, and communities themselves are continually changing and no longer provide the stable influences previous genera-tions experienced. Colleges and universities find that their "hot line" services are used with a desperate frequency. Youngsters in late adolescence, who look like adults and who are extremely competent in their studies and/or their work, may be inwardly confused and disconcerted by rapid mood shifts, persistent feelings of inferiority and loneliness, and brave attempts to achieve mastery in interpersonal relationships and over environmental obstacles. How much of this anomie results from internal conflict and how much from legitimate environmental factors is open to speculation.

Erikson (1963, pp. 262–263) states that "the adolescent mind is essentially a mind of the moratorium, a psychosocial stage between childhood and adulthood, and between the morality learned by the child, and the ethics to be developed by the adult." In order to pass successfully through this adolescent stage, Erikson feels that one needs to form the basis of an ego identity, to identify the "me" in relation to the "me" others perceive and the "me" of childhood dreams. Erikson's work forms the foundation for the commonly accepted views of adolescent development.

A significant part of this identity-formation process requires *individuation,* the separating of one's self from one's family system and forming one's identity on the basis of one's own values, beliefs, and experiences rather than simply adopt-ing the dreams of one's parents. The process of detaching oneself psychologically from parental authority, from what were really one's first love bonds, is indeed the most critical and agonizing part of the adolescent's work and lays the ground-work for future development. The adolescent may indeed adopt his or her par-ents' values and beliefs, but to truly individuate he or she must choose these values and beliefs freely rather than accepting them blindly. Remember that the adolescent is experiencing physical and mental transformations of dizzying pro-portions while enduring the loss and pain of separation. As Scarf (1980) states, "an adult, lacking the flexibility of the adolescent's unformed ego, might become psychotic if confronted with so many demands for change, all happening at once!" (p. 21).

Let us consider Erikson's fifth stage, identity versus role confusion, as the foundation for our understanding of adolescent development and early adulthood development.

IDENTITY FORMATION

The adolescent is faced with rapid physical, biochemical, and emotional changes as well as increasing social expectations for adult behavior and achievements. Thus, the adolescent has to learn to contend with changes in physical appearance, abilities, feelings, and roles all at once. Often we see these changes reflected in adolescents' increasingly uncontrolled emotionalism, self-consciousness, egocen-trism, or narcissism. As previously noted, adolescents can appear to function as adults one moment and as children the next. Reason and emotion, rationality and irrationality, are constantly juxtaposed.

Somehow, all these changes must be integrated with one's previously held child identity. By the end of adolescence, the youngster has to have made some tentative decisions about how he or she will conduct his or her life after high school regarding education, work, military service, marriage, and so on. Though such decisions are indeed provisional, they reflect at least some choices, either conscious or unconscious, regarding "who am I?" and "who do I want to become?"

> The growing and developing youths, faced with this physiological revolution within them, and with tangible adult tasks ahead of them are now primarily concerned with what they appear to be in the eyes of others as compared with what they feel they are, and with the question of how to connect the roles and skills cultivated earlier with the occupational prototypes of the day. In their search for a new sense of continuity and sameness, adolescents have to refight many of the battles of earlier years, even though to do so they must artificially appoint perfectly well-meaning people to play the roles of adversaries; and they are ever ready to install lasting idols and ideas as guardians of a final identity [Erikson, 1963, p. 261].

Over the years, this writer has asked college freshmen, college seniors, graduate students, and adults at different ages to answer spontaneously the question "Who am I?" The answer has differed, depending on developmental stage. The college freshman typically answers with assumed assuredness (for example, "I am a student," "I am a freshman," or "I am an 18-year-old man"). The college senior answers with uncertainty, reflecting the growing confusion that accompanies the process of working through the identity-formation process (for example, "I think I am a person who isn't sure what will be next year," or "I am a person who wants to find a job working with people").

Adolescents need to do much testing out of family and other authority in order to discover who they are themselves. Parents often wonder how they could have failed to teach their youngsters some form of impulse control, values, and responsibility. Those adolescents whose family and school systems do not permit such testing out may either have to delay this process or go to unusual lengths in acting out. This inevitable process must occur at some time (with or without turbulence) if growth is to ensue.

Role confusion, the opposite of ego identity, occurs when the adolescent is so overwhelmed by changes and possibilities that a firm identity is never attained. This state is apparent in some young people who are unable to determine who they are, and who go through early adulthood searching and seeking, trying new roles, and inevitably experiencing confusion and disappointment. Such individuals might change majors and/or jobs frequently and might enter and leave relationships with great frequency. They are always looking for "the right thing," the right person or job that will tell them who they are. We will see that dualistic thinking (right versus wrong) is characteristic of late adolescence and can persist into adulthood if development is retarded.

The process.   The process of identity formation continues throughout the life cycle, though the foundation is laid during adolescence. We will see as we go through the adult life cycle that each transition contains a reassessment and reformulation of identity. However, there has to be an initial identity to reassess and reformulate. The initial adolescent identity seems to develop from the integration and synthesis of self-concept, feedback from significant others, and educational, childhood, and adolescent experiences. Later identity reassessments are more heavily influenced by first-hand life experiences and intimate relationships. The adolescent identity-formation process is a period of heightened self-consciousness and reflexive introspection as the adolescent searches to answer the question "Who am I?"

The cognitive processes required for identity formation have been developing since birth but only reach a maturity appropriate for this task during adolescence. The work of Piaget (1964, 1965, 1969) elucidates this cognitive development, which involves shifts in the process by which one perceives and reasons about the world. Piaget postulates that at some time during adolescence, one begins to be able to solve problems objectively through forming propositions, hypothesis-testing, abstract reasoning, and combinatorial thinking. Piaget calls this stage of cognitive development *formal operations,* because it allows for relativistic, pluralistic thinking and complex abstract problem solving. The process of identity formation involves continuous and complex questioning, the exploration of alternate possibilities for adult life—in terms of career and family—and the development of new skills with which to meet the challenges of adult life.

Kimmel (1974) describes the identity formation process as "one in which the *I* succeeds in bringing a sense of consistency, continuity and wholeness out of the mass of *mes* that others respond to in social interaction . . . this integration could not arise in the sense of a fully formed identity prior to the development of intellectual mastery of abstract thought and sexual maturation . . ." (pp. 111–112). What we are emphasizing here is that biological and cognitive development are necessary for dealing with the psychosocial issues of late adolescence.

Perry (1970) has postulated a cognitive-development theory of college-age students based on research conducted with Harvard undergraduates from 1954–1968. His studies clarify the changes that college students seem to undergo intellectually and ethically over the four years and show the relationship of identity and intellectual development. He describes the students' cognitive processes as occurring in a series of nine "positions." Each position represents a qualitatively different mode of thinking about the nature of knowledge. Gordon (1981) simplifies Perry's nine positions into the following four stages:

1. *Dualism.* The student enters college with a simplistic approach to reasoning, perceiving counselors or teachers as authority figures with the right answers (regarding choosing a college major, say, or determining the major reasons for the decline of the Roman Empire). Little self-processing is evident at this stage, and students' perceptions of the world are absolute.

2. *Multiplicity.* Students begin to take more responsibility for their own learning, although they are still controlled by external forces such as parents, peers, faculty, and job market. They are concerned now with the possibilities of right or wrong decisions and they turn to counselors or advisors to eliminate anxiety. Multiplistic students acknowledge that evaluating all choices is part of the decision-making process.

3. *Relativism.* Students are able to synthesize diverse and complex elements of reasoning. They make decisions and are in charge of their own lives. Their life

choices are tailored to their own needs and interests and uncertainty is accepted as legitimate.

4. *Commitment*. This occurs later. These students accept a pluralistic world and make commitments to a certain area to establish an identity. They have a sense of being themselves.

Students may delay this development by temporizing, retreating, or escaping.

Like Piaget, Perry believes that growth occurs when students encounter the real world and experience conflict between their assumptions and their real-world experiences. The student's homeostatic balance is upset, causing disequilibrium and requiring him or her to accommodate to changes. How Perry's model applies to noncollege youth is not clear.

Kohlberg's work (1971) focuses on how people reason about the moral issues and decisions in their lives. He postulates that they move from egocentrism through sociocentrism to allocentrism as they move through the hierarchical stages of preconventional, conventional, and postconventional, or principled, moral reasoning. College-age students usually operate in the conventional stage, which means that they are seeking approval and obeying the rules of the social order. In other words, they are oriented toward showing respect for authority and maintaining social order for social order's sake.

The above-mentioned theories are important because they emphasize cognitive development during late adolescence and youth. The ability to seek and process information is necessary for effective decision making.

Identity statuses.   Considerable research has been conducted with college students on Erikson's identity concept. Marcia (1966, 1967, 1968, 1976) describes four types of identity statuses. The first is positive and the latter three are negative:

1. *Identity achieving:* Those who have been able to critically evaluate parental influences regarding occupation, religion, and politics, and have been able to take a firm personal stand that may or may not be consistent with that of their parents. They have strong egos and stable self-definition. Their interpersonal relationships are effective and their self-appraisal realistic. These students have resolved their identity crises and have made commitments to an occupation and an ideology.

2. *Foreclosure:* When the young person avoids confrontation on controversial issues and acquiesces to the parents' views either because of fear of disapproval or rejection or through introjection of parental standards. These people are usually accommodating and eager to please, and thereby they avoid conflicts or risks. They tend to be overly self-critical but at the same time are unrealistic in their self-appraisal and often set unrealistic goals.

3. *Moratoriums:* Wherein one is preoccupied with identity issues but unable to make any decisions or commitments. These people have many unresolved questions and vacillate in their experimenting behaviors. They tend to be extremist and like to challenge and change the system. They are not controlled or influenced by others and are unpredictable.

4. *Identity diffuse:* Where chronic indecision and lack of interest prevent one from achieving a firm identity. These people want to do only what feels good and they remove themselves from crises or confrontation. They appear to be opportunistic and are easily influenced, which leads to interpersonal problems. They have the least amount of basic trust.

Marcia believes that the process of identity formation involves two factors: (1) crises, requiring choices among alternatives, and (2) arrival at investment and commitment to whatever choices are made.

This research has been followed up with several other studies on college-age men and women (Podd, 1972; Waterman and Waterman, 1974; Schenkel and Marcia, 1972; Toder and Marcia, 1974; Schenkel, 1975; Orlofsky, 1977; Waterman and Nevid, 1977; Munro and Adams, 1977; Marcia, 1980). Gender differences have not really been resolved. However, Marcia (1980) suggests that identity resolution takes longer for women because of their two contradictory roles, as glamorous, socially attractive female, and as achiever. Men may take longer to resolve intimacy crises. These identity statuses are not types, but rather styles. They characterize the process of coping with the identity crisis in adolescence, and we do not know whether or not they generalize to adult identity processes. We do know from clinical experience that they are related to how one goes about the task of separating from one's family of origin and that those adults who have not worked through the identity formation process will have to do so at one time or another before being able to cope with adult developmental tasks. Thus, a crucial property of identity is the sense of individual separateness and uniqueness.

Developmental Tasks

To recapitulate, the major task for late adolescents is to begin to make some decisions reflecting the formation of a basic ego identity. Thus, late adolescents have to plan their lives following high school graduation, an inevitable marker event. They must decide what to do next, where and how to live, and with whom; what relationships to relinquish, maintain, or pursue; what decisions and powers are rightfully theirs; and what the ethical and moral values are that will guide these decisions.

Today's late adolescent has to make some conscious decisions about sex roles. Currently, the concept of androgyny is receiving a great deal of media attention. A large part of the identity-formation process includes decisions about which sex-role stereotypes to adopt, reject, or modify. Until recently, females were socialized to formulate their identity based on intimate relationships; it is more commonly accepted today for females to be socialized to formulate their identity prior to forming an intimate attachment. However, as Gilligan (1982) and Kegan (1982) point out, separation and attachment are both necessary for development, and males and females probably do not progress at the same levels or in the same order.

For those who continue their education, these decisions may involve which college or university to apply to, which courses to take, which major to adopt, whether or not to live on campus and with or without a roommate, whether or not to work, how to arrange for financial support, and how to maintain family involvement. Those who enter directly into the labor market must cope with the realities of job searches in an employment market unresponsive to youth, and with entry-level salaries, living arrangements and relationships. All adolescents have to renegotiate their relationships with their immediate families, their extended families, their high school peers, their neighbors, and other significant people from childhood. Further, they must begin to deal with new situations, new people, new demands, and new experiences. They are expected to behave more independently and more self-sufficiently than formerly and to be able to take some responsibility for the consequences of their actions. Finally, they are expected to have internalized moral values that will guide their decision-making processes.

We can conclude, then, that late adolescence is a period of experimentation, where one can hypothesize and conform to or deviate from society's dictates in order to test both the reactions of family and peers and the workability of the shaky identity formulations that have been tentatively arrived at. Some late adolescents in college or within an institutionalized structure such as the military have more latitude for trial-and-error experimentation than do those who are working and supporting themselves and their families.

Developmental Issues

Issues that late adolescents continue to address include sexuality, drugs, alcohol, and intimacy. People approach and deal with these issues in various ways throughout adolescence. For example, a young adolescent may begin drinking in order to go along with the peer group, and in late adolescence may continue to drink because she "feels better and more comfortable with others" when drinking and because she feels "the need to drink." Late adolescents may be every bit as confused as the early adolescent about such issues, but owing to increased freedom from restraints, they are expected to take responsibility for deciding what to do about them. Typically, late adolescents are treated differently from early adolescents for drunk driving by both their parents and the courts.

Intimacy issues begin to emerge at this time, particularly in relation to the process of separation from parents. Often, adolescents attempt to replace the primary parental attachments with relationships or series of relationships that appear to be characterized by "instant intimacy." In other words, many of these initial intimate relationships are based more on the need to replace the loss of attachment to the parents, the need to be involved in a close relationship, than on the mutual desire to be together for sharing of selves. People who find themselves locked into such a relationship during the late-adolescent period often realize later that they put themselves into a "moratorium" position and missed out on a great deal of learning about the development of intimate relationships.

Table 3-1 shows the major tasks and issues of late adolescence. These are extensions of earlier adolescent tasks and issues as well as forerunners of the tasks and issues to be achieved in youth.

TABLE 3-1. Late adolescence

Developmental Tasks	General Issues	Requisite Skills	Significant Others
Identity Formation			
Make provisional career, living, and educational decisions	Individuation Separation from family Internalized morality Self-sufficiency Sex-role clarification	Abstract thinking Problem solving Initial decision making Specific educational and career skills	Peers Family of origin School/work personnel Community members
Initial Intimacy			
Develop and maintain new heterosexual and same-sex relationships Let go of outdated relationships Renegotiate existing relationships	Relationships Sexuality Substance-abuse	Social skills Interpersonal skills Beginning conflict-resolution skills	Family of origin Old peers New peers—varied ages School/work personnel Community members

Once one's sense of self has sufficiently developed so that a core self exists that is uniquely one's own, then one can begin interacting with others in more intimate social interactions without fear of losing one's self in the other. During adolescence, people use others to increase their understanding and clarify their perceptions of themselves. In late adolescence, people are able to relate to others and see the world from others' perspectives. It is at this stage that one enters what we call youth.

YOUTH

Youth has been defined by Keniston (1971) as the middle period between adolescence and adulthood, the period when one has a stable sense of self (as opposed to the adolescent's seeking identity) but is still searching for comfortable vocational and social roles. In other words, youths are still searching for the road to take. Levinson (1978) calls this period early adulthood transition, and places it at ages 17–22. Here we consider the period of youth to fall between the late teens and mid-twenties. Youth is a period characterized by tension and ambivalence about traditional practices and values versus individualism and by a continuous struggle to try acting out the tentative decisions reached during adolescence.

Levinson (1978) refers to the critical importance of this period, stating that the process of entering adulthood is more lengthy and complex than has usually been imagined. In fact, he believes that it may take about fifteen years to emerge from adolescence, to find a place in adult society, and to commit oneself to a stable life. This implies that we need to change our expectations for members of this age group, recognizing that they are in a state of transition rather than actual adulthood. In fact, rigid expectations of adult behavior of youngsters in this stage of development result more frequently in depression and other symptoms than just about any other variable. Increasingly, college seniors, for example, are so bewildered and confused both about options and courses of action after college and about their parents' expectations that they immediately commit themselves to a career path and a stable social life.

As previously noted, many young people experience this stage of development in college or in the military service, systems that allow for further seeking, testing out, and experimentation with identity formulation. Some students go on to graduate school merely to extend this structure and context. For those young people who go straight from high school into the world of work and/or marriage, the transition from adolescence into adulthood may be abruptly and forcefully truncated. The result could be premature commitments and the undertaking of adult tasks too early, leading to other problems and issues. Premature decisions are sometimes violently reversed and overturned in later life. It is not uncommon to hear adults in their thirties and forties bitterly bemoan the fact that they had entered the adult world too quickly, without taking a period of time to explore who they were and what they really wanted to do with their lives.

Only in the past two or three decades have we come to understand development as a process. We have further realized that the transition between adolescence and adulthood does not occur automatically within a limited time period but, in fact, lasts well into the twenties and involves many trial-and-error explorations and many developmental fluctuations. Youth's ego identity is still fragile and tentative, and youths are still in the process of separating from their families and attempting to develop intimate relationships with peers.

Gould (1978) calls the age period between 16 and 22 "Leaving Our Parents' World." He says that the major false assumption of this age is "I'll always belong to my parents and believe in their world" and suggests that component false assumptions needing to be challenged and mastered are: (1) if I get any more independent, it will be a disaster; (2) I can see the world only through my parents' assumptions; (3) only my parents can guarantee my safety; (4) my parents must be my only family; and (5) I don't own my own body (pp. 47–48). Gould sees the major developmental task at this stage to be achieving physical, emotional, economic, and intellectual independence from one's parents. One learns to live away from home, to have satisfying emotional relationships outside the family, and to manage one's own finances while preparing for a full-time job or actually working. One also learns to think rationally and self-sufficiently.

Levinson (1978) posits that the developmental tasks of this early-adult transition (ages 17–22) are to resolve the issues of adolescence—namely, dependency— and to establish self-reliance. This includes formulation of what he calls a "dream"—that is, "a vision or an imagined possibility that generates excitement and vitality" (p. 91). This dream guides the occupational decision-making process and early attempts to develop potentially significant emotional relationships separate from one's family and the society in which one was raised. Levinson points out how important it is for clinicians to recognize developmental issues as distinct from psychopathology so as not to place young patients into a psychiatric sick-role identity.

Gilligan (1982) discusses the sex-role differences in terms of attachment and separation, the anchors of the life cycle. Males are socialized to separate emotionally in order to achieve a separate identity and to define and empower the self. Women are socialized to define themselves through intimate relationships, since the ongoing process of attachment creates and sustains human development. Thus, women are more likely to experience conflict between integrity and caring, attachment and separation, and helplessness and power. Women tend to describe relationships when asked to describe themselves, whereas men tend to describe power and achievements. These differences are reflected in developmental theory: for men, identity is seen as preceding intimacy and generativity in the optimal cycle of human separation and attachment, whereas for women these tasks are seen as fused. Furthermore, women are defined as deviant in a man's life cycle. Using "male" norms, women's behavior is labeled as deviant—the same behavior would be considered normal for men. Contemporary young women do indeed receive double messages about the norms for their development, and this lack of clarity results in stress-related symptoms. It is critical that we keep these sex differences in mind as we consider the developmental tasks and issues posited for youth and young adults.

Remember, youths are special—they have a unique psychology and subculture and this is sometimes very threatening to older adults (Gould, 1975). Youths are more open to new ideas about the world and are less repressive than older adults. Perhaps this is due to the tentative nature of their ego identity at this period in their lives.

Developmental Tasks

The two major developmental tasks of youth parallel those in late adolescence: (1) identity stabilization and (2) intimacy development.

Identity.   Stabilization of ego identity remains a critical task of youth. This process involves deepening one's perception of oneself as having a clearly defined self, distinct from others. In youth, the sense of self seems to fluctuate less than during the adolescent stage of development. Thus, consistency begins to characterize one's ego identity, and this trait is reflected in role commitments. Such commitments in turn lead to an increasing selectivity of experience, and social reinforcement and social interactions thus confirm the developing sense of identity. The implication is that other identities, which earlier might have seemed attractive, become less appealing as experience reinforces one's chosen roles and aspects of self. As youths explore the adult world, and participate more deeply in adult roles, they make decisions about styles of participation and combinations of roles.

For example, many of the decisions that youths make regarding lifestyle, relationships, and work are modified as a result of actual experiences "in the real world," and exposure to new people, values, and opportunities. Frequently, youths are embarrassed by the incongruity between their late-adolescent illusions and the decisions they make based on post-adolescent experiences.

The dream.   Levinson (1978) asserts that defining a dream of adult accomplishment is significant to the identity stabilization of male youths. This process involves identifying and articulating one's vision of one's self-in-the-adult-world, in terms of imagined possibilities in all aspects of life—individual, family, and work. This dream serves as a basis for the decisions one will make during early adulthood and becomes a reference point for the later assessment and evaluation of one's life.

While research about women's dreams is still under way, clinicians have found that women have traditionally dreamed about becoming wives and mothers and about implementing their husbands' dreams. More recently, women appear to dream about becoming "Super Woman," combining career, marriage, and parenthood smoothly and effectively.

Ellen Goodman (1981) describes this current female dream in her witty formulation of a typical day in the life of Super Woman: she gets up at 7 A.M. with her 2.3 children and prepares for them a Grade A, nutritionally balanced breakfast which they eat without a complaint. At 8 A.M. the children leave for school, perfectly groomed and without forgetting anything. Super Woman goes upstairs and gets dressed in her $600 Ann Klein suit and goes off to her $50,000-a-year creative, interesting, and socially useful job. At 5:00, she returns home for an hour of meaningful interaction with her children (everyone knows that quality is more important than quantity). At 6 P.M., she goes into the kitchen and whips up a Julia Child gourmet dinner. At the dinner table, the family discusses the international monetary fund without any arguments. After dinner, when the dishes are done and the children are upstairs doing their homework and preparing for bed, Super Woman devotes herself to her significant relationship with her husband. At 9 P.M. she goes upstairs and puts on a beautiful negligee and is multiply orgasmic until midnight, at which point she goes to sleep to prepare for tomorrow, another day!

Clinicians can attest to the devastating effects attempts to implement this dream can have on young women. Clients are often paralyzed by the overwhelming expectations they have of themselves, and this paralysis in turn naturally affects their relationships and career development, which in turn affect and are affected by their self-identities. Today's young women are really in a vise, attempting to develop their own achievement dreams simultaneously with developing intimacy and helping their chosen mates achieve their dreams.

The dreams working-class women have may be about achieving the very same full-time housewife/mother lifestyle that more highly educated career-oriented women are attempting to leave behind. Many working-class women work for economic reasons, not for "fulfillment" or "self-actualization."

Intimacy.   The development of intimate relationships becomes an increasingly critical issue as youths move toward adulthood. This is reflected in the need of youths to reach out to others and to develop a sense of closeness. Again, these new relationships replace their attachments to their families of origin. During this transitional period, people spend more time than before in attempting to develop intimate relationships.

Kimmel (1974) thoughtfully declares that feedback from these intimate social relationships influences identity development and that, likewise, identity development influences intimate relationships. In other words, there is a reciprocal influence between these two processes, particularly at this vulnerable stage of development. If one is successful in one's attempt to develop intimate relationships, one's self-concept encompasses the ability to give and receive caring. If one is unable to develop intimate relationships, a significant component in one's self-concept might be the inability to achieve intimate relationships. The latter can lead to a self-fulfilling prophecy. Consider the following case: John was unsuccessful in his adolescent attempts to develop and maintain intimate relationships with young women. As a youth, he does not perceive himself as capable of achieving a meaningful relationship with a woman, and viewed himself as unattractive and socially awkward. Now, he is so eager to prove to himself that he can be "one of the boys" and have a "good relationship" that he attempts intensely to develop relationships with whomever he thinks might be available and always ends up feeling rejected and disappointed. In fact, his intensity and eagerness to rush into a relationship distances the very women he wishes to attract. As this cycle is repeated over and over, his identity and intimacy issues become more and more intertwined.

Sexuality.   Youth typically involves a series of attempts to establish intimate relationships. Often during this period intimacy is confused with sexuality. Having a sexual relationship with someone does not imply an intimate relationship. Intimacy exists when one has reached the level of cognitive and moral development necessary for beginning to empathize with others' needs and for expressing care and concern for others. Those who have yet to reach this level still see others as extensions of themselves and as providing gratification for their own needs and desires. The developmental process involves the development of mutuality in sexuality, which not only affirms one's identity but also leads one closer to the attainment of intimacy.

Youths who marry right after high school may attempt to develop the capacity for mature intimacy with a spouse during this period. Whether this development requires a series of relationships or can be accomplished within the context of one relationship, the ability to develop and maintain a mature intimate relationship that includes mature sexuality is a process that takes many years. Thus, sexuality begins to mature during this stage but usually does not fully mature until later phases of early adulthood. Chickering (1969, 1973) points out that one's ability to relate to others shifts from symbiosis, where two people are alike and differences are not tolerated, to shared mutual interaction, where individual differences are valued and respected.

The process of developing intimacy is further explored in the section on young adulthood, when it becomes the paramount developmental task. Suffice it to say here that in youth the first earnest attempts occur to develop and maintain intimate relationships based on mutuality rather than on narcissism and the replacement of parental love bonds.

Developmental Issues

Many issues are associated with the developmental tasks that occupy the time and energy of youth. Some of these issues are extensions of adolescent issues and some emerge with impending adulthood.

Autonomy.   Achieving autonomy remains one of the most critical issues for youth. Although autonomy is traditionally based on male norms, the women's movement has influenced women to seek similar autonomy. And the increase in divorce has, indeed, forced many women to seek autonomy whether or not they desire it.

The term *autonomy* refers to a mature type of independence. The autonomous individual can live without the constant reassurance, approval, and affection that was needed in earlier stages, can solve daily problems and function without reminders and support, and can ask for help when it is needed and help others when appropriate. In other words, autonomy is the ability to stand on one's own feet and take care of one's needs without imposing or detracting from someone else's needs and without requiring undue propping and support.

Most youths go through periods in which they can function autonomously, reverting to more dependent behaviors during critical periods. It is not unusual for a youth to return home for nurturance and protection when recovering from a disappointing love affair or unsuccessful work experience. The process of developing autonomy is gradual, not sudden; eventually, the critical periods requiring excessive support from others lessen in frequency and intensity.

People usually make progress in separating from their families of origin during this phase, but how this separation is experienced depends as much on the family system's developmental issues as on the individual's developmental issues (see Chapter 12). For example, if the family system is comfortable with the tasks and issues of the launching stage and has facilitated the self-differentiation and individuation of its members, then the parents may actually aid and encourage the youth's separation. On the other hand, a family that fears this individuation may use subtle and not so subtle maneuvers to retain a youth within the system and to prevent this necessary separation.

The issue of autonomy, then, in part involves both individuation and alienation with regard to family and cultural mores. During the stage of youth, many people need to rebel against and react against conventional lifestyles in order to test out their identity hypotheses and seek places where they feel individuated. Alienation may be necessary to stabilize ego identity. For example, a young man may refuse to enter the family business as expected by his parents and may ignore his educational training and go off to a rural area to build houses. Whereas his parents may regard this course as an extreme rejection of their values and expectations, the whole process may well be necessary to their son—in determining who he is and what he wants to do in life.

Values and morals.   The issues of autonomy and alienation are strongly affected by one's clarification of values and morals. Youths need to reconcile competing values from competing influences so they can commit themselves to their own value and belief systems.

As mentioned earlier, Kohlberg (1969) suggests a paradigm of moral development, based on Piaget's scheme of cognitive development, that is composed of six stages:

1. Morality as punishment and obedience;

2. Morality as consisting of acts that are satisfying to self and occasionally to others;
3. Morality as maintaining good relationships and gaining approval of others;
4. Morality as showing respect for authority and maintaining social order for the sake of social order;
5. Morality as the acceptance of democratically contracted laws;
6. Morality as individual principles of conscience that govern one's behavior regardless of others' reactions.

The work of Piaget and Kohlberg indicates youth's potential for a high level of abstract moral philosophy, influenced, of course, by personal experiences, inputs of significant others, and the process of identity formation. A correlation seems to exist between levels of individuation, autonomy, and Kohlberg's progression of individual morality.

Gilligan (1982) believes that moral development occurs differently in women than in men in that the former are more likely to try to change the rules than sacrifice relationships to them. Men, on the other hand, in abiding by rules, depict relationships as easily replaceable. Thus, women see moral dilemmas in terms of conflicting personal responsibilities. Their initial moral concerns are first with survival, then with goodness, and later with a reflective understanding of care.

It is during the stage of youth that one is really held accountable for one's decisions and actions. One can no longer blame one's parents or other authority institutions for one's values and morals. In other words, youths are of legal age and are held responsible and accountable for the consequences of their choices and behavior. Thus, whether or not they adopt, overthrow, or modify the values and morals with which they were raised, they must still decide on their own morals and values at this time and take responsibility for their choices and actions.

Career choices.   Making initial job and career choices and developing the competencies to implement these choices is a process accentuated during the youth period. These competencies may be developed in entry-level job experiences, apprenticeships, or through appropriate coursework or training programs. Youths wrestle with these choices knowing that what they are doing at this stage can open or limit future options and possibilities. (This process is further elaborated in Chapter 5.)

Interests.   Another issue for youth involves the deepening of interest in activities that will affect avocational and vocational choices. Such interests may involve sports, hobbies, cultural activities, family activities, and solitary or group activities. A trend is exhibited at this time away from fleeting involvements and toward deeper commitments to fewer interests. Kimmel (1974) states that "first a person undertakes some activity which in some sense intrigues the individual; second, satisfying consequences follow from the activity; third, feelings of competence and skill also follow, which are themselves satisfying; and fourth, these feelings lead to even greater interest and deeper involvement" (p. 92). Thus, the interests of youth relate to the identity-stabilization process. As these interests crystallize, they both influence and are influenced by one's identity.

Time.   Time management becomes important for youth, since allowing for the development of different aspects of life and laying the foundation for a later balance of self, work, and family gain importance. Away from parental supervision and later from the school structure, youths frequently stumble as they learn to budget their time for study, work, play, and relationships, and still retain some time and space for their individual selves. Many college freshmen flunk out due to their inability to manage their time properly and to accomplish the required academic tasks.

Youths often have trouble managing the time structures in the work place after enjoying the freedom of the home or school. In this respect, youths may require some further values clarification and decision making with regard to their career path. Industrial management has become increasingly aware of the time-management issue, noting a marked abuse of absentee policies and disregard of daily hours on the part of the so-called "me generation" as it enters the labor force.

Another aspect of time to be considered involves the perspective youth takes on time itself. During this period, people typically feel that adulthood stretches out interminably and that time passes very slowly, permitting one to try different things, and to develop and implement one's dream. In fact, youths often seem unaffected by the passage of time and the aging process, much to the frustration of older adults.

Interpersonal relationships.   Youths form peer relationships with both sexes of various backgrounds and ages as they expand adolescent relationships. During adolescence, in contrast, most peer relationships are formed within a single age range and geographical location. The period of youth may be the first opportunity for expanding one's social network on one's own volition (rather than through accident—for example, with whomever happens to be one's roommate or live in one's dormitory). Again, a reciprocal influence occurs between the stabilization of identity and interpersonal relationships: interpersonal experiences affect values clarification and decisions just as one's values and decisions affect the range and types of people with whom one becomes involved.

As young adults, people renegotiate their relationships with their families and with other adults of both sexes, relating with maturity rather than as children. Youth is a time for letting go of outgrown relationships and developing new relationships of varying styles and at varying levels of intimacy. As one enters the world of work, one learns to develop congeniality in work relationships, casual relationships, and deeper relationships.

Authority relationships.   Learning to relate to authorities as a young adult rather than as a rebellious adolescent may cause difficulties. Despite the freedoms from restraint that adulthood implies, adults still need to be able to negotiate relationships with authority figures at work, at the university, and in the community. Adults who have not worked through their unfinished business with parental authority and have not successfully separated from their family systems may bring these issues into their work lives and act them out, causing interpersonal difficulties. Where these difficulties involve supervisors, one's career development might be affected.

Consider the following example: Henry, age 23, completed an M.B.A. degree and took a position in a bank-executive training program. From the outset, he disliked his supervisor, a 46-year-old man who expected the trainees to be grateful for their opportunities and to obey all the company policies without questioning. Henry found himself resisting every demand of his supervisor, ridiculing him to the other trainees behind his back. Simultaneously, Henry was feeling disappointed and discouraged with his slow progress in the training program. He had been certain when he began that this was the right industry and position for him, but now he was beginning to question his decision and even the values that led him to it. Henry sought some vocational counseling and learned that the issues with which he was contending had little to do with his job and a lot to do with his unfinished business with his father. Indeed, his supervisor had many traits and characteristics in common with Henry's father and elicited the same types of guilt and frustration in the young man that his dad did. With help, Henry was able to reframe his relationship with his supervisor and to understand and work through some of his authority issues in order to avoid jeopardizing his development in his chosen career.

Table 3-2 summarizes the developmental tasks and issues of youth. The table shows that the skills required and the significant others involved are expansions of those necessary for late adolescence. It is also clear that this transitional phase is critical to the successful negotiation of early-adulthood issues. Increasingly, youth is being seen as a highly stressful period in which decisions and their implementation are viewed as threatening life events that are often out of one's control.

TABLE 3-2. Youth

Developmental Tasks	General Issues	Requisite Skills	Significant Others
Development of Intimacy			
Develop and maintain mature intimate relationships	Conflicts and ambiguity in relationships	Values and morals clarification	Lover(s)
Develop mutual sexuality	Balance of individuation and intimacy	Conflict resolution	Spouse
Develop mutuality in relationships		Interpersonal skills	Friends
		Ability to express and receive caring	Children
			Community members
Identity Stabilization			
Develop the dream	Consistency	Values clarification	Lover(s)
Begin to implement provisional career, living, and educational decisions	Continued individuation	Occupational and relationship skills and competencies	Community members
	Completion of separation from family	Ability to cope with disappointment and failure	Colleagues
Commit oneself to interests	Demonstrated self-sufficiency	Appropriate time and energy management	Authority figures
	Congruence among thoughts, feelings, and behaviors		Peers

YOUNG ADULTHOOD

Young adulthood, which lasts from the mid-twenties to the mid-thirties and includes what Levinson (1978) calls the thirties transition, can best be characterized as a time when people explore adult roles, memberships, responsibilities, and relationships, and make provisional commitments to them. This is an establishment period—establishment of one's adult lifestyle or structure, one's career, and one's family. All three areas present herculean tasks and it is therefore understandable that many young adults experience stress and confusion as they try to develop these major areas of life simultaneously.

During the twenties, one is typically in peak physical condition, enjoying stamina and muscle strength, fine body shape and tone, reproductive maturity, hormonal balance, and memory peak. As one enters the thirties, however, subtle changes begin to occur that signal the beginning of a slowing-down process. While these changes may be overlooked for several years, they nevertheless take place, and they may possibly affect the reassessment and reevaluation of one's life that typify the early thirties. It is impossible to know whether the physiological changes one begins to experience in the early thirties account for identity changes or vice versa, but we do know that reciprocal influences are highlighted at this time.

Young adulthood has been characterized by many researchers as a temporary period during which one's decisions and nature influence continuities or discontinuities with the future. At this time one works out a balance between work, family, and leisure, often changing roles and continuing to keep future possibilities open. Also, as previously stated, at this time issues of personal, career, and family development may compete or conflict, resulting in an inability to completely resolve any one question or in the resolution of one only through the exclusion of the others.

Thus, young adulthood really marks one's entrance into the adult world, when one becomes more discriminating in one's relationships and establishes one's life structure and style. One sets up goals, plans ways of achieving those goals, and modifies memories and perceptions to fit them.

Gould's (1978) stage II, "I'm Nobody's Baby Now," occurs during young adulthood. The major false assumption he identifies is this: "Doing things my parents' way, with will power and perseverance, will bring results. But if I become too frustrated, confused, or tired, or am simply unable to cope, they will step in and show me the way." Clearly, Gould believes that strong parental influence prevails even though direct dependency issues have been resolved during the previous stage. Other false assumptions associated with this stage are: (1) that rewards will come automatically if we do what we're supposed to; (2) that there is only one right way to do things; (3) that my loved ones can do for me what I haven't been able to do for myself; and (4) that rationality, commitment, and effort will always prevail over all other forces. The thinking during this time is what Kohlberg would call conventional, or what Perry would call dualistic. And we must remember that this is the stage in which many people marry. Gould suggests that marital motivation and choices reflect unresolved parent/child relationships at this stage.

Developmental Tasks

Erikson (1963) and Sullivan (1953) consider the development of intimacy to be the critical developmental task in young adulthood. This task, then, assumes more importance than it did in prior stages. The implementation of initial career-development plans is another major developmental task (explored in detail in Chapter 5).

Intimacy.   In support of the importance of intimacy development, Vaillant (1977) points out that difficulty with intimacy is the dominant motif of young adults' complaints. The emotional disorders that selectively affect young adults— schizophrenia, mania, impulsive delinquency, and suicidal inclinations—all reflect anguish or protest against failures at intimacy. While Vaillant's research was with males, Scarf (1980) found that women who suffer from depression in this stage of life are also predominantly concerned with intimacy issues and are perhaps still affected by issues of unfinished separation from their families of origin.

Lowenthal and Weiss (1976) support the importance of intimacy development during this stage, maintaining that in the "absence of overwhelming external challenge, most individuals find the motivation to live autonomous, self-generating and satisfying lives only through one or more mutually supportive and intimate dyadic relationships." Levinson (1978) says that a young man in his twenties formally enters the adult world when he builds the first adult life structure by choosing an occupation and entering into love relationships, frequently including marriage and family. The distinctive character of this developmental period lies in the coexistence of these two tasks: (1) discovering and exploring alternative options, and (2) developing roots, stability, and continuity.

While our notions of intimacy and mature love are based on the work of Erikson, his definition appears to focus on heterosexual relationships that are most likely to lead to marriage. He defined mature love as the giving of self, other-centeredness, and the fusion of one's self with another into mutuality. His concept of intimacy combined a sense of mutuality, sensitivity to the partner's needs, physical closeness, willingness to share, and openness, or a lack of defensiveness, with the partner.

Erikson's concept of intimacy can be applied to any relationship involving emotional commitments between two adults, not only to those engaged in a sexual or marital relationship. Thus, one may have intimate relationships with close friends of the same or the opposite sex, and with older or younger adults within or outside the family system. The intimate sexual relationships that one may have outside marital relationships may be homosexual or heterosexual. Intimate relationships, therefore, are characterized by mutuality, sharing, individuation, commitment, emotional support, dependability, trust, mutual empathy, or understanding.

In adult intimate relationships, each person can retain his or her unique attributes outside the fusion between the two selves and still be committed to the bonds that join them. Some people have intimate relationships that endure throughout life; others have a series of intimate relationships; and still others have varying numbers of simultaneous intimate relationships. And of course, levels of intimacy vary among relationships. Thus, it is important to remember that intimacy can manifest itself in varying levels and in various styles.

The opposite of intimacy is isolation, a state which one maintains in order to avoid contacts that might lead to intimacy or to distance people who threaten to encroach on one's personal territory. Obviously, one's experiences with significant others in childhood and adolescence will affect one's ability to develop and maintain intimate relationships in adulthood. In Eriksonian terms, how one fares in passing through the previous stages of development lays the foundation for developing the capacity to form intimate relationships. Particularly important are one's previous experiences with interpersonal relationships. If one has experienced a confirmed sense that mutuality of efforts is beneficial, and if others have proved faithful in cooperative and intimate interactions and in sacrificing and compromising to maintain relationships, one will have the strength to abide by commitment to others and to share and give of self while maintaining one's own individual self. Conversely, people who have been victimized, abused, or exploited by others are likely to have a shaky sense of identity that will cause them to repudiate things foreign to self, validating experiences that involve competing rather than cooperating. Such people are likely to have difficulty in developing intimate relationships.

Consider the case of Anne, age 27, who grew up in an enmeshed family system where one was encouraged not to be an individual, but to be dependent and needy. During adolescence, Anne developed complementary relationships in which others made the decisions and led the way, and she obediently and adaptively followed. When her friends, both male and female, began to feel burdened by her dependency and neediness, they would distance themselves and eventually drop her. Anne went through late adolescence, youth, and early adulthood seeking the man who would show her the way, tell her who she was, and be her omnipotent father figure. She went from one relationship to another, always immersing herself in her partner's needs and dreams, never feeling satisfied with whatever affections and reassurances he gave. Typically, these relationships lasted only until the man found her neediness and dependency stifling and repressive. Not only had Anne failed to work through her identity issues, but she confused intimacy with symbiosis.

Vaillant (1977) suggests that once men are able to establish intimate relationships in young adulthood, they can then devote themselves to working hard and consolidating their career development. Traditionally, this certainly has been so. In the ideal reinforced by society, in his early twenties, a man sought an appropriate wife, and it was her mission to facilitate the fulfillment of the man's dream by permitting him the freedom and energy with which to develop his career (while she stayed home and raised children and handled the household chores).

Sex-role differences.   Today many researchers are reflecting on the sex-role differences in the young adulthood years and the influences of cultural changes. Traditionally, men appeared to have a greater need for achievement, whereas women appeared to have a greater need for affiliation. Needless to say, these needs affect relationship and career choices. Horner's (1968, 1972) research reveals that women fear success and often sublimate their needs for achievement. Chodorow (1978) suggests that gender identity for males and females is different because their relationships differ with their mothers, the primary caretakers in early childhood. Chodorow asserts that daughters tend to remain part of this primary relationship, identifying with Mother; moreover, attachment and separation are the daughter's major developmental issues, and she develops her identity through relationships. Conversely, sons are pushed out or push themselves out of this primary relationship to identify with Father. In so doing, they learn "individuation and a more defensive firming of ego boundaries" (p. 166). Thus, males may retreat from intimacy, fearing engulfment and the loss of an individuated identity, whereas females seek intimacy in order to develop an identity.

Women today are dealing simultaneously with great needs for both achievement and affiliation, and they often feel that one must take priority over the other. Thus, women are increasingly attempting to postpone gratification of their affiliation needs while concentrating on their career development. This accounts, in part, for the delay of marriage and parenting. However they reconcile the conflict, in general, women's identity and intimacy issues are more fused than those of men. By the same token, men are less well prepared for intimacy than women.

Levinson (1978) points out that the young man is looking for a place to "fit," searching both for a mentor and for "The Woman." Clinicians and researchers note that it is difficult to conduct a systematic study of women in early adulthood, since their lives are less orderly and predictable than those of men. Many women focus on intimacy and family during their twenties and early thirties, attempting to establish a career in their thirties. Others, who focus on their careers primarily in their twenties, having demonstrated their competence in the adult occupational world, often find themselves in their thirties focusing on their marital and maternal roles with increasing urgency.

The increasing competition for desirable career slots enhances the intensity with which young women develop and pursue their goals in early adulthood. Many feel that they no longer have control over or choices regarding their lifestyles but, rather, must choose careers that reflect the priority they have decided on—either career or family. Where they have chosen both, they feel they must be prepared to make compromises continually. Traditional "female" occupations (such as teaching, social work, library science) are shrinking, making the competition even greater between men and women for challenging, meaningful work; possibilities for time-out periods, flex-time, and shared positions, all alternatives geared toward sharing home and career responsibilities seem unavailable.

Reassessment at Age 30

As one approaches the age of 30, one begins to reassess and reevaluate the choices and decisions made in the twenties. In other words, one reviews all one's provisional commitments to career, marriage, children, interpersonal relationships, time management, energy, and other resources. This is really the first time one makes a major reappraisal, beginning to recognize the passage of time and to ask such questions as "Am I what I want to be?" and "What do I really want out of life?"

Levinson (1976) describes this period as a transitional phase between "getting into the adult world" and "settling down." One reassesses the dream of one's youth and one's relationships with mentors, one's occupational choice, and one's love relationships. One might make a major shift in life direction as a result of reactivating the sense that the dream has been betrayed or compromised. This transitional phase may be smooth or disruptive, depending on the degree of self-doubt. It is to be hoped, however, that one clarifies one's strengths and weaknesses and translates them into more obtainable goals. The motto of the 1960s—"Don't trust anyone over 30"—suddenly becomes a real barrier between the twenties and the thirties.

Vaillant (1977) claims that the most common psychiatric complaints of the thirties reflect conflicts about success (compared with the yearnings toward and retreat from intimacy manifested in psychiatric complaints of the twenties). Many young adults have difficulty in obtaining or accepting in real life the occupational success they envisioned in their dream. A decline of the defense mechanisms of fantasy and acting out seems to occur in the twenties, along with a concomitant increase in suppression. The decade from 25 to 35 is a guilty period in which defenses of reaction formation and repression are used with greater frequency.

Gould (1978) calls the period between ages 28 and 34 "Opening Up to What's Inside." The major false assumption of this stage is that "life is simple and controllable. There are no significant coexisting contradictory forces within me" (p. 153). Component false assumptions include: (1) what I know intellectually, I know emotionally; (2) I am not like my parents in ways I don't want to be; (3) I can see the reality of those close to me quite clearly; and (4) threats to my security aren't real (p. 164). Thinking becomes more relativistic and some type of re-evaluation occurs. Gould's views are similar to Levinson's in terms of the presence and outcome of reassessment conflict. Gould believes that parenthood is one of the major causes of conflict at this stage, since discrepancies exist between the parents' actual values and the values they are attempting to teach their children. Divorce increases at this stage as spouses see conflicts emerging between their own and their partners' developing values and lifestyle preferences.

We see from these theorists that part of this age-30 reassessment is the experiencing, while still defending against, conflicts between what exists and what one wants. The early thirties have been characterized by Levinson (1976) as a settling-down period. The young adult male now makes deeper commitments, investing more of himself in his work, family, and valued interests. Within the framework of this new life structure, he makes and pursues more long-range plans and goals. Thus, two aspects of this period are: (1) order, stability, security, and control, and (2) planning and striving toward goals that one wants to reach by the age of 40.

Developmental Issues

The kinds of issues that one deals with during this stage involve intimate relationships—such as whether or not to marry and/or have children—time management and time perspective, occupational commitments, energy management, leisure, self-acceptance, and reappraisal. It is hoped at this stage that autonomy is no longer a major issue, although one must always balance individuation with mutuality in a couple relationship. Likewise, values, morals, and interests have become more crystallized and stable.

Family.   The issues of whether or not to marry and whom to marry if one inclines in that direction are paramount during this stage. One needs to decide how to meet one's needs for intimacy and emotional support and, if marriage is desired, how to find a potential spouse. The latter involves integrating one's ideal image of a spouse with more adult perspectives, meeting the criteria of intimacy posited in the previous discussion.

Once married, one must go about the task of developing a couple system that does not conflict with either partner's career development. Then, one must decide whether or not to have children and, if so, when.

For people who are already married, the early thirties can represent a period for reappraising the marriage. One substitutes a realistic assessment for the ideal vision of youth and becomes able to accept one's spouse as an individual—and be accepted as an individual by one's spouse. At the same time, one is learning to accept one's children as separate individuals rather than as aspects of one's incomplete dream. In other words, one's dreams of perfection and total omniscience in terms of creating the perfect family become more realistically tempered.

Other relationships.   Often, during this stage of development, one is so pre-occupied with career and family relationships that one attends inadequately to the development of outside support systems—friends, community groups, and colleagues. Gould (1975) found that men's social life begins to fall off in the early thirties and does not rise again until the early forties. It is as if relationships outside work and the immediate family are in moratorium as one furiously races through the thirties to achieve one's dream.

One of the issues adults face during this stage is managing the potential conflict between total absorption in family or work to the exclusion of community and friends. However, relationships with mentors reach their peak during this stage and serve as models for the development of caring and supportive adult relationships.

Women tend to focus more on friendships and other significant relationships during early adulthood and are much more reluctant than men to put these relationships "on a back burner" while they establish career and family. This tendency is a clear reflection of women's socialized pattern of fusing identity and achievement with relationships.

Time perspective.   As one progresses through early adulthood, time becomes a major factor. In the thirties, if one has not heretofore developed intimate relationships, one feels pressure to do so. If one wants to get married but has always assumed that plenty of time was left in which to do so, one suddenly realizes that time is finite, and that it seems to be passing much more rapidly than it did a few years ago.

Likewise, if one, married or not, has not yet decided whether to have children, the ticking of the biological time clock exerts even more pressure. For women, the issues of marriage and parenthood become particularly critical at this time, owing to biological and medical considerations. Also, though the urgency of the time perspective increases for both men and women, it is possible that this issue differs qualitatively for men and women owing not only to reproductive factors but also to the fact that men still have more opportunities than women in their thirties for meeting and selecting possible mates.

One of the focuses of research of the 1970s has been decision making regarding family size, the timing of births, plans to attend school, and job choice. The purpose of this research was not to discern an ideal time path, but rather to consider the consequences and possibilities of alternative time paths. For example, Daniels and Weingarten (1981) found that parenting for older mothers is more stressful than for younger women. Compromises and tradeoffs are inevitable when one decides to juggle simultaneously multiple roles and responsibilities.

Time and energy management.   The early-adulthood stage is the most stressful and demanding; people in this stage are expected to be absorbed in their careers, their families (the presence of young children places extraordinary demands on both parents), and a myriad of activities. Lowenthal and Weiss (1976) see this period as the time of the greatest variety of activities and demands. Vaillant (1977) comments that men frequently choose to sacrifice play during this stage, instead working to consolidate their careers and devoting themselves to the nuclear family. He says that "they are poor at self-reflection, not unlike their grammar school children; they were good at tasks, careful to follow the rules, anxious for promotion, and willing to accept all aspects of the system" (p. 38). In other words, men in early adulthood are so focused on "making it" that they tend to conform in any way that they believe will facilitate their upward mobility.

Women face the herculean task of juggling family and career responsibilities. Despite the women's movement, most studies show that women still manage a greater share of home and parenting responsibilities than men regardless of career status and commitment. And despite many types of liberating legislation, there is still evidence that sex discrimination abounds regarding women's career opportunities, salaries, and promotions. Women may not have the luxury men do of reassessing the commitments they made in their youth; they may be too involved in the day-to-day maintenance of family and career to permit such reevaluation.

Career.   Although career considerations will be elaborated in Chapter 5, suffice it to say here that during this stage initial commitments are enacted—finding mentors, for example, and assimilating knowledge from them. This issue involves continuous self-assessment in relation to career productivity and achievements and the ability to make major changes in direction if indicated. In the early thirties, one comes to terms with one's occupational choice by (1) working hard to make it consonant with one's dream, (2) giving up a portion of the dream in exchange for security, or (3) redirecting oneself entirely. For women who have postponed entry into a career, this stage may involve tentative goal formulation and the development of the competencies for implementing these goals. Thus, women in this stage may go through the same initial establishment steps that men worked through earlier.

Leisure time. During the first part of this stage, the mid- to late twenties, maintaining leisure time and pursuing leisure-time interests and activities are high priorities. This priority is perhaps reflected in courtship stages and the initiation and development of intimate relationships. However, a shift begins to become apparent during the thirties transition, and leisure time and activities assume lower priorities. It is probable that the sense of urgency one feels as one's time perception changes in the thirties results in a rearranging of priorities so one can accomplish one's dream by age 40.

Table 3-3 summarizes the developmental tasks and issues of young adults. The continuum goes from self-assuredness and the belief that time is infinite through a doubting, questioning period, to a more focused, determined, and urgent focus on achievement and the realizing of career and relationship dreams. The major skills necessary for these tasks and issues are decision making, juggling, energy maintaining, boundary setting, interpersonal skills, and increasingly sophisticated conflict-resolution skills.

TABLE 3-3. Young adulthood

Developmental Tasks	General Issues	Requisite Skills	Significant Others
Development of Intimacy			
Clarify sex role	Commitment to mature	Decision making	Lover(s)
Develop mutual sexuality	relationship(s)	Juggling of time, energy,	Spouse
Develop mutuality in re-	Discrimination among re-	and boundaries	Children
lationships	lationships	Interpersonal skills	Extended family
Balance individuation,	Ability to share with oth-	Sophisticated conflict-res-	Friends
family, and career de-	ers	olution skills	
mands		Sharing	
Reassess relationships			
Withstand conflicts and			
disappointments within			
relationships			
Development of Career			
Enter career path to im-	Balance of career con-	Interpersonal skills	Colleagues
plement dream	text needs with indi-	Time and energy man-	Supervisors
Develop mentor relation-	vidual needs	agement	Supervisees
ships	Job reality variables	Pressure management	Mentor(s)
Develop competencies		Conflict resolution	
and skills		Assessment skills	
Reassess and redirect			
when necessary			

THE MID-THIRTIES TRANSITION

As adults approach their mid-thirties, they seem to become more aware that they are aging. Of course, the intensity of this awareness varies among individuals: some people notice physical changes—such as the thinning or loss of hair, the appearance of wrinkles, a new difficulty in weight control, a drop in available energy, and so on—sooner than others. What becomes apparent is the gradual shift of perspective regarding time and the mental and emotional preparation for the forties. The mid-thirties transition covers the period roughly between ages 35 and 40, the last period of young adulthood, but some of the developmental issues and tasks characteristic of this time may not appear until the early forties. Most adults become more aware that they are approaching middle age and that they will no longer be considered "young." Some find this development so threatening that they deny the passage of time and emphasize youthful dress and behavior. Others find this transition a challenge and are determined to learn and grow with it.

As previously contended, how one perceives and adapts to the mid-thirties will depend largely on how one coped with the earlier stages of development. Obviously, whatever choices were made at the age-thirty transition will affect one's functioning later. Also, the timing of other events will affect how one experiences this period. For example, if one has achieved desired success in one's career, family and other interpersonal relationships, and if one's identity and intimacy issues have been resolved, then one might experience this transition with relatively little disruption and urgency. On the other hand, a person who has postponed establishing a secure individual self-concept, a career, or a family might experience great stress in this period, feeling the pressure to make up for lost time before it is too late.

Gould (1975) found the late thirties to be a period of "quiet urgency," when time becomes visibly finite. He found in his sample of men that they became more concerned with child rearing at this time—hoping to influence their children, who were no longer infants, before it was too late. These men felt their personalities to be set and believed that whatever problems they had resulted from their parents' own child-rearing practices. He also found that these men were more concerned with health issues than before and were less involved in their social lives as they concentrated on career and family concerns.

Vaillant (1977) calls this stage of development the career-consolidation stage. He assumes that most of the men in his sample have completed the tasks relating to identity formation and the achievement of intimacy and at this point a last gasp of energy is focused on career development (see Chapter 5). Schein (1978) described this career-consolidation stage as a man's "coming to terms with his occupation, career—to either 'make it' or give up a portion of the dream and settle for security." Of course this same view applies to marriage: at this point people must come to terms with it, substituting a realistic assessment for the ideal vision they had during their twenties.

Jaques (1965) believes that an acute awareness of death at this time is responsible for the poignant frustration people feel at the idea that they will not achieve what they had planned. He writes that the central developmental task of a man in his late thirties is working through the depressive position to an enjoyment of mature creativeness, and to resignation rather than defeat.

We learn from these researchers that during the mid-thirties transition, one begins to grow out of one's illusions and to face the disparity between one's aspirations and achievements. One facet of this period, then, involves order, stability, security, and control. By this point in life, men have established their niches in society, and have dug in and pursued their interests within a defined pattern. Another aspect is the contrasting effort to succeed in society, to move "upward according to an inner timetable about the age when certain goals should be reached. The executive has to get into the corporate structure by age 40 or has to be earning at least $50,000 by 40; the assistant professor has to get tenure by 40 and so on" (Levinson, 1976, p. 23).

For women, we know that a constant juxtaposition of identity and intimacy issues takes place. Women, too, go through a critical reassessment period and make choices about implementing their dreams or about separating their dreams from those of their mates. However, an increasing number of women at this age are left to be single parents, and they do not always have the luxury of reassessment—or even of remembering their dreams—as they tend to their parental and career responsibilities. Consider the following example.

Marjorie, age 36, was a school teacher for fourteen years, and was married for eight years before she had her two sons. She had supported her husband, Jim, through law school and then scrimped and saved to live on a law clerk's salary, willingly postponing buying a house and having children. When her husband began to feel more secure in his profession, he urged his wife to become pregnant. After their first child, Daniel, was born, though, a marked difference occurred in the couple's relationship. Jim, the same age as Marjorie, was no longer attentive or responsive and, while he professed adoration for his wife and son, he participated in household and parenting chores only if and when he felt like it. When Marjorie considered leaving her job, he urged her to remain in it so that they could maintain their current lifestyle.

When Daniel was 2, Jim persuaded Marjorie to have a second child. Right after this baby, John, was born, Jim left home, claiming that he had married too young and needed time and space to "find himself" and to live with his mistress of three years. Three months later, he managed to be fired from his job, leaving Marjorie totally responsible for the care and financial welfare of herself and her two youngsters.

The case of Marjorie and Jim is not atypical. We have an increasing number of single-parent families in our society—some headed by fathers rather than mothers—in which the adult in the mid-thirties transition is trapped by responsibilities into trudging through each day, grateful for every penny and every free moment. These adults do not often have the option to redirect their careers or their families and individual energies. They are totally immersed in day-to-day survival.

Levinson (1978) describes two stages within the period between ages 33 and 40: what he calls (1) settling down and (2) becoming one's own man. The settling-down period is when

> a man works to fulfill his Dream, pursue his ambitions and become the hero in the scenario of his youth. At the start, he has the sense of being on the low rung of a ladder and preparing to make his way to the top. The ladder may have many rungs or few. His ambitions may be vast and burning or modestly pragmatic. The ladder may lead towards the realization of the Dream or in another direction [1976, p. 89].

Levinson points out that a man may be falsely reassured by the stability of this stage, believing that he is highly autonomous and free of his parents' influence, having decided for himself the importance and meaning of his career and his family and individual relationships. In fact, a man is always influenced by his family of origin and is never as autonomous as he desires to be. The next step in Levinson's scheme, becoming one's own man (BOOM), is the connecting link between the settling-down period and the mid-life transition.

According to Levinson (1978), the BOOM tends to occur in the late thirties. A key element in this period is the man's feeling that no matter what he has accomplished to date, he is *not* sufficiently his own man. He feels overly dependent upon and constrained by authority, as manifested in both people or organizations, and feels a sense of constraint and oppression in work, marriage, and other relationships. These feelings match exactly those of Jim, described in the preceding case study. Jim's feelings are neither atypical nor pathological. It is the way one reacts to and copes with these feelings that determines how constructively or destructively he or she passes through this developmental stage.

A critical characteristic for men of the BOOM period is the ending of the mentor relationship. After all, one does not have need for mentors after the age of 40. As Levinson states (1976),

> the person who was formerly so loved and admired, and who was experienced as giving so much, comes now to be seen as hypercritical, oppressively controlling, seeking to make one over in his own image rather than fostering one's independency and individuality; in short, as a tyrannical and egocentric father rather than as a loving, enabling mentor [pp. 21–26].

Clearly, this event reactivates and reworks previous Oedipal conflicts. However, Levinson emphasizes the importance of the mentor relationship for men in terms of achieving Erikson's ego stage of generativity versus stagnation and its attendant virtue, caring.

Rossi (1980) suggests that women during their twenties and early thirties are intimacy mentors for men and that women usually resolve their intimacy issues long before men do. But mentors for women are much more difficult to find in the career sphere than those for men, and mothers and elder sisters tend to fill the mentor role in the family sphere. By the time of the mid-thirties transition, women who have not previously been in the world of work may be seeking a mentor, while terminating their dependency on whomever has filled the role as family mentor.

Neugarten (1976) states that, according to her Midwest sample, women become more tolerant of their own egocentric, aggressive impulses as they work through the mid-thirties transition and men begin to become more tolerant of their nurturant, affiliative impulses. This finding implies a crossing of paths, as women become more achievement oriented and men more affiliative oriented.

Developmental Tasks

The developmental tasks for this period are transitional in nature. There is a tendency to consolidate one's gains in terms of career and family, and to put down roots and settle into the adult world. Simultaneously, one must come to terms with one's actual achievements and with the disparity between achievements and aspirations. This necessity requires assessment and problem-solving skills, since one must collect concrete, realistic data about one's actual achievements and about possibilities on which to base future decisions.

Another major task is reassessing one's relationships—with one's mentor, spouse and children, peers, and extended family. This reassessment involves dealing with the gradual disenchantment of relationships, terminating unrealistic relationships, and substituting one's own values for those of others in preparation for becoming a mentor oneself.

Thus, the major task of the mid-thirties is to begin to review and come to terms with the elements of one's dream, and the disparity between that dream and reality. One hopes to become aware of one's self and others as a basis for better future choices and to begin to make new choices, either to accept and seek new meaning in work, family, and self, or to head in new directions.

In Eriksonian terms, the developmental task of the mid-thirties transition is to bridge the gap between the development of intimacy and generativity—to prepare for becoming more concerned with the welfare and development of others than with "making it." This concern is predicted to come after one employs a last spurt of energy to achieve the dream before the onset of the forties.

Developmental Issues

The developmental issues of the mid-thirties are similar to those of young adulthood. They reflect an increasing urgency regarding time management and time perspective, with the allocation of energy and resources, and with the stability of relationships. Anxiety may increase during this stage as one drives oneself to reach one's goals and to prove to oneself that one is as autonomous as possible.

Issues that differ from those of young adulthood include increasing concern with appearance, health, energy, and social issues. As Levinson (1978) states, the mid-thirties transition period into middle adulthood lasts about five years and involves coming to terms with four major polarities that have existed since adolescence, conflicts in feelings that have never been resolved:

1. Being young versus being old;
2. Being destructive versus being creative;
3. Being masculine or feminine;
4. Being attached to others or separate from them.

Along with Havighurst's (1980) notion of social roles and social responsibilities, these are the major issues facing adults in their mid-thirties transition. Havighurst states that civic consciousness and community involvement are necessary issues for adults of this age.

Table 3-4 summarizes the developmental tasks and issues of the mid-thirties transition. These issues and tasks are not as clearcut as those in the previous early-adulthood stages because they reflect a transition period between early and middle adulthood.

TABLE 3-4.   Mid-thirties transition

Developmental Tasks	General Issues	Requisite Skills	Significant Others
Consolidation of Intimate Relationships			
End some relationships and begin others	Commitment to or change of family rela-	Decision making	Spouse
		Assessment skills	Lover(s)
Finalize commitments to family and others	tionships	Time-and-energy-management	Children
	Increased concern with		Friends
Prepare for generativity	parenting	Interpersonal skills	Community members
	Increased tolerance of	Conflict resolution	
	nurturing tendencies	Nurturing and caring	
	Control of individuation	Reflection and introspec-	
	vs. fusion	tion	
	Preparation for middle age		
Consolidation of Career			
Finalize commitment to career or prepare for	Last spurt of energy to implement dream	Assessment skills	Mentor
		Decision making	Potential mentees
mid-career change	Redirection if necessary	Time-and-energy man-	Supervisors or bosses
Terminate relationship	Put down roots in world	agement	Supervisees
with mentor	of work	Interpersonal skills	Colleagues
Take on social and civic responsibilities			Peers and friends
			Community members
Become one's own person in world of work			

SUMMARY

We have seen that in young adulthood the major personal issue that must be achieved is the formation of a well-integrated adult identity that permits a realistic self-perception, a realistic assessment of individual needs, well-thought-out values, a consistent set of beliefs, and immediate and long-range sets of personal, family, and career goals. In addition, during this time one must also deal with interpersonal relationships and decide how to meet one's needs for intimacy.

The work of Erikson, Levinson, Gould, and Vaillant provides a theoretical foundation for adult-development theory. As the research conducted to date has focused on males almost exclusively, we have taken pains to extrapolate what might be applicable to women and to hypothesize, based on clinical experience and the work of Scarf (1980) and Gilligan (1982), with respect to identifying some of the female issues concerning identity and intimacy. Differences based on sex-role socialization are crucial to understanding and working with adults.

The research cited has limitations. It is largely based on a white, middle-class, male sample and cannot, therefore, be generalized to females or to members of other social classes. It contains no evidence of involving control groups, which affects the research methodology. Furthermore, these theories are more biased toward Freudian theories than humanistic or systems theories, and they lack integration with cognitive theory. Interestingly, most of the work on the development of cognitive processes is based on samples of college-age or younger subjects. Throughout the literature, interesting implications arise for further research on the life span.

It is clear from the theories cited that relatively smooth, stable periods of early adulthood are interspersed with transition periods. These transition periods may be turbulent or relatively carefree. Men and women may differ in the timing and priorities of events and issues, and there are individual variations among men and women. However, both men and women are strongly influenced by their families of origin, society's expectations, and the ways in which they have negotiated and resolved earlier stages of development.

Early adulthood, then, is a period in which people become adults, forming an adult identity, establishing intimate relationships, and establishing themselves in the world of work. It is a period of peak physical prowess and psychological energy, both of which must be optimum for the enormous tasks of individuation and establishment required in all domains of life.

The rapidly changing cultural forces in our society are presenting new challenges to young adults. Many such people feel that they are pioneering new ground and that role models from previous generations are no longer valid. We might conclude this chapter by pointing out that the development of flexible, multifaceted coping strategies supported by a firm, positive self-concept and positive relationships help young adults to chart this unfamiliar territory.

REFERENCES

Chickering, A. *Education and identity*. San Francisco: Jossey Bass, 1969.

Chickering, A., & McCormack, J., Personality development and the college experience. *Research in Higher Education*, 1973, *1*, 43-70.

Chodorow, N. *The reproduction of mothering*. Berkeley, Calif.: University of California Press, 1978.

Daniels, P., & Weingarten, K. *Sooner or later—The timing of parenthood in adult lives*. New York: Norton, 1981.

Erikson, E. *Childhood and society* (2nd ed.). New York: Norton, 1963.

Gilligan, C. *In a different voice*. Cambridge, Mass.: Harvard University Press, 1982.

Goodman, E. Wellesley College commencement speech (May 29, 1981).

Gordon, V. N. The undecided student: A developmental perspective. *Personnel and Guidance Journal*, 1981, *59*, 433-489.

Gould, R. Adult life stages: Growth towards self-tolerance. *Psychology Today*, 1975, *8*, 74-78.

Gould, R. *Transformations: Growth and change in adult life*. New York: Simon and Schuster, 1978.

Havighurst, R. Social and developmental psychology: Trends influencing the practice of counseling. *Personnel and Guidance Journal*, 1980, *58*, 328-335.

Horner, M. A psychological barrier to women. Paper presented to Midwestern Psychological Association, 1968.

Horner, M. Toward an understanding of achievement related conflicts in women. *Journal of Social Issues*, 1972, *28*, 157-176.

Jaques, E. Death and the mid-life crisis. *International Journal of Psychoanalysis*, 1965, *46*, 502-514.

Kegan, R. *The evolving self*. Cambridge, Mass.: Harvard University Press, 1982.

Keniston, K. *Youth and dissent*. New York: Harcourt, Brace, Jovanovich, 1971.

Kimmel, D. *Adulthood and aging*. New York: Wiley, 1974.

Kohlberg, L. Stage and sequence: The cognitive developmental approach to socialization. In D. Goslin (ed.), *Handbook of socialization theory and research*. Chicago: Rand McNally, 1969.

Kohlberg, L. Stages of moral development. In C. Beck, B. Crittenden, and E. Sullivan (eds.), *Moral education*. Toronto: University of Toronto Press, 1971.

Levinson, D., Darrow, C. N., Klein, E. B., Levinson, M. H., & McKee, B. Periods in the adult development of men: Ages 18-45. *The Counseling Psychologist*, 1976, *6*, 21-26.

Levinson, D. *The seasons of a man's life.* New York: Knopf, 1978.

Lowenthal, M., & Weiss, L. Intimacy and crises in adulthood. *The Counseling Psychologist,* 1976, *6,* 10–16.

Marcia, J. Development and validation of ego identity status. *Journal of Personality and Social Psychology,* 1966, *3,* 551–558.

Marcia, J. Ego identity status: Relationship to change in self-esteem, general maladjustment and authoritarianism. *Journal of Personality,* 1967, *35,* 118–133.

Marcia, J. The case history of a construct: Ego identity status. In E. Vinacke (ed.), *Readings in General Psychology.* New York: Van Nostrand-Reinhold, 1968.

Marcia, J. Identity six years later: A follow-up study. *Journal of Youth and Adolescence,* 1976, *5,* 145–160.

Marcia, J. Identity in adolescence. In J. Adelson (ed.), *Handbook of Adolescent Psychology.* New York: Wiley, 1980.

Munro, G., & Adams, G. Ego identity formation in college students and working youth. *Developmental Psychology,* 1977, *13,* 523–524.

Neugarten, B. Adaptation and the life cycle. *The Counseling Psychologist,* 1976, *6,* 16–21.

Orlofsky, J. Sex-role orientation, identity formation and self-esteem in college men and women. *Sex Roles,* 1977, *6,* 561–575.

Perry, W., Jr. *Forms of intellectual and ethical development in the college years: A scheme.* New York: Holt, Rinehart & Winston, 1970.

Piaget, J. Cognitive development in children. In R. Ripple and V. Rochester (eds.), *Piaget rediscovered: A report on cognitive studies in curriculum development.* Ithaca, N.Y.: School of Education, Cornell University, 1964.

Piaget, J. *The moral judgment of the child.* New York: Free Press, 1965.

Piaget, J., & Inhelder, B. *The psychology of the child.* New York: Basic Books, 1969.

Podd, M. Ego identity status and morality: The relationship between two developmental constructs. *Development Psychology,* 1972, *6,* 497–506.

Rossi, A. Life span theories and women's lives. *Signs, Journal of Women in Culture and Society,* 1980, *6,* 1–24.

Scarf, M. *Unfinished business.* Golden City, N.J.: Doubleday, 1980.

Schein, E. *Career dynamics,* Reading, Mass.: Addison-Wesley, 1978.

Schenkel, S. Relationships among ego identity status, field-independence and traditional femininity. *Journal of Youth and Adolescence,* 1975, *4,* 73–82.

Schenkel, S., & Marcia, J. E. Attitudes toward premarital intercourse in determining ego identity status in college women. *Journal of Personality,* 1972, *40,* 472–482.

Sullivan, H. S. *The interpersonal theory of psychiatry.* New York: Norton, 1953.

Toder, N. L., & Marcia, J. E. Ego identity status and response to conformity pressure in college women. *Journal of Personality and Social Psychology,* 1974, *26,* 287–294.

Vaillant, G. *Adaptation to life.* Boston: Little, Brown, 1977.

Waterman, C. K., & Nevid, J. S. Sex differences in the resolution of the identity crisis. *Journal of Youth and Adolescence,* 1977, *6,* 337–341.

Waterman, C. K., & Waterman, A. S. Ego identity status and decision styles. *Journal of Youth and Adolescence,* 1974, *3,* 1–6.

CHAPTER FOUR

FAMILY DEVELOPMENT IN EARLY ADULTHOOD

The family life cycle intertwines with that of the individual life cycle. In fact, the perception of the family unit as an evolutionary process with a developmental life cycle of its own has its roots in the conceptual framework of the individual life cycle. Developmental theory postulates a series of stages of growth, each of which the organism must successfully negotiate in order to avoid stagnation and chronic crisis. The same applies to the family—a series of stages exists, each embracing predictable as well as unpredictable events, and each requiring successful negotiation in order to prevent stagnation and the formation of symptoms.

The nature of the structures and communication styles of the family unit determines the family's success in negotiating the various developmental stages. Conversely, the nature of the particular developmental stage through which the family is passing affects the family's structures and communication styles. Transition from one stage to another inevitably transforms family structures and communications and transformations in family structures and communications are requisites for successful developmental stage negotiation. In short, these two aspects of families are inseparable (Okun and Rappaport, 1980).

In this chapter, we will explore the beginning stages of the family life cycle, those stages that are likely to occur in early adulthood. These stages are called the beginning family, infant family, preschool family, and school-age family. Clearly, couples may not be at the same chronological ages when they pass through these stages; thus, the impact of these stages on and by their individual-development stages will vary. For example, a couple in their early twenties, youth, will experience the beginning and infant-family stages differently than a couple in their late twenties or early thirties or a couple whose partners are at two widely varying ages. Thus, the individual-developmental stages of the people involved and the differences in the developmental stages of the marital partners will affect their experience of the family developmental stage. The focus here is on the typical, not the atypical, timing in the middle-class American family life cycle. But this approach by no means implies that one type of family is more "normal" than another, or that there is an ideal ethnic type or style of family. However, since most of the research, theory, and clinical practice to-date is based primarily on middle-class American families, we use this model as a reference point in our study of family development.

Some of the questions addressed in this chapter are:

1. Why do people marry?
2. What factors influence mate selection?
3. What are the most difficult aspects of marriage?
4. How do couples decide whether or not to have children?
5. What factors enhance marital relationships?
6. Do children help or hinder marriages?
7. Are families similar or different in terms of tasks and issues?

THE FAMILY LIFE CYCLE

Although several varying models of the family life cycle have been proposed over the past fifteen years (Duvall & Hill, 1948; Rodgers, 1973; Hill & Rodgers, 1964; Duvall, 1971; Feldman & Feldman, 1975; Yorburg, 1975; Carter & McGoldrick, 1980), we are basing our model on Duvall's eight-stage model because it appears to be the most elaborate and to illustrate most easily the typical American middle-class family. As Kimmel (1974) points out, the middle-class American family is probably the "pervasive stereotype in our society that influences other family styles."

According to Duvall (1971), the eight stages through which the family typically passes in its normal cycle of development are: (1) beginning family, (2) infant family, (3) preschool family, (4) school-age family, (5) adolescent family, (6) launching family, (7) postparental family, and (8) aging family. Each of these stages has its own unique set of tasks and issues.

Terkelson (1980) delineates the normative and paranormative events associated with these stages. The normative events include marriage, childbirth, the child's entrance into school, the child's entrance into adolescence, the launching of the child into adulthood, the birth of the grandchild, retirement, and senescence. Normative events occur regularly in most family units and focus on the children of the system. Paranormative events occur frequently but not universally. They are characterized by conflict, illness, and extrinsic circumstances, and include miscarriage, marital separation and divorce, disability and death, severe illness, household relocation, changes in socioeconomic status, and extrinsic catastrophes resulting in massive family-unit dislocation. As we consider these normative and paranormative events, it is important to remember that the most pronounced effects usually occur with first events. Thus, the birth of the first child is more likely to transform the family system than the birth of subsequent children. The first child's going off to school is more likely to affect the separation anxiety level of the system than when a younger sibling enters school a few years later. Of course, exceptions occur—sometimes a particular child affects the family system more profoundly because of variables other than birth order.

As we consider the family life cycle from a systems perspective, it is important to remember two major concepts: (1) each individual's personal development is shaped by, and in turn shapes, each other family member's development; and (2) the family development of any family is influenced by the developmental experience of preceding generations of that family system. These reciprocal and multigenerational influences in family systems affect both individual and family development. For example, if Mom has never successfully separated emotionally from her mother (who, in turn, never successfully separated from hers), then Daughter may encounter great resistance to her attempts to separate from Mom during the launching stage of the family, and the entire family system may experience heightened stress during this period. A major purpose of the family system is to preserve itself as a system; most family systems foster the individual development of its members, but if a member's individual development threatens the homeostatic balance of the family system, the system's goals and welfare take precedence over the individual's goals and welfare. This concept is elaborated in later chapters, where later stages of individual and family development are covered.

The family stages discussed in this chapter are beginning family, infant family, preschool family, and school-age family. However, to lay the foundation for the beginning-family stage, we turn now to a discussion of courtship, or the premarital stage (Kimmel, 1974; Meyer, 1980).

PREMARITAL COURTSHIP

Mate selection and the process of courtship are the principal features of the premarital-courtship phase. This stage serves either to create the foundation of a couple and family system or as a period of experimentation that fails to develop further.

Mate Selection

As discussed in Chapter 3, a young adult's identity, self-concept, and family-of-origin experience influence how he or she develops and conducts intimate relationships. We have explored the reciprocal influences of identity formation and intimate relationships. Now we consider the influences of one's family of origin.

Family-of-origin influences.   A young adult's parents' marriage, his or her relationship with each parent, and his or her experiences in the sibling system are all major influences on that person's capacity for developing and maintaining intimate relationships. These early experiences influence the types of attitudes and expectations that young people develop, the sense of efficacy in interpersonal relationships they feel, and the variety of interpersonal skills that they bring to relationships. Meyer (1980) categorizes these influences as emotional, financial, and functional interconnectedness to parents and previous generations.

With regard to emotional interconnectedness, often young adults either follow the patterns established by their families of origin or choose a diametrically opposed pattern. Whatever course they take, they are still deeply influenced by their families of origin whether or not they realize it. Young adults who have been successful in separating emotionally from their parents are able to select mates on their own terms rather than in conformity with or opposition to parental wishes. Consider the following examples.

Mark, 24, grew up in a family system where managerial or professional occupations and an upper-middle-class lifestyle were highly valued. But, to the dismay of his parents, Mark switched from a business major to an education major halfway through college. After college graduation, he took an inner-city teaching job and soon met and married another teacher in his school. The two young teachers lived in a project apartment, were thoroughly engrossed in their community, work, and marriage, and, in sum, chose to have a very different lifestyle than Mark's parents. This choice was based on Mark's strong sense of self rather than on rebellious acting out. Eventually, when Mark's parents realized how happy Mark and his wife were with their careers and their shared lifestyle, they professed to a great deal of pride and respect.

Susan, 26, found herself breaking off a four-year live-in love relationship 1,000 miles away from her family of origin because she knew that her parents would be horrified if she chose a marital partner from a different ethnic group and social class. Despite her love for and successful living experience with the man involved, Susan did not feel she could tolerate or endure her parents' disapproval, even from a distance. She had taken great pains during those four years not to tell her parents about her living arrangements and to prevent a meeting between her lover and parents. Susan had not separated emotionally from her parents despite her physical separation, and still depended upon their approval and support.

In both cases, the key ingredient is the level of individuation of the adult offspring. Family influences affect decisions in all areas of life, however, not just mate selection—for example, career, residence, and lifestyle. Interestingly, most people are completely unaware of the pervasive influences of their family-of-origin systems.

Financial interconnections can be either helpful or a hindrance to separation. It is important to learn whether or not the financial dependence of adult offspring on parents is based on reality or merely represents the offspring's inability to become financially self-sufficient. The meaning of money to the family system—whether or not it is used as a means of controlling and intruding—and the terms of the financial arrangement are also important.

Mary and John, engaged for three years and in their late twenties, borrowed money from John's parents for a down payment on a home. Agreeing to pay his parents back at a specified interest rate, John assumed that the loan was strictly a business arrangement. John's parents, however, felt that the loan gave them privileges they did not have before—to insist that the couple marry and that Mary quit her job and settle down to have a baby. Heretofore, they had been quiet and reserved on this topic. Although Mary wanted to marry John and had been concerned about John's reluctance to make such a commitment, this was not the way she wanted to get married. Moreover, John was forced to decide who and what were most important to him. He eventually decided to return the loan to his parents and to marry Mary because of his own desires rather than in reaction to his parents. This was a painful process for John. Working through his separation issues required several months of intensive therapy.

Functional interconnectedness refers to the amount of energy and interest parents commit to taking responsibility for their children regarding their daily living functions such as eating, health, their activities, social life, and so on. Many parents of adult offspring still treat their children as they did years before. They expect to be consulted regularly and have little regard for their offspring's maturity or independence. A young adult who depends on his or her parents' over-attachment and/or overfunctioning is most likely to have difficulty separating and may even select a mate who conforms to or conflicts with the parents' desire. Thus, the young adult selects a mate who will allow the parents to continue overfunctioning or who will take over from the parents, or one who permits him or her to break away from the overfunctioning parents. A young adult who is able to become self-sufficient despite his or her parents' overfunctioning is more likely to select a mate based on the couple's mutual needs and desires. Some adults are able to separate regardless of whether their parents cooperate and facilitate the process, though, naturally, separation is a more difficult, painful process when parents resist. Separation under such circumstances requires a strong self-concept and much ego strength.

In describing family-of-origin influences on mate selection, McGoldrick (1980) notes that the retirement, illness, or untimely death of a parent or some other traumatic family loss often precipitates mate selection. The powerful sense of loss or aloneness can propel one to find a replacement relationship. Scarf (1980) points out that many young adults choose mates to replicate and replace the lost parent (whether lost in actuality or symbolically)—for example, the daughter who married someone "just like Daddy," to provide the nurturing and protection she no longer received from her parents.

Kimmel (1974) emphasizes that mate selection is usually based on homogamy or complementarity. *Homogamy* refers to similarity of age, race, religion, ethnic origin, social class, and education. Social and family pressures support the notion of homogamy—it is a common myth that "marrying your own kind" facilitates adjustment to marriage—and Kimmel believes that homogamy indeed contributes more often to successful marital adjustment than *complementarity*, where needs, styles, and values complement each other. On the other hand, Prosky (1979) believes that people in their teens and twenties choose psychologically complementary mates, partners who will complete or make up for what is lacking in themselves. One selects a mate, then, who will be able to do those things and manage in those areas in which one is weak. Certainly this is likely to be true for individuals with low levels of self-differentiation—that is, those who have failed to separate emotionally from their families of origin and develop their own identities.

The selection variables appear to change as people grow older. It may be that more mature, more individuated adults are more likely to select an equally well-differentiated mate in order to have a relationship that is more *symmetrical*—that is, equal and parallel—than complementary. While a need for symmetry does not necessarily correlate with chronological age, it is more likely to influence mate selection if a young adult does not go directly from being a son or daughter to being a lover and then a spouse. Those young adults who take the time to be on their own, functioning self-sufficiently with minimal environmental and relationship support, manage to develop a clearer sense of identity and a higher level of self-differentiation than those who marry out of their families of origin.

A very successful architect of about 36 consulted a therapist about his current live-in relationship with a woman. He had decided that it was time for him to marry and have a child and he was concerned about the pattern of his relationships—he had been involved in one relationship after another since age 14 and he admitted to needing the woman in his life to be completely dependent on him, completely absorbed in him, and totally supportive of his needs and goals. He could not understand why these relationships fizzled out after a while, though when he saw them beginning to disintegrate, he always had another woman lined up for replacement. In the initial consultation sessions, he admitted to a fear of being alone and of discovering who he might be without these relationships. He also described his enormous emotional attachment to his mother. He was a perfect example of a 36-year-old man who had never achieved self-differentiation or emotional separation from his parents and who always sought complementary relationships with women to replace his attachment to his mother. His terror of being without a relationship and finding out who he was as an individual was crippling. He demonstrated clearly the fact that one's psychosocial stage of development, not one's chronological age, affects mate selection.

Several variables that influence the decision to marry and that are also affected by family-of-origin influences are: (1) societal expectations; (2) loneliness; (3) parental pressures; (4) romantic literature, tradition, and social hysteria; (5) economic insecurity; (6) the desire for upward mobility; (7) neurosis; and (8) the desire to escape from family of origin, work situation, or living conditions (Okun and Rappaport, 1980). To this list might be added pregnancy, whether or not it is terminated by abortion. Recently, despite the widespread use of birth control, many young couples seem to engineer pregnancy in order to "get them off the fence" in terms of decision making about marriage. In fact, the 1979 census report notes that in the early 1970s, one-third of all first births were premaritally conceived.

Dacey (1982) cites "pull" factors for getting married, those intrinsic reasons that include love or reward seeking, sex, prestige, material possessions, childbearing, companionship, and curiosity. The "push" factors are extrinsic reasons, including escape from an unpleasant home life, conformity to social expectations, pregnancy, rebound, or avoidance of loneliness.

The changing roles of women and career-development factors affecting them certainly influence the decision to marry. Campbell (1975) believes that men are more ambivalent about marriage than women. I have found in recent clinical experience that more and more women are surpassing men's levels of ambivalence—women who are immersed in their own career paths are very concerned about whether or not marriage and career can co-exist.

Many people do not even think of getting married until after they meet someone they want to marry. Just as many people, however, decide that "it is time" to get married and actively seek potential mates. While we have no sound theory of attraction and interaction to explain people's motivations for marrying, we do know that timing and individual stage of development are important variables.

Courtship

Courtship is the phase of a relationship when people are selecting a partner and moving toward commitment. It is usually a time of magnetic romantic attraction, when each partner is trying to test out his or her own and the other's apparent expectations for the relationship. It is a time when each person puts his or her best foot forward, and a time of high idealization, energy, and motivation. This phase is also characterized by its voluntary nature—at any time either person can easily terminate the relationship.

Egan and Cowan (1980) define marital commitment as deeper than a love or emotional commitment, involving a public commitment to mutual responsibility. They describe the courtship period as developing the following competencies:

1. Interpersonal skills;
2. The ability to delay gratification in view of a higher goal;
3. The ability to engage in collaborative decision making, problem solving, and life planning;
4. The ability to develop and pursue mutual interests;
5. The ability to coordinate multiple commitments;
6. The ability to appreciate a relationship;
7. The ability to be committed to another person without being possessive;
8. The ability to develop self-knowledge;
9. The ability to understand and appreciate conflicting cultural backgrounds;
10. The ability to expect and deal with conflicts and disagreements.

One of the critical aspects of the courtship is the process of arriving at the decision to marry. The nature of their experience determines the initial rules and regulations of the dyadic system and is influenced by the individuals' motivations, needs, and expectations. Sager (1976) defines marriage as involving three motivational contracts—namely, his contract, her contract, and their interactional contract. These contracts incorporate underlying expectations of marriage, which in turn reflect internal and external motivations for marrying. There are three aspects to these contracts: (1) one that is conscious and verbalized; (2) one that is conscious but not verbalized, perhaps owing to fear or shame; and (3) one that is beyond awareness. The interactional contract is where his contract and her contract battle out their struggles to fulfill their needs and terms. The point is that each marriage begins with a contract, whether explicit or implicit, that is developed during the courtship period. Thus, each relationship has a set of rules based on expectations and reflecting individual motivations. The partners may or may not be aware of what these rules are, how they operate, and who determines them (Okun and Rappaport, 1980).

As more and more couples live together without marrying, the decision to marry becomes more threatening and fraught with anxiety. The young adult's infinite time perspective allows those in that stage to put off the decision longer and longer, until either one party, with patience worn thin, delivers an ultimatum, or pregnancy occurs, or the couple decides to have children. Or, perhaps, one party becomes involved with someone else. When the decision to marry is made reactively rather than proactively, the stage is often set for disruptions further down the line.

THE BEGINNING FAMILY

When a couple marries, the family life cycle begins. The first stage of this family life cycle is termed *beginning family*. It comprises the period that begins with marriage and continues until the first child is born. Thus, the beginning family lasts from under a year to several years. The goal of this stage is to achieve intimacy with clear boundaries—that is, to form a couple system. Once marriage occurs, the relationship becomes compulsory rather than voluntary and the major task is for two people to form a primary-couple relationship.

Learning how to function as a new dyad, a couple system, is one of the most complex and difficult tasks of the family life cycle. While this beginning-family stage is perceived as a joyous and extended romantic honeymoon, the rate of divorce is greater at this stage than at any other in the family life cycle.

Developmental Tasks

In order to join as a couple, two individuals must have completed their emotional separation from their families of origin and formed strong senses of identity through individuation. Likewise, they need to renegotiate individual and interpersonal boundaries and then learn to establish couple boundaries.

Boundary negotiation.   The couple faces many boundary issues during this stage of the family life cycle. Unlike the individual issues discussed in Chapter 3, these issues relate to establishing boundaries between the couple system and the rest of the world—siblings, friends, colleagues, extended-family members, and society at large. During courtship, the two people are pretty much left alone; parents in particular seem to voice few demands or expectations. After marriage, however, the two family systems are joined—and each brings different heritages, motivations, and expectations. Thus, the couple needs to renegotiate its relationships with both partners' families of origin. The resolution may differ for each family of origin, depending on each party's level of emotional separation and autonomy. Next, other relationships need redefinition: those with his friends, her friends, and our friends; with his business colleagues, her business colleagues, and so forth. If he does not like one of her friends, for example, she may decide to see this particular friend at lunchtime when they can be alone together, rather than having her over for dinner as she used to.

The terms *negotiation* and *renegotiation of boundaries* refer to distance regulation (ranging from enmeshment—that is, fusion or symbiotic intertwining—to disengagement and distance), to the sorting and resorting of priorities, and to the establishment of new spoken or unspoken rules about who speaks for whom. A *boundary* can be defined as "the rules and regulations that separate the system from its environment" (Okun and Rappaport, 1980). The characteristics of the boundary determine how communications are sent and received. A boundary can be highly permeable, permitting the easy exchange of thoughts and feelings, or fairly impermeable, inhibiting the exchange of thoughts and feelings or permitting the exchange only with much difficulty.

Consider Martha and Jeff. Martha loves to touch and be touched and to talk about her feelings and thoughts. Her personal boundaries are more permeable than Jeff's. Jeff is unused to physical touching except when connected with sex and is definitely uncomfortable when talking about his feelings and thoughts. The degree of permeability of a boundary has no value in itself. Martha and Jeff need to learn to negotiate their differences, to understand and accept their different styles, and to find a way of relating that is satisfying and comfortable for them both.

Boundary negotiations determine relationship structures, power dynamics, and the meaning of the relationship. And boundaries determine and are determined by the communication styles developed by the couple system.

Minuchin (1974) sees the complex process of negotiation in this primary stage of family development as occurring on three fronts:

1. The spouses must develop a series of mutually satisfying *patterned transactions*—for example, they must decide such mundane issues as who will shop and how they will share or not share a bathroom, closet, and so forth. Will the toilet seat be left up or down? Who will put the dishes away and who will take out the trash? Should they have one bank account or two?
2. At the same time, the spouses must accomplish the task of separating from their family of origin and from other family systems. This task involves negotiating new boundaries (relationships) with parents, siblings, in-laws, divorced spouses, and so forth.
3. They must decide how they will reorganize and regulate the demands of the world of work, as well as their idiosyncratic leisure activities and commitments.

Needless to say, the patterns of boundary renegotiations that begin in this stage become the foundation for the boundary renegotiations necessitated by each successive stage of the family life cycle.

Communication styles.   The resolution of the major and minor issues of this initial stage in the family life cycle may establish major patterns that will endure over the entire life cycle of the family. These patterns are reflected in the communication patterns that deal with conflict resolution and the assignment of roles and responsibilities. If the couple can learn to communicate clearly and congruently in order to make decisions collaboratively, they may be able successfully to rework their individual needs and thus avoid conflict between individual needs and couple needs.

The communication styles and patterns of a relationship indicate family rules, power dynamics, and the process of negotiation. Messages form the substance of the communications between people in relationships and, as such, are the basic element of the interactional process. Messages have two major aspects: (1) the communicational, dealing with the content of the message itself; and (2) the metacommunicational, dealing with the verbal and nonverbal messages about the message. It is metacommunication that seeks to impose behavior or to define the self and the nature of the relationship.

Steve says to Mara: "It might be nice to have a child." Mara replies, "If we had a child we wouldn't be able to go away as much as we do now. I can't wait until we meet John and Ruth at the cabin this weekend." In a couple of hours, these two are fighting about some inconsequential event, when, in fact, neither heard what the other really said in the loaded exchange. It turns out that what Steve really was saying was "I want you to want to have a child with me," and what Mara was really saying was "Let's not spoil the way things are now." By failing to hear the metacommunications, Mara and Steve were beginning a pattern of talking *at*, rather than *with*, each other.

Conflict-resolution styles and patterns are major components of the communication patterns that couples develop. Each member of the couple has learned a different way of expressing and dealing with differentness and conflict from his or her family of origin, and the two may struggle greatly to arrive at a satisfactory and effective style.

In Dad's family of origin, conflict was avoided and Dad left the scene whenever it began to emerge. Mother, on the other hand, comes from a family where everyone screamed and yelled but got the conflict out and resolved it. In the couple system the two share, when she screams and rants and raves, he is terrified, thinking she no longer loves him, and he retreats behind a silent, cold, distant veneer. She becomes more and more enraged as he retreats further and further. They end up totally distanced until one breaks the impasse and gives in to the other.

McGoldrick (1980) believes that most marital problems derive from unresolved extended-family problems and not from the specific marital conflicts on which the spouses focus. Other clinicians find that the patterns and styles of conflict resolution can take three forms: (1) effective working through of the issue leading to satisfying change and growth; (2) development of a symptom in one member of the couple system; or (3) triangulation involving a third factor, such as an in-law, a job, or even the conception of a child.

Developmental Issues

Intimacy versus fusion.   Serious intimacy issues confront the couple in this first family stage regardless of how long they have lived together before marriage. Bowen (1978) comments that "it is common for living together relationships to be harmonious, and for fusion symptoms to develop when they finally get married. It is as if the fusion does not develop as long as they have the option to terminate the relationship."

Newly married people often confuse closeness with fusion, expecting their mates to complete their selves and improve their self-esteem. Bowen (1978) believes that fusion results when couple members have failed to resolve their relationships with their parents and to separate and become emotionally independent. Satir (1967) calls this type of fused marriage a "survival pact," wherein each partner puts the other in charge of his or her self-esteem. An extreme example of a fused couple are Tom and Julie, both in their early twenties.

Tom married Julie right after they both graduated from college. They had been living together for two years, although their parents believed they each lived in a separate dormitory. They spent all their free time together, never allowed themselves to disagree, and virtually excluded friends and extended family from their life. Julie would talk about how she could not live without Tom and how she needed his advice on every decision—whether it was what to wear, what job to take, or whom to have lunch with. Tom felt that he needed to be with Julie whenever he was not at work, since he felt important and strong when he was with her. Both refused invitations from other couples, since they wanted to be alone together. They always managed to spend their time in the same room together—if he was studying, she did her sewing or her chores there. Observers could easily detect fused communication patterns: the overuse of the pronoun *we*, the assumption that one could speak for the other, the sense that each always knew what the other was thinking or feeling. In fact, the two would think and feel for each other. If Julie became upset about something, Tom too became upset, and vice versa. If Julie's mother was critical of Julie in a telephone conversation, Tom withdrew from his in-laws, feeling personally criticized.

Individuation versus undifferentiation.   As discussed in Chapter 3, one who has been unsuccessful in separating emotionally from his or her family of origin and who has not been encouraged by his or her family of origin to become self-differentiated is a likely candidate for a fused intimate relationship. Although Bowen (1978) believes that most people select mates at a similar level of self-differentiation, occasionally the less differentiated person in a couple system learns to become more differentiated within the context of the relationship.

Reality versus idealization.   Prosky (1979) believes that most conflict in this beginning stage of the family centers on both partners' fear of the dissolution of their ideal images of their mates. After conflicts arise, both partners frantically attempt to regain and reinstate their former perceptions of merged bliss and their ideal mates. Each partner appears to will the other to become the mate of his or her dreams, and anger results from repeated disappointment. Sometimes this struggle results in compromise to avoid conflict; this compromise may, in addition to sacrifice, provide the partners with an opportunity to experience a different way of being. In other words, in fearing differences many couples resist the loss of their romantic illusions and spend years trying to recapture these illusions. Failure and frustration can result from unrealistic fantasies of the "ideal marriage" as well as from the individual's experiences in his or her family of origin and from different styles of communication and negotiation. But after years of such a struggle, each partner begins to accept the fact that both partners are distinct people and neither conforms to the other's ideal. Prosky asserts that at this point couples decide to separate, to institutionalize their differences, or to continue to grow and develop in their marriage as they learn to value their differences and integrate into their own functioning the complementary functioning of the other.

Okun and Rappaport (1980) point out that when a couple reaches an impasse during this stage, they may successfully resolve it alone or through the intervention of friends, counseling, or therapy. But regardless of how they resolve it, their need in the midst of the crisis is for change and growth. If they are able to resolve the conflict, they move toward growth. An alternative solution may be separation or divorce. However, other alternatives exist; one common method of moving the dyad to "change" is to make it into a triad—that is, to have a child. The latter "solution" is usually unsuccessful. It may create the illusion of change in the family system, but it is likely that the basic problems—the failure to establish styles of conflict resolution, rules for boundary regulation, and so forth—will be merely submerged by the excitement of the pregnancy and the new baby, only to arise at a later time.

Children.   Stress in the beginning-family stage surrounding the decision of whether or not to have children is arising with increasing frequency. This choice is frightening—if one manages to make the choice, then one must willingly accept the responsibilities and consequences of the chosen alternative. In the past, people had children because they were expected to do so when they married, and it was easier to feel victimized by parenthood and society rather than to take personal responsibility for the decision to have a child.

The current responsibility to decide whether or not to become a parent presents a true dilemma. After all, parenthood requires an even deeper commitment than marriage—once a child is born, the decision is irreversible. Likewise, the decision not to have a child becomes biologically irreversible with time. In fact, as pointed out in Okun and Rappaport (1980), many couples in their thirties, feeling the press of biological time, reactively decide to have a child because they cannot decide not to have one.

As with the decision to marry, the changing role of women affects the decision to have a child. As more women wish to remain in the work force, many fear their spouse's lack of actual participation, of sharing parental responsibilities, and of having to assume the ultimate childcare responsibilities. As pointed out in Chapter 3, many women who focus on their career development in their twenties become obsessed with marriage and parenthood in their thirties.

One of the issues that emerges with delaying the decision to have children is that of fertility. Women in their thirties who do not get pregnant easily feel the pressure of the biological time clock. This pressure can augment stress and anxiety, which in turn can lessen chances for successful conception, and so forth. Infertility problems can add tremendous stress to the couple system.

If the decision to have or not to have children is not resolved to both members' satisfaction, the marital relationship may not survive. It is amazing how many couples avoid dealing with this issue in their twenties and then are shocked at each other's expectations and attitudes in their thirties as they wrestle with this decision.

Childlessness.   McGoldrick (1980) notes that couples who do not have children, whether voluntarily or involuntarily, go through the family life cycle even though those aspects dealing with childrearing do not apply to them. They still need to go through the process of renegotiating relationships with their families of origin, friends, colleagues, and so forth, in each successive life stage. Many childless couples meet their needs for generativity and continuity in their relationships with nieces and nephews or the offspring of close friends. Some concern has been raised about these couples in the elderly years now that geographical mobility has separated family systems. We will consider these issues in a later chapter.

Cultural issues.   In the past decade, couples are marrying later and, as noted, as a result of the changing role of women, family patterns are changing. It is more acceptable today for individuals from vastly different ethnic or cultural backgrounds to marry, and couples are less strongly bound than previously by family traditions. Improved contraception allows couples to decide if and when to have children, and social distances between family members often allow couples more privacy and autonomy than in the past. Two-career families are becoming more the norm than the exception. Obtaining a divorce has become easier and an increasingly large number of single-parent families are in existence. Also growing is the number of babies born to single parents who never do marry.

It is clear that couples in the 1980s will contend with cultural and economic issues unknown to couples in the 1960s and 1970s. In a precarious economy, job choice and mobility become more restrictive, affecting both individual and family choices.

Table 4-1 shows the major developmental tasks and issues of this stage in the family life cycle. The critical importance of successfully negotiating the challenges of this first stage in the family life cycle cannot be overestimated. Couples who manage these initial challenges may look forward to the next stage in their family life cycle by planning for children.

THE INFANT FAMILY

The infant-family stage begins with the first pregnancy and the birth of the first child and continues until that child becomes a "preschooler," usually between ages 3 and 5. The couple's goal at this stage is to clarify the boundaries in order

TABLE 4-1.   The beginning family

Developmental Tasks	General Issues	Requisite Skills	Significant Others
Join as a couple	Intimacy versus fusion	Negotiating	Friends
Negotiate boundaries	Individuation versus	Conflict resolution	Families of origin
(between couple	undifferentiation	Clear, congruent	Relatives
members)	Reality versus	differentiated	Colleagues
Renegotiate boundaries	idealization	communications	Employer
with others and	Sex	Expressing affection	Neighbors and
between self, spouse,	Children versus	Compromising	community members
and career	childlessness	Decision making	
	Cultural		

to become a three-person system. As Bradt (1980) points out, there may be space for a child in the family system, there may be no space, or there may be a vacuum the child is intended to fill. The marital relationship is now characterized by an even less reversible commitment, and pressures and limitations on the couple system increase, often causing an increase in dissatisfactions.

In addition to learning to function as a couple system, now the couple members need to learn how to function as parents. These new roles require new rules and regulations and, again, renegotiation of boundaries that may be so recently formed that they are still not firm or stable. The infancy stage requires a great deal of physical and emotional energy. The couple system necessarily revolves around the needs of the infant, who is completely dependent upon the parents for physical and emotional nurturance. The parents' level of confidence in their ability to understand the infant's needs and to respond to those needs with ease and affection will affect their experience as parents. They must continually redefine their expectations and responsibilities.

Developmental Tasks

The major task for the couple is one of expansion: to make space for a new member in the system, to establish a parent hierarchy within the system, and to continue to replenish the couple system. The infant-family stage is a crucial turning point in the life of the family. Persons who had the single role of spouse must now assume the double role of spouse/parent. Responsibility as providers for each other becomes responsibility as provider for "all of us."

If the marital system has not had the time to stabilize and if earlier issues have not been worked through, the couple's anxieties and tensions may be deflected onto the child. The presence of the infant depletes the couple's time and energy for the marital relationship, and this requires more concrete determination and the mutual assignment of areas of competence and responsibility.

Boundary negotiation.   Shifting from joining to expanding and renegotiating their intimacy boundaries are critical tasks at this stage. Much of this boundary negotiation will be influenced by the initial motivation and decision-making process regarding the birth of the child, by both parents' preparation for childbirth, and by the experience of both during the actual birth. Research and clinical experience show that couples who have planned and prepared together for a baby have an easier time renegotiating their intimacy boundaries than couples in which the male has not shared and participated in the pregnancy and delivery experiences.

It is not uncommon for a temporary enmeshment to occur between mother and baby (Minuchin, 1974) in the early months following birth. Again, how the father handles this temporary distancing may depend both on his motivation for parenthood and his preparation for it, and on how fully developed the couple system was before the onset of parenthood. It is not unusual for the husband to feel that his wife is devoting too much time to the new member of the system and for the wife to feel suddenly restricted to one member of the family and tied down to the borders of the family while the husband is free to come and go as he pleases. Couples need to find some ways to refuel their individual selves and the couple system during this period. They need to be supportive of each other to facilitate this refueling process.

During this stage, the couple begins to clarify their roles as parents (who will do what, when, and where); as workers (who will work, when, and where); as economic providers (who will be responsible for what); and as individuals (who will have free time when, where, and how). The partners need to determine how they can keep their roles as parents from interfering with their roles as spouses. In addition, they need to bond with the infant. This is often easier for the mother, who bonds biologically with the child. How she includes the father and facilitates his bonding separately with the infant will be critical to the development of the family.

Another boundary task is to begin to create clear boundaries between the child and the parents—that is, to create a parent hierarchy. Again, couples who have established clear couple-system boundaries are more successful at this task than couples who have no clear boundaries and who need a child to resolve their issues. By *parent hierarchy* I mean a parent subsystem that naturally has more power and authority in the family system than the child or sibling subsystem will have. Haley (1980) has found that lack of this parent hierarchy inevitably results in child and adolescent acting-out symptoms later on.

Again, at this stage, the couple needs to renegotiate boundaries with extended family, friends, colleagues, and the outside world. The issues surrounding the grandparents can become stressful now, as the couple decides how much to include or exclude them. In some family systems, in-laws are not at all demanding or intrusive until they become grandparents, and then boundaries need to be firmed. Some couples find that including their families of origin into their nuclear family system allows a greater variety of triadic relationships to form and relieves stress on the parent system. Other couples find that their own unfinished business with their parents resurfaces and gets played out with the grandchildren.

Obviously, couples need to deal with the restrictions on their time, energy, and space once they have a child. Their social lives will be affected: having a drink with the guys after work or just picking up and going somewhere spontaneously become more difficult. Further, in two career families, the boundaries between the couple system, the parent system, and the world of work need to be renegotiated.

At present, many women are seeking mates who will participate actively in parenting, and many couples are choosing to share jobs, arrange for flex-time schedules, or limit their career aspirations to give priority to their parenting roles.

Florence and Mel were married for seven years before having their first child, when they both reached the age of 30. Each had been successful in career development and they had devoted the decade of their twenties to graduate school and establishing their careers. Florence was a social worker and Mel was a lawyer in a large, prestigious firm. After the birth of their baby, they decided to modify their careers. Florence cut back to a three-day-a-week job, and Mel cut back his law practice to four days a week (an unprecedented move in his firm), knowing that this decision would affect his chances for advancement in his chosen field. This modification worked out very well for this particular couple and strengthened their marital relationship as well as their parent system. In fact, they decided to have a second child two years later and continued to feel very committed to their concept of shared parenting.

Communication styles.   Although a couple's communication patterns are established in the beginning-family stage, they too may need to be renegotiated in this stage. The couple must decide how their family system will share power, affective feelings, and other resources, how and why they will fight, and what they need to do to implement their personal and family goals.

Even though infants cannot speak, they communicate, affecting their parents' couple system. If an infant's needs intrude disproportionately into the couple's communications, the latter may be irreparably damaged, reemerging as a major symptom of family dysfunction years later. An example of this delayed reaction is the King couple.

The Kings are in their late thirties and have several young children. They had been married for three years before the birth of their first child and they described a smooth, relatively open-style marital relationship during those preparenthood years. Once their first baby was born, however, their marital relationship was put far in the background as each parent began to communicate through the baby (and later on through the other children). Without realizing it, the Kings came to focus all their anxieties and tensions onto their children and to stop talking to each other except through their children. This pattern was traced back to the infant-family stage: their first baby was a difficult baby and required so much attention and energy during its first few months of life that the communication patterns the parents had developed during the first three years of marriage gradually disappeared, to be replaced with a triangular form of communication.

Developmental Issues

Parenting styles.   Each parent comes to this stage of the family cycle with a different history and set of experiences. Both have distinct expectations of themselves and each other and of the child. If these matters are not discussed and negotiated, they can be a source of great conflict over the years. Parenting styles will affect the influence and power dynamics that develop in the parent system, specifically the success of conflict-resolution techniques and of goal achievement.

Issues that can lead to parenting-style conflicts are whether the infant gets picked up whenever he or she cries, or whether the child is allowed to sleep in the parents' bed or is taken out with the parents, and so on.

Grandparenting styles.   The attitudes and expectations of the grandparents with regard to raising the infant often become an issue in the infant-family stage. The parents may expect more babysitting and other types of help from their parents than they actually receive. Or conflicts may arise regarding parenting styles—the grandparents may be particularly critical or controlling, offering many suggestions. It will be important for the parents to establish and clarify a grandparent hierarchy and to see that its boundaries remain clear by clarifying the rules, regulations, and expectations associated with grandparenting. Another possible issue is competition between the two sets of grandparents to have the most contact with the baby and the greatest amount of input into the childrearing. Again, it is important that the parents take responsibility for negotiating these boundaries by establishing the appropriate hierarchies.

Time and energy management.   Because the infant-family stage places inordinate demands on the family system, determining who is available for whom, when, and where may become a source of conflict. For example, for a few months after the birth of the baby, owing to her enmeshment with the infant and her excessive fatigue, the wife may no longer be able to take breakfast with her husband. A husband who resents this rebalancing and fails to understand that it must occur will only exacerbate the situation. The wise use of time that enables husband and wife to replenish the couple system (leisure, individual, and couple time) requires skillful management and good collaboration.

Sex.   The wife may be unavailable sexually for a few months after the birth of the baby. Again, it is important that the husband understand why this is so and relieve the pressures on his wife by sharing as much of the parenting as he can. The presence of a child can deprive parents of energy as well as privacy; sex can become more pressured (with the parents always listening for the baby's cry), and more hurried so the partners can get what sleep they can. Also, some men find their wives less sexually attractive after childbirth. It is as if they confuse their wives at some level with their mothers and feel incestuous if aroused by a maternal woman. Other men find that they resent sharing their wife's body with the infant, with the infant suckling the wife's breasts that were heretofore reserved for lovemaking. Perhaps the wife loses interest in her husband, too, as she focuses on the baby and lavishes all her attention on him or her. Thus, the sexual relationship needs to be renegotiated after childbirth—albeit temporarily—and the couple needs to understand that growth and change mean that things cannot stay the same.

Careers.   Where both parents are involved in a career, they will have to decide how to manage this difficult transition in their lives. One parent may choose to take a leave of absence from work, or the couple may decide to obtain the services of a nursemaid, to share childcare with friends or kin, or to find infant daycare. Most likely, they will need to reconsider plans made during the pregnancy, since they are likely to find that their feelings and thoughts have changed after the actual birth. Both parents will have to renegotiate their career involvements in order to manage their new parenting responsibilities.

Economics.   If one parent cuts back on work, the family income will be reduced just when the expenses escalate. Thus, the couple will need to reallocate their funds to meet infant expenses—for babysitting so that the couple can get out alone as a couple sometimes, and perhaps even for more spacious housing. This financial strain could augment stress in that the breadwinner might feel the full brunt of the family's economic pressures. If both parents continue to work, they may find that so much income is going to childcare that the family's style of living must be drastically changed. Frequently during pregnancy, the woman chooses to wait to decide if and when she will return to work. The couple might find, however, that their economic situation gives them no option for making decisions, and that the woman must return to work despite her desire to remain home with the child. Further, they may find that the additional expenses burden their budget even with two incomes. Money often becomes a great problem in this stage and can stress the entire family system.

Friendships.   Many young couples are surprised at the changes that occur in their friendships once they have a child. Many of their former couple friends who do not want to have children seem to drift away, feeling uncomfortable with the accommodations the new parents have to make. The parent couple may begin to feel uncomfortable about their new parenting roles with their nonparent friends and frequently drift into friendships with other couples who have young children.

Nowadays, young families often live far away from extended families or move frequently due to job transfers. Peer-support systems, therefore, have become increasingly important. Friends can serve as parenting models for each other, as sounding boards in the airing of frustrations and difficulties, and as resources for carpooling and sharing babysitting. In other words, they can be "parent mentors." As more and more women go to work after childbirth, neighborhoods are no longer affording a natural support system for new parents. Young couples are finding that they must deliberately seek out such relationships to help them deal with the requirements of this stage.

Table 4-2 outlines the developmental tasks and issues of this stage of the family life cycle. We see that these involve a careful renegotiation of the rules, roles, and resource allocations first negotiated in the previous stage.

THE PRESCHOOL STAGE

The preschool stage of family development occurs when the oldest child in the family is between 3 and 5 years old. Although children are entering school earlier than in previous decades, this family stage begins after the couple and their child have adjusted to the initial challenges of the new triad, and it ends when that

TABLE 4-2.   The infant family

Developmental Tasks	General Issues	Requisite Skills	Significant Others
Expand intimacy boun- daries to include infant	Parenting styles Sex	Providing nurturing infant care	Grandparents Pediatrician
Learn parent roles	Time and energy	Negotiating	Nonparenting friends
Renegotiate roles, rules, and boundaries of the couple system	allocation Division of labor Career involvement	Inclusion Renegotiating Decision-making	New friends as possible models/mentors Colleagues
Renegotiate boundaries with significant others	Financial planning	Budgeting Reassessing priorities	Babysitters Neighbors
Renegotiate boundaries with career			
Ensure direct communi- cation with spouse, and separate couple and parent subsystems			

youngster begins attending school full time. The major goal of this stage is to provide a transition from the expansion of the previous stage to the progression of the next stage, the School Age stage.

In this stage, both the physical exertions and the gratifications of the parents increase. The couple must be constantly on the alert, protecting and supervising their youngster as he or she begins to explore and wander out of the narrow confines of infancy. The child's verbal ability increases, allowing parents to begin to supervise and protect on a more verbal level.

Developmental Tasks

The major developmental task is that of socialization. This involves the genera- tional transmission of values, attitudes, and ideals in all aspects of childrearing. The parents attempt to socialize their child and, in the process, are socialized by the child. Again, important boundary renegotiations must occur.

Boundary negotiation.   First, the boundaries between the parent system and the child must be renegotiated. The child has more mobility than in the previous stage, when one could put an infant in the crib or playpen and he or she would remain there. Young children are another story: they are always demanding, into just about everything, and probably at their most intrusive stage. The parents have to work out their rules with regard to disciplining and providing affection, intimacy, and nurturance without detracting from their own needs as individuals and as a couple. They also have to renegotiate their roles and responsibilities as spouses and parents—that is, the rules of their relationship. Furthermore, each parent has to negotiate separate boundaries with the child: the child has separate relationships with Dad, Mom, and the parents together.

Also, just as the couple had to renegotiate its boundaries with the outside world, extended family, friends, and colleagues, so the triadic (three-person) fam- ily must do likewise at this stage. Of particular import now are relationships with neighbors and with the child's friends and their parents. Parents who both work often feel frustrated by their inability to reciprocate hospitality to their child's friends and to neighborhood children. This situation often, of necessity, remains unbalanced. Also, the couple system will have even less time and energy than before and the partners will have to make conscious attempts to protect and replenish their marital relationship. The careful renegotiation and protection of boundaries are ongoing tasks.

Communication styles.   As mentioned earlier, the child becomes more verbal during this stage. The child's own communications will be simpler and clearer than those of the parents, but the child will nevertheless be sensitive to the metacommunications of the parents' messages. The parents will thus have to modify their patterns and styles of communication to include, and sometimes exclude, the child.

Children at this stage often reflect and mirror their parents' styles of communication in a way that shocks their parents, often causing them to think hard about restructuring old patterns. For example, if Mom and Dad overhear their 4-year-old screaming into the toy telephone at "her pretend husband," they will be forced to take seriously their child's perception of their communication style.

Other patterns of communication have to do with some of the rules in the family system. For example, the 3-year-old may learn that in order not to have to go to bed he can ask Dad for another story despite Mom's admonishments. Who speaks to whom about what becomes part of the pattern.

Developmental Issues

Parenting styles.   The major issue of this stage relates to dilemmas at the individual and couple subsystem levels about duplicating, modifying, or reacting against each partner's parenting styles. Many parenting challenges arise now; psychoanalytic theory and many other theories of child development see this stage in the child's life as involving much significant emotional growth that sets the stage for what occurs in later life. Our systems-theory perspective suggests that the child not only passes through and attempts to resolve certain psychosexual conflicts, but that in the process the parents relive and perhaps finally come to terms with some of their unresolved developmental problems.

Differences in parenting styles often become the focus of conflict in a family. For example, Mom may be quite permissive with the child, allowing him to leave toys all over, to eat when he wants to, and to keep irregular bedtime hours. Dad, on the other hand, may feel very strongly that the youngster should put away each toy after he finishes playing with it, should not eat between meals, and should go to bed at a regular hour. If, within the couple system, the two have worked out effective conflict-resolution strategies, then they may be able to negotiate their differences without triangulating in the child. If not, they formulate a pattern in which they play off against each other through the child when such childrearing matters arise. Conflict-avoiding parents practice what Wynne and associates (1958) call pseudomutuality—the appearance of closeness, sameness, and agreement that hides the distance between the two and the mutual lack of recognition. Often the result is that one parent—usually the mother—assumes a disproportionate amount of the parenting function. In Kantor and Lehr's (1975) terms, the mother may become the "mover," or the initiator, the child the "opposer," and the father either a "follower" of the mother or of the opposing child.

Power struggles.   As the child learns to speak, one of the first words to come out of his or her mouth is "No!" The immediate result is a power struggle between the parents and the child, which, if not handled in accordance with a parent hierarchy within the system, can become a permanent struggle that endures throughout the family life cycle.

If the couple is engaged in a couple-system power struggle, it is very likely that the child will be triangulated into this struggle to reduce conflict and tension. Usually, in such cases, the child ends up with some kind of symptom to prevent the parents from having to deal with their own conflicts. For example, if Dad feels that his needs for affection are not being met by his wife, he may find that being with his adoring little girl assuages his loneliness. The little girl might encourage Dad's affection even if Mom seems annoyed by it, since she will sense that it keeps things on an even keel—that is, maintains the homeostasis. Years later, Daughter may have her own difficulties with men and with expression of affection, in part owing to her overinvolvement with her father at this stage.

Childcare.   For dual-career families, childcare is a paramount issue. The major types of childcare are: (1) in-home care; (2) family day care; and (3) daycare centers. The first, in-home care, involves either live-in or day help. Anxieties arise around day help when the helper is ill, or unable to arrive on time, or fails to show up at all and to provide enough time for the parents to make other arrangements. With live-in help, another person is present for the family system to absorb and interact with on a day-to-day basis. Family daycare involves taking the child to someone else's home, where the child is incorporated into another family system during the day. Daycare centers are formal, licensed programs where several children from different families are tended by professional staff.

Childcare is becoming a more common option as mothers remain in the work force after childbirth. Many issues arise in relation to nonparent childcare—economic, power, and affectional. Childcare can also produce tension within the couple system if the parents disagree about the type of care their child should have. In most areas of the country, it is still very difficult to locate suitable daycare and this can be a source of great frustration and anxiety to both parents. They may need to decide how to handle emergency situations when the child is too sick to leave home or when the nonparent caretakers are ill and unavailable. I have seen many couple systems erupt into serious power struggles over the issue of who will stay home from work in such situations.

Economic issues.   Again, the economic pressures on the family continue to increase. Children's expenses grow as they grow and daycare is most expensive during this stage. Living arrangements may need to be renegotiated, for a child of this age can't be placed in a corner as can an infant, and there must be room for toys and play.

Other children.   In many families, a second child is born in this stage. This means that the whole system now becomes a four-party system, recycling through the boundary renegotiations and issues described above. While this process is usually not as traumatic as the first time around, different tasks and issues may cause varying levels of consternation for different families. It appears that families who absorb their first child into their family system with relative ease will have an easier time with their second child than families who are still struggling to incorporate the first. Again, much will depend on how adaptable and responsive the baby is. For example, some families have exceptionally "good" babies the first time around and marvel at the ease and joy of parenting, only to have a more typically fussy baby the second time. Such parents, with a young child in addition to a new baby to care for, can feel their patience and tolerance severely tested and their family system heavily stressed.

With the birth of a second child, a new subsystem, called the sibling subsystem, is created, and the two youngsters begin to establish the pattern and structure of their own relationship. The parent system has a great deal of influence over the formation of sibling subsystem patterns in modeling the sharing of family resources and facilitating nurturance. Writes Bradt (1980, p.132), "that siblings inevitably create 'a trauma' for one another seems more a function of availability of caring adults than of the inherent rivalry of children."

The birth of a second child can further strain the couple relationship. The parent role may become more dominant than the spouse role, and marriage may seem less fulfilling and more tedious. Frequently, one or both parents seek intimacy in an outside relationship or absorption in a career—both outlets outside of the marriage—as each feels the other slipping away from what used to be closeness.

Single parenting.   This is probably the most difficult stage for single parents, particularly in situations where the single parent works full time to provide economically for the family. If the absentee parent is available, and if the terms of the marital separation permit, both parents may still be involved in the actual parenting. But if one parent has full custodial rights and all childcare responsibilities, this is indeed a strenuous time. Even visitations are difficult, since it is hard for the separated parent to take young children out for too long, and uncomfortable if that parent's living situation is inappropriate for the child. Thus, visitations often occur in the custodial parent's domicile, which intrudes on his or her privacy and causes stress for all. Also, young children are not often aware that they should have a strong relationship with the absent parent, since they may be too young to remember the separation or divorce. Thus, the child may consider life with one parent to be normal.

The single parent in this stage is fortunate if he or she has a minute alone during the day. The effects of task overload will depend on the level of organization already existing in the family as well as on the economic resources, extended family, and friend support systems in place. Without support from friends, the extended family, or neighbors, the stress and strain on a single parent can result in social isolation causing serious family crises.

Children under 5 years of age seem to have greater difficulty adjusting to parental divorce than children over 5 (Wallerstein & Kelley, 1980). Beal (1980) points out that normal children aged 2½ to 3½ may regress in cognition, behavior, and self-control during the first year after divorce. Normal children aged 3¾ to 4¾ may experience self-blame, low self-esteem, and disruptions in their sense of order and dependability. Young children are susceptible to developmental disruption when their environment presents them with sudden or major changes.

It is not unusual for the single parent either to overinvest in or to disengage from parenting during the first year following divorce. Overinvestment may lead to enmeshment between the parent and at least one child, and this can retard development and cause regression or fixation. Disengagement can result in a lack of parental controls, causing chaos that requires intervention by an outside agency or an extended family. The situation of Marilyn is an example.

Marilyn, aged 22, is the single mother of three children under 4. Marilyn has been on welfare since her boyfriend left her two years ago and lives with her mother and two teenage sisters. She has been aggressively seeking help from her social worker and is angry that no one will take responsibility for her children. Her mother and sisters go about their lives as if the children were not there, despite the constant fighting and yelling. In her parenting behavior, Marilyn vacillates between overcontrol and laissez-faire. She wants her social worker to find her childcare so she can get a job. She complains constantly and picks fights with whomever will engage with her. Marilyn's social worker is working to help her individuate to a level where she will be able to take responsibility for herself and her children without depending excessively on her mother or the social worker. Only now, at the age of 22, is Marilyn beginning to consider the "who am I" issues she previously ignored. At the same time, she is learning some new communication patterns and parenting strategies that will help her manage more effectively at home.

In his review of the literature on single-father families, Pichitino (1983) notes the increasing trend for males to take on this responsibility. His review indicates that single fathers undergo considerable intrapersonal stress and pressure: (1) to prove their competency as parents; (2) in terms of changing relations with friends and colleagues; and (3) with regard to their need to relate firmly but intimately with their children. Single fathers are characterized by adaptive coping capacities in dealing with financial and domestic problems. They were actively involved parents prior to their marital separation and, on the whole, are competent and confident with the nontraditional role of single father. They tend to delay cohabitation or remarriage, giving priority to their parenting role and responsibilities. Since this group comprises only 10 percent of single parents in this country, it is likely that their motivation and commitment to parenting is higher than the norm of the entire single-parent group. Obviously, one must have strong determination and confidence to undertake and achieve this role successfully in today's society.

TABLE 4-3.   The preschool family

Developmental Tasks	General Issues	Requisite Skills	Significant Others
Differentiate couple-system and parent-system boundaries	Parenting styles Childcare (daycare, preschool) Power Economics Additional children Resource allocation	Negotiating Renegotiating Sharing Disciplining Nurturing Decision making Problem solving Budgeting	Daycare and babysitters Preschool teachers Grandparents Child's friends and their parents Pediatricians Neighbors Friends Colleagues Relatives
Learn appropriate preschool parenting roles			
Socialize children			
Replenish the marital relationship			
Balance self, family, and work roles and responsibilities			
Differentiate communication styles between couple and parent systems			
Renegotiate other relationships and commitments			

Table 4-3 outlines the developmental tasks and issues of the preschool stage of the family life cycle. In this stage, everyone in the family does some changing and growing and the energy level is at its highest.

THE SCHOOL-AGE FAMILY

The school-age stage begins when the child enters school full time and ends when the child reaches puberty. The major task of this stage is progression, as opposed to stagnation (the lack of growth or change). To accomplish this progression, it is necessary to maintain the system's homeostatic ideal without ignoring or denying the individual needs of the family members.

When the child enters school, the parents usually experience relief at having them in school for part of the day, but they are also faced with giving up total control of the child. Now they must share their influence with other authorities. Thus, both the couple and family systems, and their attitudes, values, and actions are now open to speculation and evaluation by outsiders.

Developmental Tasks

The major tasks of the family in this stage are to accommodate the influences of the outside world and to facilitate the child's first major leave-taking of the security and control of the family system. Both tasks require major boundary negotiation between the family system and the outside world.

Boundary negotiation.   In addition to renegotiating the couple-system boundaries, family members must renegotiate the parent-system boundaries and both systems' boundaries with friends, colleagues, extended families, neighbors, and so on. Radical changes are often necessary. First, the child must begin to negotiate his or her boundaries with the outside world—with a new teacher, who often becomes a type of surrogate parent, new classmates, the crossing guard in front of the school, and all of the other new people in his or her life. If the child has been successful in a preschool or daycare situation, he or she might manage this negotiation more smoothly than if going off to school is the child's first venture away from home. And the parents' facilitation or lack thereof will affect his or her success at this task.

The parents, too, must negotiate their relationships with these new outside forces. Teachers, for example, can become significant role models to the child; further, they often provide feedback to the parents about the child's achievements and productivity, which can be gratifying or threatening. The degree of permeability of the family system's boundaries with the outside world will affect the difficulty they will have in this integration with their community. Their values and attitudes will be subject to scrutiny by outsiders and their children may be exposed to conflicting beliefs and values.

A renegotiation of the boundaries will take place within the family system as well. The process of self-differentiation will become more pronounced as the young child goes off to school and becomes more self-sufficient. The couple system may have more time and energy for replenishment and the couple will reevaluate their couple and family ideals and renegotiate parental roles and responsibilities. The sharing of resources will increase as the child grows older.

Communication styles.   During this stage of the family life cycle, it is not uncommon for a child or family to be referred to therapy. The reason is usually symptomatic social, emotional, or learning behavior on the child's part. Frequently, a family assessment will provide useful information about the communication patterns that underlie the problems. The family system needs to modify its communication patterns during this stage—to clarify the new rules for incorporating outside-world influences and to provide the opportunity for each member to express clear communication in congruence with the system.

Developmental Issues

Individuation issues.   In this time of the family life cycle, couple members may experience individual identity-crisis issues. Childrearing responsibilities dominate so much of a parent's life where a young child is involved, that frequently the parent feels that parenting is all he or she does. Now, with some free time, parents find that they have to decide how to protect their individual and couple boundaries. Many mothers, in particular, become so used to thinking of themselves as parents that they forget they are also individuals and wives. Parents of school-age children need a great deal of emotional support—from each other as spouses, from friends, and from extended-family members and neighbors.

Couple issues.   Power struggles frequently develop in parenting and/or marital systems as less energy is devoted to the couple system and more goes to the parenting system. The degree of the couple's success in working through these issues in previous stages will determine their success with the challenges of this stage. Many couples find that they need to become more careful in managing their time, energy, and resources in order to strengthen their couple systems, working harder to share responsibility for parenting and economic support. Couples who attempt to avoid these tasks by communicating and negotiating through their children only manage to postpone confronting them rather than avoiding them altogether.

A child's problem at school can escalate at home into a couple-system power struggle. One parent may blame the other for the child's difficulty, and conflict over parenting styles may arise. Often, however, the child's problem at school serves to mask a deeper conflict in the couple system and to provide a focus for the parents' relationship that allows them to avoid their own issues.

Time management.   The fact that the child is away from home for considerable lengths of time can require significant system adjustment. If there is a younger child, for example, he or she will no longer have a built-in playmate and may become more demanding of the parent at home. A mother who stayed home through earlier stages may now decide to work, to go back to school, or to pursue some avocational or leisure interests. If the mother has been working right along, the family is likely to have to make new childcare arrangements, some type of after-school daycare. Again, depending on what part of the country the family resides in, finding adequate care can be a difficult and tense process. Also, where the school has no lunch program, the family must make those arrangements too, and if the child is unable to walk to and from school, transportation arrangements will be necessary. If the mother goes back to work or continues to work, a rebudgeting of time will be necessary—the sharing of chores and the economic responsibilities must be scheduled. And decisions will be necessary regarding childcare during vacations and holidays. Finally, since more women are leaving teaching for the occupations traditionally reserved for men, their hours and vacations are becoming more traditionally "male" as well, no longer coinciding with those of school-age children who are still too young to be home unattended. All these details require shifts within the couple and the family.

Divorce.   A very high incidence of divorce occurs in families at this stage of the life cycle (Beal, 1980). In certain locations, divorce is so common that school-age children from divorcing or divorced families receive much automatic support in school; in other parts of the country, the child of divorced parents feels stigmatized, like an outcast, and no support is forthcoming. The impact of divorce on children in this stage of family life is influenced by the intensity of the parents' emotional attachment, the level of conflict between the parents, and the degree to which the child has been triangulated into the marital conflict. Children experience many fears and insecurities during and after the divorce of their parents, some of which go unnoticed by the custodial parent, who has personal issues of emotional separation to deal with. The stress associated with parental divorce is often manifested in school-related problems, which serve to attract the necessary attention and, it is hoped, lead to treatment.

For the custodial parent, the first year of separation contains many transitional readjustment difficulties, such as social isolation and loneliness, anger, depression, and lack of parenting control (Wallerstein & Kelley, 1980). These difficulties must be considered developmental rather than pathological. The single parent needs time to work through the process of separation, to mourn the loss of the old relationship and way of life, and then to restructure the new family system, establishing appropriate new boundaries and communication patterns.

Single Parenting.   The issues for single parents in this stage are similar to those in the preschool stage. The child's involvement in school will allow the single parent some space to tend to his or her own individual issues and to make new friends and develop a more active social life. The school-age child is old enough to visit the separated parent or other relatives and friends, and the single parent is less likely now to feel totally overwhelmed by the burdens and responsibilities of single parenthood than in the preceding stage.

As in the preschool stage, however, the single parent may overinvest in the children during the period of adjustment. Or the single parent may disengage too much, appearing to abandon parenting responsibilities. Many inconsistencies and insecurities will challenge all members of the family. The power structure might have to be made more democratic to ensure cooperation and sharing. If the custodial parent works, then the children will have to pitch in more with routine chores to protect the single parent against becoming overloaded. Power-structure changes may require changes in communication patterns.

An advantage for single parents in this stage is that the school environment provides some constancy for the children. Elementary school teachers and counselors are particularly sensitive to students' family issues and are likely to provide support to children of divorcing parents, and perhaps to the single parents themselves. A great benefit here is that the single parent has a chance to communicate with another adult about the child—a built-in part of marriage that is lost with the divorce.

Remarriage.   Remarried families begin after the former family system(s) have already started a course of development and then dissolved. Thus, they "carry the scars of first families" (Carter & McGoldrick, 1980, p. 206), to say nothing of unresolved issues from each spouse's family of origin. One cannot erase or give up former ties, and predictable emotional issues in remarriage may therefore include the following (Carter & McGoldrick, 1980, pp. 268–270):

1. Complex, conflicting, and ambiguous new roles, relationships, and loyalties;
2. Boundary difficulties regarding membership (who are the "real" members of the new family? his old family? her old family?), space (what space in this new home is mine? where do I really belong?), and regarding authority (who is really in charge? of discipline? money? decision making?);
3. Anger, guilt, and other emotions;
4. A tendency of the family toward pseudomutuality or fusion, to be perfect in order to compensate for past failure and to overcome an increasing sense of vulnerability to failure.

Carter and McGoldrick (1980) cite some factors often associated with the poor adjustment of children in remarriage situations. These include: denial of the importance of prior loss; too little time between marriages; failure to resolve intense relationship issues with the first family, including extended family and friends; expectations that remarriage will be easily accepted by the children; and poor preparation for the changes that will occur.

Visher and Visher (1979) believe that preschool children adjust most easily to blended families. School-age children have more difficulty with membership in two households; visitations and children's fantasies of their natural parents reuniting (despite remarriage) often exacerbate these adjustment problems. Also, school-age children often maintain a sense of guilt over causing the divorce longer than younger children.

The nature of the divorce process—whether it is conducted agreeably by the couple or on an adversary basis—and the decisions regarding custody, visitations, and new lifestyles affect the quality of adjustment to a new family system. The important thing to remember is that, for a reconstituted family system, evolving into a functional system—with appropriate boundaries, rules, roles, and communication patterns—takes longer than for a family system that begins with just two spouses. The process for the former is more complex and requires much adaptation and renegotiation.

TABLE 4-4.   The school-age family

Developmental Tasks	General Issues	Requisite Skills	Significant Others
Renegotiate boundaries with the outside world	Emotional separation and individuation	Negotiating Conflict resolution	School and community staffs
Facilitate the child's entrance into school	Educational philosophies Parenting styles	Disciplining Nurturing	Child's friends and classmates
Renegotiate relationships with the school-age child	Triadic power Resource, time, and energy management	Teaching Communicating	Neighbors Extended family
Reevaluate couple roles and responsibilities	After-school care	Sharing Modeling	Babysitters
Renegotiate parental roles and responsibilities			
Balance the couple and parent subsystems			
Balance the self, family, and work			

Table 4-4 shows the developmental tasks and issues of this stage of the family life cycle. We see that the boundaries must necessarily expand to include community institutions and friends.

SUMMARY

These first four stages of the family life cycle are the most demanding; however, they can be the most exciting and gratifying. So much change occurs so rapidly, it is a miracle that as many people as do survive.

The first four stages of the family life cycle are most likely to occur during the early-adulthood period. In these stages the following processes take place: becoming a dyadic couple system; expanding into a three-party family system composed of two parents and a baby; and socializing the children and progressing in the family life cycle. The major developmental tasks involve boundary negotiations and renegotiations: between the individual partners as they merge into a couple system; among the couple system and the partners' respective and joint friends, families, careers, work colleagues, and the outside world; between the couple and their infant; and among the newly formed triadic family system and extended family, friends, colleagues, neighbors, and the outside world. Eventually, the outside-world negotiations become more critical as the young child goes off to school. At each stage of development, boundaries need renegotiation and communication patterns need restructuring.

The typical issues affecting families during these stages are: intimacy; parenting styles; economic issues; childcare (in or out of the home); time, energy, and space management; single parenting; career–family integration; and so forth. Cultural changes affect these issues, and families of the 1980s and 1990s are likely to contend with issues that differ from those of earlier decades.

Most people have some issues to work through with their families of origin in terms of attitudes, values, needs and expectations about parenting. Most adults have to face the issue of children in some way or another—whether or not to have them and how to meet whatever parenting needs they may have. Marriage and parenthood involve major commitments to other people; and these commitments impose constraints, requiring the constant renegotiation of relationships, the differentiation between needs and desires, compromises, self-sacrifice, the postponement of gratifications; and the will to work past difficult obstacles. These commitments are not only emotional and moral, but are also supported by our legal structure and cultural mores.

REFERENCES

Beal, E. Divorce and single parent families. In E. Carter and M. McGoldrick (eds.), *The family life cycle: A framework for family therapy.* New York: Gardner Press, 1980, pp. 241–264.

Bowen, M. *Family therapy and clinical practice.* New York: Aronson, 1978.

Bradt, J. The family with young children. In E. Carter and M. McGoldrick (eds.), *The family life cycle: A framework for family therapy.* New York: Gardner Press, 1980, pp. 121–147.

Campbell, A. The American way of mating. *Psychology Today,* May 1975, p. 37.

Carter, E., and McGoldrick, M. (eds.). *The family life cycle: A framework for family therapy.* New York: Gardner Press, 1980.

Dacey, J. *Adult development.* Glenview, Ill.: Scott Foresman, 1982.

Duvall, E. *Family development.* Philadelphia: J. B. Lippincott, 1971.

Duvall, E., & Hill, R. Report of the committee for the dynamics of family interaction. Prepared at the request of the National Conference on Family Life. Mimeographed. 1948.

Egan, G., & Cowan, M. *Moving into adulthood.* Monterey, Calif.: Brooks/Cole, 1980.

Feldman, H., & Feldman, M. The family life cycle: Some suggestions for recycling. *Journal of Marriage and the Family,* 1975, 37, 277–284.

Haley, J. *Strategies of psychotherapy.* New York: Grune and Stratton, 1963.

Haley, J. *Leaving home.* New York: Grune and Stratton, 1980.

Hill, R., & Rodgers, R. H. The developmental approach. In H. T. Christensen (ed.), *Handbook of marriage and the family.* Chicago: Rand McNally, 1964.

Kantor, D., & Lehr, W. *Inside the family.* San Francisco: Jossey-Bass, 1975.

Kimmel, D. *Adulthood and aging.* New York: John Wiley, 1974.

McGoldrick, M. The joining of families through marriages: The new couple. In E. Carter and M. McGoldrick (eds.), *The family life cycle: A framework for family therapy.* New York: Gardner Press, 1980, pp. 93–121.

Meyer, P. H. Between families: The unattached young adult. In E. Carter and M. McGoldrick (eds.), *The family life cycle: A framework for family therapy.* New York: Gardner Press, 1980, pp. 71–93.

Minuchin, S. *Families and family therapy.* Cambridge, Mass.: Harvard University Press, 1974.

Okun, B. F., & Rappaport, L. J. *Working with families: An introduction to family therapy.* Duxbury, Mass.: Duxbury Press, 1980.

Pichitino, J. P. Profile of the single father: A thematic integration of the literature. *Personnel and Guidance Journal,* 1983, *61,* 295–300.

Prosky, P. *Some thoughts on family life from the field of family therapy.* Unpublished paper, 1979.

Rodgers, R. H. *Family interaction and transaction: The developmental approach.* New York: Prentice-Hall, 1973.

Sager, C. J. *Marriage contracts and couple therapy.* New York: Brunner/Mazel, 1976.

Satir, V. *Conjoint family therapy.* Palo Alto, Calif.: Science and Behavior Books, 1967.

Scarf, M. *Unfinished business.* Garden City, N.Y.: Doubleday, 1980.

Terkelson, K. G. Toward a theory of the family life cycle. In E. Carter, and M. McGoldrick (eds.) *The family life cycle: A framework for family therapy.* New York: Gardner Press, 1980, pp. 21–53.

Visher, E. B. & Visher, J. S. *Stepfamilies: A guide to working with stepparents and stepchildren.* New York: Brunner/Mazel, 1979.

Wallerstein, J. S., & Kelley, J. B. *Surviving the breakup.* New York: Basic Books, 1980.

Wynne, L. C., Ryckoff, I. M., Day, J., & Hirsch, S. I., "Pseudomutuality in the family relationships of schizophrenics." *Psychiatry,* 1958, *21,* 205–220.

Yorburg, B. The nuclear and the extended family: An area of conceptual confusion. *Journal of Comparative Family Studies,* 1975, *6,* 73.

CHAPTER FIVE

CAREER DEVELOPMENT IN EARLY ADULTHOOD

The foundations of career development are, like those of family development, laid down long before adulthood. By the time people reach late adolescence, they already have a well-established orientation toward work, a sense of work's meaning, and attitudes, values, and beliefs about work. The interrelationships among individual, family, and career development are critical, but this chapter will identify and describe the separate stages, tasks, and issues relating to career development.

Like mate selection, occupation selection involves individual control. Even though one's career is subject to external influences, he or she has influence over the decisions involved in career development, and career changes are often easier to negotiate than family changes. Whether or not one chooses to take advantage of all possible options, many alternatives exist to be considered.

For the purposes of this text, the terms *career* and *occupation* are used interchangeably. Thus, one's career could be a *job* or could involve many jobs within a well defined, well planned developmental career path. While variations clearly exist within and among occupations, here the purpose is to deal with common variables. The following are some of the questions addressed in this chapter:

1. What is the meaning of work?
2. What are the effects of social and cultural forces on career development?
3. What are the effects of work on one's identity?
4. Does work influence personality processes?
5. Are the patterns of career development different for men and women?

The early-adult stages of career development are correlated here with the developmental stages of early adulthood:

1. Initial Choice—occurs in late adolescence;
2. Entry into the work world—occurs in youth;
3. Establishment—occurs in youth and young adulthood;
4. Career consolidation—occurs in young adulthood and mid-thirties transition.

Again, these parameters are relative and depend on career variations. For example, physicians are most likely to be in their late twenties or early thirties when they begin to establish their careers, considering the length of medical training. A factory worker, on the other hand, may have already worked up the organizational hierarchy to become a foreperson by the age at which the young physician is just starting out.

THE MEANING OF WORK

Obviously, work means different things to different people. Occupational choice determines one's own self-definition and one's lifestyle and position within the community. Likewise, self-definition, family's lifestyle, and position within the community affect occupational choice and attitudes toward work. Family variables in particular have the potential to impose significant constraints on when and where one goes to work and the type of job one takes. Consider the following example.

Tom, 25, had gone to work on the training program of a multinational corporation and was rising nicely in the organizational hierarchy. He foresaw a secure, successful career path for himself in this company, which was located in a major Midwest city. Tom was married to Ann, and they had one child, aged 2. Tom considered himself happy with his family and career. But his youngster had asthma, and as it became increasingly acute, Tom and Ann grew more and more anxious. Finally, their physician suggested that the boy would suffer far fewer major attacks if they lived in a different part of the country. Tom realized that he would be unable to find a similar job elsewhere, for his industry was tied to the Midwest. Finally, after much soul searching and discussion, he and Ann decided that Tom would resign and that the family would move and find some other way to make a living. Tom ended up selling insurance and real estate and working on his own. While he will always regret the necessity of making this decision, he nevertheless discovered that he could shape a new lifestyle and follow a new career direction.

The meaning of work can involve any one of any combination of the following factors: prestige, social recognition, self-respect, sense of worth, social opportunity, social participation, service to mankind or the community, enjoyment of a particular activity, securing a certain kind of lifestyle, creative self-expression, and so forth. Moreover, personality characteristics, such as the needs for achievement, security, autonomy, and conformity, are formulated in childhood and affect the meaning of work.

Cultural Influences

The meaning of work changed radically during the countercultural revolution of the 1960s as values were reassessed and reformulated. No longer were job stability and job security viewed as the major priorities in adult life. Organizations were no longer allowed total control over individuals' life decisions, such as how and where individuals lived. Rather, the emphasis was on the "socially useful" aspect of work, the aspect of doing something that contributed simultaneously to one's self-worth and to society. Meanwhile, young people's growing distrust of government and business organizations led them to choose smaller businesses and professions that allowed them more autonomy. Previously recognized patterns of career development, such as those promulgated by Super (1957) and Miller and Form (1951), became outdated.

The 1970s saw a proliferation of human-service types of occupations—social work, teaching, counseling, youth work, public law, and so on. In addition, a growing number of young people adopted trades and artistic endeavors; they were interested in creative self-expression and aspired only to make enough money to live on. It is not unusual today to meet highly educated young people from affluent families who are "working the land," building ships, or doing woodwork for a living. Upward mobility was scorned when they were making their career choices, and there developed a tendency to ask "What's in it for me?" rather than "What can I do to help develop the organizational system?"

Needless to say, this change in the work ethic often conflicted with the values and orientations of the parent generation and resulted in family struggles, with the generations pitted against each other. In many cases, the disruption served as a catalyst in strengthening family relationships, but in others, family systems were more permanently broken.

Prior to the late 1960s, it was generally assumed that adults would look for occupational niches that gave meaning and importance to their lives by implementing their self-concepts. They had the option to choose which part of the country to settle in, which particular job (of many) to take, and which kind of lifestyle to seek. A myriad of options came into existence as new fields opened up, and new opportunities seemed endless. Work was considered to be the most important aspect of life, and family and individual sacrifices made in the pursuit of work were assumed to be necessary. But during the 1970s, many people decided to question these assumptions and to reassess their priorities. Thus, for many, work became a lower priority, a means to an end, a way of supporting a particular lifestyle or avocation. People no longer felt the push to translate their interests into a career—if one worked out, fine, but if not other choices were available. This new attitude was reflected in more frequent job changes and more persistent demands by workers for modifications in working conditions and job opportunities.

The kinds of factors that are likely to influence one's work values include the following:

1. Individual needs, as formulated by Maslow (1943)—the achievement motive, the need for affiliation, the need for power, and the need for psychological well-being and meaning;
2. Interpersonal needs regarding the type of organizational system in which one feels comfortable (for example, working alone and unsupervised versus working collaboratively with people, with or without structured supervision), and regarding communication styles and socialization possibilities;
3. Intrinsic and extrinsic rewards, such as excitement, challenge, salary, and fringe benefits.

Economic Influences

The latitudes and freedoms discussed above can only occur in an expanding economy. For example, the huge amounts of money and governmental services earmarked for human service programs created a vast array of jobs for the increasing number of young adults and youths interested in them. Thus, in the 1970s, we saw more men than ever before enter the fields of teaching, social work, counseling, and nursing, just as we saw women begin to enter engineering, finance, and other traditionally male occupations.

With the 1980s, some changes began to occur. The effects of a reduced birthrate following the postwar boom began to show up as reduced enrollments in the public schools across the land; thus, the teaching profession became restricted. Human service programs began to dry up, which resulted in an abundance of experienced workers joining the unemployed, to say nothing of the younger people who planned to enter the social service field. Whereas college graduates used to have their choice of jobs, they were fortunate now simply to find a job even remotely related to their major field of study. Meanwhile, the medical, law, social science, and academic professions became overcrowded, and there developed a greater demand for engineers and other technological occupations. As colleges and universities began to compete more earnestly for the rapidly dwindling student body and as inflation began to spread uncontrollably, attitudes and demands regarding education and training changed.

The competition grew fierce for entrance into professional schools, and many began to question the efficacy of an expensive college education, particularly as more and more college graduates found themselves unemployed, driving cabs or tending bars. Those high school graduates who went on to college began to demand that their training have relevance to career development; therefore, the value of an undergraduate liberal arts education was seriously questioned except in a dozen or so of the nation's elite colleges and universities. In a desperate attempt to recruit and retain students and thus to remain in existence, many colleges quickly tried to develop prevocational training programs.

Thus, we are now seeing the return of the serious college student who is aware of the real competitions and restrictions in the occupational world. While today's young adults have more choices than their counterparts of a generation ago, many options have disappeared. Near-desperation invades young people as they assess work possibilities and opportunities. They see work now as necessary to survival—no longer can young people assume that they will surpass their parents' socioeconomic statuses or lifestyles. In fact, the usual phenomenon of each generation automatically surpassing the preceding one appears to have died.

While young people today hope for the opportunity to have a career they enjoy and find meaningful, many realize that they cannot count on achieving that luxury. Today's young adult generation has been raised in more affluence and with more permissiveness and stimulation than any preceding American generation. Perhaps, because these young people have had so much, they will not be as hungry for more, or as driven as were their depression-scarred parents and grandparents to gain complete security. On the other hand, media coverage and accessibility may have heightened their expectations more than ever before, and those expectations may well collide with reality.

The word of the 1980s seems to be *compromise.* In the context of this book, compromise means negotiating career choice along with personal and family choices, and finding an occupational niche that allows one dignity and integrity without requiring the sacrifice of autonomy and control.

THE INITIAL CHOICE

One usually makes one's initial career choice during late adolescence. The stage characterized by this choice is called by Super the *specification stage,* by Ginzberg the *realistic stage,* and by Levinson the *entering-adulthood stage.* Career choice becomes a conscious process during the last years of high school, when one begins to make post-high-school plans—whether to continue one's education or training or to enter the labor force directly. There are many influences on this choice.

Influences

Family-of-origin influences.   A young person's attitudes and expectations have already been formulated by the experience of growing up in a particular family system. Parents' occupations—what they did, how they felt about their work, and how that work affected the family and the individuals within it— provided first-hand data for a youngster to consider. Some parents prescribe a particular career path for a youngster, and this may differ for boys and girls. Some families encourage what is known as the development of occupational awareness, helping to expose their children to a wide variety of possibilities and opportunities. Others prefer to restrict their children's exposure, hoping to retain control longer, and perhaps influence their youngsters into making decisions that will keep them close to home.

Thus, parents' expectations, attitudes, values, and beliefs about their own occupations, about what work is desirable, and about life's priorities will inevitably affect youngsters' choices, though whether the result will be conformity or opposition is another matter. A young person's ability to make an occupational decision based on an individuated self-assessment will depend greatly on the degree of self-differentiation and emotional separation from the family he or she has achieved.

Part-time jobs.   Many young people hold part-time jobs as they are growing up. Their experiences in working, earning money, and being responsible for a particular job will affect their attitudes toward work in adulthood and will perhaps stimulate their interests and attitudes about a particular type of work. The following examples illustrate this point.

One young woman, named Jan, reported to her counselor that the waitress jobs she held for two summers while in high school convinced her that serving of any kind was not what she wanted to do for the rest of her life. She learned that she wanted more autonomy than might be available to her in a service-type occupation and that she preferred to work more independently—she liked being alone rather than with people. This was valuable information for her in making her initial occupational decisions. And a young man, Jack, discovered after he had completed his Ivy League university education, that he was happiest during the summer, when he worked with a house builder constructing summer homes. He decided to return to that kind of work, and his career development took a totally different path than he or his parents had anticipated.

Peers and community.   We cannot underestimate the influence of peers and the type of community in which one is raised. Both factors affect the scope of one's exposure and the development of one's occupational awareness—after all, you can't consider an occupation that you do not even know exists. For instance, if you live on a seacoast, you might be exposed to many types of occupations that you might not consider if you lived inland.

Since adolescents are in a stage of life development in which the opinions and acceptance of their peers are critical, they might select an occupation that heightens their acceptance and approval rather than threatens it. Many youngsters with peer systems that do not value higher education or social institutions, for example, find that they totally lose the support and acceptance of their peer system if they go on with their educations or choose such careers as military or police work. Until they are able to develop a new peer system that approves of their occupational choices, they may feel alone and bereft.

By the same token, peers can increase the possibilities one is exposed to. The issue of conformity versus nonconformity becomes critical, and again is dependent on the young person's degree of self-differentiation.

Teachers, ministers, and other significant role models in the community can often foster one's career awareness and exploration. It is not at all unusual for a dedicated teacher to take on a mentor role in helping certain students develop appropriate career aspirations.

Larger organizations and institutions. The prevailing economic system clearly increases or restricts the opportunities open to young people. In addition, government policies can regulate access to particular occupations, salary levels, and future trends in particular fields. Likewise, professional organizations and labor unions affect access into particular fields and regulate advancement. And, of course, the admissions policies of educational and training institutions affect entrance into occupations requiring specific educational and training credentials.

Another important factor is the organizational context of a particular field. If one grows up in what Kantor (1975) refers to as an open-family system, one might be appalled at the prospect of working in a closed-system type of organization, such as the government, a large corporation, or the military service. An open system is characterized by lateral power and authority, permits universal participation, encourages dissent, expects loyalty to the system's individualistic and collective ideals, expresses and shares affect openly, and values uniqueness and differences. In the closed model, power might be organized vertically, rules are clear and hierarchical, opposition is discouraged, and strong, unquestioned loyalty is expected.

Cultural influences. One's ethnic and cultural heritage automatically invests one with certain attitudes and values about occupational choice. These may or may not be in accord with the attitudes and expectations of the family of origin.

Sex-role stereotypes are a major cultural influence today. These stereotypes have been changing very slowly since the 1970s, although much discrimination against women still exists in the work place, as reflected in their smaller salaries and promotion opportunities compared with those of men. Two major setbacks to the dissolution of sex-role stereotypes occurred, first in 1981, when the United States Supreme Court ruled that women could not be registered or drafted, and then in 1982, when the Equal Rights Amendment, prohibiting sex discrimination, failed to be ratified.

Most vocational-development theories have been based on men. This model reflects the traditional societal expectation that, for women, work outside the home is of secondary importance and may even be in contradiction to a woman's role. The traditional sex-role distinctions of women's occupational patterns have been so subtle and pervasive that the majority of women today have been affected by them whether or not they are aware of the fact.

For example, Hennig and Jardim (1978) found that men focus on achieving long-range goals whereas women focus more on short-range goals. Many women, therefore, make their career decisions late, perceiving and fearing risk-taking as being equivalent to loss rather than to challenge or gain. A possible explanation is that men grow up knowing they will have to work for the rest of their lives, whereas women grow up in a cloud of ambiguity—they may or may not work and may have some say over how long they will remain in the work force. Thus, women have more variables to consider when making an occupational choice—

family needs, timing, and so on. Furthermore, women apparently have to prove constantly that they are seriously committed to their careers, whereas men are assumed to be focused and committed.

Men, too, are influenced by traditional sex-role stereotypes. They are expected to compete successfully in the working world and to prioritize their achievement motivation in a typically male-oriented occupation, giving their parenting role a lower priority. It is to be hoped that as men and women continue to redefine their roles to share more equally the family and occupational responsibilities, sex differences will become negligible in determining the choice and course of an individual's career development.

Social class.   Social-class variables affect occupational choice, although these boundaries have become more permeable since World War II and the increasing accessibility to education and mobility. However, these variables still contribute to the shaping of expectations and the formulation of identity and one's dream, which, in turn, influence the choices of jobs and lifestyles. The meaning of work for many youths in low socioeconomic classes is strongly associated with the physical and economic lower-level needs postulated by Maslow. Thus, many of their job decisions are based on immediate needs rather than long-range planning. People who are concerned with basic survival do not have the luxury of seeking fulfillment, gratification, and challenge. Interestingly, the economic realities of the 1980s may force many people in higher socioeconomic classes to change their expectations.

Military service.   A major factor that influenced vocational choice during the 1970s was the abandonment of the military draft. Conscripted military service served a number of purposes in our society. First, it provided a "growing-up period" for young men who had not yet discovered who they were or who they wanted to be and who needed help in separating emotionally from their families of origin. Second, the military provided both an extraordinary opportunity for occupational awareness and exploration and superior vocational education. It served to weaken social-class boundaries in occupational choice. Now, with the draft eliminated, many young people who might have found a satisfying occupation through their experiences in military service are floundering, searching for whatever type of employment seems to be available.

However, for those young people who do choose to serve in the military, the benefits still exist. Many make occupational choices, receive training and attain career development that they would never have aspired to outside of the service. Some elect to remain in the service, and many find that their military experiences open up employment opportunities in the civilian world.

Developmental Tasks

The major developmental task of this stage is to make an initial career choice. This process involves both making a decision about what one is going to do and discovering what one must do to implement this choice.

Decision making.   Making the decision involves several steps:

1. Discovering one's own needs, interests, abilities, and talents;
2. Finding out about different occupations from role models, the media, school studies, and other sources;
3. Using whatever data are available from school guidance programs such as testing and counseling;
4. Seeking out reliable sources of information about possible occupations to discover the work roles and conditions involved;
5. Learning more about one's attitudes, values, and aspirations;
6. Making appropriate educational decisions;
7. Performing well enough in high school and college to keep as many career options open as possible;
8. Learning about oneself from extracurricular activities and social life;
9. Exploring the world of work with part time and summer job experiences.

Early influences.   The process of making this initial choice really begins when one is a child, fantasizing about being a grownup and experimenting with different roles in school and in the community. When the youngster enters high school, he or she makes one decision that is part of the larger choice process—namely, the type of high school program to follow—business, vocational, general, or college preparatory. Perhaps the individual makes the decision even earlier on the basis of prior academic performance, family pressures, or emerging interests.

Every time the person reaches a particular choice point, some options are kept open and some are closed. Guidance counselors and teachers, it is to be hoped, aid a youngster in keeping as many options open as possible. The importance of guidance at this stage is illustrated in the following example.

Ben came from a working class family in which the son was expected to obtain a minimal education and work with his parents in the factory. Ben automatically attended a regional trade school from seventh to ninth grades. In the ninth grade, he took a required general science course and had a particularly inspiring teacher who took a special interest in him. At the end of the school year, this teacher, in conjunction with the guidance counselor, approached Ben and his parents and urged them to place him in the academic high school, since they believed Ben had high academic skills. Ben's parents agreed and he transferred to the academic high school, graduated in the top tenth of his class and won a full scholarship to a major university.

High school influences.   One's academic performance in high school affects the next series of choices. For example, if one is taking a business curriculum, the types of jobs available after graduation will depend upon one's job experiences and academic performance in high school. Vocational training might prepare a youngster for entry level in a particular trade or for specialized technical training after graduation. A general curriculum is probably the least advantageous, leaving the graduate at the mercy of the prevailing opportunities in the labor market. One's academic performance in a college-preparatory program will determine choice of college or university and concomitant financial aid. Some students know early in their high school career just exactly what their occupational path will be, and they follow this course without wavering. More commonly, though, high school students become less and less certain about their goals and attempt to keep all options open as they continue a more liberal type of education. By high school graduation, however, the late adolescent is beginning to have a strong sense of self and some ideas about his or her abilities, needs, and interests. These will influence the type of occupation he or she seeks or the type of college program selected.

As we understand more about the vicissitudes of individual development in late adolescence and early adulthood, we can better appreciate the wavering occupational choices, the confusion about lifestyle directions, and the psychological manifestations of stress characteristic in young people. Career choice is no longer conceived as a linear task, but rather as a complex one that continues throughout life.

College influences.   One unfortunate ramification of the intense competition in colleges and universities today for managerial and professional training is that students tend to select safe courses to maintain high grade point averages, and, therefore, they are reluctant to take courses totally removed from their previous experience for fear of risking lower grades. Thus, students fail to expose themselves to possible new interests and abilities. At the end of the sophomore year in college, most students are required to select a major. Some do so with a particular career in mind; some select the most liberal major, figuring that they can select a career later on. Some select the subject they feel the most secure and competent with to ensure a high grade point average; still others select what is the most interesting to them, regardless of whether or not it is their "best subject." Although a college major is not a final career choice, it often is interpreted by college students as a narrowing of the options.

College years are critical years for all aspects of development and whatever experiences (social, work, academic, community) one has during these years affect the choices made for postcollege life. Some students select a field of work and go straight into graduate school or specialized training. Others decide to go to work to earn money and to see what it feels like to be in the work world, hoping that such exploration will lead to some type of career direction. Still others take time out before making this initial choice. They may travel, "bum around," or do volunteer work such as the Peace Corps. For some, taking a job in a particular industry or organization puts them on a career ladder in terms of their functional and technical career development. Consider the example below.

When Don was 22, he majored in economics because he liked the subject and had a vague interest in banking. During the summers, he worked in restaurants in summer resorts and his interest in banking remained intact only because some of his friends had the same interest. His university career services office suggested he apply for a training program with one of the large banks. He did so and, because of his outstanding academic record, was offered a high-level training position with a prestigious bank. Don had no long-term career goals at this time, though he was eager to become financially self-sufficient and to live on his own without the academic pressures of college or parental pressures. He was really concerned only with the gratification of short-term needs and figured that some day he would make a satisfactory living, get married, and have a family, car, home, and vacations. However, Don found that he liked working at the bank; he liked the atmosphere and people. He was fortunate in that he moved up the organizational hierarchy regularly and smoothly. Fifteen years later, he was still with the same bank, in an upper managerial position. If you were to ask Don how he got to where he is, he would shrug and reply that he was "lucky"—he happened to find the right job when he left school that afforded him the opportunity for advancement.

The point of Don's story is that one's initial career choice may or may not correspond to the job one ends up with years later. Most likely, there is no one best career choice (just as there is no one perfect mate); one can do well in and enjoy more than one situation. However, people's initial career choices do affect later career development by helping them collect first-hand data about what they like, want, and need. The initial career choice may be largely determined by luck, by happening to be in the right place at the right time, or by being born into a family that affords certain opportunities. For many, however, initial career choice is determined by clearly defined interests or abilities, by whom one marries, and by options created by conscious, serious planning and evaluation.

Major Theories of Choice Recapitulated

To further understand initial career choice we turn to the major vocational-development theories. As noted in Chapter 2, Holland presents a comprehensive model that attempts to relate personal and job typologies: realistic, conventional, enterprising, investigative, artistic, and social. Holland and Gottfriedson (1976) note that person–job congruence leads to increased job satisfaction, which, in turn, leads to stable careers. The initial job choice, then, is based on an attempt to seek this congruence. One's typology can change over time, however, depending on life events and experiences.

Super and associates' (1963) self-concept theories assume that career choice is determined by people's ideas of themselves. He postulated five vocational life stages: growth (birth–14); exploration (15–24); establishment (25–44); maintenance (45–64); and decline (65 on). Each stage is characterized by a series of vocational tasks and behaviors that society expects an individual to accomplish. Super et al. (1963) identify these tasks as crystallizing a vocational preference, specifying it, implementing it, stabilizing in the chosen vocation, consolidating one's status, and advancing in the occupation. One's self-concept may be subject to change over time, although Super believes it to be relatively stable. Although Super's work is influenced by Erikson's, it is hard to know if one's self-concept develops as a consequence of career choices and achievements or is necessary for making choices or gaining achievements. In other words, is one's self-concept an antecedent or outcome of career choice? I believe that adult-development theory postulates a continuously developing self-concept and that the stability Super refers to is no longer a viable concept.

Krumboltz (1979) proposes a social-learning model of career choice. This theory recognizes career preferences, occupational skills, and all choices of courses, occupations, and fields of work as a composite of many past and present experiences as well as the anticipation of future experiences. These experiences are composed of four general factors: (1) genetic endowment and special abilities; (2) environmental conditions and events; (3) specific learning experiences; and (4) a set of "task-approach skills." The genetic endowment and special abilities include race, sex, intelligence, muscular coordination, and music and art skills. The environmental conditions and events include the number and nature of job and training opportunities, social policies, selection procedures, the rate of return for various occupations, and family, social, educational, technological, labor, and natural variables. Specific learning experiences include instrumental ones, such as the consequences of actions in the past, and associational ones, such as stereotypes, beliefs, and values. Task-approach skills include problem-solving skills, work habits, performance standards and values, and perceptual and cognitive processes.

An important model of cognitive career development was formulated by Knefelkamp and Slepitza (1978), based on Perry's (1970) model of the intellectual and ethical development of college students. As noted earlier, Perry proposed that college students' thinking develops from dualism through multiplicity and relativism to commitment. The dimensions of cognitive change important for college students in the process of selecting an occupation are:

1. Locus of control (from external to internal);
2. Integrative ability (ability to foresee cause–effect relationships);
3. Cognitive complexity (ability to synthesize);
4. Openness to new ideas;
5. Awareness (self-processing);
6. Ability to assume responsibility;
7. Ability to take on new roles;
8. Ability to take risks with self.

While this view identifies the cognitive processes involved during the college years with occupational decision making, it does not formulate satisfactory measures of these processes or concomitant counseling interventions. Also, this approach has not been tested on noncollege youth. Nevertheless, this work does focus attention on the importance of the development of cognitive processes in effective decision making.

Tiedeman and O'Hara (1963) define career as "the imposition of direction into the vocational behavior of a person which is subject to his comprehension and will" (p. 295). They say that one is confronted at many points in one's life with environmentally caused "study and work discontinuities" or transition events requiring career-related decisions (for example, selecting a college and choosing a college major). These writers identify seven stages of career decidedness, which require the processes of differentiation and integration in problem solving:

1. Exploration (14–18 years), where one is vaguely anxious and considering career options but lacking information about self and careers;
2. Crystallization (18–21 years), where one is collecting data and evaluating options but is still not ready for public commitment;

3. Choice (18–25 years), where one is experiencing varied uncertainty but planning action and experiencing relief from the planning;
4. Clarification (also 18–25 years), where one has well-thought-out plans;
5. Induction (21–30 years), where one is entering one's occupational choice and experiencing the reality of the choice:
6. Reformation (also 21–30 years), where one is deciding whether or not to pursue the initial choice or to modify it or make an altogether different choice;
7. Integration (30–40 years), where one integrates one's career choice and experiences into one's identity and lifestyle.

This delineation seems to match most closely the developmental model presented in this text in that it reflects an ongoing decision-making process throughout early adulthood.

Regardless of which theory one subscribes to, it is important to consider psychological, sociological, and economic variables. We know that working itself socializes one and influences personality processes, and we can assume that one's experiences with initial career choices will affect one's later career development. People are defined by their work roles in our society more than by any other social roles. When people meet each other socially, one of the first questions they ask is "What do you do?" or "What does your mom do?" or "What does your spouse do?" Rappaport (1972) states that one's self-concept is influenced by one's occupational choice and commitment in three ways: (1) through the daily routines and activities associated with a job that affects the periphery of the self; (2) through social relationships and socioeconomic status; and (3) through values or beliefs associated with a particular type of occupation. If cognitive dissonance exists between a person's values and job, the person is more likely to change the values than the job without necessarily realizing it. Thus the age-old question arises: Does the person make the job or does the job make the person? Surely, mutual socialization occurs with the job, and organizational socializing influences are stronger, in many cases, than one's individual personal values. Perhaps, then, a self-selecting process exists that occurs at the outset of the occupational choice. At some level, one knows the type of person and lifestyle associated with a particular field of work and seeks to fulfill one's dream of what life is to be.

Developmental Issues

A young person must consider several issues when making this initial occupational choice. Obviously, these differ among occupations.

Realistic socioeconomic constraints.   As tuitions rise and student loans decrease, certain types of occupations may automatically close to a larger number of young people. The family's socioeconomic circumstances, the ability of a young person to work while in school, and the escalating costs of post-high-school education can place a realistic constraint on someone's choice. Another aspect of this issue is learning about the realistic possibilities of making a living in one's chosen field.

Laura, 20, was a gifted musician who wanted to major in music and pursue a career as a symphony player. Halfway through an undergraduate program in a leading musical school of a large university, she realized, through discussions with peers and faculty, that the possibility of her eking out a living as a professional musician was indeed slim—not because of her lack of talent, but because of the intense competition for the declining number of symphony positions predicted well into the 1980s and 1990s owing to the dwindling funds for the arts. Laura's parents urged her to switch into a science major, as she had always shown aptitude for science and math subjects. With sadness, Laura finally decided to pursue music as an avocation and to protect her employability by majoring in chemistry. Laura knew that she would need to support herself upon completion of college and that she would not be able to afford further musical training without a satisfactory income.

Basic work-world skills.   Many employers have said loudly and clearly that they are not as concerned with a prospective employee's technical and functional skills as with his or her ability to work with people and to be punctual, reliable, and dependable. Likewise, many counselors and therapists know that for many of the people who experience difficulty at work, inappropriate or deficient interpersonal skills and personal habits are the foundation for these work difficulties. Therefore, one issue that young people need to consider is how they can develop the basic skills and habits needed in the world of work. While it is true that some occupations require more interpersonal skills than others, a base level is required for just about every occupation at some point. One must decide what one can do and what one is willing and unwilling to do in terms of choosing an occupation. For example, if regular work hours are a requirement for a particular person, he or she might eliminate certain occupations, such as a career as a pilot or an obstetrician. And if one knows that he or she cannot stand being confined to an office, working with the same people day in and out, and being closely supervised, he or she will be more likely to select an occupation that requires travelling and autonomy, such as a career as a sales representative or a visiting nurse.

Realistic appraisal of opportunities.   A critical issue in initial career choice is obtaining realistic information about conditions, salary, and growth opportunities within a particular occupation. Along with this information, one must project the likely possible impact of a particular career choice on lifestyle and aspirations for family development. In the Northeast, for example, a person who wants to become an elementary school teacher today would be well advised to consider moving to another part of the country. Interestingly, people deny much realistic data along this line. For example, the American Psychological Association surveyed doctoral students in clinical psychology programs across the country in 1979–1980 and found that most of these students aspired to become university or college professors. Most of the students realized that projections showed that only 10 percent of the doctoral candidates would find academic jobs in the succeeding decade. More than 85 percent of the respondents, however, believed that they would be among the 10 percent. In reality, a large number of doctoral-level psychologists are currently unable to obtain academic or clinical positions and are being forced into private practice and part-time jobs to make a living. This is not to suggest that someone with a burning desire to enter a particular occupation should give up that desire on the basis of a weak prognosis for the future. Rather, one must take these data into consideration and be aware of the possible need to remain flexible and to consider alternate options.

Obtaining appropriate training or education.   It is amazing how many times young people select a career direction and then choose an unsatisfactory or inappropriate type of training or education. Perhaps poor preparation is a way of expressing ambivalence about one's choice; or perhaps it results from poor guidance from counselors, teachers, and parents. Ideally, young people should visit training and education sites, talk with interested people, and make appropriate choices based on what they have learned.

For example, consider Jonathan, who as a junior in high school decided to become an engineer and began applying to engineering schools. He had already taken the college board achievement tests in biology and mathematics and thought that he had only one more to take, the required English composition test. It was only after he received college catalogues from engineering schools that he realized that most engineering schools required either a chemistry or physics college board achievement test; fortunately, he was able to take a fourth test during his senior year to keep open the possibility of being accepted into engineering school. Likewise, many young people find that the curricular paths they are pursuing do not lead to their goals and discover late that they must take additional courses to meet requirements for a particular career.

Sex-role issues.   The type of career a woman selects will determine the kind of integration she can achieve between work and family commitments. Many women choose traditionally female occupations, such as teaching, social work, or library science, with this factor in mind. However, the opportunities in these fields are now dwindling, and women who wish to integrate careers with families must seek new ways of doing so.

The choice between a traditional and a nontraditional career reflects a woman's identity and is a source of continued influence as she goes through her adult development. A woman who chooses what Wolkon (1972) calls a pioneering type of career, something heretofore associated with males, may cut herself off from the support of other women and from alternative family options. This result of a nontraditional choice creates a genuine dilemma for women today. In high school and college, late-adolescent women feel torn between their needs and desires to be simultaneously family oriented and career oriented. Many feel that the choice is an either/or one, and that integrating career and family is impossible. The lack of successful and significant role models adds to women's anxieties connected with these decisions. Scarf (1980) points out that most young women today are still receiving double messages from their families and the culture at large: they are told both to succeed in a man's world and to remain feminine, nurturing, and adaptive so they can marry and have children.

Young women today still feel ambivalence about achievement and success, as Horner (1972) found in her pioneering studies on this subject. They are very concerned with the timing of their plans—whether to develop a career first and then plan for a family, or vice versa, or whether to do both simultaneously, and they feel intensely that they are subjected to more discrimination and to more burdens than their male counterparts.

Doris, aged 32, had completed medical school, a rigorous internship, and a residency in a specialization dominated by men. She was considered a "hot ticket" in the medical-research field and had many high-level job offers to consider. However, Doris knew that she wanted to marry and have children and that her absorption in her career along with her long hours and weekend commitments precluded this possibility. After much soul searching, Doris decided to leave her specialty and to move to another city, where she would have the opportunity to meet new people and to take a 9-to-5 clinical staff position. Her colleagues and supervisors thought she was "insane" to give up what she had already pursued (although she did not tell them the real reason), but once Doris made this decision, she adhered to it. Her rationale was that she at least needed to take steps that would open up opportunities for meeting men before it was too late to consider having children. This decision worked out very well for Doris. She married within the next year and had two children while retaining her clinical staff position. Thus, Doris managed to integrate the two areas of her life. However, she was intensely aware that men do not have to make these kinds of choices and that therein lies the sex-role difference.

The earlier women confront such issues, the more appropriate are their choices likely to be. Too often, a woman in her early twenties refuses to deal with these issues and is thrown into a panic in her early or late thirties, when her biological time clock forces some kind of confrontation with these realities.

Thus, the period of initial choice is one of anticipation, tentative exploration, and attempts to narrow down options to a realistic choice that is consonant with one's emerging identity. All these aspects require an awareness of self—of one's interests, values, and capacities—and an awareness of the world of work and the possibilities therein. Table 5-1 shows the tasks and skills associated with initial choice, the first stage in adult career development.

TABLE 5-1.   Initial choice

Developmental Tasks	General Issues	Requisite Skills	Significant Others
Decide on an initial career choice	Family-of-origin influences	Self-assessing	Teachers
Develop a plan	Peers and community influences	Data collecting regarding self, occupation, and world of work	Counselors
Take steps to implement the plan	Organizational-context influences	Appraising data	Parents
	Cultural influences	Evaluating options	Occupational and lifestyle models
	High school and college influences	Fantasizing	Peers
	Socioeconomic influences	Checking out	Employers
	Sex-role issues	Exploring	
	Realistic constraint issues	Maintaining flexibility	
		Decision making	
		Planning	
		Basic work-world skills	
		Reassessing	

ENTERING THE WORLD OF WORK

The actual entrance into the work world usually occurs during the period of youth. This stage is similar to Super's implementation stage and Levinson's early-adult transition. Some professions, such as medicine and law, require extensive training, internships, or clerkships, thus postponing actual entry into the work world until young adulthood.

During this stage, one develops a new role, that of a worker in a particular job or field. Typically, the first years on a job for anyone are a kind of trial and error, as one attempts to implement ideas and dreams of a job or career and develop a self-concept as a worker in a particular field. Troll (1975) quotes Becker (1964) as describing these years as a "period of initiation, accompanied by fears about one's competence and self-worth and by the use of such coping strategies as rehearsal and strict adherence to rules." When one makes a choice or decision, one anticipates possible outcomes. Entering into the world of work involves assessment of one's decision-making skills and checking to see whether predicted outcomes of the choice are realized. Since a person is still finding out who he or she is at this time of life, a faulty initial occupational choice may result from an incomplete sense of self rather than a faulty sense of self resulting from a faulty initial occupational choice.

Developmental Tasks

The overall task of this period is to test out the world of work to decide whether one's initial choice warrants the efforts and energy of formulating a career. The specific tasks are these:

1. Learning how things are actually done on the job and how to perform effectively—in short, acquiring occupational skills, values, and credentials;
2. Learning how to accept responsibility for one's job functions and tasks;
3. Accepting a subordinate status within an organization or profession;
4. Learning how to get along with a boss and with peers;
5. Demonstrating that one can keep the job and improve and progress;
6. Finding a mentor or sponsor;
7. Negotiating the boundaries between the job and outside relationships and interests;
8. Reassessing the initial choice so one can pursue this type of work in terms of the feedback that one receives and the actual outcomes of the work experience and opportunities;
9. Dealing with feelings of disappointment, frustration, success and/or failure.

The task can be seen as one of initiation and socialization into one's chosen career. One learns from co-workers and supervisors the rules and regulations of the organization or profession. In short, one first learns how to behave and then chooses whether this mode of behavior is congruent with one's self-concept or personality typology. Thus, one masters the routine contents and functions of the job as well as the more subtle lifestyle, social, and organizational factors.

Consider Alan, who received a Ph.D. in economics from a major west coast university and was able to attain a position as assistant professor at a small college in the Midwest. Alan's major goal was to become a college professor, and he chose the field of economics because it interested him and because he excelled in those studies. After six months as an assistant professor, Alan went to see a therapist to explore his increasing dissatisfaction and depression. It turned out that Alan's dream of academia had been rudely shattered by some of the machinations he had been unable to avoid within the college. He had initially rejected a business career because he believed that business was a cutthroat pursuit, too competitive and too lacking in humanistic values. Now he found himself in a department where the autocratic chairman expected junior faculty to follow orders automatically and to bow down to the senior faculty. It was made very clear that the route to tenure involved "playing the game" according to the whims of the administration more than teaching and scholarly competence. This was a valuable learning experience for Alan: he discovered early that he was not comfortable in this work setting and that the actuality conflicted with his self-concept. After finishing out the academic year, he obtained a research position with a large corporation and found the organizational climate and rewards much more to his liking.

In contrast, many people thrive on the socialization process and become valued employees because they find satisfaction in their choices and congruence between the work they have selected and their self-concepts. Henry (1971) found in his study of mental health professionals that their training and socialization into their profession led them to share beliefs, ways of behaving, and a common ideology very different from that projected in their original education. They ended up using work and leisure time similarly, and exhibiting similar patterns of work interests, social behavior, belief systems, explanations for behavior, and the kinds of patients they treated. In other words, their work socialization extended into their personal and social lives. It is not uncommon, both in large metropolitan areas or small company towns, to find members of professional or occupational groups socializing with each other more than with those in other occupational groups.

Measuring the anticipated outcomes of an initial career choice partly involves evaluating the returns (benefits and rewards) of the job. These returns may be immediate or longer range, and may include earnings, prestige, power, autonomy, associations, social benefits, and personal growth. Such returns can function as motivations or as discouragements when one is deciding whether to continue on. Some returns may be more important than others, depending on one's personal values. Likewise, as one's needs change, one may find that one's priority of returns changes. Sometimes such changes eventually result in career changes.

If one finds that one's first job is unsatisfactory, which is frequently the case, then it is important to reactivate the decision-making process and decide what to do about it. Some people fear making a change, particularly if their investment of time and preparation in a particular career path has been extensive. A critical variable is learning what contributes to the dissatisfaction—it may be misperceptions of the work environment as in the case of Alan, faulty self-assessment in terms of competencies and abilities, or a changing self-concept that requires a different choice. Is it the work place or the nature of the work that needs to be changed? In such a case, the developmental task is to move on and decide how to do so—whether to stay within a particular career field or to enter a new field.

Developmental Issues

The kinds of issues that one deals with at this phase of career development include those discussed in Chapter 3, in conjunction with family development.

Responsibility and commitment.   The ability to accept responsibility for fulfilling successfully the tasks and duties associated with a job requires the following commitments: to completing a task, to the rules and regulations of the work environment, and to the ethics and loyalties existing in the chosen field. Many young people find making such commitments more difficult than they thought, and discover that meeting deadlines, finishing projects, or following tasks through from inception through implementation to evaluation are too difficult. For example, some people find that they need very structured work environments: where they know exactly what is expected of them; when, where, and how they are expected to perform their work; and where close supervision is provided. Others find that they perform better if left alone and allowed to proceed in their own style and at their own pace. The task is to integrate one's own needs and styles with the demands of the job and the organization, finding ways to meet both one's own needs for self-worth and self-respect and the needs of the job and/or profession. Depending on past experiences, the individual may or may not have anticipated these issues.

Skill development.   Another common issue relates to the development, not only of occupational skills and values, but also of political and organizational skills necessary for promotion in the field or for lateral career growth into other areas. People run into job difficulties most often because they lack the interpersonal skills necessary for working in an organizational or professional structure regardless of their specific technical and functional competencies. Thus, the socialization skills learned from peers, superiors, clients, or customers can enable one to function within an occupation or organization and keep the options open for growth and development.

Balancing individual needs with organizational restrictions.   Most people have some need for independence and find that being subordinated to an organizational or professional structure heightens their dependence rather than independence. It is necessary for the worker at this stage to try different ways of balancing these needs in the effort to find a satisfactory resolution. Recent issues of *Time, Fortune,* and *Business Week* refer to the "arrogance and impatience" of young college graduates who defy the initial period of subordination at this stage of career development. Such an attitude is largely related to unresolved authority issues, as discussed in Chapter 3.

Decision making.   An important ingredient is now added to the decision-making process, that of first-hand knowledge. Once one has actually experienced a type of work, one has important data with which to assess the wisdom of the initial career choice. This knowledge differs from that gleaned from books or other sources of occupational information and relates as much to one's self as to the nature of the job and the world of work. Thus, the issue is deciding whether to remain in an occupation or organization or to seek a better match between one's own needs and occupational or organizational constraints and opportunities.

Finding a mentor.   Finding a mentor or sponsor is a developmental task, according to Levinson (1978), and if he is right the task can indeed be a difficult one. Interpersonal skill and the ability to be dependent are requisites. In addition, an individual seeking a mentor must clarify expectations to ensure that the relationship is helpful rather than destructive. Skovholt and Morgan (1981) point out that entering the occupational world of one's career field without a mentor is like traveling without a road map; the journey toward one's goals will take longer and may be more circuitous than when a mentor is along to offer guidance.

Sometimes, one finds a mentor outside the particular organizational setting in which one works. Such a mentor can be as effective in helping one learn the ropes of a particular occupation as one on the job site. This is particularly true if the beginner is more interested in developing the skills and competencies of a particular field of work than in learning a specific job at a particular site and is merely using a particular organization as a way of gaining experience and credentials within the field at large. The following story elaborates.

Martha, a young personnel worker who aspired to personnel management, found that the only entry-level job she qualified for was in a retail organization. She did not like this particular type of organization, but was so determined to gain experience in personnel work that she took the job and relied upon a mentor to initiate her into this line of work. After three years on the job, she was able to move into a higher level of personnel work in a public relations firm, an organization more akin to her values and liking.

Women often have difficulty finding mentors, particularly same-sex mentors, although the research shows that male mentors for females can be just as effective, if not more effective, than female mentors. Many women deliberately shun female mentors, perceiving males as more powerful and therefore able to provide greater opportunity for advancement. Two sex-role issues tend to reduce the likelihood of solid mentor relationships for women: (1) male competitiveness, and (2) the difficulty of finding a mentor in a nontraditional field. Women, however, are sometimes more skilled in seeking out the nurturing possibilities within a work organization and sometimes find mentors whom males would have failed to recognize as such.

Clearly, great latitude exists in this stage of career development. This is a time of experimentation, of discovering who one is and what one's job is really like. It is acceptable at this point to reassess and change direction. In other words, this is not an evaluative period during which one determines whether he or she made the right initial choice. Rather, one determines that whatever the initial choice, the choosing was a valuable learning experience in that it led to a testing of the choice. If one wishes to revise one's initial choice, one has learned first-hand that the job did not meet anticipated expectations, a lesson as important as learning that a job is satisfactory and fulfilling.

TABLE 5-2.   Entry into the world of work

Developmental Tasks	General Issues	Requisite Skills	Significant Others
Begin a job in the field of choice (initiation and socialization)	Responsibility and commitment	Dependency Learning Self-assessing	Mentors Bosses Colleagues
Acquire occupational skills, values, credentials	Interpersonal relationships Individual needs versus	Refining work habits Refining occupational, functional, and	
Accept a subordinate position	organizational restrictions	technical competencies	
Get along with colleagues and boss	Sex-role issues		
Find a mentor			
Negotiate boundaries between job demands and outside relationships and interests			
Assess on-the-job feedback			
Deal with disappointments, frustrations, success, and failure			
Assess experiences continually			

Entering the world of work also affords one the opportunity to reassess the meaning of work and one's own commitment to the chosen career. All the new self-knowledge and awareness that results from this work experience reflects growth and change and, therefore, enhances development. Table 5-2 summarizes the tasks and issues of the entry stage.

ESTABLISHMENT

The establishment of a career involves full membership in one's chosen career and usually occurs during young adulthood. This stage is similar to Super's stabilization stage and to Levinson's entering-adulthood and settling-down stages. Establishment may occur earlier for men than for women, particularly if the latter have taken time out to have a family.

Developmental Tasks

The major task of this stage is choosing a specialty or a way of making a contribution in a special area. One becomes more committed to the field and/or organization and is no longer considered a learner or an apprentice. Thus, one spends energies and efforts in developing and demonstrating competence and in looking for ways to make a special contribution in order to gain tenure or be promoted. One has passed through the initiation tasks of the previous stage and is now focused on finding a niche and becoming a valued member of the profession and/or organization. The reciprocal influences of career achievement and self-concept are heightened during this stage of stabilization. If there is congruence, one's life satisfaction is likely to be high; if not, one may go through a period of stress leading to alternate choices.

Other developmental tasks of this stage include the following:

1. Attaining some measure of independence and thus reducing the degree of supervision and monitoring necessary;
2. Learning to develop one's own standards of performance and self-confidence;
3. Carefully assessing one's motives, talents, and values to determine whether to become specialized or to remain a generalist;
4. Carefully assessing the organizational and occupational opportunities in order to make valid decisions about one's next steps;
5. Developing credibility and relationships within the field but outside of the particular work setting.

These tasks, then, involve developing more independence on the job and more visibility as a knowledgeable and competent worker within a field, though not necessarily as an organizational person. Levinson (1978) describes these tasks as the development of a more differentiated occupational identity and establishment within the chosen world. He points out that some men stay narrowly within a single track or try several directions before settling firmly on one. During this stage, the process involves overcoming inner conflicts and inhibitions, and struggling with opposing external pressures and career demands. Vaillant (1972) refers to this period as one in which the worker performs tasks well, carefully follows rules, and is anxious for promotion and willing to accept all parts of the system. Thus, we see that independence as well as conformity are necessary attributes for the successful negotiation of this career-development stage.

Developmental Issues

The major issue involves finding a way to be accepted as a valued member of the organization or profession and deciding again how committed one wishes to be to this aspect of life. Within the field itself, the important issue involves finding one's niche.

Specialization versus generalization.   Depending on external forces, it may be important to develop a specialization to find a niche. Likewise, in some circumstances, remaining a generalist will enable one to move toward management or administration. Deciding which alternative is best requires a realistic assessment of the best way to achieve one's goals in accordance with future and emerging societal needs, economic and marketing needs, and professional or occupational trends and needs.

Making the move from specialization to generalization or from generalization to specialization requires decision-making skills that utilize data not only from past and present work experiences, but also from family and personal development and from formal and informal sources of information about occupational trends and opportunities. Since the goal is to establish oneself by securing a niche, whatever decision leads toward that goal will be satisfactory. Still, one must consider all consequences of any decision—for instance, whether a specialty will transfer to another job or field.

Continuing to learn.   It is sometimes difficult to remain technically competent and continue to learn in one's chosen area or in a new, emerging area. It is important for one to be realistic in terms of short-range and immediate needs and goals while still remaining in touch with outside sources and retaining a long-range perspective that accounts for future possibilities. In short, those becoming established in their fields are well-advised to keep options open to permit the future transferring of skills, knowledge, and competencies should the opportunity or need arise.

Projecting a competent image.   Many workers find that their competencies go unrewarded because they are unnoticed. An important part of establishing oneself is to project a clear identity in the organization or occupation by becoming visible—in popular terms, by maintaining a high profile. In other words, one must be responsible for one's personal public relations. This effort may reflect one's interests and competencies, as one volunteers for committees and task forces, for instance, and attends meetings and cultivates important contacts. During this stage of career development, it is important to learn about the total field or the larger organization rather than remaining focused on the routine content and tasks of a particular job. It is also helpful to be able to relate jobs to other functions and jobs, looking beyond the confines of one's particular area of work.

Supervision.   Very often as one becomes established in a career, one takes on not only more responsibilities but also responsibilities of a higher order. These may include responsibility for the work of others as well as one's own. Supervising others requires effective supervisory skills—one must learn how to facilitate productivity and enhance others' self-respect and commitment to work. One learns these skills in large part from models—remembering what types of supervision were effective for oneself, for instance—and by learning different styles and modes of working with different types of people. Most people are promoted to supervisory positions on the basis of their technical and functional competencies, but, without effective interpersonal and supervisory skills, they often have difficulty with this type of responsibility regardless of their technical and functional capabilities.

Improving satisfaction and productivity. If the returns of the work are unsatisfactory, productivity is likely to be lowered and establishment or development in one's career retarded. Thus, it is important for one at this stage to prioritize returns, to find ways of replenishing the satisfactions (both intrinsic and extrinsic) of the work, and to find ways of avoiding burn-out or falling into a deadly routine that precludes growth and change. Many people fear establishment, equating it with stagnation. It is up to workers themselves to find ways to meet their needs without stagnating, to find niches that are satisfying and that have the best chance of fulfilling their youthful dreams. Taking outside courses, attending conferences, reading, and traveling are some ways to replenish energy and enthusiasm for work.

It takes several years to establish oneself in a field of work. Some people do not live up to the promise of the first couple of years, and others develop slowly. It is important to remember that individuals have varied styles of entering the world of work and establishing themselves: some do it steadily and quickly, while others take circuitous routes and move at slower paces. Also, the notion of establishment differs for individuals: some equate it with reaching the top of their chosen field, some with acquiring a steady job and income and feeling settled, and still others equate it with liking what one does regardless of the rewards. Table 5-3 summarizes the tasks and issues of the establishment stage of career development.

TABLE 5-3.   Establishment

Developmental Tasks	General Issues	Requisite Skills	Significant Others
Choose special contributions in order to become a valued member of the occupational work place	Mentor relationships	Interpersonal	Organizational peers
	Specialization versus generalization	Supervisory	Nonorganizational occupational peers
	Continued learning and training	Skill in occupational area	Supervisors
Project a competent image	Personal public relations	Decision making	Supervisees
	Supervision	Public relations	Affiliates in the wider occupational context
Work more independently	Occupational satisfaction		
Internalize organizational or occupational values	Work/family/personal boundaries		
Plan the next career steps			
Assume higher level and broader responsibilities			

CONSOLIDATION

Consolidation occurs during the latter part of young adulthood and the mid-thirties transition. Super (1963) points out that this stage involves the reweaving and embellishment of a vocational direction. Levinson (1978) calls it the period of settling down and becoming one's own man. Vaillant and McArthur (1972) describe this period as one of assimilation, wherein men assimilate all their experiences to date and are able to revise their priorities and focus on new ones. In this period, establishment becomes stabilized, and a deeper balancing of aspirations and achievements takes place.

Developmental Tasks

One of the major tasks of this stage is, as Levinson (1978) puts it, to become one's own person, to work through one's relationships with mentors, and even to prepare to become a mentor to others. This involves establishing oneself as an independent, self-sufficient, and contributing member of the organization—in short, becoming included in the profession or organization. Thus, it involves taking full responsibility for one's productivity and achievements and striking out on one's own. At this stage, the individual has, figuratively, passed the apprenticeship and can now be trusted to go it alone; another way of expressing it is to say that the individual has grown up and assumed adult status within the organization. Often, this stage is unsettling to an individual, as he or she becomes more aware of the younger people in the profession or organization at the entry and establishment stages. One is likely to become more aware of one's age at this point, of the time pressures on one and the need to think more in terms of present goals and rewards than distant future goals and rewards.

Other developmental tasks at this stage include the following:

1. Renegotiating the boundaries among increased responsibilities at work, family, and self-concerns and needs;
2. Dealing with feelings of failure if performance is poor, tenure is denied, or the challenge is lost;
3. Deciding on goals for the next decade and on strategies for attaining these goals;
4. Consolidating one's knowledge about oneself, one's competencies, one's aspirations, and one's chosen field into a workable, long-range career plan.

In a sense, the consolidation stage is like the calm before the storm. One is finally beginning to feel like an adult, secure and competent in one's chosen occupation. If one has started a family, one may feel secure and settled in that arena also. If not, one may rush to catch up in the family arena now that one is settled in the career arena. Adults are approaching the mid-life stage of questioning, where they consider whether or not this is what life is all about. At this time they need to feel and experience a period of consolidation in order to assess realistically the mid-life issues.

Developmental Issues

The major developmental issue in the consolidation stage revolves around stability versus change. This means developing one's long-range career plan in terms of ambitions, progress, and targets against which to measure progress.

However, at this stage it is impossible to consider stability versus change in the career dimension apart from the individual and family dimensions.

Risk.   One must decide at this stage how much risk one wishes to incur in terms of developing and implementing a long-range plan. Some paths may entail higher risk than others, and one's personal disposition plus such external variables as family and the nature of the field may affect the level of risk one chooses to take. As the individual consolidates, he or she still keeps options open while eliminating some alternatives and sharpening the focus on clusters of those retained. In other words, one attempts to narrow alternatives rather than expand them.

The issue of risk is different at this stage of development than earlier. A person who has a family and related financial responsibilities may feel unable to take the risks necessary for a radical career shift or to achieve desired satisfactions. For example, a person who works for a company that requires transfers along with promotions may feel unable to turn down a transfer to another geographical location even though the disruption of moving could be catastrophic for the family. Particularly in a declining economy, people feel controlled by organizational demands more fully than in an expanding economy, in which job changes can be effected more readily. At this point in the career-development process, many variables must be carefully weighed in the assessment of risks, whereas in earlier stages only oneself might have been affected. Now it is possible that an entire family may be involved.

Mobility.   At this stage, one may feel that one cannot or will not continue to change jobs or move around too much. Thus, the decision arises as to whether advancement within a particular field or organization warrants transfer or whether it is time to settle down and become a full member of a particular organization rather than continuing to be an entrant into a new job or organization even where the job is at a higher level. Since many people have families at this time of their career development, they feel that their mobility options are limited.

Mobility is also affected where one's spouse has a career. If one spouse is in the consolidation stage, for instance, and the other in an earlier stage, conflicts can arise that demand the clarification of family priorities. If both spouses are in the consolidation stage and one wishes to accept a transfer, the other spouse may have to revert to an earlier stage of career development. Careful negotiation and accommodation are often necessary between spouses in two-career families in order to preserve family and career solidarity. Many companies are finding that when transferring their executives, they must find jobs for their employees' spouses that equal the latters' current jobs. Many couples are commuting, to allow both partners career autonomy and the chance to develop at work; and often one spouse works in an autonomous, freelance style to enable the other to take advantage of advancement opportunities. Some couples today are forced by employment layoffs and limited opportunities in their field of work to separate so that one partner can accept employment in another geographical location. When this situation is involuntary, the stresses on individuals and their family can be enormous. Table 5-4 summarizes the tasks and issues of the consolidation stage.

TABLE 5-4.   Consolidation

Developmental Tasks	General Issues	Requisite Skills	Significant Others
Take on full membership in an occupation	Risks	Reassessing	Organizational peers
	Realistic constraints	Appraising	Nonorganizational
Consolidate knowledge and experiences about self, competencies, occupation	Personal/work/family issues	Independent functioning	occupational peers
	Two-career family issues	Planning	Supervisors
		Decision making	Supervisees
Plan goals and strategies for the next decade			Affiliates in the wider occupational context
Renegotiate boundaries among self, work, and family			
Appraise risks			

CONCLUSIONS

As we review the tasks and issues of the early adulthood and career development stages, it is important to remember that each stage builds upon the tasks and issues of the preceding stages. Furthermore, the tasks and issues of earlier stages remain, to a lesser degree, as challenges in later stages. For example, responsibility and commitment to the job involve the organization, the field, the family, and the community. These are always developmental issues but take on a different meaning depending upon the individual's particular stage of development.

From this discussion, we can conclude that career development today is not necessarily an orderly progression of sequenced events. Changes often occur faster than can be predicted or fully appreciated, and individuals must continually reassess the meaning work holds for them. Thus, no single universal meaning of work exists in our society—for some work is an end in itself, and for others it is a means to an end. The major conclusion that one can draw for counselors and therapists is that it is absolutely necessary to help people remain flexible and able to tolerate changes and adapt creatively. This means teaching basic interpersonal and occupational skills that keep options open both for short-term and long-term changes.

SUMMARY

The stages of career development in early adulthood require a complex process of decision making and interpersonal skills. In this chapter, we have delineated the developmental tasks and issues associated with the first four stages of career development: (1) initial choice, during the period of late adolescence; (2) entry into the world of work, during the period of youth; (3) establishment, during young adulthood; and (4) consolidation of career, during young adulthood and the mid-thirties transition.

While it is impossible to consider career development as separate from individual and family development, we have shown the reciprocal influences of these dimensions and of the psychological, sociological, and economic factors affecting career development. We have focused mostly on tasks and responsibilities that the adult can assume in terms of self-assessment: the appraising of occupational information, work experiences, and organizational variables; planning; deciding on and implementing goals; and continuing to learn, grow, reassess, plan, and decide. Part of this process involves assessing and making decisions about realistic external constraints.

In discussing career development in early adulthood, we have explored the meaning of work in the past decades and the effects of current social, cultural, and economic variables on today's worker. We have suggested that the effects of work influence one's self-concept and identity just as the latter influence one's occupational selection and work experiences. We have also highlighted the differences in career development for men and women. While much of the theoretical work on career development has been predicated on men's development alone and on an expanding economy affording possibilities for choice and occupational satisfaction, we have tried to consider the possible effects of a declining economy and the special issues that women face in today's society.

REFERENCES

Becker, H. S. Personal change in adult life. *Sociometry*, 1964, *27*, 40–53.

Erikson, E. *Childhood and society* (2nd ed.). New York: W. W. Norton, 1963.

Erikson, E. *Identity youth and crisis*. New York: W. W. Norton, 1968.

Ginzberg, E. et al. *Occupational choice*. New York: Columbia University Press, 1951.

Hennig, M., & Jardim, J. *The managerial woman*. New York: Simon and Shuster, 1978.

Henry, W. E. The role of work in structuring the life cycle. *Human Development*, 1971, *14*, 125–131.

Holland, J. L., & Gottfriedson, G. D. Using a typology of persons and environments to explain careers: some extensions and clarifications. *The Counseling Psychologist*, 1976, *6*, 20–29.

Horner, M. Toward an understanding of achievement related conflicts in women. *Journal of Social Issues*, 1972, *28*, 157–176.

Kantor, D., & Lehr, W. *Inside the family*. San Francisco: Jossey-Bass, 1975.

Knefelkamp, L. L., & Slepitza, R. A cognitive-developmental model of career development—An adaptation of the Perry scheme. In J. M. Whiteley and A. Resnikoff (eds.), *Career counseling*. Monterey, Calif.: Brooks/Cole, 1978, pp. 232–247.

Krumboltz, J. D. *Social learning and career decision making*. New York: Carroll Press, 1979.

Levinson, D. *The seasons of a man's life*. New York: Knopf, 1978.

Maslow, A. A theory of human motivation. *Psychological Review*, 1943, *50*, 370–396.

Miller, D., & Form, W. *Industrial sociology*. New York: Harper, 1951.

Perry, W., Jr. *Forms of intellectual and ethical development in the college years: A scheme*. New York: Holt, Rinehart, & Winston, 1970.

Rappaport, L. *Personality development: The chronology of experience*. Glenview, Ill.: Scott, Foresman, 1972.

Scarf, M. *Unfinished business*. Garden City, N.Y.: Doubleday, 1980.

Skovholt, T. M., & Morgan, J. I. Career development: An outline of issues for men. *Personnel and Guidance Journal*, 1981, *60*, 231–237.

Super, D. *The psychology of careers.* New York: Harper, 1957.

Super, D., Stavishesky, R., Matlin, N., & Jordan, J. P. *Career development: Self-concept theory.* New York: College Entrance Examination Board, 1963.

Tiedeman, D. V., & O'Hara, R. P. *Career development: Choice and adjustment.* New York: College Entrance Examination Board, 1963.

Troll, L. *Early and middle adulthood.* Monterey, Calif.: Brooks/Cole, 1975.

Vaillant, G., & McArthur, C. Natural history of male psychological health. *Seminars in Psychiatry,* 1972, *4,* 415–427.

Wolkon, K. A. Pioneer versus traditional: Two distinct vocational patterns of college alumnae. *Journal of Vocational Behavior,* 1972, *2,* 275–282.

CHAPTER SIX

IMPLICATIONS FOR COUNSELORS: CASE STUDIES

The preceding chapters show clearly that clients in early adulthood are likely to present issues that are concerned with identity, emotional separation from the family of origin, intimate relationships, career choice and management, mate selection and marital adjustment, lifestyle, and whether or not to have children. Such developmental issues may either be apparent or underlie other presenting problems. Counselors sensitive to developmental issues will perceive both the underlying issues and the presenting problems and will consider young adult clients in the contexts of individual, family, and career development. Counselors can then formulate interventions that not only help the client to resolve presenting problems but also provide opportunities for growth, autonomy, and the development of problem-solving and coping strategies.

In this chapter, we consider some representative case studies of young adults. No particular strategies or techniques are advocated here as panaceas. The suggestion is, rather, that incorporating the systems and developmental perspectives into the assessment process in therapy can maximize the effectiveness of existing therapy techniques.

CASE 1: BELINDA

Presenting Problem

At the suggestion of a friend, Belinda, 22, went to the counseling center at her college for career counseling four months after college graduation. An art history major, she had decided during her senior year to find a job in a large city bank. This decision was based on the experience of a former boyfriend, who was doing very well financially after one year in the banking business. Belinda graduated, then, with the determination to find immediately a high-paying, prestigious position. Two months later, she was very discouraged by her lack of success. Her parents were suggesting that she return home and she was experiencing depression and anxiety, which only retarded her job-seeking activity. Belinda requested career testing; she wanted confirmation of her decision to enter banking and hoped to elicit more parental support. She was eager for a "right answer" and for a clear-cut guide on how to get what she wanted.

The Client

Belinda was attractive and well-groomed. She appeared to have self-confidence and poise. She conversed easily and exhibited satisfactory interview behaviors except for anxious motions of her hands.

The Individual Context

When asked to talk about herself, Belinda described herself as the oldest of three girls from an upper-middle-class southern family. She had been a top student in high school, had been elected prom queen, and felt that she was the prettiest and the most popular of the three sisters. Belinda reported that she was always successful in achieving her goals, getting whatever she wanted whenever she wanted it. She was used to receiving constant admiration and adulation from her peers, teachers, and family.

Belinda loved the first two years of college. The last two years were harder, though, and she felt restless throughout them, but she thought this feeling might have been related to her boyfriend's graduation. Currently, she was going with a boy a year younger than herself and still in college. She expressed satisfaction with this relationship, although she only saw the boy a few weekends a term now. Belinda's major concern was finding a job that would enable her to live the way she was accustomed to living. She assumed that she would eventually marry, but felt that she would probably never have children, as "the world is too rotten to bring children into."

Although not artistic, Belinda had majored in art history because it held her interest and because she received high grades in courses in that field. She reported that she had done well in college courses she liked and not as well in those she did not like.

When asked about friendships, Belinda became more nervous. She talked about needing admiration and explained that she worked hard to be the center of attention in groups. She was eager, enthusiastic, and open to new kinds of fun. She felt she was a leader and initiated most activities whenever she was in a group. She was puzzled, however, as to why she had been unable to maintain friendships with girls in college. Every time she felt she had found a close friend, the relationship petered out and she ended up feeling resentful. She had no difficulty finding boyfriends, and had been in two long-term relationships during college.

Belinda described herself as a perfectionist. She would obtain extensions for her papers in college because they were never "good enough" and she never felt satisfied with them. She resented demanding pressures or anything unpleasant; often she would use her need for an active social life to justify avoiding other responsibilities (such as handing in assignments on time in college or working on her resume).

It became apparent to the counselor that underneath Belinda's veneer of self-confidence and poise were many doubts and feelings of inadequacy. As the counselor began to explore with Belinda some of her underlying feelings about herself, Belinda's defenses weakened and she became aware that she really was unsure of what her interests, strengths, and weaknesses were. She began to express confusion regarding who she really was as opposed to who her mother thought she was. This led to a focus on Belinda's family system.

The Family Context

As noted above, Belinda was the oldest of three girls. Her father was a successful attorney and her mother had been an elementary school teacher prior to Belinda's birth. The family lived in an affluent suburb of a southern city and were active in the community.

Belinda described her parents as being concerned about their image in the community. She felt that they were permissive parents and very involved in their daughters' lives. They were always eager to help out. They were proud of Belinda's eastern college education and, she believed, they had high aspirations for her. Her father called her "princess" and always gave in to her demands. Often, Belinda's mother accused her father of indulging their oldest daughter, sparking arguments. On the one hand, Belinda described everything as "perfect" at home, but on the other hand, she expressed anxiety about her parents' pressures for her achievement and their bickering about discipline. Still, Belinda asserted that family members never got truly angry with each other and implied that it was important for everyone always to have a great time and be "fine."

Belinda was becoming vaguely disturbed by her mother's suggestions that Belinda begin to support herself. Nothing had actually been said outright, but her mother did talk about how someone with the type of education Belinda had received should really be able to find a top-notch job. Thus, Belinda's sense of urgency about finding a prestigious job originated more with her mother than herself. Belinda reported that she and her mother had frequent disagreements about clothes or friends or privileges, but that she was closer to her mother than was either of the two sisters. Belinda liked her sisters and considered herself close to them too, but, upon further questioning, it turned out that they rarely saw each other and never wrote or spoke to each other on the phone. Belinda was so self-absorbed at this point in her life that it was hard for her to consider others except peripherally.

The picture that Belinda painted of her family was one of underlying tensions and pressures with a surface appearance of ease and happiness. As Belinda continued to talk about her family, she became more aware of the dissonance between her feelings and her words as evidenced by such questions as "All families are like that, aren't they?" and "Don't you think my sisters and I are as close as other sisters?"

Career Context

As a child, Belinda used to dream of becoming a famous actress, of being the "star." She assumed she'd marry an attractive, wealthy man and have a lovely home and children who would be raised by servants (as she had been). She aspired to a life similar to her mother's and did not think much about what her future would really bring. Throughout high school, her major aspiration was to be popular and to get into a "good college." Her father got her summer jobs in a law office and during college she traveled to Europe during the summers and worked in his office as a secretarial assistant.

When Belinda arrived at college, her goal was to obtain a liberal arts education, and she did not intend her major to be career oriented. She assumed that she'd get a job after college and probably marry, but she really did not think about what type of job she should look for until her senior year. By this time, Belinda had been thoroughly exposed to "career-oriented" women and she felt that she should style herself in this way too in order to retain the approval and status she craved from her parents and peers. During her senior year, she experienced a great deal of anxiety accompanied by depression (evidenced by excessive eating and sleeping) as she listened to her classmates talk about their career plans and actions. It took her seven months to prepare the first draft of her resume; it was a laborious task for her and she still expressed dissatisfaction with the product. She managed to avoid campus interviews, always being too busy with schoolwork or her boyfriend, and she did not begin actual interviewing until after graduation. It had never occurred to her that she would not obtain a job immediately, and the first two rejections were devastating. Gradually, she began to realize that she was delaying follow-ups and answering ads and that she was beginning to forget to make phone calls and send out resumes. The rejection–discouragement cycle increased, until she was avoiding all job-seeking activity.

Belinda's parents started urging her to return home where they could find her a job. She was continually having to ask for more money to support herself and, while she was still claiming that it was "unfair" that she hadn't found a job, she was beginning to wonder if she was really on the right track. When queried about her interviews, she reported that she thought they had gone very well, which added to her dismay when they did not pan out. She felt she was clear about her requirements for a beginning salary and interesting work and assumed that with her credentials, she would be "snapped up."

When asked to imagine where she would like to be in five years in the work world, Belinda was unable to respond except to quote a high salary and a top-level managerial position. She did mention that she liked to take lots of vacations and long weekends and hoped that she would be able to find a job that would afford her that type of flexibility. It was hard for Belinda to think about the future, given her overriding concern with the immediate present.

Assessment

Although Belinda had sought out career counseling, the counselor realized that issues of identity and emotional separation from her parents, not to mention more education about occupations, were equally important. Belinda was still perceiving herself as Daddy's princess, and had not yet decided who she was apart from her parents' perceptions. Some of her negative feelings about her family that she had not yet admitted to herself were confusing her, and she needed to renegotiate her boundaries with her parents as an adult rather than as a child. Thus, Belinda would have to undergo some self-processing (introspection, self-analysis) as she began clarifying some of her values and learning to appreciate herself as different from her mother and her mother's perceptions. Her poorly developed self-processing skills, affected by her dualistic thinking, were retarding her development.

At the same time, Belinda needed to reconsider her career aspirations in light of her real feelings and values, not those of her peer group, which was emphasizing "careerism" or prioritizing career over other aspects of life. Not until she had done so would she be able to muster the resources to choose an occupation and to implement her choice.

Goals

The major goal of counseling was to facilitate Belinda's self-differentiation—that is, to help her understand that emotional separation from her parents was both necessary and desirable and that it did not necessarily entail angry rejection. She also needed help in differentiating herself from her peer group so that she could do her self-processing and problem solving in terms of occupational selection and immediate living decisions.

Interventions

The self-differentiation goal was achieved through an individual, client-centered type of counseling. Belinda was encouraged to choose some short-term goals to facilitate this self-differentiation. Meanwhile, she decided to become a hostess in a local restaurant to become financially independent while she gave further thought to the direction of her career. The counselor also applied cognitive-restructuring techniques to help her question some of her irrational beliefs and take responsibility for developing a more rational belief system. The counselor also gave Belinda some behavioral assignments to help her feel in control of her destiny and to develop symmetrical relationships outside the counseling relationship, such as some reading assignments (bibliotherapy), writing assignments, and research and group activities centering on growing up into adulthood.

When Belinda had reached her short-term goals, the counselor began to help her with problem solving relative to her career dilemma. First, it was necessary for Belinda to acknowledge that she herself was not as career oriented as she felt she should be, that she really wanted a job that would be enjoyable rather than career oriented, and that such a criterion was perfectly acceptable. Belinda talked extensively about the pressures today on young women to put their career interests ahead of personal or family interests. She admitted that she would feel guilty if she did not conform to this pattern. As she began to know and appreciate her own individuality, she felt more comfortable about making a short-term rather than a life-long occupational choice. The counselor encouraged her to fantasize, to brainstorm, and to consider all possible options, researching them both by interviewing people and reading pertinent material. The counselor also urged her to consider the results of career-interest and aptitude tests and to consider short-term and long-term payoffs and consequences. These strategies helped her to think with more multiplicity and relativity.

Simultaneously, Belinda received some feedback on her resume and interview behavior, and was taught general and specific job-seeking skills. Using role playing and rehearsal, she came up with a written plan for herself. She decided to broaden her scope for a job search, and after one month of dedicated looking, she accepted a job in the travel office of a large stock brokerage firm. This job probably represented a dead end job within the firm, but it afforded her the travel, glamour, and salary that she desired for now, and provided training in important job skills that would be transferable to other industries.

Outcome

The counseling lasted for four months. By the end of that time, Belinda was employed and financially independent from her family, though she was still in close contact. She felt better about herself and her relationships and considered herself more satisfied with her life than she had been since high school. A six-month follow-up found that she had already been promoted, had broken off her relationship with her college boyfriend, and was currently seeing a man at work. She reported that she was working harder and enjoying work more than she ever had anticipated. She found herself becoming more career oriented. She was surprised and pleased with her newfound self-confidence and she felt that it benefited her relationships with her family.

Comments

Although Belinda came to counseling believing that her only problems were in the career domain, she realized quickly that those problems were intertwined with her own personal and family development issues. Perhaps she had been overindulged and spoiled by her parents and teachers, and perhaps she had failed to receive coherent career guidance throughout the years. Nevertheless, she was ripe for some coaching and counseling that would enable her to finish the launching process and make decisions she could live with.

Belinda exemplifies the young college graduate who is expected immediately upon graduation to assume adult responsibilities and roles with little actual preparation, and who may be overwhelmed by being thrown "out of the nest," whether it be the family or college. Developmental counseling, whether in response to acute symptoms or vague uneasiness, facilitates the transition of the young adult from a dependent student or offspring to a self-sufficient adult. Belinda found that her relationships with her family became more enjoyable and genuine as she learned to relate as an independent, successful adult. As an extra bonus, she was able to play mentor to her younger sisters when they went through this inevitable transition.

CASE 2: STEVEN

Presenting Problem

Steven, aged 27, was referred to counseling by a colleague owing to his devastation over a broken love affair. A successful account executive with a small advertising firm, Steven found that since his woman friend had returned to her husband, he was obsessed with her; he was unable to concentrate on his work or to sleep and had lost weight and cried frequently. He could not understand what had happened or why it had happened, and he had lost interest in everyone and everything save his lost romance. His presentation was most dramatic and romantic as he went over and over the details of this affair.

Six weeks had elapsed since Steven had last seen the woman, Debbie, though he spoke to her on the telephone daily (she now lived 2,000 miles away). He had taken excessive time away from work and was in danger of losing his job if he did not pull himself together quickly. His parents were distraught over his unhappiness and, since he was living at home, he found that their concerns heightened his own discomfort; thus, a circular type of reaction was in place. The more upset and depressed he became, the more concerned his parents grew, which intensified his upset and then theirs, and so on.

Steven described this romance as "the perfect love." He had only been in love once before, during college, and when that love affair had ended with the girl's rejection of him, he had sworn to himself that he would never again risk putting himself in that position. Thus, until he met Debbie a year ago, he had not had any serious involvement but had instead devoted his energies to career attainment. He was more successful than he had dreamed of being by this age and was enormously satisfied with his job, his salary, his lifestyle, and his prestige. In fact, the only thing that was missing was the "right partner," and in Debbie he felt as if he had found this missing part of his life.

Steven had met Debbie at a conference. She was an artist who was married to a physician, and while their initial involvement was strictly business that evolved into a casual friendship (occasional cocktails and lunch), eventually Debbie began to confide in Steven that she was unhappy in her marriage because of her husband's preoccupation with his career. Their friendship evolved into an affair, and, after a couple of months, Debbie left her husband and moved in with her parents so she could spend more time with Steven. During the next few months, Steven and Debbie became closer, and considered themselves engaged to be married, supposing that Debbie would divorce her husband. They spent every weekend away together, spoke on the phone several times daily, and were totally immersed in each other. Upon close questioning, however, it turned out that at many points during this time Debbie would vacillate, talking about her obligations to her husband, her remaining feelings for him, and the desirability of being married to a physician. Her husband had two more years of residency and then the payoffs would begin. Steven pushed these incidents out of his mind and continued to fantasize about the "perfect love" and the "ideal marriage" he was going to embark on. He felt very possessive of Debbie and was unaware of how he consumed and controlled her. Abruptly, Debbie phoned one evening and said that she had returned to her husband and was leaving for another part of the country that evening. Steven's world came crashing down. He claimed he had no warning and he blamed Debbie's husband, considering Debbie the innocent victim of some "Svengali" type person.

Description of Client

Steven was short, stocky, and relatively attractive. He dressed expensively in three-piece suits (which he later referred to as his "suits of armor"), drove an expensive car, and carried an expensive attaché case. His walk was almost a strut, and he gestured dramatically as he relayed his story. In fact, the manner in which he relayed his story was like an actor telling a melodramatic romantic story.

Individual Context

Steven portrayed himself as the only son and eldest of two children of immigrant parents. His father had never been financially successful—he was currently a shopkeeper, but he had lost a few shops along the way. His mother performed bookkeeping for his father. The family lived in a working-class suburb of a metropolitan city, and the boy was close both to his extended and nuclear family. Steven had been the favored child. He was in a gifted program from the time he was in second grade and considered himself to be extremely bright and intellectual. His peer relationships had always been strained; he felt that he was always doing favors for others and that he got rejected a lot. He blamed much of this on his being shorter and smarter than the other children.

As Steven talked about his childhood and adolescence, he came in touch with the pressures he had felt to achieve, to be "the best." As a child, if he did not bring home an "A" on his report card, his parents always wanted to know why. He was not encouraged to go out with friends, as the family preferred to do things together. There was some distrust of people who were not related, particularly of different ethnic types.

Steven referred to the rich fantasy life that helped him through the loneliness of childhood and adolescence. His fantasies concerned becoming successful and rich and showing everyone that he was better than they. He was always self-conscious about being short, although he could not recall being teased by other children. He felt that he had none of the athletic prowess of other boys, and he compensated by excelling in academics until midway through high school, when he felt his academic prowess was working against him with his peer group. He then took great pleasure in achieving good grades, not by working, but rather by ingratiating himself with teachers and other manipulative strategies.

Steven valued status and prestige highly and his greatest disappointment occurred when his father went bankrupt during his high school senior year and he had to withdraw his application to an Ivy League college. In counseling, he got tears in his eyes as he talked about this incident and he related it to Debbie's preference for her husband who was tall, handsome, and a graduate of an Ivy League college and medical school. Steven worked his way through the city college, obtaining a degree in business and a master's degree in marketing.

When he began counseling, Steven still maintained an active fantasy life, much of which he tried to act out. An important fantasy was that of becoming a successful, famous novelist. He had written several short stories and two romantic novels that he was attempting to sell. He perceived Debbie as the heroine of his latest novel, and talked often of how they were collaborating on another novel. He used his salary to take luxurious vacations and to take dates to expensive restaurants and shows. In other words, he was attempting to live out his fantasies.

Family Context

Steven's family of origin was a close-knit, traditional family system. His parents apparently had a companionable marriage, and, while they were concerned about their adult children, both of whom have reached their late twenties without marrying, they were currently preoccupied with their own issues (relating to health and care) and not really intrusive into their children's lives. Steven still lived at home, although at one period in his life he maintained a separate apartment until he found that the expense was too great. He was free to come and go as he pleased at home and he seemed to have an easy relationship with his parents. His parents' current concern about him was related to his withdrawal at home—he began to stay in his room, refusing to eat, and they often heard him crying. They had met Debbie and, assuming things to be as Steven reported, were thrilled that their son was finally going to marry. Now they were naturally worried and disturbed by his evident distress.

Steven claimed to be closer to his father than to his mother. He often found himself irritated with his mother's concerns about his welfare and, while he felt himself to be much more successful than his father, his bitterness was mingled with fondness. He was aware of his need for his parents' approval, to be looked up to and admired by his parents and their relatives. Upward mobility was important to Steven. He felt that his parents were always supportive and giving, and his current concerns with them were over their health issues. His father had some medical problems, and his mother depended upon Steven to cope with these (he took his father to the doctor and picked up medicine), and Steven was beginning to think that perhaps he needed to move out of the house so that his mother would learn to deal directly with his father's medical issues.

Steven's sister lived in an apartment in a nearby town and came to visit once a week. The two siblings had never been close, because the parents played one off against the other; they talked to each other occasionally, but Steven's sister found her brother too controlling, and Steven himself was aware that his need to control caused difficulties with interpersonal relationships.

In short, Steven did not feel that his parents were preventing his leaving home. They were not a major concern of his, and he came to realize that he was relying on their dependency on him as a safe crutch, so he could feel needed and important.

Career Context

As previously indicated, Steven had a very strong drive for achievement from his early years. It was important to him to be successful—by that he meant having a prestigious job that yielded a high salary and fancy lifestyle. He had worked from high school through college and had excellent references that enabled him to start at a high level immediately after college graduation. At one time in his youth, he had entertained the notion of becoming a lawyer. However, by the time he was midway through college, he decided that the business world would be a faster route to success. He received his master's degree at the city college and that year resolved someday to attend an Ivy League university for an M.B.A. degree to compensate for missing the chance to attend an Ivy League college as an undergraduate.

Steven stayed in his first job for two years and then moved on to a national advertising firm. The firm recruited him, and he was very pleased with the opportunity. After one year, however, by mutual agreement, he left that firm. It turned out that he had alienated one of the senior partners so completely that remaining there was impossible. After three months, Steven found his current position, which he considered the "perfect job in the perfect company." The firm was small, which allowed him many of the glamorous perquisites he desired. In addition, this firm had suggested that it might pay his tuition to an Ivy League part-time M.B.A. program in lieu of an annual bonus. Thus, it seemed to Steven that he had everything going for him—the perfect lover and the perfect job along with his long-time dream of getting a prestigious M.B.A. degree. The owners of the firm seemed to like and appreciate Steven, and he felt successful and strong.

Steven described his peer relationships at work as being satisfactory. He perceived himself to be the most successful individual in the firm and often bragged of holding the firm together and being its most significant contributor.

Assessment

It was clear to the counselor that Steven's self-concept was weak and character-ized by grandiosity. He was continually striving to compensate for his short stat-ure and working-class origins with achievement and fame. Because of this shaky self-concept, or identity, he had difficulty in developing and maintaining intimate relationships at all levels and he took refuge in elaborate, excessive fantasy. He seemed to have remained in his family system longer than necessary. Certainly, with his salary, he could have afforded to live on his own, but he clung to his parents' "need" of him as a safe anchor. He also seemed to have some difficulty in dealing with authority figures, and while Steven usually maintained strong control over his impulses, he had let go of his control during one period of employment and ended up in difficulty. It was possible that his grandiose self-concept and his projection at his current place of employment could lead to more interpersonal difficulties.

When he entered into counseling, Steven's defenses were weak as he tried to cope with his crumbling world. It was important to take advantage of this crisis to aid Steven in reassessing himself, his life, and his choices.

Goals

The immediate goal of the counseling was to develop a safe, trusting, empathic relationship so that, in an appropriate setting, Steven could ventilate his dejec-tion, resentment, and frustration at losing control over his life and to enable him to regain his equilibrium at work. The next goal was to aid Steven in looking at himself, his defenses, and his relationships so that he would feel that he had the power to make choices, initiate and develop relationships, and renegotiate his boundaries with his parents. This would require a painful, close examination, not only of his relationship with Debbie, but of previous significant relationships. The counselor knew that that process would be slow, since Steven would be strongly resistant to looking too closely at the discrepancies between his fantasies and the realities he had experienced.

Interventions

An individual type of client-centered counseling was the major strategy for the first part of the treatment. During that time—about four months—Steven needed a great deal of help in separating fantasy from reality, and Gestalt role-plays and writing assignments helped him first to ventilate and then begin to recognize differences between his desires and what had really occurred. He continued to talk with Debbie daily on the telephone and to obsess about her, but he was able to bring this obsessing into the counseling sessions and out of his office and home settings. Thus, he quickly returned to an effective level of functioning at work. This was important, since Steven needed to feel in control, successful, and impor-tant in some area of his life. He clung tenaciously to his fantasy of Debbie, claiming that he would never love again, and acted out symbolically many fantasies of flying out and "rescuing" her from her ogre husband, even though in reality she had freely chosen her own destiny. This became a ritual fantasy. The prescription of acting the fantasy out in a sculpture or in a psychodrama in the counseling sessions after each phone call with Debbie facilitated the working through of Steven's anger and overwhelming desire.

Midway through the counseling, another catastrophe occurred in Steven's life. The firm where he worked went bankrupt. Steven claimed that the senior partners had lied and cheated the employees, and he knew that his days in that firm were numbered. This crisis was helpful to the treatment, for it provided Steven a chance to examine and use his problem-solving skills, to examine his choices, and to see firsthand how he avoided important signals when they failed to meet his fantasy needs. It turned out that signals abounded regarding the impending disaster at work that Steven could have picked up from colleagues at the office and contacts in the field as well as from clients. Therefore, the second part of treatment focused on Steven's problem-solving skills in addition to his self-processing. However, another repeat of history occurred—for the second time Steven lost the chance to attend an Ivy League university.

Toward the end of the counseling, Steven's parents and sister came in for some joint sessions. In a caring, supportive manner, these family members were able to communicate to Steven their admiration and approval as well as their willingness for him to be independent and lead his own life. His mother seemed to be willing to take full responsibility for his father's health issues and Steven realized that no one was holding on to him, but that he was the one reluctant to be fully launched. Some family sculpture techniques were used to realign the structures and boundaries of this family, separating the sibling subsystem from the couple subsystem, and showing that the outer boundaries of the family were indeed more permeable than Steven had thought.

Outcome

The counseling treatment lasted eight months and consisted of weekly, and, during periods of crisis, twice-weekly sessions. During this period, Steven developed insight into his compensatory defenses and was able to begin clarifying some of his values. He realized that he distanced people by bragging and that he was terrified of rejection, and he began to take steps to risk relationships rather than to avoid them. He began to distance himself emotionally from Debbie, although he still phoned her often and entertained the fantasy that some day she would return to him and all would be "beautiful." The resolution of this affair was still incomplete. However, he did take some definite steps to begin to develop a social life, meeting and dating new people, and he joined a sailing club and reactivated some previous relationships.

In his job search, he considered moving out of town, but he ended up taking a position in a large, national firm in the city in which he currently resided. This firm was a competitor of his previous national firm, and he was able to reexamine the earlier experience and make some choices about how he could avoid a similar situation. The new firm offered him the possibility of the same M.B.A. program after a two-year period, and his salary enabled Steven immediately to begin looking for his own apartment. While Steven had doubts about this job and this firm, he felt it was the best he could do at the moment and he thought that "being a small fish in a big pond" might be better for him than being "a big fish in a small pond." He believed that he was more realistic about this choice than he had been in the past and his cautiousness about the outcome was a welcome relief from his cocksure, absolute optimism. He was willing to risk making mistakes; things no longer had to be "perfect" or "devastating."

The immediate goal of treatment, crisis intervention, was accomplished in this case. The goals of self-assessment were not completely accomplished but were initiated and some progress was made. Steven himself commented on the value of developing a trusting relationship with another person and knowing that the counselor would not collude with his fantasies, but would be kind, firm, and supportive in helping him deal with the differences between his dreams and realities. The door was left open for further counseling at any time. As Steven gained some strength, some of his defenses were remarshaled, although many were dented enough to permit him to use his new self-processing and problem-solving skills and to return for consultation if and when necessary.

Comments

This case started out as crisis intervention. However, it was important to consider the presenting crisis in all contexts and to discern the similar patterns in individual, career, and family development. While most of the counseling focused on a particular love relationship and a certain career crisis, the dynamics of the two crises were similar, involving faulty perceptions and ultimate rejections, and a transfer of learning occurred from one to the other.

Labeling Steven "narcissistic" or "a borderline personality" might have led to a long-term, traditional type of psychotherapy, but there is no reason to suppose that the outcome would have been any more favorable. In other words, while Steven still had grandiose notions and still strutted around, he did grow somewhat in terms of his identity, his desire to attain intimacy, and his problem-solving skills. Marshaling family resources for support, rather than conflict, freed him to focus on his own issues and allowed him to realize that this support was always available to him even if he did not live at home.

CASE 3: CAROLE AND MARK

Presenting Problem

Mark, aged 37, phoned for an appointment for couple counseling for himself and Carole, aged 30. They had "been together" for two years, with a four-month separation, and they felt that their relationship was stuck. Mark was eager for counseling so that they could get off the fence, either developing or ending their relationship. He was referred for counseling by a friend. Carole was slightly reluctant to enter counseling, but agreed to an initial session.

During the first session, Mark said that he "adored" Carole, and wanted to live with her in a "truly intimate" relationship. He was hurt and confused because she kept him at arm's length, refusing to live with him and seeing him only on weekends. She appeared to be entirely satisfied with the status quo. Mark had been married for two years at the age of 30 and had no children. While he was not pushing for marriage, eventually he hoped to "marry and settle down." He claimed that he was getting too old for the dating scene and that Carole was the only woman he'd ever met who really satisfied him in every way.

Carole described herself as put off by Mark's aggressiveness and frightened by his controlling and intrusive behavior. She was involved in her career as an oncological nurse practitioner and claimed that she was too drained during the week to have to deal with "heavy personal relationships." She had never been married, but had been heavily involved with one man from age 20 to 26, and she still had not worked through that relationship. She liked Mark but didn't know if she really was "in love" with him. He followed her around wherever she went and, while he was "good and caring," it was almost more than she could bear.

The couple described their four-month separation as initiated by Carole. After four months, Mark initiated their reconciliation and Carole went along. She felt guilty and uncomfortable about distancing herself from Mark and was concerned that her feelings were beginning to affect their sexual relationship, since she now found that she was rarely able to become sexually aroused by him.

Carole's goals were to maintain the status quo of the relationship. She did not see marriage or children in her future, she was unsure where she wanted to live in the future and even whether she wished to stay in nursing. She understood Mark's desire to settle down but felt that they were in "different life stages." She liked having him available, but she did not want the responsibilities of an intimate relationship.

As the couple talked, it became apparent that they were simultaneously attracted and frightened by the vast differences between their values and ideologies, turning their conflicts into power struggles over "the right way" and "the wrong way," or "the mature way" and "the immature way." Carole thought that their differences meant that they should not be together and Mark thought that one of them should change for love of the other. They identified as the strengths of their relationship the genuine care they had for each other, the satisfying sex they had most of the time, and the intrigue each felt for the other's lifestyle.

Description of Clients

Mark, 37, was a tall, attractive, energetic man who verbalized easily, expressed affection with gestures, and was eager and enthusiastic about everything. Carole, 30, was quiet, somewhat withdrawn, extremely attractive in a natural way, and very contemplative. It was clear that Mark was the initiator and Carole sometimes the follower and sometimes the quiet, subtle opposer. Mark seemed to need more open intimacy whereas Carole seemed to be more self-contained and guarded.

Individual Contexts

Mark described himself as the older of two children of immigrant parents. He grew up in a suburban working-class environment and his family was very close and religious (Jewish). His mother was ill most of her life and the family centered around her needs. Mark considered himself a "good boy," always eager to please and willing to do whatever was asked of him. He had put himself through college and was very proud of his independence and self-sufficiency, considering himself a "self-made man." He felt that his adolescence had been fairly smooth. As a young adult he went into military service and then on to college to get a business degree. He still had three or four close friends from his college days and his other current relationships consisted of casual business acquaintances. Mark considered himself energetic, outgoing, intelligent, warm, caring, exuberant, and fairly conventional. He was the kind of man who decided what he wanted and then went out and got it, and he was frustrated by his inability to penetrate Carole's barriers.

Thus, Mark seemed to have a good sense of himself and was satisfied with what he had achieved in life. He considered himself "straight," "typically middle class," and "easy to get along with." He had never rebelled or acted out in any unconventional way, and he felt truly comfortable about his lifestyle.

Mark described his interests as people, fine wining and dining, reading, and working along with people. He did not believe that he had had any major adjustment difficulties growing up, and he felt that he had worked through his "unfinished" business with his parents before they died. He described his brief marriage as "without passion," just sort of a trial-and-error event that ended without hard feelings or much distress on the part of either member. Since his divorce, he had been successful in the "singles' world" but was delighted by the immediate attraction and fascination he felt when he met Carole at a party.

Carole, on the other hand, described herself as the older of two children from a rigidly fundamentalist (Lithuanian) midwestern family. Both her parents worked for their parochial college, and Carole grew up in a repressive, small-town environment. She attended a parochial college, where she dated "the right kind of guy" from her parents' perspective whom she abandoned right after college graduation. Her parents still regret that she did not marry this man and return home. After college, she went to Europe for two years to visit relatives, where she engaged in casual love affairs and began to "sow her oats" and to throw off the shackles of her background. When she returned home, she found that she "did not fit" and she moved to another city where she got a job and engaged in a type of "flower-child" lifestyle.

Carole considered herself a remnant of the hippie culture. She was most comfortable with nonconforming people who had had similar drug and sexual experiences to those she had had in her past, and she currently lived in a commune with several gay friends. The idea of marriage or living with a mate was too "middle class," and she felt the need to separate her life with Mark from her day-to-day life at home. As Carole talked, she became very weepy and sad about the "old days" when everything seemed both sure, safe, fun, and dangerous. She was very concerned about not hurting Mark, so she refrained from discussing past relationships. She described her life as being at a standstill and herself as feeling mostly pleased but vaguely uneasy. She felt unable to give any thought to what she might do in the future, and to who she wanted to be or what her aspirations were.

Carole described herself as caring, agreeable, conscientious, and not terribly intelligent. She said that she gets along well with people and has a hard time saying "no." She was used to people telling her what to do and she considered herself a follower. She rarely got angry although she did get depressed (evidenced by sadness and an inability to sleep) and she believed herself to be more of a loner than a social person.

Family Contexts

Mark came from the type of family system where he really had to take care of himself, since his mother was preoccupied with her health and his father with providing for the family. He learned early to be self-sufficient and felt that he had a "normal, okay family life" while growing up. He reported that his parents seemed to genuinely care for each other and he recalled few conflicts or disagreements. He felt that the rules in his family were fairly relaxed and that he never had any difficulty in getting what he wanted, but he pointed out that his demands were few and mostly reasonable. He characterized his family as being kind and rational, with fairly distant boundaries enabling everyone to do his or her "own thing." His parents had been dead for several years when counseling began, and he was very close to his sister (a nurse) who lived nearby with a male friend. In fact, Mark's sister and her boyfriend were the only couple with whom Carole and Mark socialized as a couple.

Carole, on the other hand, came from a much more controlling family, and she needed to react against it strongly in order to break away. Interestingly, her family never tried to prevent her from leaving, and she maintained cordial relationships with family members, making annual visits home. Her parents chose not to know anything about her postcollege life and family interactions focused on the parents' lives and issues (as well as relatives' and neighbors') rather than on Carole's. During counseling it became clear that Carole saw her life at a standstill and assumed that eventually she would return home to care for (nurse) her parents. Her mother's current illness (multiple sclerosis) caused Carole to give more thought to this possibility. Her brother (aged 39) still lived at home and had never engaged in any long-term intimate relationships.

Carole reported that her childhood was "bland." She always felt fat and unattractive, although the photographs she brought in of her childhood show her to be unusually pretty and of normal weight. She remembers having to hide her fears and concerns about her sexuality and her relationships outside the family. She tried to please her family by being a "good little girl." She spent a lot of time alone in her room reading, and she perceived her life as normal and satisfactory. She did not feel that she did any rebelling until she left college, and then she went far away from her family in order to protect them. Life in her small town revolved around close family and religion, and the rules were rigidly clear. Affection was not expressed but there was always a sense of commitment and caring.

Career Contexts

Mark found that he automatically gravitated toward a business career. He was a successful sales manager of a large drug company and he remembered that as a youth he aspired to a job that would provide security and financial growth and that would not require him to sit at a desk all day. He majored in business at college and had several jobs in the drug industry, first as a salesman and later as an assistant manager, leading to his current job as a manager. Mark said that he realized early on that he would want to travel, to meet new and interesting people. He knew that he was gregarious and that he got restless if he didn't get out and move around. He was satisfied with his current job and its rewards and felt that, since he had stabilized his career, he wanted to stabilize his personal and family life. He felt that he was realistic in his self-assessment and aspirations and that he wanted to put less energy into his career and more into a "meaningful relationship."

Carole received a liberal arts education at college and did not have any career aspirations. She did not work during the two years she was in Europe, but concentrated on learning the language and culture of her relatives. When she returned home, she worked briefly at the local college (where her parents worked too) and then moved to another state where, owing to the influence of new friends, she spent several years working as an aide on a ward in a mental institution. During this time, she fell in love with another aide and she lived with him for several years. She followed him to nursing school, enrolled herself, and went with him out of state to a nursing position. She felt that she had never really made a career choice of her own but rather had merely followed someone else's lead. However, she liked her work and felt that it would serve her well when she returned home to care for her parents. Still, she wondered if in the future she ought to make some more proactive choices for herself. She was aware that her intimacy needs were met through her relationships with patients, where she was always in control and did not have to fear being "swallowed up" or abused.

Assessment

Carole and Mark did indeed come from different backgrounds and were indeed in different life stages in terms of their needs and aspirations. Their couple conflict centered around a power struggle to determine the nature and extent of their relationship, but underlying that were Carole's struggle to find out who she was and to separate emotionally from her family and Mark's need to stabilize an intimate relationship and settle down. Carole was having difficulty with intimacy, particularly with a caring rather than an abusive lover (as her former lover had been), and Mark was exacerbating this difficulty by his need to control and ignore her boundaries. Mark was fairly clear about his life goals; Carole foreclosed on that issue and never proactively worked through who she was and what she wanted to do with her life.

Goals

The first goal in this case was to reframe the couple relationship in order to alleviate the power struggle and postpone any final decision making. The couple and the counselor agreed that a major antecedent goal to working on the couple relationship would be helping Carole to work through her own issues regarding identity, emotional separation from her family, and intimacy. Included in this work with Carole would be some career assessment and an exploration of possible alternative directions for her to ponder. She needed to reassess her life and to make some choices and decisions proactively, to learn to be an initiator rather than a follower. The next goal would be to help the couple enhance their relationship by exploring its pluses and minuses as well as to make some structural changes—for instance, regarding roles and boundaries. Finally, the plan was to help them decide what they wanted to do with and about their relationship.

Interventions

The counselor first reframed their couple relationship, showing them that they could respect rather than fight over the vast differences in their backgrounds and lifestyles. They were relieved at this perspective and could then begin to look at themselves and each other with more tolerance and consideration. Next, the counselor gave Mark some directives to help him refrain from placing demands on Carole that would cause her to distance herself. For example, he was directed not to initiate sex but to allow Carole to become the initiator so that he could learn to follow. The couple was directed not to talk about their relationship when together and to see that each weekend included an activity initiated by each of them. They were also directed to begin to seek out other couples so that they were not always alone together. In short, the counselor encouraged them to reduce the intensity of their relationship so that individual work with Carole could begin.

The individual work with Carole was precipitated by her obvious reluctance to discuss her past in front of Mark. It was clear to everyone that her past relationship was interfering with her ability to develop any relationships at this time. During the individual sessions, she developed a trusting relationship with the counselor and enthusiastically embarked on a self-exploration process so she could "catch up" on the development that she had delayed. Much of this work involved assessing her relationships with her parents and her former lover, who had abused and hurt her dreadfully and then abandoned her for a gay lover. She had accepted this abuse and final rejection without anger and had never questioned it. Subsequently, she had gravitated toward other abusive heterosexual relationships. Mark was the first kind, caring, thoughtful lover she had known. For the first time in her life, she began to allow herself to express anger (several Gestalt and Rational Emotive Therapy strategies were used for this purpose), and she learned to become more assertive at work and in other relationships as she began to value herself.

After fifteen sessions of individual work, the counselor met with Mark and Carole as a couple. Mark had felt left out during that period of time, but he had followed his directives and cared enough about Carole to learn to give her more space. By this time, the couple relationship was on a more positive, even keel, with each party feeling some hope that the relationship had a possibility of growing, owing to both partners' increasing experience of comfort and relaxation within the relationship. After three couple sessions, it was decided that counseling would be terminated for six months so that the relationship could take its own course and Carole and Mark could put what they'd learned about each other into the context of the couple relationship.

Outcome

Eight months later, Carole and Mark were still involved with each other and reported that their relationship was slowly developing. Neither had the inclination to see other people in love relationships or to terminate their relationship with each other. Carole was actively researching other types of nursing careers, and she was finding that she trusted Mark and no longer felt guilty about being treated lovingly. The two still saw each other only on weekends but reported that they had made new friends and were enjoying their time together more. Carole reported that she was able to let Mark know when he became too intrusive or controlling, and Mark reported that he had developed more interests and friendships of his own with which to fill his weekday evenings. They both reported an improved sexual relationship.

Carole felt that her personal growth during the counseling sessions had been "fantastic" and that she had gained a great deal of insight into her life patterns and styles. She was, for the first time, taking active responsibility for her own life and giving a great deal of thought to who she was, who she wanted to be, and what type of life she wanted for herself at present and in the future. Her thinking had borne fruit in the career context; she was able to assume more leadership responsibilities and initiated and managed a three-day in-service training program for her own and other hospital staff in the city. Mark said that he was pleased with Carole's development—although he had feared he would be threatened—and that her self-sufficiency made it possible for him to spread out his energies and become more involved with others. He turned some of his excessive energy into community work.

Comments

This case is a good example of a couple situation in which each party is in a different stage of adult development. Fortunately, one party here was patient and willing to wait for the other to do some growing, and both worked together rather than against each other. Interestingly, Carole proved eager and willing to deal with her personal issues despite her initial resistance to couple counseling. She later mentioned that she had often thought of getting some counseling. Carole's situation exemplifies how career demands (such as oncological nursing) can drain one's energies from a more conflict-ridden area of life and help one to avoid dealing with those other issues.

Although Carole claimed that her career choice was reactive and accidental, it had really been no accident that she became a nurse. She chose a career that allowed her to relate to people from a nonthreatening, distanced vantage point in a field where she could be used and controlled by physicians and where she could continue to be the good little girl seeking approval by doing "good," as she had been at home. It also turned out that she had chosen this particular type of nursing as a reaction to a family secret that had terrified her during her childhood—that her grandmother had cancer, the worst thing, in Carole's family, that could happen to anyone. Although Carole did not find this out until recently, in some part of her mind she was aware of her thought that by nursing cancer patients she would insure herself against getting cancer.

Whether or not Carole and Mark stayed together was not the issue. Were they later to decide that they had gone as far as they could go together and needed to separate, they would do so with honesty and integrity, knowing that they had tried in a mature fashion to develop a relationship. In other words, they would be proactive rather than reactive, and they would be able to acknowledge sadness rather than the bitterness and resentment that result when relationships fail because of a power struggle and impasse.

Again, the techniques of reframing the problem and active directives to restructure roles and boundaries were helpful for this couple. Many techniques from individual counseling modalities (see Okun, 1982) were helpful to Carole.

CASE 4: DON, VICKY, JOEL, BERNARD

Presenting Problem

The Masur family was referred to therapy by an elementary school counselor. Bernard, aged 5, was having difficulties in kindergarten. He had a poor attention span, had difficulty obeying his teacher, and fought with the other children. In other words, he was disruptive and required too much attention from the teacher. Joel, aged 2, was in a daycare situation, since Vicky, 32, worked as a second grade teacher, and Don, 34, worked as an engineer in a technological firm. The initial session was a family assessment in which the entire family assembled for two hours with the counselor. During this session, the family performed several structured activities (see Okun and Rappaport, 1980) so that their structures and communication patterns could be assessed. In addition, Don, Vicky, and Bernard were asked to describe their perceptions of the problems.

Don stated that he felt Bernard's problem stemmed from Vicky's inability to enforce discipline and her inconsistent rules. He expressed a great deal of anger at her, stating that one minute she was too rigid and narrow in her rules and the next minute her rules were nonexistent. He said that he was very busy at work, aiming for a large promotion that would "make or break" his career, and that he did not have much tolerance for the noise and bickering that went on at home. He was annoyed at the school, since he felt that a "good kindergarten teacher" would surely be able to handle a little boy as good as Bernard. He had never had any trouble with him at home.

Vicky felt constantly tired from dealing with thirty-one 7-year-olds all day and her own two children the rest of the day and evening. She tried to be a patient, loving kind of parent, and worried about her lack of patience and tolerance at home. She had always found Bernard to be a very trying child. She just did not know how to get him to listen to her. Joel, on the other hand, was much easier to deal with, and never caused any difficulties. Vicky tried to be fair in her dealings with the children in order to give equal attention to both, but she felt that she was always trying to catch up, never quite making it. Don's criticisms and lack of support hurt her very much. She claimed that he was never available to her and that he was always using his work as an excuse for staying away in the evening. She never knew if he would be home for dinner (leaving her with the sole responsibility for bathing and putting the kids to bed); many nights he did not come home until the early hours of the morning, never even phoning to tell her he would be late. She felt that Don would help out with the kids only if and when he felt like it and only on his own terms. Weekends were particularly trying: each wanted some free time, and each refused to take full responsibility for the kids.

Bernard reported that his teacher did not like him, but that in general school was "okay." He liked hearing stories and playing with the trains. He did not like the way Mommy and Daddy were always fighting, and he wished Joel was older so he could play more and do more things with him. He really did not like the lady who took care of him after school, and he wished Mommy was home more and not always busy with her lessons when she was home. But now that he was going to school, it was better than when he went to the "baby school" (daycare). Bernard said that when his teacher took him by the hand he listened, but that sometimes he had trouble hearing what she said.

Joel did not talk, but sat contentedly on his mother's lap playing with a toy. During a family drawing activity, he allowed his father to help him participate.

Description of Clients

The Masur family presented themselves as an attractive, verbal, and energetic young family in the preschool/school-age stages of family development. Don, 34, was easily in control of the family, as was obvious in his directing of everyone to seats and in activities. He was of medium height, attractive, well dressed, and very charming and outgoing. Vicky, 32, appeared more scattered, and was dressed more casually. She was soft spoken and diffident and she looked to Don for most answers. Bernard was average size for a 5-year-old and appeared to have an average amount of poise and social skills. Whether or not he was immature in terms of his attention span remained to be seen, but he certainly appeared to be within the normal limits for a 5-year-old boy. Joel, 2, held on to his mother and sat on her lap and sucked his thumb. He smiled a lot and seemed pleasant, but was definitely the bystander in this family of four. When Vicky and Don disagreed, it was Bernard who diverted their attention onto him by making noise with a toy or attempting to tease Joel. Thus, the major configuration consisted of a triangle, with Bernard at the apex and Don and Vicky at the two other ends.

Individual Contexts

Don was the middle of three children of college-educated parents in a southern rural community where his father was a factory manager and his mother a housewife. He excelled in school and other community activities and he was used to being set apart from his peers and admired by the entire town. His family was in the top socioeconomic stratum in this small town. Don graduated first in his high school class and was also class president. He won a full scholarship to an Ivy League college. At college, he had a great deal of difficulty adjusting to his roommates and the peer culture and he took off two years for military service, an acceptable alternative path at that time. He also found that he didn't want to work too hard at his studies and he was alarmed by his low, borderline grades. He really was unsure who he was and what he wanted and this frightened him. He met Vicky when he returned to college for his senior year. She was at a neighboring college. They married upon his graduation, as he wanted "to show his folks that he really was grown up so they would stop worrying about his floundering." He had had minimal dating experience and no long-term intimate relationship before Vicky.

In terms of individual development, Don felt that he was "trapped" and "stuck" in an upwardly mobile career and family. The joy had gone out of life for him by the time he married and, although he and Vicky were married for seven years before they had Bernard, he now reported that whatever good was in family life had been covered over by responsibilities and chores. In other words, he felt that Vicky and the children had deprived him of his own self, of any freedom and space. Because he married so young, he felt that he had never really acted out or played around. Don talked about how he had refused to make choices, since he could not stand to be confined. He allowed things to happen to him—college, military, jobs, marriage—and refused to take responsibility for the consequences. He described himself as "confident," "verbal," "strong," "bright," and "needing lots of freedom and space."

Vicky, on the other hand, was the older of two daughters of a federal-government employee at a department-head level. Her mother was a housewife until Vicky entered high school and then she took an office job. Vicky reports her childhood as "ideal," with no fighting and everyone pitching in to help and caring for each other. She herself liked school and had lots of friends. Whenever she was upset or had a problem, her parents were very supportive. She had wanted to be a teacher from early childhood, since she liked kids and thought that teaching would be a good career to combine with having a family (in terms of hours and vacations). Her major dream was to get married and have an "ideal family life" along with a career. She knew exactly what was needed to have this "ideal family life," and she was determined that everyone would play the role as she directed. Vicky described herself as "kind," "loving," "creative," and "energetic." She felt that she had been fun-loving until she became overburdened with childrearing responsibilities. She accepted these responsibilities and was concerned by Don's inability to accept his share.

When they talked about their families of origin, it became apparent that Don's had been a more random system than Vicky's; in her family, the rules were clear, although benevolently administered, and it was rare that anyone failed to cooperate. In his family, it was unclear what the rules were, and arguing and resisting were considered acceptable. Their power struggle included their families of origin, in that each one disliked the other's and both tried to bring their own families into their shared family system.

Family Contexts

A major characteristic of the Masur family was the conflict between the parents over what type of system to have, random or closed. The random type of system advocated by Don won out over the more orderly system that Vicky desired but was unable to implement, since Don really held the power. He had the choice of when to come and go and whether or not to participate in the parenting. When the two were together, they argued a lot about who had done or had not done what. During these arguments, it was easy to see that Bernard became upset, putting his hands over his ears and trying to distract his parents by creating his own disturbances or engaging one of them in conversation. However, the two did not spend much time together owing to Don's business hours.

A family history revealed that the marriage had had serious difficulties before Bernard was born and that, in fact, the decision to have Bernard was predicated on the couple's belief that a child would hold the marriage together. Just prior to Vicky's first pregnancy, Don had had an affair for six months. He was ambivalent about whether or not to stay in the marriage, but he felt that his parents would disapprove if he left. Vicky was so determined to have her marriage and family, to fulfull her "dream," that she put up with whatever came her way and, while she argued, her resistance was not very strong. She would, in fact, smile and giggle like a little girl whenever she confronted Don, so he did not take her very seriously. Fighting about the child enabled the couple to diffuse their hostilities toward each other. Occasionally they had good sex together and often they were able to socialize with other young families at the same stage of family development. It was during one of the "good periods" that they decided to have Joel, hoping that another child would make life easier for Bernard so that he would not make so many demands on them.

Affection and emotional resources were definitely scarce in this family, and time and energies were strained. The tension level was high, but the family managed it in a somewhat civilized manner, and their engaging appearance made the family seem to be a group of likeable children rather than two adults and two children. Not until several sessions had passed did data about wife-hitting, excessive drinking, and marijuana smoking on Don's part come to light.

Career Contexts

Don was quite content with his position. He was now in a managerial position, and he was allowed the autonomy that he desired, more as an internal consultant than in a staff engineering position. He related well to his colleagues and frequently went out for drinks with them. He had difficulty with supervisors and authority, but he had learned to control and circumvent these problems over the years. After college, he had had no difficulty finding a job, and his move up the career ladder was orderly and predictable. Things always came along for him and he never had to seek out an opportunity. He had one more hurdle to cross and then he would head his own department and, as far as he was concerned, that was where he would stay. He liked his salary, although he never seemed to have enough money to buy everything he wanted, and the family always had to be careful about spending. He felt that he had shown his parents that he was successful; he had security and sufficient status and prestige.

Vicky was finding that teaching was losing its fun and joy as the "back to basics" movement spread. She was beginning to experience what is known as burn-out in the teaching field and was fantasizing about some other type of career, such as owning and running a children's clothing store. She had learned that she needed to work and that she did not like being at home; in fact, she often took weekend and summer jobs to avoid being an "at-home mother." She felt somewhat guilty about this but knew that she needed some of her own space and freedom. Don was becoming impatient with her career dissatisfactions and kept urging her to start looking around and find out what other possibilities there might be. The problem for Vicky was that she would not be able to replicate her salary and benefits in another area—at least not for some time—and she wasn't sure they could really cut back, since they lived on their combined earnings and had nothing left over for savings.

Assessment

Although the presenting problem involved Bernard's school difficulties, it became evident fairly quickly that the underlying problem was in the couple system. The power structure needed to be equalized and some room for fun and spontaneity recreated. The system's goals were unclarified and each new developmental stage was causing more stress and disequilibrium than growth. It also became clear that Bernard's acting out in school was his way of protecting his parents from fighting each other. As long as Don and Vicky could worry about him, they would not have to deal with the issues of their marital conflicts that might tear their marriage apart. Somehow, children can sense the effectiveness of diversion, and they often develop symptoms to protect the family system.

The school counselor perceived that the difference between the home and school systems was confusing for Bernard. His classroom was strict, authoritarian, and closed, very different from his random family system. He did not know how to negotiate a closed type of system, and he was reacting as he did at home when the tension became too great—by tuning out "mother" or "teacher" and becoming increasingly helpless, distracted, and restless.

In terms of the couple conflicts, it was clear that Don resented being married, but was having difficulty allowing himself to acknowledge his resentment. Vicky, sensing this resentment, reacted in a terrified manner by trying harder and harder and ending up more and more harried. Don was fantasizing about his lost youth and opportunities, and Vicky was yearning for the security and stability she had perceived her parents to have and that she believed automatically came with adulthood. Both were disappointed and confused.

Goals

The first goal of therapy was to alleviate the presenting problem by helping the parents deal more consistently with Bernard at home. In addition to some directives and bibliotherapy about parenting, the counselor taught Don and Vicky how to set up a behavioral contract with Bernard and his teacher. Each day that Bernard brought home two out of three stars for good conduct, Vicky spent half an hour alone with him doing something he wanted to do. At the end of that week, if he had brought home sufficient stars for the week (75 percent of the total possible), Don and Bernard did something special together without Vicky and Joel. The purpose of this contract was to give Bernard some of the time alone and emotional security he craved with each parent, apart from the usual family tensions.

The next goal was to work with Don and Vicky on their couple issues so that they could look at their marriage and decide what they wanted to do about it. They were very willing to do so when the counselor pointed out to them that their own dissatisfactions were affecting the children. At some level, they knew that they were in trouble and that they could no longer cover up and pretend that everything was all right.

Interventions.

As previously mentioned, behavioral contracts and parenting directives were applied to meet the first goal, that of dealing with Bernard's school problems. The parents were encouraged to take charge of their child, to talk with him about school, and to urge him to have a positive experience there. The behavioral contract helped them to understand the value of a clearly defined structure with a child of that age, taking the focus off what was wrong with Bernard and placing it on the process of facilitating Bernard's school adjustment. The parents were taught about typical 5-year-old behavior and the wide variations in children's physical, social, emotional, and cognitive development.

The couple's work included the use of conflict-resolution strategies, and paradoxical directives (a clinical intervention whereby a therapist gives a client [or family] a directive he or she wants resisted; the change then occurs as a result of defying the therapist). However, before these strategies could be used, the counselor devoted several sessions and homework assignments to teaching clear communications. Vicky and Don had not really listened to each other for years and each had really lost touch with the true identity of the other. They needed to learn to rephrase what they had heard from each other, to differentiate between "I feel" and "I think" messages, and, above all, to check out misunderstandings and interpretations. Two examples of the paradoxical directives used follow:

1. When Vicky complained about how she couldn't sleep and how she worried when Don did not come home at night, she was instructed to stop trying to sleep and to sit up all night in a chair until Don came home. Eventually she became so tired that she went to sleep and stopped worrying, since she began to realize that she could not control his comings and goings.
2. Since Don never told Vicky whether or not he was coming home for dinner and he resisted all her attempts to "pin him down," he was told to come home for dinner no more than one night a week under any circumstances and to give Vicky six hours notice of which night he would be there, so she could fix a special dinner for him. After two weeks, Don started coming home more than once a week because he found that he enjoyed the special dinners without the nagging.

The couple was told to consider the possibility of separating, something that neither had allowed him- or herself to do except in secret fantasy. Once this possibility was out in the open, they could begin to assess their marriage in terms of its positive and negative aspects, and to communicate more clearly their desires to each other, in order to decide what they wanted to do.

Outcome

The six months of couple's therapy in this case were turbulent. The issues with Bernard were resolved fairly quickly and the school reported vast improvement in his classroom behaviors. However, the couple counseling proceeded slowly and with many setbacks. Often, Don did not attend sessions and his behavior changes at home were short lived. During this time, however, Vicky became stronger and more competent in her parenting and teaching, and she eventually got to the point where she told Don that she did not want to continue in the marriage this way, and that if he really did not want to be married to her and to partake in family life, she did not want him to stay. This was quite a shock for him, since heretofore Vicky had professed that saving the marriage in spite of everything was her foremost goal. When she stopped pursuing this goal and developed more of an individual life, he had to stop resisting and decide whether he wanted to stay in the marriage. Although he had denied any extramarital involvements since Bernard's birth, he finally admitted that he had been involved with another woman for two years and that he was conflicted about which woman to choose. Vicky was furious and told him that he could not live at home as long as he kept up this other liaison. Thus, he moved out and they eventually began divorce proceedings. Interestingly, when he left Vicky, he lost his job due to excessive absenteeism over the preceding few months, and he remained unemployed for many months before finding a lesser type of position. Vicky was unaware of any job difficulties until the time of his firing.

Vicky remained in counseling for another 12 months while she restructured her life as a single parent. Bernard's behavior continued to improve in school and he was having a positive experience in first grade, despite the separation of his parents. Vicky found that her life really changed little after Don left. At least she no longer was concerned about whether or not he would come home and her childrearing responsibilities were just about the same as prior to his leaving. She regretted the demise of her marriage and came to understand her contribution to it—her denial of the signals, her controlling imposition of her dream onto Don without negotiating with his dream, her inability to recognize Don's reluctance to take on family responsibilities, and her blind insistence on having children and going on as if there were no problems.

Vicky's attorney was successful in negotiating a financial settlement that allowed her to begin to study for a master's degree in marketing and to prepare for a career change. She was very happy about these opportunities and commented on how good it felt to finally grow up and take responsibility for her own life. She was fortunate in having a large support system formed by family, friends, and colleagues to aid her during the separation process, and her physical appearance and manner improved as her self-confidence and self-esteem increased.

Don returned to the counselor for a referral several months after the divorce came through. He had had several affairs and was considering marrying the woman with whom he had been involved during his marriage to Vicky. He did not see his sons much, calling the experience "too difficult." He was somewhat bitter about the financial settlement that Vicky received and his visitation agreement and he was confused and upset about the decline of his career. Thus, he thought that some individual pyschotherapy was in order before embarking on another marriage; the counselor encouraged him to pursue that path. Like Vicky, he felt that divorce had been the most desirable outcome for that particular situation. He also regretted that it had taken so long for them to confront their marital issues.

Comments

This was a case of two young people getting married before they really had worked through their identity issues. Unfortunately for them, marriage served to impede their development rather than enhance it. When children entered the family, Vicky was forced to grow up and assume responsibilities since Don would not. He hid in his career and she had to juggle her career and family demands. The more responsible Vicky became, the more hostile Don became, perceiving her demands to be entrapments, like his mother's demands had been. The two had to deal with the reality of two little boys and, while Vicky earnestly attempted to work through her marital difficulties, Don withdrew without telling Vicky and became involved elsewhere. Eventually, the couple had to decide what to do about it, and they chose divorce.

It is not the purpose of counseling to moralize about divorce and marriage. The outcome of couple counseling is whatever the couple responsibly and proactively chooses. Divorce is as valid an outcome as a renewed marriage. It is always sad to see a family break up, but, in this case, it was exhilarating to see Vicky grow and blossom as she acknowledged her competencies, strengths, and new interests.

This was another example of how family issues can affect career issues. On the surface, Don's career status was secure. However, his increasing anxiety about his duplicity and the demands of two simultaneous relationships detracted from the time and energy he could put into work. The strain also caused him to drink and smoke more. While he thought he could get away with it, eventually his limited resources caused a disaster and he lost both his family and his coveted position. All these serious difficulties were covered up by concern over a 5-year-old child's adjustment to school.

Besides considering individual, family, and career development, we must also determine the meaning of the presenting problem to the individual and to the family. In this case, Bernard's difficulties served to protect his parents, diffusing the tensions he sensed in his family system. The meaning of the presenting problem to Vicky was that something was wrong with her child; to Don the meaning was that something was wrong with the kind of mothering the child was receiving. Each member of a system perceives and interprets the presenting problem in accordance with his or her own needs. It is up to the counselor to disentangle these perceptions and to view the presenting problem both as serving a function for and being maintained by the system.

SUMMARY

The case studies in this chapter deal with issues common to people in early adulthood. These issues often concern self-identity, emotional separation from family of origin, intimate relationships, career choice and establishment, marital selection and management, and parenting. As early adulthood is a time of great variation in terms of attained development, each person must be considered separately, and chronological age cannot be considered the major variable. Many of the people in their early thirties described in this chapter were at the same level of individual development as some people in their early twenties. They were not sick or pathological, but underdeveloped and stuck. However, the tasks and issues of early adulthood depend on resolution of the tasks and issues of late adolescence, and people must work through earlier unfinished business in order to continue growing and developing.

Interventions from any modality of individual and family therapies can be effective, as can pertinent career assessment and planning strategies. A major point about working with adults is to help them mobilize and utilize whatever resources are available to them—from within themselves, and from peers, institutions, and the community. Young adults do not generally know much about their stage of life, and they often feel that their parents were inadequate role models in terms of today's unique stresses and problems. They are confused about others' expectations of them and by their expectations of others. Therefore, education and exposure to relevant reading and media materials can be a useful adjunct to counseling. It is important as well to encourage and facilitate the development of young people's friend and peer support systems. Often, an overdependency on one's immediate family for emotional support cuts the individual off from the outside resources that can foster new ideas and potential styles of living. Young adulthood is a time of expansion, when all possibilities are to be considered before the narrowing selection process takes place.

Young adulthood is a difficult time when you consider that one establishes oneself as an adult and builds a career and family. These activities require enormous energy and perseverance, and it is no wonder that so many people falter in some way at some time. However, this is also a period when people are eager for help, eager to assess how they are doing and how their accomplishments mesh with youthful dreams and aspirations. People have a tremendous capacity for growth during this period as they begin to live independently of their family of origin.

Individual, group, and family counseling modalities can be successfully used with young adults. The particular strategies that may be effective, in addition to more conventional strategies from individual counseling (see Okun, 1982), include: (1) reframing the presenting problem into a developmental and systems perspective; (2) prescribing the symptom; (3) paradoxical or straight directives; (4) family sculpture to realign boundaries; (5) behavioral contracts; and (6) bibliotherapy.

REFERENCES

Okun, B. F. *Effective helping.* 2nd ed. Monterey, Calif.: Brooks/Cole, 1982.

Okun, B. F., & Rappaport, L. J. *Working with families: An introduction to family therapy.* North Scituate, Mass.: Duxbury Press, 1980.

PART THREE

MIDDLE ADULTHOOD

"Life begins at forty!" For years, this homily has provided comfort to those entering their fourth decade—reassuring them that there still is opportunity and enjoyment after the loss of youth in a society traditionally dominated by a youth orientation. Perhaps, however, this homily covers the anxiety surrounding the underlying message that forty is closer to death.

Recently, the media have given great attention to "the mid-life crisis," highlighting stereotypical conceptions of men in their forties shedding their jobs and families for young, nubile women, and of women in their forties racked by menopausal depression and "the empty-nest syndrome." Most of the serious literature on the middle years acknowledges that some type of mid-life transition occurs, but the exact timing and nature of this transition can vary. And the issues that arise during the middle years may indeed involve the mourning of youth and open-ended opportunities, but they may also present new challenges and opportunities for creative growth. We know that, in this country and many other industrialized nations, changes occur during middle life, but, media images aside, these changes have positive as well as threatening aspects.

This part explores the years of middle adulthood, roughly the ages 40–60. We begin our exploration with a study of the mid-life transition, which can occur in the late thirties or early forties. We then turn to the issues and tasks of the late forties and the fifties, noting that they depend on the satisfactory negotiation of the mid-life transition, a period of reappraisal and renegotiation between the more stable periods of young adulthood and middle age. Social class, gender, cultural, and ethnic variables all influence the timing and duration of this mid-life transition, and we focus on the common themes and issues.

The major personal issues of middle adulthood involve the reappraisal and reformulation of life's priorities, goals, and relationships and a restructuring of one's time perspective as well as a preparation for the loss of family, friends, hopes, fantasies, youthful vigor, and the roles and status of youth. Those in middle adulthood also grapple with their own mortality. All these issues involve a reexamination and restructuring of major developmental issues from early adulthood, mainly of identity and the formation and development of intimate relationships. One may have achieved a satisfactory sense of self and developed satisfying intimate relationships during earlier years; mid-life is an opportunity again to question and examine, albeit from a more experienced perspective, the same attitudes, values, beliefs, and choices considered earlier. How one has coped with these issues during the earlier course of life will no doubt influence how one copes with them later on in life.

Chapter 7 covers the stages, tasks, and issues of individual development, the biological/social/emotional aspects of the life cycle. Chapter 8 focuses on the middle stages of the family life cycle, and Chapter 9 on the tasks and issues of career development in mid-life. The events and issues from each domain influence the others, and we must remember that the age cohorts are relative. In Chapter 10, we present case studies and implications for treatment in middle adulthood.

CHAPTER SEVEN

INDIVIDUAL DEVELOPMENT IN MIDDLE ADULTHOOD

One's fortieth birthday seems to be a definite boundary between youth and old age. In our society, being old is laden with unpleasant emotional connotations. Older adults—and many people consider middle-aged adults to be old—are perceived as declining steadily in the areas of physical prowess, sensory perceptiveness, agility, health, intellectual capacities, sexual vigor, and so forth. At the same time, middle-aged adults are expected to be "stable," "settled," "mature," "committed," and "responsible." They are also expected to be productive workers and responsible citizens and family members. Yes, the middle-aged are "over the hill," but they still hold leadership positions in families, work, and the community.

There is no turning back from middle age. Who can recapture his or her youth, no matter how hard he or she tries? This realization is difficult to accept. Thus, at this stage, we may have to question the value of our youth and wonder about the value of aging. It is at this point that we begin to question the myths and the stereotypes, to decide for ourselves what is valuable and not valuable for making the transition into middle age. As several adults have commented, "passing the age of 40 is nowhere as difficult as the dreadful anticipation of it." The bark of the middle years is worse than their bite.

As life expectancy increases, middle age becomes a lengthier, more well-defined period with its own developmental tasks and issues that serve as a broad transition between early adulthood and late adulthood. In other words, middle age has become more clearly delineated and has come to last longer as increasing numbers of people live through it to enter older age.

In the past two decades, as the population bulge has begun to shift toward middle age, this period has come under the scrutiny of social scientists, physicians, psychological writers, journalists, novelists, poets, and dramatists. The results of this attention indicate that important changes do indeed occur during middle age, and that many of these changes involve complex transformations rather than the simple decline of capacities. Thus, middle age is a time of change, involving gains as well as losses, and affording the same opportunities for growth and development and for stress and crisis as other phases in the life cycle. The possibilities for growth and change in middle age are as pervasive as in adolescence and in early adulthood.

We begin our study of middle adulthood by exploring the mid-life transition from early adulthood into middle adulthood. Although the concept of mid-life transition has become a popular preoccupation, we attempt here to separate the myths from the realities as we consider the characteristics, challenges, and potentials of this transitional period. Following our treatment of this transitional stage, we consider the late forties and the fifties as separate stages, delineating the crucial tasks and issues relevant to each stage.

Some of the questions covered in this chapter include:

1. Does everyone go through a mid-life transition?
2. Is the mid-life transition a crisis?
3. Is the mid-life identity crisis similar to the adolescent identity crisis?
4. Is there increased vulnerability to depression and psychopathology at mid-life?
5. What are the influences of social, economic, and technological factors on middle age?
6. What are the sex-role variables that affect middle age?
7. How do endocrine changes affect middle age?
8. What are the major differences between people in their forties and people in their fifties?

MID-LIFE TRANSITION

Although some writers believe that the preoccupation with the mid-life transitional experience is largely a narcissistic, white middle-class phenomenon associated with the affluence and the increased leisure and self-absorption of the 1960s and 1970s, the view presented in this book is that everyone goes through some type of mid-life transition, albeit at different times and at different levels of intensity. This transition may or may not be a "crisis" in terms of tumult and disruption. Whether or not it is depends on one's expectations and anticipations, on how one experienced earlier stages of development, and on how easily one can negotiate the tasks and issues necessitated by the transition. Those adults who manage to cope successfully with this transition appear to be more likely to cope successfully with the tasks and issues of later middle age and older age. Those who do not manage well during the mid-life transition or who do not resolve the conflicts and issues posed by this transition may be more vulnerable to stress and difficulties in later stages of life. Vaillant (1977) points out that as men get older, their ways of coping with reality crises become more mature and the quality of their sustained relationships becomes more important as predictors of later adaptation than their childhood traumas.

Most of the studies reported in the literature do indicate that a transitional period between early adulthood and middle adulthood occurs and that this transitional period may indeed be stressful. Let us review some of the major findings of these studies, remembering that the samples usually consist of white, middle-class men and that the studies themselves may well be challenged on the basis of design and methodology. We will then discuss the developmental tasks and issues commonly associated with this transition.

Major Findings

Carl Jung.   Jung (1933) was one of the first psychological writers to mention that a mid-life crisis occurs around the age of 40. During this mid-life crisis, one's psyche begins a transformation, as aspects of one's self that were repressed during early stages of identity formation emerge, requiring a reorganization of one's dominant pattern of self-identity. During the first half of life, an outward expansion is characteristic, as the individual dedicates his or her self to the task of mastering the outer world. Now, one turns inward and examines the meaning of life. This interiority is prompted by the unconscious, which seeks recognition to bring about harmony and psychic balance (Jung, 1933, pp.17–18, 62–63).

For Jung, then, it is during this mid-life transition that one begins to incorporate certain unlived or denied aspects of self—the contrasexual aspects of self—to a new, total self. Therefore, men at this time can acknowledge and incorporate their feminine aspects into their being and women can acknowledge and incorporate their masculine aspects into their being as they mediate and compromise between their own needs and impulses and the expectations of society.

Jung calls this process *individuation*, and sees it as leading toward health and growth. The tasks of individuation are: (1) to achieve a measure of psychic balance, and (2) to separate the self out from ordinary conformity to the goals and values of the mass culture and to find one's own way. Involved is the developmental task of tolerating both the changes emerging in self-perceptions and the loss of old identities while continuing to function sufficiently to cope with everyday matters. One feels inner urgings to listen to one's unconscious in order to learn about the potentials so far left unrealized. This tendency raises questions about the meaning of life.

Jung (1933) also points out that while growth during the second half of life does indeed create tensions and difficulties, the greatest failures come when adults cling to the goals and values of the first half of life in order to avoid these tensions and difficulties. To cling in this way results in what Erikson (1968) calls "stagnation."

Erik Erikson.   For Erikson (1968), a great internal choice is made at mid-life that is comparable to the basic decisions of earlier years. A mid-life crisis missed or fumbled leads to stagnation, a state in which one's essential vitality sinks too low for further development. But if the crisis is confronted and resolved, it can lead to enormous gains in perspective and creativity—namely to generativity, which is a concern for and commitment to the next generation and to the welfare of society.

Thus, in Erikson's Stage 7, the task is generativity versus stagnation. The success and sense of satisfaction one derived from one's occupation and/or family life can both resolve one's identity crisis and lead to a sense of generativity. The latter is the adult's concern for and psychological investment in younger persons (offspring or others) or the adult's desire to achieve or create ideas or products that will be of benefit to society in the future. Generativity invests one's energy and ideas in something new and involves future plans that require the development and use of one's skills and abilities. If one is frustrated and lacks a sense of fulfillment in occupational and/or family roles, stagnation may result as the adult withdraws from younger people and productivity. Stagnation leads to self-preoccupation, to a sort of vegetation where one merely performs routines of work and activities, feeling useless, unneeded, and dependent. Brim (1976) points out that this description of generativity may relate to the resolution of the mid-life transition rather than to its cause. Erikson writes:

> The generational cycle links life cycles together by confronting the older generation's generativity with the younger one's readiness to grow. This has three dominant aspects: the procreative one which gives birth and responds to the needs of the next generation; the productive one, which integrates work life with family life within the political and technological framework; and the creative one, which elaborates cultural potentials within the emerging world image [1981, p. 269].

Generativity cannot occur, according to Erikson, if identity and intimacy are not formulated and developed. Such generativity is necessary in order for one to pass successfully through the middle years and to reach the ego integrity that characterizes older age. Remember that one of Erikson's basic theses is that *every time a person enters a new stage a new chance arises for reintegrating the issues of previous stages.*

Elliott Jaques.   The British psychoanalyst Jaques (1965), studying the historical data that document the lives of great men, postulated the existence of a universal mid-life transition (which he called mid-life crisis) that requires a constructive resignation to human imperfections and to the shortcomings in one's own work. Thus, people have to decide what they can still do and, at the same time, give up their inflated, omnipotent sense of self.

Although the process of transition lasts for *several* years and the duration varies among individuals, Jaques writes that the transition begins around the age of 35 and may take one of three forms for artists: (1) the creative aspects may emerge for the first time; (2) one may burn out creatively or literally die; and (3) a decisive change may occur in one's work. Jaques was really the first to coin the concept of a universal mid-life transition for men, even though his original sample was composed exclusively of artistic men.

Daniel Levinson.   Levinson's findings are interpreted in the Jungian context. He considers the mid-life transition the first stage of mid-life and characterizes this transition as occurring between two relatively stable periods of adulthood, early and middle adulthood. For Levinson, the mid-life transition usually extends from ages 38 to 43. The major task of the mid-life transition is what he calls de-illusionment, which leads to reappraisal of one's life. Levinson (1978) states that the central task of this transitional phase is "to terminate a time in one's life; to accept the losses that termination entails; to review and evaluate the past; to decide which aspects of the past to keep and which to reject; and to consider one's wishes and possibilities for the future." This work differs from that required of youth in that it involves greater responsibility, perspective, dispassionate interest, and judgment. Levinson says that

> . . . to do it well, one must be able to care for younger and older adults, to exercise authority creatively, to transcend the youthful extremes of shallow conformity and impulsive rebelliousness. The moderate mid-life decrease in biological capacity must be counterbalanced by an increased psychosocial capacity to contribute . . . [1977, p. 31].

The three major developmental tasks of the mid-life transition, according to Levinson, are: (1) to review, reappraise, and leave the early adult stage; (2) to decide how middle adulthood should be lived; and (3) to deal with the young/old, destructive/creative, masculine/feminine, and attachment/separation polarities of life.

Thus, the individual's primary task is to draw selectively upon the past, to develop more fully one's inner resources, and to form the basis for a new life structure in middle age. Anxiety may be a dominant motif at this stage, owing to the fear that life ends rather than begins at 40. The problem, then, is to balance the worry about growing old with the futile attempt to stay young. We must outgrow our youthful immaturities and illusions in order to build a balanced life. This necessity involves reassessing the meaning of "old" and "young" and finding new age-appropriate, satisfying behaviors. Levinson's men became more in touch with their "good" and "bad" aspects and, if honest, were able to develop an awareness and to balance this polarity as well as the masculine/feminine polarity.

The attachment/separation polarity is most visible during the mid-life transition. Many divorces occur at this point, as men who are unable to resolve this polarity flee from commitments and attachments to go through a second adolescence of separation from family and the established society. During the twenties and thirties, most men were preoccupied with career and family establishment and with implementing their dream. Now they have either achieved these goals or changed them. They may need to try out new ways of living if they do not find their dream or achievements satisfying.

It becomes apparent that there are two aspects to Levinson's mid-life transition: (1) destructuring, and (2) restructuring. The first involves the de-illusionment process and reappraisal of the life structure of the thirties, in which high priority was most likely to be given to those aspects of the self oriented toward social adjustment and achievement. Restructuring involves the creation of a new structure that includes those aspects—previously not receiving a high priority—leading to a sense of reconciliation and fulfillment and calling upon dormant inner resources. Levinson found that 80 percent of his male sample experienced a tumultuous struggle within themselves, between their selves and the external world. He concluded that most men undergo a moderate-to-severe crisis as they experience more fully their own mortality and the actual or impending death of others while simultaneously experiencing a strong desire to be more creative and generative. In describing this conflict, he writes that "the powerful forces of destructiveness and creativity coexist in the human soul and man strives to integrate them in new ways" (1978, p. 89).

The kinds of questions Levinson's subjects reported considering during their mid-life transitions included these:

1. What have I done with my life?
2. What do I really get from and give to my wife, children, friends, work, community, and self?
3. What are my central values and how are they reflected in my life?
4. What are my greatest talents and how am I using or wasting them?
5. What have I done with my early dream and what do I want to do with it now?

In other words, a man must decide about his sense of disparity between what he has done and what he wants to do, and the necessity for this decision leads him to search his soul to determine what he really wants. The level of disparity and dissonance experienced will depend upon the goodness of the fit between the self and the life structure, between one's identity and one's actual accomplishments.

Both Levinson and Vaillant noted that from early adulthood through their early forties their male subjects overwhelmingly gave the highest priority to their work commitment and career progression. During the mid-life transition, these men questioned this priority and, as they came to terms with their career status, many renewed their family and friendship relationships.

Roger Gould.   Gould's (1972) findings reflected the trends noted by Levinson. He found that subjects in their forties became more aware that time is finite, as they became aware of parents' and friends' mortality through serious illness and death. They gave a high ranking to the statement "I try to be satisfied with what I have and not to think so much about the things I probably won't get." His male subjects were also involved in a process of reappraisal during the mid-life transition. They asked themselves such questions as "Have I done the right thing?" and "Is there time to change?" Many of his adults experienced a kind of desperation regarding the squeeze of time; their acceptance of the finite time left in their life span was accompanied by frustration. This frustration was often manifested in scapegoating behavior—they blamed their parents for their current problems, and their children and spouses for making unwarranted demands and pressures and for failing to appreciate and understand them.

For Gould, the major false assumption accompanying the mid-life decade, ages 35–45, is "There is no evil or death in the world. The sinister has been destroyed" (1978, p. 217). Component false assumptions that must also be challenged and mastered include: (1) the illusion of safety can last forever; (2) death can't happen to me or my loved ones; (3) it's impossible to live without a protector (women); (4) there is no life beyond this family; and (5) I am an innocent (1978, p. 219).

Both men and women have a growing sense of vulnerability resulting in a heightened sense of power and freedom as they begin to feel less controlled by the fear of others' power over them. Gould describes the mid-life decade this way:

> Mid-life, then, is not a sedentary or bucolic period. In fact, mid-life is every bit as turbulent as adolescence, except we can use all this striving to blend a healthier, happier life. For, unlike adolescents, in mid-life we know and accept who we are [1978, p. 307].

Gould found that his women subjects in the mid-life transition tended to move in independent directions, such as taking a job or more vigorously pursuing earlier non-familial interests, in order to overcome their feelings of needing a protector. In addition to dealing with their own and others' mortality, women need to confront and work through the issues of their separate individuation. The issues of mortality and individuation are intertwined. If a woman depends on her husband for protection and she becomes more aware of his mortality, she needs to think of her own potential for survivorship.

George Vaillant.   Vaillant's (1977) subjects experienced a mid-life transition parallel to their adolescent transition. For mid-life adults, it is a time of exploring and reassessing their experiences and relationships to-date, a period of arriving at an integration or consolidation of career and intimate relationship strivings. Vaillant's findings do not, however, indicate a tumultuous mid-life transition. Rather, this period consists of renewed vigor and excitement as one feels released from the constraints and demands of early adulthood.

Vaillant's subjects, seen as the most satisfied at age 47, reported their mid-life transition period to have been the happiest in their lives, as opposed to the men seen as dissatisfied at age 47, who perceived early adulthood to have been their happiest period. Stable marriages and a successful mentoring relationship seemed to contribute to a positive mid-life transition.

Bernice Neugarten.   Neugarten's (1968) subjects included both men and women. She, too, found middle age to be a major turning point. She describes the mid-life transition as involving an emphasis on introspection and reappraisal, a move toward interiority (including contemplation, reflection, and self-evaluation) and an increasing preoccupation with one's inner life. This mid-life transition, a major turning point, has both painful and gratifying aspects. It is accompanied by a shift in time perspective as adults begin to think more in terms of the time left to live rather than the time since birth. The concept of time becomes more finite— more of a double-edged sword, with challenges and opportunities on the one hand and the personalization of death on the other hand—as one works through the mid-life transition and enters middle age.

Stability in personality traits and processes is a major finding of the Neugarten studies. The findings indicate that social changes are more powerful determinants of behavior than biological changes. Neugarten found that many of her subjects felt more fully in charge of their lives than ever before as they entered middle age. They perceived themselves as more able to control the environment than younger or older people. Some also found that their changing time perspective caused restlessness and discontent, which were powerful incentives to further accomplishment for some and were brakes for others.

Neugarten emphasizes that sex, generation, social class, and cultural factors are indeed major influences on the timing and duration of a mid-life transition. She writes that whatever personality changes occur result from accumulated life experiences, some of which are role changes and some of which are not. Also, like Jung and Levinson, she found that sex-role reversals begin to occur during middle age.

The Northwestern Group. Recent research from Northwestern University (where Neugarten is now) interposes an additional middle stage to Levinson's two stages of mid-life transition (destructuring and restructuring). Stein (1980) calls Levinson's destructuring stage "separation," and describes this process as a "psychological state of alienation from the identity formed in the familial and social matrix," whereby a pulling away occurs from earlier dreams and goals, and commitment is lost to certain earlier ambitions, persons, and institutions. The result might be boredom and lethargy as one changes one's dominant pattern of self-organization and integrates the unlived aspects of self postulated by Jung.

Stein (1980) coins a new term for this new phase: *liminality,* defined as a threshold or a moratorium period between the destructuring and restructuring phases during which aspects of the self previously rejected can appear and take the time to be integrated. This is the phase between decathexis and recathexis of the psychological structures, and one might experience this stage with ambiguity, confusion, and alienation from an earlier sense of selfhood and from social structures and previous commitments. Often one's identity fluctuates between opposite extremes as it seeks to negotiate the bridge between destructuring and restructuring. Thus, the need develops for an in-between moratorium stage. Levinson's second stage becomes Stein's third stage, and Stein calls this stage *reintegration.* At this point, the new pattern of self-organization reflects more aspects of the total psyche than the earlier pattern. In other words, the individual experiences an awareness and integration of formerly denied and repressed aspects of the self that prepare the middle-aged adult for attitude, behavior, and role changes. This new self-identity is based more on personal experience and the self than on the social and cultural expectations that formed the earlier adult identity.

Cytrynbaum (1980) believes that the work of the mid-life transition is not under conscious control and that it is triggered by personal confrontation with death anxiety and the challenge of previously denied, neglected, or repressed components of the personality. He sees the major issues of the mid-life transition as involving changes in one's orientation to self and time, the experience of death anxiety and mortality, the reassessment of primary interpersonal relationships and work roles, and the emergence of previously suppressed opposite-sex personality characteristics. He believes that personality differences predispose adults to respond differentially to the mid-life transition and that one's interactions with primary systems (family, community, career) also influence one's mid-life transition.

Cytrynbaum (1980) lists the major developmental tasks of the mid-life transition as: (1) the acceptance of death and mortality; (2) the acceptance of biological limitations and risks; (3) the restructuring of the self-concept and sexual identity; (4) a reorientation to work, creativity, and achievement; and (5) a reassessment of primary relationships. If one is successful with these tasks, then one will be able to cope with the developmental tasks of the second half of life. If one is unsuccessful with these tasks, one may experience mid-life-related symptoms such as depression, anxiety, decreased appetite for food and sex, poor concentration, alcoholism, psychosomatic disorders, fear of homosexuality, or vulnerabilities and predispositions to distress as well as maladaptive symptoms later in older adulthood.

Reviews of the literature.   Rosenberg and Farrell (1976) reviewed the literature concerning the male mid-life transition and found considerable evidence that the entrance into middle age is indeed associated with some types of stress and that this stress often results in maladaptive patterns of reaction. These writers acknowledge, however, that little information is available on the specific nature of the stressors, on the differences in their impact, or on the factors associated with an individual's attempted style of adaptation to these stressors.

Brim (1976) concludes from his review of the literature that: (1) the mid-life male is likely to undergo some profound personality changes; (2) these changes will have multiple causes (endocrine changes, aspiration–achievement gaps, resurgence of the dream, family and career changes, social-status or role changes); (3) a "male mid-life crisis" will occur for some men if there are multiple, simultaneous demands for personality change—for example, if during the same month or year the man loses his last illusions about great success, accepts his children for what they are, buries his parents, accepts his mortality, and so on; (4) these changes may be stretched out over 10 to 20 years; and (5) the "growing pains" of mid-life, like those of youth and old age, are transitions from one comparatively steady state to another, and that these changes, even when they occur in crisis dimensions, bring for many men more happiness than they had found in younger days.

Most of the writers reviewed suggest that the following are causal triggers or accompanying variables of a mid-life transition:

1. A sense of bodily decline such as hair thinning or head balding, appetite change and weight loss or gain, changes in sexual appetite, changes in

seeing and hearing capacities, slowing of reaction time, diminishing physical energy, changes in physical prowess;

2. Changes in social roles and status, such as children leaving and the lessening of parenting involvement, plus changes in one's roles with older parents, health issues, career changes, and increased economic burdens;

3. The recognition of one's own mortality as parents die and friends get life-threatening illnesses and die.

These triggers induce one to acknowledge and deal with one's own process of aging and whatever issues accompany this process.

Let us now turn to consideration of sex-role differences as we consider the mid-life transition. Although less data exist on women subjects, the little that has been engendered reveals that women do indeed have mid-life transitions, albeit different from those of men.

Sex-Role Differences

It is generally agreed that gender differences exist that are as important as age variables in terms of the mid-life transition. Gutmann (1969) discusses the sex-role changes that lead to a "normal unisex of later life," describing mid-life men as becoming more sensual, more sensitive to incidental pleasures and pains, less aggressive, more affiliative, more interested in love than conquest or power, more present than future oriented, while mid-life women are becoming more aggressive, less sentimental, and more domineering. Later cross-cultural studies show that these sex-role shifts are not just peculiar to Americans (Gutmann et al., 1980).

Neugarten (1968) writes that "important differences exist between men and women as they age. Men seem to become more receptive to affiliative and nurturant promptings; women, more responsive toward and less guilty about aggressive and egocentric impulses." She points out that the onset of mid-life is perceived differently according to sex. Women, for example, take their cues from happenings within the family, such as moving to a bigger house, the maturing of children, and the leaving and marrying of children. She found that even unmarried career women discussed middle age in terms of the family they might have had. Men, on the other hand, get their cues from the outside world; perhaps a better job along with the prestige and respect that accompanies it, or the point at which younger men ask for advice or when they realize that achievement goals have been gained or missed. Neugarten also found that health changes were more of an age marker for men than women. While both men and women resort to what Neugarten calls "body monitoring" (the protective strategies designed to keep a failing, middle-aged body at a stable level of appearance and performing), men seem to go to greater lengths than women to do so. Neugarten hypothesizes that perhaps men do this at the urgings of their wives, who fear illness and widowhood. *Time* (October 27, 1981) also refers to the unusual lengths taken by men to maintain a youthful appearance, citing the increase of physical exercise and men's use of cosmetic and plastic surgery in the past decade.

Lowenthal and her colleagues (1975) and Lowenthal and Chiriboga (1973) have also found that mid-life female personality changes and trajectories are outward, away from dependency on the husband and away from providing nurturance and support to him. Women tend to move toward greater instrumentality, integrating more autonomous, independent, competitive, and aggressive qualities into their personalities, whereas men become more able to experience expressive, passive, sensuous, and dependent characteristics. These findings might explain why men become more family oriented and women more career oriented during this mid-life transition.

Scarf (1980) points out that women experience more discontinuities than men in terms of biological factors in their roles, functions, and self-perceptions. For example, the issue of physical attractiveness is more salient with women than with men in our culture and childbearing possibilities for women end long before they do for men. These discontinuities can create important pressures regarding identity reassessment and reformulation and have the potential for gain and growth as well as defeat and despair.

The issue of generativity certainly points up some role differences between men and women. If women have been primarily responsible for nurturing during early adulthood and men have been primarily involved with their career development, it makes sense that women will have preceded men into generativity and may now be ready for more achievement-oriented pursuits while men become more interested in generativity, with their children as well as with protegees, than with productivity, possibly seeking more parenting involvement just when their offspring are readying themselves for launching.

There is much speculation as to whether sex-role differences exist with regard to the timing and intensity of the mid-life transition, and whether one sex experiences more crises than the other. The best indications to date are that how one fares with mid-life transition depends more on one's past history of coping with developmental issues and transitions, one's anticipation of what is entailed in the mid-life transition, the type of support one has in primary systems, and the timing of external events than on age or sex variables. Recent evidence indicates that for women, menopause is associated not with the mid-life transition, but rather with the later forties and fifties, particularly as its onset may have been delayed by the advent of contraceptive pills. With regard to the timing of external events, Neugarten (1970) reports that on-time events are not unsettling because they are anticipated and rehearsed. It is the unanticipated events that may result in trauma. Also, external cohort stresses, such as war or economic depression, can exacerbate one's mid-life transition. Many clinicians report an increase in the number of families and individual patients in mid-life who manifest stress symptoms directly attributable to unemployment and economic hardships relating to prevailing societal conditions. These people may not have sought therapy but for the combination of external and mid-life stresses.

Gilligan and Murphy (1979) suggest that sex-role differences exist in terms of adults' orientation to morality, and that more research is needed in order to determine what types of changes may occur over the course of development.

They point out that women learn autonomy and self-esteem from men but that they integrate these characteristics into a system of values that already emphasizes their responsibility and relationship orientation. This may explain why men often appear to have a more dramatic form of mid-life transition. If a man wants to abandon his responsibilities and commitments—such as family and job—he has more freedom to do so than his wife, who typically retains the responsibility for childcare. Although more women are leaving childcare to their husbands while they leave home, societal and cultural as well as legal variables make it more difficult for women than for men to abandon their responsibility for children. It has been suggested that women may not have the luxury to act out a mid-life crisis. Someone in a couple system has to assume responsibility for childrearing and economic survival.

In her recent popular book *Pathfinders*, Sheehy (1981) found that, throughout adulthood, women had greater difficulty in determining their own identity than men. She says "it appears to take the average woman no less than a lifetime to outgrow her training to be a pleasing little girl" (p. 87). Thus, the mid-life transition for a woman may focus on her assertion of an individual identity apart from accommodating relationships. This finding is reaffirmed by studies measuring sex differences in performance levels, which are significant only for competitive tasks. Whereas Horner (1972) interpreted her findings to reveal women's fear of success, Sassen (1980) found that women feel high anxiety in competitive situations because of their interpretation of social success. They focus on preserving relationships rather than the rules and, as Gilligan and Murphy (1979) point out, they view moral dilemmas in terms of responsibilities rather than rights.

Each sex has to explore and deal with whatever anxieties, guilts, or fears result from the emergence of previously contrasexual aspects as they cope with the mid-life transition. Men will need to recognize, experience, and integrate emerging passive, dependent, intimacy-oriented parts of their personalities while women will have to recognize, experience, and integrate the more independent, aggressive, competitive parts of their personalities that emerge. In addition, people have to cope with changes in their spouses and friends, which, in turn, may result in changes of roles, status, sexual interests, occupational roles, and leisure-time activities. Such changes must be incorporated into the new dominant self-identity and existing as well as new relationships.

Dual-career couples.   With women entering the labor force in greater numbers and at all levels of professions and organizations, an increase is occurring in the "dual-career family," in which both husband and wife are full-time paid employees pursuing careers. Further research is needed to determine whether women who have been involved in careers throughout early adulthood experience the same types of personality changes as those postulated for women who follow a more traditional role, involving childrearing and the support of husbands' career development. In other words, those couples who have incorporated more androgyny into their lifestyles and who have shared more equally the family and career-developmental tasks during early adulthood may find that their mid-life transitions are more parallel than opposite.

The Major Developmental Tasks

Whereas the writers concerned with mid-life transition differ regarding terminology and emphasis, all seem to agree that some common tasks are associated with this period of life and that these tasks are approached with great variability in terms of timing, style, and amount of anxiety and stress.

Identity reappraisal.   Mid-life transition is the time of life when everything must be reassessed, when one must question earnestly whether or not one has fulfilled one's dream, and whether one has indeed become the person one wished to become twenty years earlier. Remember that this reassessment is greatly influenced by one's life experiences and by the societal and cultural changes that have taken place over the previous decades. For example, many people who might have been characterized by Whitbourne and Weinstock (1979) as "foreclosed" in the 1950s, suffered dramatic, tumultuous identity crises during their mid-life transitions in the 1970s as a result of the radical cultural changes that occurred during the 1960s, with respect to compliance, sex roles, sexuality, and lifestyles. Thus, these people often went through a kind of acting-out period during their mid-life transition, a time when they tried new and different options in an attempt to find out who they were and what they wanted for themselves. The unfortunate consequence of a tumultuous mid-life transition may be the harmful effects on family and friends, on people who are unwittingly part of a primary relationship. Whitbourne and Weinstock (1979) do point out that the adult who had a "foreclosed" identity—that which automatically accepted familial and societal directives without going through a process of self-evaluation and selection in late adolescence and early adulthood—might have considerable difficulty at this time of life. They believe that "Achieving Identity adults might progress more smoothly through the period of potential mid-life crisis, that a Moratorium Identity would be chronically in crisis anyhow and that a Diffuse adult would be unaffected by the issues involved in questioning of identity" (1979, p.139).

The 1980s seem to be a calmer period than the 1970s. It may be that the tightening economy does not allow people to act out as extremely as previous times did. Just as college students today are perceived by researchers to be more task oriented and more conforming than the earlier generation of college students, adults experiencing mid-life transitions today seem to internalize their stress more frequently than overthrowing their current lifestyles in favor of totally different ones.

Not everyone throws out an old identity to take on a new one. Some find themselves quite content with who they have been and who they are; they determine to continue along the route they have chosen. Others modify or expand their new identities slightly by incorporating those aspects of self previously denied or not attended to. Outcomes differ, but the process of reappraisal is the commonality that cuts across adults in mid-life transition. It seems that the ease with which one reappraises one's identity is linked to the amount of emotional separation and individuation that occurred in early adulthood as well as to the events in one's life and the type of support one has available from primary relationships. Thus, in addition to cultural, social, ethnic, and economic variables, identity reappraisal is also influenced by intrapsychic variables, the timing of events in one's life experience, and the types of intimate relationships that have developed.

Women who have followed a fairly conventional lifestyle may find themselves experiencing more dissonance than men in terms of their identity reappraisal. The reason is that many women never really achieve the goal of individuation, going from the role of daughter to that of wife and then to mother. Mid-life may be a time in their lives when they are finally relatively unburdened by the mother and wife roles and can begin to individuate psychologically and find a sense of identity. Some clinical evidence shows that the women who allow themselves to acknowledge stress and dissonance in this period may have the greatest opportunities for making choices and decisions that offer possibilities of satisfaction and fulfillment in the second part of their lives. The level of stress may be an incentive toward proactive rather than reactive choices and decisions.

The point is that everyone goes through some type of identity reappraisal in mid-life. For some, this reappraisal results in radical behavioral and role changes, while for others it results in no change. For some, the process is stressful and for others it is easy. One's anticipation and perceptions of the process will influence how one actually fares. Avoidance of the process is more likely to result in eventual stress than approach to it, as is the case for adolescence identity formulation.

The recognition of mortality and the change in time perspective.   When one is young, one never thinks about how much time remains in life. Time seems endless and plentiful. Unless one has been personally touched by the death of a significant other, death is a phenomenon that happens to others. More likely than not, by the time one reaches mid-life transition, death becomes closer; one may have by this time experienced the death of a friend, a sibling, or someone of the same generation. And, as surrounding deaths increase in frequency, one becomes slightly uneasy and more consciously aware of one's own health and physical stamina. Some people notice their increasing interest in the details of others' deaths and in reading the obituaries.

This recognition of mortality and the conscious thought given to death is associated with a change in the way one thinks about time. Now one begins to consider the time that is left to achieve goals, to implement one's identity, and to develop intimate relationships. One seems to become more aware of the effects of time on family and career systems. There may or may not be time to redo some things, to reformulate lifestyles and relationships.

Although, traditionally, men have incurred a higher rate of stress-related diseases (for example, hypertension and ulcers) in their forties and fifties, women are now becoming affected by the same diseases as they add stress to their lives by attempting to integrate family and career roles. Men still die earlier than women in our society and men tend to become more anxious about the loss of time than women, whose pursuit of outside or occupational interests and roles often does not begin until this period of life. A shifting of roles becomes affected by the passing of time and each gender experiences losses and gains.

The reappraisal of relationships and commitments.   Men and women find themselves reappraising their earlier commitments to people and to systems along with their own identities. Particularly if they reformulate their self-concepts, they may need to restructure some of these relationships and commitments. Potential changes are also affected by changing time perspectives; because there may not be time and because economic factors may act as constraints, totally altering roles and responsibilities may not be feasible. However, regardless of individual parameters, all of us can change to some degree if we want to. Many people in mid-life transition find these change possibilities exciting and challenging.

Not only can we expand existing relationships and commitments, we can also develop new ones. The risk involved is related to making dramatic and premature changes in one's primary relationships or career without the identity reappraisal and reformulation required by any transition. While precipitous changes can provide temporary relief from stress, they usually turn out to be inappropriate or maladaptive solutions to problems that require slower, more deliberative changes. Wadner (1979) points out that transitional relationships can help one move through this phase by providing support, reality testing, the chance to explore ambivalent feelings, and the validation of the emergence of frightening aspects of the self. Discussing the issues and problems involved in this transition with new friends is one means of undergoing such a transition successfully.

Obviously, the reappraisal of relationships and commitments will be affected by how well someone has developed intimate relationships earlier in adulthood. Maintaining intimate relationships differs from initiating them in terms of requirements of mutual trust, support, acceptance, and nurturance. Those adults who feel that they have been unsuccessful in maintaining intimate relationships may find themselves seeking harder and more desperately to acquire new, lasting relationships. Consider the following example.

Roger, 41, presented himself to therapy in a panic. His woman friend had walked out on him after a six-year relationship characterized by passion and conflict. Within a two-month period, Roger had lost more than 30 pounds and was agitated and confused. He kept reiterating "I'm over 40 and should be settled into a relationship by now." Further discussion revealed that he had never been able to sustain a satisfactory relationship and that his identity formulation was weak and shaky. Roger felt worse than he had as an acting-out adolescent and it took some months of intense insight therapy to help him work through unfinished developmental tasks and issues so that he could make decisions appropriate to his time of life. A firm sense of self combined with full individuation will enhance existing relationships and the development of new ones. Many people who have put attachment and intimacy needs in the background during early adulthood while they focused on career development, find that mid-life transition is tumultuous as they attempt to "catch up" and settle down in some kind of primary relationship such as marriage or parenthood. Those who have focused on secure, safe career patterns or invested themselves in family relationships find that now they can take some risks in terms of career changes, finding support from strong personal relationships.

Another area of relationship reappraisal and reformulation involves rejoining the family of origin. During mid-life, one's parents are in older age and dealing with tasks and issues of that age group. While it is appropriate for young adults to separate emotionally from their families of origin, in mid-life they need to reformulate their relationships vis-à-vis their siblings and parents as they move from the role of dependent to caretaker. Thus, one of the developmental tasks of middle adulthood is what Blenkner (1965) calls *filial maturity,* involving the changing of relationships between generations. This task is not role reversal; rather, it represents mutuality and shared responsibility whereby members of the older generation forego their characteristically condescending attitudes toward their adult offspring and grow sufficiently to accept help willingly from them. The middle-aged offspring, in turn, forego their earlier relationships with their parents (fear of overdependency, perhaps, or rebellion) and are able to take on caretaking functions. This renewed interaction with one's parents might reactivate conflicts around independence and dependence or around acceptance and rejection that arose before launching and were never resolved. Further, old conflicts might continue or new ones develop. The same may be said to occur with sibling relationships, as sibling systems negotiate care responsibilities for elderly parents. Competitive sibling relationships that had been in a moratorium during the increased individuation of early adulthood may be reactivated and cause conflict and pain at this time. On the other hand, such renewed contact may be centered around the common bond of caring for parents and may result in newly found intimacy as siblings become reacquainted. Whatever the result, the changing roles and relationships with one's family of origin are important to the reassessment and reformulation of intimate relationships that occur in mid-life transition.

This reappraisal of relationships and commitments involves choices that provide opportunities for generativity. Generativity is closely akin to the recognition of mortality and the change in time perspective as one begins to consider how one can contribute to society via the community, or the younger generation, or through some type of creative productivity. One's involvement in social systems expands now as one feels more secure individually, and it might even be said that one's narcissism or self-absorption can be transferred to preoccupation with society, children, or protegees.

Again, the major developmental tasks described above are affected by social and cultural variables, personality differences, sex roles, past experiences with developmental tasks (identity formation and intimacy), timing of life events, and anticipation and rehearsal. Other variables are the support provided by primary relationships and the fulfillment and satisfaction experienced from primary relationships and commitments.

Developmental Issues

Particular issues clearly emerge during this transition as adults struggle with their developmental tasks. While some of these issues arose earlier and will arise again later, their importance increases at this time.

Health. As adults begin to become more aware of their mortality and bodily changes, they become more consciously concerned with their own personal health. They become more aware of the loss of reserve capacity that has been depended upon to provide backups in times of stress or physical dysfunction. Physicians report an increasing preoccupation with health issues by patients in this age group resulting in more hypochondria and psychosomatic complaints. It used to be thought that women presented these complaints more frequently than men. However, it now appears that while there are sex-role differences in the types of complaints, both men and women tend to be more aware of their own bodies, symptoms, and changes. Men seem to present symptoms in the cardiovascular and ulcer area while women typically present digestive and headache-type symptoms. Cytrynbaum (1980) suggests that there is evidence of increased frequency in the mid-life transition group of: paranoid ideation and psychosis; psychosomatic disorders and hypochondriasis; sexual difficulties; depression associated with weight loss, gastrointestinal, and sleep disturbances; and marital, family, and work-related disturbances.

Other manifestations of the preoccupation with health issues are the increased interest mid-life adults take in aerobic and other types of physical exercises and sports and their increased attention to nutrition and preventive health measures. Many adults take to exercise with such ardor and vigor that they overdo it and create unnecessary, painful physical problems, such as muscle, joint, or back injuries. It appears that both men and women become aware of their greater vulnerability to stress and physical illness at this time. An increasing number of reports in the media raise the possibility of significant correlation between stress level and the onset of major disease (such as diabetes or cancer, which occur most commonly in mid-life).

Psychopathology. Freiberg (1976; 1983) reports that adults in their early forties compose the group most frequently admitted to psychiatric units. Their major illnesses are alcoholism, organic brain syndrome, schizophrenia, and depression. Of these, depression is the most frequently treated disorder. Scarf (1980) confirms that more women than men in this age bracket experience depression. It is clear that little attention has been paid to the relationship between adult development and psychopathological symptoms, other than to acknowledge that social crises, physical stamina, personality predispositions, and endocrine changes may have a reciprocal, circular influence on each other that may be reflected in psychological distress.

Many writers on the mid-life transition suggest that this period of development increases one's vulnerability to distress. Some people will obviously cope adaptively with the tasks and issues of this period whereas others may find themselves "stuck." The latter show symptoms of disturbance perhaps for the first time, possibly similar to symptoms manifested during earlier transitional periods of development. Gutmann and his colleagues (1980) suggest that unsuccessful integration of formerly suppressed aspects of personality, the opposite-sex components, can precipitate psychological problems for both men and women. Cytrynbaum (1980) suggests that trouble is more likely to result if spouses go through the mid-life transition at different times.

Sex.   Whether or not adults actually experience a shift in their sex drives, they become more aware of the possibilty of such a shift. Mythology emphasizes both sex-appetite and performance changes in mid-life. There appear to be some sex-role differences, in that men seem to experience more fluctuations in their sex drives while women seem to increase their interest in and desire for sex. Whether these changes are related to hormonal factors has not yet been determined. Both sexes may entertain active fantasies about varied and/or outside sexual relationships, and these fantasies could serve to excite existing relationships or to inhibit them if fear and guilt ensue from the fantasies. Sexual relationships often become more important during this transition—perhaps to alleviate tension, perhaps to recapture lost opportunities of youth, perhaps to catch up as former priorities recede.

One's sexual identity and consequent sexual relationships are greatly affected by how one incorporates the contrasexual opposite components of personality. For example, a woman who has heretofore been passive and dependent may allow herself to act more independently and aggressively in a sexual relationship. Likewise, a man who has been more aggressive and independent may find himself behaving more passively and dependently. If these transitions are accompanied by guilt, fear, and anxiety, they may result in disruption. If they are accepted and integrated, sexual relationships may in fact become more fulfilling and satisfying.

Changing sexual mores and practices certainly influence whatever changes occur in mid-life. These changes are highlighted by the media, and it is often during the mid-life transition that adults first have the opportunity to act out and try new types of sexual behavior. It has been suggested by some clinicians that when the youth of the 1960s hit their mid-life transitions, their sex issues will be different from those of preceding generations, since they will have already experienced their "revolution."

Religion.   Perhaps owing in part to their recognition of mortality, adults often find themselves reconsidering their attitudes, values, and involvement with religion at this time of life. For some, this reconsideration results in the reaffirmation of their previous attitudes; others find that they want to redecide what their beliefs and positions will be. Many writers refer to the increasing affiliation of adults with religious organizations as they enter mid-life. Again, on this issue too, mid-life adults decide proactively rather than reacting to parental or societal imperatives. Also, as adults are socialized by their children, many find that their mid-life reassessment in this area is influenced by their children's religious views and needs.

Caretaking roles.   As the children become launched, adults find that their physical caretaking responsibilities for their children lessen while their emotional caretaking responsibilities may actually increase. At the same time, however, adults may find that their relationships with their parents and siblings begin to change. It is usually during mid-life that adults first come to terms with their changing roles vis-à-vis their aging parents. They are no longer dependent sons or daughters. They may now have to take active responsibility for the physical, emotional, and financial welfare of their parents, and this necessity can cause difficulty if there is much unfinished business between parents and their adult offspring. Thus, as adults move into middle age, their children simultaneously move into adolescence and their parents move into old age. The complex intertwining and reciprocal influences of the generations—each with its own cultural and historical perspectives and competing demands—can affect the process of mid-life development.

Conflicts may arise between adults' responsibilities to their aging parents and those to their current family system. Conflicts may also arise between siblings regarding who is responsible for what. Such conflicts may in turn affect the nurturance, intimacy, and individuation needs in the couple relationship of the mid-life adults. In dual-career families, when both spouses are absorbed in their occupations and the children are more or less self-sufficient, unpredictable crises with elderly parents can cause much conflict. The following questions arise:

1. Whose job is most important?
2. Who should take care of whose parents?
3. How can we afford for one of us to take time off or to hire substitute care?
4. How can we support each other emotionally and still protect our own jobs, parents, and selves?

These issues require clarification—of responsibilities and the boundaries between adults and their families of origin and current families—and a reworking of continuing, new, and reactivated conflicts. Guilt and resentment that feed each other in a circular manner are commonly associated with caring for elderly parents. There is little government or social support available to families of the elderly and the frustration resulting from attempts "to do the right thing" can disrupt marital and other subsystems of the family unit. Recent research (Horowitz, 1982; Silverstone et al., 1982; Troll, 1982) reaffirms that being a caregiver to elderly parents takes an emotional toll on the adult child. Many adult children experience the following problems: sleeping difficulties, guilt, feelings of loss of a source of strength as the parent becomes more impaired, time and financial pressures, and a personal sense of growing older. Income, age, and gender seem to be more significant indicators of morale regarding this issue than ethnicity.

The reassessment of individual, family, and career boundaries.   As one experiences mid-life transition, often one simultaneously experiences a family-system transition as the launching of the children begins. Also, occupational choices and changes may be occurring along with these major transitions. Thus, reassessment and reformulation may be needed in all areas of life, and these needs in themselves can be confusing and disruptive. People need to reassess: (1) the fit between their current and projected needs for the second half of life, (2) the reality of their family and work roles, and (3) their personal identities. Issues of individuation and autonomy continue to need clarification, which requires a reassessment of limitations and possibilities in personal, family, and career choices.

For example, a man may decide that he has come to terms with his career achievement and wants to focus more on his family relationships. However, he may discover that this decision is at odds with his wife's move from the family to a career and his children's first moves out of the family system and their increasing individuation and autonomy. Clearly, in such a situation, marital conflict can result as family members redefine their boundaries in distinct ways.

Leisure. There may be more or less leisure time as the family members individuate and attempt to implement their revised choices. Mid-life is often a time in which adults consciously develop leisure-time activities that may involve new relationships or new commitments. Again, this tendency relates to the changing time perspective—one who has always wanted, say, to learn how to sail but has been too busy in the past, realizes that it is now or never. Part of one's identity reassessment involves using leisure time as well as individual, family, and work time.

Money. Money can become a critical issue in mid-life as one becomes more realistic about achievement–aspiration gaps. At this time of life, one begins to question whether and how much one's income is likely to change and what the costs of any changes might be. Further, one must think about how to finance the children's education and, perhaps, provide financial support to elderly parents. Many adults in mid-life, who already have mortgages and other financial commitments, are currently finding that their spouses must work to maintain their current lifestyles or even a more modest lifestyle. At this writing, more and more mid-life adults are facing layoffs and unemployment for the first time and are wondering, in a genuine panic, how they are going to meet their financial responsibilities. Thus, whatever types of psychological reassessments are occurring, they must include consideration of financial matters.

Table 7-1 summarizes the developmental tasks and issues of the mid-life transition. Of course, other issues affect many mid-life adults. Those discussed in this section are considered to be the most common major issues that affect adults to some extent.

TABLE 7-1.   Mid-life transition

Developmental Tasks	General Issues	Requisite Skills	Significant Others
Reappraise identity	Health: physical, mental	Self-assessing	Spouse
Recognize mortality	Sex	Appraising environment	Children
Change one's time	Religion	Data collecting	Parents
perspective	Caretaking of elderly	Data evaluating	Siblings
Reappraise relationships	parents	Decision making	Old friends
and commitments:	Personal/family/career	Self-caring	New friends
spouse, children,	boundaries	Caretaking	Colleagues
friends, family of	Leisure	Interpersonal	Supervisors
origin, career	Civic responsibilities		Supervisees
	Money		Community

THE FORTIES—ENTERING MIDDLE ADULTHOOD

We turn now to the late-forties stage, which follows the transition and which Levinson (1978) calls entering middle adulthood. This stage may last into the early fifties. If one has come out of the mid-life transition with a restructured life pattern, one will most likely find the next phase of life relatively calm and stable, having reached a new equilibrium. At this point, the stresses and pressures of the transitional phase are alleviated. Levinson (1976) states that there seems to be a three- to four-year period at around age 45 during which the mid-life transition ends. At that time, a new life structure begins to take shape and to provide a basis for middle adulthood. The issues of the mid-life transition are still being absorbed, although perhaps less acutely. Now one is focusing more on the upcoming tasks and issues.

Developmental Tasks

In the subsections below, we consider those developmental tasks that differ from those of the mid-life transition.

Interiority.   One of the major tasks of this stage is to continue to develop interiority: to examine inner experiences, fantasies, values, beliefs, conflicts, and attitudes (Neugarten and Gutmann, 1968). This introspection helps mid-life adults to reformulate their lifestyles in accordance with the choices and decisions they made during the transitional phase. There seems to be more acceptance of the aging process now, as compared with the resistant struggle that is common to the transition phase. However, although individuals reach stable plateaus at which they maintain stability and equilibrium when a developmental or historical task appears to be completed, these developmental and historical tasks are never really fully completed. At that moment when completion seems to be achieved, new questions and doubts arise from systems' feedback. However, during this phase, the individual accepts and copes with new questions and doubts in a relatively calm, stable manner rather than fighting them in the turbulent style characteristic of the transitional phase. Perhaps, for example, in this stage one will decide to have cosmetic surgery—that is, to take action rather than agonizing over a changing physical appearance and the feelings such changes precipitate. Now, too, we often find people interacting more passively with the environment, rather than frantically attempting to "change the system," as they did earlier. Havighurst (1953) noted that middle-aged adults devote more energy and effort to mature social and civic responsibilities in leadership or consultation roles than to revolutionary or disruptive strategies. Those in their forties thus join the "establishment," rather than fight it. Maturity often seems to bring an improvement in the exercise of judgment and impulse control. Nevertheless, some observers feel that these changes are evidence of "selling out."

Interpersonal relationships.   Another task of the middle-adulthood stage is to reassess and restructure interpersonal relationships. Having friends and loved ones seems to be valued more, and the energy invested in interpersonal relation-ships is deemed more worthwhile. Money, status, and achievement now appear to be downplayed as involvement with others assumes a higher priority. Remember, with increasing age, perspectives lengthen, leading to attitude and behavior changes. Lowenthal and Weiss (1976) reported that close interpersonal relation-ships served as resources with which to face life's crises for middle-aged adults and that "the salience of intimacy waxes, wanes and waxes again across the life course . . . the rhythms vary between sexes" (1976, p.17). These investigators found that their middle-aged female subjects, although acknowledging their need for mastery and competence beyond their family sphere, wanted a renewal of intimacy with their spouses. The middle-aged male subjects, on the other hand, needed close interpersonal relationships in proportion to the amount of stress they were experiencing. Men who rated themselves "overwhelmed" by stress rated themselves low on the capacity for intimacy and mutuality. Thus, these researchers believe that initiating, developing, and maintaining satisfactory inter-personal relationships are necessary for coping with stressful experiences.

Gould (1972) supports this emphasis. He found an increased interest in an active social life for his subjects (all male) in their late forties. This increase was reflected in more church and club activity and more participation in family gather-ings and career-related social functions. Le Shan (1973) points out that we spend several decades building assumptions about ourselves, depending on illusions to maintain our self-esteem. We define our relationships in terms of these illusions. Now we need to establish relationships where "the heavy burden of our masks" can be dropped, and where we can implement our new life structures. Thus, identity and intimacy issues are intertwined.

Many adults in this stage of life find that they once again focus on relation-ships—with siblings, neighbors, and friends. They enjoy sharing the same life-stage experiences, perspectives, and feelings, and gain support and comfort from such sharing. Now that they are no longer preoccupied with younger and adoles-cent children, they have time for friendships and different kinds of leisure activi-ties. Somehow, peer relationships do not seem to be as competitive as in earlier years.

Leisure-time activities become more important now. These activities are often associated with social relationships. Not too surprisingly, Freiberg (1976) finds that there seems to be a decrease in energy expenditure—for instance, more involvement in relatively unrigorous sports. However, many studies on middle-age leisure activities indicate that adults' interests and attitudes usually reflect those undertakings preferred in the past and those that can be shared with friends and family.

The climacteric.   Both men and women undergo endocrine changes that af-fect their moods as well as their sexual behavior. The term *climacteric* is used for men who show a substantial drop in hormone level during the forties and early fifties (some men's lowering of testosterone secretion drops steadily from age 18; it is possible that these men do not experience a sudden drop at any one particu-lar period of time). Although the same term can be applied to women, the cessation of menstrual periods is an overt sign that allows them to know for sure that they are experiencing *menopause*. We will discuss the climacteric in more detail in the next section, but it is important to mention it here as a challenge and a developmental task with which every adult must come to terms.

Developmental Issues

Danielson and Cytrynbaum (1979) note that male blue-collar workers seem to have the same middle-aged themes and preoccupations that middle-class subjects have. These are:

1. Concern with job security and boredom, monetary preparedness and future retirement;
2. Commitment to the future development and launching of children;
3. Awareness of a shortening life span;
4. Preoccupation with losses of varying magnitudes, including lost opportunities to relate to "empty-nesting" children;
5. Self-assessment and reassessing of primary relationships;
6. The significance of the dream;
7. The importance of past military service in shaping occupational goals and opportunities.

We can see how these concerns emanate from the tasks and issues of the mid-life transition. Further, we can appreciate how these tasks and issues remain even after the individual undertakes the transitional reassessment and reformulation of his or her identity and primary relationships and commitments.

The themes and issues denoted by Danielson and Cytrynbaum are similar to the crucial issues of middle age identified by Peck (1955), which follow.

1. Valuing wisdom versus valuing physical powers. As physical powers decline in the forties, adults are likely to emphasize their mental abilities as a primary resource, favoring activities that stress mental skills and capacities rather than those that emphasize physical ones.
2. Socializing versus sexualizing in human relationships. As men and women individuate and become more autonomous, their relationships with spouses and opposite-sex friends are apt to become more symmetrical and to include a greater depth of understanding and companionship. In other words, while their sexual relationships are indeed important, other aspects of their relationships are allowed to flourish and to take an equal or superior priority over the sexual component.
3. Cathectic flexibility versus cathectic impoverishment. There is a shift in emotional openness and relationships as parents die, as old circles of friends are changed by health, death, or geography, and as children become adults. Adults become better able to reach out and take advantage of their widening circle of possible friends and to learn to formulate new relationships with their adult children and their families.

4. Mental flexibility versus mental rigidity. Many middle-aged adults are able to be more open to new experiences and new interpretations rather than to cling to past answers and roles. This ability perhaps follows from Item 1 above.

Thus, we see that interiority, interpersonal relationships, and a type of opening up or mellowing are likely to prevail during the later forties and the early fifties. However, health, the availability of financial and social-support resources, and cultural variables influence the potency of these issues. When adults are concerned with their day-to-day survival and do not know where their next meals are coming from, they will be more concerned with basic survival issues, such as food, clothing, shelter, and safety than with more general matters affecting the quality of life.

Physical changes.   Obviously, vast individual differences exist with respect to adults' physical changes. It is difficult to assess one's age on the basis of physical appearance at this stage of life. Some adults in their late forties and early fifties have smooth skin, appear healthy and active, and have full heads of hair. Others have wrinkled skin, grey hair, or bald spots. And, regardless of outer signs, some in this age group are in peak health while the health of others has deteriorated.

A common variable, however, is a general slowing down of physiological functions with a gradual decreasing capacity for tissue regeneration. Bones lose some of their density and resilience. As cartilage between vertebrae starts to degenerate from normal wear and tear, the vertebrae become compressed, causing the spinal column gradually to begin to shorten. This change constitutes a gradual, often unnoticed loss of height. With aging, other joint cartilage has more limited regeneration and muscle mass, bulk, and strength decline. The respiratory, heart, and circulatory systems become less elastic. Breathing capacity decreases, sometimes from smoking or other long-term environmental factors. These conditions and changes cause a lower cardiac output per minute per square meter of body surface, which in turn leads cumulatively to a loss in elasticity of arteries and results in higher blood pressure. The digestive process becomes less efficient, which may lead to weight increase and constipation if diet is not adjusted. Skin loses its elasticity and produces less sebum, which leads to more pronounced wrinkles and new creases as well as thinning and drying. Also, hearing and visual acuity diminish. For most people, these physiological changes occur gradually and may, in fact, remain unnoticed for a long time. Often, it is someone else who points out that one's hearing or vision seems to be changing.

Health.   We know empirically that chronic diseases and fatal illnesses increase with age. However, it is important to remember that genetic predispositions to diseases, lifestyle changes (related to alcohol, drugs, cigarettes, food, and exercise), immune responses, and the utilization of available medical resources all influence the onset and course of diseases. As mentioned earlier, increasingly the literature suggests that stress is related to a wide array of illnesses. The stress of coping with families, careers, and aging also influences the onset and course of diseases.

Freiberg (1976) cites the five leading causes of death between the ages of 45 and 64:

1. Heart disease
2. Cancer
3. Blood vessel diseases (other than heart)
4. Accidents
5. Cirrhosis (liver disease related to alcohol)

She suggests that men are more often felled by disorders involving bones, joints, and digestive conditions, whereas women more frequently suffer from disorders involving joints, high blood pressure, and digestive symptoms. Adults in this age group seem to be particularly aware of the causes of death in their own parents, siblings, and other relatives. They are slowly becoming more conscious of their own responsibilities with regard to preventive health measures.

The most prevalent types of psychological disorders in this age group are depression, alcoholism, and suicide. In fact, many of the suicides in this age group are related to depression and/or alcoholism. Boyd and Weissman (1981) found that women seek help far more easily than men and that women's rate of depression levels off at age 50 whereas the rate for men increases. For both sexes, social isolation, loss, emotional deprivation in childhood, and a difficult family history heighten the risk for middle-aged depression. Alcoholism is more prevalent among men and in lower social classes. Men commit suicide more successfully and more often than women, and widowed and divorced men are more frequent suicides than married men.

The climacteric.   For women, menopause is a definite rite of passage, marking the end of menstruation and the end of childbearing capabilities. However, the menopause is only one part of the climacteric, which includes a whole spectrum of hormonal changes that occur in middle age. These changes may occur over several years, even if the actual menopause period lasts only a few months or a couple of years. Nevertheless, many women fail to realize that they are in a period of change, the climacteric, until they experience the actual menopause.

Some symptoms of the climacteric appear to be caused or triggered by the decline in production of certain sex hormones, whereas others are suspected to stem from the hormones themselves. Pronounced alterations in behaviors and outlooks can be associated with these physical changes. Remember, however, that these hormonal shifts are subtle and gradual and occur over several years. Some people may be unaware of them and others may experience them with varying intensity. The physical and psychological conditions of an adult may compound hormonal effects. Likewise, the physical and psychological effects of hormonal decline may exacerbate the pattern of the hormonal decline.

It is now thought that both men and women go through a climacteric period in their middle years, although only women experience menopause. Both men and women may exhibit increased nervousness, irritability, depression, indecisiveness, upheaval, and feelings of helplessness and futility. In addition, women may endure vasomotor disorders such as "hot flashes" as well as sharp mood swings. Although more is known about the biological changes of women than of men, there has always been disagreement in the literature about the implications of male and female sex cycles for psychological behavior. We do know, however, that hormone levels and fertility are unrelated to the ability of men and women to engage in satisfying sexual relations. Obviously, the effects of shifting hormones in both women and men are influenced by individual differences in personality and physiological changes along with satisfactions about personal, family, and occupational roles, the cognitive meaning of aging and the climacteric period, as well as general coping abilities.

Colarusso and Nemiroff (1981) conclude from their review of the literature that, more than physiological changes, health and social and cultural factors along with past levels of sexual activity account for most of the sexual-activity changes seen with aging.

Menopause. Menopause is caused by an apparently age-programmed change in the ovaries, which normally respond to hormone-borne instructions from the pituitary gland in the midbrain. When the time comes, although the pituitary continues to secrete two sex hormones—follicle-stimulating hormone (FSH) and luteinizing hormone (LH)—the ovaries no longer respond to these hormones and the reproductive processes slow to a halt. In other words, the ovaries, which have been gradually shrinking since the late twenties, begin responding less to the pituitary hormones and begin producing less estrogen and progesterone of their own. As the ovaries slacken in their function, so does the release of ripe ova, and eventually fewer and fewer ova are left to be released and fewer to ripen. At the same time, the lining of the uterus no longer thickens with extra blood cells. And as estrogen and progesterone production lessens, menstruation (endometrial bleeding) lessens. In many women, menstrual periods become irregular for a period of time and then eventually stop altogether. However, some women experience a gradual slowing of their menstrual flow with no irregular timing and still others simply experience an abrupt cessation of their periods. It is important to remember that the actual menopause may happen suddenly or over several years.

The reduction of the ovaries' secretion of estrogen and progesterone is related to some of the physical symptoms associated with menopause. The estrogen decline brings on such symptoms as "hot flashes" and "sweats," a period of warmth, flushing, and perspiration occurring when the body's temperature-regulating system, usually monitored by estrogen, goes temporarily out of adjustment. Other physical symptoms include: an increased flabbiness of the breasts; looser skin; eye pouches; backache; dry vaginal lining, which may cause painful urination and painful sexual intercourse; nausea; vomiting; constipation or diarrhea; indigestion; appetite change; dizziness; headaches; insomnia; breast tenderness; and finger and toe numbness. Eventually, the reduction of estrogen will be manifested in hair thinning on the scalp and genitalia and the generation of facial hair.

These bodily changes and physical symptoms will affect most women's self-concepts and attitudes and behaviors. However, there is conflicting evidence as to how much these hormonal changes and resulting symptoms can be held accountable for depression and other mid-life psychological and emotional distress. Neugarten (1968) found that menopause was rarely an actual crisis for women, and that more women found dread in its anticipation than in its experience. In fact, many of her middle-aged subjects did not rank menopause as a high fear. Rather, they found it a relief not to have to worry any longer about pregnancy or birth control and not to bother with monthly periods. Scarf (1980) believes that hormonal changes have been unfairly scapegoated as causes of mid-life depression. Other variables, such as role and status changes as well as previously unresolved issues, are more likely causes of mid-life psychopathology than actual hormonal changes.

It is certainly understandable that attitudes and anticipation will affect the experience of hormonal changes and psychological events. It is possible, however, that the changes caused by hormonal effects may be triggers for distress and disruption—or perhaps one type of trigger among many. It is important to include hormonal changes among the variables that influence one's experience of mid-life.

Recent attention to the reality of premenstrual syndrome (PMS) and its effect on the feelings, thoughts, and behaviors of women at certain times of the month are causing physicians to reconsider the impact of women's menopausal changes on the mid-life experience. Many women today are so confused about what is "psychological" and what is "biological" that their stress is deepened by conflicting opinions and prescriptions. Consider the following case.

Ann, 47, was a psychiatric nurse who sought therapy after being treated with Valium by her gynecologist for seven months. Ann had been feeling depressed and anxious for close to a year and she could not attribute these feelings to any event in her life or family. She was very frightened by her inability to control her morbid thinking and by her preoccupation with irregular periods and continuous premenstrual symptoms. For example, she had swollen, sore breasts for the two weeks between her periods and she found embracing her husband painful. This curtailed her sexual desire and their relationship. She sought help from a therapist who allayed her fears by reframing her symptoms developmentally and by educating her about the process of menopause. She was referred to a gynecologist who specialized in premenstrual syndromes and menopause and, after three weeks of hormonal treatment, Ann's symptoms vanished and she resumed her previous lifestyle to her complete satisfaction.

Estrogen replacement therapy is sometimes used for short periods of time in acute cases of menopausal distress. There is some controversy about the possible correlation of estrogen replacement with cancer; however this therapy is now recommended for women under the careful supervision of a physician in order to prevent osteoporosis (brittle bones) in later life. Many woman are finding that knowing more about the climacteric and being able to discuss it with friends is easing their adaptation to this process, just as adolescents are adapting more easily to the onset of puberty now that the mystery and secrecy about the process have been dispelled. Nevertheless, there is so much misinformation about this process that it is difficult to keep up with new findings.

The male climacteric. The term *male menopause* is sometimes used to describe the psychological distress that some men experience during their forties. We know surprisingly little about this phenomenon, other than the fact that men, too, seem to experience a gradual decline in their hormone production. Men may experience psychological symptoms in mid-life, but we know too that declining production of androgen may result in delayed erection time, reduced ejaculatory volume, and a gradual loss of facial and body hair. Likewise, men experience a decrease in muscle strength and increases in wrinkles, greying or balding of the hair, fat accumulation, and digestive disturbances.

We also know that anxiety in middle-aged men can cause a drop in testosterone, the testicular hormone. However, unlike in women, a drop in this hormone production is not related to a man's fertility. But, a correlation exists between sexual capacity and testosterone level. While probably not more than 10 percent of all men will experience severe distress or disruption, many more may nevertheless experience the shifting mood swings and slower erectile regaining typically associated with the climacteric.

Men's hormonal decline may be so gradual that its effects are unnoticed. It is important, however, to keep in mind that men too experience endocrine changes and that, while we do not know as much about men's hormone-related changes as we do about those of women, it is indeed possible that some of the stress we see in middle-aged men is similarly affected by hormonal change.

TABLE 7-2.   The forties: entering middle adulthood

Developmental Tasks	*General Issues*	*Requisite Skills*	*Significant Others*
Develop interiority	Physical changes	Self-care	Spouse
Reassess and restructure	Health	Introspection	Children
interpersonal	Menopause/male	Interpersonal skills	Children's friends/lovers
relationships	climacteric	Self-acceptance	Old friends
Cope with the	Social and civic	Caretaking	New friends
climacteric	responsibilities		Siblings
	Elderly parents		Parents
	Launching children		Physicians
	Personal/family/career		Colleagues
	boundaries		Supervisors
			Supervisees
			Neighbors
			Community

Table 7-2 summarizes the developmental tasks and issues of the forties, entering middle adulthood. We turn now to the fifties and see what new tasks and issues evolve for this stage of life.

THE FIFTIES

For many adults, the fifties are years of peak status and power, of peak personal and marital satisfaction. Now one may reap the benefits of years of dedication and hard work—recognition and respect for past accomplishments, respect and caring from adult children, increased earnings along with decreased expenses. In this period of life one may be perceived as wise, mature, and showing good judgment. Overall, the fifties are a stage of a new equilibrium, a new stability (Barnett & Baruch, 1981; Sheehy, 1981; Campbell, 1980; Freedman, 1978; Levinson, 1976).

Gould (1972) reported that many of his male subjects in their fifties experienced a relief from internal conflict at this stage but felt that "the die was cast" and that this closure was a bitter pill to swallow. Frustration was liable to result from a lack of upward mobility; simultaneously, seniority could provide a type of security. His subjects reported more interiority as well as more self-acceptance, self-approval, and self-reliance. Gould wrote that they "look within themselves at their own feelings and emotions, although not with the critical time pressure of the late 30s or with the infinite omnipotentiality of the early 30s but with a more self-accepting attitude of continued learning from a position of general stability."

Neugarten (1968) found subjects in their fifties to be very reflective, self-evaluative, and contemplative. She made a point of differentiating this type of reflection from the reminiscing of older age. Unlike Yankelvich and Gurin, she found that people in their fifties felt more in charge of their destinies than ever before as they revised their self-concepts along with their concepts of time and death. They seemed to have a decreased concern with external and social and environmental constraints and an increased focus upon internal interests and internal dynamics. Neugarten and Gutmann (1968) found that both men and women move from active mastery to passive mastery in orientation. Like men, women become more constricted and more detached from the active mastery of their environment and less inhibited about expressing aggressive feelings.

Kimmel (1974) suggests that the development of the personality system progresses from a period of maximal expansion in early adulthood through a period of relative balance between internal processes and external demands in middle age to an increasing focus on internal processes in old age. Thus, people in their fifties would be involved in learning this balance by beginning to focus more on internal processes. His interactionist perspective views personality as determined by environmental variables and individual behavioral dispositions. Thus, cognitive processes, personality traits, and environmental factors reciprocally influence one another.

Sheehy (1981, p.228) lists the following new potential and special strengths characteristic of the fifties:

1. Relaxation of roles;
2. Greater assertiveness in women;
3. Greater expressiveness in men;
4. The freedom to say what you think;
5. The freedom to pick up and go again;
6. More time and money for self;
7. More tolerance for others;
8. Greater opportunities for companionship with mate;
9. The chance to meet children again as friends;
10. The possibility for contributing to community, history, culture.

Sheehy's data, gathered from extensive interviews around the country, reflect clinical impressions and the findings of developmental researchers. The fifties may indeed be one of the more satisfying phases of adult life if earlier tasks and issues are resolved and health is retained.

Developmental Tasks

The major developmental tasks of the fifties involve the renegotiation of relationships and roles, beginning preparation for retirement, and health care.

Relationship renegotiation.   Most adults in their fifties are entering or are in the postparental stages of the family life cycle. While this will be discussed more fully in Chapter 8, it is important to mention here that new relationships with adult offspring, daughters- and sons-in-law, the families of in-law offspring, and grandchildren are in order. These new relationships require tact and skill and their quality will depend on the state and degree of satisfaction with the marital relationship.

Social roles and roles in the community continue to be developed during this decade. In addition, adults in their fifties need to work on their relationships with aging parents. Both Neugarten (1968) and Gould (1978) report that people in their fifties are more mellow and develop warmer, more sympathetic feelings with their own parents than earlier. They exhibit more warmth and affection and less blame for their problems. During this decade, responsibility for aging parents often increases—involving housekeeping, shopping, transportation, financial aid, and holiday-preparation chores. Neugarten (1968) also reports that elderly people are more likely to seek help from their daughters than from their sons. The demands of the older generation will doubtless affect the adult offspring's marriage, especially when they are burdensome and detract from the spouse. Relationships with siblings also undergo a transition now, as people's responsibilty for their aging parents increases. This transition may lead to closer or more distanced sibling relationships, depending on current issues and the past history of the sibling subsystem.

Preretirement planning.   It is important for people in their fifties to begin thinking about and planning for retirement, which now looms ever closer. These plans will affect the lifestyle as well as relationships, roles, and social status. While this issue will be fully explored in Chapter 9, it is important to recognize it as a developmental task. Anticipation and preparation for role changes—whether for retirement from a job, widowhood, or relocation—influence the actual experience of these inevitable changes.

Health care.   With increasing age, illness becomes more likely. Preventive medicine also becomes more important, requiring greater individual responsibility. For example, there is a higher incidence of gum diseases in the fifties, which can result in serious dental problems. Early diagnosis and treatment can alleviate the ravages of such diseases and, perhaps, impede their onset. Likewise, in the fifties there is an increasing possibility of cataracts, glaucoma, and retinal diseases. Again, early detection and treatment can prevent and impede the course of these diseases. Adults in this stage of life cannot rely on their parents to provide the impetus for self-care, and can no longer depend on youthfulness to protect them from the vicissitudes of life; nor will the medical system ensure that they care for themselves. A person's level of self-care may be indicative of how successfully he or she has worked through the tasks of the mid-life transition and the late forties and how firm the self-concept is.

Developmental Issues

Physiological changes.   While physiological changes continue to be gradual, they are more extensive than in the forties. Muscles begin to diminish more noticeably in terms of their strength, size, and reflex speed. Bones lose their mass and density, break more easily, and heal more slowly. Skin continues to lose its elasticity, becoming drier and more wrinkled, and hair continues to thin and grey. People become aware that their vision and hearing are less keen than before. They are also likely to experience more frequent digestive disorders and to gain weight if they do not change their diets. Diminishing energy becomes more apparent. Again, the rate and degree of one's physical decline are greatly affected by lifestyle, psychological states, exercise, diet, health, coping strategies, personality, and genetic predispositions.

Sex.   A change in sexual interests and activities may or may not occur in the fifties. Many women report a renewed interest in sex after menopause and a new tendency to behave more aggressively and less inhibitedly. Men may feel a gradual waning of their sexual interests and may try to compensate for this by intensifying their sexual activities. Sexual interest and activity is more a reflection of past history, current relationships, and health and life satisfaction than aging. Remember, it is important to check out hormonal functioning in cases of male sexual problems. In studying sexually impaired men, Spark and White (1980) found that impotence in half the subjects was traceable to medication or a disease such as diabetes and that it was thus treatable. Since more men in this age bracket may be in treatment for disorders than men in earlier age groups, it is important to keep this in mind.

Many people in their fifties report very satisfying sexual relations, characterized more by tenderness and caring than by prowess and performance pressures and experienced as more sensuous and deeper than at earlier times of their lives. Adults who understand that the rate of sexual performance may diminish often consider such a change to be a benefit rather than a hindrance, often reporting sex to be "in slower motion with greater sensitivity to the actual feelings and the actual process."

Intellectual processes.   Many studies report no significant decline in intelligence scores in middle age. Furthermore, those changes that are reported may relate to the nature of the tests rather than the intelligence of the subjects. Many researchers believe that the nature of intellectual processes changes with age. For example, whereas verbal subtests show no declines with age, performance tests may, since a reduction occurs in motor skills, such as eye-hand coordination and reaction time. Kimmel (1974, 1980) concludes that any intellectual decline related to age is a result of a slowing down in performance speed and problem-solving abilities with respect to new problems where past experience is of no help. And Botwinick (1967) believes that one's intellectual functions in middle age are more dependent on motivation, education, experience, intellectual activity, and intellectual stimulation than on age.

Evidence of changes in creativity and thinking is inconclusive, though they seem to be related more to health conditions than age. However, some writers believe that creativity reaches its peak during the forties and fifties (Neugarten, 1968; Gould, 1978). Dacey (1982) points out that there is a lack of agreement on how to define and measure creative productivity that hinders research. He cites two theories as to how the mind of a creative person works: (1) associationism, by which the parts of a problem are synthesized in new, innovative ways; and (2) structuralism, in which whole problems are restructured in their entirety. The studies he reviewed are inconclusive but certainly leave open the possibility of heightened creativity during the mid-life years. It may be that adults in mid-life who have successfully resolved the tasks and issues of early adult life are freer to think and produce creatively.

Adults normally function intellectually until the day they die, which means well into old age, developing compensatory skills as needed. Their short-term memories and speed skills may change, but these changes only suggest that teaching must be specifically geared to the learning styles of middle age in adult education classes. Whereas Baltes and Schaie (1976) argue against intellectual decline, Horn and Donaldson (1976) believe the following:

1. That inductive reasoning improves until the late forties or early fifties and then begins to decline;
2. That spatial relations improve to forty and then plateau through the mid-fifties before beginning to decline;
3. That verbal meaning rises until the fifties and then plateaus;
4. That numbers do not decline until late adulthood;
5. That decline in psychomotor speed begins around fifty;
6. That motor-cognitive rigidity plateaus in the early fifties;
7. That there is no decline in verbal fluency.

These writers point out that the declines they identify may be associated more with health status than with age.

Colarusso and Nemiroff (1981) refer to the concept of neural plasticity, which suggests that the adult brain continues to change in response to stimulation from experiences in living. This concept challenges the traditional belief that the adult brain is static and incapable of structural change.

We can conclude from the research that older people process information and behave differently from younger people. The literature suggests that older people differ in their capacities to attend to, perceive, encode, and remember information in performing tasks ranging from simple perceptual decision making to complex problem solving. However, in certain cognitive areas no age differences are found; thus, a hypothesis of a deficit of intellectual capability in late middle age does not hold. Yet to be determined is the extent to which age effects are not irreversible deficits but changes in cognitive strategy used to perform tasks (Smith, in Poon, 1980).

Table 7-3 summarizes the developmental tasks and issues pertinent to middle age, which comprises the late forties and fifties.

TABLE 7-3.   The fifties

Developmental Tasks	General Issues	Requisite Skills	Significant Others
Renegotiate relationships	Social and community	Self-care	Aging parents
Learn new roles	activities	Launching of children	In-laws
regarding in-laws;	Physical changes	Interpersonal skills	Grandchildren
grandparents	Health	Planning	Spouse
Make pre-retirement	Sex	Negotiating	Adult offspring
plans	Intellectual functioning	Caretaking	Friends
Take self-health-care			Colleagues
measures			Supervisees
			Community

Middle age is a time when perspectives lengthen and behaviors and attitudes change. It is a time when one can make decisions based on past experiences and on self-perceived needs and values rather than in conformity with parental imperatives and institutional demands. This is possibly the time of the greatest independence and autonomy, and the greatest personal power and prestige. On the other hand, it is a plateau period involving the reassessment and reformulation of life goals with a finite time perspective and a glimpse of the realities of the aging process. Thus, like any other stage of life, middle age is fraught with both potential gains and losses.

SUMMARY

This chapter covers first the transition from early adulthood to middle adulthood. Much has been written about the mid-life transition, and here we summarized the research to date, along with findings from clinical practices and interviews. The mid-life transition is primarily a period in which identity and relationships, commitments and goals are reassessed and reformulated. The process may or may not be tumultuous; it has the potential for stress and conflict as well as for growth and change.

After the mid-life transition, the later forties appear to be relatively stable. In this period, the choices and decisions made during the transition are implemented and the major focus is on socialization issues, coping with the climacteric period, and a new use of time, energy, and leisure activities. How stable and satisfying this period is will depend on how successful one was in resolving the tasks and issues of the mid-life transition. Remember, these tasks and issues are never fully resolved. They are worked through until they are no longer dominant, controlling issues.

The fifties may be both a peaceful and an exciting period as people feel more autonomous and less burdened with the responsibilities of parenthood and career and family establishment. One has usually completed one's painful reassessment, so one can begin to take better care of oneself and prepare for older age. Many people find this stage satisfying because they are no longer working so hard to establish themselves, prove themselves, and seek others' approval. They are more accepting of their achievements and of themselves, and they tend to want to enjoy life while they still can.

We have delineated the likely physical changes during the stages of middle adulthood. While acknowledging individual differences and variations, these physical changes affect one's self-concept and relationships, which in turn affect one's life experiences. The climacteric is a major physical change emanating from hormonal declines that influence psychological feelings and behaviors; likewise, the hormonal decline can be influenced by psychological states.

REFERENCES

Baltes, P. B., & Schaie, K. W. On the plasticity of intelligence in adulthood and old age. *American Psychologist,* 1976, *31,* 720-725.

Barnett, R., & Baruch, G. Multiple role strain, number of roles and psychological well being. Unpublished paper, Wellesley College Center for Research on Women, 1981.

Blenkner, M. Social work and family relationships in later life, with some thoughts on filial maturity. In E. Shanas and G. Streib (eds.), *Social structure and the family: Generational relations.* New York: Prentice-Hall, 1965.

Botwinick, J. *Cognitive processes in maturity and old age.* New York: Springer, 1967.

Boyd, J. H., & Weissman, M. M. The epidemiology of psychiatric disorders of middle age: Depression, alcoholism and suicide. In J. G. Howells (ed.), *Modern perspectives in the psychiatry of middle age.* New York: Brunner/Mazel, 1981, pp. 201-221.

Brim, O. G., Jr. Male mid-life crises: A comparative analysis. In B. B. Hess (ed.), *Growing old in America.* New Brunswick, N.J.: Transaction Books, 1976.

Campbell, A. *The sense of well-being in America: Recent patterns and trends.* New York: McGraw-Hill, 1980.

Colarusso, C. A., & Nemiroff, R. A. *Adult development: A new dimension in psychodynamic theory and practice.* New York: Plenum Press, 1981.

Cytrynbaum, S. *Adult development theory and research: Implications for faculty development.* Paper presented at the American Educational Research Association Annual Meeting, April 7-11, 1980, Boston, Mass.

Dacey, J. S. *Adult development.* Glenview, Ill.: Scott, Foresman, 1982.

Danielson, K., & Cytrynbaum, S. *Midlife development for blue-collar working men: Preliminary findings.* Unpublished manuscript, Northwestern University, 1979.

Erikson, E. *Identity: Youth and crisis.* New York: W. W. Norton, 1968.

Erikson, E., & Erikson, J. M. On generativity and identity: From a conversation with Erik and Joan Erikson. *Harvard Education Review,* 1981, *51,* 240-278.

Freedman, J. L. *Happy people: What happiness is, who has it, and why.* New York: Harcourt, Brace, Jovanovich, 1978.

Freiberg, K. *Human development.* No. Scituate, Mass.: Duxbury Press, 1976.

Freiberg, K. *Human development,* 2nd ed. Belmont, Calif.: Wadsworth, 1983.

Gilligan, C., & Murphy, J. M. Development from adolescence to adulthood. In D. Kuhn (ed.), *Intellectual development beyond childhood.* San Francisco: Jossey-Bass, 1979.

Gould, R. The phases of adult life: A study in developmental psychology. *American Journal of Psychiatry,* 1972, *129,* 521-531.

Gould, R. *Transformations: Growth and change in adult life.* New York: Simon & Schuster, 1978.

Gutmann, D. The country of old men: Cross-cultural studies in the psychology of later life. In W. Donahue (ed.), *Occasional papers in gerontology.* Ann Arbor: University of Michigan, 1969.

Gutmann, D., Grunes, J., & Griffin, B. The clinical psychology of later life—Developmental paradigms. In N. Datan and N. Lohmann (eds.), *Transitions of aging.* New York: Academic Press, 1980, pp. 119-131.

Havighurst, R. J. *Human development and education.* New York: Longmans, 1953.

Horn, J. L., & Donaldson, G. On the myth of intellectual decline in adulthood. *American Psychologist,* 1976, *31,* 701-719.

Horner, M. Toward an understanding of achievement related conflicts in women. *Journal of Social Issues,* 1972, *28,* 157-176.

Horowitz, A. *The impact of caregiving on families of the frail elderly.* Paper presented at American Orthopsychiatric Association Annual Meeting, San Francisco, March 29-April 2, 1982.

Jaques, E. Death and the mid-life crisis. *International Journal of Psychoanalysis,* 1965, *46,* 502-514.

Jung, C. *Modern man in search of a soul.* New York: Harcourt, Brace, 1933.

Jung, C. The stages of life. In J. Campbell (ed.), *The portable Jung.* New York: Viking Press, 1971.

Kimmel, D. C. *Adulthood and aging.* New York: Wiley, 1974.

Kimmel, D. C. *Adulthood and aging.* 2nd ed. New York: Wiley, 1980.

Le Shan, E. J. *The wonderful crises of middle age.* New York: McKay, 1973.

Levinson, D. *The seasons of a man's life.* New York: Knopf, 1978.

Levinson, D. Middle adulthood in modern society: A sociopsychological view. In G. DiRenzo (ed.), *We the people: Social change and social character.* Westport, Conn.: Greenwood Press, 1977.

Levinson, D., Darrow, C., Klein, E., Levinson, M., & McKee, B. Periods in the adult development of men ages 20-45. *Counseling Psychologist,* 1976, *6,* 21-25.

Lowenthal, M. F., & Chiriboga, D. Social stress and adaptation: Toward a life-course perspective. In C. Eisdorfer and M. P. Lawton (eds.), *The psychology of adult development and aging.* Washington, D.C.: American Psychological Association, 1973.

Lowenthal, M. F., Thurnher, M., & Chiriboga, D. *Four stages of life.* San Francisco: Jossey-Bass, 1975.

Lowenthal, M. F., & Weiss, L. Intimacy and crises in adulthood. *Counseling Psychologist,* 1976, *6,* 10-15.

Neugarten, B. L. (ed.). *Middle age and aging.* Chicago: University of Chicago Press, 1968.

Neugarten, B. L., & Gutmann, D. Age-sex roles and personality in middle age. In B. L. Neugarten (ed.), *Middle age and aging.* Chicago: University of Chicago Press, 1968.

Neugarten, B. L., & Gutmann, D. Dynamics of transition to old age. *Journal of Geriatric Psychiatry,* 1970, *4,* 71-87.

Peck, R. C. Psychological developments in the second half of life. In J. L. Anderson (ed.), *Psychological aspects of aging.* Washington, D.C.: American Psychological Association, 1956.

Rosenberg, S. D., & Farrell, M. P. Identity and crises in middle aged men. *International Journal of Aging and Human Development,* 1976, *7,* 153-170.

Sassen, G. Success anxiety in women: A constructivist interpretation of its source and its significance. *Harvard Education Review,* 1980, *50,* 13-24.

Scarf, M. *Unfinished business.* Garden City, N.Y.: Doubleday, 1980.

Sheehy, G. *Pathfinders.* New York: William Morrow, 1981.

Silverstone, B., & Poulshock, W. *A survey of families caring for the elderly in Cleveland: Focus on stress and effects.* Paper presented at American Orthopsychiatric Association Annual Meeting, San Francisco, March 29-April 2, 1982.

Smith, D. B., Thompson, L. W., & Michalewski, H. J. Averaged evoked potential research on adult aging: Status and prospects. In L. W. Poon (ed.), *Aging in the 1980s.* Washington, D.C.: American Psychological Association, 1980.

Spark, R. F., & White, R. A. Impotence is not always psychogenic. *Journal of American Medical Association,* February 22-29, 1980.

Stein, J. Developmental phases during midlife. Paper presented at American Educational Research Association Annual Meeting, April 7-11, 1980, Boston, Mass.

Time, October 27, 1981.

Yankelvich & Gurin cited in the New York Times, January 20, 1965.

Troll, L. Health of oldest family member and affect of self, child and grandchild. Paper presented at American Orthopsychiatric Association Annual Meeting, San Francisco, March 29–April
2, 1982.
Vaillant, G. *Adaptation to life.* Boston: Little, Brown, 1977.
Wadner, D. Object relations theory as a function for the dream and transitional partners in mid
life. Paper presented at Symposium on Midlife Development: Recent Work on Gender, Personality and Social Systems Influence, Illinois Psychological Association, Decatur, Ill., 1979.
Whitbourne, S. K., & Weinstock, C. S. *Adult development: The differentiation of experience.* New
York: Holt, Rinehart & Winston, 1979.

CHAPTER EIGHT

FAMILY DEVELOPMENT IN MIDDLE ADULTHOOD

Middle adulthood is characterized by alternate periods of transition and stability, beginning with a crucial transition period, the mid-life transition. As seen in Chapter 7, this particular transition often generates intense pain and conflict as well as heightened levels of autonomy and multipotentiality. The adolescent and launching stages of family development, which typically occur during middle adulthood, are likely to be the most tumultuous and disruptive periods in family development. The upheaval in these periods stems from the fact that parents are undergoing individual mid-life transitions and, perhaps, turmoil while their adolescent offspring are undergoing turmoil and having identity crises of their own.

Most adults in middle adulthood who married and had children in early adulthood are entering or preparing to enter the adolescent stage of family development. It is possible that, owing to the increasing tendency to delay parenthood, middle adulthood will increasingly be associated with the preschool and school-age stages of family development. Even so, families that delay the onset of parenthood will experience the adolescent and launching stages of family development some time before they leave middle adulthood.

We note that middle-aged adults are faced with differentiation of and launching their children from their family systems, whereas adults in earlier stages of family development are faced with joining and inclusion of new members—that is, children—into expanding family systems. So, family systems deal with joining and expanding in earlier stages and differentiating and constricting in later stages.

Remember that the dramatic changes in family membership and relationships experienced during middle adulthood occur simultaneously with the major mid-life reassessment of identity, intimate relationships, and career development. Just as the twenties may be overwhelming in requiring the establishment of career, adult self, and family, the forties may be overwhelming in requiring the reassessment and renegotiation of self, family relationships, and career plans.

Some writers have suggested that it is ironic that adults experience a renewed identity crisis in mid-life just as their children are beginning to grapple with their adolescent and early-adulthood identity crises. The process for parent and child may indeed be comparable as each attempts to negotiate developmental transitions. It has also been suggested that the sexual and identity issues of parent and adolescent have a reciprocal influence—one stirs up current or unfinished business of the other, and a mutual escalation can result. Thus, the way adults in mid-life perceive and deal with their individuating, differentiating children will be affected both by the way they individuated and separated emotionally from their parents in their late adolescence and early adulthood and the way they are currently experiencing and resolving the issues of their own mid-life transition. Braverman (1981) observes that parents often experience the differentiation of adult children as tantamount to ego loss and that the parents' attempt to deal with the resulting inner conflict can create a marital crisis even after a relatively stable long-term marriage. In other words, marital crises can appear for the first time in this stage of family development and may, in fact, be the symptomatic manifestation of one or both parents' reactions to the adult child's separation.

In this chapter, we will consider the adolescent, launching, and postparental stages of the family life cycle. During these stages, the family system constricts. This process parallels individual development, which is less expansive and higher in interiority during middle age. Obviously, individual and family development are closely intertwined.

Some of the questions we will attempt to answer are the following:

1. How do parents' mid-life crises affect adolescent offspring?
2. Is it advantageous to be young, rather than old, when you have adolescents?
3. Why do so many families experience crises during adolescent periods?
4. Do acting-out adolescents have gender issues?
5. Why do so many offspring have difficulty leaving home?
6. How does the "empty-nest syndrome" affect families?
7. Do families very often break up because the children grow up and leave?

DELAYED PARENTHOOD

Before beginning to discuss the family stages of middle age, it will be useful to consider the implications of delayed parenthood. As previously noted, there is an increasing trend in our society for two-career couples to delay entering the infant stage of family development until their middle and late thirties. Thus, more and more couples are entering the preschool and school-age stages of family development in their forties. More research is needed to assess the mutual impact of mid-life and early stages of family development. An obvious topic to begin with is that of fertility, as it pertains to delayed parenting and middle adulthood.

Fertility.   If a couple delays trying to have a child until their thirties or early forties, they are more likely to experience fertility difficulties than those who start earlier. A woman's most fertile years are her twenties and women who wait until their thirties to have a child face increased risks with respect to conceiving, carrying, and giving birth to a healthy child. Women must contend with their biological time clock. Even minimal anxiety about fertility and pregnancy can lead to a vicious cycle: of anxiety causing infertility, which causes more anxiety, which results in continued infertility, and so forth. Such an anxiety cycle can have a deleterious affect on the marriage and on the sexual relationship, possibly spawning the woman's resentment regarding the relative limitations on women's fertility compared with men. Consider the following case.

Andrea, 37, was a successful public relations account executive and Martin, 38, a successful accountant. They had been married for fifteen years and had enjoyed affluent, satisfying career development and a mutually satisfying marriage. After deliberating and agonizing for a long time over whether to disrupt their lifestyle by having a baby, they decided that they did not want to miss out on that experience and, admitting to some ambivalence, attempted to conceive. After six months of being disappointed, they began to attend an infertility clinic, where they went through several assessments and procedures that turned up no organic causes for their infertility. Stress and strain escalated in all aspects of their lives. Finally, they entered therapy. They were almost ready to relinquish the hope of becoming parents and wanted help with their frustrations and resentments about their infertility and its spillover into their marital relationship. Every time Andrea got her menstrual period, she experienced feelings of depression, inadequacy, and repressed resentment, followed by a renewed vigor in the timing of sexual relations. This was followed by hopeful optimism and then by bitter disappointment.

The therapy focused on the strengths of this couple's marriage and the partners' careers, on restoring spontaneity and enjoyment to their sexual relationship, and on diminishing anxiety about conception, since that appeared to be beyond their range of control. Several months after the therapy began, after Andrea and Martin had let go of their desperation to have a child, they somehow managed to conceive and Andrea experienced a relatively anxiety-free pregnancy. However, their experience of the infant stage of parenting was very anxiety-provoking, despite their good fortune at having a healthy, relatively adaptive infant. It seems that the issues underlying their original ambivalence and anxiety about whether or not to have a child and the subsequent experience of infertility had resurfaced. These issues had to be worked through in conjunction with their mid-life transitions so as to enhance their experiencing of parenthood.

A second case provides another view.

Marie, aged 39, and Tim, aged 41, had been married for seven years and were both well-established physicians before they first attempted conception. During that seven-year period, they too had agonized over the decision to have a child and the timing of birth and, like Andrea and Martin, they experienced infertility. Marie's pregnancy was fraught with anxiety due to miscarriage threats. But the pregnancy remained viable and, after a difficult caesarean delivery, Marie and Tim settled into the infant stage of family development. Their infant was sickly and underweight, but he slowly regulated himself, becoming more manageable. Marie and Tim were as anxious about their parenting as were Andrea and Martin, but they were more accepting of the parenting role, enjoying it more than the other couple. They attributed their tolerance and management of the stress to the increased desire to parent they felt as a consequence of the difficulty they experienced in becoming parents.

These two cases show that when an older woman experiences infertility or anxiety regarding pregnancy and delivery, this anxiety may resurface once the child is born. But the initial anxiety in such a case has a real cause: the older a woman is when she begins to attempt conception or when she miscarries, the less time will be left to her to bear a healthy child.

A recent breakthrough for older parents was the development of amniocentesis, a diagnostic procedure performed routinely on pregnant women aged 35 and older. This procedure, which involves the removal and analysis of amniotic fluid during the fourth month of pregnancy, allows for the detection of chromosomal defects, such as Down's Syndrome, more likely to occur with older women. If they receive a negative report from this procedure—that is, if the fetus is determined to have chromosomal abnormalities—the couple may consider the option of abortion.

Advantages. Many older parents feel that the advantages of delayed parenthood far outweigh the disadvantages. They feel that they have had the time and opportunity to establish and develop their marriages and careers and in both areas have withstood the tests of time that result in stability and maturity. In other words, they have passed through the establishment phases of career and marital development. Further, men at this time may be more supportive and collaborative in parenting. Also, the couple may have greater financial resources than earlier, thus feeling able to use auxiliary services more freely. They may also consider their careers well enough established to allow time off for the parenting of babies and young children.

Bird (1979) found that where couples became parents late, they were most likely to share the parenting responsibilities equally when they had equal incomes and/or equal job status. Other studies emphasize the beneficial effects of mature adulthood on childrearing practices, noting that older parents are able to focus more than young parents on the psychological aspects of child development because they have experienced both the struggles and the stable plateaus of adult development. And it is possible that, owing to the greater age differences between parents and children, the role confusion between parents and children is reduced and the rules and roles are clearer.

Wilkie (1981) found that older parents are more likely to encourage verbal behavior in their children and to discourage dependency, are less likely to use physical punishment or ridicule as disciplinary strategies, and are better able to handle the competing demands of work and family, feeling more secure financially and maritally. She also noted that disagreement about childrearing was less prevalent in older parents. She pointed out that "the most noteworthy consequences of later parenthood is its contribution to a new stage in the life course between childhood and adulthood" (p.588). Compared with younger parents, older parents prepare more for parenthood (with positive attitudes), have more patience with and tolerance for their children, experience greater satisfaction as parents, and, of course, have a smaller number of children per couple.

Many clinicians have found that those adults who have worked through their own issues of mid-life transition are better able to view their adolescent offspring's struggles with sensitivity and compassion than are younger parents, who are usually simultaneously wrestling with the same types of issues. However, it is possible that the level of differentiation of the parent, rather than the actual age or life stage, is the distinguishing factor between young and older parents.

Disadvantages.   Gluck, Dannefer, and Milea (1980) point out that older mothers may experience stress owing to their relative lack of physical energy and to the social isolation deriving from being out of step with friends and peers whose children are already in adolescence. Another factor, noted by Wilkie (1981), is that older parents are less likely to receive help from their own parents, who might be well into older age.

Daniels and Weingarten (1981) mention the stress older mothers experience in combining work in high-level occupations with the responsibility for the care of young, demanding children. This overload may be particularly stressful for the older woman because changing energy levels and physical changes can reduce tolerance. (The age of fathers appears to matter less than that of mothers.) However, these researchers found that for the couples who had their children early, there was less time to build couple intimacy before childbearing began, and for the couples who had their children late, there was less energy and malleability for children. Thus, they concluded that people who marry early enjoy their children and people who marry late enjoy each other. All of their subjects (86 couples in their thirties, forties, and fifties) basically agreed that it is best to raise children when you have the combination of energy, insight, maturity, education, financial security, and social support that most people achieve between 30 and 40.

One can postulate both advantages and disadvantages with respect to the increasing tendency to delay parenthood. We must remember that the reciprocal influences between the older adulthood stages and younger family stages will be different, though not necessarily better or worse, than those related to more conventional life styles.

THE ADOLESCENT STAGE OF FAMILY DEVELOPMENT

By the time the children have entered adolescence, parents are aware of the strong power of the peer system competing with them for their adolescents' allegiance. The balance of power in the family system has begun to shift during preadolescence as children begin to argue and question their parents' values, pronouncements, and authority. Triangulations are often accentuated in pre-adolescence, and the parents' unresolved issues about sexuality, control, and individuation begin to emerge then. As the child's bonds with peer groups become stronger, the couple system often finds itself separated by turmoil and arguments if the preadolescent, along with the peer group, pit one parent against the other. Concurrently, the parents are typically dealing both with their own development and with the pressures and demands of their parents who are entering older age. Thus, the adolescent stage of family development is often characterized by imbalance and disequilibrium, requiring the continuous adaptation and renegotiation of rules, roles, regulations, and boundaries.

The major process during this stage is that of individual differentiation, as everyone in the system experiences erratic growth and change. *Differentiation* here means individuation, whereby each member of the family learns to function as a more self-sufficient, autonomous person while still interacting and relating with the others with respect to clearly defined boundaries. Thus, two major issues of this stage are autonomy and control, issues that are constantly raised, challenged, and tested by adolescents seeking their own identities, limits, rules, and regulations and the values and meaning of their lives.

In this stage, family size is largest, and many changes transform the established system, often as resolutions to crises. Also, during this stage, the expense of maintaining the family is at its highest, since adolescents wear adult size clothing, which costs more than children's size clothing, eat enormous amounts of food, and are usually indiscriminate in their use of water, electricity, and telephones.

As pointed out elsewhere (Okun and Rappaport, 1980), the way in which the critical tasks of communication and boundary negotiations have been resolved in past stages of family development will influence the resolution of challenges at this stage. It becomes evident that the previously accepted rules, roles, regulations, and boundaries no longer work, and the patience and tolerance of all family members are tested as new rules, roles, regulations, and boundaries are negotiated. The adolescent often functions as the "opposer" in the system, testing everyone's mettle with new styles, new language, new mannerisms, and new values for behavior—perhaps through rebellious acting out. As stated in Chapter 3, the adolescent alternates between over- and underfunctioning. This mix of child and adult can confuse other family members as they interact with the adolescent.

Ackerman (1980, p.154) summarizes the three major aspects of family organization that are regularly and simultaneously being shifted in families with "ordinary" adolescents:

1. The balance of responsibility along the overfunctioning–underfunctioning axis of each relationship seesaws;

2. The marked shifts of intensity of interaction in some relationships with concomitant compensations in others;
3. A great surge of exchange with the community at large, with input from the adolescent and friends as well as teachers, other parents, work, camp, and community personnel.

Perhaps this time may best be characterized by its intensity, by the instability resulting in unpredictability, and by the forced permeability, or opening up, of family-system boundaries with the larger community. This stage can be one of the utmost despair and frustration on the one hand and hilarity on the other. It requires humor, endurance, and forebearance on the part of all family members.

Of the total population of clients of family therapists, families with adolescents form the greatest portion. This is a primary time for symptoms to flare up in the adolescent, in a marriage, or in one of the parents. The issues facing families with adolescents may indeed trigger the reemergence of unresolved issues in a parent or in the marital relationship as the balance of power and boundaries require renegotiation. The following case illustrates the type of renegotiation required in this stage of family life.

Mr. Lee phoned the therapist requesting an immediate session. A professional photographer, aged 44, he was concerned about his 15-year-old daughter's refusal to attend high school for the two days past. Jane, the daughter, had refused to get out of bed, stating that she had been worrying all night about school, could not sleep, and was therefore too tired to go to school during the day. The therapist agreed to see the entire family that evening. The family consisted of Mr. Lee, Jane, Mrs. Lee, 39, a piano teacher, and Randy, 12. When the family presented itself that evening, it was interesting to observe that Jane sat between her parents and Randy was off to the side. Jane explained her worry and fatigue: this was her first year in senior high school and she found the demands for homework burdensome. Mr. Lee appeared to be the initiator in this family system. He explained that he did not believe children should do what they did not wish to and he had never required anything of them. He was puzzled by Jane's inability to function in school. Mrs. Lee claimed that she had given up trying to instill motivation or self-discipline in her children. She did not agree with her husband but had ceased trying to influence him or the children several years earlier, since she had begun to get backaches and headaches that distracted her from her music and the rigorous discipline required for teaching. Jane was obviously the mediator between her parents. She argued with her father on behalf of her mother and empathized with her mother while expressing scorn and disappointment with the older woman's lack of assertiveness. Randy tried to get a word in edgewise but was always ignored. The school issue was critical, for the school adjustment counselor had informed Mr. Lee of the consequences of continued unexcused absences.

Realizing that the symptom had to be eliminated to permit treatment of the underlying family issues, the therapist used a paradoxical intervention, suggesting that Jane change her idea that she needed to sleep at night and that she stay up all night to worry, but still go to school the next morning. Mr. and Mrs. Lee were instructed to ignore Jane in the morning and not to acknowledge whether or not she went to school. Jane went to school the next day and continued to do so and the family returned for treatment. In the second session, when the parents finally began to argue directly with each other, Mr. Lee refused to discuss his marriage and Mrs. Lee retorted bitterly that "that's the problem," whereupon Jane arose from her seat between them, moved over to sit by her brother, and said "I got you folks in here, now you do something about your problems."

This example illustrates the fact, true in all families, that family rules must change when the adolescent naturally assumes more power, disrupting the old homeostasis. In this case, the adolescent's symptom and increased verbalization were constructive in that they provided a mechanism for the family to receive necessary help. However, the developmental issue that emerged concerned individuation and separation. As Jane began to grow up and to take steps toward her own individuation, the tension between her parents increased. She was leaving the triangle that had served to stabilize the marital relationship. Randy, it turned out, was already too closely allied with Mrs. Lee to replace Jane effectively in the triangle. The marital tension increased to a point where Jane felt threatened and needed to act out.

Further work with this family focused on the parents' issues—individual, career, marital, and parental. Mrs. Lee's mid-life transitional reassessment was another trigger for Jane's symptom, in that she began to be more open about her disappointments and resentments toward her husband. As the couple focused more energy on their marital relationship, the family tensions decreased and Jane experienced no further school difficulties.

Perhaps a more typical family in the adolescent stage is that of the Conns.

Mr. Conn, 50, was a high school principal. Mrs. Conn, 44, was a first-grade teacher. They had two children, Lisa, 17, a senior in high school, and Todd, 15, a sophomore in high school. The family was referred to family therapy by the school counselor. Lisa had excessive school absences and was doing very poorly in school. She did not attend the school where her father was principal. Todd also had academic difficulties and was in private school, where he appeared to be coasting along. Mr. and Mrs. Conn had felt a lack of control for several years and were aware of their children's acting-out drug and sexual practices. They were terribly distressed and did not know what to do.

It emerged in therapy that until Lisa entered adolescence the family had managed to hide disagreements and cover up problems by always being busy with activities and functions. Mr. Conn ruled the family rather autocratically and had allied with Lisa against Mrs. Conn, who was seen by the children as ineffectual. As Lisa entered adolescence, she began to rebel against her father's strict rules and to seek her mother's permission for more latitude. This resulted in marital fighting, and the youngsters became angry and frightened. Lisa's decision was to ally with acting-out peers and to see if she could "get even" with her father by shaming him with her behavior. Mr. Conn was genuinely confused. He had always obeyed and pleased his own father and had expected his children to do the same. That they could reject his values and take opposite ones appalled him. He blamed his wife for having been too indulgent when the children were younger. She in turn expressed resentment that he had always put his career first and, until recently, had failed to deal directly with the children at all. Now that the children were old enough to be related to verbally and in more adultlike styles, he wanted to become the controlling parent.

Clearly, the rules and roles in the family were necessarily changing and the unresolved marital issues were now beginning to resurface as Lisa's leavetaking approached. Both parents had had difficulties emotionally separating from their own parents, and it was not unlikely that Lisa's issues centered around that very same topic.

Regardless of who bears the symptom or what the symptom is, families with adolescents share in common the necessity for changing old patterns in order to progress through this stage. We turn our attention now to the particular tasks and issues that all families in this stage need to renegotiate.

Developmental Tasks

The major tasks involve the process of differentiation, not just for the teenagers but also for the parents. The parents need to begin to think of themselves as other than the teenagers' parents and to reassess their own self-concepts in order to renegotiate these relationships successfully. This differentiation is a prelude to the task of separation, which is crucial to the next stage of family development, the launching stage.

Boundary negotiations.   The major boundary renegotiations concern those between the adolescent and the parental subsystems. It is important that the adolescent be able to move in and out of the family system, and this new mobility is often accompanied by marked shifts in the intensity of existing family relationships. For the shifts to occur with minimal disruption, the parents must be able to understand the adolescent's need for mobility and to allow and even encourage the adolescent to experience the ups and downs that accompany them. If the parents fail simultaneously to redefine their relationship and their intimacy needs, they will be less able to facilitate the adolescent's development. Couple issues often surface as a result of the adolescent's increasing verbal criticism. Some research suggests that marital dissatisfaction tends to peak during this stage (Rollins & Feldman, 1970; Lowenthal et al., 1975).

These boundary changes will be evidenced in changes in the parenting roles. Parents who find it difficult to allow their adolescents age-appropriate freedoms in terms of decision making and responsibility are usually expressing resistance to this change in parenting roles. For example, the mother who demands to know everything about her adolescent daughter's social life and friendships and who needs to maintain rigid control over her daughter's activities may be reliving her own unmet adolescent desires vicariously through her daughter. She may also be clinging to her daughter to avoid intimacy with her husband, or she may be reluctant to give up parenting as her primary role and means of identification. Overcontrolling as well as undercontrolling in the parenting subsystem indicates resistance to inevitable changes. Likewise, a father who refuses to let his adolescent son drive or attend peer social functions may be reliving his own adolescent issues with impulse control. The father-son battles may serve to distance the spouses from each other and escalate the adolescent's acting out.

The family system also needs to renegotiate its boundaries with the outside community, particularly with the adolescent's peer system, which becomes more and more important to the adolescent. In some situations, the peer system becomes triangulated into the conflict between parent(s) and adolescent, serving to escalate tensions and conflicts and remaining a no-win situation for all parties. Many parents in this stage of development find that attending to their own community affiliations increases their ability to maintain a reasonable perspective vis-à-vis their adolescent and the adolescent peer system. In other words, maintaining some type of involvement in the community can help a parent to retain an awareness of the issues and events affecting adolescent peer systems and to receive and give support to other families in the same stage. Some parents make a point of volunteering their services—for instance, as drivers or chaperones to teenage functions or, with other parents, to provide activities and outlets for their offspring.

Another necessary type of boundary renegotiation takes place within the sibling subsystem. The adolescent now pulls out of the sibling system to move more freely in and out of the family system, and younger siblings may find this unsettling. Concurrently, the parents need to redefine their boundaries with the younger siblings, particularly where they interface with the adolescent's boundaries. Such boundary renegotiations will include those with grandparents and other extended-family members, with long-time family friends, and with rituals. It is sometimes difficult for parents to learn new parenting roles and behaviors with their oldest children as they move into adolescence while still playing appropriate roles and exhibiting appropriate behaviors with the younger children.

While the family is experiencing major boundary renegotiations, the parents are, both individually and as a couple, reassessing their own self-concepts and their primary relationship as an intimate dyad.

Communication styles.   In order for these boundary renegotiations to occur, communication styles must become clearer, more differentiated, and more symmetrical. As mentioned earlier, adolescents can verbalize with more ease than younger children. These older offspring can sound like mature, reasonable adults one moment and like whining, insecure children the next. At this point, there may be a greater gap than ever between the content of the message and the metacommunication—the message about the content of the message. Parents and adolescents need to become more sensitive to these incongruities and learn to check them out.

A most common difficulty in this stage is a lack of clarity in family rules as those rules change. Typically, each party assumes that everyone else understands and agrees that new, implicit rules are in force, although the new rules have never been clarified explicitly. A common example involves the adolescent's abuse of the curfew hour. The parents assume that the adolescent understands that midnight is the time agreed upon for return home. The adolescent knows that the parents want him or her home by midnight, but has never agreed to it and is unaware of the consequences of ignoring the rule. In this way, the whole issue of power becomes clouded, owing to unclear communication styles. Where parents in such a family have been using discipline as an arena for their struggles, their struggles may become heightened as the issues become more serious. For example, if the parents have always argued between themselves over the rules, with one favoring strictness and one permissiveness, then the adolescent may try to clarify matters by testing the limits, possibly ending up in serious difficulty with the school or the law or some other agency within the community. This trouble, in turn, could increase the family system's vulnerability to outside evaluation and affect the parents' self-concepts in terms of their efficacy as adults and as parents.

Family members inevitably need to learn new strategies for resolving conflicts at this stage. Moreover, negotiations typically become more verbalized than before and involve more participation and compromise from all members. Parents who refuse to negotiate with their adolescents and who attempt to retain unilateral control are more likely to inspire their adolescents to rebel strongly enough to differentiate and later to separate. Differentiation in these circumstances is likely to lead to a painful, angry kind of emotional separation that leaves lifelong scars. In actuality, parents no longer have the resources with which to retain unilateral, authoritarian control. Their adolescents can receive nurturance and support from their peer groups, whereas in earlier stages of childhood they were more dependent on their parents for this type of caring. Adolescents can obtain jobs to earn money and they are too big to be physically restrained. The increasing incidence of adolescent runaways and pregnancies attest to the futility of unilateral, authoritarian parental control.

Developing differentiated communications characterized by more "I" messages, as opposed to "we" messages, will allow for the differentiation of feelings and thoughts and will foster some respect for differences in family members' values, attitudes, and beliefs. Communicating in this way may be difficult for parents who have not yet themselves worked through these issues and who cannot tolerate their children having values, attitudes, and beliefs that differ from their own. On the other hand, many parents, who remember their own adolescent struggles, become more attuned and responsive to their adolescent's struggles and recognize that the extreme testing out represents a period of values clarification for the adolescent and a necessary stage for his or her individuation.

Differentiated communications also include a "checking out" process, whereby family members do not assume that they know what the others are thinking and feeling, and where they take the time and make the effort to check out each other's perceptions—what they *think* they are hearing—as well as whether their own meaning is getting through.

The communication of affection is an important consideration in this stage of family life. Adolescents need physical affection from both parents even when they appear to resist it. Many parents are uncomfortable with this need, particularly in light of their adolescent's burgeoning sexuality, and they focus on other issues as a way of avoiding this aspect of communication. Parents in this stage often verbalize their assumption that teenagers no longer need hugs and kisses, and teenagers, in turn, frequently wonder why the hugs and kisses from parents have stopped after puberty. Rather than ceasing altogether, the expression of affection needs to find new forms.

Developmental Issues

In addition to the adolescent's individual issues, discussed in Chapter 3, we will consider those issues that affect the entire family system in this stage of family development.

Individuation.   The goals of the family system take precedence over the individual goals of the members. Thus, a major developmental task of the family is to find ways to permit its members to move toward individuation without destroying the system. Since systems resist change, it is not surprising that the families often resist an adolescent's attempts to pull away from the family mass. However, in order to work through this stage successfully, the family system needs to learn how to expand and constrict its boundaries as necessary. Families have to protect adolescents in their reach for individuation, while developing their own resiliency in order to change and grow. Thus, the developmental issue becomes a double one of promoting and fostering individuation while changing the way the system functions and thus enabling individual members to function both as individuals and as family-system members.

Parental authority.   Parents need to feel effective as parents; but adolescents, in addition to feeling effective as growing teenagers, need permission to test the limits and to participate in the negotiation of rules and roles. Therefore, family systems that have been able to move from power-influence systems which rely on the children's identification as "good son or daughter" and on fearful compliance with parents' rules because of parental power to power-influence systems based on internalization—where children have internalized parents' values—will be able to manage adolescents more easily than those who still rely on strategies that worked with younger children. Internalization, in turn, depends on the parents' credibility as role models to their offspring, rather than on their authority.

Coping with adolescents is rarely easy, since reason and emotion, rationality and irrationality are constantly juxtaposed. Parental confusion manifests itself in the unclear and inconsistent setting of limits, in the withdrawal of physical affection, and in the making of confusing, unclear expectations and demands. This pattern can result in more adolescent acting-out behavior, which, in turn, leads the parents to feeling less and less effective. Such parents apply more stringent controls, which again fail to work, and which exacerbate the cycle just described. Thus, parents have to learn how to alter and modify demands and expectations that are no longer appropriate for this stage of family development. They need to reconsider their priorities and to realign family resources. It is difficult for many parents to recognize that they no longer have the power to demand what they want from their children, and that their children are becoming separate individuals with their own separate aspirations and motivations. Many parents feel cheated if their aspirations and expectations are not met through their children. In addition to blaming the youngsters, they blame the schools and other institutions of society.

Freedom and responsibility.   As cultural changes confuse people's perceptions of the norms of adolescence, generation gaps often occur in terms of appropriate and inappropriate rules and behaviors. Issues of freedom and responsibility are closely allied to those of individuation and parental authority. Parents need to negotiate between themselves to determine what they consider appropriate freedoms and concurrent responsibilities, rather than using the adolescent in acting out their own issues with each other.

Sometimes parents have difficulty distinguishing between allowing freedom and setting standards and limits that they are willing to take responsibility for enforcing. Parents can no longer consider themselves responsible for their adolescents' behaviors; they cannot control these behaviors. For example, parents who say to adolescents "you are not allowed to drink, smoke, or to have intercourse" are fooling themselves, since there is no way to enforce this rule except by locking their children up. An enforceable condition, however, is this: "You cannot drink, smoke, or have intercourse in this house, and if you come home under the influence of alcohol or pot you will no longer have the freedom to go out in the evening or to use the car."

Parents who attempt to control their adolescents by restricting their freedom to come and go usually succeed in enmeshing the adolescents in their families rather than encouraging them to separate. Parents need to think through their separation from the adolescent just as the adolescent needs to attempt emotional separation from both parents. The parents also need to understand that adolescents must take responsibility for their own behavior and that parents can only enforce certain consequences and support and encourage responsible decision making on the part of the adolescent.

Drug and alcohol abuse, sexuality, delinquency, and academic problems. Adolescent problems involving drug and alcohol abuse, destructive sexual acting out, alienation, academic failure, career-planning failure, delinquency, cognitive disorders, and psychosomatic complaints are particularly apt to occur in families with unresolved conflicts. These issues are sometimes scapegoated by the system. Rather than acknowledging and dealing with unresolved conflicts, the family blames the child's peers, the drug culture, or the confused mores of society. Thus, attention gets focused on the content issues rather than on the family-process system. However, the content issue is often the manifestation of some developmental and family-system issues that require careful assessment and renegotiation.

It is not always the adolescents who experience difficulties with these issues. The adolescent family stage is a time when marital sexual dysfunction may be heightened, perhaps because the parents' unresolved issues are awakened by the adolescent's emerging sexuality. The parents may be in a stage of development in which they want to act out by trying new sex partners or attempting drug use as they try to come to grips with their own identities, the aspiration–achievement gap, or their relationship to these adolescent activists.

Resource management.　The family's time, energy, and money resources need to be reallocated during this stage. The family is likely to be strained financially. Adolescents wear adult-size clothes and shoes, as mentioned earlier. Ticket fares and other expenses are likely to rise dramatically. The parents may be planning for higher education expenses. Residential space becomes tighter as children grow, and the number of cars the family owns may cause conflict. Disputes may arise over the adolescent's earnings, how and when they are spent. There is never enough time in the day. In high school, schedules are irregular and after-school activities may signify that the family is rarely together for a dinner during the school week. People always seem to be running in and out, and family life is hard to plan, impossible to predict.

Because of the irregularities and excesses of energy and time, the couple system is often pulled in many directions. In families at this stage, you often hear the spouses talk about getting away from it all, wishing they, rather than the adolescents, could leave home. The adults often feel as if their space and privacy are continuously intruded upon and they marvel at the limitless, boundless energy of their adolescent offspring.

Dual-career couples.　Dual-career couples in this stage of family life face peculiar challenges. Usually, by this time the couple has been employed for 15 to 30 years and are fully established in their careers. Their salaries may be high and they are no longer concerned about physical childcare and financial pressures. However, they now have to deal with the power and discipline issues associated with adolescence—they cannot depend on surrogates such as babysitting or day-care personnel. If their adolescent offspring are not unusually trustworthy and self-sufficient, they may be unable to handle too much freedom. Emotional intensity in the family system is at its peak now, and often parents, preoccupied with career roles, fail to realize that they are making unrealistic demands on adolescent offspring—for example, in caring for siblings or doing household chores—and that adolescents still require emotional support and supervision.

"Maternal employment can be viewed as setting legitimate limits on the otherwise endless, often conflicting demands of the wife and mother roles" (Barnett and Baruch, 1981). If the adolescents get into any kind of trouble, one parent may accuse and blame the other parent for not devoting more energy to parenting, and couple conflict may escalate. By the same token, competition between the couple may surface at this time as the partners assess discrepancies between career aspirations and realities. Maples (1981) points out that commitment to equity is one of the primary requirements for successful dual-career couples. This equity is particularly important in parenting responsibilities.

Barnett and Baruch (1981) point out that career women who feel a sense of mastery in their work are better able to handle conflict or difficulty than women whose mastery is low, and who feel less in control and more victimized. Thus, multiple roles, while stressful, can lead to high levels of mastery and attachment and can result in higher levels of satisfaction with life regardless of multiple pressures and conflicts.

Divorce.   Although divorce deserves a chapter of its own, it is necessary to mention its special impact on a family in this stage of development. If divorce occurs during this stage, it is usually a 15- to 20-year marriage that is breaking up. The longer the couple has been married, the more vulnerable may be their respective self-concepts and senses of identity to this type of disruption. Divorce always disrupts the system. However, one can postulate some advantages and some disadvantages for it occurring at this stage rather than earlier. For example, most adolescents have more freedom of movement and are more able than younger children to distance emotionally from family conflicts via their peer relationships and activities. Also, adolescents are more likely to have a say in custody decisions and are better able to retain independent contact with both parents. On the other hand, the normal adolescent developmental tasks may be intensified and telescoped owing to the system disruption, and this could hamper necessary individuation.

Single-parent families.   Single-parent families with adolescents seem to have more potential for difficulty than do intact families. The single-parent circumstance is an additional complication at a difficult time in family development. Perhaps conflict exists owing to the fact that both adolescent and parent are simultaneously trying to establish heterosexual relationships. Whereas pursuing similar tasks can be mutually rewarding in terms of shared sensitivity and empathy, it can also be mutually anxiety provoking. If there is insufficient distance between the parent and adolescent, the parent may regress across necessary generational lines, with adolescent and parent competing in the area of dating, sexual attractiveness, and so forth. Hetherington (1972) found that daughters of divorcees had more problematic heterosexual relationships than daughters of widows. She attributed this problem to distance-regulation difficulties.

Single mothers typically report increased stress and conflict with their adolescent offspring. Without support, single parents often find themselves helpless in renegotiating rules and roles, managing discipline, setting appropriate limits, and simultaneously building a satisfactory life for themselves. An imbalance exists in the hierarchical organization of the family system, and the single parent often feels powerless and completely at the mercy of the adolescent offspring. Also, during adolescence, relationships with the noncustodial parent can become a problem, in that the custodial parent no longer has control over the adolescent's contacts and communications with the other parent. Where unfinished business remains between the couple and they have not completed their emotional separation from each other (despite the number of years they have been divorced), the adolescent may find him- or herself triangulated into parental conflict.

Weltner (1982) summarizes the structural problems of the single-parent family as follows:

1. Time and motion placing overwhelming demands on the single parent precludes adequate responsiveness to all of the demands;

2. Lack of validation to the single parent from another adult in the house particularly with regard to discipline and management;
3. Lack of clear generational boundaries, particularly with adolescent sons and single mothers;
4. Enmeshment, or symbiosis.

These structural problems are additional burdens for the normally difficult adolescent stage of family development.

Table 8-1 summarizes the major developmental tasks and issues of the family system during the adolescent stage.

TABLE 8-1.   The adolescent family

Developmental Tasks	General Issues	Requisite Skills	Significant Others
Differentiate Negotiate boundaries: adolescent/parents; adolescent/siblings; siblings/parents; family/outside world; family/work/self Clarify communications	Individuation Parental authority Freedom/responsibility Drug and alcohol abuse Sexuality Resource management: time; energy; money; space/privacy	Conflict resolving Negotiating Symmetrical-power relationship skills Communicating affection Clear, congruent, differentiated communicating	Peers of offspring Community Friends, relatives Neighbors

THE LAUNCHING STAGE OF FAMILY DEVELOPMENT

The launching stage of family development marks a period of gradual disengagement from active parenting as children begin to leave home for extended periods of time, whether to serve in the military, to go to college in another town, or to live in an apartment in the same city. This change is naturally unsettling for a family system, for the departure of the first offspring is the beginning of a major adjustment for the family system that has spent many years becoming a unit with cohesive membership. Major changes are necessitated as the family system contracts—and possibly expands again.

Although the tasks of the earlier stages of family development focused on joining and inclusion, the tasks of the later stages focus on differentiation and separation. In families where levels of self-differentiation of members are high and where children have experienced separation attempts earlier, such as going away to summer camp or being left by parents for substantial periods, the preparation for launching has probably already occurred. In families where this preparation has not been encouraged, and where, in fact, it is resisted, the launching may result in real crisis, such as illness or some other event to prevent the offspring from leaving.

Once the first offspring leaves home for a period of time, an irreversible change occurs. The family system can never revert to the way it was, even if the youngster returns home for periods of time. When the first child leaves home, there is a hole, a gap in the family system. There is unused emotional and physical energy in the system, which needs to be reallocated. The remaining members of the family experience a period of loss and, as a result, also experience the pangs of mourning. In time, the system will transform into a new and different system if it allows this launching to occur. If it resists, it becomes stuck with this hole which it attempts to fill by binding the lost member back into the system. In such families, the offspring sometimes gets "sick" in order to return home or distances further to avoid the possibility of entrapment.

There are many tensions that arise due to changing relationships. These tensions affect the offspring, the offspring's spouse, the parents and the younger children, if any, who remain in the family system. Some view this stage as an exciting opportunity to explore new possibilities and new roles, and others view it as a catastrophe, a precursor to the disintegration of life's meaning.

Many studies show that marital satisfaction is lowest at this stage of family development (Campbell, Converse and Rodgers, 1976; Burr, 1970; Rollins & Feldman, 1970). The process of launching is never smooth and even. Just when the family system that accepts the launching appears to have recalibrated to the new system, and just when the family and the launched child have developed some satisfying modes of communication (such as letters, telephone calls, and short visits), Christmas vacation comes around and the child returns. The reappearance is disruptive, despite the family's pleasure and delight in being together again. The child expects to find the family system as it was before the launching, but he or she actually returns to a different system, one that has been transformed through its reaction to the launching. Perhaps this is what Thomas Wolfe meant when he wrote *You Can't Go Home Again*. Tensions may arise, causing everyone to feel disappointment and guilt, and, although relief may sweep the family when the child returns to school or work, guilt and fear also surface as to what these ambivalent feelings really mean. Families who understand these dynamics are often heard to say "I love it when they come home and I love it when they leave again."

The Cartwright family consisted of Mom, 41; Dad, 45; Jonathan, 18; Mary, 16; and Benjamin, 12. When Jonathan first left home to attend the university in a neighboring state, the family was excited and proud. They were surprised by the feelings of loss they experienced in the weeks following Jonathan's departure. Everyone was pretty cranky and they all spent much of their family time together talking about Jonathan, the missing member, and wondering how he was, what he was doing, and so forth. They counted the days until Christmas vacation, and Mom fantasized about preparing Jonathan's favorite meals and the feelings of "wholeness" she would experience at having her family together again. Mary, who had shared many activities and interests with Jonathan, found herself becoming depressed and having little energy for school activities and friendships. Her listlessness was unusual and noticed both at school and at home. Mary wrote to Jonathan several times a week and eagerly anticipated his weekly phone calls. Benjamin enjoyed the additional attention he received from his parents and sister and, while he missed his older brother, he did not appear to suffer much. Dad missed Jonathan too, but he managed to keep busy at work and found that he was enjoying spending more time with Benjamin. In fact, Dad was experiencing some relief over Jonathan's departure, for their continuous arguments and struggles over "school and home responsibilities" were absent, and Dad now had time and energy for the other two children.

Shortly before Christmas vacation, Mary's first-term grades came out and she and her parents were shocked to see how much they had fallen. The family felt considerable dismay, for, in their system, high achievement was a major goal and much attention was focused on monitoring Mary's activities to ensure that she had adequate time for homework and study. Mom began to compare Mary's achievements with Jonathan's, causing Mary to feel some resentment toward her brother for the first time. Jonathan, meanwhile, was adjusting very satisfactorily to university life. He was looking forward to the Christmas vacation, to see his family and friends again, but also to gain some relief from the pressures of academic work and final exams. In reaction to their stress at Mary's difficulties, the whole Cartwright family intensified their anticipation of Jonathan's return—somehow, they felt everything would revert to the way it had been and be resolved when Jonathan came home.

The family's actual experience when Jonathan returned for Christmas vacation was very different from that which they had anticipated. Jonathan spent the first three days sleeping to catch up on all the sleep he'd missed during the first term, and Mom and Mary were disappointed that he was not available to them. He did not seem to share as much of his life with them as he had before he left, and he spent more time than they liked talking to his friends on the telephone and going out with them. He was sympathetic to Mary's difficulties, but he did not become too involved, although he did suggest to his folks that they leave her alone and stop harping on her grades so much. Benjamin was disappointed because there was never enough food around—it seemed to him that all Jonathan did when he was home was sleep, eat everything in sight, and talk on the telephone. Jonathan was confused by the bickering and squabbling in his family. Somehow he had forgotten about that aspect of his family life. While he was away, he had idealized his family, and he found himself resenting the implicit demands for his involvement.

In short, each member of the Cartwright family experienced surprise and disappointment over the Christmas vacation. Jonathan was relieved to go back to his new life at school, though he felt guilty about these feelings, since he truly did care for his family. Mom, Dad, Mary, and Benjamin also felt relieved. They did not understand their feelings, but somehow sensed they could manage their tensions better without Jonathan criticizing them for bickering. They did, however, feel the need to seek counseling to find out if their "bickering" could be diminished. It took time for the family system to develop new rules, roles, and regulations, and to find a way to manage without Jonathan and still appreciate him when he did come home. They had to learn to adjust to Jonathan's comings and goings.

This example is fairly typical. The Cartwright family experienced a "normal" stress period while adjusting to a difficult developmental transition. They found themselves stuck a bit, and they benefited from some help in getting unstuck. It is likely that they would have weathered the storm without professional help, albeit a bit slower and with more anguish. The point is that the Cartwrights were neither "sick" nor "deeply disturbed," they were merely adjusting.

The launching stage is a time of letting go rather than one of binding. Many parents fail to realize that one of the major tasks of parenthood is to facilitate, rather than hinder, this letting go—to give children "wings as well as roots" so they may separate appropriately and learn to lead their own lives. The degree of self-differentiation the young adult has achieved by the time of launching, the complexities of whatever triangulations exist within the family system, and the double binds and enmeshments—all come to the forefront as parents and children prepare to take leave of each other. How each parent experienced his or her own launching and the multigenerational themes regarding emotional separation also affect the handling of this process. Remember, the interactional patterns that young adults learn within the family system determine the type of interactions they achieve with people outside the family system and, later, in their own newly created family systems (Okun and Rappaport, 1980).

Minuchin (1974) uses the term *family cutoff* to describe emotional separation during the launching period. The way this cutoff is accomplished determines whether the young adult will take a responsive (choosing) position or a reactive (obligated) position in relation to the family of origin. Also affected will be the type of interactions the launched offspring maintains with his or her family of origin. Given an appropriate, effective launching, the young adult may be able to visit home without anger at "having" to do so. Or the young adult may interact only minimally with the family of origin and still not feel guilty about it. Obviously, an effective launching enables the young adult to view his or her family from a relatively objective, distanced perspective, to integrate perceptions of his or her strengths and weaknesses without undue self-blame, and to recognize and accept his or her difficulties and problems without feeling responsible for solving them.

If the launching is difficult and involves resistance, however, major problems may ensue. For example, a youngster may not leave when appropriate and may become physically or emotionally ill in order to avoid leaving home. And the child's failure to leave may, in fact, protect the parents from having to deal with their own individual and couple issues and renegotiating their marriage. Or a parent may develop a symptom and insist that the youngster stay home to provide care and support. Avoidance and resistance of the launching process will result in family-system symptomology sooner or later as the system becomes stuck in the process of individual and family development. Harkins (1978) found that a woman's adjustment to launching was correlated with the timeliness of the launching. If the child's leaving was delayed or the child was unsuccessful in launching, the mother was more likely to experience physical and psychological symptoms than if the launching succeeded at the appropriate time.

Certain sex-role factors affect expectations of daughters' individuating as compared with the individuating of sons. Some therapists or theorists today (Gilligan, 1982; Chodorow, 1978; Low, 1978) question the psychological theory that favors detachment from one's family of origin for both males and females. They claim that female offspring have not been socialized to separate, and that emotional separation should not be considered a norm for health. My view is that individuation and emotional separation are necessary steps toward achieving psychological maturity but that these objectives need not require a "cut off" from one's family system and from attachments within that system. Rather, launching requires that one pull away sufficiently to become one's own self, learning to be self-supportive rather than family supported and learning to clarify one's own values, attitudes and beliefs. One then renegotiates one's relationship with one's parents as an adult. Mothers and daughters are caught up in fusion, and daughters cannot expect their mothers to teach them to become individuals. Daughters must do it themselves and the goal is for daughters to take a nondefensive "I" position with mother without attacking or rejecting her (Carter, 1982).

Developmental Tasks

The major developmental tasks at this stage involve letting go and renegotiating the relationships, rules, and roles, both within the family system and with the launched member. This task is often accompanied by some degree of ambivalence and time is necessary for the readjustment of these relationships. The parents' individual developmental issues are closely intertwined with how they accomplish this stage of family development: parents must deal with their own aging, their mid-life identity reassessments, and dramatic changes in their own self-concepts and major roles while their children are being launched.

Boundary negotiations.   As the parenting role changes and diminishes, emotional energy must be redistributed among fewer people in the home than before. Thus, it is necessary to shift and strengthen the alliances in the couple and sibling subsystems.

Couple renegotiation.   Couples who are reluctant to deal with their own relationship tend to redistribute their emotional energy into their remaining children and attempt to prolong the launching process. If the first child has been triangulated into the couple relationship, the parents may seek to draw another child into the empty place. If this is impossible, they may seek a job, activity, lover, or elderly parent to fill the empty place.

Other couples see the first launching as an augur of what is yet to come, and begin to reassess their couple relationship in order to determine whether it should continue and, if so, how. Since they will no longer be able to maintain the view that they must stay together "for the sake of the children," they must look anew at their relationship to decide whether or not it is worth the investment of the rest of their lives. Many couples, of course, find that their commitment to their marriage is heightened at this time, and that, with renewed vigor and attention, they can develop a more satisfying, fulfilling relationship (Okun and Rappaport, 1980).

The marital reassessment may focus on various issues. For example, women who are moved to explore the world outside the family and to focus on their own achievement issues may find their husbands beginning to focus more on relationship issues, seeking more intimacy and companionship just when they are about to look for gratification and satisfaction outside the family system (Levinson, 1978). The couple who is able to resolve these differences, by meeting the needs of each without giving up individual interests and senses of autonomy, is likely to endure. On the other hand, women who have been overinvolved with their children and who now become interested in renewing their marital relationship may find that their husbands have distanced from the family long ago and are not interested in a renewed relationship. How the couple works through these differences will determine whether or not the marriage survives. Each spouse's individual issues with identity, intimacy, and career development will influence the outcome of the couple-system renegotiation.

It is during this stage of family development that the failure to resolve the tasks of the early-marriage stage exacts its toll. If either spouse has failed to establish a separate identity within the marital relationship, and if both have used the children to avoid intimacy with each other, they are likely to experience strong disappointment and resentment at this stage and may feel at a loss as to how to renegotiate the relationship or how to leave. An increasing number of couples are separating during this stage and attempting to find new lives for themselves while there is still time. Still, many couples find that if they can weather the storm and negotiate their differences, they can gain even greater satisfactions than they expected. Involved is a reconciliation between their idealization of their couple system and the disenchantment they have actually experienced—a working through of the initial joining phase.

Couple renegotiation with launched offspring. If the partners are successful in renegotiating their relationship, they need also to renegotiate their relationships with their launched offspring, formulating adult–adult relationships that have clear generational boundaries. In other words, they must decide how to be supportive of their offspring without being intrusive and how they can facilitate the launching process while refraining from "rescuing," "leading," or "overprotecting" their child. This role involves acceptance of the launched offspring as a separate individual with the right and responsibility to make decisions, fail, and succeed. The offspring has to learn, to grow, to develop, and to experience pain as well as happiness. Parents will always feel pain when their offspring are hurt, but they can learn to acknowledge that such pain is their own feeling rather than a controlling mechanism to influence their offspring. To do so requires that they increasingly accept the worth of the offspring's independent pursuits.

Couple renegotiation with elderly parents, friends, and the outside community. Other boundaries the couple system needs to renegotiate are with their elderly parents and with the outside community. Many couples find that some of their released emotional and physical energy can be transferred to old and new friendships. Some of these friendships may have been "on hold" for several years while the couple was more involved with adolescent and launching offspring. It is likely that these friends were involved with their own adolescent and launching offspring, and the renewals of relationships may therefore be mutual.

As the couple's elderly parents experience a drop in time and energy, they may make more demands on their middle-aged offspring to provide care and attention. They may also exacerbate the situation by expressing critical judgments of their launching grandchildren and their offspring's parenting capacities and outcomes.

Again, their input will be influenced by the previous history of emotional separation and launching in the multigenerational family system.

Sibling-system renegotiation.   The parents need to renegotiate their relationships with the siblings remaining at home, deciding on rules and roles appropriate to the ages of these youngsters. Likewise, sibling-subsystem members must renegotiate their mutual relationships—with siblings not yet launched, the parents, and with the launched sibling or siblings. This process involves letting go of old dependencies and expectations and learning to appreciate differences in styles and choices. Remaining siblings may enjoy increased attention or may find their new position burdensome, feeling pressures to fill the gap created by the launched siblings. New feelings of ambivalence may surface about the launched sibling, who has gained new freedoms and has left the others behind. The older sibling's launch, however, may be an effective model for the younger siblings' impending launchings, and it can motivate the younger siblings to grow up and seek the same benefits.

The launched member, of course, must renegotiate his or her boundaries with the family system (discussed in depth in Chapter 3). Needless to say, the success of this particular set of renegotiations depends on the effectiveness of the family system's renegotiations with each other and with the launching member during this stage.

Communication styles.   The communication styles within the family system must be made even clearer, more differentiated, and more symmetrical. As the launched member finds new ways to communicate with the family, the members of the family system need to find new ways of communicating with the launched member. One common difficulty is agreeing on the frequency of communications between family and child and on who is to be the initiator. Many families, for example, insist that their offspring write letters or telephone at certain intervals. If the requirement is arbitrarily set by the family, the launched child may feel anger and guilt at being obligated to make contact rather than being allowed to choose.

When the launched member returns home for visits, the rules of the visits must be clarified, since the system will have changed and the old rules will no longer apply. For example, the launched offspring will be used to coming and going and entertaining guests freely, and, upon visiting the family home, will have to realize that he or she is neither in the new home nor in the family home as it was. The child will need to consider and respect the parents' rules and wishes unless these rules have been successfully renegotiated. As parents and offspring renegotiate their relationships, it is important that they make concerted efforts to listen to each other's views and learn to recognize and accept differences rather than engage in win-or-lose power struggles.

Power, support, and other rules of the relationship need to be clearly communicated once they have been decided on. The parents must identify and express their opinions and beliefs, offer advice rather than make demands, and refuse to be maneuvered into taking responsibility for the offspring's choices and decisions.

Developmental Issues

Some of the issues discussed pertain exclusively to the period during which the first child is launching and other children are at home. Others pertain to the time after all the children have gone.

Sex-role issues.   Obviously, the departure of grown children from the family system produces a void that must be filled. There appear to be some differences in the ways mothers and fathers cope with this void. Clinical data show that, compared with women who have developed more self-differentiated self-concepts and compared with men, women who have based their sense of self-worth on caring for and nurturing others more often experience crises in dealing both with their offspring's launchings and with the loss of spouse or parent through divorce or death. We also know that the age of the mother and father at the time of launching is an important factor in determining the situation that parents face at this stage. A woman in her early forties, for example, may now be ready to think about a new career or the expansion of an existing one by further education or training. Her situation differs from that of the woman whose children leave when she is in her fifties, and who is thus more likely to be concerned with health problems, retirement, and use of leisure time than with career issues. Likewise, a woman who has plans for a new life after the launching period may find herself constrained by the sickness or disability of an aging parent or spouse. Thus, some women may find themselves forced to continue caring for and ministering to the needs of others, causing resentment and leading to considerable marital stress.

Many women who have postponed their own career plans find that just when they finally have the time and opportunity to branch out of the family system, job opportunities have dried up and their career development is restricted. Their level of resilience and their ability to reallocate their time and energies in gratifying ways will be influenced by the coping strategies they have developed in the past and by their level of self-confidence. Also significant will be the support they receive from their spouses and significant others. During the 1960s and 1970s, women were encouraged to reenter or to enter for the first time the expanding labor market. Many returned to earlier professions, such as teaching, social work, or library science. During the 1980s, in a tighter, declining labor market, many women are finding that their previous training and experience are irrelevant and that the competition for the remaining jobs and fields is very keen.

A variety of studies show that, contrary to popular mythology, most women do not anticipate or experience the "empty-nest syndrome" (Neugarten, 1968; Lowenthal, 1972; Harkins, 1978; Okun and Rappaport, 1980). This launching stage permits preparation for the postparental stages. It is a time when women can begin to experience changes in their roles and to think about and try out different ways of living, expanding their opportunities and personal interests. There is no research reporting the effects of launching on fathers. Men obviously feel the effects of this major change but may deal with it through their occupational and/or other family investments.

Resource management.   If offspring are launched by means of higher education, this period may be one of financial stress for the family, and the mother may feel obliged to earn money however possible. While on the one hand financial stress may be a problem, on the other it may serve to keep the family system focused on the goal of providing higher education for the offspring (tuitions seem to rise about 20 percent per year), and it may facilitate the avoidance of relationship issues. The amount of financial support parents can give to launching and launched offspring is an issue that must be considered and negotiated; otherwise, such support can become a mechanism for avoiding launching and for controlling and interfering with the autonomy of young-adult offspring.

Multigenerational issues.   Clinicians are aware that issues arising from the parents' own experience of the launching stage as offspring affect their ability to cope with this stage as parents. Often, it is important for parents, the middle generation, to renegotiate simultaneously their relationships with their elderly parents and with their adult offspring. By changing their roles and rules as adult offspring, they are able to effect change in their roles as parents of adult offspring. For example, a man who is able to accept himself and his parents as separate, autonomous individuals with differing needs and values will be better able to view his offspring autonomously than one who still perceives himself as controlled by his parents and as obliged to relate to them in a prescribed manner. Thus, the multigenerational perspective can facilitate the process of launching for all participants.

Parental authority.   From the adolescent stage of family development on, the parents continue to renegotiate their authority relationships with their offspring. This process may take several years, as the parents learn to hand over the reins of power to their youngsters and to allow the youngsters to accept the responsibilities and consequences of early adulthood. This does not mean that parents must refrain from voicing their opinions, beliefs, and concerns; rather, they learn to do so without making demands and imposing their personal opinions, beliefs, and concerns on their offspring.

New relationships.   During the launching stage, offspring may develop intimate relationships with new friends. How open the family system is to welcome these significant others of their offspring and how much they share in the lives and relationships of their offspring will vary with the family system. It is during this phase that the family system first prepares itself for the inclusion and/or exclusion of current and new members. How well the family can regroup to include new or lost members is a major predictor of how well they will prepare themselves to incorporate changing alliances and relationships in the future with in-laws and ex-in-laws.

Divorce.   When divorce occurs during this stage of family development, the family system is disrupted in many ways, both "natural" and "unnatural." The divorce may hasten or impede the launching—for example, the launching offspring may be drawn back into the family system to try and restore the marriage or may distance him- or herself further to avoid entanglement and having to take sides. Beal (1980) points out that, whereas the death of a parent may draw the surviving parent and adult children together, the divorce of parents has a tendency to polarize the relationships of parents and their adult children. Often, the spouse most resistant to the divorce wants one or more of the adult children to fill the gap left by the divorcing spouse, and the emotional separation process between parent and child thus may become troublesome. The greatest problems occur for those spouses emotionally cut off from their extended families. The divorce itself may precipitate emotional cut-offs from both family and friends, leaving older divorcing adults without supportive resources at a critical period in their lives.

Single-parent families.   Single-parent families will experience varying levels of stress and/or relief during this stage. Again, what happens will depend on the level of self-differentiation of the single parent—how well she or he has worked through the marital separation and career development tasks and issues. Where the single parent is enmeshed with the offspring and terrified at the prospect of launching, the offspring may feel compelled to resist launching in order to care for the single parent. However, often both single parent and offspring welcome the launching as providing opportunities for further growth and development.

Table 8-2 summarizes the developmental tasks and issues of the launching stage of family development.

TABLE 8-2.   The launching stage

Developmental Tasks	General Issues	Requisite Skills	Significant Others
Let go	Power	Time managing	Adult offspring
Renegotiate boundaries:	Multigenerational themes	Adult–adult relationship	In-laws
couple system;	Parental authority	skills	Elderly parents
parents/launched	New relationships of	Caretaking	Old friends
offspring; couple/	offspring	Decision making	New friends
friends; elderly	Sex	Listening	Community
parents; community;	Lifestyle	Encouraging	Grandchildren
parents/remaining	Use of time, energy, and	Renegotiating	
siblings; launched	money		
offspring/siblings			
Restructure			
communications:			
power; rules			

THE POSTPARENTAL STAGE OF FAMILY DEVELOPMENT

The term *postparental* is really a misnomer, since one never ceases being a parent. The relationship between parent and child is altered, not terminated, once the offspring are launched. The parent relationship with the offspring is always a psychological bond, regardless of the age of the offspring. However, this is the stage of the family life cycle that occurs after the youngest child has left home and in which the parents begin to function again as a couple system. The offspring do not come and go as frequently as they did during the launching stage, when they were in the process of leaving. They have now left and established their homes outside the family domicile.

As noted in previous sections, this period may be one of rediscovery or disappointment. The couple reassesses and redefines the marital relationship and prepares for the offspring's marriages (and the introduction of in-laws into the family system), for becoming grandparents (and the introduction of grandchildren into the family system), and for changing their lifestyle in anticipation of retirement, health changes, and the death of elderly parents and peers.

At this stage in their relationship, the middle-aged partners may find themselves on the other side of the same boundary they negotiated years ago when they first became a couple. Their children are now negotiating the boundaries of their own couple or relationship systems and, in doing so, are moving the middle-aged couple out of the parenting relationship. Later, with the birth of grandchildren, the boundaries of the new family systems may be altered to include the couple as grandparents. But more importantly, the middle-aged couple must now attend to the boundaries of their own marital relationship, which they may have neglected for years. In making this reexamination of their relationship, the partners can be twenty or thirty years older than when they formed the relationship, and, thus, they are likely to be two quite different people.

In the folk myth of our culture, this stage is where "the empty-nest syndrome" occurs. The implication is that members of the couple, now alone and childless, find themselves considerably dissatisfied with each other and their relationship. As mentioned earlier, the research in the field actually indicates the contrary. McCullough (1980) reviewed the literature and found three competing descriptions of what can occur in this stage:

1. The empty-nest syndrome, positing problems for one or both parents;
2. The curvilinear model, positing increased freedom and independence for the couple;
3. Varieties of the above.

Increasingly, the research is finding greater incidences of (2) than (1). In fact, many couples at this stage report that they are relieved not to have turbulent adolescents and young adults living at home and not to have the financial burdens; this feeling far outweighs the loneliness or bereavement they may experience at the loss of the parenting function. Mean standard scores on marital satisfaction at each stage of an eight-stage family life cycle, measured by no fewer than three reputable inventories of marital satisfaction (Rollins and Cannon, 1974), indicate that both men and women experience more marital satisfaction as they move from the adolescent-family stage to the launching stage, and they experience another increase in satisfaction as they move from the launching stage to the postparental stage.

Recent literature suggests that people who are in reasonably good health and who are relatively free of financial burdens find this period of life to be one of the most expansive and autonomous. Obviously, the state of one's health, one's career satisfaction, one's economic status, and the well-being of one's launched children all affect the quality of experience at this stage of family life.

Developmental Tasks

The major developmental tasks involve two major role changes, both requiring boundary renegotiations. One concerns the older generation, the couple's parents, and the other involves the newest generation, grandchildren. In addition, the partners need to define their relationships with their sons- and daughters-in-law and with these newcomers' respective families.

Boundary negotiations.   The major boundary negotiations are those of inclusion—incorporating in-laws and grandchildren into the family system, and defining roles and rules. Also, at this time, the couple's own parents are usually old enough to require care. Therefore, just as the couple finally steps out of the child-care role, it may find itself stepping into a parent-care role. This role will eventually lead to exclusion—dealing with the death and loss of parents—which, at any age, constitutes a major step into adulthood.

How couples in this stage fare with their elderly parents will be affected by the range and scope of their "unfinished business" with their parents. If the partners have failed to resolve relationship difficulties while focusing on the younger generation, they may now find that these problems require some type of attention. This may be reflected in dependency/independence issues between the middle and older generations as well as in power and control issues. The middle-generation adults may have to take the responsibility for changing their behaviors in order to work through these issues and accomplish whatever caretaking tasks are required. The ability to individuate and accept the older generation's differing perceptions, behaviors, and beliefs—as with the younger generation—will help family systems to maintain balanced, supportive, and nondefensive mutual relationships. When the elderly die, the middle-aged parents themselves become the older generation, and this in itself requires a reassessment of identity, roles, and rules.

Grandparenting.   Even more than dealing with in-laws, grandparenting requires delicate boundary negotiations. In fact, in-law issues often fail to emerge until grandchildren are born. Having renegotiated the boundaries between themselves and their children when the children first left home, and then married, parents must now negotiate new boundaries in order to enter their children's family systems. How they negotiate these new boundaries will be affected by the history of their relationships with their children and by the manner in which they themselves passed through the previous stages of the family life cycle.

Grandparenting can produce its own set of stresses and strains. The grandparents and parents may relive some of their own unresolved parent-system conflicts, resulting in the triangulation of the grandchildren. Grandparents often feel the need to indulge and nurture their grandchildren, and this may conflict with the parents' needs to control and determine their own style of parenting. On the other hand, grandparents who do not become involved with their grandchildren, owing to absorption in their own interests, may also create conflict by failing to meet their children's expectations of them as grandparents. Finally, competition may occur between two sets of grandparents and between the adult children vying for the grandparents' attentions.

Neugarten and Weinstein (1964) pioneered a reconceptualization of this stage. They identified five distinct styles of grandparenting:

1. The *formal* grandparent, who leaves parenting to the parent but has the prerogative of special times with or performing special favors for the grandchildren;
2. The *surrogate* parent, most often the grandmother, who is allowed parental responsibility for the child by the parents;
3. The *reservoir-of-family-wisdom* grandparent, who retains a position of authority, dispensing special "wisdom" or skills;
4. The *funseeker* grandparent, frequently in his or her late forties or early fifties, and not old by our current standards, who actively joins with the grandchildren in play;
5. The *distant-figure* grandparent, absent on most occasions, who has sporadic and peripheral contact with the grandchildren.

The first three types of grandparenting roles are relatively traditional, and are associated with past generations. The last two are found increasingly in modern family systems, as more and more middle-aged women enter the labor market and as geographical mobility becomes a way of life.

Robertson (1977) developed the concept of four styles of grandparenting, which are dependent on one's personal orientation toward grandparenting and on one's perceptions of the social and normative meanings attached to grandparenthood: (1) remote; (2) individualized; (3) symbiotic; and (4) apportioned. A variety of styles and attitudes exists toward grandparenting, and much depends on how the middle generation, the parents, define the relationships (George, 1980).

Colarusso and Nemiroff (1981) found that grandparents idealize their grandchildren to serve several defensive purposes: (1) denial of aging; (2) a chance for magical repair of one's parenting through the grandchild; and (3) denying the imperfection of self by selectively identifying with particular qualities in the grandchild. The grandparent usually enjoys the continuity and meaning of life that multigenerational ties bring. One's recognition of death enhances one's appreciation of how one's self lives on through one's creations and offspring. Thus, grandparenthood reinforces generativity.

Other boundary negotiations concern outside interests and socialization affiliations with outside roles. In other words, the renewal of previous relationships and activities and the development of new relationships and interests require individual as well as couple-boundary renegotiations.

Communication styles.   The tasks involving communication carry over from the previous stage of family development. Communication patterns and information processing must be clarified and changed as people physically separate and the number and age-span of family members change. For example, protecting older parents from disturbing news by not sharing critical material can, in fact, cause more disruption and pain in the system than sharing relevant information directly. Likewise, it is important that spouses and adult children not be triangulated into other relationships. If a mother is upset that her daughter-in-law is choosing to spend Thanksgiving with her own parents, she needs to express her feelings directly to her daughter-in-law rather than through her son or a grandchild. Regulating the communication patterns and checking out meanings and intentions can save family systems much distress and unhappiness.

Developmental Issues

The major issues of this stage involve lifestyle discrepancies, the death of close friends and parents, physical separations, changes in financial and occupational status, health, preretirement, physiological and sexual changes, and the accommodation of emerging needs and interests.

Lifestyles.   In earlier stages of family development, adolescents and launching offspring often engage in alternate lifestyles as a means of separating emotionally and of sending messages to their parents about their own individuation. While this behavior is indeed distressing to the parents, it is often viewed as temporary acting out. In the postparental stage, however, an alternative lifestyle choice may have stabilized and the parents can no longer rationalize it, expecting their offspring to conform. Parents have few choices. They can accept their offspring's lifestyle, although they disapprove, in order to maintain some type of relationship; they can engage in a no-win power struggle with their offspring that will impede the actual launching; or they can disengage completely, choosing not to retain relationships with their offspring. Most parents choose the first option, reserving discussion of their feelings and judgments for their spouses, and maintaining some type of relationship with their adult offspring. Nevertheless, the pain and disappointment such parents feel are real and are often manifested in another arena, such as an illness, for example, or overinvolvement with another offspring or a grandchild.

Loss and death.   If a couple has reached this stage of life without experiencing the death of a significant other, they are indeed unusual. However, they cannot expect to continue for long in this way and must prepare for their own and others' demise. Obviously, the death or serious illness of any family member disrupts the family equilibrium and may result in regression or fixation in individual or family development. According to Herz (1981), the degree of disruption to the family system is affected by many factors, including the following:

1. The timing of the death or serious illness in the individual's life cycle;
2. The nature of the serious illness or death;
3. The openness of the family system;
4. The family position of the seriously ill, dying, or deceased member(s).

Illnesses or deaths that occur early in the individual or family life cycle, prolonged illnesses and painful deaths, reactions to radical surgery or treatment, the effectiveness of communication patterns, and the dependency of the system on the ill or dying member all naturally intensify the system's disruption and reactions to loss. How the system has dealt with symbolic and lesser losses in the past provides the foundation for the system's coping capacities with major loss.

Widowhood begins to occur more frequently during this stage of family development and, while this phenomenon will be elaborated upon in Chapter 12, it is important to mention it here as affecting one's role and status. As remarriage is likelier the younger the widow or widower, adjustment to remarriage might be a factor for many people in this stage of life. Gluck, Weiss, and Parkes (1974) found that relatively young and middle-aged widows and widowers tended toward five patterns of adjustment:

1. Movement toward remarriage;
2. Movement toward an intimate relationship but no remarriage;
3. Organizing life around children or other relatives;
4. Independent lifestyle;
5. Disorganized, chaotic lifestyle.

The choice of pattern depends on individual issues as well as the experiences and history of the individual within a family system.

The physical separation of children and grandchildren requires careful planning and strategies for maintaining relationships, such as telephone calls, letter writing, and short or extended visits. The latter require careful planning and negotiation of roles and rules. Often, for example, power struggles emerge as to who will visit whom where, for how long, and under what rules.

Changes in financial and occupational status.   Although financial matters are discussed in Chapters 9 and 13, certain changes in financial and occupational status have a bearing on lifestyle changes for the middle-aged parents. These lifestyle changes may be either chosen or necessitated and, therefore, they can be viewed either optimistically or pessimistically. Changes will affect the couple's individual and couple identities as well as their attitudes toward and goals for their relationship. If, for example, there are now two incomes rather than one and the couple has fewer financial obligations for the offspring, the partners may choose to travel more, to fix up their home, and to be more expansive in their financial outlay. Sometimes adult offspring are startled by their parents' sudden "looseness" with their money and resent never having experienced such an attitude when they lived at home. Or, a single parent may find that she receives less financial aid now that she no longer has dependent children and that she must work, whether or not she wishes to, in order to maintain her lifestyle.

Preretirement.   Again, although these issues will be elaborated upon in the next chapter, the way the couple plans for retirement and formulates expectations, needs, and new interests will affect how they experience this milestone. Is the couple allied and working together or is retirement a topic that escalates their existing power struggle? Recent data show that retirement is more likely to be experienced positively if anticipated and planned and if the couple relationship has achieved a satisfactory level of intimacy and interdependence without sacrificing individual differentiation. Thus, a couple that is united and working collaboratively is more likely to enjoy retirement and benefit from preretirement planning than partners at odds with each other.

Health and physiological changes.   People must accommodate to physiological changes and declining health. If both partners are at the same life stage, they may not view these changes as issues. If, however, they are in different stages of the individual life cycle, they may view the discrepancies in their changing needs and energies as threatening to their relationship.

Sex.   Sexuality may take on a new dimension for the couple at this time. Many women report an increased interest in sexuality, possibly related to genuine but unfounded fears of losing sexual satisfaction during menopause or to the new freedom from pregnancy fears and birth control concerns. Men may become anxious about their sexual prowess and fail to understand their changing performance. How couples resolve their sexual issues depends on the current couple relationship—the history of their sexual relationship, and its meaning to them individually and as a couple. If the couple relationship results in an invigorated bonding, this period may be one of the happiest in the partners' sexual life, since they can relate to each other without the pressures of time and children. Where the bond is weak, the sexual relationship may dwindle and disappear altogether. Many couples rationalize this disappearance by claiming that "they're too old for sex" or that "sex is not important after middle age."

Differentiation.   Differentiation continues to be an issue in this stage of family life as dependency/independence issues continue to emerge. Preparing for the inevitable loss of a spouse and for more distanced relationships with adult children, as the latter become more involved with their own growing families, individuals in the couple system must continue to develop interests and relationships that will afford support and sustenance when necessary.

The postparental stage is a time of consolidation and may result in heightened marital satisfaction and individual functioning. The major responsibilities of childrearing are over, the major financial burdens have lifted, and now, with many years still left, the partners have the opportunity to reorganize their lives and their life experiences. The negative image of this stage of life is giving way to the realization that the postparental time may indeed be one of the most satisfying stages, when one reaps the benefits of years of hard work. This realization is becoming more and more widespread, as people in our society experience and speak out about the pleasures and advantages of this stage of family life. Table 8-3 summarizes the developmental tasks and issues of the postparental stage of family development.

As the greatest proportion of our population moves into middle age, we will find that understanding and sensitivity increase to the issues of families in mid-life.

TABLE 8-3.   The postparental stage

Developmental Tasks	General Issues	Requisite Skills	Significant Others
Create new roles: with elderly parents; with grandchildren Renegotiate boundaries: with in-laws; grandchildren; adult offspring; elderly parents; friends and community Restructure multigenerational communications	Alternate lifestyle choices Loss and death Financial and occupational status Preretirement Health Physiological changes Sex Differentiation Mid-life career issues Time, energy, and other resources management	Grandparenting Negotiating Planning Self-caring Couple intimacy	In-laws Adult offspring Grandchildren Friends, old and new Community Elderly parents Siblings

And as people continue to live longer, three- and four-generation systems will not be uncommon; thus, we need to learn how to help families cope with the increasing complexities of wider spans of development. For example, one recent phenomenon is the return of already launched offspring, who have come to live at home for economic reasons. Such a development may precipitate a recycling from postparental stages to, say, a new stage rather than back to the launching stage. In such a case, the disruption requires careful negotiation and clarification of rules, roles, and regulations.

SUMMARY

These three stages of the family life cycle may be the most turbulent and unsettling. Change is intense and unpredictable, requiring active boundary renegotiations and limitless patience and energy. But for those families passing through these stages, there are gains as well as losses.

In this chapter, we elaborated the fifth, sixth, and seventh stages of the family life cycle: the adolescent family, the launching family, and the postparental family. These stages are most likely to occur during the middle-adulthood period and are periods of differentiation, launching, and consolidation, respectively. The major developmental tasks are boundary renegotiations and communication restructuring. Spouses need to renegotiate their own couple relationship, their relationships with their offspring and remaining siblings, and their personal relationships with their own mid-life issues, relationships, and outside interests.

Typical issues affecting families during these stages involve changing authority channels, changing relationships, inclusion and exclusion of old and new members, separation, and the reallocation of resources. Letting go is often more difficult and painful than the inclusion of the earlier stages. This process requires higher levels of self-differentiation and the ability to let others take control of their own lives.

REFERENCES

Ackerman, N. J. The family with adolescents. In E. Carter and M. McGoldrick (eds.), *The family life cycle: A framework for family therapy.* New York: Gardner Press, 1980, pp. 147-171.

Barnett, R. & Baruch, G. *Multiple role strain: Number of roles and psychological well-being.* Wellesley College Center for Research on Women, No. 73, 1981.

Beal, E. Separation, divorce and single-parent families. In E. Carter and M. McGoldrick (eds.), *The family life cycle: A framework for family therapy.* New York: Gardner Press, 1980, pp. 241-260.

Bird, C. *The two-paycheck marriage.* New York: Rawson Wade, 1979.

Braverman, S. Family of origin: The view from the parents' side. *Family Process,* 1981, *20,* 431-439.

Burr, W. R. Satisfaction with various aspects of marriage over the life cycle: A random middle class sample. *Journal of Marriage and the Family,* 1970, *32,* 29-37.

Campbell, A., Converse, P. E., & Rodgers, W. L. *The duality of American life.* New York: Russell Sage Foundation, 1976.

Carter, E. *Mothers and daughters.* Conference at Harvard University, June, 1982.

Chodorow, N. *The reproduction of mothering.* Berkeley, Calif.: University of California Press, 1978.

Colarusso, C. A., & Nemiroff, R. A. *Adult development.* New York: Plenum Press, 1981.

Daniels, P., & Weingarten, K. *Sooner or later—the timing of parenthood in adult lives.* New York: W. W. Norton, 1981.

George, L. K. *Role transitions in later life.* Monterey, Calif.: Brooks/Cole, 1980.

Gilligan, C. Why should a woman be more like a man? *Psychology Today,* June, 1982, *16,* 68.

Gluck, I. O., Weiss, R. D., & Parkes, C. M. *The first year of bereavement.* New York: Wiley, 1974.

Gluck, N. R., Dannefer, E., & Milea, K. Women in families. In E. Carter and M. McGoldrick (eds.), *The family life cycle: A framework for family therapy.* New York: Gardner Press, 1980, pp. 295-329.

Harkins, E. B. Effects of empty-nest transition on self-report of psychological and physical well being. *Journal of Marriage and the Family,* 1978, *40,* 459-556.

Herz, F. The impact of death and serious illness on the family life cycle. In E. Carter and M. McGoldrick (eds.), *The family life cycle: A framework for family therapy.* New York: Gardner Press, 1980, pp. 223-241.

Hetherington, E. M. Effects of paternal absence on personality development in adolescent daughters. *Developmental Psychology,* 1972, *7,* 313-326.

Levinson, D. *The seasons of a man's life.* New York: Knopf, 1978.

Low, N. *The mother–daughter relationship in adulthood.* Paper presented at Massachusetts Psychological Association, Boston, Mass., 1978.

Lowenthal, M., & Chiriboga, D. Transition to the empty nest. *Archives of General Psychiatry,* January 1972, *26,* 8-14.

Lowenthal, M., Thurnher, M., & Chiriboga, D. *Four stages of life.* San Francisco: Jossey-Bass, 1975.

McCullough, P. Launching children and moving on. In E. Carter and M. McGoldrick (eds.), *The family life cycle: A framework for family therapy.* New York: Gardner Press, 1980, pp. 171-197.

Maples, M. F. Dual career marriages: Elements for potential success. *Personnel and Guidance Journal,* 1981, *60,* 19-25.

Minuchin, S. *Families and family therapy.* Cambridge, Mass.: Harvard University Press, 1974.

Neugarten, B. L. (ed.) *Middle age and aging.* Chicago: University of Chicago Press, 1968.

Neugarten, B. L., & Weinstein, K. K. The changing American grandparent. *Journal of Marriage and the Family,* 1964, *26,* 199-204.

Okun, B. F., & Rappaport, L. J. *Working with families: An introduction to family therapy.* North Scituate, Mass.: Duxbury Press, 1980.

Robertson, J. F. Grandmotherhood: A study of role conceptions. *Journal of Marriage and the Family,* 1977, *38,* 165-174.

Rollins, B. C., & Cannon, K. C. Marital satisfaction over the life cycle: A reevaluation. *Journal of Marriage and the Family,* 1974, *36,* 271-283.

Rollins, B. C., & Feldman, H. Marital satisfaction over the life cycle. *Journal of Marriage and the Family,* 1970, *32,* 20-28.

Weltner, J. A structural approach to the single-parent family. *Family Process,* 1982, *21,* 203-211.

Wilkie, J. R. The trend toward delayed parenthood. *Journal of Marriage and the Family,* August 1981, *43,* 583-591.

CHAPTER NINE

CAREER DEVELOPMENT IN MIDDLE ADULTHOOD

Until fairly recently, the static view of adulthood was paralleled by a static view of vocational development. Adults had one career, characterized by stability, continuity, and advancement leading to retirement.

Millions of Americans have been inculcated with traditional career wisdom that says an individual needs to identify a career goal during adolescence or early adulthood and develop a long-range plan to achieve it. Anxiety, fear or guilt are common feelings of many people who have found their own career evolution to be incongruent with existing stereotypes of occupational choice and vocational adjustment. [Berman & Munson, 1981].

Such anxiety, fear, and guilt were seen as manifesting personal or family stress; career issues were considered as separate. Since early theories of vocational development postulated that young adulthood was a period of choice, entry, and establishment, middle adulthood and late adulthood were presumed to be periods of maintenance and stabilization in the vocational-development process (Isaacson, 1981; Zunker, 1981; Schein, 1978; Sarason et al., 1977; Super, 1977; Ginzberg, 1972).

However, our views of adult development have resulted in an understanding of the process as an ongoing one of change and growth, and recent vocational development theorists have come to recognize that occupational choice is a continuous process that lasts throughout the career development cycle. The "norm," therefore, is no longer a pattern of choosing an occupation or job in one's early twenties and remaining with it until retirement in one's sixties. Rather, people change careers, often in the middle years, and many such changes result from chance and experience rather than earlier choice. Sarason and colleagues (1977) suggest we interpose a *renewal stage* between Super's establishment and maintenance stages and Ginzberg (1972) refutes his earlier belief that occupational decision making is irreversible, although he still stresses the importance of early choices in the career-decision process.

Adults have decisions to make regarding their career development throughout the life cycle. These decisions include greater emphasis on actual experience, tried values, changing needs and proven occupational and interpersonal skills. Thus, as highlighted by Super (1977), career maturity in mid-career contains experience, attitude, and competence dimensions which were limited in youth when provisional decisions and choices were made. One's self-concept is continuously shaped by one's passages through life stages. Career decisions are also continuously shaped by this evolving self-concept.

The notions of change, growth, and flexibility within and among career paths are relatively new to career development theory. The established career theorists have not thoroughly researched or developed the aspects of their theories pertaining to middle and late adulthood. Social attitudes and economic variables have changed so rapidly and dramatically in such a short time that research and theory lags behind. As we learn more about cognitive development in adulthood, gender differences and biological factors, we will be able to learn more about adult career development.

Formerly, people who changed jobs or careers in mid-life were viewed suspiciously: "What is wrong with this person?" people asked. "He must be unstable if he wishes to make a change at his age."

In the past decade, the literature on mid-career change has grown as the phenomenon has become more normal in our society. Preretirement and retirement planning are also now accepted as significant developmental tasks. The implications are that career development is not static and that career satisfaction is inextricably interwoven with identity and intimacy issues and family life satisfaction. Obviously, we make our mid-life decisions from a different perspective than those we made earlier in life. Experience and cultural changes cannot be underestimated as major variables.

In this chapter, we will discuss the mid-life career reassessment, which involves consideration of realities versus expectations of late adolescence and early adulthood, and individual and family responsibilities and commitments. The next stage, the maintenance stage, involves the implementation of the decision arrived at in the mid-career assessment—for example, to maintain the status quo, to modify one's current career commitment, or to change fields altogether. Both internal and external variables contribute to this implementation. During the late-career stage, workers begin gradually to distance themselves from formal work and to prepare for a postemployment stage of life.

Some of the questions addressed in the chapter are these:

1. Are people who shift careers unstable?
2. Is it desirable to change careers in mid-life?
3. Do people's occupational interests and aptitudes change with time?
4. Is it too late to become successful after the age of 40?
5. Do most people have the same orientation to work in mid-life?
6. Are there gender issues in occupational development during middle adulthood?
7. Do older workers reduce their productivity?

MID-LIFE CAREER REASSESSMENT

We hear and read stories about the successful executive who gives up his lucrative job and moves to a rural community to whittle wood or run a country inn. Stories abound about the doctor or lawyer who leaves a successful private practice and affluent lifestyle to live out some persistent dream, such as playing a musical instrument or joining the Peace Corps or becoming devoted to public service. What prompts this behavior? Schein (1978) refers to the mid-career stage as "making it, leveling off, or starting over." This description summarizes the outcome of what, for some, will be an arduous reassessment process and, for others, a conscious choice to maintain the status quo. Or perhaps a basic reassessment takes place with moderate change resulting.

As we mentioned earlier, women and men entering their forties are likely to experience a transitional period of alternating depression and euphoria. Some of these people are aware of the career-related issues: their jobs no longer excite them; they feel trapped in dead-end jobs or careers; their expectations have remained unfulfilled; and they realize that they may not have made the best career choices twenty years earlier. At the same time, people are redefining who they are and what their relationship commitments are. They are often entering the adolescent stage of family life, and are therefore constantly engaged in confrontations regarding values and lifestyles. As their family roles change, their self-concepts may waver when they reconsider their personal, family, and occupational roles. Henton and her colleagues (1983) point out the significance of the wife's perceptions on male mid-life career change and the impact of these career changes on the family system. These impacts are important variables for career counselors to consider in aiding clients to understand the process of occupational decision making, assessing all the pertinent variables.

Consider the Burt family. They were referred for treatment after Don, the 17-year-old son, was caught shoplifting. The father, aged 42, was a moderately successful lawyer in a large firm. He did not expect to become a senior partner and was satisfied with his status within his firm. The mother had recently ventured out into the world of work, earning a real estate license. She thoroughly enjoyed her new occupation. Don was annoyed about being caught and resentful at the pressures he experienced from his parents about his misbehavior. The daughter, Dorothy, perceived the family problem as continuous arguing and tension between her parents.

As the therapist elicited each person's perception of the family issues, a major point kept surfacing. It seems that Dad had gone to law school straight from college at his parents' urging. He was groomed to be a wealthy, successful corporate lawyer. He was not particularly happy in law school, but he thought that no one liked the law school curriculum and that he would probably enjoy the practice of law better. When he graduated from law school, he practiced in a small firm for a couple of years, and then moved to a larger firm to make more money. He had married during law school and Don was on the way, so new living accommodations were necessary. Mom had not worked since she married. She had completed two years of college and had worked during vacations and summers. In any case, Dad found himself repelled by the politics of his law firm and turned off more and more to the practice and profession of law. However, he did not allow himself to acknowledge his disappointments, even to himself. He thought he "should" be happy, since he had everything he was supposed to want: a wife, two lovely children, a lovely home, vacations, and so on. His parents were thrilled with his upward mobility.

For the past few years, Dad had found himself feeling more and more depressed. His family had no idea that he was unhappy with his work. In fact, they considered him too wrapped up in it, as he always closeted himself off in his den at home and spent less and less time with them. After Mom went back to work, things really began to erupt in this family, and the kids felt trapped by the increasing bickering between their parents. The parents fought mainly over home and parenting responsibilities. Dad's career unhappiness was exacerbated every evening when Mom came home energized and glowing, thrilled with the happenings in her new, outside life. Not only was Dad alarmed at Mom's growing self-sufficiency, but he felt clear resentment that she liked what she was doing and had the chance to do what she wanted because she did not bear the full burden of providing for the family. But he also felt guilty about resenting Mom's "happiness," and thus retreated further into a silent shell. It was only when Don became a problem that the members of this family could get together to share their real feelings and concerns.

Once the validity and importance of Dad's career issues were acknowledged, he began consciously to reassess and discuss with Mom possible alternatives. She was delighted to be included again in Dad's life, and the tensions between the spouses decreased as their communication patterns became clearer and more direct. Don then felt freer to discuss his own issues—mainly, how frightened he was of "making a mistake that he would regret" in deciding which direction to pursue after high school graduation.

You could say that Don and his dad were going through many of the same developmental tasks and issues, albeit from different vantage points. At the same time, they were in the process of redefining their relationship as Don prepared to launch. Likewise, Mom's role change as she moved into the career world impacted upon the homeostasis of this family system, causing a disequilibrium that was manifested in Don's acting-out behaviors.

It is a premise of this book that work and career issues play a major part in one's mid-life transition. Changes may be voluntary or involuntary, but the reassessment process is, of necessity, multifaceted. The specific issues differ for men and women, and for white-collar and blue-collar workers. Men, for example, have been conditioned or socialized to equate their identities with their occupational successes so their redefinitions of self-identity during this transition often depend on attributes of achievement, power, and emotional involvements. Women, on the other hand, may now be able to choose a field that does not require the flexibility necessary for major parenting responsibilities, or they may need to reassess interests, skills, and needs in line with early adulthood life experiences in order to enter a new or different occupational field. Some studies have shown that blue-collar workers experience more involuntary mid-career changes than white-collar workers (Thomas, 1980). Whether or not the changes are voluntary or involuntary is a major factor.

Developmental Tasks

A major task of the mid-life career transition is the reassessment of one's occupational choices and roles in conjunction with one's individual and family choices, commitments, and roles. In Levinson and associates' (1976) terms, this means reappraising the dream of early adulthood, gauging the aspiration–achievement gap or the expectations–reality gap and deciding what to do about it.

One must deal with the strong influence that situational and nonpredictable factors have on both occupational choice and work environment. For example, a marked discontinuity may exist between what is perceived to be the "amorality" of the work world and a young idealist's expectations that the world of work will function by just and sensible rules (Baumgardner, 1977; Okun, 1970). One must contemplate contradictions in the environment by questioning, challenging, probing, and exploring whatever discontinuities exist. The restructuring that may result from this reappraisal can lead to compliance with the world-of-work morality (ethics and values), minor or major modifications of the person–work environment relationship, or change of job or job setting.

This reappraisal may or may not be a profound, turbulent, or stressful experience. Noticeable change may or may not result. Whatever the outcome, most adults do go through some process of questioning and reevaluation. For some, if the process proves to be too disturbing, they will make strong attempts to deny and block their uneasy feelings and to burrow deeper into the previously chosen lifestyles and occupational choices. Some such adults may develop a psychological or physiological symptom as a manifestation of repressed agonizing. Other outcomes may involve job or occupational change, priority change, expansive thinking and behavior, alienation of family or friends, or some other type of acting-out behavior.

For women just entering the world of work, the shift from the housewife/mother role requires a reappraisal of previously expressed occupational interests, earlier work experiences, studies, and plans. In some respects, reentry women start with a clean slate. Many studies have shown that the later occupational choices of women who have been out of the labor market to focus on homemaking are more heavily influenced by experiences and chance happenings during the homemaking period than by earlier occupational choices and working experiences (Okun, 1970).

Career reassessment.   The process of career reassessment occurs within the contexts of individual and family reassessment. A major preliminary task, then, is for one to focus on the balance of individual, family, and career roles and responsibilities. What are the satisfactions and dissatisfactions of these roles? Which seem to impinge on which the most? In other words, what are the current priorities and does one wish to modify or change them? Some men clearly find that their occupational roles have dominated their lives but, once having proven to themselves that they can achieve and be successful, they can change their priorities. Some women find that they have put their occupational roles on the back burner and that now is the time to give a higher priority to their career development. Other women find that they have experienced achievement and success in their career roles and can now focus on parenting and family development. An increasing number of successful career women are starting families in their late thirties and early forties (*Time,* February 15, 1982). Any changes in priorities will naturally affect other roles in one's life. Thus, a primary task is to determine the balance and allocation of one's energies and resources.

Leisure.   One significant resource-management task is the work/leisure relationship. Blocher and Siegal (1981) describe three kinds of leisure/work relationships that are psychologically relevant in career assessment:

1. Complimentary, in which the nature of work and personal relationships are associated in both a physical and social framework–for example, one's job allows activities such as conventions in resort areas, or travel for airline employees;
2. Supplementary, in which leisure rounds out the work involvement, creating a balance of fulfillments and satisfactions that are not necessarily related–for example, the teacher who values the long vacations that allow leisure pursuits;
3. Compensatory, in which the leisure activities provide escape or alleviate stresses or tensions built into family life or work–for example, the person who needs the thrill of sailing races or regular competitive tennis games as an outlet for stress or tension.

By mid-life, one has become more acutely aware of one's leisure interests and possibilities and one's changing time perspective dictates that one must actively include these leisure activities in one's lifestyle rather than put them off until one becomes more settled. Thus, people are more likely to consider leisure activities based on experience during this reassessment period than they were in late adolescence and early adulthood.

Leisure priorities become more important during mid-life as one's time perspectives and values change. One often hears "I need to learn how to be good to myself" from mid-life adults who have been task-focused in order to establish themselves in the adult world. The idea that fun and leisure are acceptable, legitimate, and necessary pursuits is often a new, suspicious dimension.

Self-assessment.   Along with the reassessment of priorities comes the reassessment of one's strengths and weaknesses and values in one's chosen field. This new look is based on fifteen to twenty years of actual work experience, as opposed to the test predictions and academic interests of early adulthood. Now is the time to evaluate the expectations–reality gap and the aspiration–achievement gap. Did the occupational choice provide the achievement and lifestyle expected? Did the nature of the actual job prove to be as expected and desired? What has the fit been between one's maturing adult values and the actual work experience? Are one's dissatisfactions associated with the field of occupational choice, the actual job, or, perhaps, another area of life? How well does one feel able to meet the changing job requirements? Do younger people in the field seem better trained and more competent? If one could live one's life over and make a different career choice, what would it be? What behavior is necessary for overcoming identifiable weaknesses? How realistic is one's self-assessment? Does it correlate with job reviews and other feedback? What are the changing interests, values, and needs one is experiencing that might indicate a change is necessary in occupational choice and/or lifestyle? Is one frightened by change or is change welcomed as a challenging opportunity?

Self-assessment includes dealing with one's time perspective, attempting to determine how one's skills and interests can be utilized in the future, and evaluation of the organizational context within which one works. This latter variable is often overlooked by people undergoing this type of reassessment, and Schein (1978) points out that the organization's needs and policies are important in assessing future probabilities and opportunities for any employee.

Often, an individual finds that he or she likes his or her type of work and actual job but that an organizational change is necessary to enhance job satisfaction. How a particular individual will fit into any organization requires knowledge of self as well as knowledge of the organizational variables.

Dan, aged 41, found that he was devoting so much of his work time to the organizational politics necessary for survival that his actual involvement in accounting, which was his primary occupational choice and the source of his occupational satisfaction, had shrunk to less than 20 percent of his time and energies. In moving from a large, multinational firm to a smaller, regional firm, he found his occupational satisfaction increasing and his stress symptoms fading. He did not change fields, but changed organizational contexts. Moreover, the self-awareness that Dan gained in assessing his expectations, roles, and behavior within a large, closed-system organization enabled him to view his family system from a different perspective and be more flexible in his roles and behaviors within that family system. He would find himself taking the role of "opposer" so frequently at work that he became stuck, and automatically transferred that role to his family, thus escalating the tension that already existed at home during the adolescent stage of family development.

John, aged 40, on the other hand, found that as much as he loved the practice of pediatrics, it was taking him away from his family too much and that he had no time or energy left for any avocations or relationships. When he realized that his marriage of 18 years was in serious jeopardy, he decided to undergo a residency in child psychiatry. His rationale was that he would be able to devote more time and energy to his wife and children and to developing his own avocational interests, since private practice in psychiatry would allow him to regulate his hours and would not require night and weekend emergency calls.

One's values in mid-life are not necessarily similar to those held in earlier life. The meaning of life, work, and family becomes clearer now, and one's mid-life interiority allows one to incorporate these evolving values into one's reassessment and decision-making processes. In other words, the inputs into the decision-making process originate in a different perspective in mid-life from that of earlier adulthood, one that is perhaps more individuated than accommodating environmentally induced expectations.

Career anchors.   Schein (1978) postulates five categories of career anchors that men can use to reassess their career issues. The career anchor serves to guide, constrain, stabilize, and integrate a person's career and consists of the interaction of one's abilities, motives, values, and self-concept. Since much of this reassessment is based on one's actual life and career experiences, it is unlikely that one would be able to become truly aware of one's career anchor before mid-life. Thus, career anchors reflect one's underlying needs or motives and one's values and discovered talents based on the experiences of early adulthood. "It is the process of integrating into the total self-concept what one sees oneself to be more or less competent at, wanting out of life, one's value system and the kind of person one is that begins to determine the major life and occupational choices throughout adulthood" (Schein, 1978).

Career anchors, therefore, consist of evolution, development, and discovery through actual experiences of the following:

1. Self-perceived talents and abilities based on actual successes in a variety of work settings;
2. Self-perceived motives and needs based on opportunities for self-tests and self-diagnosis in real-life situations and on feedback from others;
3. Self-perceived attitudes and values based on actual encounters between self and the norms and values of the employing organization and work setting.

The five categories of career anchors that Schein identifies are these:

1. Technical/functional competence—this person enjoys the performance of the task (as Dan, for example, enjoyed the tasks of accounting) and prefers

to devote the majority of his or her energy to those areas of competence, avoiding general management;

2. Managerial competence—this person has the analytical, interpersonal, and emotional competence to manage people and projects effectively and strives toward such a position;

3. Security/stability—this person has learned that he or she needs the security and stability of a safe, known job within a safe, known organization and considers those elements top priorities. Thus, this person would be unlikely to take risks with an unknown venture;

4. Creativity—this person needs the opportunity to try new things and develop his or her own ideas, and would, therefore, avoid employment in a setting that did not encourage and allow for creativity;

5. Autonomy/independence—this person has learned that he or she likes to be his or her own boss and to have control over what he or she does and when; this person is more likely to develop his or her own business rather than work for someone else or to pick a profession or freelance occupation where he or she can retain control.

We do not put a value of good or bad on any one of these career anchors. They are categories that allow one to recognize one's self and to help one make meaningful choices. Each individual must take responsibility for his or her criteria of satisfaction. In other words, if an individual chooses what someone else considers a "safe way out," that is the individual's right as long as he or she takes responsibility for that choice and its consequences. The most productive approach is to consider all possible options. These choices require a realistic assessment of the implications for the future of one's career anchor. Not everyone will be able to make a choice in full accordance with one's anchor—limited mid-career opportunities are forecast for the next decade and compromises may be necessitated by economic and employment-reality variables.

Specialization versus generalization.   The example of John above illustrated that one of the components of reassessment involves the issue of specialization, which leads to the focusing of one's contribution, versus remaining a generalist. Either choice requires the consideration of both internal and external factors—namely the awareness of one's career anchor and of the organizational or professional opportunities. Within each of the career anchors, it is possible to be either a specialist or a generalist. The labor market changes, in that generalists are in high demand during an expanding market and specialists appear to be in high demand during a declining market.

Mentoring relationships.   Both Levinson (1978) and Schein (1978) have referred to the importance of mentoring in career development. One of the developmental tasks of the mid-thirties transition involves transition from being mentored to accepting the responsibilities of mentoring. This shift involves, first, accepting that one is no longer the learner, the rising young star, but an established member of the occupation. Some people have difficulty accepting this responsibility and attempt to avoid it. Schein (1978, p.178) points out that a variety of mentoring roles exists and that the mid-career person must avoid getting trapped into mentoring relationships that do not fit his or her needs or talents. The varieties of mentoring roles identified by Schein (1978, pp.178–179) are these:

1. Mentor as teacher, coach, or trainer—a person about whom the younger person would say "That person taught me a lot about how to do things around here."
2. Mentor as a positive role model—a person about whom the younger person would say "I learned a lot from watching that person in operation; that person really set a good example of how to get things done."
3. Mentor as a developer of talent—a person about whom the younger person would say "That person really gave me challenging work from which I learned a great deal; I was pushed along and forced to stretch myself."
4. Mentor as an opener of doors—a person who makes sure that the young person is given opportunities for challenging and growth-producing assignments and who fights "upstairs" for the younger person, whether or not the younger person is aware of it.
5. Mentor as a protector (mother hen)—a person about whom the younger person would say "That person watched over me and protected me while I learned; I could make mistakes and learn without risking my job."
6. Mentor as a sponsor—a person who gives visibility to his or her "protégés," who makes sure that they have "good press" and are given exposure to high-level people so they will be remembered when new opportunities come along, with or without the awareness of the younger person.
7. Mentor as a successful leader—a person whose own success ensures that his or her supporters will "ride along on his or her coattails," and who brings these people along.

Schein points out that the teacher, role model, and developer roles do not require a high formal position or power but are, nevertheless, as powerful as the "godfather" role.

The research on mentors has focused on their work-related characteristics. It does not address the power of the mentor's values and moral integrity as a person, apart from his or her occupational role, to affect the mentee. Conceivably, some dissonance could exist that might affect the choice and course of a mentoring relationship. Or, such dissonance might be an ingredient in the mid-life renegotiation of the mentoring relationship.

Referring to Erikson's concept of generativity, it is important to remember that mentoring can fulfill an important psychological need for people who have leveled off or wish to share their learning and experience while they themselves continue to develop and grow.

Decision making.   The outcome of the mid-career reassessment will result from a decision-making process. Super (1977) points to the use of decision-making skills in the past as an index of the degree of skill in the present. Past decisions may have been faulty in terms of impulse control, rationality, the ability to consider many options, information processing, and so on. Super highlights the processes of planfulness, exploration, and information checking as important components of decision making. Thus, people often need help in learning how to develop and utilize effective decision-making skills. They may fail to realize that they have not collected enough information to make a valid decision, or that they have neglected key areas or variables, whether relating to self-assessment, accurate occupational information, or knowledge of the world of work. To make a choice—even if the choice is to make no change—one must integrate one's reassessment into the behavior that reflects one's individual and family development. The kinds of questions one needs to ask oneself, in addition to those involving the interrelationship of individual, family, and occupational roles and responsibilities, include the following:

1. How can I remain competent or learn new marketable skills?
2. How can I develop interpersonal or group skills if needed?
3. How can I develop supervisory or managerial skills if needed?
4. How can I function in a political environment from a mid-life position?
5. How can I deal with the competitiveness and aggressiveness of younger people on the way up?
6. How can I enter a new field?
7. How can I maintain a positive growth-oriented outlook?
8. How can I use learnings from past experiences to enhance my functioning in the present?

Lowther (1977) has cited several motivating forces that result in mid-career change:

1. Mid-life crises;
2. Changing social worth of occupations;
3. Changing career options within and outside fields;
4. Belief that work should be stimulating and provocative;
5. Discrepancies between expectations and realities;
6. Changing attitudes about the work ethic;
7. Changing values on leisure activities leading to a desire for less time-consuming careers;
8. Trade mastery leading to job boredom and dissatisfaction;
9. Trying to get into what had been an earlier first choice;
10. Effect of women entering or reentering the market;
11. Dead-end syndrome;
12. Early retirement;
13. External forces such as obsolescence, being fired, or being laid off in a declining economy.

These forces are either voluntary or involuntary, internal or external. Those that are anticipated tend to bring less distress than those that are unanticipated. And the amount of distress tolerated is related more to the intrinsic satisfactions of the outcome than to the pain of the decision-making process. Armstrong (1981) found a significant relationship between the pattern of decision making and the career-change goal. The more one wanted to satisfy goals rather than optimize opportunities, the more successful was the career change. In other words, personal goals are given higher priority than external opportunities. Leonards (1981) points out how important it is to prevent fear from leading to hastily concocted and immature decisions, such as taking the first job offered after being laid off from work. As Sheehy (1981) suggests, unexpected crises can result in a rational decision-making process—in which all the variables are considered and the effort is made to collect as much realistic information as possible—leading to "pathfinding" decisions that result in higher degrees of satisfaction than heretofore attained.

Zunker (1981) cites the motivational drives of the unfulfilled worker searching for autonomy, challenge, and meaning in work:

1. Change to a higher order of needs and a subsequent restructuring of the goals set at the time of the original career commitment;
2. Recognition of the disparity between the current work content and the reformulated goals;
3. A lack of conformity between personal goals and the organization's or employer's policies and goals;
4. The recognition of a disparity between self-perceived abilities and the utilization of these abilities in the current work environment;
5. A feeling of isolation resulting from the lack of conformity with the goals and values of peer affiliates or the informal organization;
6. A failure to achieve a sense of accomplishment from past work and future prospects.

These motivational drives surface during the period of reassessment, helping one to identify a career anchor and engage in a concrete decision-making process.

Developmental Issues

The kinds of issues one confronts during this process of reassessment are often the result of the impact of internal and external variables. Let us consider those not already discussed.

Values conflicts. Cultural changes involving attitudes toward life, work, leisure, and family may affect one's traditional values in all spheres of life. Contradictions in these values may surface during the adolescent stage of family development when one is confronted by the current youth culture's values. For example, as previously mentioned, a discontinuity may exist between personal morality and the morality of the work place, just as discontinuity may exist between the values of an individual and a system (family, school, work, or community). In the late 1960s and early 1970s, the values of many parents were challenged by their adolescents' countercultural involvements. These challenges influenced career-related decisions, for people were forced to acknowledge possible discrepancies between personal and systems' values. Thus, one who has given achievement the highest priority may, after such a values clash, recognize the associated costs and, upon making a values clarification, shift priorities. This shift, in turn, might result in a choice to reap the benefits of work in order to pursue family or leisure pursuits. Or, one may have a strong orientation to following a single career and find that as a new career anchor emerges, a change is suggested. As one goes through this process, considering second and even third careers is no longer unusual, although by no means are multiple careers necessary or more or less desirable than a single career path.

Sex discrimination.   Covert and overt sex discrimination may impact the mid-career assessment for women, both those just entering the labor market and those who have always been employed. Women who are entering the labor market may find certain jobs or fields closed to them because of stereotyped attitudes. Traditional, feminine occupations (teaching, social work, library science) may be closed because of declining opportunities. The federal government has piloted several training programs for displaced homemakers and women reentering the labor market to break down these barriers, hoping to train women for nontraditional careers and to reduce sex-role stereotyping as it affects women in general and, more specifically, women in the work force.

Kanter (1976) shows that in organizations in which the sex ratio is skewed and where women in management or professions are alone, or nearly alone, in a peer group of men, these women are likely to face social isolation, heightened visibility, "mistaken identity," and continued pressure to adopt stereotyped roles. Thus, they are likely to do less well than others in the group, especially if the leader is male, and they are therefore subject to mental and physical stress. And women in mid-life often find the sex discrimination more overt than younger women, perhaps due to their decreasing physical and sexual attractiveness and to the high value society places on young women. Society's expectations of middle-aged women differ from those of younger women. And women who have risen to management levels are perceived as particularly threatening by men who are leveling off or who have failed to realize their dreams and aspirations.

Myths about "menopausal" women prevail—such women are seen as unstable, "bitchy," and castrating. How a woman perceives herself will affect how she deals with these issues. It is not uncommon for a woman's suppressed rage at previous discriminations to erupt during this period if she perceives unfair and impenetrable barriers in her way. It is as if the accumulation of obstacles over the years suddenly takes its toll.

The lack of role models and support within professions and organizations does not make sex-role issues any easier to deal with. Because most mentors are men, women in management and professions are currently attempting to develop networks, to create "old girl clubs," to provide support and encouragement, and to help other women overcome these obstacles.

Cytrynbaum and his colleagues (1980) found that:

1. Gender stereotyping and devaluation of women in managerial positions (they are seen as very powerful and intimidating) are defensive mechanisms to protect subordinates from perceived authority threats.
2. During particularly stressful periods, both men and women seem to prefer a male to a female authority, owing to the defensive belief that women are more vulnerable than men during times of pressure, tension, and stress.
3. Structural components in the organization itself contribute greatly to the overall devaluation of women and to the difficulties experienced by women in authority.

The fact that women in positions of authority elicit different responses in subordinates, both male and female, than do male authority figures is also related to the powerful impact of the mother/child relationship in one's family of origin—that is, to the natural conflict between nurturing and power.

It is during the mid-career reassessment that many women in positions of authority reappraise their emotional competencies and their stress-management capacities in conjunction with their individual and family roles. For some, the attainment of authority has provided fulfillment of their aspirations, and they can then elect to relieve themselves of the concomitant conflicts and choose different types or styles of career functioning. Others find themselves challenged and energized by the conflicts and are determined to work through them. One's actual experiences of sex-role conflicts are a necessary part of the reassessment processes.

Declining or changing economy.   A declining economy is most likely to result in more limited mid-career shifting along with a minimal growth of new opportunities. Thus, there may be a large number of middle-aged workers with reduced mobility, who desire to change but are unable to find changes they can afford to make. Particularly when large numbers of public-sector employees seek private-sector jobs as public funds diminish, the competition for the available openings increases. Inflation makes it difficult for people with mortgages and family responsibilities to absorb salary cuts or to invest in their own businesses. Thus, just keeping up with the annual increase in the cost of living becomes a chronic struggle. The upshot may be a limit in risk taking, a heightening of stress and depression, and a radical alteration of family plans—for example, deciding, after a lifetime of planning, to forego higher education for the children.

A declining economy increases the number of involuntary changes made, such as firings and layoffs. Reduced unemployment insurance and social security benefits result in heightened anxieties and stress symptoms as families struggle to keep their heads above water. Increasingly, white-collar and professional workers are finding themselves the victims of such pressures. Many, never having foreseen that such an event would affect them personally, are totally unprepared, and they panic. Stress is also experienced by those who stay employed while colleagues get laid off and by those who have to do the actual firing or laying off.

The lack of available career counseling and out-placement services for adults heightens fears. This stress can spill over into every aspect of life and can require medical and psychological crisis intervention. Such stress seems to have the gravest impact in the middle years—when financial responsibilities and commitments are at their peak and when age discrimination in the job market is more of a reality.

Obsolescence.   Technological and economic changes can increase the possibility of obsolescence occurring in one's chosen field of work. Narrowly specialized workers may find themselves replaceable, with no transferable marketable skills. And those who have been generalists may find themselves replaced by specialists. The realities of the world of work may conflict with personal goals and desires.

The issues of retraining and retrenchment are difficult, owing to cost and support requirements. Unlike European countries and Japan, in the United States access to and resources for education and new employment opportunities are limited for workers. Often, workers must subordinate or relinquish their personal goals to take any job that will provide enough income to meet the pressing needs of family members. The natural results are resentment, bitterness, and depression, which affect all areas of life.

Many organizations are now taking the time and trouble to develop career-path approaches for employees to reduce the impact of obsolescence. Concepts of flexibility and transferability have gained importance in career development. We cannot predict the number or types of new jobs that will be required in the coming decades. We can predict, however, that a flexible and adaptive work force will be needed to meet emerging needs. Therefore, accurate occupational information must be readily available to new and current workers so that they may prepare for inevitable changes.

Credentialing.   We are finding that along with a declining economy and obsolescence, an increasingly complex occupational and professional certification process is emerging that often requires higher than necessary credentials for particular positions or occupations. A union card is such a credential; another example is the requirement that an accountant be a certified public accountant in order to work in a given firm. This overcredentialing can be particularly unnerving for the middle-aged worker who perceives younger people as being more highly trained and highly credentialed. It is difficult to balance experience against credentialed training, and middle-aged workers who are encouraged to continue their training and to obtain higher credentials may encounter difficulties, as cost and time requirements may be prohibitive. The issue of credentialing, then, may influence the types of choices open to those who desire to make career shifts. The changes and demands of existing and emerging careers may indeed seem overwhelming to people already committed to family and financial responsibilities.

The issues discussed here are those that typically affect middle-aged adults in their mid-career reassessment tasks. Once the reassessment process has resulted in a decision, the next stage begins, that in which the resulting decision is implemented. Table 9-1 summarizes the tasks and issues associated with the mid-career reassessment.

TABLE 9-1.   Mid-career reassessment

Developmental Tasks	General Issues	Requisite Skills	Significant Others
Reassess the career: self-assessment regarding on-the-job functioning, skills, needs, interests, aptitudes; aspiration– achievement gaps; recognition of career anchors; values reassessment; occupation assessment; world-of-work assessment Reassess personal/family/career boundaries	Specialization/ generalization Mentoring relationships Mid-life crises Changing social/cultural values Sex discrimination Ageism Economy Realistic opportunities Obsolescence Credentialing	Data collecting Assessing Planning Decision making Risk taking Mentoring	Peers/colleagues Supervisors Supervisees Career counselors Mentors/models Spouse Friends

MAINTENANCE

The term *maintenance* refers to that period following mid-career reassessment and preceding the late-career period, which usually begins in the fifties. The ages associated with the maintenance stage, approximately 45–55, bridge the latter part of what Buhler (1968) calls the culmination stage and the early part of decline and disengagement. Maintenance refers either to the earlier career decisions that may have been reaffirmed during the mid-career reassessment or to the establishment and development of a new career that resulted from a mid-career shift. Maintenance represents the highest level of occupational activity and may be accompanied by feelings of accomplishment or resignation, and high or low self-esteem. Thus, maintenance involves attaining full membership as an individual contributor to one's chosen field of work, perhaps as a manager, technical specialist, or generalist. One might say that this period represents a plateau—whereas some may rise higher into senior leadership roles, most are settling into their peak and are finding new ways to develop and enjoy what they are doing and what they have attained. People at this stage are more present-time than future-time oriented. They seem to be more realistic about their possibilities for further development within the hierarchy of their professions or organizations. Likewise, some people become "deadwood" during this stage, putting no energy into renewal and continued development and waiting it out until retirement.

Naturally, both satisfactions and frustrations characterize this stage, and individuals will perceive and respond to them differently. Super (1957) points out that the term maintenance does not necessarily imply constancy, but

. . . that perfect equilibrium is never reached, that vocational adjustment is a continuous process throughout the whole of life and that even the maintenance stage is not, as the name may be thought to imply, a period of undiluted enjoyment of the fruits of labor. Instead, the labor continues, although perhaps somewhat less arduously because its pattern is by now well established [p.149].

Developmental Tasks

The major task of this stage is to implement the decision made in the mid-career assessment, whether it be reaffirmation of an earlier choice, modification of such a choice, or entry into a new career.

Implementation.   Implementation involves a rebalancing of personal, family, and career commitments. If one is entering a new field, it is to be hoped that one is able to use past experience in the establishment process and to pass quickly through the entry-level phase. If one has chosen to focus on a particular specialization within one's chosen field, one will do what one needs to attain the technical competencies and the necessary credentials. Some people may choose to remain unchanged, and implementation will thus involve affirming this decision. One never really goes back to the first establishment period, even in a new or slightly different occupational field, for one brings the learnings and experiences of the twenties and thirties into the new field or specialization.

Very important to the implementation task is what Super (1977) refers to as *reality orientation.* This orientation requires that the individual has checked out all possible obstacles and facilitating factors during the decision-making phase and is continuing to assess these factors during the implementation process to stay fully aware of changing conditions. Often the "rules of the game" are different by the time of implementation from those that applied during the decision-making time. Thus, it is important for people to check out their interpretations of the realities of work in order not to be misled by misperceptions and misinterpretations. Consider the following example.

A 44-year-old college counselor, Ian, gave up a tenured position to enter private practice full time, believing he would double his income and be able to send his two children through the colleges of their choice. He had never had difficulty maintaining five or six private clients during his years in a salaried position and he figured that he would have no difficulty finding twenty clients per week. What he had not foreseen, or considered possible, were the changes in state licensing requirements and the increasing competition from other practitioners. In fact, Ian was unable to find more than twelve steady private clients in any given week, and, in addition to experiencing unexpected financial strain, he began to experience dissonance as he found himself hanging on to clients longer than necessary in order to meet his basic financial needs. Clearly, Ian failed to check out what steps would be necessary to develop and maintain a private practice; he assumed that the practice "would automatically occur."

Another important reality factor is how a career shift might affect personal and family relationships (as well as financial commitments).

Mr. and Mrs. Shortman found themselves experiencing serious marital stress after Mr. Shortman decided to leave a secure, high-paying engineering job to establish his own firm. While working for the large firm, Mr. Shortman's hours had been relatively stable, and he had spent evening and weekend hours with his family and pursuing hobbies and working around the house. Mr. Shortman's mid-career assessment convinced him that his career anchor was autonomy/independence and that he could meet his unfulfilled needs by working for himself. Mrs. Shortman was reluctant to give up the financial security that the salaried job provided, but supported her husband's decision. What she had not realized, and what Mr. Shortman had neglected to consider adequately, was that the establishment of a new business would require most of his time and energy. No longer was there time for customary recreation, leisure, or vacations. Mr. Shortman was thrilled with his new business and totally absorbed.

During this time, Mrs. Shortman became first depressed and then angry. After two years, she decided that she was "too old to wait around" for things to change and perhaps balance out, and she deliberately immersed herself in her own activities and relationships, which only drove the couple further apart. The next year, she left her husband. After the separation, Mr. Shortman developed hypertension and began to feel depressed. He withdrew further and further into his business and gradually lost contact with his children or anyone associated with his former life. While his mid-career shift worked out to his career satisfaction, he was angry that he had to lose his family.

Power and responsibility.   Although some people peak in terms of levels of power and responsibility in early adulthood, many reach their peak during middle adulthood. As Schein (1978) points out, when one reaches one's peak of occupational development, one has usually reached the highest levels of power and responsibility in one's work. Success in these areas is relative, of course, but it may involve learning to deal with high-level and sensitive political situations both inside and outside the organizational context. Thus, stress may reach its highest level just when power and responsibility peak and a capacity for stress management must be developed and refined. These years may also require that one grow more sensitive in interpersonal relationships as one further develops as a mentor or supervisor. At this time, one is called upon to develop necessary supervisory, management, and political skills to differentiate between emotions and intellect, and to implement strategies for coping with internal and external stresses.

Continuing education and career development.   If one is to avoid stagnation, it is necessary to keep abreast of new developments and competencies in one's chosen field. Such involvement requires one to actively seek and follow through on what is necessary. The drive for renewal and continuing development comes from within, not from without, and the attitudes of a worker reflect his or her self-concept and life goals.

Rebalancing personal resources and energies.   Remaining aware of changing personal energies and resources and reallocating them to one's advantage require continuous self-monitoring. One must recognize and acknowledge physio-logical and energy-level changes and accommodate one's desires, goals, and activ-ities accordingly. One can, for example, begin to think of ways to transfer inter-ests and capabilities to the community in order to feel generativity and a sense of self-worth or, say, to foster a younger adult's development rather than to drive oneself harder and harder.

Accepting a reduction in influence and challenge.   If the mid-career deci-sion is to level off and seek gratification and growth outside one's work, it is necessary to accept the consequences of this decision. Such acceptance may result in more enjoyment of work, a reduction in the intrinsic and extrinsic re-wards one derives from the work situation, and a reduction of power, status, and stimulation in the work place. Many people who decide to diminish their work priority continue to be valuable contributors at work, but they have transferred their priorities and find renewal from their outside interests and activities, which can serve to enhance their performance at work.

Developmental Issues

Let us now consider the issues that affect the tasks just discussed.

Organizational values.   Workers in organizational systems and members of established professions must meet certain expectations to be fully established members. These expectations involve inclusion into a hierarchical subsystem. Thus, one is expected to become more responsible for organizational welfare, and less concerned with one's personal welfare. In other words, one's contributions are to be made in the interest of the welfare of the organization or profession, and one is expected to be particularly sensitive to the role of the organization or profession in society. Thus, an established worker becomes more closely identi-fied with the organization or profession at this time. Figuratively speaking, he or she has passed through the initiation rites and is now given full membership responsibilities and privileges. With seniority come certain privileges, responsibil-ities, and explicit expectations. Workers who are unable to accept organizational or professional values have usually left or drifted into a "deadwood" role by this time. By the time one is in the forties or fifties, one is expected to remain with the firm or profession. Stability and endurance are expected and considered to repre-sent the worker's acceptance of the organizational and professional value systems.

External crisis.   As mentioned above, in a declining economy, anyone at any age or work level may be suddenly laid off. When the victim is someone who has made a long-term and long-range commitment to a particular organization or profession, the resulting predicament is particularly painful and disrupting, both to the individual and his or her family. Often workers feel that they have invested a large portion of their lives in a particular organization or profession. When they find out that the loyalty and investment is not returned, they feel anger, betrayal, and bitterness, much as if they had been rejected and abandoned by a spouse.

Further, people who have failed to achieve a satisfactory level of self-differentiation have usually failed, too, to prepare for such an event and have reserved no options or resources for such emergencies. The meaning of their lives is then taken away and it is hard for them to recover from this loss. It is clear that one's personal issues of individuation and independency/dependency affect one's ability to deal with external crises that may occur during this phase of development. Likewise, the capacities of the family system to cope with crisis and adversity influence the individual's coping capacity at this time and vice versa.

Changing physical, mental, and emotional resources.   Health and physical changes certainly affect individual work choices and performance. For example, someone might find him- or herself tiring more from extensive travel and might need to change jobs in order to spend more time at home than on the road. Others might find that teaching and supervising are more suited to their mid-life stamina than actually practicing their profession.

The realities of middle age are important considerations where work management is concerned. Athletes, for example, know that they must choose a second career during mid-life, and some prepare themselves to do this while others remain oblivious. Many people fail to anticipate the effects of aging on work performance. Therefore, they are surprised and caught off guard when they first begin to experience these effects. Some feel trapped and unable to make a job change. They become dependent upon "medical excuses" for changing their ways of work.

Sex-role issues.   For men and women who have always been part of the work force during adulthood, the sex-role differences may appear to diminish during this stage of career development. For women who have reentered the work force within the past decade, however, sex-role issues may be quite prevalent as they seek to "catch up" with their male counterparts and to ascertain how much they will be able to develop before they reach the retirement stage. In other words, as men begin to rebalance their energies and plan to transfer work satisfactions to other areas of their lives, women who have recently become workers are readying themselves to go "full speed ahead" and may be more preoccupied with their occupational roles than men who have lived with their occupational roles for several more decades.

Many women find that the interpersonal and management skills they developed during their homemaking years have prepared them to make unique contributions to their chosen fields of work. Real estate sales is an example of the type of occupation that homemakers are able to enter successfully, transferring their skills and knowledge from earlier roles and responsibilities. As there is no motivating force like success, these women bring as much enthusiasm, excitement, and energy to their work in their fifties as men did in their twenties and thirties. Thus, it seems safe to say that women may be putting more energies into work than men at this time.

Table 9-2 summarizes the tasks and issues of the maintenance stage of career development. This stage leads into the late-career stage, which is a preparation for deceleration and disengagement from the preoccupation with work.

TABLE 9-2. Maintenance

Developmental Tasks	General Issues	Requisite Skills	Significant Others
Implement the mid-career reassessment decision: reality assessment; power and responsibility acceptance; stress management	Organizational values Professional values External crises Changing physical, mental, and emotional resources Sex role issues	Stress managing Supervising/managing Organizational/political Interpersonal Assessing Implementing	Colleagues/peers Spouse Friends Supervisees Offspring Community
Continue education and training			
Rebalance personal resources and energies			
Accept changing influences and challenges			

LATE CAREER

Late career is the period of the fifties and early sixties. The two major tasks here are gradual deceleration and preretirement planning. Obviously, different people start these processes at different ages, and some never start at all. However, societal pressures to make preretirement plans have highlighted the necessity for preparing for this approaching major transition.

Developmental Tasks

Deceleration.   The process of deceleration involves a gradual distancing from one's job and requires acquiring a new perspective about the meaning of work in one's life. Even someone at his or her peak in terms of responsibility and status can be aware that time is definitely limited and that retirement is around the corner. Owing to declining energies, the continued participation of people at this stage in both occupational and social spheres may become increasingly limited. How family and other relationships are renegotiated at this point will affect the ability to renegotiate occupational roles and commitments.

Deceleration leads to disengagement. This does not mean pulling away from work or lessening productivity during the fifties and early sixties; in fact, these years might see one's greatest contributions and productivity. However, one now begins to consider other ways of defining one's identity, learning to envision and prepare to manage a life that is or will become less dominated by work. Such preparation might involve finding new sources of satisfaction in hobbies, family, social, leisure, community, and political activities. It may involve using work competencies in performing independent consulting, free-lance assignments, or volunteer work. Chiriboga (1975, p.98) found that "getting rid of unwanted duties and obligations and settling for ease and contentment . . . as a way of life may represent one of the major tasks" for preretirement adults. For some, the processes of deceleration and disengagement will include learning to accept reduced levels of power, responsibility, and centrality, and to accept and develop new roles based on declining competence and motivation. A key variable here seems to be "control." The worker who feels in charge of the disengagement process can turn it into an enhancing, positive experience, in contrast to the worker who feels controlled and defeated by the aging process and the changing needs of the occupation.

Preretirement planning.   As with any other major transition, anticipation and preparation help to ease the disruption that accompanies preretirement planning. Retirement is a major transition that affects many aspects of life. Status, role, position in life, and one's reference group will all change. In society, retirement as a role is unclear, and one has little guidance in forming expectations and rules. For some, retirement is equated with death; it is feared and avoided, particularly if formal work is the primary focus in life. For others, retirement is regarded as a challenge, a time to develop heretofore untried interests and activities. One's success at entering and leaving other family systems in one's life cycle, and in dealing with inclusion, exclusion, and loss, will determine how well one can begin to disengage and plan for retirement.

George (1980) points out that retirement is an event (the end of formal work), a role (involving behavioral expectations), and a process (involving the recognition, negotiation, and resolution of the consequences of retirement). Preretirement consists of two phases, remote and near, which are characterized by anticipation and planning respectively (Atchley, 1976). Much attention has been paid to such anticipation and planning in recent years.

In the prevailing weak economy, a surplus of workers exists relative to the positions available. An interesting double bind is the direct result. Several years ago, the federal government (in the 1967 Age Discrimination in Employment Act) outlawed mandatory retirement at age 65 in certain areas because Americans were living longer than ever before and, as work is socially and often economically desirable, it was necessary to reduce age discrimination. Now, however, if all the workers choose to stay on in their jobs until they are 70, there will be a huge increase of unemployed and underutilized workers in early and mid-adulthood. Some of these younger workers may, in fact, be better trained and qualified and more highly motivated than some of the older workers. Nowhere is this double bind better illustrated than in American universities and colleges. As tenured positions dry up and student enrollments decline, faculties are characteristically composed of older professors who received tenure long ago (often under outdated criteria). Thus, in the late 1980s, the average age of most university and college professors will be the late fifties. The result will be that students will fail to be exposed to the varying perspectives and role modeling that faculties with a wider age range would provide.

Inflation naturally affects retirement plans. With cost-of-living increases eroding savings and downgrading pensions, many retirement programs are no longer realistic. Although social security pensions now have a built in cost-of-living increase, most private pension plans do not. Therefore, although most people might prefer earlier retirement, many feel unable to afford it. Yet many fields are glutted with workers, and simply do not need the large numbers of older workers attempting to retain their jobs. Some organizations are offering attractive early-retirement incentives—at 50 percent, say, of regular salaries, hoping to reduce their payroll and staff in that way rather than through forced layoffs. Workers, on their part, seem to prefer earlier retirement, but must grapple with realistic concerns about financial solvency. Because of these uncertainties and rapidly changing societal and economic factors, it becomes imperative for people in their fifties to begin thinking about and specifically planning for their retirement in order to retain some control over their destinies.

Determining the meaning of retirement is the first primary task. To perform it, one must become aware of one's particular orientation and attitudes toward work. Before one can begin to plan for retirement, one must reappraise its meaning and decide on some retirement goals. What are the myths and experiences I associate with retirement? one must ask oneself. What are the resources and supports available in my organization to help me develop my skills and competencies for use in my retirement? And, in addition to the necessary financial requirements, one needs to consider the interpersonal support systems that will facilitate later retirement—for example, one's intimate relationships, family unit, reference groups, and friends network. What kinds of health facilities will be required and what kind of physical setting (with respect to climate, location, neighborhood, living arrangements, opportunities for part-time or volunteer work) can be planned for? In general, the types of questions that people need to consider as they assess their lives to date and prepare for retirement include: What should I do now and after retirement to be useful? to help others? to have friends? to stay mentally alert? to keep healthy and physically active? to relax? to have a good family life and to be able to afford to live in the style I choose?

Mr. Jenkins, 57, was a successful sales representative for a conglomerate of manufacturing firms. For twenty-three years he traveled the midwestern territory, returning home for weekends and summer vacations. Mrs. Jenkins, 55, was a school teacher. Together the couple had raised four sons. The Jenkins lived in a midwestern metropolitan city where Mrs. Jenkins had family and friends. They had a close-knit circle of friends with whom they played cards and vacationed, and they considered themselves to be blessed with health and good fortune. However, for some time Mr. Jenkins had been feeling bored and tired. He found that he was restless and was fantasizing about quitting his job and moving farther north. During this time he was diagnosed as having diabetes, and his physician suggested that he consider changing his lifestyle, since the constant travel required by his job made controlling his diet difficult.

That was all the "permission" Mr. Jenkins required. He and Mrs. Jenkins spent several months looking into possibilities and finally sold their home and moved to northern Wisconsin, where they bought a restaurant–gift shop in a resort area. Their sons and friends were shocked and questioned their rationality. Their oldest son was particularly disturbed, expressing his concern about their financial solvency. But the Jenkins were convinced that they were doing what they needed to do. They struggled for the first two years before breaking even. They were amazed at their new physical energy as they renovated and restored their new property. They had thoroughly researched the conditions and requisite competencies necessary, and four years after buying the shop, they themselves, their sons, and friends all agreed that making the purchase was the best thing they could have done. Mr. Jenkins expected to manage the place actively for four years and then to turn over the business to his middle son, who moved up north to join his parents. Another son was considering the same move. This family felt that they were closer and enjoying each other more than ever before.

Mr. Jenkins had always thought that he and his wife would retire to the Southwest. In retrospect, he realized that the planning he had done in his early fifties showed him that his pension benefits and social security payments would not afford him the opportunity to retire fully without working part-time. But opportunities for part-time work in the Sunbelt were scarce at the time of his research. So he transformed his earlier expectation into a new dream, that of owning his own business in the northern country. Without the preretirement planning, he probably would not have reached this fortuitous decision.

Developmental Issues

The kinds of issues that continue to influence task negotiations in the preretirement stage are highlighted in the following categories, designated by Schlossberg (1981).

Psychosocial competencies.   Evidence from Lieberman (1975) and Lowenthal (1975) suggests that the particular coping mechanisms and personality characteristics that facilitate planning and adaptation to change may be life-stage specific. Thus, it is possible that the preretirement and disengagement processes involve the identification of both those psychosocial competencies that have been useful in the past and those that need to be developed to permit the successful negotiation of the forthcoming transition. Letting go, active planning based on information adequately discovered and processed, positive self-esteem, and the need to control one's life are all attributes that may permit the successful negotiation of the tasks associated with this stage.

Sex-role issues.   Some research has shown that women who have not had full-time careers prior to their husbands' retirement experience noticeable role changes when their husbands change occupational roles. Regardless of whether or not one is happy with this role change, one's preretirement planning must include the needs and inputs of the nonworking spouse to permit both members of the couple to achieve optimum satisfaction. Likewise, where both spouses are working and one plans to retire earlier than the other, they must consider these differences. In such cases, early retirement is often a possibility for one spouse owing to the other's income or pension benefits. The quality of the spouse relationship will determine how carefully the couple plans and how fully each partner participates. In couple systems where the power has been unilateral, the powerful spouse might take full responsibility for the planning without consulting the other. If the nonparticipating spouse does not mind, all will be well. But if the nonparticipating spouse feels that his or her needs have not been considered, conflict may result.

Research has not shown whether gender differences exist regarding the planning process required at this stage. Traditionally, women have been more concerned with family roles and transitions and men with economic and lifestyle decisions. However, couples in a symmetrical, two-career relationship—an increasingly familiar pattern—have to balance each spouse's individual, family, and occupational needs, roles, and interests in order to agree on a timetable for retirement and a style for life after work.

Health.   Obviously, the physical well-being of oneself and one's spouse is critical, even if the health of both is good in the preretirement stage. During the fifties and sixties, preoccupation with health increases in both subjective and objective aspects. Shanas and his colleagues (1968) compared self-ratings of health with degree of actual incapacity of people in this stage and classified them as *health pessimists, health optimists,* and *health realists.* Chiriboga (1975) suggests that noncomplainers, likely to be health optimists, who repress and deny their health problems, may exact a physical toll. Thus, it is important for people realistically to assess current and likely future health states in their retirement planning.

Values orientation.   Our values about life, relationships, self, and work are obviously important components of the disengagement and preretirement planning processes. One's adaptability to changing value orientations will affect how one views retirement, and the compatibility of spouses' values will affect the values and attitudes each holds about aging and the future. Sheehy (1981) believes that people in the process of disengagement from work value independence and moral integrity more highly than others. She comments that a retreat from work is toward independence and away from valueless or value-violating work and is healthier than withdrawal from work as a place of uncertainty and change. This view supports that of Schlossberg (1981), which stresses that values may be either helpful or dysfunctional, and that a value system contributing to adaptation at one life stage may be dysfunctional at another. Thus, people at different life stages tend to emphasize different values. For example, one who values membership in the work group may profit from the value in early stages of career development and suffer from it when facing disengagement and retirement.

Previous experience with transitions and planning.   The quality of one's experience in weathering changes and losses of roles and relationships in the past will influence one's ability to anticipate and prepare for the loss of the work role. Again, types of interpersonal supports as well as the issues described above will affect how one deals with the current tasks. Attitudes and experiences regarding one's past planning will influence whether one dreads and avoids this planning process or accepts it as a challenge.

Table 9-3 summarizes the tasks and issues of the late-career stage. The planning process intensifies as one moves closer to retirement. Social and economic changes may cause one constantly to reassess and modify earlier plans. This ongoing anticipatory planning process will influence how one experiences this developmental transition.

TABLE 9-3.   The late-career stage

Developmental Tasks	General Issues	Requisite Skills	Significant Others
Decelerate: find alternative ways of determining self-identity; find new sources of satisfaction; transfer competencies; gradually distance work priorities Make preretirement plans: appraise the meaning of retirement; plan the budget; consider all options	Sex role issues Different couple-life stages Health Values orientation Control Independence/ dependence Previous experience with transitions	Information seeking Information processing Financial planning Assessing Decision making Negotiating Compromising Reality testing Self-caring Values clarifying Adapting	Spouse Employer Accountant/lawyer Offspring Peers/colleagues Friends Community

SUMMARY

In this chapter, we have regarded the broad spectrum of career development in mid-life. We began by elaborating the mid-career reassessment process, which requires that one rebalance individual, family, and career roles, responsibilities, and commitments and that one consider the validity of earlier career choices and whether or not one's expectations and anticipations have been met. We suggested that people try to determine which career anchor best suits them and utilize this knowledge in the decision-making process. We considered specialization versus generalization, mentoring relationships, and decision-making skills. Information seeking and reality testing are necessary for determining possible options or directions available within the career field, the employing organization, or a new field. We also considered the appraisal process that women undergo upon entering the world of work after years of homemaking. We identified the issues that affect the mid-career reassessment as values conflicts, sex discrimination, the declining economy, job obsolescence, and credentialing.

The next stage in career development is the maintenance stage, which typically encompasses ages 45–55. The major tasks of this stage are to implement the decision of the mid-career reassessment and to learn to handle the work required during this period, which usually sees the highest level of career attainment. One is a full member of one's organization or profession now and the expectations placed on one regarding responsibilities and contributions may be affected by the organizational or professional values structure, external crises, the changing physical, mental, and emotional resources of the worker, and sex-role issues.

The maintenance stage leads into the late-career stage, whose two major tasks are deceleration, or disengagement, and preretirement planning. These tasks are closely related to changing family roles and relationships and may require the development of new psychosocial competencies, a sharpened awareness of changing health states, a change in value orientation, and the transfer of learning from earlier planning experiences.

The overall goal of the middle-career stages is to continue to maintain optimum productivity and contribute fully to one's chosen field of work while continuing to replenish one's energies, broaden one's activities and interests, and allow oneself to continue the individuation and separation processes.

REFERENCES

Armstrong, J. C. Decision behavior and outcome of midlife career changers, *Vocational Guidance Quarterly*, 1981, *29*, 205–213.

Atchley, R. C. *The sociology of retirement*. New York: Wiley, 1976.

Baumgardner, S. R. Vocational planning: The great swindle. *Personnel and Guidance Journal*, 1977, *56*, 17–20.

Berman, J. J., & Munson, H. L. Challenges in a dialectical conception of career evolution. *Personnel and Guidance Journal*, 1981, *60*, 92–97.

Blocher, D. H., & Siegal, R. Toward a cognitive development theory of leisure and work. *Counseling Psychologist*, 1981, *9*, 33–45.

Buhler, C., & Massarek, F. (eds.). *The course of human life: A study of goals in the humanistic perspective*. New York: Springer, 1968.

Chiriboga, D. Perceptions of well-being. In M. Lowenthal et al., *Four stages of life*. San Francisco: Jossey-Bass, 1975.

Cytrynbaum, S., Dubowsky, L., Gilbert, D., Pawelski, T., & Wadner, D. *Implications of social systems stress for women in positions of authority*. Paper presented at American Educational Research Association Annual Meeting, Boston, Mass., April 7–11, 1980.

George, L. K. *Role transitions in later life*. Monterey, Calif.: Brooks/Cole, 1980.

Ginzberg, E. Toward a theory of occupational choice: A restatement. *Vocational Guidance Quarterly*, 1972, *20*, 169–176.

Henton, J., Russell, R., & Koval, J. Spousal perceptions of midlife career change. *Personnel and Guidance Journal*, 1983, *61*, 287–291.

Isaacson, L. Counseling male mid-life career changers. *Vocational Guidance Quarterly*, 1981, *29*, 324–331.

Kanter, R. M. *Women and organizations*. Englewood Cliffs, N.J.: Prentice-Hall, 1976.

Leonards, J. Corporate psychology: An answer to occupational mental health. *Personnel and Guidance Journal*, 1981, *60*, 47–52.

Levinson, D. *The seasons of a man's life*. New York: Knopf, 1978.

Levinson, D., Darrow, C., Klein, E., Levinson, M., & McKee, B. Periods in the adult development of men: Ages 18–45. *Counseling Psychologist*, 1976, *6*, 21–26.

Lieberman, M. A. Adaptive processes in late life. In N. Datan and L. H. Ginsburg (eds.), *Life-span developmental psychology: Normative life crises*. New York: Academic Press, 1975.

Lowenthal, M. F., Thurnher, M., & Chiriboga, D. *Four stages of life*. San Francisco: Jossey-Bass, 1975.

Lowther, M. A. Career change in mid-life: Its impact on education. *Innovator*. Ann Arbor, Mich.: University of Michigan School of Education, 1977, *8*.

Okun, B. F. A study of the variables affecting the occupational choice of women 12–20 years after college graduation. Unpublished dissertation, Evanston, Ill.: Northwestern University, 1970.

Sarason, S. B., Sarason, E. K., & Cowden, P. Aging and the nature of work. In H. J. Peters and J. C. Hansen (eds.), *Vocational guidance and career development*. New York: Macmillan, 1977.

Schein, E. H. *Career dynamics*. Reading, Mass.: Addison-Wesley, 1978.

Schlossberg, N. K. A model for analyzing human adaptation to stress. *Counseling Psychologist*, 1981, *9*, 2–19.

Shanas, F., Townsend, P., Wedderburn, D., Friis, H., Milhoj, P., & Stehouwer, J. *Old people in three industrial societies*. New York: Atherton Press, 1968.

Sheehy, G. *Pathfinders.* New York: Morrow, 1981.

Super, D. E. *The psychology of careers.* New York: Harper & Row, 1957.

Super, D. E. Vocational maturity in mid-career. *Vocational Guidance Quarterly,* 1977, *25,* 297–309.

Thomas, L. E. A typology of mid-life career changes. *Journal of Vocational Behavior,* 1980, *16,* 173–182.

Time, February 15, 1982, p. 68.

Zunker, V. G. *Career counseling.* Monterey, Calif.: Brooks/Cole, 1981.

CHAPTER TEN

IMPLICATIONS FOR COUNSELORS: CASE STUDIES

The types of issues that clients in middle adulthood present include those concerned with reassessment of identity, family, and career commitments, and the planning and implementation of the decisions made during this process of reassessment. People who are currently in their middle years are not particularly prone to consulting counselors for their own issues. Many were brought up during an era when "seeking help" was considered a sign of weakness. Therefore, many adults in their middle years come into treatment indirectly, either as the result of an adolescent youngster's problem that has escalated family stress and affected everyone's lives, or in response to a physical or psychological symptom such as depression, headaches, sexual dysfunction and so on. Even when the presenting issue is clearly related to career concerns, those in middle adulthood often show reluctance to seek professional help except from a placement agency. Often, adults with career problems do not come for professional help until the situation has developed into a bona fide crisis.

Another problem with respect to the middle-aged client is the age and life stage of the counselor. As adults become older, they grow ever more suspicious of younger helping professionals, preferring the comfort of same-generation helpers who are more likely to share cultural and generational perspectives. Counselors must be sensitive to these feelings as well as to the ebbs and flows of development during the middle years in order to assess effectively the reciprocal influences of developmental issues and the presenting problem(s).

This chapter presents some representative case studies of adults in their middle years. Again, we are not advocating any particular strategies or techniques here. Rather, the suggestion is to reframe presenting issues into a developmental perspective and to use family-system members as participants in treatment whenever possible, since significant relationships play an important role during these years. In early adulthood when individuation issues predominate, individual treatment may often be more appropriate than treatment with the family of origin. Obviously, therapy consists of a blend of the therapist's theory of use and style of relating and the type and style of the client and his or her presenting issues.

CASE 1: MARIANNE

Presenting Problem

Marianne, 41, came to see a counselor requesting a divorce. She had been married for twenty-two years, had three children aged 17 through 21, and felt that now it was time for her to "live a little." She was angry that her husband, Stanley, 44, refused to move out of their home and would not even consider a divorce.

When asked to describe her feelings about her marriage, Marianne reported that she had spent years being a "good wife and mother," that she was no longer attracted to her husband, and that he was too tied up in his career to pay much attention to her anyway. She expressed envy of other women in her neighborhood who worked or had affairs, and she felt isolated and forgotten in her homemaker position. Two of her children were away at the state university, and her youngest was to graduate from high school and go off to the university shortly. Marianne was not interested in couple work. She wanted support and help in carrying out her decision to leave Stanley, mainly to force Stanley out of the house. She insisted that he leave the house and provide her with enough money to open up a children's toy shop, an idea she had been considering for several years. Her decision to seek a divorce was sudden and unilateral, by her own admission.

Description of Client

Marianne was attractive and looked several years younger than she was. She dressed well, was well-coiffed and made-up, and exhibited charm and poise, despite her nervous finger tapping and wavering eye contact. She was hesitant when describing her feelings and thoughts, however, and had difficulty talking about herself rather than her husband and children.

Individual Context

Marianne described herself as the second to oldest of four daughters in an urban Italian immigrant family. She felt that her childhood was average and happy. Her mother was a homemaker and her father a factory worker who was domineering and controlling at home. Dad was the undisputed boss, and the entire household revolved around his needs. The rules were very strict, and Marianne resented not being able to play more with other children. She had many household and babysitting responsibilities and she remembers fantasizing about growing up, getting married, and having her own babies. Her family referred to her as "the dreamer." Because of her dreaming, she was often forgetful and was accused by her mother of being selfish, forgetful, and irresponsible.

The four girls attended a neighborhood parochial school and were not allowed to date during high school. Their models of women were conventional. Marianne described her mother as "hardworking, thrifty, obedient, and a good cook." Mom and Dad never fought, since Mom always gave in to Dad before a fight could develop. That was what women were supposed to do.

Marianne was a good student in school and remembered no health problems. She went to work in an office right after high school graduation, still living at home under her parents' rules. She had little money of her own, since she turned most of it over to her father. Some of her fantasies at that time included obtaining control of her own money and being able to spend it as she wished.

When asked how she felt about herself as a young girl, Marianne replied that she was "heavy and awkward." She used to worry about whether other kids, particularly boys, would ever find her attractive, and she went to the movies frequently to stimulate her fantasies about beauty and love. She felt confident about her academic abilities but never considered going to college as the family rule was that "you went to work and helped support the family until you married." Marianne could not remember her early interests, except for the movies. She liked taking care of the younger children and particularly enjoyed reading romantic fairy tales to them.

Marianne's current fantasies were also romantic. Recently, she had been fantasizing a great deal about falling in love with a "wealthy, attractive man" (no one she knew) who would allow her to realize all her other fantasies. Prior to her decision to divorce, her fantasies increased in frequency and intensity.

Family Context

It is clear that Marianne grew up in a closed-system, traditional family. When she was 18, her father brought home Stanley, the nephew of one of his factory friends. Stanley was then 21, and was graduating from the state university with an honors degree in business. Her father indicated that Marianne could spend time with Stanley, and she immediately fell in love with him. He was attractive physically, quiet, and Italian, all desirable attributes. They began to date with the full approval of both sets of parents. Six months later, they decided to marry. Marianne would go with him when he entered military service.

Marianne described her wedding as the happiest day of her life. All her dreams were now going to come true. She and Stanley spent their first two years of married life away from home in the military service. During the first year, Marianne worked on the base and enjoyed her traditional housewife role. She had her first baby in the second year of her marriage and she stopped working. It was like playing house and she remembers being preoccupied with her baby. Stanley was not home much, and he socialized with his army buddies. It never occurred to Marianne to resent Stanley's absences, since she had her baby. Marianne did describe her early married years as being sexually disappointing. In retrospect, she realizes that Stanley was inexperienced and awkward and not at all concerned with her sexual satisfaction. Having babies alleviated that disappointment somewhat and Marianne spent the next three years having two more babies.

By the time Marianne and Stanley moved back to their home city, they had established a routine of living together without intimacy and of communicating mostly about the children. Stanley went to work for a large corporation and steadily worked his way up the corporate ladder. At the time Marianne began therapy, he was a vice president of finance for a large publishing company. Marianne enjoyed the perquisites of a steadily increasing salary and spent much time and energy designing and decorating her suburban home. She was finally able to buy the clothes and other things she had always desired. She was very involved with her children's activities, always volunteering and car pooling. The family took vacations together and spent much of their recreation time together, although many times just Marianne and the kids went places together, since Stanley was tied up with business affairs.

According to Marianne, Stanley assumed that his marriage and children were "stable and permanent" and that everything had worked out the way it was supposed to. Marianne claimed that she began to resent her marriage several years before entering therapy. She said that the women's movement and the concomitant media coverage caused her to rethink her ideas about life and that she began to feel anger toward her husband and father ("two peas in the same pod") for controlling her and taking her for granted. Then, as she saw her neighbors and the mothers of her children's friends reenter the world of work, she began to feel left out and cheated. For several years, she compensated for these feelings by being the "super stay-at-home mom," always volunteering to serve and provide. As her children began to leave home, she began to experience headaches and tension and she found herself wanting to be away from Stanley.

Three years before entering therapy, Marianne joined a women's group. Stanley openly derided her new activity. However, Marianne began to take herself more seriously and to resist some of Stanley's controlling moves. With the support of her new friends, she also began to resist her father's controlling strategies. As a result, her father and husband joined together to ridicule and tease her about "women's lib." Her mother and sisters provided no comfort or support, adhering to their more conventional philosophies and lifestyles. In fact, everyone in her family seemed to be offended by her desire to become more of her own person except her oldest daughter, who encouraged her to think about opening up her own store and confronting the overbearing men in her life.

Marianne began to feel more anxious as her children left home. She found herself fantasizing more about other men and feeling sexual stirrings that she had not felt since her youth. She realized that she was in trouble when she found herself clinging to her youngest daughter, not wanting her to grow up and leave home. After months of discussing these feelings with her group, she confronted Stanley one day and told him she no longer wanted to live with him and that he had to leave. She was afraid that if she waited any longer, she would lose her looks and youth. Stanley was upset. He reacted to her as if she were an "hysterical female" and suggested she consult a psychiatrist. Thus, Marianne called her family physician, who made a referral. Marianne was convinced that the issue of divorce was nonnegotiable. She wanted support in her battle against Stanley and her family of origin.

As Marianne talked about her families, much repressed rage and fear surfaced. She was overwhelmed by these feelings and tried to choke back her tears and anger. When encouraged to let go and sob, she expressed fear of losing control. This brought back images of the "good little girl" who had always been obedient and pleasing to the men in her life. Soon she was able to get in touch with her feelings of anger toward her mother and sisters, who had never supported her attempts to stand up to her dad, and who, in fact, seemed angrier with her than her father did. A great deal of strength emanated from Marianne as she became aware of her early decision to help her children grow up to be more independent and self-sufficient. She was definitely the primary parent, and was thus able to accomplish this goal with little interference from Stanley. However, it was just this phenomenon that was now eliciting so much pain. Her children were, in fact, leaving as self-sufficient adults and she was left to deal with many unresolved issues related to her early family and her marital situation.

At the counselor's insistence, Stanley accompanied Marianne to the third session. He was a very handsome man and presented himself as much warmer and less arrogant and domineering than Marianne had described. In fact, he was openly verbal about his distress and confusion. He said that he had always adored Marianne but that she was always in her own world and he could never reach her. He stopped trying so hard after their last child was born, when he realized that she was more interested in the children than in him. He admitted to an "old fashioned" upbringing, with fairly traditional and stereotyped family sex roles but he surprised Marianne with his awareness of changes in these roles and his readiness to become more "modern."

Career Context

Marianne had no trouble gaining a job as a file clerk in an import–export firm upon high school graduation. She had no career ambitions then, and was merely seeking a stable, well-paying job to keep her going until she got married. She enjoyed working—not because of the actual work, but because of the contact with the other girls in the office—and she felt grown up going into an office building and out to lunch every day. She was happy that she did not have to work in a factory, and that she had acquired business skills in school.

After marriage, when Marianne accompanied Stanley to various military bases, she was able to obtain civilian part-time clerical positions. These jobs kept her occupied and she had some extra money to spend as she wished. When her first baby was born, Marianne assumed that she would never work again. She enjoyed homemaking and developed sewing, knitting, and cooking skills. She found child-rearing pleasurable and she particularly enjoyed reading to and playing with her children.

Marianne first began to think about opening up a children's toy shop when her children were completing elementary school. She missed being around young children and found herself advising friends and neighbors on suitable toys and games for school-age children. She also became aware of the need for a suburban specialty store as her friends and neighbors constantly complained about having to go far away to the mall for birthday gifts. Occasionally, she would verbalize her dream to Stanley, who did not take her seriously.

As Marianne listened to her two oldest children (a son and a daughter) talk about college majors and career choices, she began to feel as if she had missed out. She knew that she was tired of and finished with volunteer activities (mostly in the schools) and that she needed to have something to do with her time and energies.

Stanley professed to be proud of and pleased with his career development and current position. He considered himself to be a steady riser and felt that he had achieved a higher occupational level than he had dared to hope for. He liked the company he worked for, liked his coworkers and the status and prestige of his position, and he expected to remain with this firm until retirement. He was just now beginning to think about other aspects of his life since he now felt more secure than he had in the past. His goal, then, was to maintain his current job level rather than aim for anything higher or for another position. He had been thinking about taking up sailing and doing some kind of physical exercise in order to stay in shape.

Assessment

Both Marianne and Stanley were experiencing mid-life transitions, and Marianne in particular was dealing with sudden role changes. Her primary "mother" role was no longer feasible and she now had to return to previously unresolved issues—namely, her relationship to her family of origin, her marital relationship, her sexual relationship with her husband, and her current desire to choose a career path. Marianne had participated in the formulation and development of a traditional, complimentary marital contract, and she now needed to engage Stanley in a renegotiation process to determine whether or not the marital relationship could change and develop into a more satisfying one. This would require self-reassessments for both parties as well as a mutual decision as to whether they would renegotiate their relationship. Divorce was, of course, a possible outcome of this decision-making process. Regardless of the final outcome, it was important for both Marianne and Stanley to take responsibility for reassessing their identities, their career and lifestyle choices, and their relationship.

Goals

The goals for individual assessment were to help Stanley and Marianne understand themselves, their earlier choices, and their current aspirations. The goal for them as a couple was to help them through the decision-making process so they could determine whether or not a new relationship contract could be developed that would be mutually satisfying.

Interventions

The counselor suggested to Marianne that she needed to utilize this period of transition to find out who she was apart from "daughter," "wife," "mother." She further encouraged Marianne to postpone action regarding a divorce until she had reviewed her life up to now and could decide proactively how she wanted to live the rest of her life. It was necessary that the reassessment process include her couple relationship, particularly since Stanley had expressed willingness to work with her. Both their needs for mid-life reassessment were reframed as a normal developmental process, and Marianne and Stanley were encouraged to consider their current difficulties as normal and understandable.

Individual client-centered counseling sessions were conducted with each member of the couple. Marianne was encouraged to develop a clearer conception of who she was, to define her strengths and weaknesses, and to become more assertive (not aggressive) in her relationships. She was directed to dialogue in Gestalt fashion with her parents, sisters, husband, and children during the counseling sessions so she could become more aware of her feelings and integrate them into behaviors. At the same time, she was confronted with many of her "irrational" ideas, which resulted in her feelings of low self-worth. To help her become more comfortable with her feelings and thoughts, she was given homework assignments involving interactions with significant others.

When Marianne became more aware of her identity and her personal goals, she was instructed to collect data about possible options by interviewing divorcees, other women leading lifestyles she envied, and proprietors of suburban retail shops. During this period, Stanley was seen individually, so that he could become more aware of his need to control and of his insecurities. He was very responsive to a client-centered approach and became more aware of his love for and emotional dependence on Marianne. He was coached to become a "follower" at home, allowing Marianne to be the "initiator."

After three months of individual sessions, Marianne and Stanley were seen as a couple. By this time, they were both open to the possibility of staying in the relationship. The counselor pointed out that they needed to make that decision themselves and that, before doing so, they needed to consider carefully all alternatives, including divorce. They might then be able to clarify what each would need in order to grow within the relationship. Their fears about aging were openly discussed and they talked about their sex life. The interventions were largely based on a communications approach to couples work. They were taught to listen to each other, to differentiate between the literal and metacommunicational messages, and to send "I" messages as opposed to "you" messages. They were then taught some sensate-focus exercises and other behavioral exercises to improve their sexual relationship. They were also given specific homework reading assignments.

Marianne began to report that Stanley was more attentive and caring than before and that she was beginning to "like him" again. The couple was urged not to make a final decision too quickly, and to expect things to get worse again before they got better.

After ten sessions of couples work, Marianne and Stanley decided to take a three-month period without counseling to see how they would function on their own. During that period, Marianne decided to work as an assistant in a children's toy shop in a neighboring town to see how she felt about it and to determine what it really involved. Stanley was supportive, although he resented the low salary that she would be getting for her many hours of work. However, he agreed to reserve judgment on the feasibility of her seriously considering her own store.

Outcome

Three months later, Marianne and Stanley returned for a follow-up session and reported that they had decided to stay together and work on their marriage. Marianne felt stronger as a person and, for the first time, she realized that Stanley also had vulnerabilities and was not necessarily the "ogre father figure" she had needed to perceive him as. She was now able to see the little boy in him and to respond playfully and nurturingly. They decided that they knew each other's strengths and weaknesses and that they could work things out without one totally capitulating to the other. They still had a way to go in terms of developing intimacy in their relationship, but they both agreed that, for the first time, they were really communicating with each other rather than through their children or their families of origin.

Marianne enjoyed working but realized that she would not be likely to make a success of her own retail operation. She did not want to make the required investment of time, energy, and capital. She took a job in the children's department of a large department store. She was happy there because she had flexible hours and she could thus still pursue her personal interests. Marianne also mentioned that her two younger sisters were beginning to approach her for advice as they began to emerge from their full-time mother roles. Stanley reported that he no longer wanted to invest so much of himself in his career and that, in fact, to do so was no longer necessary. He was hoping that Marianne would take sailing lessons with him so they could find new ways of enjoying each other's company.

Comments

It was clear to the counselor that impulsive, unilateral decision making of any kind could lead to more pain than the current stressful situation. Particularly sensitive to the issues relating to mid-life transitional stress, the counselor sought to consider Marianne's individual, family, and career issues in a developmental framework. Doing so necessitated that Stanley be involved in the actual counseling process, and this proved to be the turning point for determining goals for treatment. Stanley's actual part in the problem was quite different from that as described by Marianne.

The counselor had no investment in whether or not the couple decided to remain together. However, the counselor did have an investment in urging both members of the couple system to engage in reassessment and decision-making processes in order that each could take proactive responsibility for input into the final outcome. Proactive decisions take longer than impulsive reactive resolutions of power struggles. During transitional disruption, it sometimes seems to the parties involved that impulsive resolution will alleviate the discomforts associated with the disruption. Counselors need to help clients accept the pain of the transitional stress and work through a careful decision-making process.

Note that the units of treatment changed in this case. Originally Marianne entered for individual counseling. However, since her marital relationship was a major part of her presenting issue, it was impossible to assess (much less treat) that issue without the presence of her spouse. In this case, Stanley was agreeable and cooperative. However, even if he had not agreed to participate in the actual treatment, it would have been necessary to engage him for at least one session so as to assess accurately the nature of the relationship. A counselor observing two or more members of a relationship system interact can learn more accurately and quickly just what the dynamics and nature of the relationship really are than by listening to hours of description.

CASE 2: BERNARD

Presenting Problem

Bernard, 46, went to see a counselor because of his concern about his wife's relationship with their 19-year-old son, a high school dropout. Bernard felt that it was "abnormal" for his wife, Annette, 45, to "dislike" their son and to insist he move out of their home and support himself. Annette had, in fact, delivered an ultimatum: either their son Joshua leave or she would. Bernard was feeling "depressed" and did not feel that this ultimatum was fair. He wanted to keep his family together and wanted the counselor to tell him what to do to "solve Joshua's problems." Bernard believed that Joshua should live at home until he "grew up," but he was unclear as to what that really meant.

Further discussion revealed that Bernard and Annette had two children: a 22-year-old daughter, who was graduating from college and who had recently declared herself to be a lesbian, and Joshua, who had experienced behavioral difficulties from early childhood, had been in and out of psychiatric treatment, and had dropped out of school abruptly in the middle of his junior year of high school. Joshua had held sporadic jobs since dropping out of school, and spent most of his time at home closeted up in his room. When he did have a job, he depended upon his mother to wake him every morning and get him off to work. Bernard was very distressed about his children's problems and believed that Annette was largely responsible. If she had been the "right kind of mother," he thought, the children would have turned out differently. He felt himself to be caught between his wife and son and he resented Annette's attempts to disentangle herself from this obviously triangulated situation.

Annette had returned to school two years earlier, and was now working toward a degree in accounting. She planned to take a full-time job after completing her program. During the two years she had been in school, she had worked in three cooperative-education assignments, and she found herself delighted with the world of work. She was becoming more independent and developing a positive, competent self-concept. She wanted Bernard to cooperate with her attempts to individuate rather than to pull her down.

Bernard's hurried consultation was precipitated by his finding drugs in Joshua's car and learning that Joshua was being sought by the police for passing a bad check. According to Bernard, Annette was furious and she believed that Bernard covered up and made excuses for Joshua. Bernard always refused to participate in any type of counseling except for the three sessions he had had several years ago with a psychiatrist because of "depression." Bernard reported that Annette was angry and resentful that he never participated in family therapy over the years. Now, when he is ready to participate, she "has had it." Bernard only wanted to protect his son by being a "good father" and wanted Annette to be a "good mother."

The presenting issue for Bernard, then, was how to satisfy his wife and son simultaneously, without having to choose between them. In actuality, Bernard was resisting change and wanted to retain the status quo. He was desperate, even threatening Annette with another bout of "depression."

Description of Client

Bernard was casually dressed, rather overweight, and obviously low in energy. He appeared to be vulnerable and confused. His speech was slow, containing intermittent stammers, and his voice was low. The counselor had to utilize responsive listening to elicit his slow, long-drawn-out description of the presenting issue.

Individual Context

Bernard described himself as merely "existing." He could not remember ever being particularly happy, nor did he expect to be. In fact, he did not even know what "being happy" might mean. His view of life was that you go along day by day and accept whatever comes along with a minimum of fuss. He had gone to college and put himself through law school at night. He never practiced law, since he thought it would be "too hard." Currently he manages a small shopping center that Annette's family helped him to purchase. He could not think of any special interests, other than his family, and he spent most of his time at home watching television and reading magazines. Once a week, however, he played cards with Annette's father and brother, his business partners.

Bernard was the older of two boys of immigrant parents and he grew up in a lower-class urban environment. His memories of his early family life were negative. There were no affection or warmth at home, and he left after high school to join the Marines and escape an abusive father. Life had always been hard and difficult. His parents were now deceased, but he had had only minimal contact with them during his adulthood. He had no contact at all with his brother. When he came home from the service, he used the GI bill to attend college, where he met Annette. She represented all the good things—beauty, class, and an appropriate religious and family background. They "truly loved" each other and he felt lucky for the first time in his life. His expectations were few and, except that his children had disappointed him, things had worked out pretty much as he had thought they should. He really was confused about his children. He believed he had made a real effort to be a different kind of father from his own father.

Over the years, Bernard said, he had learned to insulate himself from Annette's nagging about his lowly occupation and his "lack of involvement" with the children. He felt he had been a "good" father, but that it was the woman's role to raise the children. Until they reached high school age, he left childrearing to Annette. When Joshua was referred for psychiatric treatment in nursery school, it had been more than Bernard could bear. He had just blocked it out by watching more television and reading more magazines than usual, leaving it all to Annette. He had really resented her wanting him to be part of the family therapy, refusing to acknowledge that there might be any serious problems. Surely the child would outgrow his difficulties.

Bernard described himself as moody and tired a lot. He said that the person he cared most about in this world was Annette. She was a marvelous housewife and cook and up until recently he had assumed she was a wonderful mother. However, the outcomes of his children's lives showed that he had been wrong. He was confused now by Annette's demands. He failed to understand her involvement and enthusiasm for her work. "A job is a job," he thought, and one is not supposed to like what one has to do. He made adequate money and did not understand why she wanted to work.

It was very difficult to get Bernard to talk about himself. He kept returning to his concerns about Joshua and Annette. He had no friends, considered himself an introvert, and was totally preoccupied now with his family problems. The counselor suggested that Annette come in for the next session. Bernard was not sure if he could convince her to come, but agreed to try.

Family Context

In front of Annette, Bernard described the grim realities of his family background and how determined he was not to lose his cool and fight with the kids. Annette talked about her close, controlling family and how she still felt "put down" by her parents' demands. Because Bernard worked with her father and brother, she was often caught up in a situation that she would have preferred to avoid. She resented their business relationship and felt that her father and brother had prevented Bernard from becoming a lawyer, which would have been more socially accepted and in keeping with the type of lifestyle she had presumed she would have in marrying Bernard.

Annette presented herself as self-confident and determined. She was obviously very angry with Bernard, but there were overtones of affection and caring. She remembered meeting Bernard and falling in love with him because of his gentle, laid-back manner (as opposed to her father's aggressive, domineering ways). She had been impressed by Bernard's attempts to better himself by going to law school. She and her father had both contributed to his law school tuition. She worked until he completed school and then had their daughter. They both had agreed to have this child and had been pleased with her arrival. Now, however, Bernard claimed that he only went along with the decision to have a baby to please Annette, since he had not really been ready to share her with a baby. Bernard and Annette agreed that Bernard had opposed a second pregnancy, but Annette had insisted on having two children. This time, Bernard refused to participate in the pregnancy or delivery and he never helped her with the new infant as he had with their daughter Diane. Soon after Joshua's birth, Bernard had begun to distance himself. He found the household and the demands of two toddlers overwhelming and he escaped by working long hours.

Annette was immersed in childrearing and homemaking, but she was also aware of her growing resentment toward Bernard. He never consulted her about his career plans and would not listen to her concerns about their relationship or the children. When Joshua first developed social and emotional problems in nursery school and Annette was urged to consult a family therapist, she tried in vain to get Bernard's cooperation. Now she admitted that she had never been able to forgive Bernard for withdrawing during her pregnancy with Joshua and for refusing to help her deal with Joshua's problems. She felt that this abandonment of her and the children at that point had led to their current problems.

Joshua presented problems from the beginning. He was a difficult infant and became more of a problem as he grew. Annette was always running to schools, interfering with teachers and other school personnel, and trying to rescue her son. Many family tensions and unhappinesses arose and Bernard refused to get involved. Diane was close to Annette and a source of much pleasure and pride, which had developed into mutual comfort and support. After Diane left for college, Joshua announced that he was dropping out of school. At this point, Bernard became activated as a parent and tried in every way to dissuade his son. When Joshua would not change his mind, Bernard took responsibility for getting him jobs and Annette took responsibility for seeing to it that he got to work every day. At the same time, Annette returned to school and became aware of her own career potential. Thus, she began to experience conflict between her own school and family demands and pressures.

The situation with Joshua went from bad to worse. He was unable to keep a job for more than a few weeks. He slept all day, expected to be waited on, and caroused with his friends all night. Whenever he ran out of money, he was successful in wheedling it out of his father. That behavior inevitably precipitated a fight between the parents. Bernard felt guilty and unable to say "no" to his son.

Annette was angry and, though she wanted Joshua to grow up and take responsibility for himself, she continued to infantilize him out of her own guilt feelings. Joshua was now openly antagonistic to his mother, telling her that if she were a "good mom" she would let him have his way as does his "good dad." Bernard agreed with Joshua, and kept assuring Annette that things would work out all right in time. At this point, Annette was determined that Bernard would have to throw their son out and follow through if she was going to remain at home. She was negotiating for a job as an accountant and she would be capable of supporting herself if she had to. She was "fond" of Bernard and felt sorry for him, but she could not go on this way any longer. She did not know if she still loved or respected him.

As Annette became more assertive, Bernard became more depressed, and he reminded Annette that he would become *truly* depressed if she continued on the way she was. Annette seemed to waver at these threats and to back off from her clearcut demands, becoming more vague and hesitant about timelines for Joshua's departure. However, she insisted that she would not continue on indefinitely and that as soon as she went to work full time, things would have to change. She would no longer sit around and wait for Bernard to get ready to do things. She had a lot of catching up to do and she intended to do it. Diane was giving her much support and encouragement. It was clear that there was a boundary between the men and the women in this family.

Career Context

Bernard never took responsibility for determining his career path based on planned goals and self-assessment. His goal was to provide a lifestyle that was comfortable for his family with as little work and effort as possible. While still in law school, he realized that practicing law would be too much effort for him. Because of the GI benefits and Annette's desires, he completed his course of studies—"it was the easiest way to go." He was delighted when his father-in-law offered to invest in a shopping center for him to manage "while he got his bearings." He has been managing this center for more than twenty years and he had managed to scrape together a living with the least amount of effort and output. Most days he sat in his office and read magazines. He had other deals (a source of legal and moral concern to Annette) to supplement his income. He expected to work as long as he had to. He really did not understand how or why people expected to like their jobs. When asked what he would like to do if he had a "magic wand," he replied "nothing." He had no desire to change or do anything differently. Everything was okay the way it was, according to Bernard.

Annette, whose earlier bookkeeping experiences had helped her through college and Bernard through law school, had not worked since Diane's birth. She had never anticipated returning to work but, at Diane's urging, returned to earn her B.S. degree when Diane left for college. At school, she found herself receiving respect and praise for her own self. She turned out to be an excellent student and found that she loved the involvement and demands of going to school. The more excited she became about her activities, the more morose Bernard became about his work. When Annette went out on co-op assignments, she received excellent evaluations and much encouragement. She felt now that she had "found herself" and that she had much to contribute to a career over the next twenty years. Since she could not depend on Bernard for vicarious achievement and success, she was determined to achieve and succeed on her own and she felt like a "new woman." Thus, she resented the attempts of Bernard and Joshua to keep her at home and involved in their difficulties.

Assessment

This couple—like Marianne and Stanley, described above—were in the final launching stage of development in the family life cycle. Bernard was in identity "moratorium," whereas Annette had reassessed her life and priorities and taken some steps to develop and implement a new identity and concomitant career and family commitments. Bernard had been diagnosed as neurotic depressive by a psychiatrist with whom he consulted several years ago. The couple system was indeed unbalanced, and Joshua was serving his lifelong function of holding them together by escalating his difficulties. However, this disabling sequence no longer worked. Annette's new sense of individuation caused her to abandon her former role, that of placator and mediator. In fact, she was now eager to let go and let whatever would happen occur for Joshua so that his launching would be complete. Annette was signalling Bernard that he could either let go and grow along with her or stay stuck with Joshua while she went on her way. The couple power struggle was being played out to the finish. All the pain that had accumulated during their married life was being reactivated as each struggled to define the nature of the couple relationship. The see-saw had been accelerated—when one was up, the other sank down.

Goals

The first major goal for this family was to detriangulate Annette completely. Bernard would then have to decide what to do. Thus, the parent system was the first locus of treatment and the goal was to facilitate the parents to work cooperatively in launching Joshua. This goal required that the couple be educated about the appropriateness of launching at this time. It was appropriate and necessary for Joshua to learn to fend for himself if he ever was to grow up. The next goal was to help Bernard and Annette, as a couple, to reassess their relationship and determine whether or not it could survive without either one having to give up his or her sense of self. This involved encouraging Annette to pursue her career and Bernard to consider ways of learning to enjoy his life more—in other words, allowing them to separate emotionally in order to achieve higher levels of self-differentiation. The marital power struggle had to be reframed so that Bernard realized that his threats of becoming "depressed" were indeed power plays. He had to choose whether or not he wished to become depressed. If he did choose to do so, he would have to live with the consequences. Likewise, if he chose not to invest in a satisfying career, that did not mean that Annette had to do the same.

As the couple system became less enmeshed, the partners could learn to accept their differences rather than engage in power struggles over who was right and who was wrong. If they were successful in separating, they would be able to renegotiate their relationships with Annette's family of origin so that they felt less controlled by them. A further goal would be to help Annette and Bernard, either separately or as a parent subsystem, to renegotiate their relationships with their launched adult children.

Intervention

The first major intervention was cognitive restructuring—that is, educating the parents about the launching stage of the family life cycle and about their mid-life transitions. The two were taught to question and correct some of the "irrational" assumptions that maintained their disappointments and unhappiness. Another intervention was reframing the presenting problem to enable them to view Joshua as a "good son" who was protecting his parents from having to confront their marital issues. Joshua was giving Bernard a *raison d'être,* a meaning for his life, and allowing him to compensate for his previous lack of involvement. For the first time, Bernard was feeling powerful and important as the protective parent. The therapist then helped the couple to describe the possible catastrophes that they imagined might occur if Joshua was let go and left to fend for himself—for example, jail, drugs, and poverty. The parents were informed that they could not protect Joshua from himself indefinitely. Sooner or later, the therapist pointed out, the boy would have to face himself and take responsibility for the consequences of his actions. When this reframing succeeded in alleviating some of the prevailing tensions and opening up couple-system communications, Annette was able to state clearly and directly to Bernard that she really meant business and that in continuing to aid and abet Joshua with secret money he was hurting Joshua as well as the rest of the family. Bernard was finally able to hear this message, and the two of them began to cooperate for the first time in planning their approach to Joshua. The therapist encouraged them to reenact their problems in the therapy sessions and to practice collaborative, supportive strategies for dealing with their son.

Between the next two sessions, Annette and Bernard confronted Joshua, telling him that he must prepare to leave home and that they would no longer give him money or let him come between them. Much to their surprise (and relief), Joshua seemed to accept this ultimatum, responding by making plans to leave the city despite the warrant out for his arrest. He did attempt several times to undermine his father's resolve, but Bernard had finally realized that he could not change Annette's mind and that it was more important to him to keep his wife than his son. Bernard decided not to return to therapy, but Annette continued for several more weeks.

In the subsequent sessions with Annette, she worked very hard to understand her unfinished business with her family of origin and how she brought these issues into an enmeshed type of family situation. As she began to feel even stronger, she was able to separate emotionally both from her parents and her husband. She hoped Bernard would opt for "growth" rather than "stagnation," but she decided that she could not pressure him and she would have to continue to grow while he worked out his own choices.

Annette obtained a desirable job and Bernard, while professing to be simultaneously proud and resentful of her, decided that he too might begin to consider other ways of spending his time. Without Annette's pressures or protection and without the children at home, Bernard was in fact freer to consider his own life choices. Joshua did indeed leave the state and telephoned often to request funds from his father. Bernard went through agonies refusing to rescue his son, but he kept his word not to bail him out and this fostered mutual support in the couple system. Now, when Bernard became depressed, Annette responded affectionately, without taking responsibility for Bernard's depression. She no longer "mothered" him and she verbalized (as practiced in many role plays with her therapist) that he could consult a doctor if he got depressed or he could choose to "get off his duff" and start living with her. Thus, many of the interventions included teaching the couple differentiated communications, assertiveness, and structural moves to clarify roles and boundaries.

Outcome

Three months later, Joshua was still out of town, claiming that he would never return. He had run through his own meager funds and his parents were not sure how he was supporting himself. His requests for money ceased, owing to a lack of reinforcement, and his phone calls became much more adult and less beseeching. Annette was happy in her job and Bernard was beginning to think that maybe he could find more interesting activities. In fact, he telephoned the therapist to request a referral for vocational testing, claiming that he was considering some options as part of pre-retirement planning. The couple reported that they were more comfortable with each other than they had been in many years. Annette still feared that Joshua would get into serious trouble and return, and that Bernard would once again become involved. They found Joshua's absence to be a tremendous relief, and the boy seemed to be functioning better than he had at home. Annette was still not completely sure that the marriage would survive but she seemed to believe it was improving. The couple suggested they come in for follow-up sessions every three months. Bernard, interestingly, initiated that suggestion. This was the first time he had been willing to engage in any type of therapy.

Comments

Obviously, the final outcome for this couple was still to be determined. However, the two were able to get over their impasse, and the fact that they were still together indicated that some positive bondings existed in their relationship. It is important to remember that the marital issues in this case were put on hold from the beginning of the marriage, and that the children served as the focus of the couple's interactions while Bernard's job choice was seen as the scapegoat in the system. Both Bernard and Annette had unresolved identity issues and, because of their low levels of self-differentiation, enmeshment was the likely result. Bernard naturally resisted the changes that Annette initiated with her mid-life transition, and he was secretly gratified when Joshua stepped into the fray to provide a focus for their interactions. The scared, dependent little boy in Bernard needed protection, and when Annette withdrew her protection and replaced it with anger, Bernard became depressed, anticipating abandonment. Joshua's leaving alleviated much of the tension, and, as Annette ceased nagging and went about living her own life and developing her own interests and activities, Bernard found himself, for the first time, beginning to consider some of the issues that he had neglected several decades earlier. While he had not yet committed himself to change and growth, he seemed to be getting unstuck, and he was making tentative moves that Annette found encouraging.

Short-term therapy can be very effective in such cases. When the presenting client refuses to continue directly in treatment, note that, if another member of the family elects to continue, the structural moves that affect the presenting problem can be administered through the family member involved in treatment. If Annette changed her behavior at home, Bernard would have to respond to her differently, and this response in turn would change his behavior.

CASE 3: THE WILLIS FAMILY

Presenting Problem

The Willis family, consisting of Mark, 55, Melanie, 48, and their fourth daughter, Irene, 20, were referred by Irene's college counseling center because of Irene's anorexic symptoms. She had been losing weight since she had gone away to college. Now, she was living at home and attending a local college for her last two years. The older three daughters were married and all lived away from home.

Irene was not, nor had she been, in an acute stage of anorexia nervosa, but her refusal to eat and her steady weight loss were of concern to her physician and her parents. Melanie reported that Irene, the "baby" of the family, had been reluctant to go away to school, but since her older sisters had, it was assumed that she would. Irene was very homesick and came home every weekend. She seemed to crave parental nurturing and care. Until the end of her sophomore year, Melanie and Mark did not realize that Irene had a "problem." But Irene's dormitory advisor had alerted the college health service to the possibility that the girl might have an eating disorder, and a physical examination indicated excessive weight loss along with other manifestations of anorexia nervosa. Melanie and Mark decided, when so informed, that Irene should come home so they could take care of her and feed her. Their family physician explained the nature, course, and possible consequences of anorexia nervosa and strongly recommended family therapy.

Description of Clients

Melanie and Mark Willis were a well-dressed, well-educated, upper-middle-class suburban couple. They were both articulate and expressed concern about their lifestyle and the importance of presenting a "good image" to the community.

They believed that they never had any real problems in their family. Irene's current difficulties were a shock for them and kept them concerned and preoccupied.

Mark had worked his way into the upper management of a technological firm and Melanie considered herself to be a traditional housewife. They belonged to a country club, led an active social life, and traveled frequently for business and pleasure. They considered themselves lucky in maintaining their current lifestyle and attributed it to the rewards of their hard, conscientious work over the years. Mark described himself as the son of immigrant parents and Melanie explained that she was the daughter of hard-working country school teachers. Mark went to college on the GI bill and credited the military service for offering him opportunities to achieve upward mobility.

Irene was very thin and pale, but quite a pretty girl. She spoke quickly and nervously and gestured intensely with her hands. She sat between her parents and allowed her mother to talk for her. Her most animated behavior accompanied any reference to her eating difficulties. Most of the time, she looked from mother to father as they spoke about her.

Individual Contexts

Mark considered himself a self-made man who had moved upward in his life. He described himself as "conscientious, a good family man, a good worker, always calm and in control." He was known at work as a "good thinker." His leisure activities included golf at the country club and whatever social activities Melanie arranged.

In talking about his childhood, Mark referred to an early decision that he must become successful and recognized in order to avoid the financial insecurities and humiliations he experienced as a youngster in an immigrant family. As a boy he delivered newspapers in a wealthy section of his home town and he always yearned for a nice house and a fancy car. After high school, he went into the service, and it was not until he returned that he realized that he could actualize his dreams. His motto was always "if you want it badly enough, you can get it with hard work and focused concentration." He reported that he was even-tempered and that he rarely got angry. When he was upset, he kept it to himself, since he never wanted to worry his family and he believed that he could wait things out. He remembered no conflicts or changes in his life course. He always vigorously pursued a consistent path and never had any reason to question or reassess it.

Melanie felt gratification at being a wife and mother. She resented the media for encouraging women to work rather than staying at home and tending to their children. Her dream had been to marry and have children and a nice comfortable life, and that is just what she did. She loved entertaining and cooking and her major hobby was gardening. She enjoyed the country club and the social life there and was pleased with the way her marriage and her children had turned out. She was, however, puzzled by Irene's difficulties. She had never realized that Irene was getting "too thin" and at first she resented the fuss the college was making. She admitted that she had felt a little lost after Irene went off to college and that she had looked forward to her weekend visits. Now that Irene was home, everything was fine and she really enjoyed having someone to take care of. Melanie claimed that she had always appreciated and been happy with her marital and lifestyle choices and that she could never understand other people who seemed to agonize over decisions, regret choices, and make themselves miserable. "Family stability" was her highest value and she believed that she had come as close as possible to creating the "ideal family."

Irene indicated that she was not sure who or what she was. She did not particularly like college. She found most of the courses meaningless and did not know why she selected them. She did not like dormitory life, where there was no privacy and everyone minded everyone else's business. She reported that she had never been as popular or as outgoing as her sisters. Her mother interjected here to comment that "Irene was the stay-at-home girl—my special helper." Irene responded that she liked to help her mother cook and garden. She liked her time alone with her mother. They went out to lunch and to shop. Irene had no idea what she would do after college. She supposed she would get some kind of job. Irene had dated very little. She went along with friends on casual group outings, but she had never felt any romantic attachment.

Family Context

Neither Mark nor Melanie maintained much contact with their family of origin. As the Willises moved up the socioeconomic ladder, their interests changed and they no longer felt comfortable visiting their parents' homes or having their parents visit them. With further exploration, it turned out that Mark was really the one who felt this way and that Melanie missed her parents and would have liked more contact with them. However, as she became busier with her own children and activities, her feelings about her parents receded. She had been thinking about them more since her own children were grown and she was now telephoning them and worrying about their aging and declining self-care capacities. Mark seemed surprised to hear this and suggested that perhaps after Irene got well Melanie could visit her parents. Melanie replied that she herself had been thinking about that.

Melanie and Mark met six months after Mark returned from service and entered the university where Melanie was also an undergraduate student. They began to date steadily, and after six months they became engaged. Melanie finished college first and did secretarial work while Mark finished up. They timed their first baby to coincide with Mark's graduation. He was hired immediately by a large manufacturing firm. They moved four times in the thirty years of their marriage and each move involved a promotion and financial reward. They had been in their current residence for twelve years and felt rooted there, not intending to move again.

The four daughters were easily conceived and delivered and presented no problems in terms of childrearing. There were no untoward school or behavioral difficulties. Both parents agreed that Melanie was an "excellent mother" who always put her family's needs first. All the daughters exceeded their parents' expectations. The parents reported that Irene was probably the most spoiled of the daughters and the most "clingy," but they enjoyed that quality and agreed that she probably did receive more of their time and attention than the others. The three agreed that Mom was the family manager, although most of the rules were declared by Dad, who passed them on to Mom. Irene had never seen her parents disagree or argue and she considered them to be "super" parents. None of the daughters ever went through any adolescent rebellion other than some arguing about curfews.

This family was also at the end of the launching stage, and again we see that a symptomatic youngster can delay the process of this stage, which would require major role and boundary changes involving couple renegotiation. This was a family with a "be perfect" family script—no problems whatsoever were allowed. They presented an ideal image to the world at large.

Career Context

Surprisingly, it was in the career area that the "family secret" emerged. Neither Melanie nor Irene had even begun to consider their own career goals, so Mark was the major focus in terms of career context. Mark felt that he had been very successful at work and that he had deserved his steady rise up the career ladder. He had only worked for two companies since college graduation and he believed he was one of the most valued executives in his company. He considered himself to be loyal and dedicated and never refused a company request to travel, relocate, or work later or harder than usual. The pay and benefits were always satisfactory to him and he and Melanie were careful to obey the implicit company rules and to entertain and associate with the "right" people. He felt that he was respected at work; he tried to remain uninvolved personally and emotionally with peers.

When the counselor commented on the impact of the declining economy on technological firms, even giants such as those he worked for, Mark blanched and then murmured that there had been recent layoffs across the board. It then emerged that three people on Mark's level had been let go and that several departments were up for consolidation, including Mark's. During this dialogue between the counselor and Mark, Melanie kept interjecting comments such as "Don't worry so much dear; I'm sure they'll never let *you* go." The anxiety and evasion that this topic caused was sufficient to alert the counselor to a serious threatening issue. It finally emerged that both Melanie and Mark knew that a strong possibility existed that, if things did not turn dramatically for the better businesswise in the next few months, Mark was one of the people most likely to be laid off. While he would receive a generous severance and partial-pension paycheck, his employability was doubtful at his age and with the economic situation as it was. This issue was so painful for this couple that they had great difficulty even discussing it. They preferred to deny it, as they had all unpleasant or difficult issues. They could not conceive of what a layoff might mean to them in terms of their lifestyle or how they might prepare and plan for such an involuntary change.

Further probing revealed that Irene had overheard her parents talk about a colleague who had been laid off, describing the disastrous results for this man's family. Mark and Melanie were surprised that Irene even knew about this possibility and hastened to reassure her, telling her not to worry or think about it. The focus was again transferred back to Irene's problems, and both Melanie and Mark closed up on career issues.

Assessment

This family was a very frightened system defending itself against inevitable changes. Melanie did not want to lose her primary role as "mother," and was working hard to keep Irene needy. Mark was afraid of being forced to take early retirement or start all over again, and refused to allow himself to plan for likely changes. Irene, the self-sacrificing daughter, was rescuing her parents from their fears by refusing to grow up and leave home and by presenting them with an all-consuming problem to focus upon. Each member of this family was confused as to identity and the enmeshment of all three protected them from having to confront these identity issues. They banded together for safety and security, and it was only when Irene's attempts to protect got out of hand and outsiders (physician and college personnel) were brought in that they were forced to seek help and expose their neediness and problems. Since this family was better versed in denial than in coping, the members had a lot of catching up to do to deal with the developmental issues they could no longer stave off.

Very often in family systems, the members' attempts to solve a problem result in more problems than solutions. In this case, the Willises' strategies to solve their problems with enmeshment and caring resulted in raising the ante, escalating the solution (the anorexia, which would protect the parents from dealing with more frightening issues and Irene from having to grow up and leave home) to life-or-death proportions. This coverup only increased the anxiety level and the family's defensive strategies. Eventually, a crisis was inevitable and the system was bound to experience major disruption.

Goals

The primary goal of therapy was to cure Irene's anorexia by detriangulating her from her parents, helping her to individuate and prepare for launching. Simultaneously, Mark and Melanie were targeted to remove some of their energies from Irene and to focus on their couple and career issues. Another goal involved dealing with unresolved issues from their families of origin and using this learning to help them renegotiate their relationships with their adult offspring.

Interventions

Interventions were utilized to disrupt the homeostasis of calm, denial, and perfection, and to introduce some structural changes so that the system could recalibrate. The first intervention involved dealing directly with the presenting symptom, anorexia nervosa. First, the problem was reframed so that Melanie and Mark could see how Irene's problems protected them from having to acknowledge, much less deal with, their individual, couple, and career issues. The therapist called Irene a "good daughter" and told her that she was no longer going to have to work so hard or to sacrifice herself by staying a child. The therapist educated the parents about the seriousness of Irene's illness and gave them specific behavioral instructions on cooperating to get Irene to eat. It was their responsibility as parents to see to it that their daughter eat and they were to accomplish this any way they could. Some new rules were established:

1. In between meal times, no mention of food or eating was to be made;
2. Melanie and Mark were not to weigh Irene;
3. The family physician was to monitor Irene's weight.

Alternative ways of dealing with eating times were role played during the therapy sessions. Family sculpture was also employed so that each member of the family could express personal perceptions and desires for closeness and distance.

Simultaneously, Irene was given several assignments to help her to learn more about her possible interests and desires and to help her to become more involved with college peers. She was directed to her college counseling center for career testing and to her church for youth-group activities. Likewise, Melanie was encouraged to identify interests and activities she could pursue without Irene. With increasing free time as her children left, she had to find new ways to occupy her time. In other words, the counselor gave Irene tasks that would enable her to take more responsibility for age-appropriate activities, and taught Melanie and Mark to refrain from interfering and rescuing her. The goal was to formulate clearer rules about parent–offspring interactions. Melanie and Irene were taught to practice differentiated communications so that infantilizing mother–daughter disabling sequences could be disrupted.

When the presenting problem of anorexia began to abate, the therapist saw Irene individually to work on her individual identity and career issues. The therapist saw Mark and Melanie as a couple so that they could deal with their couple and career issues. There were three weeks of struggling for this family. They were being forced to change some ingrained patterns and they naturally resisted change. Every time Irene began to eat, the tension escalated as Mark and Melanie began to panic about her leaving and about their probable career crisis. Irene, feeling the tension, would then backtrack and stop eating, and, as her parents refocused on her eating difficulties and on feeding her, the tension level was reduced. Since the family was directed to deal with the eating only at meal time, it was important to measure the lengths of meal times. If meals grew short because Irene was eating, tensions increased; then Irene would begin to resist and meals grew longer, leaving little time for other issues to surface. The therapist continued to give specific directives and to confront and reframe the system's resistances and gradually Mark and Melanie lowered their defenses and admitted that they needed to face up to some things.

Another intervention was bibliotherapy. Mark had always been too busy to read nonbusiness-oriented materials and the therapist suggested that he read some popular trade books on mid-life issues, preretirement, and career choices. Melanie was directed to read specific books about women's mid-life years and the types of changes that might occur. Cognitive restructuring was ongoing as the therapist attempted to change the partners' thinking about growth and to teach them that growth and change are potentially positive rather than negative and fearsome.

Outcome

After three months of treatment, the family physician determined that Irene's eating disorder was definitely improving. Her weight had stabilized in an acceptable range. Irene decided to take a year off from college to try some work experiences. She thought that it was a waste of time and money to go to college when she did not like it or know what she wanted to do. She said that she would probably remain at home for a while, but she hoped to earn enough money to move. She seemed relieved once she had made this decision. She hoped to find herself and to return to college when she knew how to use it. Mark and Melanie were disappointed at first by her leaving college, but they were also relieved at the financial implications. They supported her decision after expressing their initial reservations. Irene still needed to work on peer relationships, but she was making attempts to socialize more with friends now that she could no longer count on her parents to include her in their activities.

Melanie was finding that she liked her own pursuits. She was beginning to think of ways that she might be able to help out financially if Mark indeed did get laid off. During this period, Mark and other executives in his firm had to take a 15 percent salary cut, a difficult situation but one that Mark hoped would preclude further drastic action. He and Melanie could not talk about the threats to his job security, however, without taking it as a personal failure, though Mark was beginning to talk to associates about other possibilities. The couple began to plan how many years they needed to work and what their financial and living requirements were likely to be in ten years. At last they were acknowledging the approaching retirement stage, whether it would be early or on time, and what kinds of options they might have should a forced retirement occur early. One thing that was helpful for Mark was learning about his company's outplacement counseling policy, which had proven successful for other executives of Mark's age and background. This policy provided six months of career counseling, help with actual job searches, and follow-up. As the couple began to focus more on their own issues, Irene was freed to focus on hers. Mark and Melanie could now share their fears of aging and loss, and this new freedom in communication strengthened their bonds.

Comments

The presenting problem in this case, anorexia nervosa, was cleared up fairly quickly and easily. The anorexia nervosa was apparently not severe and served as a protective mechanism to cover up more frightening issues in the family system.

Strong, directive interventions escalated the homeostatic disruption that allowed the family to change. Supportive interventions encouraged change, and once movement occurred in one area, with the presenting symptom, change was fostered in other areas.

As with many families, members needed to learn about the phases and issues of development. Reframing problems helps to convey this knowledge, and bibliotherapy and exposure to other people sharing similar concerns reinforce the teaching that occurs during sessions. When the problems and issues are reframed as developmental happenings, people can see that they are stuck rather than sick and they are more encouraged to grow and change.

Again, we see that the reciprocal influences of individual, family, and career issues underlie the presenting problem. It is not unusual for a youngster to be the identified patient with the presenting symptom, with this configuration viewed as a more acceptable way of dealing with the parents' mid-life issues.

CASE 4: ANNA

Presenting Problem

Anna, 57, was referred for therapy by her physician. She visited him regularly with vague physical complaints. He was unable to find any organic basis for her complaints and felt that she was depressed and lonely. He referred her to a therapist. She was compliant and immediately followed through on his referral. In fact, she went to great lengths to do so, since she had to take a two-hour bus trip each way in order to see the therapist he recommended. Anna presented herself as always feeling nervous and jittery, claiming that she had difficulty getting along with her co-workers and that she now fights continuously with her 83-year-old mother, with whom she lives. In therapy, she spent a great deal of time talking about how other people irritate her and how she feels they always look down on her and talk about her behind her back. She expressed guilt about resenting her mother's controlling demands. Life seemed very hard and dull to Anna and she was frightened. She said that she needed to relax and feel better in order to go on living.

Description of Client

Anna appeared to be quiet, timid, neat, and orderly. When she smiled, she loosened up and was quite attractive. Most of the time she had a pinched, anxious look about her and her eyes darted around the room. Her voice was low and well modulated and her vocabulary indicated that she was intelligent, alert, and well read. Her posture and body language fit that of a depressed person. Anna said that she always had low energy and felt vaguely unhappy. She was getting worried because her bitterness and sharpness seemed to be increasing with age and sometimes got out of control with co-workers, as indicated by her last job evaluation. She snapped nastily, expressing impatience and resentment, and this behavior tended to alienate others in the office.

Individual Context

Anna described herself as "quiet, conscientious, dependable, and a loner." She was a high school graduate, having majored in business, and she entered the world of work immediately after high school, working herself up from entry-level clerical jobs to a senior bank clerk. She was always shy and lonely. She was the older daughter and middle child in a Middle Eastern immigrant family, and always lived in an ethnic section of town where family life centered around the church. Although she attended public school, she had few friends now and remembered no close relationships in her lifetime. She remembered her childhood as family-centered. She was a good student and she read and fantasized a lot. Her mother still calls her the ethnic term for "bookworm." Her sister and brother were more sociable and outgoing and Anna did not mind that. She believed that she was her father's favorite. However, he died when she was 9, and she then had to assume more household responsibilities while her mother went out to work. Thus, Anna was a good girl who never gave anyone any trouble. She was obedient and never allowed herself to express anger although she was aware of inner resentments over her mother's demands. She dreamed of getting married and having her own family. However, she has never dated or had a relationship with a man except in fantasy. She mentioned several relationships but exploration revealed that they had never gone beyond an initial meeting because Anna was "afraid that he would want more than I could give." It was pretty clear that Anna had tried to repress her sexual impulses and that now her fantasies and desires were becoming irrepressible and causing her a great deal of anxiety.

For the past thirty-seven years, Anna had lived a stable, predictable, dull life. She was the only sibling who never married and, while the decision was never discussed or openly acknowledged, she was the one who took responsibility for living with Mom. Her nonjob life always revolved around her house, her mother and her mother's friends and relatives, and solitary pursuits such as cooking, sewing, and shopping.

Anna had never really liked working. She had a history of unsatisfactory relationships with co-workers and supervisors but had never been fired. She always managed to find another job and leave before the interpersonal issues erupted into a full-blown crisis. She claimed that her relations with unfair supervisors caused her problems. Until the age of 50, she had not stayed on any job longer than a few years. She had been working at a bank for the past seven years and she felt that she had to stay there because of her age and accumulated pension benefits.

Anna's life was regularly scheduled. She cleaned house, sewed, cooked, watched television, or took walks in the evenings, and enjoyed shopping on Saturdays (usually alone but occasionally with her sister). Sundays were family visiting days and Saturdays were the days that Anna shopped and ran errands. She never took vacations or trips but she was thrifty enough to have saved up money "for a special occasion."

Several years before entering therapy, Anna had an emergency gall bladder operation and she remembers that period of time as the "happiest" in her life. She enjoyed her hospitalization, where she was nurtured and taken care of and she enjoyed the attentions of her family and co-workers during her convalescent period. She wanted to learn how to make friends and she was feeling a need to get involved in new interests and more sociable activities. When asked why at this time she wanted to make these changes, she replied that she was beginning to realize that her mother would not live forever and that, since she would not be able to work forever, she would have to find some meaning in her life. Her mother's health was remarkably good. However, Anna saw other people her age involved in families and/or activities and was feeling more and more left out of the mainstream of life.

In terms of the individual developmental life cycle, Anna was another example of the "moratorium identity" suffering a delayed mid-life transition. She never had decided for herself who she was or what she wanted out of life. She merely continued to be the devoted daughter and to plod through life, escaping into fantasy and hoping that someone or something would rescue her. Her physician was perceptive in recognizing her bids for attention via psychosomatic complaints. The psychosomatic complaints coincided with the onset of menopause and it was possible that menopause served as a trigger for escalating accumulated anxieties.

Family Context

Anna's older brother had married and moved across the country many years ago. His contact with his sisters was infrequent, although he phoned his mother once or twice a month. There were rare visits. However, Anna's mother still doted on her only son and held him up as the favorite child. Anna's younger sister lived at home until she was in her late twenties, whereupon she met her husband at a church function and moved to a neighboring city with him. She has two children and works full time.

Anna said that her family never expressed warmth or affection to each other and that verbal communication was nonexistent. She visited with her sister on Sundays and occasionally her sister came in to shop with her, but they did not have a close relationship. Anna said that she did not want to "bother her sister" with her concerns and that it would not occur to her to share her feelings. Her sister offered to take their mother so that Anna could go away for a vacation, but Anna always found an excuse as to why she could not do this.

Anna felt that her mother had always been critical and cold with her. She was pained by this, as she perceived herself as obedient and considerate. In the couple of years before therapy began, their bickering had escalated into loud arguments—over how loud the television was, who left a dirty plate on the table, and so on. Anna complained that her mother wanted her to do as she bid and that if, for example, Anna went into the kitchen to bake and her mother wanted to watch television, she would nag Anna to come watch television with her. Her mother told her how "nervous" and "difficult" she was to live with and said things like "no wonder you have no friends; I'm the only one who can stand to be around you."

Career Context

Anna was bored with her job but felt that she had no choices in terms of her age and the economy. She felt that she got the detail work that no one else ever wanted to do and she resented the fact that other people in the office socialized with each other and enjoyed themselves. She definitely felt left out and she expressed a great deal of her antagonism to her co-workers. Anna felt that her salary and pension benefits would be adequate. Because she did not drive, she was appreciative that she worked for a bank located on her bus line.

When Anna was in high school, she hoped to become a personal secretary to an important executive. However, she found that she had difficulty talking to men at work and she ended up in a stenographic pool. Eventually she got into book-keeping and accounts payable work, more or less by chance. In actuality, she could think of nothing she would rather do. She reacted poorly to pressure and deadlines and she preferred to work alone without any distractions. She was, in fact, transferred to a lesser job after complaining about the distractions of answering the office telephone.

Assessment

Anna was indeed clinically depressed and reaching a stage of life where she could no longer evade making some decisions. Her fantasies no longer worked for her as defensive strategies. The pain of her loneliness and alienation and her years of growing bitterness and anger erupted through these defensive strategies and she selected the only way she knew to get help: developing a physical symptom. Anna needed to understand her feelings about her mother and to separate emotionally from her so that she could continue to live with her and care for her but, at the same time, develop some kind of social life for herself. She also had to plan for her retirement and for living alone.

Goals

Because of limited finances and the need to stay within the range of insurance benefits, Anna and the counselor decided on time-limited therapy. A first goal was to teach Anna how to relax physically and to gain control over her muscles, so she would feel fewer physical manifestations of anxiety. A second, and simultaneous, goal was to establish a trusting relationship so that she could openly explore her negative feelings about herself and others. The point was to use the therapeutic relationship as a basis for self-understanding and changing interpersonal relationships. A third goal was to involve Anna in some structured activities and help her achieve the concrete goal of taking a vacation by herself.

Interventions

A trusting relationship between Anna and the therapist developed easily. She was so eager for attention and empathy that she worked very hard to cooperate in the therapy. An interesting phenomenon occurred after the second session, during which Anna was being taught muscular relaxation techniques: Anna fell and broke her hip while taking the bus home from work and she was hospitalized for four weeks and confined at home for another six weeks. Because of the efforts she had made and her desperation for help, the therapist continued the sessions by visiting Anna in the hospital and at home. For Anna, this hospitalization was a bitter disappointment. She was not nurtured this time and no one paid much attention to her. In fact, the nurses perceived her as too demanding and went out of their way to avoid her. On one particular night Anna rang and rang and no one came, so she telephoned the hospital operator and reported that the nurses were having a party and ignoring her. Needless to say, the staff did not take to this kindly. However, upon the therapist's investigation, it turned out that Anna's report was fairly accurate. Her disappointment was translated into antagonism, which further alienated the staff and continued the rejection–resentment cycle. In addition, Anna was disappointed because she did not get cards or visits from her co-workers. This hospitalization experience was quite different from her earlier one.

The therapist continued the relaxation exercises and spent much time eliciting exploratory comments from Anna, while reframing many of the thoughts and perceptions that Anna presented. Utilizing role plays and switching roles between Anna and significant others, Anna came to understand the kinds of distancing and double messages she sent to people and how she thought for them rather than allowing them to think for themselves. For example, she defensively decided that someone did not like her, so she acted on that presumption without checking it out or giving the other person a chance. It was not difficult to understand why people left her out. She sent out messages that she was proud and did not need anyone's friendship, though in reality she was urgently pleading for attention and friendship.

Anna's mother was present at several home sessions, and they focused on opening and clarifying direct communications and boundaries. Anna was surprised to learn how much her mother cared for her and how concerned her mother was about Anna's loneliness and what will happen when she inevitably is left alone. These sessions proved very helpful for both women in fostering mutual understanding and consideration.

Between sessions, Anna was given structured assignments, such as inviting someone for tea, sending away for adult education brochures, and opening up certain topics for conversation with her sister. Anna always performed these tasks eagerly and conscientiously.

Outcome

As soon as Anna was able to return to work, she noticed a difference in her relationships with co-workers. She was able to cognitively restructure her old internal sentences and to approach people rather than evade them. She registered for two adult education courses that met right after work. She chose one group experience entitled "How to Meet Other People" and found the first few sessions very threatening. Still, she stuck it out and succeeded in making a couple of friends. She reported that she and her mother were fighting less and that she was surprised to find that her sister had always wanted to be closer to her. She was unsuccessful in her attempt to find a friend to take a vacation with, but she did sign up to take a four-day bus tour alone. She wrote the therapist a letter nine months later and reported that she had fewer feelings of depression and was continuing to work on making friends.

Comments

Many deeper issues could have been worked through with Anna, but the nature of the presenting symptoms and the limited number of sessions possible indicated that a short-term, problem-focused therapy was the most realistic choice of treatment for this client. Anna was basically very lonely and frightened, and she had never successfully achieved emotional separation from her mother. She was still fighting with her as an adolescent, and she was so angry she could not allow herself to see the fears and insecurities her mother was experiencing with increasing age. When Anna was able to see this, she was able to relate better to her mother and even to move closer to her sister. Rather than prolonging a dependent counseling relationship, it was important to help Anna develop other relationships. Much of the therapy focused on her finding compatible people who would become a network for her in her later years.

This case is a good example of how effective a short-term, problem-solving type of treatment can be with an adult client in later middle years. Anna had many strengths and talents that needed to be activated and developed. Teaching her about the tasks and issues of her stage of life and her mother's stage of life proved to be beneficial in mobilizing her resources.

SUMMARY

The four cases presented in this chapter dealt with an array of issues common to middle adulthood. We noticed how unresolved issues from early adulthood—namely, insufficient emotional separation from one's family of origin—can affect adult functioning in the middle years in family and other interpersonal relationships. We also noted that the reassessment of earlier career and relationship commitments is necessary. This reassessment may be tumultuous and may coincide with the leaving home of the youngest child or with an adolescent's own turbulence.

Interventions from many individual, group, and family therapies may be effective with adults in their middle years. Reframing the presenting issues in a developmental perspective is a common strategy that allows the client(s) to understand that they are stuck rather than sick. This is particularly helpful in those cases where the identified patient is a youngster. Little is known by most parents about facilitating the launching process and renegotiating the parent-adult-offspring relationships; thus, working with adults in this stage of life includes reeducation. This type of teaching may be reinforced by bibliotherapy and group experiences.

Other interventions include stress-management-skills teaching, career decision making and planning, preretirement planning, and dealing with grief and loss. Challenging and changing assumptions as part of cognitive-restructuring strategies are important in helping adults cope with difficulties and problems. Supportive relationship skills are necessary for making cognitive, behavioral, and structural strategies work. Thus, the major strategies and techniques include teaching, reenactment of problems during therapy sessions, homework assignments, reframing, family sculpting, and paradox (prescribing the symptom).

Many adult clients in their middle years mention that they prefer to work with a therapist who is in the same generation rather than one who is twenty years younger. This implies the importance of peer-support relationships, whether they be familial, professional, friendship, or work-related. Adults in middle and late adulthood have historical perspectives and experiences to share.

People in their middle years are often caught between the demands and needs of the younger and the older generations. While middle adults vacillate between change and stability, these years are enriching and require particular sensitivity on the part of the therapist to the individual, career, and family tasks and issues concomitant to that stage of life.

PART FOUR

LATE ADULTHOOD

The study of late adulthood, geropsychology, is relatively new. Many people are reluctant to delve into this area of study because of their irrational fear of aging. This is the same fear that causes us to distance ourselves psychologically and physically from having to think about or deal with the elderly. Our irrational fears have produced the phenomenon of *ageism*, the stereotypical negative and hostile attitudes that prevail about older people and the aging process. Common stereotypes include beliefs that older people are poor, rigid, reactionary, ill, unhappy, isolated, lonely, senile, and prone to mental illness. In truth, a 1981 Harris Poll showed that older people are perceived as being in much worse shape than they really are. Other studies show a higher degree of life satisfaction among the elderly than among younger adults. Nevertheless, stereotypical beliefs even affect the way older people perceive themselves and the process of aging.

Demographic data reveal that because the elderly population is living longer it has more than doubled during this century and will continue to increase. Thus, as the older population grows larger and demands more goods and services, it will demand higher status and will constitute a larger portion of the counseling clientele. As life expectancy continues to rise in this country, medical and technological advances are beginning to help us differentiate between the effects of aging and the effects of disease.

The purpose of Part IV is to identify and explore the years of late adulthood, from 60 on. We will divide this population into two groups: senior citizens, age 60–75; and the elderly, age 75 and above. This arbitrary differentiation will enable us to clarify the developmental tasks and issues facing older adults while acknowledging that the elderly will experience more disabling effects of disease than the senior citizens.

Let us remember that, while we can highlight some common developmental tasks and issues, the aging process does vary. In fact, most investigators find increasing diversity with age in terms of gender, health, role, and environmental issues. We will attempt to identify the psychological, physiological, social, and environmental variables that affect the aging process. Again, how one has coped with previous developmental tasks and issues will affect how one copes with those tasks and issues pertinent to late adulthood. Thus, aging is shaped by past developmental stages as well as by heredity, nutrition, disease, and factors related to socioeconomic status. The aging person draws on experience in adapting to biological changes from within and to the social changes from the environment.

Chapter 11 identifies and discusses the individual developmental tasks and issues of late adulthood. In general, these concern: disengagement from formal roles, relationships, and organizational systems; selective intense activities; and adaptation to inevitable changes in one's personal life circumstances. The postparental family stages, including the loss of one's spouse and formation of alternative relationships, are explored in Chapter 12, as are grandparenting and other independency/dependency issues. Chapter 13 covers the issues of retirement and postretirement and approaches to work and leisure. Chapter 14 presents case studies and discusses the implications for treatment and social service.

CHAPTER ELEVEN

INDIVIDUAL DEVELOPMENT IN LATE ADULTHOOD

We know that in late adulthood psychological, physiological, social, and environmental changes occur. These changes include both losses and gains. They differ among individuals in terms of their onset and impact. Some of the changes may even be modifiable or reversible, whereas some require positive adaptation. It might also be said that some of the changes appear to originate more in expectancy—as "self-fulfilling prophecies" resulting from the cumulative effect of mythological beliefs and stereotypes—than from aging or disease.

Thus, adults' expectations, anticipations, and preparations for late adulthood have an enormous impact on their transition to an actual experience of this stage. Many adults have no role models for late adulthood, owing to the early death of their own parents and grandparents. Only in recent years has popular media coverage of the "greying of America" served to raise our consciousness and educate us about the process of aging and the opportunities as well as changes that await us in late adulthood.

Birren (1983) states that there are two faces of aging in our society: optimistic and pessimistic. The optimistic faces concerns the competent elderly who enjoy a high quality life and who want new services, products and opportunities for personal growth. The pessimistic face concerns the poor, unhealthy and lonely elderly who have multiple health, social and psychological needs and dependencies. While as counselors and therapists we may see more of the pessimistic elderly, we need to remember that the other type exists and aim our interventions and objectives toward the optimistic face of aging.

The purpose of this chapter is to highlight the major findings of current studies of late adulthood and to identify and discuss the common developmental tasks and issues. In so doing, we will address the following questions:

1. What is aging?
2. What are the differences between aging and disease?
3. What are the physiological, psychological, social, and environmental variables affecting the aging process?
4. What are the effects of aging on sexual behavior? learning? creativity?
5. What are the role transitions pertinent to late adulthood?
6. What kinds of identity issues do older people face?
7. What kinds of interpersonal relationships are necessary in late adulthood?
8. What cultural factors affect the aging process?

We begin our discussion with a study of the aging process itself. We will consider the physiological, cognitive, and behavioral changes associated with this universal process. Next, we will study the current data about late-adulthood disease and its effect on the aging process. We will then look at the developmental tasks and issues for senior citizens, aged 60–75, and for the elderly, aged 75 and above. Whereas some of these tasks and issues continue throughout late adulthood, emphases and foci vary among individuals.

THE AGING PROCESS

Our view is that aging is a universal, complex, life-span phenomenon. We begin to age from the moment of conception, although we are more likely to term the process *maturation* in the early decades. This process embraces our physiological, psychological, and social functioning. Likewise, there are biological, psychological, and sociological aspects of aging. Whereas no single theory of aging is universally accepted, we will recapitulate some of the main findings of the major views about the aging process.

Biological Theories of Aging

In later years, biological aging involves physiological changes that increase our susceptibility to illness and then to death. These physiological changes affect the functioning of all our organic systems—for example, our digestive, neurological, cardiovascular, and endocrinological systems—as well as our cognitive, psychological, and social functioning. The cumulative effects of the aging process that manifest themselves more acutely in the later years make it appear as if the physiological, psychological, and social changes had a rapid onset when, in truth, they had begun slowly many years earlier. The changes are, however, multiple and profound as well as varying in intensity.

Biological theories of aging cover a wide range, from alterations in DNA structures to errors in cell division to defects in immunological systems. Basically, there appear to be two major schools of thought: (1) the programmed theory, which assumes a preset for every species; and (2) the accumulated-insults-to-the-body theory, which assumes a kind of wearing out as the body goes through the normal wear and tear of life and then becomes more susceptible to disease.

Kimmel (1974) points out that gerontology has been unable to determine whether aging results from an evolutionary necessity for survival of the species, accumulated effects of "wear and tear," or a natural process of cellular aging and physiological change. Macione (1979) refers to the difficulty of distinguishing between changes caused by aging and those caused by time-related diseases. The homeostatic view has been explicated by Comfort (1970), who defines aging as

> . . . the process or group of processes which cause the eventual breakdown of mammalian homeostasis with the passage of time. The timing of these processes, although it shows some genetic scatter, is uncommonly stable. It is the universal experience of man that while we may die sooner from single causes, between 70 and 90 years of age homeostasis declines across the board, causes of sickness accumulate and causes of death become multiple [p. 228].

This implies that the capacity of homeostatic mechanisms to restore equilibrium in the organism decreases in efficiency with age. As one becomes older, one is less likely to tolerate stress and strain and to bounce back. Because of this decreased homeostatic efficiency, disease, seen as physiological stress, and emotional stresses such as loss of spouse or environmental changes, could then increase the risk of death for the elderly as compared with the young.

Regardless of which parts of which theories cause the aging process, we do know that aging leads to a growing inability to adapt to the environment and to survive. We can also assume that hereditary and environmental factors impact physiological aging. Recent concern has focused on environmental factors, such as the effects of radiation on the life span, and the effects of continuous sun exposure on the aging of skin. Let us review some of the common physiological changes associated with the aging process.

Physiological changes.   Physiological changes associated with the aging process include changes in one's physical appearance, losses in sensory modalities, and neurological and sensorimotor changes. Some of the specific changes associated with late adulthood include the following:

1. Diminished hearing, particularly the ability to hear higher frequencies.
2. Diminished sight, including the ability of the eye to adjust its focus between near and far objects and its ability to adapt to light and dark.
3. Declining sense of smell; the brain's ability to recognize the taste of food is blunted as taste buds degenerate.

4. Decreasing maximum lung capacity; a reduced amount of air coming into the lungs during heavy breathing alters one's athletic capacity.
5. Hair loses it color as pigment-producing cells die.
6. Hair thins and grows more slowly.
7. The duration and quality of sleep changes owing to neurological changes. Sleep is less deep and contains fewer dreams. How long one sleeps in older age, however, seems to be related to the amount of sleep one needed as a younger adult.
8. Height decreases 1 to 3 inches as the vertebrae become smaller and undergo increased pressure. Stooping is caused by wedging of spinal bones.
9. Bones lose their calcium and become less dense, more brittle, and more susceptible to fracture.
10. Skin wrinkles as it becomes thinner and less resilient through a weakening of a protein called elastin. This process is accelerated in sun-exposed skin.
11. Muscles become weaker and less coordinated. The lean body mass and skeletal muscle decrease as the percentage of body fat increases.
12. Cardiac output diminishes, meaning that the amount of blood the heart pumps lessens.
13. Renal (kidney) blood flow diminishes to fifty percent of its original capacity. Since kidneys eliminate drugs from the body, their decline means that older people are more susceptible to drug intoxication.
14. Decreased capacity to fight infections as the effects of the immunological system are reduced.
15. Hormonal balance changes affecting physical appearance—for example, women grow hair on their faces—and affecting orgasm frequency, particularly of males, and arousal time in both men and women.
16. Arteries become thicker and stiffer and less responsive, thus slowing the blood flow. The regulation of the circulatory system is less effective and blood pressure control less accurate.
17. Regulation of body temperature is impaired, leading to more vulnerability to extremes in temperature. Sweat glands and subcutaneous tissue atrophy, leading to decreased ability to perspire.
18. Teeth become worn or lost, which affects food intake.
19. Digestive enzymes and gastric acids decrease qualitatively and quantitatively, leading to less efficient digestion. Digestive tract muscles weaken and shrink, resulting in more sluggish bowel functioning.

Remember, individuals vary regarding the degree and age of onset of these changes. As we think about these physiological changes, we can perhaps better understand some of the stresses originating with them, stresses that might show up in altered behaviors and that might cause confusion in the diagnosis of illness vis-à-vis physical or mental aging. Likewise, we can see how these physiological changes are reciprocally influenced by the social, psychological, and environmental experiences of older adults. People who have always valued their physical appearance and who begin to worry about their attractiveness as these changes become more pronounced will undoubtedly be affected in their self-concepts, relationships with other people, and attitudes toward the world at large.

Psychological Theories of Aging

It is difficult to consider the psychological aging of older adults apart from the physiological, social, and environmental contexts. Let us look briefly at what is currently known about personality types and aging and the intellectual functioning of older adults. Much of the research is inconclusive, but we are interested in whether or not there are likely to be recognizable changes.

As Neugarten (1968) pointed out, psychological differences increase with age. In other words, while it is easy to generalize about the behaviors and traits of children at the primary-grade level or at preadolescence, it is much more difficult to generalize about the behaviors and traits of adults in later adulthood. Perhaps the reason for the differences is related to variations in the life experiences of individuals and to health, financial, and longevity variables as well. Significant differences also exist regarding surviving kin, intrafamilial communication patterns, and other significant relationship-support networks. And certainly much diversity among individuals is to be found in terms of lifestyles and life circumstances.

In their review of the literature, Whitbourne and Weinstock (1979) concluded that older adults perceive the environment as more complex and dangerous than adults in midlife, and that they have moved from an outer-world to an inner-world orientation. Certain personality characteristics remain consistent over the life span while others change. Overt qualities, those purposive and subject to conscious change, do not change, whereas covert, intrapsychic qualities, such as impulse control and inner-world orientation, become more pronounced. Some studies have attempted to identify personality types in later adulthood.

Personality types.   While controversy surrounds the effects of aging on personality types, Buhler (1968) found that most of the older people she studied in the 1920s and 1930s fell into one of four distinct personality types:

1. Those satisfied with their past lives and content to relax;
2. Those who would not sit back but felt they must strive to the end;
3. Those who were dissatisfied with their past lives and sat back with an unhappy air of resignation;
4. Those dissatisfied with their past lives who continued to experience regrets, frustrations, and guilt to the end.

She concluded that one's life experiences combined with life-long personality traits and patterns lead to one of these formats. We can see that there is an approach–avoidance continuum, which is probably likely to remain constant over the life span. Simultaneously, the satisfaction–dissatisfaction continuum also seems to remain fairly constant over the life span. Such consistency might lend some credence to the view that one's predisposition to perceive things as positive or negative might be a fairly constant pattern, as might be the tendency to actively engage with the world or to passively resign oneself to the problems of life.

Neugarten and her team (1968) predicated their four major personality types of older people on the Chicago and Kansas City studies (upon which her books, particularly the 1968 book, are based):

1. Integrated personalities: people who faced up to their emotions, had rich inner lives, and either pursued focused activities or were contented to sit back in their rocking chairs;
2. Armor-defended personalities: people who restrained their creativity and carefully held their impulses and emotions in a tight harness;
3. Passive–dependent personalities: people who were less satisfied with their lives and were either apathetic or excessively dependent on others;
4. Unintegrated personalities: people with low activity levels characterized by dissatisfaction and disorganization.

Again, the continua emerge of satisfaction–dissatisfaction with past lives and approach–avoidance regarding engaging in life activities (as with Buhler, 1968). Neugarten is careful to point out that the origins of these personality types are established by middle age. In other words, she found remarkably consistent patterns of coping and adjustment over the life span, indicating that personality continuities definitely existed over time. Kastenbaum (1971) supports these findings in his research and concludes that many of the psychological changes and patterns associated with aging began many years earlier.

However, it is important to remember that with advancing age, one's familiar environmental niche typically changes, and this causes a shift in the fit between the individual and environment. These shifts, in addition to the psychological changes that they typically bring, add stress to one's personality system as it seeks to maintain its fit, or homeostasis, with the environmental niche. It is not unusual for internal and external stresses to overwhelm the personality system, leading to some type of psychopathology.

An interesting study by Maas and Kuypers (1974) found sex-role differences as well as individual differences in the personality types of middle-class white subjects (all parents) ages 60–82. Remember that elderly subjects today were raised in a culture much more rigidly sex stereotypical than our own and that the sex-role differences in this group are likely to be more pronounced than in younger age groups, which have benefited more directly from changes in sex roles. This research team found that women fell into four types of personalities:

1. Person-oriented mothers, who were giving, sympathetic, warm, and well-liked;
2. Fearful-ordering mothers, who were withdrawn, reassurance-seeking, and anxious, with little personal meaning in their lives;

3. Autonomous mothers, who were more involved with formal organizational systems (clubs, work) than with their families;
4. Anxious-asserting mothers, who were histrionic, self-dramatizing, moody, hostile, or talkative.

Men fell into three types:

1. Person-oriented fathers, who, while still less socially poised than the person-oriented mothers, were warm, sympathetic, giving, and popular;
2. Active-competent fathers, who were power conscious, aloof, verbal, and charming;
3. Conservative-ordering fathers, who were overcontrolling, repressive, and conventional.

Most importantly, these researchers found that not all of their subjects in later life had the same personality types as they did in earlier life and that the changes they exhibited depended upon environmental, physiological, and social variables.

Maas and Kuypers (1974) also looked at the lifestyles of these subjects and found that those of the women tended to be less continuous than those of the men. The six lifestyles they identified for women follow:

1. Husband-centeredness, where the woman was more interested in her husband than in anyone else;
2. Uncentered mothers, where the woman lived alone, usually in poor health and with meager financial resources;
3. Visiting mothers, where the women had frequent social interaction with their peers, churches, and/or clubs;
4. Work-centered, where the woman was usually widowed or divorced and working full or part time and living alone in relatively good health;
5. Disabled-disengaging, where the woman was in poor health and lived with others, but in a withdrawn, dependent manner;
6. Group-centered, where the woman was well educated, financially comfortable, and active in formal social organizations and functions.

The predominant elderly male lifestyles identified were these:

1. Family-centered fathers, where the major involvement was with wife, adult children, and grandchildren;
2. Hobbyists, where leisure interests and activities were the major interest;
3. Remotely sociable fathers, where formal organizations and functions were the major interest;
4. Unwell-disengaged fathers, where the man was isolated and withdrawn.

Many of the sex-role differences have been constant over the life span.

These lifestyles reflect both circumstances and personality types and they indicate much diversity as well as stability and continuity among the elderly. Perhaps merely our awareness of this variety and diversity, and of the constant interplay between stability and change, will dispel some of the stereotypical myths that prevail about the elderly population. Obviously, no such thing as a single "old personality" exists. But, in truth, older people have more changes and stresses to cope with and fewer resources to call upon for coping with them than younger adults.

Intellectual changes.   Changes in cognitive functioning associated with the aging process are also characterized by marked individual differences and are usually more gradual, less widespread, and more subtle than generally imagined. Most studies that deal with intelligence changes in later adulthood report on changes in measured IQ scores. These studies have found that traditional IQ tests are indeed inappropriate for elders, who consistently do less well on tests requiring manual dexterity, speed, and visual acuity (Botwinick, 1978; Eisdorfer & Cohen, 1961; Wechsler, 1958). In addition, questions from traditional IQ tests such as the WAIS are geared to predict adult success in learning various academic subjects and are, therefore, irrelevant to the concerns of the elderly. Other factors are likely to influence IQ test results, such as neurological deterioration, physical limitations, physiological factors, test anxiety, boredom, lack of motivation, cautiousness, self-defeating attitudes, inefficient problem-solving tests, terminal drop, and a lack of continued intellectual activities.

Kimmel (1974) points out that while typical elderly people may be somewhat slow at intellectual tasks and exhibit some impairment at mastering new problems where past experience is of no help, they are relatively unimpaired in many aspects of ordinary intellectual functioning. Memory loss does appear to be prevalent with advancing age, and whether this decline results from acquisition, retention, or retrieval of the memory is as yet unclear. It is true that younger people have better short-term memories and that memory loss with age results from increasing difficulties with organizing material and from the diminishing ability to retrieve information from memory. Gallagher and her associates (1980) point out the interrelationship of memory loss, organic pathology, and depressive and paranoid reactions, and they suggest a multimodal assessment in order to understand fully and treat concerns about memory and the elderly.

However, elderly people are certainly capable of learning when interesting, relevant material is presented at an appropriate rate. Learning and memory are interrelated and older people can learn new skills and information if it is presented slowly, at length, and over a relatively long period of time with appropriate intervals between exposures (Kastenbaum, 1971). Health, education, fear of failure, and individual differences may be much more important variables than age in terms of learning capabilities in the older adult. Another issue is how continuous learning and intellectual functioning have been throughout the life span of the older adult; one who has continuously engaged in such pursuits is more likely to have an easier time learning new material in later adulthood than one who has not engaged in such activities. Willis and Baltes (1980) identify three sets of interacting influences on development: (1) age-graded; (2) history-graded; and (3) nonnormative critical events. They propose that the intellectual capacities of the elderly can be practiced and preserved in varied appropriate ways if one considers these influences.

Skinner (1983) suggests, from his own aging experience, behavioral techniques that can directly reduce problems associated with sensory and motor deficiencies, memory loss, motivational changes and mental fatigue. These include use of reference books, use of productive leisure to control mental fatigue, rehearsal of what you're going to say, use of cues and so forth. He reports that his intellectual functioning in late adulthood is different but is just as effective as in earlier adulthood.

No data exist to show that there is a universal decline in creativity among the elderly. It is possible that, regardless of the way one defines creativity, functioning in this area is more the result of noncognitive factors than intellectual changes. It may also be true that younger people bring a fresher perspective to problem solving and that older people are more trapped by habitual patterns. On the other hand, one could argue that older people have the benefits of accumulated experiences and knowledge that could allow them broader creative freedoms. Many creative older people live in our society—some have always been creative and some have only recently begun to express their creativity.

Older people's intellectual functioning is interrelated with their self-identities and environmental opportunities and their satisfactions with various aspects of their lifestyles. Biological and environmental variables interact. Remember that, just as children and young adults learn to compensate for their learning disabilities, older people can learn compensatory strategies for whatever deficits their natural aging processes bring about.

Sociological Theories of Aging

The sociological theories of aging deal with the status of the aged in our society, and this status depends on the proportion of the population that is aged. As the aged population continues to grow, its status, needless to say, constantly changes. In the mid-twentieth century in this country the elderly have characteristically been held in low regard and been granted low status relative to other cultures in which the elderly are revered, given leadership roles and high status, and seen as the major source of wisdom and transmitters of the cultural mores. The economic implications of the status of the elderly in this country are hard to ignore. An expanding society, with plenty of jobs and services for all, would tend to view the elderly more liberally and to provide more services for them. But a constricting economy tends to be suspicious about resources taken away from younger adults and children and distributed to the elderly, and thus tends to devalue the elderly. Prevailing social, economic, and political policies reflect these views.

In a constricting economy, one tends to find the disengagement theory promulgated. According to this view, as stated by Cumming and Henry (1961), people in older age are considered well adjusted and successfully aging when they graciously withdraw from society. In fact, society and the aging withdraw from each other mutually—there is no resistance to retirement or to isolated residential living, and the elderly are supposed to be "seen and not heard," and to accept the biological and psychological changes they undergo as intrinsic, inevitable, and necessary for aging. This withdrawal is seen as a developmental process and is accompanied by an increased preoccupation with one's self and a decreased emotional investment in others and world affairs. Gradually, the disengagement leads to death, the final isolation and withdrawal.

In a more expansive economy, an activity theory of aging becomes more popular. This view maintains that the elderly should maintain their normal, usual level of activities and engagements, and that the more active one is, the more successful one's aging process will be. The normal activities referred to may be informal, formal, solitary, or group-oriented. In this viewpoint, too, biological and psychological changes are not intrinsic and inevitable but, rather, result from the influences of one's past lifestyle and socioeconomic forces. If one chooses isolation (living alone and liking it versus going to the old folks' home), that is fine as long as one continues to utilize whatever personal and environmental resources are available.

More recently, a third sociological view has been proposed, the social-reconstruction theory (Bengston, 1973). This viewpoint suggests that self-concept and the ageist social environment interact negatively to produce dysfunction. The theory proposes an ethic of feeling, sharing, surviving, enduring, and caring to be promoted by ongoing social services and programs designed to enhance self-concepts of the elderly—by improving housing, economic, and health resources, and by encouraging autonomy as much as possible. In other words, society is to provide programs and services to counterbalance the negative interaction between the elderly and the environment.

These approaches to the aging process—the biological, psychological, and sociological—all highlight vital components that mutually affect the older adult. From a systems perspective, we must consider their interrelationships with particular individuals and an individual's anticipations and unique interpretations of these issues and forces. The philosophical views of the individual overlay the interactions of the biological, psychological, and social variables, resulting in the humanistic aspect of development. Now that we have reviewed some of the natural characteristics of the aging process, we must consider the nature of disease and its particular impact on late adulthood.

DISEASE IN LATE ADULTHOOD

During late adulthood, individuals become more vulnerable to stress, disease, and complications of the aging process. It is therefore often difficult to distinguish between the effects of aging and those of disease. Particular degenerative changes and chronic diseases do increase in incidence with age, and older adults are more likely than younger adults to have multiple health problems or precipitous changes in their health status. The effects of aging and disease do indeed compound each other.

Chronic, rather than acute, diseases seem to prevail during late adulthood. The course of severe illnesses such as cancer and diabetes are much slower in their onset and progress in later adulthood than in earlier adulthood, and are more often considered chronic than acute. Thus, illness presents special problems for the elderly in that a given illness is superimposed on an assortment of preexisting chronic illnesses and on organ systems that have lost their wide margin of reserve capacity.

Herr and Weakland (1979) state that "most people by the time they are 65 are suffering from at least two chronic diseases" (p. 233). The most prevalent chronic diseases in late adulthood are high blood pressure, heart disease, arthritis, rheumatism, emphysema, diabetes, glaucoma, osteoporosis, and kidney disease. As previously mentioned, chronic impairments such as visual, hearing, or body-limb dysfunctions also increase with age.

The most important issue in the therapy of late-adulthood clients is how disease affects their quality of life. Obviously, individual differences mark how older adults handle and interpret their ailments. Many expect aging to be associated with the onset of disease and they respond with hypochondriasis and excessive attention to symptoms and ailments. "Elders' responses to health problems of all kinds will be influenced by their social and emotional interactions with their friends, families and health service providers" (Herr & Weakland, 1979, p. 233). Thus, human interactions and physical illness are intertwined.

An example is Mr. Jepson, 73, who had always been healthy and active, though emotionally distant from his adult children and grandchildren. His late-adulthood personality type was "active-competent father," and his lifestyle was "remotely sociable," his major interests being in formal and informal social organizations and activities (Maas and Kuypers, 1974).

When he was 73, Mr. Jepson experienced the onset of two diseases: glaucoma and angina. While neither condition was considered acute or particularly dangerous, Mr. Jepson was in the hospital for a few days for diagnosis and medication control and was advised to slow down his activities and adhere strictly to a medical and dietary regimen. Frightened and unused to restrictions of any kind, since he had never had to be concerned about his own health before, Mr. Jepson's behavior changed so dramatically that his children and grandchildren began to stay away. He withdrew more than necessary from his normal activities and he frightened away friends and family by obsessing continually about his symptoms, doctors, and medications. Any attempts to distract or reassure him were firmly resisted.

Mrs. Jepson found herself tiring of her nursing role after several months and began to complain to her children that she could never leave him without him complaining and whining. Two multigenerational family therapy sessions were conducted to enable Mr. Jepson to discuss his fears and express his needs and concerns directly to his family. They, in turn, developed more sensitivity to his vulnerabilities and were able to provide more support in their interactions with him.

This example illustrates how aging can be confounded by disease and its consequences. Many of the behavioral changes that result probably originate more from disease and its consequences than from aging per se.

Major Diseases

Let us briefly consider the major illnesses associated with late adulthood.

Cardiovascular diseases.   It is common for some hardening of the arteries to occur in late adulthood. If, however, this becomes a chronic disability, it is termed *arteriosclerosis,* the most frequently documented form of heart disease in late adulthood. Arteriosclerosis appears to have a number of causes, including heredity, diet (excessive high-cholesterol foods), lipid-metabolism dysfunction, smoking, pollution, and lack of exercise (Freiberg, 1976). The condition can affect the flow of blood throughout the body, causing clotting and acute myocardial infarction, angina pectoris, arrhythmia, congestive heart failure, and cerebral stroke.

Arteriosclerosis may cause psychological dysfunctions typically confused with the aging process. Such dysfunctions may include memory loss, a narrowed range of interest, and emotional reactions. One of the most devastating symptoms of arteriosclerosis is cerebrovascular stroke. The majority of strokes in the elderly are caused either by cerebral embolisms, hemorrhage, or cerebral thrombosis. Treatment is aimed at the primary cause—at preventing complications and recurrences and at restoring as much physical functioning as possible. Anticoagulant or antihypertensive drugs may be used. The restoration of functioning after such a stroke depends on the extent of the physical impairment, the part(s) of the body affected, the kinds of therapy available, the interpersonal supports, and the patient's will to live and personality traits.

Cerebral diseases.   Senile brain syndrome, or dementia, is the cerebral disease most closely associated with older age. There seems to be a national tendency to assume that all elderly people become demented as part of the aging process (Henig, 1981). In actuality, only 4 to 5 percent of the elderly population has the disease called dementia (Butler, 1977; *Boston Globe,* 1982). The term *dementia* refers to an illness characterized by such symptoms as mental failure, and the loss or reduction of memory, reasoning skills, orientation, social skills, emotional control, judging ability, calculating ability, and attention span. Sometimes these symptoms of dementia (confusion, disorientation, memory loss) are really the results of reversible conditions other than dementia, such as poor nutrition, diabetes, adverse drug reactions, depression, or boredom. Thus, when dealing with the elderly, it is important to distinguish between benign and malignant forgetfulness, and between true dementia and pseudosenility.

However, incurable dementia, commonly known as senility, does exist. The most common forms are multiinfarct dementia and Alzheimer's disease. (Alzheimer was a German neurologist who first described this disease in the early 1900s.) The former is a series of multiple strokes that cause the widespread deterioration of the brain tissues. The second, the more common, is found in 50 to 60 percent of all elderly people who develop severe intellectual impairment. While the term Alzheimer's disease was once used to refer to the mental impairment of people under age 65, it is now used to describe such a condition at any age. This devastating disease begins with the loss of memory and leads to the inability to perform even the simplest chores. It is incurable, although some of its behavioral symptoms can be reduced through highly concentrated doses of a substance called lecithin. Usually within ten to fifteen years from the onset, the disease renders the patient so incapable of functioning that the presence of any other illness is liable to cause death. There is no prevention for this disease and the exact causes are unknown (LaBarge, 1981).

The impact of Alzheimer's disease on the families of its victims is enormous. Elderly patients require round-the-clock attention and bear no resemblance whatsoever to the people they once were. Guilt, fear, and desperation are common reactions of family members, who may need to use all their financial and energy resources to contend with this illness.

Drug abuse.   Drug abuse for the elderly is different from that in adolescents and young adults. A common health problem of the elderly concerns the cumulative effects of inappropriate or unprescribed drugs. This problem cuts across socioeconomic classes, although it is recognized that some people receive a higher quality of health care than others. Drugs are often carelessly prescribed or purchased over the counter or passed among peers also preoccupied with ailments and health concerns. A major problem is the lack of careful monitoring and follow-up. As mentioned previously, due to physiological changes, the elderly are more susceptible to drug abuse than the younger populations and they require careful, ongoing monitoring.

Alcoholism is another type of drug abuse found in the elderly. According to Zimberg (1974), there are two types of elderly alcoholics: those with a long history of alcohol abuse who continue drinking excessively into late adulthood, and those reacting to one or more stresses of aging who begin to drink in late adulthood. Alcoholism in older adults may involve serious vitamin and protein deficiencies, liver dysfunction, and bone demineralization. Gross and Capuzzi (1981) point out that the manifestations of addiction to alcohol mimic those of the aging process, a situation that can confound diagnosis and treatment of the alcoholism. These problems may be less reversible and less treatable in late adulthood than in earlier stages of the life cycle.

Malnutrition.   The incidence rate of malnutrition in the elderly is alarmingly high. There is some question as to whether this rate is related to inappropriate drug usage, anemia, obesity or the reduced income of old age resulting in improper nutrition. It is important, then, to ascertain whether the malnutrition is primary or secondary.

Many human service workers who work with the elderly find that recent information about proper nutrition has not really been absorbed by this segment of the population and that these people cling to lifelong eating patterns that are not always conducive to good health. For example, many of the elderly refuse to cut down on cholesterol, sugar, salt, and other known contributors to cardiovascular disease. They are not convinced that it makes sense at their age and they have seen too many faddish trends in their lifetime to put much stock in those of today.

Psychopathology.   Whereas the aged seem to have the same range of psychopathology as the young and middle aged, it is important to remember that certain physical illnesses and social traumas can precipitate psychopathology in later life. With advancing age, a person's environmental niche changes and he or she may struggle to regain former comfort and familiarity and to resist all changes. Therefore, whereas depression and suicide are prevalent in late adulthood, the psychological, social, and physical factors affecting older adults vary in their onset, intensity, and effects. Busse (1969) suggests that depression in old age differs from that in younger adults in that it is precipitated in older people by a loss of self-esteem related to aging whereas it originates in young adults with the turning inward of hostility. Scarf (1980) confirms that depression in the elderly is related to loss of self-esteem. She finds that men suffer a more violent type and a higher rate of suicide than women because their losses of self-esteem and satisfying roles—namely, career roles—are more devastating than for women.

It appears that the way elderly people adjust to changes and losses will depend on their physical health, personality traits (including defense mechanisms and learned coping strategies), philosophical views of life, earlier life experiences, societal supports, and current living conditions. These issues seems to be at the root of psychopathology that is not directly related to illness or drugs.

The negative evaluation of the elderly by our society can certainly result in feelings of loneliness and low self-esteem that can contribute to depression. Thus, a mutually reinforcing cycle between societal attitudes and one's feelings of self-worth can maintain depression. Kucharski, White, and Schratz (1979) report that older patients are less often urged to seek psychological assistance than younger patients. Whereas younger patients with obvious psychiatric symptoms are referred to mental health workers, older patients with such symptoms are referred to neurologists or other physicians and are given psychotropic drugs. Many professionals believe that the elderly cannot be helped by counseling or therapy and do not consider referral to mental health workers a viable alternative.

The aging process and the types of disease affecting this process are such important issues for late adulthood that we have highlighted them separately from the developmental tasks and issues of this stage. We turn now to a delineation of these tasks and issues for senior citizens and the elderly. Please remember that our chronological indices are mere approximations and that extreme variation and diversity exist among late-adulthood individuals in terms of their experiences and interpretations of older age.

SENIOR CITIZENS

Most adults between the ages of 60 and 75 are relatively active, healthy, and involved in relationships. They consider themselves to be middle aged rather than elderly. People in this category prefer to be known as *senior citizens,* and are quick to point out that the *elderly* are more passive, irritable, and disabled than they are themselves. So categorizing themselves as senior citizens may be a defense mechanism against negative attitudes associated with the elderly. Sheehy

(1981) reports the discrepancy older adults feel between the way they look, what their bodies permit, and the way they feel inside. They feel like the same young, energetic people they always were and are surprised when they see old images in the mirror and angry when they cannot perform tasks as easily as they used to.

Havighurst (1972) suggested the following as the developmental tasks of later maturity, over the age of 60:

1. Adjusting to decreasing physical strength and health;
2. Adjusting to retirement and reduced income;
3. Adjusting to the death of the spouse;
4. Establishing an explicit affiliation with one's age group;
5. Adopting and adapting to social roles in a flexible way;
6. Establishing satisfactory living arrangements.

These tasks all involve the concept of adjusting to loss or decline and are so broad that they do not allow us to differentiate between the beginning stages of (or transition to) late adulthood and the later stages. Also, because of the increased diversity among older adults, it is impossible to overemphasize the individual variations in environmental, physiological, social, and psychological changes. Here we attempt to select those developmental tasks and issues considered to be the most general and prevalent in this stage of life. Remember that each of these tasks and issues is influenced by the aging and disease process inevitable in all older adults.

Developmental Tasks

In general, the developmental tasks for this stage of life involve a conservation of strength and resources and the adaptation to social, psychological, and physiological changes and losses. As pointed out by developmental theorists (Erikson, 1963; Gould, 1978; Levinson, 1978; Neugarten, 1968; Sheehy, 1976, 1981; Vaillant, 1977), past experiences with developmental tasks and issues lay the foundation for how one copes in late adulthood.

Identity.   Always present in the life cycle is the task of reassessing and redefining one's self-concept and self-esteem in accordance with social, physical, and environmental changes. This periodic adaptation is perhaps just as critical for the senior citizen as for the adolescent, in that both are faced with rapid physical changes affecting appearance and feelings of well-being and with major role changes. As the adolescent is expected to establish an adult identity, career, and family, so senior citizens are expected to detach themselves from their work roles by retiring, to forego a primary parenting role as their adult children move toward middle age, and to give up status, power, and leadership roles. Age 65 in our society is a definitive marker event: senior citizens receive identification cards entitling them to receive reduced rates for transportation, theaters and other entertainment, hotels, and restaurants. They begin to collect social security and Medicare and become eligible for other social services.

Thus, whether or not they wish to, at 65, people begin to move away or to be pushed away from the mainstream of our society, and this movement is often reflected in power struggles with colleagues and children. Some senior citizens accept these changes, but others resist vigorously. In recent years, many organizations and services have developed to help senior citizens rebound from these role changes with new orientations to relationships and activities. For example, the American Association for Retired People (AARP) has become an active political, economic, and social force. Retirement villages have provided alternative living arrangements attuned to elderly needs in several areas. The Grey Panthers, for some, has become an organized lobbying force. Such organizations subscribe to the activity theory of aging rather than to the disengagement theory, and they help senior citizens to seek out substitute relationships and activities so they can maintain a sense of meaning and productivity in their lives.

We know that the senior citizen's self-concept depends largely upon health, psychological, social, and physiological variables. It also depends on philosophical development: how one views the meaning of life and the meaning of aging. Self-concept, in turn, affects how a person interacts with others and deals with the other tasks of late adulthood. A common saying, "You're only as old as you feel," indicates the real correlation of self-concept and environmental factors.

Mutran and Burke (1979) found that late in life one's personal feelings related to identity are influenced by one's earlier feelings and life experiences. Feelings of usefulness and low self-worth in late adulthood are deepened by loneliness, poor health, low income, singlehood, unemployment, and low educational level. High levels of self-esteem are related to good health and social integration. Linn, Hunter, and Perry (1979) found that feelings of personal control were important contributors to positive self-esteem and positive identity reappraisal in older age, which confirms Neugarten's findings. Some gender differences were reported by Turner (1979) in that women were found to be more self-critical and to have lower self-esteem than males. This finding may be associated with the fact that women usually suffer a greater loss of income and more women than men lose their spouses and suffer more major losses of health. Turner suggests that increasing assertiveness and masculinity are associated with positive self-esteem among older women. Thus, the concept of androgyny may become a crucial factor in the self-esteem of the elderly.

Social adjustment.   Many role changes are experienced by senior citizens in terms of work, family, and the community. The senior citizen must adapt to the increasing loss of friends, family, and colleagues, and must adapt by forming new companionships and reestablishing previous relationships to fend off isolation. As one moves out of Erikson's generativity stage, where the focus is on contributing to the welfare of the younger generations or to the culture at large, one becomes more centered on one's inner self and the changes one is experiencing. One transcends former roles as one reaches new levels of development. The generativity impulse thus may become more focused on senior-citizen issues and peers. The ability to form and maintain new relationships and new forms of companionship may therefore affect the type of social adjustment that one makes during these years. Underlying these relationships is the knowledge that continuous loss will inevitably occur as people become ill and die. Also, one's perception of and needs for interdependence change as one becomes more aware of potential loss and the limitations on personal autonomy.

Personal preference is really the major issue regarding social adjustment. For a person who has always chosen isolation or individual activities, this preference is not likely to change in old age. If one makes such a choice as a defensive reaction, because of hurt and anger, one is more likely to develop dissatisfaction or some type of dysfunction. Involuntary isolation can lead to heightened loneliness, which itself can negatively affect both one's feelings of personal worth and one's general functioning. Many writers note the increasing importance of informal social support systems (for example, friendships and neighbors) in later life (Cantor, 1979; Conner et al., 1979; O'Brien and Wagner, 1979; Palmore et al., 1979). It may be that friends and neighbors provide a kind of emotional support for the elderly that is more helpful than that supplied by adult offspring and grandchildren.

Sex-role differences are apparent regarding the social adjustment of senior citizens. Typically, women have had more experience dealing with interpersonal relationships and do not experience as many traumatic changes in their lifestyles as men do when they are forced to relinquish their work roles and their concomitant social relationships. These differences will be discussed further in Chapter 13.

The reallocation of energy and resources.   This important task concerns physical, social, financial, and psychological energies and resources. As stated earlier, senior citizens become more aware of decreasing physical vigor, time constrictions, and changing activity orientations, and must learn to balance needs, desires, and possibilities. For example, senior citizens learn how to distance themselves from many of those life activities that absorbed their time and energy during the middle years, and to find satisfaction in relationships and activities that are more feasible with respect to their physical and emotional vigor. Likewise, financial planning and economic considerations are very important in that they either force or allow restrictions and changes. Dependency/independency issues come into play with respect to finances as senior citizens discover how realistic their planning was and how consistently they can maintain their old style of life, given their limited financial resources and such uncontrollable environmental factors as inflation.

Stress management.   Elders who failed to develop adequate stress-management skills and strategies in earlier stages may be forced to learn some effective ones rather quickly during this period of life. Many of the identified changes and losses of old age assault individuals suddenly, sometimes overwhelming them. We know that conditions conducive to the adjustment to social stress differ from one life stage to another and that such adjustments are harder in later than earlier life stages because we have less reserve and resiliency when we are older. Though in our discussion we can conveniently distinguish among somatic, cultural, economic, social, and psychological stresses, in real life, stresses are often multiple, interactive, and cumulative, and the overall effect can be an overload on the senior citizen's homeostasis. Coping strategies depend on personality traits, past experiences, the nature, perception, and interpretation of the stressor, and on the possibilities and feasibilities of alternative resolutions.

The senior-citizen stage can be viewed as a transition from middle age to old age, just as we saw the twenties decade as a transition from late adolescence to early adulthood. People in this stage are struggling during a transitional period with many changes in expectations and roles, and they are attempting to anticipate and prepare for the more critical role changes likely to occur in older age. Stressful life events include retirement, serious medical problems, widowhood, and the last child's departure from home. The favorable effects of health, psychological, and socioeconomic resources on adaptation to life were demonstrated by Palmore et al. (1979). Better levels of health, psychological, and social resources mitigated the stressful impacts of retirement, illness, and widowhood.

Developmental Issues

In addition to the physiological, psychological, and social changes already discussed, other considerations are likely to surface during this life stage.

Dependency/independency issues. These issues may be manifested in power struggles with adult children, social service providers, or others in society or government who seem to advocate that the senior citizen relinquish power and withdraw from active participation in society. Obviously, economic and health variables will affect the timing of retirement, living arrangements, and the daily functioning of the senior citizen. Whereas most people in this life stage continue to work part or full time and have full control over their lifestyles, some are beginning to think about their limited futures and how they are going to manage. They particularly fear losing control over decisions affecting their lifestyles and their well-being. Thus, the threat of becoming more dependent with increasing age may be a heightened source of distress, since the possibility of health and role loss is continually present. Senior citizens are constantly faced with evidence of potential loss as they see lifelong friends and acquaintances succumb to illnesses and sudden role losses.

Time structure. People who retire from their primary roles must change orientations toward leisure and avocations in order to continue to enjoy enrichment experiences. Many of today's senior citizens were socialized to "work before play." Therefore, they feel guilty about indulging themselves in leisure or avocational pursuits. This segment of the population survived a major depression, a world war, and several other "skirmishes." Many senior citizens today need help in developing positive attitudes about leisure and a willingness to engage in new and different activities that may offer the potential of satisfaction.

Because their physical and emotional energies are diminishing, seniors need to learn to manage their time differently. Their time perspective becomes more foreshortened with the realization that the end is nearer, and thus short-term, present-oriented planning predominates.

Health. The senior citizen with poor health must adapt to the "sick role" and all that entails, participating as much as possible in decision-making and self-care. The loss of health, along with increasing dependency, can give rise to depression. As noted, support and time from friends, family, neighbors, and physicians can alleviate depressive symptoms. In the absence of a specific disease, heightened awareness of preventive health measures becomes increasingly important. This includes responsibility for proper diet and exercise, early attention to medical problems, and a willingness to compensate for impaired sensory modalities with, say, hearing aids or bifocals.

Sexuality. Despite negative attitudes toward sexuality in the two phases of late adulthood, and despite a drop in the opportunities for sexual gratification, sexual needs are as important in senescence as they were during earlier life stages. Senior citizens need information about their particular sexual needs and abilities. They need to learn about opportunities for gratification, such as masturbation or alternative partners. The work of Kinsey (1948), Masters and Johnson (1966; 1970), Comfort (1976), and Finkle and Finkle (1977) confirms the fact that the sexual capacity remains intact throughout life, despite some changes in sexual performance. Some of these changes include slower arousal patterns, sensitivity and loss of lubrication in a female's genitalia, and lowered needs for ejaculatory release in men. Botwinick (1978) notes some gender differences in patterns of change with age. Males change gradually whereas females rarely change until after age 60. The changes in sexual behavior are related more to frequency and vigor than to kind and quality.

It is important to note that most sexual dysfunction reported in late adulthood is related to disease, drug utilization, or psychological factors, not to organic factors. Capuzzi (1982) summarizes common medical problems that affect sexuality of the elderly, pointing out that abstinence owing to illness need only be temporary and that physicians must communicate carefully with their elderly patients to prevent misunderstandings and misinformation. In other words, illness and drugs can certainly affect sexual functioning in late adulthood, but these effects are often temporary and can usually be remedied.

Cognitive functioning. As adult education becomes more accessible, senior citizens are finding alternative ways of obtaining intellectual stimulation and new learning. Since they have more time, they are applying for such programs as Elder Hostel, university and college summer courses available to this age group and specifically geared to their learning styles, interests and needs. Despite the seniors' decreasing efficiency in acquiring new information and their slower processing speed, their judgment and experience can compensate in seeking out stimulation and learning. Many senior citizens have used this time of life to venture into new fields, learn new skills, and gain new knowledge, adding new meaning to their lives and activities.

Death and bereavement. With increasing age, death and loss become increasingly likely—both one's own impending death and that of one's spouse or significant others. However, many researchers have found that most people in this age group, except where a life-threatening illness is present, are really not preoccupied with death. They utilize much of their energy and resources to adapt to role and lifestyle changes. In fact, middle-aged adults think more existentially about death than do older adults, who see death as inevitable and who have foreshortened their time perspective to more immediate concerns and issues (Freiberg, 1976; Kastenbaum, 1972; Kimmel, 1974; Whitbourne and Weinstock, 1979).

Attitudes toward death seem to be correlated to personality type more than life stage (Busse and Pfeiffer, 1977; Lowenthal et al., 1975; Maas and Kuypers, 1974; Neugarten, 1968; Schneidman, 1976). One researcher (Riley, 1979) found educational background to be more of a factor than age, and suggested that the awareness of aging is a step in the subsequent recognition of one's own vulnerability to death. Elders personalize death more, beginning this process in middle age.

Nevertheless, a substantial number of senior citizens lose their spouse and this is seen by most stress researchers as the most critical loss in one's life cycle (Holmes and Rahe, 1967; Lazarus, 1966). Since loss of spouse will be further discussed in Chapter 12, suffice it to say that the senior citizen may be more vulnerable to this loss than younger adults and it could be the ultimate assault on top of many other major losses during this stage and could compound and complicate one's adaptation to late adulthood.

Therapy with a focus on grief is necessary for working through the effects of loss, whether loss of a person or a symbol, such as a work role or a fantasy, is involved. Anticipatory grief is common in the senior citizen phase of life. Where one has not yet lost a significant other, one knows nevertheless that the inevitable is coming ever closer.

Some common phases in anticipatory grief are depression, a heightened concern for significant others, rehearsal in one's mind of the expected loss, and rehearsal of attempts to adjust to the loss (Fulton, 1977). The meaning an individual gives to death and loss will influence the course of grieving, and the person's coping strategies, cultural practices, available support systems, and self-concept are also critical factors.

Grief and mourning normally last for one to two years after the death precipitating them, and several writers have identified stages in the process. Bowlby (1960) identifies the characteristics of these stages as follows:

1. The mourner gives thought and directs behavior toward the lost loved one;
2. The mourner feels hostility toward the lost loved one or toward others;
3. The mourner appeals for help and support from others;
4. The mourner feels despair, withdrawal, regression, and disorganization;
5. The mourner reorganizes behavior around a new love object or a new direction in life.

Bowlby points out that passage through these phases is not steady and that periods of regression may occur frequently during the first year or two. Kübler-Ross (1969) has identified the following stages in the reaction to dying and loss:

1. Stage 1, denial and isolation;
2. Stage 2, anger;
3. Stage 3, bargaining;
4. Stage 4, depression;
5. Stage 5, acceptance.

The mourner has three tasks to achieve (Cassem, 1978):

1. To experience and reflect upon feelings toward the lost object during life and the feelings evoked by death;
2. To review the history of the attachment;
3. To examine personal wounds and confront the task of continuing to live without the lost person or object.

It is obvious that mental health workers need to understand the nature and process of grieving, since it is such a common occurrence in late adulthood. Many different styles and experiences of grieving exist, and often just being with people, allowing them to remember the loved one and vent their pain, and reassuring them about the normalcy of their grieving is helpful.

Table 11-1 summarizes the developmental tasks and issues for senior citizens. We turn now to the elderly, the last phase of late adulthood.

TABLE 11-1.   Senior citizens

Developmental Tasks	General Issues	Requisite Skills	Significant Others
Redefine identity: physiological, psychological, social, and economic changes	Dependency/ independency Health Sexuality Time structure Cognitive stimulation Death/bereavement	Letting go Adaptation Stress management Interpersonal Self-care Caretaking Trying new activities	Peers Family: spouse, offspring, grandchildren, extended family Neighbors Community Medical personnel
Adjust socially: friends, family, and community			
Reallocate energy and resources			
Manage stress			

THE ELDERLY

In the latter part of late adulthood, from age 75 on, the imminence of illness and death is the major differentiating factor from earlier life stages. Jung (1933) was one of the first theorists to recognize the importance of senescence as a major life stage. He viewed old age as a period for introspection and for inner directedness, and his work paved the way for Erikson's eighth and final stage of development, ego integrity versus despair. This last stage of Erikson's represents the fruition of the previous seven stages, even though it is his least well-defined developmental concept.

Erikson's Eighth Stage

Erikson's concept of integrity involves acceptance of one's life as meaningful, as something that had to be. Such an acceptance involves the accepting of one's origins and all other aspects of one's life (Erikson, 1950). Thus, elders who have achieved integrity accept who they are and what they have become, including all the mourned losses and integrated pains and sufferings of the past, the meaning and worth of life, and the gap between dreams, goals, and accomplishments. Erikson's eighth stage is considered applicable to people nearing death regardless of their chronological age. It is triggered by the anticipation of death and the acceptance of the finiteness of time. It is discussed in the context of the elderly only because this is the time when death is inevitable.

In Erikson's scheme, the opposite of integrity is despair, which Erikson defines as a refusal to accept one's life and fear and depression resulting from the awareness that the time left is too short to start a new life over or to try out alternate routes to integrity. If we refer back to the personality types described by Neugarten, Buhler, and Maas and Kuypers, we see that some of the types fit with the concept of integrity and some with the concept of despair. The identified types who are characterized by general satisfaction, chosen isolation, or activity are achieving integrity, and those who are disengaged and unhappy fall into the despair category.

Older people who have achieved a sense of integrity about their lives, as Erikson defines the term, feel that life has been meaningful and they are thus able to accept the disease and death that are inevitable without fear of succumbing helplessly. Those who despair, on the other hand, are preoccupied with what might have been and are bitter about their disappointment. For these people death is fearsome, for it symbolizes emptiness.

Peck. Erikson's eighth stage has been further refined and expanded by Peck (1968), who attempts to specify the developmental tasks implied by Erikson. He describes three specific developmental processes for older adults:

1. Ego differentiation versus work-role preoccupation. The retired person who once found meaning and focus in his or her vocational role now has to find new and satisfactory roles in ways previously ignored or unthought of. In other words, the task is to try to enjoy new functions, roles, and activities. Making this successful role transition could mean the difference between enjoying late adulthood and mourning the sense of loss of meaning in life.

2. Body transcendence versus body preoccupation. As one becomes more aware of physiological changes and decreasing physical vigor, one can learn to value mental and social resources more than physical well-being. In other words, one can learn to accept physical discomforts and not let them influence unduly one's relationships and activities. As handicapped people of any age must do, elders can learn to compensate for physical limitations and not allow them to control their lives.

3. Ego transcendance versus ego preoccupation. If one can learn to feel a sense of meaning and self-worth in one's life and take steps to clear up unfinished

business with significant others, the prospect of death is not feared but is accept-ed as inevitable. Again, time is present-oriented and the most is made of each available day.

These steps are more or less ideals for the elderly to attain. Some do so innately and others need help to achieve these tasks. Let us now consider the specific tasks and issues that originate in these three general objectives.

Developmental Tasks

In late adulthood, environmental events may at any time cause a sudden critical transition that requires a recycling of previously achieved tasks and issues. The major developmental tasks facing the elderly follow.

Identity. As personal and social losses as well as internal and external changes become more pronounced, the elderly must differentiate between identi-ty issues and reality experiences. In other words, they must integrate the changed physical "me," internal experiences, the past "me," and all the current internal "me's." Whitbourne and Weinstock (1979) believe that people with achieving-status identities are able to attain the integrity that Erikson (1968) describes and that they can feel comfortable and nondefensive with the identity of "old people." People with foreclosed-status identities are more defensive about their pasts, however, wanting to forget mistakes and to dwell only on accomplishments. Such people might appear to accept the inevitability of death but, owing to their denial of internal conflicts, might experience severe crisis when illness or other inevitable debility appears. Those with diffused and moratorium identity statuses are more likely to exhibit despair than integrity and may experience varying levels of stress in coping with old age. These writers point out that while these different identity statuses may change over the life cycle (that is, the identities are not stable), they depend on external as well as internal issues and changes. One's internal pattern is likely to remain stable although subject to varying influences from internal and external factors. The elderly's identity will be influenced by health and financial resources, which directly affect feelings of control over living arrangements and life management.

Emotional separation and death. Emotional separation from family, friends, and one's own previous major roles is an ongoing developmental task of the life cycle that becomes as critical in late adulthood as it was in early adulthood. To perform it late in life means coming to terms with the whole process of emotional separation—from significant others, roles, attitudes, values, and beliefs. People who were unsuccessful in gaining an emotionally separate identity in early adult-hood will continue to have difficulty adapting to change and letting go throughout the life cycle. In late adulthood, when faced with death, these people are likely to cling to life, since death represents to them the ultimate emotional separation and is therefore unbearable. Separating oneself from life is the ultimate self-differentia-tion that accompanies one's growing inner orientation. Preparing for one's own death, then, becomes more paramount. This preparation may have been repressed in earlier stages and the need to do it now becomes more difficult to deny and avoid. It may manifest itself through depression and withdrawal, both of which include fear, sorrow, and anger.

Disagreement still prevails regarding the existence of stages of dying, such as those described by Kübler-Ross (1969; 1975; and Warshaw, 1978). Certainly cultural and ethnic variables affect the meaning death has for one. Also, the type of illness one has and the circumstances affecting the death as well as the kind of support available will affect how one deals with the process of dying. An individual's response to his or her own dying is too complex to fit into any one linear model.

Summarizing the research on discussions of death among the elderly, Wass and Myers (1982) report that, in general, both institutionalized and noninstitutionalized elderly think about death and are likely to talk about it when given the chance. A variety of death fears, anxieties, and death-related attitudes exist that are interrelated with philosophical, gender, ethnic, health, living-arrangement, religious, and other demographic variables.

Bereavement.   Some of the factors that correlate positively with the elderly's adjustment to loss and grief include high economic status, high educational level, good living arrangements, and strong social support systems (Wass and Myers, 1982). It is important to differentiate between normal and neurotic grief reactions, and one can make this assessment by monitoring the intensity and length of normal reactions such as crying, sleep and eating disturbances, and depressed moods.

The elderly have different grieving reactions than younger adults. Grief is only one of the many stresses they experience and it may be more diffuse than in younger adults (Cumming and Henry, 1961). Burnside (1969) reports that in institutional settings, grief reactions of the elderly are often misdiagnosed as symptoms of organic brain syndrome.

Maintaining body integrity.   As the body continues to weaken and fail, it becomes increasingly important for the aging individual to maintain as much autonomy as possible over body functions and self-care. This includes health and nutritional care and responsible control over realistic possibilities and restrictions in terms of physical activities.

Suicide is an increasing risk for the elderly. Many suicides in this stage are related to depressive reactions resulting from loss, grief, loneliness, and despair (Butler and Lewis, 1977). As mentioned above, in addition to coping with the deaths of loved ones, the elderly have to cope with other significant losses such as physical strength and stamina, income, independence, social status, and prestige as well as customary occupational and social roles.

Accepting the loss of personal autonomy and competence.   In terms of daily functioning and activities, as people go through the last stage of adulthood, they must inevitably learn to deal with their own increasing frailty and to accept aid from others. This means that they must relinquish full control and power over their daily lives, financial management, and possibly all aspects of their lives. A reversal of roles may also be involved—becoming dependent upon children, grandchildren, or health care providers. Such a dependency may be physical, financial, and/or emotional, and it may involve the loss of privacy and the ability to select activities and companions.

The major task is to conserve strength and resources carefully and consciously in order to ensure an optimal level of activity, participation, and control over one's own life as long as possible.

Social adjustment.   Losses of friends and family members continue to abound now, and it is important for elders to find new affiliations in their own age group and to come to grips with the transitory nature of such relationships as disability and death become more prevalent. Required are skills in achieving new ties, engaging in activities where these new relationships become possible, and sharing feelings and sense of worth with age mates. Constant adjustment is also necessary in terms of relationships with younger generations. A balance of relationships with people of varying ages is a goal that ensures a continued sense of meaning and worth in life. The nature of these relationships changes—from the intense intimacy of earlier years to sharing in the present that is expected to be transitory.

Developmental Issues

The effects of ageism.   The elderly experience the deepest effects of ageism at the time in their lives when they feel least capable of overcoming the obstacles imposed by stereotypical beliefs and values. Older people are denied access to certain places, denied participation in certain activities, frequently ignored and isolated, and are taken advantage of by others in the community. They are increasingly vulnerable to consumer frauds, street crime, and molestation and abuse by family members, neighbors, and other members of the community. Because they are not highly valued in our society, they do not receive much protection or consideration from people in the community, and their efforts to function self-sufficiently often go unrecognized. Social issues such as transportation, safety, and health care for the elderly abound, and have become serious issues for the entire society.

Residence.   The residence issue is singled out because voluntary or involuntary changes of residence in late adulthood can cause major stress, affecting identity and social adjustment. Familiar life routines may be disrupted, meaningful social and family relationships may change, and emotional attachments may be severed by a residence change. In other words, the security of familiarity and continuity may be broken and a new residence may require major adjustments. How much distance is involved in relocation and the reasons for the relocation are other potentially stressful variables.

George (1980) identified the following factors as affecting elders' adjustments to residential relocation: social status variables, personal resources, and situational factors. Where the move is to an institution, she adds the variables of personality factors and socializing experiences. In particular, she reports that residential relocation is less stressful if the person has strong social support systems and a high level of education, if the physical and social characteristics of the new residential environment are pleasant, if there is a high proportion of age peers in the residential area, and if the relocation is voluntary. Some factors facilitating institutional relocation are physical health and social support by family members and friends, an aggressive and demanding personality, and preparation for relocation. In both cases, voluntary relocation facilitates adjustment in contrast to involuntary relocation.

Social issues such as nursing care, financial resources, nutrition, and social adjustment are all related to residential issues. For the elderly, living arrangements must include health care and social services. An older person's needs may range from total care at one extreme to the provision of situations allowing maximum independence and self-determination at the other. Most elderly people prefer to live in relative freedom as long as they can. Eventually, most wish to have a more protected and supportive—and affordable—living situation available when and if needed. Social issues have implications for policy planning and implementation and for advocacy efforts of mental health workers, often necessary as part of the treatment process with the elderly. Currently, alternative living arrangements may include group living, semistructured residences, foster home care, residing with family, and nursing homes.

Barry (1983) concludes from his review of the literature that older people should be able to choose among a variety of alternative living arrangements, that the relative financial costs of different arrangements are unclear, and that most older people are happier and healthier living independently in their own homes as long as they are able to do so. Counselors may have to be active in seeking out feasible alternatives and helping the elderly and their families to make decisions.

Table 11-2 summarizes the developmental tasks and issues of the elderly.

TABLE 11-2.　The elderly

Developmental Tasks	General Issues	Requisite Skills	Significant Others
Redefine identity: ego integrity, ego transcendence, and body transcendence	Health	Self-care	Peers
	Death/bereavement	Dependency	Family
	Dependency	Interpersonal	Caretakers
	Ageism	Introspection	
Separate emotionally	Residence	Adaptation	
Maintain body integrity			
Accept loss of personal autonomy and competencies: conserve strength and resources, accept dependencies			
Adjust socially: to loss of peers; to transient, fluid relationships			

SUMMARY

We are learning more about late adulthood as more researchers devote their efforts to this segment of the life cycle. In this chapter, we studied the aging process from biological, psychological, and sociological perspectives. We examined the inevitable physiological changes and considered some of the environmental issues that interact with these natural changes. We emphasized the variation and diversity of the aging process and mentioned heredity, disease, environmental, psychological and social factors, and one's own philosophical values and views as influencing this process.

The nature and impact of disease in late adulthood intermingle with the aging process and often confuse identification of problems and issues in older adults. We described the most common diseases to affect late adulthood and mentioned relevant health issues that affect this age group. Because the elderly are living longer than ever before, they experience more disability, which affects their lifestyles. In any case, health care issues become more pronounced in late adulthood.

In the latter part of the chapter, we reviewed late-adulthood developmental theory and considered the developmental tasks and issues for senior citizens in the 60–75 age range and for the elderly, from 75 on. These tasks and issues include recycling of previous developmental tasks and issues as well as a gradual disengagement from major life roles, transcendence into newer roles and lifestyles, and adaptation to changes and stress. Preparation for death and adapting to multiple types of loss are major tasks of late adulthood.

Late adulthood is viewed as a time for reflection and integration, which are seen as the sources of great change, enabling the person to reap multiple losses and gains. How one adapts to these changes is affected by personality traits, past experiences with coping strategies, perceptions and interpretations of the changes, and possible alternative resolutions. Family relationships and work and leisure activities are major components of late adulthood and will be explored separately in subsequent chapters.

One major variable affecting late adulthood is the qualitative aspect of social interactions. Same-age relationships may be more significant supports than adult offspring and grandchildren. Feelings of personal control in one's life are another major variable affecting the experience of development. The quality of life in late adulthood is enhanced by money, work, health, friends and social support, cognitive capacities, and opportunities for creative expression.

The ultimate goal of late adulthood is to complete unfinished business and prepare for death. Cultural influences in addition to physiological, psychological, and social influences occur, and the only universal findings of research are that change is inevitable and that many different ways exist to achieve the ultimate goal of death.

REFERENCES

Barry, J. P. Alternative living arrangements for older persons. *Personnel and Guidance Journal,* 1983, *61,* 267–268.

Bengston, V. *The social psychology of aging.* New York: Bobbs-Merrill, 1963.

Birren, J. E. Aging in America: Roles for psychology. *American Psychologist.* 1983, *38,* 298-300.

Boston Globe, January 20, 1982.

Botwinick, J. *Aging and behavior* (2nd ed.). New York: Springer, 1978.

Bowlby, J. Grief and mourning in infancy and early childhood. *Psychoanalytic Study of the Child,* 1960, *15,* 9-52.

Buhler, C. The developmental structure of goal setting in group and individual studies. In C. Buhler & F. Massarek (eds.), *The course of human life: A study of goals in the humanistic perspective.* New York: Springer, 1968.

Burnside, I. M. Grief work in the aged patient. *Nursing Forum,* 1969, *8,* 416-427.

Busse, E. W. Theories of aging. In E. W. Busse & E. Pfeiffer (eds.), *Behavior and adaptation in later life.* Boston: Little, Brown, 1977.

Busse, E. W., & Pfeiffer, E. (eds.). *Behavior and adaptation in later life.* Boston: Little, Brown, 1977.

Butler, R., & Lewis, M. *Aging and mental health.* St. Louis: Mosby, 1977.

Cantor, M. H. Neighbors and friends: An overlooked resource in the informal support system. *Research on Aging,* 1979, *1,* 464-480.

Capuzzi, D. Sexuality and aging: An overview for counselors. *Personnel and Guidance Journal,* 1982, *61,* 31-35.

Cassem, N. Treating the person confronting death. In A. M. Nicoli, Jr. (ed.), *The Harvard guide to modern psychiatry.* Cambridge, Mass.: Harvard University Press, 1978.

Comfort, A. Physiology, homeostasis and aging. *Gerontologia,* 1970, *14,* 224-234.

Comfort, A. *A good age.* New York: Crown, 1976.

Conner, K. A., Powers, E. A., & Bultina, G. L. Social interaction and life satisfactions: An empirical assessment of late life patterns. *Journal of Gerontology,* 1979, *34,* 116-121.

Cumming, E., & Henry, W. H. *Growing old.* New York: Basic Books, 1961.

Eisdorfer, C., & Cohen, L. D. The generality of the WAIS standardization for the aged: A regional comparison. *Journal of Abnormal and Social Psychology,* 1961, *64,* 520-527.

Erikson, E. *Childhood and society.* New York: W. W. Norton, 1950.

Erikson, E. *Childhood and society.* 2nd ed. New York: W. W. Norton, 1963.

Erikson, E. *Identity, youth and crisis.* New York: W. W. Norton, 1968.

Finkle, A., & Finkle, P. How counseling may solve sexual problems in aging men. *Geriatrics,* 1977, *32,* 84-89.

Freiberg, K. *Human development.* No. Scituate, Mass.: Duxbury Press, 1976.

Fulton, R. General aspects. In N. Linzer (ed.), *Understanding bereavement and grief.* New York: Yeshiva University Press, 1977.

Gallagher, D., Thompson, L. W., & Levy, S. M. Clinical psychological assessment of older adults. In L. Poon (ed.), *Aging in the 1980s.* Washington, D.C.: American Psychological Association, 1980, 19-41.

George, L. K. *Role transitions in later life.* Monterey, Calif.: Brooks/Cole, 1980.

Gould, R. *Transformations.* New York: Simon & Schuster, 1978.

Gross, D., & Capuzzi, D. The elderly alcoholic: The counselor's dilemma. *Counselor Education and Supervision,* 1981, *20,* 183-193.

Havighurst, R. *Developmental tasks and education* (3rd ed.). New York: McKay, 1972.

Henig, R. *The myth of senility.* New York: Doubleday, 1981.

Herr, J. J., & Weakland, J. H. *Counseling elders and their families.* New York: Springer, 1979.

Holmes, T., & Rahe, S. A social adjustment scale. *Journal of Psychosomatic Research,* 1967, *11,* 213-218.

Jung, C. *Modern man in search of a soul.* New York: Harcourt, Brace, 1933.

Kastenbaum, R. Getting there ahead of me. *Psychology Today,* 1971, *5,* 52.

Kastenbaum, R. *The psychology of death.* New York: Springer, 1972.

Kimmel, D. *Adulthood and aging.* New York: Wiley, 1974.

Kinsey, A., Pomeroy, W. B., & Martin, C. E. *Sexual behavior in the human male.* Philadelphia: Saunders, 1948.

Kübler-Ross, E. *On death and dying.* London: MacMillan, 1969.

Kübler-Ross, E. *Death: The final stage of growth.* Englewood Cliffs, N.J.: Prentice-Hall, 1975.

Kübler-Ross, E., & Warshaw, W. *To live until we say goodbye.* Englewood Cliffs, N.J.: Prentice-Hall, 1978.

Kucharski, L. T., White, R. M., & Schratz, M. Age bias referral for psychological assistance and the private physician. *Journal of Gerontology,* 1979, *34,* 423-428.

LaBarge, E. Counseling patients with senile dementia of the Alzheimer type and their families. *Personnel and Guidance Journal,* 1981, *60,* 139-143.

Lazarus, R. S. *Psychological stress and the coping process.* New York: McGraw-Hill, 1966.

Levinson, D. *The seasons of a man's life.* New York: Knopf, 1978.

Linn, M. W., Hunter, K. I., & Perry, P. R. Differences by sex and ethnicity in the psychosocial adjustment of the elderly. *Journal of Health and Social Behavior,* 1979, *20,* 273-281.

Lowenthal, M., Thurnher, M., & Chiriboga, D. *Four stages of life.* San Francisco: Jossey-Bass, 1975.

Maas, H. W., & Kuypers, J. A. *From thirty to seventy.* San Francisco: Jossey-Bass, 1974.

Macione, A. R. Physiological changes and common health problems of aging. In M. Ganikos (ed.), *Counseling the aged.* Washington, D.C.: American Personnel and Guidance Association, 1979, pp. 47-59.

Masters, W. H., & Johnson, V. E. *Human sexual response.* Boston: Little, Brown, 1966.

Masters, W. H., & Johnson, V. E. *Human sexual inadequacy.* Boston: Little, Brown, 1970.

Mutran, E., & Burke, P. J. Feeling useless. *Research on Aging,* 1979, *1,* 187-212.

Neugarten, B. L. (ed.). *Middle age and aging.* Chicago: University of Chicago Press, 1968.

Neugarten, B. L. Personalism as a component of old age identity. *Research on Aging.* 1979, *1,* 37-63.

O'Brien, J. E., & Wagner, D. L. Help seeking by the frail elderly: Problems in network analysis. *The Gerontologist,* 1979, *20,* 78-83.

Palmore, E., Cleveland, W. P., Nowlin, J. B., Ramm, D., & Siegler, I. C. Stress and adaptation in later life. *Journal of Gerontology,* 1979, *34,* 841-851.

Peck, R. Psychological developments in the second half of life. In B. L. Neugarten (ed.), *Middle age and aging.* Chicago: University of Chicago Press, 1968, 88-98.

Riley, M. W. (ed.). *Aging from birth to death.* Boulder, Col.: Westview Press, 1979.

Scarf, M. *Unfinished business.* Garden City, N.Y.: Doubleday, 1980.

Schneidman, E. S. (ed.). *Suicidology: Contemporary developments.* New York: Grune & Stratton, 1976.

Sheehy, G. *Passages.* New York: Dutton, 1976.

Sheehy, G. *Pathfinders.* New York: Wm. Morrow & Co., 1981.

Skinner, B. F. Intellectual self-management in old age. *American Psychologist,* 1983, *38,* 239-245.

Turner, B. F. The self-concepts of older women. *Research on Aging,* 1979, *1,* 464-480.

Vaillant, G. *Adaptation to life.* Boston: Little, Brown, 1977.

Wass, H., & Myers, J. Psychosocial aspects of death among the elderly: A review of the literature. *Personal and Guidance Journal,* 1982, *61,* 131-138.

Wechsler, D. *The measurement and appraisal of adult intelligence* (4th ed.). Baltimore, Md.: Williams and Wilkens, 1958.

Whitbourne, S. K., & Weinstock, C. S. *Adult development.* New York: Holt, Rinehart & Winston, 1979.

Willis, E. L., & Baltes, P. B. Intelligence in adulthood and aging: Contemporary issues. In L. W. Poon, (ed.), *Aging in the 1980s.* Washington, D.C.: American Psychological Association, 1980, 260-273.

Zimberg, S. Two types of problem drinkers: Both can be managed. *Geriatrics,* 1974, *29,* 135-138.

CHAPTER TWELVE

FAMILY DEVELOPMENT
IN LATE ADULTHOOD

The term *family development* almost seems to be a misnomer for this stage of life in that constriction and exclusion, rather than expansion and inclusion, are the major processes. Perhaps the term *family life* would be more appropriate. However, we will continue to use the term *development* to connote growth and change, which continue until death.

Many people in our society do not consider the elderly in the context of a family system. They focus on middle-aged parents and their adolescent or young adult offspring when they conceive of adult family systems (Herr and Weakland, 1979). Elderly relatives are considered peripheral appendages, out of the mainstream of the nuclear family. The prevailing stereotypical myth pictures the elderly as alienated and isolated from their families, often pining away in nursing homes or other institutions. If there is contact, it is imagined to be infrequent and obligatory. This myth perpetuates the fear of aging, the belief that older people are useless, forgotten, and preparing to die. The truth is that, despite a preference for maintaining separate households and despite geographical separations, most elders and their middle-aged children have frequent contact, at least through letters or by telephone, and they have reciprocal emotional ties (Walsh, 1980). Their relationships with grandchildren and great-grandchildren fluctuate and depend on both the system's attachment values and the developmental stages of the younger generations.

Many diverse patterns and styles of interactions occur between the elderly and other members of their families, as Chapter 11 made clear. Much of this diversity is influenced by ethnicity, economics, geography, health, and past family interactional patterns. As in other areas of development, each family's response to the challenges of late adulthood evolves from earlier family patterns, which characterized their responses to the challenges of earlier life. How families have cared, coped, and adapted to changing roles, rules, and boundaries in the past affects how they will care, cope, and adapt in later life. Certain established family patterns that were once functional may indeed become dysfunctional with the changing life cycles of any or all generational members (Howells, 1975). For example, as younger generations become assimilated by marriage with other ethnic groups or adapt alternative lifestyles, they may break the heretofore customary interactional patterns between adult generations in their family systems, since attempting to maintain them creates too much tension or stress.

Developmental issues may serve as a trigger for changing the roles, rules, and boundaries that have worked for the family system in the past. When this occurs, the family system undergoes a *developmental crisis* in that the homeostasis is disrupted by a normative demand precipitated by an event associated with a developmental task or issue. A family that may never have experienced major dysfunction in negotiating developmental crises before may be surprised by the turmoil and pain experienced in a later life stage and may require some help and education in understanding the developmental processes of family life throughout its developmental cycle.

Consider the Robinson family. Mr. and Mrs. Robinson, both in their 60s, were devoted, helpful grandparents, as their parents had been when they were in the early family development stages. They helped their children with down payments for their homes, offered to babysit frequently, and provided vacation care for their grandchildren so that their children could take annual trips. The Robinson children were accustomed to this type of service and made lifestyle choices accordingly. When Mrs. Robinson's father died at the age of 84, her mother began to show signs of senility. Mrs. Robinson felt torn between her obligations to care for her mother, who was requiring more constant attention, and her assumed obligations to her children and grandchildren. Out of necessity, she withdrew from her usual babysitting tasks to assume full responsibility for the care of her mother. This put a great deal of strain on her marriage, since Mr. Robinson was adapting to retirement and enjoying his freedom and his grandchildren just when new obligations appeared. While Mr. and Mrs. Robinson argued over the merits of institutional care for Mrs. Robinson's mother, the Robinson children felt resentful about the withdrawal of attention and care focused in their direction. For months, angry, resentful feelings accumulated, which eventually led to a distancing in the couple system and in the parental and grandparental systems and an enmeshment between Mrs. Robinson and her elderly mother. It took the onset of disease in Mrs. Robinson to engender a referral to family therapy.

It seems clear that earlier patterns of attachment as opposed to patterns of conflict or filial obligation are usually the best predictors of mutually supportive interactions between the elderly and their offspring (Cicirelli, 1981). In the case of the Robinsons, it is possible that if their children had been taught to provide as well as to consume, and if Mrs. Robinson had been less stuck in the providing role, this family would have weathered its crisis with less pain and stress. Family members who are unsuccessful in negotiating changes necessitated by development in early stages are usually likely to be unavailable to each other in helpful ways in later life, whereas family members who maintained their attachment as they struggled with earlier developmental issues are usually more likely to be available to each other in later life.

Both an approach–avoidance continuum and a helpful–unhelpful continuum seem to characterize the interactions between the elderly and their offspring. Because of the ambivalent attitudes about families and the elderly in our society, it is not unusual or difficult for adult family members to separate emotionally as well as geographically and for detached family systems to exist in large numbers. It is this latter group that sometimes is generalized to be the norm upon which many of the myths are based, and there is no evidence whatsoever that isolated, detached adult family members exist in larger numbers than caring, attached family members.

Lest we misinterpret geographical and physical separations, however, let us consider two terms developed by Rosenmayr and Kockeis (1963) that apply to the elderly and their families: (1) *intimacy at a distance* refers to the ability of family-system members to sustain meaningful relationships in the absence of frequent interactions; and (2) *revocable detachment* refers to dormant emotional ties between family members that can be mobilized whenever needed. In the past forty years adults have become increasingly mobile, older people have migrated with increasing frequency to warmer climates, and a trend has emerged toward urban rather than rural residence. Members of many extended families often never see each other except at weddings or funerals. Whole branches of families often lose touch completely with the rest of the family. The two styles of interaction just described may have arisen in response to these societal trends.

In this chapter, we again look at the postparental stage of family development as it pertains to older adults. Many families do not launch their last adult child until in late adulthood, and the tasks and issues of launching can be experienced differently then from launching in middle age. Finally, we consider the last stage, the aging family stage, which begins after the last child has been launched and ends when the original couple ends, with the death of a spouse. We consider here the relationship of the surviving elderly parent with the rest of the family members.

Some questions addressed in this chapter are the following:

1. Can the elderly make significant contributions to their family systems or are they as helpless as they were when they were children?
2. Are the issues of the aged in families more or less transitional than in earlier stages?
3. What is the impact of widowhood on the aged?
4. How does prolonged longevity affect family systems?

As noted in Chapter 11, role changes in late adulthood, accompanied by physio-logical and psychological changes, can be multiple and profound. The stresses on family systems and the necessary role changes within these systems are complicated by the aging process and the likelihood of serious illnesses. Cultural changes further compound the stresses experienced by the elderly and their families.

A growing number of blended families are in existence through divorces and remarriages and, while they increase extended family networks, these families may also stretch already meager psychological and social resources. For example, if there are several sets of grandparents owing to divorces and remarriages, spending holiday time with specific grandparents may become difficult and less frequent.

On the other side of the coin, there is a definite increase in the number of adults choosing not to marry and/or not to have children. This shift will result in an increasing number of older people without grandchildren and great-grandchildren, which may or may not be seen as deprivation by the elderly. We can only speculate at this time about the effects of alternative lifestyle options on the future elderly and their families. However, it is important to remember that the older adults today have grown up and been socialized in a different world than their middle-aged children or young grandchildren. Their generation's cultural and social variables have shaped their attitudes, values, and beliefs, which differ in many regards from those of later generations.

THE POSTPARENTAL STAGE OF FAMILY DEVELOPMENT

As discussed in Chapter 8, the boundaries and communication patterns must be dramatically changed during this stage of family development as the roles and rules for family members change. Many people in late adulthood find this stage to be more traumatic than people who went through this stage earlier, because they are dealing more consciously with the effects of the aging process than they were a decade earlier. Senior citizens who are ending the launching of their offspring naturally experience this stage differently from senior citizens who are just begin-ning the process. Likewise, an increasingly common phenomenon in this stage of life is the reappearance in the family home, ostensibly for economic reasons, of adult offspring after divorce (with or without children) or after living away from home singly for several years. The point is that the other role changes and physiological changes associated with individual development in this stage of life may cause greater stress in late adulthood for the family system as it struggles to renegotiate its roles, rules, and boundaries.

Developmental Tasks

The major developmental tasks in this stage involve renegotiation of the couple-system relationships, the relationships with adult children, and the formulation of relationships with in-laws and grandchildren.

Boundary renegotiations.   Letting go and separating emotionally as well as physically from adult children may coincide with the loss of elderly parents. Thus, as filial and parenting roles become less prominent, spouse roles, if one is still married, become primary. If the spouse roles have been ignored and deemphasized over the course of the family life cycle, this refocusing may be difficult. If, on the other hand, the spouse roles have been valued and nurtured over the years, this refocusing may be anticipated with pleasure and relief. Other factors affect the couple system at this time; usually one or both members are retiring and this affects the roles, rules, and boundaries of the couple system (see Chapter 13). Thus, how the senior-citizen couple experiences what has been seen in the fifties decade to be a highly satisfactory stage of marriage will depend on adaptation to retirement and leisure, financial resources, residential location, and support available from family and peers as well as health, gender, socioeconomic and educational factors. Another important variable will be the ease and success of the launching process for the adult offspring. Senior citizens who believe that their adult offspring are managing their lives satisfactorily are less inclined to worry and hang onto their offspring than are senior citizens who feel continuously drawn into their offspring's life struggles. Likewise, senior citizens who disapprove and are distressed by their offspring's lifestyle choices are likely either to withdraw more energetically into a "new life" in order to avoid being confronted by their disappointment, or to engage in recriminations with each other over "whose fault it is," thus hampering their marital relationship.

The couple system.   Thus, the major arena of adaptation in this stage of family life is the couple system. No longer is the couple distracted by the demands and needs of children. The couple may be pulled by the needs and demands of aging parents, however, and this may provide the source for maintaining the status quo and avoiding renegotiation. However, the couples who weather changes with the most facility and creativity usually have patterns of role flexibility and conflict approach rather than patterns of conflict-resolution avoidance. If, over the years, the couple relationship has not stagnated or been defused by raising children or caring for parents, the couple will find that there has been a gradual couple-system socialization leading to the development of similar norms and values and a shared view of the world and life experiences. This bonding can provide the couple with a foundation for further growth and development as the partners face a future free of the distractions involved in the parenting process. If, on the other hand, the couple system has been maintained by the triangulation of the children, the couple may find themselves in marital difficulty at this stage and embittered by the sense that it is too late to change their lifestyle or marital-satisfaction level. The latter situation is typical in those instances when one or both parents attempt to hang on to at least one adult child to keep the homeostatic balance that existed in previous stages. This is the situation that an increasing number of senior-citizen couples describe when they file for divorce at this stage of life.

As time and energy resources change owing to retirement, the partners need to renegotiate their boundaries with each other and their affiliations with the outside world. In other words, a resocialization takes place for the individual members of the couple system, for the couple system as a dyad, for each individual member in relationship to extended-family members and people outside the family system, and for the couple as a dyad with extended family members and people outside the family system. The partners may decide to utilize their increased time together in shared avocational interests, in increasing their individual interests with their individual friends, as a couple with other couples, and so on. It is to be hoped that a rediscovery will occur of mutual aid, nurturing, and support in the couple system that can enhance each member's self-esteem and life satisfaction without one member having to accommodate totally to the other. Negotiating closeness–distance is just as critical for the couple in the postparental stage as it was in the first stage of the family life cycle and depends on one's self-differentiation as it has developed over the years (Okun and Rappaport, 1980).

Thus, the major tasks of members of a couple system in this stage are to rediscover individual and shared strengths and to seek new fulfilling ways of relating to and experiencing each other and others, both as individuals and as a couple. Couples who are unable to rediscover or focus on their bonds are likely to experience disappointment with each other and with life in general, which is apt to be manifested in stress-related symptoms and a clinging to the past rather than in concentration on the here and now.

Adult children.   Because senior citizens are usually in good health and just as vigorous and active as adults in their fifties, they often exercise the same power or are seen to have the same power as they did in earlier stages of the family life cycle. This may be a transitional period, where the senior citizens are passing on the "baton of power" to their adult children, who are becoming the middle generation, while still making contributions and remaining involved in patterns of mutual aid and resource exchange. People in this stage possess wisdom and experience and they must learn neither to overfunction nor underfunction for their adult children. This learning process may be delicate, requiring many trial-and-error runs on the parts of both generations. In other words, the establishment of new generational roles between parents and their adult offspring is a reciprocal process and requires active work by both generations. It is sometimes difficult to understand which generation is having difficulty letting go, as the following example illustrates.

A 35-year-old divorced female client, Janet Koren, brought her 64-year-old mother, Ethel Gordon, to therapy for a joint session. Mrs. Koren felt that her mother was intrusive, controlling, and reluctant to allow her daughter to separate emotionally. She claimed that her mother phoned too frequently (they lived several hundred miles apart), was always giving advice, and was disappointed that her daughter had not remarried (she had divorced eleven years earlier). In the session, Mrs. Gordon became very angry at her daughter and told her for the first time that she dreaded her visits home, where she was criticized continuously about her housekeeping, the way she dressed, her interactions with her husband (Mrs. Koren's father), and just "everything." Mrs. Gordon told her daughter to "grow up" and to stop reiterating all the things she believed her mother did wrong in raising her (which the mother says she surely must have) and to go on and lead her own life without being so needy and emotionally dependent.

Mrs. Koren said that she had heard all this before from her mother and did not believe her mother meant it. She complained that she worried about her mother all the time and that her mother would never be able to manage when or if her husband died before her. Mrs. Gordon smiled ruefully and said to her daughter, "I am 64 years old and I'm a lot tougher than you think. Of course I love your dad and we have a satisfying marriage despite what you think. But I know I'm strong and that I can handle whatever will come." Mrs. Koren was surprised to hear this message from her mother in a setting where she had to listen to and later process it.

The members of this mother–daughter dyad misperceived each other and both remained fixed at earlier levels of their relationship. It is likely that Mrs. Gordon failed to facilitate her daughter's emotional separation when her daughter was in her twenties and that she was indeed intrusive and controlling. However, Mrs. Gordon was now in a different stage of her own life and was more than willing to let go and lead her own individual and couple life. Mrs. Koren, on the other hand, was not quite ready to let go and needed her mother to blame for her own emotional neediness. This case exemplifies how letting go (emotional separation) is a mutual process.

As noted earlier, it is becoming more common during this stage of life for adult offspring to return to the family nest after what was apparently a successful launching. In fact, the launching may have been successful and the senior citizens may have developed a satisfying lifestyle as a couple. But divorced or single offspring often return home to live because they need help with childcare or, more often, because of financial pressures. Where this occurs suddenly, without adequate preparation, the disruption for both generations can be painful, and there may be many hidden resentments that become less and less hidden as time goes on. The adult offspring may feel that they have a "right" to return home, while the senior citizens may feel intruded upon and guilty about feeling this way. An increasing number of such "reconstituted families" are entering family therapy, and the treatment involves clear explicit negotiations of roles, rules, and boundaries. Understanding and compromise are necessary on the parts of all family members, and mechanisms for problem solving and conflict resolution need to be determined. Family systems that have long-established patterns for working through these issues are finding this phenomenon to be a "mixed blessing," providing happiness as well as stress, whereas families who have in the past or are currently experiencing difficulties coping with these issues consider this phenomenon to be a "necessary happening" without much mutual benefit.

Grandchildren.   Grandparents' relationships with grandchildren change as the latter enter different stages of child and adolescent development. Such changes are affected by earlier styles of grandparenting, by the developmental issues of the grandparents, and by the relationship between the grandparents and the parents. Some senior citizens find that they wish to participate more as grandparents after retirement, when they have more time and energy. Others find that their increased time and energy is better spent on avocational and social activities with same-generation peers. Whatever the preference, the roles, rules, and boundaries among the three generations are always fluctuating and need continuous adaptation and renegotiation by the three generations. There are a variety of grandparenting styles, and these may fluctuate within a family system over the life cycles.

In-laws. At this time in the family life cycle, membership is always changing. As adult offspring become launched, they are likely to marry, divorce, and remarry, and senior citizens include and often exclude various members of the family system. They also negotiate relationships with the extended families of their sons and daughters in-law, and this process involves sharing grandchildren and off-spring.

A painful matter for the older generation is the loss of in-laws and grandchildren owing to divorce and remarriage. Often, the older person is genuinely fond of the in-law that leaves and feels regret at the rupture of the relationship that is often necessitated by the divorce and subsequent relocation of various family members. Conflicting loyalties and demands often emerge that cause more disruption of family systems than anticipated. Such stresses may affect individuals as well as relationship systems. Recent court decisions have enforced grandparents' visitation rights, legitimizing this relationship even in divorced and remarried families.

The outside world. Senior citizens are becoming one of the most widely travelled and social groups in our society. Given their increased time and energy and the distancing of immediate family members (geographically as well as emotionally), seniors turn to same-generation relationships for sharing, emotional support, and pleasure. Thus, they need to determine which relationships they want to continue, discontinue, or reestablish. There also seems to be a trend for senior citizens to reconnect with their own extended families—recontacting siblings and cousins who may have been distant for many years. One's own generation can be invaluable in providing comfortable social relations among people who share perspectives and life experiences. Such social experiences can add to feelings of membership and sharing as well as to the meaning of life. Each year, more and more senior citizens elect to leave their homes (often the only homes they have ever known) and move to retirement or senior-citizen residences in order to join social networks that serve as a sort of replacement for the family system. These new relationship systems are proving invaluable in providing mutual peer support and can alleviate some of the stresses on the family system.

Survivorship. Senior citizens are increasingly likely to be widowed during this stage of life. Losing a spouse during this particular stage may be particularly stressful, since major renegotiations and adjustments may just have begun to occur. It may seem to the surviving spouse that the couple went through all the hard stages of life and came apart just as the relaxation and fun were about to begin. Widow- or widowerhood is painful at any stage of life, but it may be particularly stressful for senior citizens who are already feeling abandoned by their launched offspring and bereft of their work role. Moreover, economic and residential decisions may force an abrupt change in lifestyle resulting in feelings of uprootedness and disorientation.

Communication styles.   Major changes in communication styles occur in the couple and parent systems. The changes in roles, rules, and boundaries are both reflected in and shaped by concomitant changes in communication styles and patterns.

Couple system.   In the postparental stage, the couple becomes more conscious of its communication styles, since there are no longer offspring around to defuse or mediate the interrelationships. For some couples, it is the first time they are forced to deal directly with each other and they may need painstakingly to learn to communicate *with* rather than *at* each other. Other couples, who have always maintained and developed their communication patterns, may barely notice the transition to more focused couple interactions. Increased time and energy allow couples to listen to each other more carefully and bonding enhances their sensitivity to each other's moods and needs. As partners spend more time together alone, they often find that they need to develop more effective conflict-resolution strategies that may sharpen their differences as well as their similarities.

Adult children.   Learning how to communicate with one's offspring on adult–adult levels as opposed to adult–children levels can be a difficult process. Adult children are particularly sensitive to implied criticism or controlling during their launching, and much misinterpretation and distortion can occur. For example, one young man, James, in his late twenties, reported to his therapist that he could never tell his parents anything about his personal life or relationships because his parents immediately responded with directives and advice. During a family session with his parents, his father explained that every time he said anything about his thoughts or feelings his son retorted with "Don't tell me what to do." The father insisted that he was only trying to have a discussion with his son and was only expressing his feelings with no intention of issuing directives. Both parties were frustrated by their inability to communicate with each other and by the "old baggage" they were carrying into this stage of their relationship. Learning to send differentiated messages—for example, by using "I feel"—and learning to check out the real message or command are important tasks for families in this stage of life. The boundaries are fragile during the launching process and both generations need to experiment with communicative behaviors that keep the door open while maintaining appropriate distance.

Many adult children complain that they are unable to communicate with their senior-citizen fathers except through their mothers. Where this pattern exists historically in a family, some sensitive reconstruction may be necessary in order for the adult offspring to develop direct, clear communications with each parent as an individual, in addition to their communications with the couple system. A triangulated communication pattern may extend downward, in that the senior-citizen parents communicate to their offspring through the in-laws or vice versa. The pattern of triangulated communications may be a learned family style that automatically gets generalized to future generations.

Grandchildren.   Seniors citizens' communications with their grandchildren often reflect the styles they utilized with their own children during early stages of development. The middle generation is usually a major force in determining the communication patterns between grandparents and grandchildren, and sensitivity to the patterns in the in-law's family system may alleviate distress. All of us have been socialized in our own families of origin and each time a new person marries into a family a merger and accommodation of family-of-origin styles occurs.

Developmental Issues

The kinds of issues that affect the family systems of senior citizens in the postparental stage are similar to those discussed in Chapter 8, with the exception of the factors related to retirement.

Retirement.   With retirement, income usually becomes fixed and time and energy are increased. Now the senior citizens may be freed to become more involved with launched offspring at the time when the latter want to put more distance between themselves and their aging parents. Thus, disappointments can result where expectations and anticipations have not been freely discussed. Adult offspring may resent their parents' diminished contribution in terms of financial support, childcare, or emotional support, or they may resent what they perceive to be their parents' increasing intrusiveness. On their part, senior citizens may feel a kind of ambivalent overattachment—they may want to experience and relish the "fruits of their labors" and make themselves available when and how they choose.

The couple system may be affected by retirement; wives may experience reduced freedom after their husband's retirement because of increased accommodation to their husband's needs. On the other hand, some wives find these restrictions offset by increased opportunities for companionship and nurturing (Keating and Cole, 1979). Many factors affect the outcome of retirement—previous family patterns of relating, inclusion or distrust of the in-law, perceptions of each other's well-being and satisfactory adjustment to life, and dependency–independency issues.

Dyadic alliances.   Frequently during times of vulnerability, previous dyadic alliances resurface, disrupting the equilibrium of the family system. If the couple is not adjusting to this stage of life, one partner may ally with an adult offspring, preventing either the senior citizen or the adult offspring from successfully negotiating respective developmental tasks. Or, if an adult offspring is experiencing marital difficulties, the senior citizen parent might ally with a grandchild or the offspring's spouse, thus unwittingly prolonging the marital difficulty.

In later stages of life, dyadic alliances can become more desperate and people can become stuck in them, contributing to some sort of crisis in order to become unstuck. We are all familiar with the stereotype of the meddlesome mother-in-law who contributes to the breakup of her offspring's marriage by constantly interfering and clinging to her offspring. Of course, her offspring will not have been able to separate emotionally, and the fact that he or she is stuck will be the major contribution to the breakup of the marriage.

Cross-generation symbiotic relationships are most likely to erupt in some type of family dysfunction, whether through an inability to separate, a divorce, or some type of illness. Same-generation symbiotic relationships are likely to result in enmeshed marriages less apt to dissolve than the conflicted or disengaged marriages resulting from one's spouse's overinvolvement with a parent or offspring.

Power.   Differences in values, attitudes, beliefs, and experiences can exacerbate generational power struggles. It requires an effort to listen, learn, understand, and appreciate differences, all of which are necessary in bridging vast differences in generational socialization issues. If senior citizens wield their power inappropriately, their adult offspring may choose an alternative lifestyle to deride their values and achievements. Power that is wielded directly is easier to deal with than that used indirectly, and it is often the latter that results in the most stressful power struggles between generations.

Remarriage.   More and more widowed senior citizens than ever before are choosing to remarry or to live with lovers. Usually these marriages are based more on needs for companionship and sharing than on passion and financial need. Remarriage in this age group appears to be just as troublesome for adult offspring as for younger offspring. Several variables appear to be operating:

1. The offspring's desire to believe that the surviving parent will remain loyal to the deceased parent;
2. Fear that financial resources will be depleted before they are inherited;
3. Resentment of an "outsider" taking away the surviving parent;
4. Belief that romance and sexuality are not appropriate for senior citizens;
5. Reluctance to share the surviving parent with others, suggesting that the senior-citizen parent is more emotionally separated than the adult offspring and that the death of a spouse and subsequent remarriage may push to the surface unresolved dependency–independency issues on the part of the adult offspring.

Mrs. Woolin, age 66, began counseling in puzzlement and distress after she had told her two sons and daughter (in their thirties) of her intention to marry an old family friend (a widower) two years after her husband's death. She expected her offspring to be happy for her and pleased at her independence, and was dismayed by their shock and resentment. She intended to pursue her plans, but she felt angry that she was receiving no support from her own family. She felt that this situation was particularly unfair in light of her supportiveness and efforts to include their own spouses when they married. Her children claimed that she would end up nursing Mr. Gray, as she had their father, and she would only be hurt. They wanted her to "adjust to being older" and participate more in the community senior-citizen center and take turns visiting them and being available for babysitting. They had known Mr. Gray for many years and had always liked him; now they were saying "dreadful things" about him.

The counselor requested a session with the three offspring and their spouses as well as with Mrs. Woolin and Mr. Gray. During this session, the offspring focused on their need for this elderly couple (if they insisted in going on with this "foolishness") to draw up an explicit financial contract so that they would not lose out on their father's resources. After much exchange of angry recriminations, the counselor was able to get the adult offspring to share some of their underlying concerns, their fears for having to help their mother through another painful bereavement, and some of their own unfinished mourning for their father. Mrs. Woolin was able, for the first time, to share with her offspring her feelings and concerns, her loneliness and desires, and to show her offspring how much she had worked through her own bereavement and been able to reorganize her life and desires. Mr. Gray remained in the background during this session although his caring and support for Mrs. Woolin were evident. This one session enabled these family members to communicate directly with each other, to work through the vestiges of their mourning, and to express their concerns and needs to each other. The counselor was also able to educate the family about the commonalities across the life stages for relating, intimacy, and sharing. All of the family members felt reoriented and ready to move on in a supportive rather than an opposing manner.

Table 12-1 summarizes the tasks and issues of this stage of family development.

TABLE 12-1.   The postparental stage—late adulthood

Developmental Tasks	General Issues	Requisite Skills	Significant Others
Renegotiate boundaries: parent/adult offspring, parent/in-laws, parent/grandchildren, spouse/spouse, couple/outside world, couple/friends	Retirement Dyadic alliances Power Remarriage/divorce Offspring's lifestyle choices Bereavement	Letting go Couple bonding Conflict resolution Negotiation Grandparenting Self-care	Spouse Adult offspring In-laws Friends, old and new Grandchildren Neighbors Community
Differentiate communications: couple system, adult offspring, grandchildren			
Survivorship			

THE AGING FAMILY

We move on here to the last stage of the family life cycle, the aging-family stage. In this stage, the major process is aging until death. The physiological, psychological, and environmental variables affected by and affecting aging and disease have major effects on the family system. The primary focus in the aging family is first on the couple system and then on the surviving spouse. Patterns developed during the previous postparental stage characterize the roles, rules, and boundaries for this final stage. Increasingly, however, external factors along with physiological and disease changes assume a greater power to influence individual and family developments. Couples with control over the external changes imposed upon late adulthood—over the timing, onset, and course—will naturally feel more in control of their lives than couples who are controlled by happenings and who are forced to adapt, sometimes all too abruptly, to the onset of multiple changes and difficulties.

Developmental Tasks

Boundary renegotiations.   For couples who survive into late adulthood, the major task is to come together as a couple in order to let go. This is what we mean when we talk about aging until "death do us part." This critical developmental task includes the process of retrospection, whereby it is hoped that previously unfinished couple-system issues are worked through at least to understanding, if not to resolution. A gradual detachment from the couple system occurs as one works through dependency-independency issues and there is an acceptance of mortality and preparation for a final letting go of the spouse.

Obviously, the nature of the final illness(es) involved, the amount of time available to prepare for loss, and the tasks involved in final caretaking will affect how the surviving spouse experiences the impending loss, the actual loss, and the mourning process. Often couples in late adulthood find the caretaking period helpful in resolving previous difficulties and invaluable in preparing for the grieving and bereavement that are inevitable for the survivor.

Mr. and Mrs. Zenker were in their late seventies when Mrs. Zenker developed congestive heart failure. At the onset of the disease, her activities were not severely curtailed, so she was able to maintain her established couple-system patterns. The Zenkers went out frequently with friends, entertained often in their home, and traveled near and far to visit children, grandchildren, and great-grandchildren. In addition, they pursued their individual avocations. Mr. Zenker had never fully retired and continued to work three days a week as a financial consultant, while Mrs. Zenker was very involved in rugmaking and needlework. Throughout the family life cycle, Mr. Zenker had been the "provider and distant parent and spouse." Mrs. Zenker had long given up desiring more intimate care from her husband and most of her emotional needs had been met by her large extended family.

As a couple, the Zenkers were happy with their mutual and separate interests and activities. Their offspring served as the focus of their shared interests and discussions, as did their mutual friends. They also attended concerts, plays, and art showings together.

Two years after the onset of her illness, Mrs. Zenker began to experience dizziness, confusion, and weakness. She had to give up driving, which restricted her mobility, and she began to falter in social situations (forgetting what she was going to say midway, stumbling over words and incidents). She definitely required more careful attention. The Zenker offspring, in their fifties, arranged for household help and frequent visits to ensure their mother's welfare. Neither Mrs. Zenker nor her offspring expected Mr. Zenker to be able to understand what was happening or what was necessary in terms of attending to her needs and care as she became increasingly invalided.

However, once Mr. Zenker realized that his wife's illness was progressing and that changes were necessary in their lifestyle, he surprised his wife and children by taking over her care in a most sensitive, affectionate, and competent manner. He managed to provide the right amount of attention without overfunctioning for her. Mrs. Zenker remarked to her eldest daughter that she had never before felt so loved and cared for by her husband. Mr. Zenker made similar comments to his son-in-law. His increased sense of marital satisfaction and the strengthening couple system not only continued to develop but actually succeeded in slowing down the course of Mrs. Zenker's illness. No one in this family system could have predicted the capacity of this couple system to adapt so positively to an aging crisis.

On the other hand, consider the case of Mr. and Mrs. Bowen. He was 82 and she 75 when he suffered his first stroke. Mr. Bowen had always been the follower in the marriage and the supportive, caring parent, whereas Mrs. Bowen, who had never achieved emotional separation from her mother, went through her adulthood years whining, complaining, and trying to manipulate her family for her own narcissistic gratification. The Bowen adult children barely tolerated their mother, but were supportive and attentive to her primarily out of affection for their father. They had talked among themselves for years about the difficulties their father must have endured in this marriage, wondering at his seeming adoration of his wife throughout her temperamental, irrational scenes and rejections.

When Mr. Bowen was first hospitalized, Mrs. Bowen panicked and fell apart, making strenuous demands on her children to rally around and support her. She seemed to be usurping all their energies and resenting their concern for their father. They tried to be responsive to her needs while brainstorming with the hospital social worker regarding alternative forms of convalescent care for their father. All three offspring lived in other states and it was not feasible for any of them to move back to resume care of their elderly parents.

Mrs. Bowen insisted that her husband return home after his hospitalization and that she, and she alone, would assume full responsibility for his care. Her insistence was so strong that it had to be obeyed. Eventually, Mr. Bowen was released to the care of his wife, with visiting nurses and speech therapists scheduling regular home visits. After one week, the visiting nurse telephoned the eldest son to report that Mrs. Bowen was so furious at her husband for being sick and not recovering quickly enough that she was physically abusing him. She became frustrated when trying to feed him and ended up throwing the food in his face; she left him in soiled pajamas and sheets. At the same time, she refused to consider placing Mr. Bowen in a nursing home and went into diatribes over the telephone with her offspring about who was in control of his care. In this case, the couple system could not withstand the crisis and a showdown was inevitable.

The Bowen offspring had to forcefully remove their father from his home and place him in a nursing care facility. Mrs. Bowen interpreted this act as a repudiation of her as a mother and a preference for their father. Her anger was so fully unleashed that her offspring feared for her well-being. They sought out family therapy to learn how to deal with both parents and to meet their conflicting needs.

The contrasts in these two cases indicate different developmental patterns. The Zenkers were more distanced because of communication difficulties—they had not learned how to air and bridge their differences through discussion and negotiation, and each had gone his and her own way while maintaining some shared connection. However, a foundation of affection and caring existed as did mutual respect in their couple relationship even though these qualities had not been directly communicated. The Bowens had a history of overt as well as repressed conflict and of denial and capitulation, but they did not share the underlying mutual caring and support that could facilitate adaptation to change and crisis. Mrs. Bowen had had difficulty throughout her life adapting to change and crisis, and the "abandonment" by her husband was the ultimate blow to her fragile ego.

Clearly, the boundary negotiations in the couple system in the aging-family stage require working through of unfinished issues and preparation for letting go, a kind of balance of involvement and gradual distancing.

Adult children.   Aging parents need to establish new generational roles as they become the elderly members of the family system. By this time, they have passed the "baton of power" on to the middle generation and the elderly parents have attempted to retain as much independence and involvement as the system allows. It is not uncommon for the adult offspring to expect a kind of role reversal, where they become the caretakers and their elderly parents the receivers. This can be distressing to the elderly couple if they do not perceive this need and wish to lead more independent lives. Ambivalence may be reflected in over- or underattachment, and it is important to assess the realities of everyone's perceptions of need.

Generational differences due to cultural factors affect one's expectations of relationships between the elderly and their middle-aged offspring. The elderly may expect the reverence, devotion, and excessive attention that they remember giving to their elderly parents, while the middle-aged offspring may resent their feelings of obligation and begrudgingly accommodate their elderly parents' demands, feeling equally stressed by the pressures put on them both by their adolescent offspring and their elderly parents. Or the middle-aged parents may expect their elderly parents to accommodate totally to their family systems, to move in under their rules and to give up their own autonomy. Whatever the conflicting expectations and perceptions, they can disrupt relationships between elderly parents and their offspring. Remember, parent–offspring relations usually reflect earlier patterns. Manipulative parents are likely to become more manipulative in later years.

Issues of power, control, financial resources, health, and residence are major influences on the relationships between the elderly and their offspring. Historical patterns of the attachment–distancing continuum will affect how these issues are worked through.

Social and economic changes have altered the nature of the American family and the care of the longer-living elderly. Today's elderly raised their families during the Depression, having fewer children than did their own families. With more women working and with increased mobility resulting in scattered families and smaller domiciles, adult children are often overwhelmed with caretaking demands and confused by their guilt, shame, and ambivalence. They do not know how to provide for their elderly parents without losing their hard-won autonomy. The elderly may fear their dependencies and feel useless and discarded, thereby demanding unreasonable proofs of love. The elderly have been likened to adolescents: "they want to be independent, but they are physically unable to act on what they want to do. Like adolescents, many elderly people just aren't able to judge their own limitations. They get angry because restrictions are put on them by, of all people, their children" (Weiss 1983, p.34). The elderly may, in fact, perceive their children as intrusive rather than helpful, and this can fuel the cycle of frustration within a family system.

Grandchildren.   Perhaps because of current school assignments stressing genealogy and "roots," many elderly people report taking greater satisfaction in their relations with their older grandchildren than younger ones. Again, this phenomenon may be developing in spite of the middle generation (parents), inclusive of the middle generation, or unrelated to the middle generation. How grandparents have related to their sons or daughters-in-law will affect their opportunities for relating to their grandchildren. Some adolescents and young adults who are feeling alienated from their own parents may seek comfort and support from their grandparents. Likewise, some elderly who feel hostile toward their adult offspring may seek to hurt these offspring by forming alliances with their children. As the grandchildren become older, they can control their contact with others, whereas the middle generation has complete control over the interactions of younger children with their grandparents.

Many elderly grandparents find that they can serve a useful function as mediators between adolescent grandchildren and middle-aged offspring. It is helpful if the elderly couple can be sensitive to the developmental issues of both younger generations to avoid over- or underfunctioning.

Great-grandchildren.   We are seeing more and more four-generation families. How the elderly interact with their great-grandchildren naturally depends on the family structure and patterns of interaction with the grandchildren. Being the head of a four-generation family can bring with it excitement, love, and a heightened sense of generativity, which in turn can enhance the elderly's sense of life's meaning.

The outside world.   Same-generation relationships are as important for the elderly as for any other age group. Many residential communities for senior citizens and the elderly are finding that peer group support is more conducive to adapting to stress and change and to working through the mourning process than the support of adult offspring. An article in the *Boston Globe* (1983) reported on a survey of the elderly showing that they derived more satisfying support and understanding from peers than from adult offspring. The elderly may need help in understanding the necessity of establishing and maintaining peer relationships and help in finding such opportunities. Many older adults avoid forming same-generation attachments because of the fear of loss.

In addition to same-generation relationships, it appears that different-generation relationships are also necessary for satisfactory living in late adulthood. Whereas extended family may provide some outlets for the cross-generational relationships, other opportunities may be helpful. One of the major tasks of service providers to the elderly is to help locate and create resources for both same-generation and cross-generation relationships.

Survivorship.   Inevitably in late adulthood, or by the time of late adulthood, one has been widowed or one dies before one's spouse dies. Whereas preparation for death was discussed in the previous chapter, here we will focus on widow- and widowerhood.

The loss of a spouse at any age has been shown to produce the greatest role stress in the life cycle. It causes an immediate identity change—one is no longer a spouse—as well as loneliness and social isolation. Our society is structured around couples, not singles, and widows and widowers find that their friends sometimes retreat after the mourning period. In late adulthood, however, so many peers share the same experience that much support is available from peers where desired.

Whereas all survivors, regardless of their life stages, experience reduced morale and a low sense of well-being at the death of a loved one, the elderly are often abruptly faced with immediate decisions about residence, economics, and family relationships.

The first stage of survivorship is the grieving or bereavement period. The adaptation to mourning is influenced by whether or not there has been anticipation and preparation for the mourning. This may depend on the cause and nature of the death—a sudden, abrupt death may result in a more severe shock reaction than a drawn-out terminal illness. Remember, the elderly have reduced stamina and homeostatic mechanisms, so they can suffer prolonged effects of a shock reaction.

Most authors agree that the grieving process varies greatly in intensity and duration from one individual to another and is influenced by situational factors. Also, emotional, structural, and social losses associated with widow- or widowerhood vary for individuals. Socially isolated survivors tend to adjust less satisfactorily than those with access to social and emotional support (George, 1980). In late adulthood, the shock and disbelief may not be as predominant as during earlier life stages unless the death is totally unexpected. Whereas the elderly experience the same type of loss and grief as younger adults, the element of tragedy is absent, since the elderly are expected to be closer to death than younger adults.

Guilt and anger are common experiences during bereavement, and depression or health deterioration may ensue. Often the guilt and anger are displaced toward surviving friends and relatives, offspring, and even grandchildren. Remember that the elderly are more vulnerable to stress and disease than younger age groups, and the loss of a spouse is stressful enough to trigger the onset of a major health deterioration of the survivor.

Research shows that recently bereaved people are more vulnerable to disease than nonbereaved people, especially when the death is sudden. A significant number of widowed elderly die within six to twelve months following loss of spouse (Wass and Myers, 1982). It is suggested that grief may serve as a mediating process between a conjugal loss and an ensuing illness or death (Jacobs and Douglas, 1979). This supports other research on stress-related topics showing loss of spouse as the most severe stress (Holmes and Rahe, 1967).

Whereas younger and middle-aged widows and widowers tend to remarry, older widows and widowers typically do not. The latter are more able to accept the end of their spouse identity. There are multiple patterns of successful adjustment to widow- and widowerhood, and these are influenced by gender, age, race, ethnicity, income, social and family support, education, personality type, coping strategies, and the nature of the marital relationship. For the elderly, issues of dependency and their impact on lifestyle decisions will be crucial factors in adjusting to the loss of a spouse.

Survivors who, because of the loss of a spouse, are forced suddenly to relocate or to alter their lifestyles and patterns are more likely to experience prolonged stress than survivors who are able to stay in their places of residence and resume their usual relationships and daily functioning. The loss of a spouse requires emotional support, allowing for a period of readjustment to the loss that will culminate in a reorientation and remobilization of one's resources and energies. Many elderly people never complete the mourning process. Some propel themselves toward their own death and some remain fixated in the midst of the mourning process. Others complete the mourning process and succeed in creating a new life for themselves.

It is impossible to predict how long the mourning process might last. Some people never finish mourning, as previously mentioned, and some are able to continue to live satisfying, albeit different lives. Lopata's work (1973) indicates that older widowed persons seem to adjust more satisfactorily than younger widowed persons. Although there are more widows than widowers in our society, we do not have clear-cut evidence that one gender adjusts more satisfactorily than the other. The critical variable is more likely to be success at individuation and emotional separation than gender.

Dr. Horn, 76, lost his wife, 86, four months earlier. They had no children and Mrs. Horn had devoted her entire life to caring for and protecting her physician husband. After Mrs. Horn's sudden death, Dr. Horn was devastated. He had never lived alone in his life and he was lost without someone providing for his every need and mediating between him and the world. He frantically began reconnecting with old friends and was quite forthright in his intent to remarry. He was looking for a woman to take his wife's place, to come into his home and fulfill the roles and functions of his wife. He became increasingly angry that the women he approached were not interested in his offer; he claimed that he did not have the time to "court" or "woo" such women, to consider their needs other than their financial security, which he could well afford. Dr. Horn had never emotionally separated from his mother or his wife, who had taken over the mothering function. His difficulty in adjusting to widowerhood was more closely related to his unsatisfactory emotional separation than to his gender.

Another type of survivorship that the elderly are increasingly likely to face is the death of an offspring or grandchild. Death of a child at any age is a major stress. If it occurs after widowhood or widowerhood it may be more devastating than if one can share the bereavement with a spouse.

Renegotiating relationships with family as a survivor.   An elderly widowed parent needs to renegotiate his or her relationships with adult offspring and grandchildren as part of the mourning process. Remembering that the adult offspring and grandchildren have lost a parent and grandparent helps the family system to share in the mourning and bereavement process. Obviously, the past history of the survivor's relationships and interactions with the family will influence this renegotiation, both positively and negatively. If the more distanced parent is the survivor, the loss may force the survivor and adult offspring to deal more directly with each other. Conversely, the death might result in a greater distancing, since the lost spouse is no longer there to mediate and negotiate. Situational and health factors will also influence this renegotiation.

The family system is under stress during the mourning period. After the initial funereal rituals, the survivor is apt to turn to his or her offspring for increased emotional support. The renegotiation of boundaries between the generations cannot occur effectively until termination of the mourning process. As previously stated, since many elderly never achieve this goal, the heightened stress on the family system may remain until the survivor dies.

Often during this mourning period a symptom develops that requires outside help. Facilitating opportunities for same-generation relationships to provide social and emotional support is a way of alleviating some of the emotional pressures the survivor places on adult offspring. Often, the adult offspring unwittingly hamper the survivor's success at working through the mourning process. Just as the elderly parent needs to avoid over- or underfunctioning for adult offspring, so do adult offspring and grandchildren need to avoid over- or underfunctioning for elderly parents.

Communication styles.   The elderly are often confused by the realization that apparent communication difficulties exist between themselves and their adult offspring and grandchildren. Many of these problems derive from generation gaps influenced by cultural and social changes. Hampered further by physiological changes and illness, the elderly must often develop compensatory communication behaviors. Just as younger adults sometimes express relief when they return from visiting elderly relatives who have difficulty hearing and understanding, so the elderly sometimes express relief when they are left to each other's more appropriate expectations and demands. Patience, tolerance, and acceptance are necessary for all parties in order for communication patterns to be renegotiated.

Developmental Issues

Some of the developmental issues previously discussed become more prominent and critical in late adulthood.

Health.   Obviously, the health of either or both elderly parents becomes a more central issue with advancing age. Preventive measures are no longer very effective and health-related decisions often involve trade-offs. Frustration and distress can result from attempts to retain responsibility for self-care and for the care of the ill spouse, and access to satisfactory health care may become a life-or-death issue. Many physicians have no understanding of the elderly and avoid caring for them. Health issues may become the major focus of intergenerational communications, becoming the focal issue for the family. Health care costs money. No matter what health-care route a family chooses, the emotional and financial costs reverberate throughout the entire family.

Dependency/independency.   Final loss of autonomy and having to accede control for one's life is a major issue in this life stage. If both spouses are alive, they may be able to bolster each other's sense of control for a longer time than a surviving spouse would be able to do alone for him- or herself. Whether one feels comfortable giving over control for one's life and livelihood to offspring or to an institution depends on situational factors as well as past family relationships. How one deals with this issue also depends on one's cultural conditioning in terms of the meaning and perception of dependency/independency issues to the particular individual. An individual who has always maintained an independent lifestyle may have more difficulty giving up independence owing to external events than one who has been able to experience more interdependence over the life cycle. This critical issue affects how one perceives and experiences illness and survivorship and strongly affects how one works through the grieving process and the renegotiation of family relationships.

Scapegoating.   Some family systems have a history of scapegoating in that throughout the family life cycle one person has always played the role of identified patient, the "sick one" who has caused all the family problems. Increasingly, we are seeing elderly family members (perhaps the one who in earlier stages modeled scapegoating behaviors) being excluded by their family systems or scapegoated and abused, whether physically or emotionally. As the elderly are more vulnerable and less well equipped than younger adults to defend themselves from abuse, this situation may go unnoticed by others for prolonged periods of time. The elderly parent is often unable to resist scapegoating owing to financial, residential, and emotional dependence on adult offspring.

Regardless of who the scapegoat is and despite his or her age, family systems operating in this manner undergo stress and dysfunction that express everyone's pain. Whereas they believe that the scapegoat is responsible for all their difficulties and that "if only he or she would change, everything would be all right," the reality is that the family system needs a scapegoat in order to maintain its homeostasis and that it is only a matter of circumstance who fits the scapegoat role when. The elderly surviving parent, in particular, is quite vulnerable to being placed in this role because of dependency factors.

Institutionalization.   Although institutionalizing the elderly is a social rather than a developmental issue, in late adulthood it is hard to separate developmental and social issues. At some point, most elderly people require some type of health care and, while it may be provided in their own residence, more typically it is provided in an institution or in the home of an adult offspring. This final development of the family system has been forming throughout the life cycle, and the way one deals with the residential issue depends on all the variables discussed in this book: historical family relationship patterns, health issues, psychological factors, economic factors, social factors, emotional factors, environmental factors, and developmental issues of all the generations of the family system. It is true that some elderly people are abandoned by their families to chronic care facilities, others are reluctantly institutionalized, and still others are maintained by their families either in the family residence or in their own homes.

George (1980) points out that the very old, who are most likely to be widowed and whose children might be relatively old, are more likely to be institutionalized than those with social support systems. Being institutionalized, whether voluntarily or involuntarily, is the ultimate acknowledgement of dependency, of admitting to the world that one can no longer care for oneself. Obviously, such an admission affects one's self-concept as a fully functioning adult. One gives up total autonomy in return for the security of an environment that will provide total essential services. It is likely that the process of becoming totally dependent on others for care and medical attention affects one's self-esteem and identity but that the impact may be secondary to that resulting from the health and self-care deterioration.

Adjustment to institutionalization in late adulthood is affected by many variables, among them social status, personal resources, coping strategies, socializing experiences, and situational factors. Relationships with family members and friends provide a sense of continuity that can positively affect adjustment. These family relationships determine the type of decision-making process resulting in institutionalization—shared, unilateral, eager, regretted, and so on. Whether or not the decision was voluntary, the types of alternatives that existed, and how the decision was implemented all influence the adjustment both of the institutionalized person and of other family members. Thus, the institutionalization of an elderly parent requires still another type of boundary renegotiation among family-system members. And, as always, communication styles need to be recalibrated as the family rules change. Often, institutionalization occurs to protect the interests of one part of the total family system over another. There is no "right solution" to the problem of an ill elderly parent, and the ways members adapt to the decision to institutionalize will affect the pattern of family relationships for the rest of the family life cycle.

Mr. and Mrs. Nunnally were in their sixties when Mrs. Nunnally's 87-year-old father, who had been widowed three years earlier and who was living in a group home for the elderly, became terminally ill with cancer. The group home could not provide adequate medical care, and Mrs. Nunnally and her two brothers were informed that they would have to make other arrangements. Mrs. Nunnally's relationship with her father had always been hostile; she perceived him to have been critical and rejecting of her. Her brothers were completely detached and wished to have nothing to do with the family.

Mrs. Nunnally felt that her adored mother would have wanted her to take Mr. Nunnally into her home for this final period, and she decided this was the best solution. Mr. Nunnally, who had never liked his father-in-law and who had always resented the way he had treated Mrs. Nunnally, was appalled. He had just retired and was looking forward to traveling and pursuing long-awaited leisure activities.

Mr. Nunnally was open and clear about his reluctance to take on the care of his father-in-law, so Mrs. Nunnally felt that she was forced to locate a suitable institution for her father. She resented her brothers' detachment, her husband's lack of agreement (although he was supportive in terms of locating an appropriate institution), and her father's neediness.

Mrs. Nunnally's father did not want to leave his current residence and the friends and lifestyle to which he had grown accustomed. He perceived Mrs. Nunnally as the perpetrator of the move and was most uncooperative and unresponsive. As a result, his adjustment to the new institution was poor, resulting in a quicker health decline than might have occurred under other circumstances. Mrs. Nunnally found herself conflicted and resentful of her husband, her father, and her brothers. Her resentment was manifested in the appearance of hypertension and migraine headaches, which prevented her from traveling with her husband. It was only after a referral to therapy by her physician that she was able to work through the impact of her decision to institutionalize her father and her relationships with the men in her life.

Death.   The death of the surviving elderly parent leads to the final dissolution of the original family system. With this death, the middle-aged or senior citizen offspring become the elder generation of several different family systems.

Increasing attention is being paid to the role of the family in the dying process experienced by the elderly and other terminal patients. The hospice movement is one way of providing emotional support to the dying patient and his or her family. Some families choose to bring elderly parent(s) home to die. Families are involved with euthanasia decisions, with both the feasibility and the morality of health care practices, and with the type of death experiences patients can have. It may be the final task of a family system to help its members achieve a peaceful death in much the same manner as we attend to a more natural, painless birthing process today.

TABLE 12-2.   The elderly family

Developmental Tasks	General Issues	Requisite Skills	Significant Others
Renegotiate boundaries: spouse bonding and letting go; parents/ adult offspring; grandparents/ grandchildren; parents/great- grandchildren; couple/ friends; couple/outside world	Health Dependency/ independency Scapegoating Residence (institutionalization) Death/bereavement Social/political/economic	Caretaking Self-care Adaptation Decision making Problem solving	Adult offspring In-laws Grandchildren Great-grandchildren Caretakers Neighbors Friends/peers Community
Cope with survivorship: mourning process; renegotiation of relationships with family; renegotiation of relationships as survivor with friends and outside world			
Readjust communication patterns			

The "right to die" issue is one that families increasingly face. Many elderly, faced with prospects of total dependence as a result of chronic, painful, and terminal illnesses, choose suicide rather than endure what to them is an intolerable situation (McCartney, 1978). The role of the family in these decisions needs further consideration. There is conflict between the medical, legal, and family systems with regard to aggressive medical treatment for terminally ill older people (Wass and Myers, 1982). Often, close family members do not know their elderly parents' views or wishes about these matters and hesitate to take responsibility for such decisions. Or old conflicts between siblings can resurface and take on devastating proportions.

Table 12-2 summarizes the tasks and issues of the elderly family stage.

SUMMARY

We have seen in this chapter the impact of the aging process on family relationships. Throughout the family life cycle, roles, rules, and boundaries need to be renegotiated as family members move into different stages of life, requiring a new set of developmental tasks and issues. Along with these boundary renegotiations occur communication-pattern renegotiations. Both mutually influence each other and allow a family system to move on rather than stagnate in a stuck position.

Role transitions necessitated by diminishing family size in the later stages need not be viewed negatively. These transitions are a challenge, a source of contentment as well as stress, and they allow one to continue to grow and change. The major differences between the nature of the changes in later family life in contrast to earlier family life lie in (1) the exchange of power—the fact that it is passed down from the elderly to the middle generation—(2) the increasing influence and importance of external factors—forced retirement, death of a significant other, fixed income, declining resources—and (3) internal factors—aging variables and health issues. As the shift of power occurs—usually taking place gradually rather than suddenly—the family focus shifts and the elderly begin the process of distancing and letting go to prepare for their final emotional separations.

It is likely that the elderly of tomorrow will be radically different from those of today, because the cultural changes have been so sharp and rapid in the past forty years. Our society is still ambivalent in its attitudes toward and policies for the elderly, and a lag may exist for a long time between the need for appropriate support services and the types of services actually provided. Family systems bear the greatest responsibilities for their elderly and need social support as well as economic support in periods of crisis. However, we must remember that many families do not experience a negative type of crisis in the later stages and that they often demonstrate resilience and the capacity to maintain high levels of personal well-being and self-sufficient functioning. Perhaps we need to concentrate on providing services to families spanning several generations in order to help them remain intact as long as possible.

It may be that as families shrink in size in the next few years, we will have more elderly single adults than family groupings containing elderly members. We can learn from the family-system perspective to help single elderly adults develop social-network systems that provide the type of caring, belonging, and mutual support found in healthy family systems.

REFERENCES

Boston Globe, February 1, 1983.

Cicirelli, V. G. *Helping elderly parents*. Boston: Auburn, 1981.

George, L. K. *Role transitions in later life*. Monterey, Calif.: Brooks/Cole, 1980.

Herr, J. J., & Weakland, J. H. *Counseling elders and their families*. New York: Springer, 1979.

Holmes, J., & Rahe, S. A social adjustment scale. *Journal of Psychosomatic Research*, 1967, *11*, 213–218.

Howells, J. G. (ed.). *Modern perspectives in the psychiatry of old age*. New York: Brunner/Mazel, 1975.

Jacobs, S., & Douglas, L. Grief: A mediating process between a loss and illness. *Comprehensive Psychiatry*, 1979, *20*, 165–176.

Keating, N. C., & Cole, P. What do I do with him 24 hours a day? Changes in the housewife role after retirement. *Gerontologist*, 1979, *20*, 84–89.

Lopata, H. Z. Self-identity in marriage and widowhood. *The Sociological Quarterly*, 1973, *14*, 407–418.

McCartney, J. R. Suicide versus the right to refuse treatment. *Psychosomatics*, 1978, *19*, 548–551.

Okun, B. F., & Rappaport, L. J. *Working with families: An introduction to family therapy*. No. Scituate, Mass.: Duxbury Press, 1980.

Rosenmayr, L., & Kockeis, E. Propositions for a sociological theory of aging and the family. *International Social Science Journal*, 1963, *15*, 410–426.

Walsh, F. The family in later life. In E. A. Carter & M. McGoldrick (eds.), *The family life cycle: A framework for family therapy*. New York: Gardner Press, 1980, pp. 197–221.

Wass, H., & Myers, J. E. Psychological aspects of death among the elderly: A review of the literature. *Personnel and Guidance Journal*, 1982, *61*, 131–138.

Weiss, R. Cited in D. Moore, America's neglected elderly. *New York Times Magazine*, January 30, 1983.

CHAPTER THIRTEEN

CAREER DEVELOPMENT IN LATE ADULTHOOD

Just as individual and family development are lifelong processes, so is career development. The issues of career development in late adulthood focus on retirement (the end of a formal work role) and the subsequent use of time, interests, energies, and skills in another type of work role (part-time or second-career, volunteer work), and/or in leisure activities. Usually people in this phase of life do not come into counseling presenting career-development issues; rather, the presenting problems are often related to finance, health, or bereavement. However, the counselor who understands and can assess the career issues will be better able to help clients work through existing presenting issues.

Only in the last few years has much attention been paid to the process of retirement, as opposed to the event and status of retirement. Whereas the psychological processes of retirement are still secondary to the practical and pragmatic issues, they nevertheless are closely intertwined and cannot be ignored. This increasing attention to the process of retirement has resulted in opening up increased options and possibilities for senior citizens and the elderly. Society's attitudes toward aging, retirement, and postretirement continue to change, and these broadening, more accepting (albeit still ambivalent) changes, plus economic and health factors, affect current retirement policies and practices.

As mentioned earlier, some developmental theorists believe that the retirement process parallels the young adult's launching process in that both involve leaving a familiar setting (retirement involves leaving the familiar work place and launching involves leaving the familiar family system) and moving out into the unknown world. Both involve giving up familiar roles for unknown roles. One major difference, however, is that for the young adult, time is infinite and possibilities limitless, whereas for the retiree, time is finite and possibilities are limited by aging, health, and societal factors. The transition process, however, may indeed be similar in that both require role losses and gains, status changes and adjustments to new environments, people and social relationships, and a reformulation of self-concept (identity) and intimate relationships.

In this chapter, we consider the tasks and issues associated with retirement itself as an event, status, and process, and with planning and leading a postretirement life. There are many individual differences in the experience of and adjustment to retirement, as with any other transition in the life cycle. The quality of one's particular experience will depend upon past experiences with transitions and change, anticipation and preparation for this transition, family relationships, social supports, economic resources, health, aging and personality variables, to say nothing of gender issues. Much of the research on adjustment to retirement and factors affecting this adjustment is inconclusive, but we will highlight some of the implications that seem to be borne out by clinical experiences.

Some of the questions we will address in this chapter are the following:

1. What are the variables that enhance the transition into retirement?
2. Do men respond to retirement differently than women?
3. Can one predict adjustment to retirement based on previous transitional experiences?
4. How do older people occupy themselves after retirement?
5. Why do some older people appear to be so much more adaptive and productive after retirement than others?
6. Is retirement planning really helpful or is it just a fad?

CAREER DEVELOPMENT THEORY

Career development theorists have traditionally viewed retirement as the "end" of the career development process. More recently, they have highlighted the importance of preretirement planning during the ten-year period prior to the actual event of retirement. However, texts and courses on career development do not typically devote much time to the discussion of the psychological process of retirement and of postretirement life. Rather, most texts and courses focus on the decision-making process and how it can be utilized in planning for retirement. It is as if career choices, growth, and change abruptly end with the event of retirement. Perhaps this is because conventional career development theories do not integrate personal and family issues into their consideration of career development and, therefore, when occupational work is not a primary role, they see career development as at an end.

Some of the major career development theories can be extended throughout retirement and postretirement if we view work and leisure as integrated dimensions of lifelong productivity and fulfillment. A theory such as Super's (1957) could be applied to postretirement leisure planning by focusing on the congruence between self-concept and perceptions of the environment. One's self concept may not change as drastically as the environmental constraints at this time, and the work may focus more on one's perceptions of the environment than on one's awareness of self-concept.

Likewise, Holland's (1966; 1973) differential typology could be just as relevant to leisure as it is to work. It could be utilized to identify activities for postretirement that are congruent with the personality types postulated in the theory. Again, the choices of activities would need to be modified according to personal and environmental constraints. Perhaps social-learning theories of career development are most conducive to utilization for postretirement because of their provisions for environmental limitations that are not adequately considered by Holland and Super. Decision-making theories have major relevance for retirement and postretirement in that, regardless of the nature or content of the decision, the requirements for information processing and cognitive processes are critical for any decision-making process.

LEISURE COUNSELING

Proponents of a relatively new subspecialty of counseling called *leisure counseling* are stereotypically seen as aiding retirees to use their work skills, interests, and aptitudes in nonwork-related activities to fill their increased time and to provide further learning and self-fulfillment. Leisure counselors seek to balance work and leisure planning throughout the entire life cycle. Yet is difficult to see how leisure counseling and career counseling could be considered separate entitites if one believes that work, leisure, family, and personal issues are reciprocally intertwined. Bordin (1979) and Kaplan (1981) argue that lifelong planning in balancing work, leisure, and other aspects of life are the necessary goals of all career and leisure counselors. We will discuss the concept of leisure in a later section.

Certainly the self-knowledge, intrinsic and extrinsic satisfactions, and decision-making skills developed in earlier stages of career development can facilitate the adaptation to retirement. Let us now look at some of the current thoughts about retirement and consider the concomitant tasks and issues.

RETIREMENT

Most writers view retirement as a major transition marked by the end of one's formal work role and the beginning of an expanded period of relative leisure. The most frequently cited definition of retirement is Atchley's (1976, p.1): "A condition in which an individual is forced or allowed to be employed less than full time and in which his income is derived at least in part from a retirement pension earned through prior years as a job holder." Thus, retirement marks the termination of a formal occupational career.

We can consider retirement as a shift from work to nonwork. One goes from less free time to more free time, from more money to less money, from a structured environment to a less structured environment. These shifts involve significant changes characterized by losses and gains in terms of roles, status, power, and self-concept. Carp (1966) differentiates among the event, status, and process of retirement.

Retirement as an Event

As an event, retirement traditionally occurred at age 65. Increasingly, this age varies. The Social Security Act of 1935 mandated retirement at age 65 in most businesses, although some professions and the self-employed were exempt. In 1978, the United States Congress passed an act banning mandatory retirement before age 70 for workers in the private sector and at any age for federal government workers. In the 1980s, economic factors and high unemployment pressure workers to choose early retirement, while, at the same time, forcing many to work as long as physically or organizationally possible. Thus, a double-bind exists for many senior citizens today. Many have planned for retirement and want to retire, only to find these plans and wishes disrupted by runaway inflation and insecurities about pensions and social security benefits. This double bind is exacerbated by increasing resentment among younger workers, who are themselves deterred by older workers' seniority privileges and the elimination of job openings, while older workers remain stuck in the fewer existing positions. We may have an increasing number of adults who will work (whether through necessity or choice) throughout their life span, whether in primary, secondary, and/or part-time late adulthood occupations.

Nevertheless, retirement is a social event marked by ceremony and recognition in some organizations, families, and communities. It is accepted as a normal life event with no particular fanfare in others. It is an event that is dreaded, eagerly anticipated, tolerated, enjoyed—there are as many views about the meaning of the event as there are varieties of individuals. Attitudes toward retirement reflect attitudes about the meaning of work, occupational satisfaction, and occupational commitment. They also reflect family relationships—meaning family commitment and satisfaction—and other lifestyle factors. People whose identities are primarily dependent on their work roles are more likely to dread retirement than people whose meaning of life is derived from a more balanced integration of work, family, and leisure roles. Attitudes and views toward retirement translate into a continuum of dissatisfaction and satisfaction with postretirement life.

Retirement as a Status

The status of retirement has to do with behavioral expectations and experiences. Retirement involves the loss of one's formal primary work role and this certainly affects one's identity. This loss will also impact family and social roles.

What this means is that retirement contains unique roles, expectations, and responsibilities, and is, therefore, a social role. As discussed before, typically there is a reduction in one's number of roles and a decline sometimes occurs in one's standard of living due to reduced income. Atchley (1976, p.4) suggests that retirees have specific rights and responsibilities that characterize their social role. Their rights include economic support without a job and without social stigma. Their responsibilities include managing their personal lives without assistance and making appropriate lifestyle decisions. Not all retirees are able to understand and utilize these rights and responsibilities. It takes preplanning as well as flexible adaptation to ensure a successful transition. Also, environmental variables may change abruptly, upsetting long-range plans.

This changing role status may be experienced negatively despite the decreased role demands and increased leisure time, or it may be experienced positively with increasing responsibilities and a creative use of leisure changes. Cultural attitudes traditionally value work and productivity and devalue leisure status activities and volunteerism. Thus, society does not consider retirees to have a highly valued status. They lose self-esteem as they continuously interact with a devaluing society.

Retirement as a Process

The process of retirement deals with the consequences of the event, how these consequences were anticipated, and how they are recognized, negotiated, and experienced. The process of retirement does not necessarily imply an end to one's productivity. Havighurst (1979) found that male social scientists who were independent and highly productive prior to retirement continued their productivity by publishing after retirement, whereas those with less self-reliance had a problem in continuing to publish without the structure of a job. For some, then, productivity is dependent upon job structures, whereas for others productivity is independent of job structures.

Let us consider some of the major factors affecting the process of retirement.

Biological factors.   As discussed in Chapter 11, the aging process along with health issues affect the process of retirement. If one is unable to travel or to enjoy leisure because of illness, one's satisfactions, roles and status are negatively affected. Consider the case of Mr. Price.

Mr. Price, 70, was a successful middle-level executive in a multinational manufacturing firm. He had worked for his last employer for more than twenty years and was satisfied with his occupational role and status and with his family and personal life. For many years, Mr. and Mrs. Price had devoted their leisure time and activities to their second home, a large farm in the country two hours away from the city where they lived. Mr. Price loved working on the farm—managing the property, restoring the farm house and guest house, and absorbing himself in necessary and elective maintenance and construction projects. As far as he was concerned, his occupation was a means to an end, a way of making possible the time and money to spend on his farm with his wife. His children had grown up spending summers and holidays on the farm, and now, in adulthood, they returned every summer with their families.

Mr. Price looked forward eagerly to retirement at age 65, when he and Mrs. Price would sell their city home and move permanently to the farm. He had become accepted in the community with respect and affection, and he expected no difficulty in making this transition. His retirement event was indeed cause for celebration, and friends and relatives came from afar to attend the company party.

Shortly after moving to the farm, Mr. Price began to experience serious health problems for the first time in his life. He underwent extensive surgery and treatment. Because of weakened resistance to infections, he was ill most of the time. For the next five years, Mr. Price had to assume the role of a chronic patient rather than that of a farmer. His disappointment, bitterness, and depression steadily mounted. He felt cheated—as if all his dreams had soured and there was little he could do except suffer and complain. He watched his beloved gardens deteriorate, since he had little energy with which to attack daily chores, but he refused to hire others to work for him, owing to his intense pride and perfectionism and his difficulty in accepting his own physical limitations. Thus, biological factors in the form of illness disrupted a well-planned, eagerly anticipated retirement and resulted in disappointment and resentment that affected the entire Price family.

Sociocultural factors.   Other factors affecting the process of retirement are such sociocultural issues as one's occupational status, the meaning of retirement, whether or not retirement is voluntary or forced, and the level and satisfaction of one's lifetime work. The Cornell Study of Occupational Retirement (Streib and Schneider, 1971) found that prior attitudes about retirement correlate more positively with retirement satisfaction than any other variable. One's attitudes can be influenced or shaped by the attitudes of job associates, neighbors, members of affiliated social and professional organizations, spouse, family of origin, and so on. The stance of the employing organization is an important variable influencing attitudes, and organizational preretirement programs attempt to foster a positive attitude about this inevitable process. As stated earlier, one's attitudes are also influenced by family life and occupational meaning, satisfaction, and commitment.

The needs of society affect policies and practices of retirement. Currently, there appears to be a trend toward encouraging earlier retirement to free up jobs for unemployed middle-aged and younger adults. Some economists predict, however, that older workers will be needed in the future to offset the effects of a decreasing population. Domestic and foreign economic and political policies definitely influence the needs of society with respect to older workers. Kaplan (1981) points out that the effects of the cost of a larger retirement population, improved health leading to longer and greater worker capacity, and inflation are all factors prohibiting retirement. Also, race, sex, ethnic group, education, and class differences can inhibit or enhance the event and process of retirement.

Economic factors.   Economic factors are probably the most important regarding the process of retirement and the adjustment to postretirement life. If we consider that perhaps 90 percent of our population works in a fairly structured environment and is struggling for existence, we can see that preparation for retirement will differ more for this group than for the more affluent, more highly educated group which has enjoyed more leisure throughout life and which is permitted more choices about the timing and nature of retirement as an event and postretirement life.

Many researchers consider economic factors to be the key to a satisfactory retirement. The bottom line is how much money the retiree will have for what may amount to one-third of his or her life span without customary income. With rapid inflation and questions about the future viability of social security, retirees can no longer assume that their retirement income will be sufficient. There is obviously a correlation between one's financial security and one's retirement satisfaction. For those with money, retirement can be viewed as a time for travel and leisure, and new and renewed social relationships. For those without money, retirement is viewed as the loss of a job, and a loss of necessary income resulting in increased insecurity about meeting basic life needs such as food and shelter, and in a continuous struggle for existence. What may have been considered satisfactory as a retirement income a few years ago may not be so now; likewise, it would be hard to predict today what a satisfactory retirement income will be even two years from now.

Psychological factors.   One's own evaluation of one's contributions to work and family is critical to one's sense of satisfaction, productivity, and accomplishment. If one feels satisfied, one is able to let go with a more positive attitude than if one feels stagnant and frustrated. Letting go of power, status, and security relates to how one has let go in the past—of the power, status, and security of parenting and other former primary roles. The availability of supportive relationships also influences one's experience of retirement. Many people have depended upon the daily human contact at work to satisfy their needs for interpersonal relationships and have not developed satisfying relationships outside work. Such people are likely to experience a greater sense of loneliness and uselessness than those who have developed and maintained relationships outside of work. Again, we see the increasing importance of social interactional systems in late adulthood.

Reichard, Livson, and Peterson (1974) cite five personality types, three associated with good adjustment to retirement and two associated with poor adjustment to retirement. Those associated with positive adjustment to retirement are:

1. *Mature personalities,* who accept conditions and find enjoyment in activities and personal relationships;
2. *Rocking chair personalities,* who are more passive yet accepting of existing conditions;
3. *Armored personalities,* who are active and who deliberately avoid or suppress feelings of anxiety over personal decline.

Those types associated with poor adjustment to retirement are:

4. *Angry personalities,* who are bitter over past failures and who blame others for what they are;

5. *Self-hater personalities,* who, like the angry personalities, are bitter over past failures but who blame themselves for what they are.

Personality types and coping capacities during times of transition and crisis have been fairly well developed by the time of retirement and are just as important for this transition as they were in earlier stages of the life cycle. Cognitive styles reflected in decision-making skills, rigidity/flexibility factors affecting identity, and relationship reformulations are other psychological factors influencing the retirement process.

Gender factors.   The Cornell Study of Occupational Retirement (Streib and Schneider, 1971) found that women were often less willing to retire than men. It has been suggested by several reviewers of this study that this finding may relate to the fact that many women enter the occupational world later than men and take a longer time to rise up the career ladder and to achieve a level of satisfaction or success. Also, women may not have accrued sufficient pension funds and may feel that they have not had the opportunity to develop their occupational roles as fully as they desire. The data in this study also revealed that single and married women were more likely to retire earlier than divorced or widowed women, although both men and women with higher incomes, education, and occupational satisfaction worked longer. Again, this may reflect degrees of satisfaction and support in other areas of life vis-à-vis meaning and commitment to work.

An interesting study by Longino and Lipman (1981) compared married and spouseless men and women in planned retirement communities and found gender differences in terms of utilized support networks. First, married males and females had more primary relationships than nonmarried males and females. However, married females had more primary relationships than married males, and spouseless females had more than spouseless males. Their findings showed that among the spouseless, females received significantly more emotional, social, and instrumental support from family members than males. Thus, the greatest informal resource deficits were found among unmarried males. These findings validate much of the data attributing gender differences to socialization processes. Women have always placed a higher priority on interpersonal relationships and have been trained to develop and value interpersonal relationship skills. Women have always been allowed to express their dependency needs, whereas men have typically been taught to develop their self-sufficiency and independence. It is not surprising, therefore, to find that there are gender differences in the utilization of support networks and interpersonal relationships.

Levy (1980–1981) studied the effects of chronic ill health and attitudes toward retirement of older women. She found that more female retirees than male retirees were chronically ill but also that women were seemingly better able to surmount the effects of bodily disease and to adapt to the requirements of these role transitions. There appear to be gender differences in attitudes toward ill health and in adaptation to the dependent role of chronic patient.

Neugarten (1973) found that the process of retirement was indeed different for men and women. Older men tended to relate to their environment in a more cognitive manner, and older women tended to relate to their environment in a more affective manner. Thus, men sought more concrete types of tasks and leisure-time activities and expressed a greater need for affiliative, nurturing relationships. Women resisted these dependency needs of men and demanded more personal time and space for themselves. Perhaps the stereotype of the needy, demanding male retiree and his exasperated, frustrated spouse has some validity. He is ready to stay home and be cared for, and she is ready to expand herself and finally achieve some independence without needing to respond to the emotional demands of children and others for nurturance and care.

Another issue that may be reflected in gender differences is the spouse relationship. Retirement of one or both spouses refocuses attention not only on the nature and demands of the employment but also on the nature and quality of family relationships. If the spouse relationship has been and is of poor quality, retirement may increase the strain and end up in divorce. Or if one spouse retires earlier than the other, there may be a great deal of relationship stress until the new roles, rules, and boundaries can be negotiated to the satisfaction of both parties.

When Mr. Johnson retired at age 65 and Mrs. Johnson continued to work, the couple experienced more conflict in the marriage than ever before. When she came home from work, he was eager to see her and to socialize. She was tired and just wanted to relax quietly at home. When he wanted to travel and she couldn't go, he felt rejected. Six years later, when Mrs. Johnson retired, she wanted to engage in her hobbies and club work with her friends. By this time, Mr. Johnson wanted to sell their home and migrate to Florida. It took two years of hassled negotiating before they could work out a satisfactory solution to their differing needs and expectations.

Thus, there may be gender differences in the expectations of the retirement process and this may affect the actual transition. Women may have been slower than men in defining their self-identities by their occupational roles and statuses and they may, thus, be less willing to give this up at retirement. On the other hand, they may never have identified primarily with their occupational roles and may in fact find it easier to give up those roles than their mates did. Obviously, much more research is necessary on gender differences, and such research must also consider the context of generational differences. Tomorrow's female retiree may be more similar to today's male retiree because she spends a longer time in the occupational world, attains higher levels of status and other benefits, and achieves greater degrees of commitment and satisfaction. Sociocultural changes affecting childhood socialization may also reduce gender differences in future years.

Family themes.   Multigenerational family themes certainly influence one's attitudes and expectations about retirement. These themes may be subtle or overt. One's memories of parents' and grandparents' experiences affect one's attitudes and expectations, whether emulation or repudiation is the outcome. Some families, for example, have a multigenerational rule of "working until death." People with this script may avoid retirement, equating leisure with idleness and sinfulness. They may not recognize where this script comes from and may be surprised at the intensity of their feelings and attitudes. Other families may have this multigenerational rule: "live it up after 65, since you can't take it with you." In these families, people have permission to retire and to do all the things they deprived themselves of during their career life. In between these two extremes are many moderate alternatives.

Still another type of multigenerational script may be that "when you retire, you go live with your children." The Howe family typifies this script.

Mr. and Mrs. Howe, in their mid-seventies, sold their suburban grocery store five years before entering therapy, after operating it for more than fifty years. They had accumulated enough financial resources to sell their home and to purchase a condominium in Florida. They lived in Florida for six months of the year and then moved in with their son, daughter-in-law, and two granddaughters for the other six months of the year. Mr. Howe's parents had lived with him, his wife, and two sons after their retirement until their respective deaths. In this family, the meaning of retirement was that you no longer worked. You were financially independent, but you lived with your middle-aged children and grandchildren in a powerful, leadership position.

The Howes' children and grandchildren knew that this was the expectation and the middle-aged offspring passed this rule down to their teenage children. Another important multigenerational rule in this family was that the oldest generation had all the power no matter whose house they lived in. Thus, when the older Howes were living with their son and his family, they moved the furniture around to their liking, ordered their daughter-in-law and granddaughters around, decided on the thermostat setting, when meals would be served, and so on. Moreover, they expected the middle-aged offspring to devote all of their nonworking time to their elderly parents The granddaughters, thus, received directions and admonitions from two parents and two grandparents.

The elder Howes had two sons. The younger son escaped to the Far East during the Korean War and never returned. He married a Korean woman and lived and worked in Korea. The older son, therefore, automatically assumed all responsibility for his parents. He had informed his wife before their marriage of these expectations and informed his daughters in many direct and indirect ways of his expectations of them.

During the five years since they sold their store, the Howe family experienced stress and difficulty during the six months that the senior Howes lived with them. The middle generation believed that they had to abide by their parents' expectations to help them feel needed and loved: obviously, the older Howes lived only for their family and could only be happy when they were together. The granddaughters were not allowed to express their feelings or individuate in any way because "it would hurt Grandma and Grandpa's feelings."

The situation came to a head when the daughters entered adolescence and began to demand their own social lives with their peer groups, and some freedom for leisure. The four adults in the household resisted these demands and attempted to block them in every way. This resulted in school failure by one daughter, and runaway attempts by the others. The family was referred to family therapy and everyone's unhappiness with the situation came to light. The grandparents admitted to feeling useless and dependent. The son expressed confusion, as he thought this was the way families were supposed to be. The daughter-in-law finally expressed her long-repressed anger about having all of the work responsibilities, while her daughters wanted only to play and have fun. It became apparent that the multigenerational script—on which all members of the family colluded—prevented, rather than helped, the senior Howes adjust to retirement and develop lives of their own as a couple, which they had never done before and never realized was necessary. In therapy, the meaning of retirement and the attitudes toward retirement were carefully reassessed by all three generations and many lifestyle changes resulted. Most importantly, the older Howes realized that they could choose to settle in Florida, with new friends and new activities. They were just as unhappy with the old script as the other family members, but no one in this system realized there were alternative options.

Adjustment to retirement.   George (1980) cites the following as factors affecting retirement adjustment: (1) occupational status; (2) gender and marital status; (3) personal resources, including income, health, and social supports; (4) personality characteristics; and (5) socializing experiences. In her review of the literature, she found that for the most part retirement appears to have little significant impact on broad levels of social adjustment and identity. She found that an individual's reaction to retirement is dependent on three types of variables: (1) the degree to which retirement is perceived as stressful; (2) the effectiveness of the coping responses utilized; and (3) the impact of a variety of conditioning factors such as those mentioned above. However, she did discover that two groups of people were most likely to find the retirement process stressful. The first group is composed of those individuals who retire from high-status jobs, who miss the intrinsic satisfactions derived from work, and who have unfavorable attitudes toward retirement. These people are the least likely to seek out relevant socializing experiences. Their social needs were probably met primarily through their work relationships and work was really the major source of their personal identity. George points out that these people usually adjust eventually because they have enough money to do so and to find substitute satisfactions and gratification. The second group is made up of people with low-status jobs, for whom loss of income is an economic hardship. These people are definitely at a disadvantage economically, which may put them at a disadvantage in terms of receiving adequate health care and social support resources.

Thus, an important variable concerns whether or not one's basic needs become the focus of postretirement life, precluding possibilities for self-fulfillment or self-actualization. Obviously, people with ample resources can afford to consider leisure activities and a wide array of options for achieving postretirement satisfaction, whereas those who need to utilize all their energies and resources to obtain food, shelter, and basic health care have more limited options and possibilities.

Walker, Kimmel, and Price (1980–1981) formulated the following typologies for retirement style: (1) reorganizer, (2) rocking-chair, (3) holding on, and (4) dissatisfied. These styles correlate with health, income, occupational status, preretirement feelings, and attitudes about retirement and are predictors of overall retirement satisfaction. The major variables these researchers found contributing to retirement satisfaction were satisfaction with income and postretirement activities. These typologies are similar to the personality types described earlier, but it is important to note that they may not necessarily be lifelong typologies. In other words, retirement adjustment may be difficult for people who have weathered earlier transitions adaptively and vice versa. Health and/or other personal and environmental constraints may contribute to retirement adjustment difficulties. It is difficult, therefore, to predict retirement adjustment without considering all the contexts affecting the retiree—for example, family, living arrangements, economics, social support, and health.

O'Brien (1981) found that the attributes of work associated with job satisfaction did not necessarily correspond with the attributes of leisure activities associated with retirement satisfaction. The most significant factors associated with retirement satisfaction were the number of leisure activities and the number of leisure interactions involving people; health and financial satisfaction were the other most significant factors. However, O'Brien did find that satisfaction with postretirement activities was the only significant predictor of postretirement life satisfaction. This implies that planning for activities to be performed after retirement must begin earlier, in middle adulthood.

A telephone survey of 514 retirees was conducted by Research and Forecast in 1980. Fifty-one percent of the interviewees reported themselves to be in good or excellent health and cited economic support as the major variable contributing to their postretirement satisfaction. An overwhelming majority of the interviewees considered inflation to be their major concern, citing the declining value of their retirement income and the curtailment of services and benefits available to improve their lives. This study classified their respondents into three groups:

1. The *enjoyers* comprised 27 percent of their respondents. These were predominantly well-educated males in good health with high assets and a household annual income of more than $8,000.

2. The *survivors* comprised 53 percent of their respondents. This group coped more or less successfully. There were an equal number of males and females in this group and they reported fair to good health, less than a high school education, and a middle range of assets and income.

3. The *casualties* comprised 20 percent of the respondents. This group was hardest hit by retirement. They were predominantly female, poorly educated, reported fair to poor health, and had low assets and household income.

Again, we see that levels of income, education, health, and occupational status contribute to the well-being of our elderly population. With a reduction of services accompanying rapid inflation, we will most likely see greater numbers of retirees in the latter two categories.

Phases of the retirement process.   Atchley (1976) refers to the *honeymoon phase* which occurs immediately after the retirement event. This phase includes feelings of relief and freedom and hopes for many opportunities. This period is often followed by a *disenchantment phase,* a period of disillusionment or emotional letdown experienced as some of the negative realities of retirement sink in. Atchley describes three subsequent phases which characterize adjustment to retirement: (1) the *reorientation phase* in which people negotiate the realities of retirement as opposed to planning for retirement, based more on anticipation than realities; (2) the *stability phase,* which includes the implementation of the negotiated routines of retirement lifestyle; and (3) the *termination phase,* wherein one relinquishes the role of retiree, perhaps to death or to the role of patient or to some type of institutionalization. Atchley takes care to point out that not everyone goes through all of these phases and that the duration and order of the phases may vary.

Atchley's process phases are most likely influenced by the timing of the event and the degree of control experienced by the retiree. These phases also need to be considered within the broad sociostructural context of our society, since race, sex, education, and class differences obviously have effects.

It is clear that retirement is an adjustment or transition process similar to earlier such processes. Retirement includes identity reformulation, reevaluation of relationships, and losses and gains of roles, status, and power, and it is experienced differently by long-term retirees than by more recent retirees. For the majority of the population, government policies and practices are major shapers of the retirement experience, and rapid and sudden changes in these policies and practices can heighten anxieties and insecurities with regard to the event, status, and process of retirement.

Tasks of Retirement

Basically the developmental tasks associated with retirement are: (1) formulating a new identity; (2) financial planning; (3) physical health care; and (4) lifestyle planning.

Formulating a new identity.   When one's primary role is no longer that of a worker, a gap exists that needs to be filled. Some people have begun to disengage from their worker identity earlier and are only too willing and ready to assume the role of retiree, having already decided how they will utilize their newfound leisure time. Others flounder, feeling depressed and at a loss—they have not developed compensatory interests, relationships, or activities and feel as if the entire meaning of their lives has disappeared. One must remember that usually more than fifty years of adult life have been goal directed and structured by the occupational or professional identity structure, in keeping with the notion "I am what I do." This has been particularly true for today's retirees, who have lived through a major Depression and world war, and who have rarely participated in the leisure activities that their children and grandchildren take for granted. Today's retirees' attitudes and values make this transition difficult. They were raised to give a high priority and value to structured work, to earning what they get, and to expecting to be self-sufficient and independent as long as they can remain working. They were raised to devalue leisure and to equate nonworking with idleness.

Retirees who have continuously reassessed their identities, and who have been able to adjust and adapt their lifestyles over the life span, will most likely experience an easier reformulation of identity than those with foreclosed identities, who have avoided this developmental task all along. As in earlier stages of the life cycle, one's capacity to reformulate a personal identity mostly depends on family and social relationships, attained level of self-differentiation, and health and aging issues.

Identity reformulation includes acceptance of oneself as a senior citizen or elder, as one who is unlikely to contribute further in a major way to one's occupation or profession and who is unlikely to be considered necessary or pivotal to one's employing organization. Some liken this development to being put out to pasture; others find pleasure in passing down the baton of power and responsibility to younger colleagues.

Financial planning.   If money is the key to successful retirement, then preparation by careful budgeting must have occurred during a period of years preceding the onset of retirement. There is evidence that retirees who have planned in advance for their retirement live much better than those who have not. Actually, financial planning for retirement takes precedence over lifestyle planning, since the kind of retirement lifestyle and leisure activities one can afford depends on the amount of money available. Most retirement experts advocate that people calculate their current income and expenses and weigh these against projected retirement income and expenses. As retirees' incomes are normally less than half as large as those of younger adults, this may be a shocking revelation. The kinds of items that need to be calculated in this budgeting process are food, clothing, housing (mortgage, taxes, maintenance), housing utilities, automobile costs (gas, license, repairs), medical and drug expenses, recreation, insurance premiums, income taxes, and miscellaneous expenses.

When such data are collected, it is important for retirees to consider alternative options for cutting down on living expenses and to estimate accurately postretirement income. This process may involve determining which living expenses are likely to be reduced after retirement and which increased. It is also important for retirees to review their life and health insurance policies to ensure adequate coverage. This data collection and analysis is essential if retirees and their families are to consider possible options for their postretirement lives. Those senior citizens who consider this assessment a challenging necessity are more likely to experience a satisfactory adjustment to postretirement than those who avoid this assessment and then find themselves dismayed and overwhelmed by financial realities.

When these data are analyzed, senior citizens can then consider how much income they can earn working without losing social security or pension income and what other options are available, either in remaining an active worker or supplementing income. In other words, ways of compensating for income reduction may be important considerations and may provide viable options.

Physical health status.   As important as financial planning is a careful assessment of physical and mental health needs and care. Some constraints on one's accustomed range of physical activities are likely, and it is incumbent on senior citizens and the elderly to take responsibility for preventive and curative health care. They must watch their diet, get adequate daily exercise and rest, seek medical care when necessary, live within their physical and sensory limitations, and take care to accident-proof their homes and the environment. Again, these factors will influence the choices that they make about work, activities, and lifestyle.

Lifestyle planning.   One's lifestyle definitely changes after retirement, if for no other reason than because more time is available. Retirees still need to be useful, to help others, to socialize, to learn and stay mentally alert, to relax, and to keep healthy and physically active, and these needs can be met in a variety of ways. Multiple options exist for the use of time—leisure activities, volunteerism, alternative careers, education, and/or increased participation in the family. The process of lifestyle planning comprises the evaluation and possible reordering of personal goals, plus the discovery of some ways of substituting for the meaning, time, socializing, feeling useful, productivity, and rewards one derived from work and of a way to retain a sense of continuity in the life cycle. Thus, one's lifestyle might remain similar, change dramatically, or represent a modification between these two extremes. The point is that one must take responsibility for making whatever choices are available and feasible within realistic personal and environmental constraints.

Alternative options involved in lifestyle planning are further explored in the following discussion of leisure, its meaning, and its implications for time use.

LEISURE

As previously mentioned, leisure counseling is a relatively new specialty. In fact, an entire issue of a 1981 American Psychological Association publication, *The Counseling Psychologist*, is devoted to the topic of leisure counseling. Most writers in this speciality contend that leisure should be conceptualized in the same way work is. That is, the purpose of leisure planning is to develop feelings of self worth, social status, and individual potential that lead to self-discovery and to a better quality of life. These objectives are identical to those of the career counselor in facilitating a client's occupational choice and development.

Definition of Leisure

Leisure can be defined as activities and interests that have no external constraints on the use of time and in which the participation and direction are basically controlled by the individual. Blocher and Siegal (1981) describe three types of leisure:

1. Complementary leisure, where there is free choice and some relationship to one's job. An example is the librarian who spends her leisure time writing

novels or the auto mechanic who uses his leisure time restoring antique cars. Another example is people who work and play with the same people or who use their occupational membership to pursue a leisure activity, as in attending a convention for their vacation or joining a country club for which the employer pays the membership fee.

2. Supplemental leisure, in which the purpose of the activity is to fill out or balance one's life and which is somewhat opposed to the nature of work. Examples are the physician who regularly plays golf for relaxation and renewal or the accountant who races cars for excitement and challenge.

3. Compensatory leisure, in which activities are used to escape or alleviate stresses or tensions in work or family life. Examples are athletics, art, fishing, and so on.

One needs to examine the psychological relationship between work and leisure activities in order to help people integrate and develop both important areas of life. Whether leisure and work activities are similar or opposite, they have a reciprocal influence.

Attitudes Toward Leisure

For today's retirees, leisure may well have a negative connotation. Remember, they were raised and have lived in a work-oriented society where nonwork is associated with nonproductivity, idleness, and sinfulness. Thus, for many senior citizens today, leisure evokes negative attitudes and guilty feelings. It is interesting to note that many of today's retirees have opted to relocate into retirement communities, often in the Sunbelt. These communities are like summer camps in that they provide structured leisure activities for their members. Since this generation of retirees rarely had the opportunity to attend summer camp while growing up (except, perhaps, for "boot" camps) and since their adult lives did not customarily include recognized or valued leisure activities, many of them respond to these new opportunities with enthusiasm and vigor. The structure of the recreational programs in these communities resembles the structure they have been used to all their lives, though it exists in a totally new environment. Thus, with peer support, today's retirees are able to overcome their guilt and anxious attitudes toward leisure activities. Adults today in their twenties, thirties, and forties, who are more likely to have attended camps and participated in extracurricular activities in school or on vacation and who have always viewed leisure activities as an important part of their everyday lives, have different attitudes about the meaning of work and leisure; they may very well have different needs and attitudes about retirement, avoiding the lifestyle choices that appealed to their parents.

Thus, the lifelong meaning of leisure and choices having to do with time and leisure activities are important influences on retirement choices. Other influences are, of course, health, environmental limitations, funds, availability of transportation, and socioeconomic background. Atchley (1977) suggests that socioeconomic factors definitely affect leisure choices. Upper-middle-class retirees tend toward sports, reading, and gardening activities. Middle-class retirees tend toward crafts, reading, and television, and lower-class retirees tend toward visiting friends and relatives.

Another factor to consider is the individual's state of mind. One person's play is another's work. The main distinction seems to be between motives, whether the activity is an end or a means to an end, and whether it is a free choice. For many, something that is freely chosen is perceived as leisure and something that is involuntary is perceived as work (Bordin, 1979). Individuals vary in how much they can and want to integrate work and play. Some people keep them distinct, others integrate them fully, and there are many varieties in between. There does seem to be a psychological chemistry of effort, spontaneity, and compulsion that affects one's choices of leisure-time activities, and this psychological chemistry may differ from that affecting occupational choices.

Leisure Choices

In lifestyle planning, retirees need to learn to value their leisure time and to use it creatively toward continued self-actualization regardless of their particular choices. This is more difficult than it may sound because the creative use of time is not automatically socially sanctioned as work is, and few cultural guidelines exist for using one's time freely for self-fulfillment.

McDowell (1981, p. 5) distinguishes between work and leisure as follows:

Work	*Leisure*
Time	Timelessness
Effort	Relaxation
Reason	Intuition
Boundedness/focus	Unboundedness/non-focus
Activity	Experience

The major differences between work and leisure appear to involve structure, effort, choice, and rationality. Certainly, we have all been socialized to focus on and value work more strongly than leisure.

For the retiree, these differences may involve the following:

1. More free time and less free time (free time may become less valued as it increases and becomes more readily available);
2. Free choice rather than compulsion (being able to do what one wants rather than what one must in order to retain work participation);
3. Thinking and planning versus spontaneous feeling and doing;
4. Structure versus nonstructure.

Some of the options that today's retirees elect have only relatively recently become available. Many are government funded or sponsored in an attempt to provide some resources for the growing "grey population." Perhaps the government is motivated to enhance retirement experiences in order to encourage the retirement process and open up jobs for younger workers.

Hobbies.   Many retirees look forward to their retirement as a time when they can devote more energy and time to lifelong or new hobbies. Senior citizen centers exist in most communities that encourage hobby selection and development, and groups of hobbyists may share and pursue their activities together.

Hobbies may have to be modified according to physical and environmental constraints. For example, those who have looked forward to retirement to do more intense sewing and knitting may find that their vision has declined, precluding additional work of this nature. Or the fisherman may find that he can only manage the fishing boat with some kind of assistance.

Avocations.   Avocations differ from hobbies in that they could be occupations, but are not. However, after retirement they may indeed become second careers.

Mr. Findley retired from the garment industry at age 65. Since his second marriage ten years earlier, he had become very interested in Cordon Bleu cooking and immediately upon retirement he went to England to take a year-long course in Cordon Bleu cooking. Prior to this, cooking was his avocation, in that he spent much leisure time preparing dinner parties for family and friends and attending professional cooking meetings and exhibitions. When his job permitted, he took adult education courses in cooking. After his Cordon Bleu course, he returned to this country and volunteered his services to local civic groups. At the age of 69, he decided to open and manage a small seasonal Cordon Bleu restaurant in a popular resort. Thus, he managed to turn his avocation into a second career and for several years (until health issues forced him into a second retirement) he diligently pursued this direction. Unfortunately, however, the time and energy Mr. Findley devoted to his restaurant placed a severe strain on his marriage and his health declined just in time to save his marriage from dissolution.

Jobs for retirees.   Many retirees seek jobs after retirement to fill their time or to supplement their incomes. This is usually difficult, because prejudicial employment practices definitely exist in our society. For example, senior citizens are often subjected to medical examinations, educational-credential requirements, interviews, and standardized tests that make it difficult for them to compete with younger adults.

Many retirees are certainly capable in every way of holding down a job and some government programs now allow for retraining and job placement. One such program is the Foster Grandparents Program, which employs people over 60 and below the poverty level to work with neglected and deprived children in and out of institutions. Many school districts employ senior citizens as classroom aides to read to children or help them with their play. Another government-sponsored program is the Senior Aide program, whereby senior citizens are hired to facilitate other senior citizen programs and to fill community social-service positions. Some institutions allow retirees to fill temporary or part-time positions.

Mr. Denning retired as a buildings and grounds employee of an urban university at age 65 with some physical disabilities. After two years at home, Mrs. Denning begged him to find a part-time job in order "to get out of her hair." He was able to secure a four-hour-a-day job as a dormitory receptionist at the university where he had worked before. This job required no undue physical activity. Mr. Denning loved his new job, which involved socializing with students and answering the telephone, and he was thus better able to utilize and enjoy his nonworking time with his wife.

Kaplan (1981) discusses alternative work options for older workers. She cites part-time, part-year, job transfers (lateral and demotion), modified jobs and flex-time options as solutions to the prohibitive costs of retirement. Perhaps these options will become more feasible and available as the population bulge shifts.

Volunteerism.   Harris (1975) reports that 22 percent of today's retirees are actively engaged in some form of volunteerism. Some of the volunteer activities reflect job skills, hobbies, or avocations, and some are life-long volunteer activities. Senior citizens and the elderly may be seen volunteering in health, mental health, transportation, civic affairs, social services, and many other areas.

One national program is Retired Senior Volunteer Program (RSVP), which recruits elders and provides training, transportation, meals and part-time placements in a variety of settings, such as schools, courts, museums, libraries, hospitals, or nursing homes. Opportunities for such workers are increasing as more and more service positions are eliminated by economic restraints.

Another growing national program is the Service Corps of Retired Executives (SCORE), started by a business consultant in Boston. This service utilizes former executives as free consultants to government, small businesses, and other needy organizations. The wisdom and experience of SCORE volunteers have meant the difference between success and failure for many new or faltering businesses.

Other national volunteer programs utilizing retirees include the Telephone Reassurance Program, the Friendly Visitor Program, Meals on Wheels Programs, and the Bereavement Counseling Programs. Some of these programs are federally sponsored, whereas others are sponsored by local civic or religious organizations.

One problem of volunteerism is that workers often feel somewhat slighted in providing services without pay. A fine line exists between altruistic volunteerism and exploitation, and retirees must keep it in balance with other leisure activities.

Lifelong learning.   Butler (1975) refers to the redistribution of education, work, and leisure over the life cycle to provide lifelong learning. The Elder Hostel program for senior citizens and the elderly was described in Chapter 11. More and more educational institutions are now offering learning programs for the elderly, considering tuition waivers, and adapting the style and pace of presentation to the needs of the elderly. Of course, this new orientation stems from these institutions' needs to survive in the face of declining enrollment by traditional students.

Nonetheless, many retirees are taking advantage of educational opportunities in all fields. They are not returning to school for vocational reasons, but are pursuing subjects and courses in avocational and leisure-time interests. Courses in liberal arts, fine arts, music, and social sciences seem to be the most popular and instructors of senior citizens find older students apt, highly motivated, and challenging.

Leisure Counseling

Leisure-time pursuits, economic factors, residence, social supports, health issues, aging issues, family issues—all these factors are components of the decision-making processes that senior citizens and elders are constantly engaged in. All decisions are possibly reversible. In fact, some people choose to return to work from retirement, like Mr. Denning, described above. Others reverse their lifestyle decisions—regarding activities, relationships, places of residence, and so on. It is not uncommon for people in this life stage to live "one day at a time," knowing that factors outside their control can erupt at any time, necessitating further assessment, evaluation, and decision making. The pursuit of meaning, usefulness, self-fulfillment, and self-satisfaction, as well as productivity and achievement are with us throughout the life cycle, and the decline or termination of one's formal occupational activity does not mean that one must stagnate, become unproductive, or useless.

Sinick (1976) suggests several considerations and emphases relevant to counseling retirees. He points out that retirees face decreased status, closed minds, and negative attitudes in our youth-oriented society, all of which make a mockery of the increased leisure time that accompanies retirement. Thus, counselors need to deal with the mundane matters previously discussed—income and finances, housing and living arrangements, health and nutrition, consumer education, personal safety, legal arrangements—as well as with the creative use of time leading toward continued self-actualization. Environmental factors may produce as many psychological difficulties as do intrapsychic conflicts. The counseling of retirees should cover role adjustment and use of time as well as those mundane matters related to retirement.

Another relevant factor is that counselors of senior citizens and older adults have their own age biases (Troll & Schlossberg, 1971). All individuals have their own styles of mourning over losses, and they must be encouraged to choose their own ways of developing a new appreciation of life and a satisfactory style of living. Counselors need to be aware of their age biases, so as not to inadvertently impose them on their clients.

As will be discussed in Chapter 14, peer counseling and formal community-based planning programs are proving effective in helping retirees become aware of their options and in acknowledging that losses and gains associated with retirement are as much a part of the normal developmental process as any other milestone or transition. Understanding the interplay between individual, family, and career issues is essential in formulating effective strategies for helping retirees plan their late-adulthood lifestyle.

Alternative retirement practices and styles are likely to emerge in the coming years, and workers who have the opportunity to plan and choose a style that meets their unique needs are more likely to enjoy retirement than workers who are forced to submit to a preprogrammed style. The outcome is related to one's degree of control. People who feel they have some control over their lives are more highly satisfied than people who do not. Obviously, feelings of control are related to the meaning one perceives in life.

TABLE 13-1.   Retirement

Developmental Tasks	General Issues	Requisite Skills	Significant Others
Reformulate identity: new roles, let go of old roles	Gender	Budgeting	Peers
	Health	Self-care	Neighbors
	Finance	Avocational	Spouse
Make financial plans: current budget, projected budget	Companionship	Interpersonal	Friends
	Family		Financial advisors
	Residence		Medical
Plan health care	Aging		Social service
Plan lifestyle: leisure; volunteerism; alternative career; lifelong learning; family; restructure energy, time, resources	Leisure		
	Hobbies		

Table 13-1 summarizes the developmental tasks and issues of the retirement stage of career development.

SUMMARY

In this chapter, we have focused on the event, status, and process of retirement as marking the termination of one's formal occupational role. We have discussed this transition from a developmental perspective and delineated the major developmental tasks as including: a reassessment and reformulation of one's identity; reevaluation of existing, new, and old relationships; financial planning; physical and mental health care; and lifestyle planning.

The transition into retirement was compared to earlier transitions and similarities in the psychological process were highlighted. We have considered the health, environmental, sociocultural, economic, gender, and psychological factors that affect one's attitude toward retirement as well as multigenerational family themes, and one's attitudes, orientation to, and commitment to work. We have highlighted certain variables that appear to enhance satisfactory adjustment to retirement, such as degree of choice and control, financial resources, social support resources, level of occupation, family commitment and satisfaction, and enjoyment of postretirement activities.

In the second half of the chapter, we considered the meaning and definition of leisure and the possible options retirees have for using their increased leisure time. We emphasized that attaining a sense of productivity and fulfillment is just as necessary after retirement as it is during earlier adulthood stages. There is a variety of ways to achieve these ends. The concept of leisure as a lifelong component of career development was posited. We discussed the relationship of leisure-time activities to work interests, attitudes, and skills, and denoted the reciprocal lifelong influences of leisure and work choices and pursuits.

This developmental perspective of retirement and postretirement life emphasizes the need for counselors to be aware of the changing environmental realities as well as changing personal (health and aging) constraints in order to facilitate clients to choose a satisfactory way of engaging in life, and of continuing to feel useful, productive and contributory to society.

REFERENCES

Aging in America: Trials and triumphs. New York: Research and Forecast, 1980.

Atchley, R. C. *The sociology of retirement.* Cambridge, Mass.: Schenkman, 1976.

Atchley, R. C. *The social forces in later life* (2nd ed.). Belmont, Calif.: Wadsworth, 1977.

Atchley, R. C. Issues in retirement research. *The Gerontologist,* 1979, *19,* 44-45.

Blocher, D. H., & Siegal, R. Toward a cognitive developmental theory of leisure and work. *Counseling Psychologist,* 1981, *9,* 33-45.

Bordin, E. S. Fusing work and play: A challenge to theory and research. *Academic Psychology Bulletin,* 1979, *1,* 5-9.

Boston Globe, February 1, 1983.

Butler, R. A. *Why survive? Being old in America.* New York: Harper & Row, 1975.

Carp, F. M. *A future for the aged.* Austin, Tex.: University of Texas Press, 1966.

George, L. K. *Role transitions in later life.* Monterey, Calif.: Brooks/Cole, 1980.

Harris, L. *The myth and reality of aging in America.* Washington, D. C.: National Council on Aging, 1975.

Havighurst, R. J. Social change: The status needs and wants of the future elderly. In B. R. Herzog (ed.), *Aging and income.* New York: Human Science Press, 1979.

Holland, J. L. *The psychology of vocational choice.* Waltham, Mass.: Blaisdell, 1966.

Holland, J. L. *Making vocational choices: A theory of careers.* Englewood Cliffs, N. J.: Prentice-Hall, 1973.

Kaplan, B. H. Alternative work options for older workers. *Aging and Work,* 1981, *4,* 145-161.

Levy, S. The adjustment of older women: Effects of chronic ill health and attitudes towards retirement. *International Journal of Aging and Human Development,* 1980-1981, *12,* 93-110.

Longino, C. F., & Lipman, A. Married and spouseless men and women in planned retirement communities: Support network differentials. *Journal of Marriage and the Family,* 1981, *43,* 169-177.

McDowell, C. F. Leisure: Consciousness, well-being and counseling. *Counseling Psychologist,* 1981, *9,* 3-33.

Neugarten, B. L., & Datan, N. Sociological perspectives on the life cycle. In P. B. Baltes & K. W. Schaie (eds.), *Life span development psychology: Personality and socialization.* New York: Academic Press, 1973.

O'Brien, G. E. Leisure attributes and retirement satisfaction. *Journal of Applied Psychology,* 1981, *66,* 371-384.

Reichard, S., Livson, F., & Peterson, P. *Aging and personality.* New York: Wiley, 1962. Cited in D. C. Kimmel, *Adulthood and aging.* New York: Wiley, 1974.

Sinick, D. Counseling older persons: Career change and retirement. *Vocational Guidance Quarterly,* 1976, *25,* 18-25.

Streib, G. F., & Schneider, C. H. *Retirement in American society.* Ithaca, N.Y.: Cornell University Press, 1971.

Super, D. *The psychology of careers.* New York: Harper & Row, 1957.

Troll, L., & Schlossberg, N. How age biased are college counselors? *Industrial Gerontology,* 1971, 14-20.

Walker, J. W., Kimmel, D. C., & Price, K. F. Retirement style and retirement satisfaction. *International Journal of Aging and Human Development,* 1980-1981, *12,* 267-281.

CHAPTER FOURTEEN

IMPLICATIONS FOR COUNSELORS: CASE STUDIES

Elders do not commonly present themselves for counseling. They usually fail to recognize the need and have been socialized to be distrustful of talking about their personal lives to "outsiders." Rather, they are usually brought in by a relative or referred to a social service agency for some type of crisis intervention. The crisis may involve bereavement, health, lifestyle, or residence. The types of issues that senior citizens and the elderly present have to do with independence and dependency, reactions to illness or physical infirmity, reactions to the death of spouses and friends, reversals of roles with children and grandchildren, companionability versus isolation and loneliness, and the postretirement structuring of time and energy. Many of these issues are reflected in elders' attitudes toward and preoccupation with recent and distant past events versus the present and future. In other words, people in this stage may dwell on past happenings rather than present and future planning and they may resist attempts to help them focus on the here and now.

Working with the elderly is different from working with younger populations. The elderly may prefer to use the counselor as a friendly companion, or captive audience. They are usually older than the counselor and may feel distanced by that fact. Often they come from different geographical and cultural segments of society. Their values, attitudes, and beliefs may conflict with those of the counselor and with those of the times in general, hindering effective relating. For example, if a young counselor is too casually dressed or groomed, an elderly client may take personal offense and be reluctant to disclose much. In such circumstances, it may take a long time to establish a supportive, empathic relationship. Communication differences may arise owing to the client's diminished hearing, seeing, and memory functions. The counselor needs to be particularly attentive to such losses, perhaps sitting closer, enunciating more clearly, and respecting the client's shorter attention span by structuring flexible sessions.

In general, counseling with the elderly focuses on providing support and cognitive understanding of whatever issues are presented. The counselor should know about retirement and late adulthood developmental tasks and issues in order to provide accurate information, educate clients about the differences between the myths and realities of aging, provide continuing, problem-focused counseling either directly or indirectly, and serve as a change agent in the community in terms of advocating and locating necessary and desirable services.

To be effective, counselors need to examine their own attitudes and biases about aging, deterioration, dependency, and mortality. If they are able to distinguish their personal issues from those of their clients, they will be less likely to intellectualize and more likely to communicate a deep compassion and empathic acceptance of elderly clients and their problems. Much of the treatment, then, needs to be problem solving, directive, and active. The goal is to clarify options and choices, not to give prescriptions for solutions. Further objectives are to mobilize family and community support by clarifying communication patterns and restructuring boundaries, and to energize all the client's assets and strengths so that clients can take control of their own lives and decision making.

Thus, in addition to sensitive communication and problem-solving skills, counselors need to expand their knowledge about late adulthood and its tasks and issues, and about community resources, legislation, and the roles of other caretakers. Further, they need to help elderly clients with practical matters, such as financial management, transportation, food stamps, collecting social security checks, residential decisions, obtaining adequate medical care, and so on. They must do these things in a way that fosters no dependency but enhances self-sufficiency, personal freedom, and the privacy of the elderly client.

The cases discussed here will illustrate some of the counseling techniques found to be particularly useful with adults in this stage of life.

CASE 1: MR. MARTIN

Presenting Problem

Mr. Martin, 64, was referred to counseling by the personnel manager of the food-service firm where he worked. He was preparing to retire in another year and was in the process of grooming his assistant to take over his job as advertising director. Mr. Martin began exhibiting signs of depression—increasing tardiness, and forgetting to return phone calls, follow up assignments, and attend meetings, a distracted attention span and a noticeable distancing in his relationships with colleagues. The personnel manager had stopped by for a chat with him and learned that Mrs. Martin was ill and that Mr. Martin was preoccupied with the sudden change in his wife's health status and its possible impact on his retirement plans. The personnel manager suggested that Mr. Martin "talk with someone" just to "get it off his chest." Thus, the presenting problem was that Mr. Martin was worried about his wife's health and upset about the possibility of having to change his retirement plans.

The retirement plan that Mr. and Mrs. Martin had agreed to ten years earlier involved purchasing land and building a home in the country where they had summered for twenty years. They planned to live there year-round after retirement. Over the past five years, Mr. Martin had been totally absorbed in building this home. He, himself, had done all the construction possible, only receiving help from locals on those tasks too difficult for him to do alone and from electricians and plumbers for their specialized work. Each weekend and vacation for the past five years, Mr. and Mrs. Martin had camped out in what developed into their new home. While Mr. Martin worked, Mrs. Martin knitted and prepared meals. Mr. Martin was thrilled with this project and his pleasure and pride were evident as he described it. Mrs. Martin was not as committed as he to this project. She complained increasingly about Mr. Martin's devotion to the new home, calling it his "mistress." Mr. Martin thought that she would be happier when the home was completed, so he worked even harder to achieve this goal.

Mrs. Martin did like taking responsibility for designing the kitchen and selecting the furnishings for the house. She helped with the interior painting and wallpapering. She selected the tiles and appliances and she seemed much more involved during the latter half of the project.

Three months earlier, just as the house was nearing completion, Mrs. Martin began to complain about headaches and frequent colds. Her physician diagnosed hypertension and a continuous upper respiratory infection. Mrs. Martin attributed the latter to spending so much time in an unheated shell of a house. She convinced Mr. Martin that they should take a vacation in Florida. During their vacation, she told her husband that she wanted to retire to Florida, where all her neighbors and friends were moving. In fact, she knew exactly where she wanted to live in Florida. When they returned from Florida, she went to see her physician and came to tell her husband that "the doctor thinks I should live in the south to stay healthy."

Description of Client

Mr. Martin looked very fit and trim for a man his age. He was suntanned, stocky, and appeared to have a lot of physical stamina and energy. He spoke clearly and was particularly enthusiastic about his building project. Its completion seemed to precipitate a let-down, and he was distracted by the sudden turn of events with regard to his retirement plans.

Mr. Martin described himself as "artistic," "sensitive," and "a loner." He loved being off by himself in nature and spent most of his leisure time oil painting and doing crafts.

Individual Context

Mr. Martin described his lifestyle as "conventional and successful." He had been the oldest of three boys and was doted on by both parents. Always artistic, his parents had encouraged him to study art and sent him on to art school after high school graduation. His father liked to paint and draw in his spare time. He was a construction worker for most of his adult life. His mother was a home-maker.

Mr. Martin felt that he had a "normal" upbringing. His parents died when he was in his twenties and he married shortly afterwards. He liked his brothers but did not see much of them since they lived a long distance away. He believed that if his parents had lived, the brothers would be closer.

Mr. Martin believed his life to be stable and no different from his anticipations and expectations. He felt that his overall life satisfaction was moderate. The last few years, while involved with his house and since the children had been gone, had been his happiest.

There were no health problems. Mr. Martin experienced some depression around the time he was forty. He was considering leaving his firm and opening his own advertising firm. Mrs. Martin convinced him to stay with his job for the security and fringe benefits. He acquiesced and he did not think about it much any more. He considered himself somewhat of an introvert and he allowed Mrs. Martin to organize their social life and activities. He did not have his own close friends and he did not feel that need. His companionship needs were met at work with colleagues.

Family Context

Mr. and Mrs. Martin were married for nearly forty years. They met at a mutual friend's wedding and were married ten months later. Mr. Martin had lost his parents in an automobile accident shortly before meeting his wife and he was eager to find a woman whom he could trust and love. He found her to be warm, attractive, and very much "like his mother." They had their first child, Bob, now 36, a year later, and Elizabeth, now 32, was born four years later. Both children were married with children when Mr. Martin entered therapy. Elizabeth lived in the same town as her parents and Bob lived 2,500 miles away.

Mrs. Martin was the primary parent and Mr. Martin the provider. Except for their summer vacations in the country, Mr. Martin really did not have much direct contact with his children—he always related to them through his wife at home. During the summers, the family spent time together without distracting obliga-tions, and Mr. Martin took his children for walks, fishing, and swimming while Mrs. Martin sunned and socialized with friends. However, there was always a strain in Mr. Martin's relationship with his son. The boy, he said, was a "mama's boy" and did not seem interested in any of the things his father cared for. On the other hand, Elizabeth seemed to be more artistic and seemed to enjoy doing things with her father more. Mr. Martin did not appear to mind that Bob was living so far away and was so infrequently in contact with his parents. Even though Elizabeth lived nearby, Mr. Martin had little contact with her and did not seem particularly involved with his grandchildren. In fact, Mr. Martin seemed distant from all the members of his family, and very much wrapped up in his house and his art interests.

According to Mr. Martin, Mrs. Martin was very unhappy with her offspring. She had devoted most of her energies to raising them and she wanted to be much more involved in their lives than they were willing to permit. Much of her complaining dealt with her grief about the children, and Mr. Martin successfully tuned it out. Mr. Martin believed that the reason Mrs. Martin supported buying the land and building the house was as an inducement for getting the children and grandchildren to vacation with them; the whole family remembers the summers as the best times in their family life together. But, to date, the children had refused to come visit during the summer.

Mr. Martin described his marriage as no different from anyone else's. He cared for his wife and acknowledged that it had been difficult for her to cope with his moods and silences. He did not seem to talk with her as much as she wanted him to and he was often impatient with her bids for attention. He was perfectly content to let her "rule the roost" and to make the decisions. The only area that he stubbornly insisted on for himself was the construction of his "dream house," admittedly, an "obsession." To appease Mrs. Martin, Mr. Martin, without any difficulty, turned over to her all of the interior design and furnishing.

The reason that Mrs. Martin seemed to have become unhappier in the couple of years preceding counseling was that Elizabeth went back to work full time and the grandchildren were in school. Earlier, Mrs. Martin spent time babysitting and helping out, and this kept her feeling useful and needed. Now Mrs. Martin had more time on her hands and she was feeling more and more unhappy as her friends migrated south. Also, the community in which the Martins raised their family was changing and they were no longer comfortable there. Mr. Martin believed that Mrs. Martin had always been something of a "hypochondriac" and he was not at all sure how real her current sickness was. While he was angry and disappointed, he was also concerned, and felt obliged to try to please his wife.

Career Context

Mr. Martin had been focused on an artistic field throughout his adolescence and adult life. He assumed more and more responsibility throughout adulthood and was quite pleased with his progress and achievement. His job allowed him sufficient free time to pursue his painting avocation. He also enjoyed acting as mentor to his assistant and he was pleased that his recommendation for his replacement was adopted by the president of his firm. In fact, Mr. Martin derived more gratification from this mentoring relationship than he did from his relationship with his son.

Mr. Martin was looking forward to retirement. He planned to putter around his house, paint, socialize with summer friends who were retiring in the same place, and just relax and enjoy his time. He meticulously planned his retirement budget and felt that his lifestyle would not need to substantially change.

Assessment

Mr. and Mrs. Martin had very different dreams and expectations for postretirement life. They also had different styles of relating, and once the children were grown and launched, Mrs. Martin felt vulnerable and needy, useless and discarded, whereas Mr. Martin felt absorbed in building his home and life and was actively involved in his career and hobbies. Neither had a high level of self-differentiation; both clung to different types of activities for security—she to her children and husband, he to his job and hobbies.

This couple did not develop direct communication patterns. During their marriage, Mrs. Martin was preoccupied with the children and Mr. Martin with career and avocational pursuits. Though both liked their summers in the country, the perceptions and needs underlying their enjoyment differed: Mrs. Martin saw it as a way of keeping the family together and under her control, and Mr. Martin saw it as a relaxing refuge away from the pressures of work and home. The children and the career and art interests were what kept this couple's power struggle from erupting earlier. Now that they were about to undergo a major transition in their lifestyle, the power struggle was emerging. Mrs. Martin was resisting the only way she knew how—by developing physical symptoms to gain control.

The issues in this intense power struggle were who would decide what their postretirement life would be and how the decision would be made. The children no longer served their function of defusing the parental power struggle. This was the first time Mr. Martin had held out for something he wanted. Heretofore, he had always allowed Mrs. Martin to make the rules and his opposition, if any, had been subtle, in the form of withdrawal. Now old ways were no longer working.

Goals

Since Mr. Martin was adamant that he did not want Mrs. Martin to come into counseling with him, the goal was to help Mr. Martin gain some understanding of this conflict and to help him decide how he wanted to deal with it and then implement his decision. His goal was to experience less friction and tension with his wife, and to stop feeling selfish, guilty, and pulled between his and his wife's desires.

Interventions

Mr. Martin was coached to respond empathically to Mrs. Martin when she complained about her ailments. He had been ignoring them, which only served to escalate her complaining. The counselor reframed Mrs. Martin's symptoms as pleas for his attention, and this reframing enabled him to practice different ways of responding to his wife during role plays. As he learned to respond with state-ments such as "I'm sorry you're feeling so badly; I wish I could help you to feel better," the immediate arguments and bickering were defused. As Mr. Martin became more supportive and expressed some understanding, Mrs. Martin's need to complain and nag diminished. Mr. Martin was actually attending to her and expressing caring, which was what she had been trying to get all along.

Mr. Martin was given the homework assignment to write down and study carefully all his possible options about postretirement life. He was asked to con-sider possible compromises and then to discuss his findings with the counselor. They then role-played, discussing the alternatives with his wife. During these role plays and discussions, Mr. Martin began to consider his underlying feelings about his family, job, and lifestyle. He was able to decide for himself that his wife's well-being was his primary priority and that he could not be happy if she were unhappy. He also began to express more sensitivity to her needs and issues and to understand her need of his attention. He admitted that perhaps he had taken her for granted over the years and allowed her to care for him just as his mother had done, without giving much back in return.

The counselor served to facilitate Mr. Martin's developing self-understanding, options, and possibilities during these sessions. Mr. Martin was encouraged to proceed slowly and cautiously, not to make any decisions prematurely. He was given some books to read about retirement issues, and was urged to visit his family physician for his own checkup and to discuss his wife's health condition. Once he had collected and evaluated all these data, he could begin to make some decisions.

Outcome

After seven sessions, Mr. Martin broached the subject of retirement with his wife. Mrs. Martin was surprised that the subject was still open for negotiation. Mr. Martin proposed several alternative options and found that his wife was willing to engage in this discussion with him as long as the possibilities could be mutually discussed. He returned to the counselor for a follow-up session and reported that after much discussion, which proved to be enjoyable as well as productive, he and his wife had decided to rent their second home for half the year and live there for the other half. The rental proceeds would enable them to purchase a small condo-minium in Florida—not in the village Mrs. Martin desired, but close by. In this way, they would both have their dreams partially fulfilled.

The process of working together to reach a mutually satisfying decision was more important than the outcome. Mr. Martin spoke warmly and caringly of his wife and appeared to be much more relaxed and at ease. He reported that he was attending better at work and was much less distracted.

Comments

Although there were many deep, underlying family issues that could have been explored during these sessions, the selected goal was symptom focused and prob-lem solving. Mr. Martin really needed an objective listener, someone who could help him with the problem-solving process in a supportive manner and with cognitive skill. He needed to consider his wife's viewpoint, to learn the steps of problem solving and conflict resolution. As he gained skill and sensitivity in these areas, his wife changed her behavior and the couple became less polarized and more responsive to each other's issues. They were able to learn to listen more to each other and to engage in a cooperative, collaborative decision-making process. Coaching one partner can facilitate change in the other partner. Role plays, rehearsals, and homework assignments are all techniques conducive to coaching.

At first, Mr. Martin appeared to be the victim of a powerful, controlling wife. Upon looking closer, one could see that Mr. Martin had unwittingly set his wife up to look this way by doing what he pleased and allowing her to carry the brunt of the responsibility until it no longer suited him. With respect to a "persecutor–victim" relationship pattern, it is important to remember that both parties contribute to the pattern and both are equally responsible for it.

Obviously, there was some mutual bonding and caring in this couple system, despite the long-established communication difficulties. This was evidenced by the couple's willingness to negotiate and eagerness to reduce the tensions. Actually, each wanted to please the other, although at first the desire appeared to be grudging and not particularly gracious.

CASE 2: THE SWIFT FAMILY

Presenting Problem

Marcia Swift, 14, was referred to a counselor by her junior high school counselor. Marcia had been a good student in school and had displayed no behavior problems until three months earlier, when she had begun to skip classes and fail to hand in her homework assignments. A conference with Marcia and her parents resulted in an outside referral for family therapy. Mr. and Mrs. Swift were very concerned and confused by this sudden change in their only child.

Description of Clients

Marcia was an attractive teenager. On her first visit, she was dressed neatly in blue jeans and a turtleneck sweater. Her hair was pulled back into a long pony tail and she looked especially nice when she smiled and revealed her braces. Her manner was reticent and polite. She responded when spoken to and seemed nervous and uncomfortable being in the session. Mr. and Mrs. Swift were anxious, concerned parents. Both in their early forties, they were teachers in a neighboring school system. They were attractive, neatly groomed, and soft-spoken, and they appeared to be in accord with each other. They spoke equally and seemed to support each other in their descriptions of what was happening at home.

Mr. and Mrs. Swift sat close to each other, glancing at each other frequently for confirmation of what the other was saying. They gestured affectionately with each other. Marcia appeared to be disinterested in what her parents were saying. However, she did look at her mother with disdain intermittently. Mrs. Swift said that Marcia's behavior at home had been changing, and that Marcia was more argumentative and resistant to helping out than she had been before. This caused Mrs. Swift to get annoyed and irritable and she was becoming distressed that what had always been a smoothly functioning household was now experiencing strain.

At this point, Mr. Swift mentioned that Mrs. Swift's widowed father had recently come to live with them. He had just been diagnosed as having cancer and he was not expected to live for more than another year. Although he now seemed to be in fine shape, deterioration and invalidism were expected. Mr. and Mrs. Swift had always been close to her family and had been especially attentive to her father since her mother's death three years earlier. As there were no siblings with whom to share the responsibility of his care, they had no reservations or qualms about taking him into their home.

It had never occurred to Mr. or Mrs. Swift that this sudden change in their living arrangements might be related to the onset of changes in Marcia. Their mention of it was casual, and it was only at the counselor's probing that they began to consider what affects this might have on her. Marcia gave up her basement playroom so it could be made into her grandfather's bedroom. When this point came up in the session, Marcia became more energized and spoke up. She said that while she loved her grandfather, she was annoyed with him because he always followed her around when she came home from school, wanting to know what she was doing every minute, to whom she was talking on the telephone, and so on. Then, when her mother came home from her job, her mother spent more time with the grandfather than with Marcia. Before Grandpa came to live with them, Marcia and her mother had spent the late afternoon hours talking and visiting, giggling and sharing. Now, not only did Marcia feel she had no privacy in the house, but she did not have any time alone with Mom. When Dad came home, it was more tense than before, as Mom was worried about her father.

What Marcia said appeared to surprise Mr. and Mrs. Swift. They did not seem to realize that the tension level had noticeably increased at home. After their first surprise, their concern was evident. They listened very carefully to Marcia. At this point, the counselor suggested that they bring Grandpa with them to the next session and they readily agreed. The problem was reframed to show that there had been a lot of sudden changes in the family system that seemed to be causing some stress for everyone. The focus was taken off Marcia's school problems and the family seemed to experience some relief with this reframing.

Individual Contexts

Marcia was entering the adolescent stage of development. Her new argumentativeness and reluctance to relate to her parents as before were, thus, a normal developmental happening. One moment Marcia seemed to want Mother's full attention; the next moment she resisted all efforts by her mother to make contact and wanted to be off brooding by herself. Marcia had always been the focus of her parents' attentions. She had been pleasing and obedient both at school and at home and she was used to praise and approval by teachers and her parents. Now she was trying out some resistant behaviors and she, herself, appeared to be confused as to what the limits were and what she really wanted.

Mrs. Swift was in the mid-life transition stage of life. Now, for the first time, she was admitting to a lack of confidence and to feeling confused about her roles and responsibilities. She was used to an orderly, smoothly functioning professional and family life, and heretofore she had been able to handle her multiple responsibilities with ease. Now, she was feeling worried, fragmented, frustrated, and tired. She no longer felt she had control over all the aspects of her life and this was very unsettling to her. As a result, she experienced heightened annoyance with both her daughter and husband. Mrs. Swift had been an only child and she had always expected to obey the family rule: to care for her parents in their old age. She was particularly devoted to her father, and was pleased to have him all to herself now, and to be able to care for him and return his affection and devotion in kind. She seemed intent on focusing on the "good daughter" role for the next few months and resented distractions from Marcia and Mr. Swift.

Mr. Swift had been orphaned in his childhood and was raised by his maternal grandmother. When he married Mrs. Swift, he felt as if he were getting parents as well as a wife. He had always liked his parents-in-law and they had all gotten along well together. There were times when he felt his wife was too "attached" to her father. Sometimes she compared him unfavorably and he did not like that. However, his father-in-law had always seemed genuinely fond of him and the two enjoyed doing things together. Mr. and Mrs. Swift were the same age. They had met in college and entered the teaching profession together. Mr. Swift was surprised to hear his wife express annoyance with him, since he felt that he was very supportive of her efforts to care for her father. He, too, was upset about her father's illness and was trying his best to be particularly helpful and considerate at home. He tried to help more with Marcia. Recently, he was feeling as if he were bearing the brunt of everyone's frustrations—Marcia's moods, Mrs. Swift's withdrawal and tension, and her father's moping about.

Mr. Pine, Mrs. Swift's father, was in his early seventies. He, too, had been a school teacher all his life and he had planned to travel and study botany upon his retirement. He had done so for two years with his wife before she became ill. She was ill for two years prior to her death. During that time, he took care of her in the house in which they had lived for fifty years. He had always been in good physical shape and he managed to maintain his gardens and continue reading during her illness. He believed in being independent and he had never wanted to live with the Swifts. His own illness was a shock in that he did not yet exhibit any symptoms. His illness was discovered during a routine physical examination. At first he did not really understand the nature of his illness, but when he began to realize what it meant, he became frightened, and with reluctance he agreed to move away from his hometown to his daughter's home. Mrs. Swift had convinced him that he could help them out by looking after Marcia when she came home from school. Since both Mr. and Mrs. Swift worked, Mr. Pine felt that he could be useful around the house and he was looking forward to the companionship of his only grandchild.

Mr. Pine was worried about what would happen to him as his health deteriorated. He talked about going to a nursing home, since he did not want to be a burden on his daughter. Mrs. Swift became upset every time he mentioned this possibility and repeated that she needed to care for him and that he was no trouble. Mr. Swift agreed with his wife, but it was clear that he was uneasy about how much stress his wife could handle.

Family Context

The Swift family system was a close-knit triad with all of the parental attention focused on their only child, Marcia. She had fit into their couple system without any difficulty and had enhanced their symmetrical relationship by giving them both much pleasure and gratification.

Mr. and Mrs. Swift met and married while in college. Mrs. Swift's parents were pleased that she was getting married and relieved at her "safe" choice. Marcia was born three years later and birth complications precluded the possibility of more children. This was not upsetting to the Swifts, since they wanted a child but did not want to have to readjust their lifestyle too much. Marcia was such a "wonderful baby" that they always felt another baby would be disappointing. Now they were entering into the adolescent stage of family development and they were unsettled by the changing roles and rules.

Whereas Mrs. Swift had always been closely tied to her parents, geographical separation made this less of a problem than it might have been had they lived in the same town. As Mr. Swift did not have any extended family, there was no competition. The Swift family increased their visits and telephone contacts with the Pines during Mrs. Pine's final illness. Mrs. Swift was prepared for her mother's death and she had hoped her father would come to live with her when her mother died. She was disappointed when he chose not to. When Mr. Pine became ill, Mrs. Swift insisted immediately that he come to live with them. This all happened so quickly that the implications were not discussed with Marcia and she picked up most of her information from overhearing her parents' discussions. So, Marcia was left to her own imagination and fears about her grandfather's illness. This was unusual for this family, who usually discussed their issues openly and sought consensus in their decision making. Both Mr. and Mrs. Swift were absorbed in Mr. Pine's crisis, and they therefore missed out on the cues Marcia was sending to express her own guilts, fears, and confusions.

Mr. Pine expressed hurt and disappointment that Marcia did not want to be with him every day after school. He not only felt as if he were failing in his part of the "agreement" to care for her, but he felt lonely and rejected. Marcia perceived him as being intrusive and her parents as failing to understand her reluctance to be supervised continuously. It seemed to Marcia as if everything revolved around her grandfather right now—she was never supposed to "upset Grandpa." Since she was not used to sharing her parents' attention, this was an abrupt change in the family functioning. Also, her family was failing to recognize that she no longer required after-school supervision, and that she was old enough to be more independent.

Thus, this family had moved into the adolescent stage of family development without realizing it. The crisis of the grandfather's illness and move had exacerbated the changing roles and rules, which were shifting faster than family members could grasp.

Career Contexts

Mr. Pine had loved being a school teacher and regaled his family with tales of the one-room schoolhouse in which he had begun his career. He had anticipated retirement eagerly, as the permissive, disorganized changes in the school system were very distressing to him. His wife had served as his faithful sounding board, agreeing with his criticisms of public education and providing much support and solace. They were in agreement about postretirement life, and he felt saddened and abandoned when she became ill before they had a chance to fulfill all their plans.

Mr. and Mrs. Swift each loved their respective jobs and the profession of teaching. Mrs. Swift had wanted to be a teacher as long as she could remember. This may have been due to her attachment to her father, but it was also the most feasible occupational choice for her in terms of combining career and family. She had taught various grades in elementary school and had taken only a few months off for Marcia's birth and early infancy.

Mr. Swift had decided to become a teacher in high school. He felt his decision was influenced by a favored social studies teacher and he has worked his way up to department head (social studies) in the junior high school. He was satisfied with his achievements and had decided several years before not to enter educational administration, but to remain in teaching. One of the things he liked best about teaching was the opportunity to take summer trips and to attend local auctions with Mrs. Swift. They both stripped and refinished the antique furniture they bought there.

Both Mr. and Mrs. Swift were concerned about the cuts being made in public education. However, they both had tenure and seniority and were not at all concerned about their job securities. Teaching had fulfilled their dreams and they enjoyed sharing this common profession with each other and with Mr. Pine.

Assessment

This family was in the adolescent stage of family development and was experiencing the changing power structure, roles, and rules associated with this stage of development. The onset of Mr. Pine's terminal illness served to exacerbate these changes. Thus, there were abrupt changes:

1. A new member had been added unexpectedly to the family;
2. This new member required considerable attention from one of the primary providers, Mrs. Swift;
3. Mr. Swift experienced stress owing to his wife's preoccupation with her father and, though he attempted to provide support, he felt lost and resentful;
4. Mrs. Swift was dealing with the impending loss of her adored father and, thus, many of her earlier feelings about him and about loss were resurfacing;
5. Marcia was angry and guilty about losing her parents' attention and unsure about the turbulent feelings she was experiencing; she chose the one sure family rule to violate, that of doing well in school;

6. Mr. Pine was frightened and feeling disoriented by his sudden uprooting from his familiar surroundings; in addition, he was facing his own mortality, anticipating more loss, and feeling useless and stripped of his usual independence.

Goals

The goals for the treatment of this family were multiple. The first was to restore some sense of equilibrium by helping the family to negotiate new roles, rules, and boundaries. Another was to problem solve with the family alternative ways of handling Mr. Pine's final illness stages. And still another was to help Mr. Pine establish a life for himself in these new surroundings.

Interventions

The first intervention was to reframe the problem of Marcia's school difficulties to show that Marcia was trying to alleviate the family tensions by causing her parents to focus on her problem rather than on Mr. Pine's illness. This reframing enabled the family members to communicate more directly with one another about their fears and to clear up some of their misperceptions about one another. Mr. Pine needed the opportunity to discuss his worries and Marcia needed to hear them. Sculpting was utilized during the sessions to reveal each person's current perceptions of the family functioning and what they wanted to change. From the sculpting emerged some comprehension of each person's problems—such as Mr. Pine's loneliness and Marcia's confusion. The counselor was then able to prescribe some specific tasks: (1) each day Marcia and Mr. Pine were to spend one-half hour together after school visiting or playing a game together; (2) Mr. and Mrs. Swift were to spend some out-of-work time together each day sharing whatever they wished as long as they did not focus on Mr. Pine or Marcia; and (3) Marcia and Mrs. Swift were to take turns preparing dinner and were to spend some time alone together visiting prior to this preparation. In addition, Mr. Pine was directed to the Senior Citizens' Community Center for morning hours so that he could make new friends in the community and become involved in his own activities and interests.

A major intervention was to help this family to research alternative health care arrangements for Mr. Pine as his illness progressed. After discussing possible options, the counselor arranged for the Swifts and Mr. Pine to interview some hospice staff and some staff at a local nursing home. They also considered the feasibility of visiting nurses and other home care services. This was a family venture that involved individual tasks and weekly family meetings. Marcia attended these meetings so that she was kept fully abreast of family happenings.

Outcome

Marcia's school difficulties disappeared as quickly as they had appeared as attention came to be focused on family system issues. A new routine developed in the family as the new roles, rules, and boundaries became clarified. Marcia was able to let her grandfather know when she needed her privacy; she was also able to be more responsive to his loneliness. Mrs. Swift relaxed more as she came to understand her father's viewpoint and the nature of his illness. This helped Mr. Swift to relax and provide more empathy and support to his wife, and this in turn enhanced her relaxation. Mr. Pine became involved in the Senior Citizens' Community Center. He was able to put his teaching skills to good use by volunteering to run political-affairs discussion groups, and he became quite an activist for elderly affairs in the center. Through these activities, he developed friendships that made him feel less dependent on the Swifts and that restored his feelings of belonging and productivity. Fortunately, his illness did not cause him much discomfort, so that most of the time prior to the final months he was able to function fully.

After researching possible health care alternatives, Mr. Pine decided to participate in the community hospice. This would involve moving into the hospice facility for the final six to eight weeks of his illness. The most important aspect of this decision was Mr. Pine's participation in the process. Mrs. Swift was a bit disappointed at first that he wanted to move into the hospice. But when she realized that this was her father's choice and that she would be able to visit him as often as she chose and participate as actively as she wanted to, she felt better.

Comments

The most important objectives were to provide opportunities for family members to share their fears and feelings with each other and to include Marcia in the information processing and Mr. Pine in the decision making about his illness and treatment. Everyone in this family meant well and cared for the other members. However, all were immobilized by the impact of the crisis and they needed some help in getting unstuck. Marcia's acting out at school was exacerbated by family tensions and by her exclusion from information sharing. Everyone needed to be educated a little about the tasks and issues of adolescence. While Marcia continued to argue with her mother, her mother learned to understand this adolescent behavior. Marcia no longer needed, then, to hurt herself by acting out at school.

CASE 3: MRS. WILSON

Presenting Problem

Mrs. Wilson, 81, was referred to counseling by the visiting nurse. Mrs. Wilson lived alone in an efficiency apartment. She was in good health for a woman her age but she kept complaining of ailments for which her physicians could find no organic basis. She had lived in this city all her life but was without family or friends. The former lived out of town and the latter had either moved or died. Mrs. Wilson had been widowed twenty years before and had retired from her career as a bookkeeper at age 65. She was in close contact with her adult children by telephone and was always telling them how sick she was and that she did not think she could last much longer. Two of her children would come to visit at her beseeching requests, and they would leave in anger when they saw that she really was not that sick. The visiting nurse thought that she was a hypochondriac and hoped that the counselor would "get her off her back."

Description of Client

Mrs. Wilson was frail and looked every bit her age. Her attention wandered and most of her conversation focused on her symptoms, her children's neglect, the fact that she did not really know her grandchildren, and how terrible it was to grow old alone. She was indeed argumentative and unpleasant. Her hearing was somewhat impaired and she always answered a question with "What's that? What's that again?" The counselor had to repeat questions and answers frequently and had to help Mrs. Wilson focus on the matter at hand.

Individual Context

Mrs. Wilson had been very healthy and active until her retirement at 65. She had not even considered her husband's death four years prior to her retirement to be a crisis. She had been dependent on her employing organization for companionship, for a sense of meaning in her life, and for positive reinforcement. She had been a conscientious, devoted worker for more than forty years, had been held in high esteem in the bookkeeping department, and had received annual merit raises.

Mrs. Wilson had prided herself on her independence, strength, and competence. She had never been sick or needy, and she had been the "strongest" member both of her family of origin and her own nuclear family. She was very attentive to self-care, walking vigorously each day, eating nutritious meals, and always getting eight hours of sleep a night. She had never had much in common with her contemporaries, as she could always manage alone and she had worked throughout her adult life.

After retirement, she was disappointed to learn that she had to cut back on her lifestyle more than she had anticipated. Her husband had been careless with finances and she had had to pay off many of his debts. Her offspring never offered to help her out. In fact, they seemed only too happy to move away. She felt they did not appreciate how hard she had had to work to feed and clothe them and that they resented the fact that she could not pay them the kind of attention that nonworking mothers paid their children.

As her few friends from work began to move away or die, Mrs. Wilson began to feel isolated and bored for the first time in her life. She then began to complain of various symptoms and went from doctor to doctor seeking aid. She began pestering her children, plying them with news of her ailments and begging them to visit her before "it was too late." They came for a while, but soon began to respond to her more grudgingly. She became more and more frustrated and ended up alienating everyone who came around with her constant complaining.

Mrs. Wilson described herself as the oldest of five daughters of an alcoholic farmer and his wife. She had quit school in the eighth grade and went to work in the town factory. Her father used to beat her and her dream was to get away from the farm in any way possible. At the age of 18, she was offered a job in the office of the factory and she learned bookkeeping skills. She fell in love with a handsome traveling salesman, married him, and moved away. She began having children immediately after marriage. She really did not want to have children; she had been responsible for taking care of her younger sisters and she did not enjoy childcare.

Mrs. Wilson's husband turned out to be an alcoholic drifter. Thus, she became the provider, the primary parent. Occasionally her husband would drift back for a few weeks and then take off again. Mrs. Wilson had nothing but scorn for him. She did not expect anything from him and she was totally absorbed in keeping her children fed, clothed, and sheltered.

Retirement was a dreaded prospect. Mrs. Wilson did not know how she would manage when she was forced to retire. She had developed no friendships or hobbies over the years. Her relationships with her children had always been strained. Until retirement, she had not paid too much attention to them.

Mrs. Wilson experienced her first illness shortly after her retirement. For the next fifteen years, she focused on her symptoms, on obtaining medical care and appropriate drugs, and on managing her meager finances. She was always "too ill" to visit her children and grandchildren. When they came to visit her, she would complain bitterly about her illnesses and the work they caused her by their visits. She was embittered and alienating, as well as alienated, at the time of her referral to counseling. In terms of Erikson's stages, she had never achieved intimacy, generativity, or ego integrity, and was still determining her own identity.

Family Context

As mentioned, Mrs. Wilson was the sole provider in her family, except when the children contributed as they became old enough to do odd jobs. Mrs. Wilson was very bitter about the men in her life. She had tried to escape the burdens of an alcoholic father and responsibility for younger siblings and she ended up with an absentee alcoholic husband and four children to raise.

Mrs. Wilson's negative feelings had certainly been communicated to her offspring, resulting in an early distancing. As long as Mrs. Wilson could work full time, be healthy, and remain in full command, everything was fine. She was proud of her children's self-sufficiency and was actually relieved when they moved away from home. She was also relieved when she received news of her husband's death. She was now free to live her own life without encumbrances.

Thus, Mrs. Wilson was in her late sixties when she began to reach out to her children for attention and caring. By this time, they had long since given up their desire to have affectionate relationships with their mother and they were involved in their own lives. The four children were all dutiful, however, and kept in touch. They soon began to find their mother's beseeching demands unreasonable. Thus, an intergenerational power struggle developed over what kind of relationships were going to exist between Mrs. Wilson and her offspring. Out of guilt and fear, they reluctantly acceded to many of her demands. But this only fueled their resentments, and they thus initiated even fewer contacts, which caused Mrs. Wilson to feel more self-righteous about being "abandoned" and to make more demands, more stridently, on her children.

Career Context

Mrs. Wilson was very proud of her career development. She was aware that she had been a "pioneer" for her generation in being a "working mother," though she had had no choice or other desire. She resented the fact that she had had to work because of her husband's ineptness, but she was actually pleased to have had this excuse, since she detested housework and staying home with her children. She felt important in a business setting.

Mrs. Wilson felt she had been lucky as well as competent. She had had no idea she would relish bookkeeping until she accidentally fell into it. Work was really her major source of gratification in life and she put everything else in a secondary position. Thus, if she could not attend to all her children's desires, it was because "work came first." She was dismayed by her children's more cavalier attitudes toward hard work and she tried to influence them by working harder and exhorting them to work harder. She did not realize that the more devotion and involvement she displayed toward her work, the more she was alienating them. Her children turned out to attain moderate levels of career stability.

Mrs. Wilson did not allow herself to think about postretirement life. She had made no plans for activities or involvements. The loss of her work role was the most traumatic crisis in her life span.

Assessment

Mrs. Wilson was self-absorbed and disappointed by her postretirement life. Because she was so old, it was difficult to consider her a true hypochondriac, since some of her ailments could indeed have had some medical origins. These ailments were the basis for what communications she had with her offspring and she was afraid to let go of them for fear that she would be totally abandoned and rejected by her children. She was lonely and frustrated, and she covered up her fear with abrasive, annoying behaviors that served only to distance people further. She had never developed the interpersonal skills necessary to maintain companionable relationships outside the work place. Time hung heavily on her hands and she was at a loss as to what to do with herself. In short, Mrs. Wilson was underoccupied.

Goals

The first goal was to establish a trusting, empathic relationship with Mrs. Wilson. This was necessary to teach her how to experience a trusting relationship and to provide the support necessary for her to take some risks. The next goal was to change the nature of her relationships with her offspring, in order to try to foster some reciprocal caring. A very important goal was to involve Mrs. Wilson in some continuing group activities so that she could gain support, learn interpersonal skills, and share concerns and feelings with age cohorts. Mrs. Wilson's energy needed to be mobilized more constructively.

Interventions

The counselor used responsive listening skills to establish a trusting relationship. It was important to provide comfort and empathy without fostering dependency. Mrs. Wilson was encouraged to reminisce about her life experiences and achievements. The counselor conscientiously reinforced all the positive reminiscences to enhance Mrs. Wilson's self-concept. This reminiscing, or life-review strategy, served to develop the trusting counseling relationship necessary for the subsequent prescriptions.

When a satisfactory relationship was established, the counselor (with Mrs. Wilson's permission) established contact with the offspring by telephone to explain the work that she was doing with Mrs. Wilson. She reframed Mrs. Wilson's complaints as mechanisms for maintaining relationships with her offspring and she told them to expect more calls in the immediate future. She then suggested that Mrs. Wilson telephone each of her children twice a day to complain to them about her ailments, a strategy called prescribing the symptom. However, the counselor had previously coached the offspring over the telephone to reply to these phone calls with a message communicating caring and empathy, such as "I'm sorry you're ill. I would like to come visit you but I care too much for you to watch you feel badly, so I would rather wait until you're feeling better and we can enjoy a visit." As anticipated, the changing responses of the offspring did affect Mrs. Wilson, who gradually began to change the nature of her messages.

Simultaneously, Mrs. Wilson was introduced to a group of peers in the neighborhood who met three times a week with a gerontologist. Mrs. Wilson was reluctant to participate in a group and the counselor accompanied her to the first three meetings. She then agreed to go alone and she gradually became more participatory than she had before.

The visiting nurse was instructed to remain neutral when Mrs. Wilson complained of being ill, but to provide clear verbal reinforcement when Mrs. Wilson reported doings unrelated to illness, such as attending a group meeting or talking to a neighbor. The counselor maintained regular telephone contact with the oldest offspring, who served as the spokesperson for the sibling system.

When some changes in Mrs. Wilson's behavior became more stable, the offspring were instructed to invite Mrs. Wilson to their homes for various holidays. At first, Mrs. Wilson claimed she was not well enough to travel, but with the support of her group, she began to decide that she felt well enough to think about it. Her offspring reduced their trips to visit her but clearly communicated that they cared about her and wanted to have her visit them and get to know their children. Mrs. Wilson found that her preoccupation with her "group," her new friends and reference group, helped her to be more reasonable in the demands she made on her family.

Outcome

While Mrs. Wilson's somatic complaints did not completely disappear by any means, they did diminish. Mrs. Wilson turned her attentions to her new friends, joined several activity groups, took long walks with new friends, and began to experience more satisfaction with her postretirement life. She maintained an on-going supportive relationship with the counselor, who was attached to the Senior Citizens' Community Center. Over time, Mrs. Wilson developed some effective interpersonal skills, which she was able to use with her offspring. Once the bitter complaining no longer dominated her relationships with her offspring, she was able to maintain more genuine, although by no means intimate, relations with them without bitterness or resentment on either side.

Mrs. Wilson was introduced to an oral history group at the Senior Citizens' Community Center. This group taperecorded their life histories and various anec-dotes, and the members sent these tapes to their grandchildren. This also fostered some contact between those two generations that proved to be mutually satisfac-tory. Mrs. Wilson's needless complaining about symptoms diminished as she de-veloped interests in activities and peers. She became much more agreeable and easier to be with.

Comments

Mrs. Wilson was not an easy client to relate to. She required a great deal of tolerance and forebearance on the part of the counselor. It took time to establish a trusting relationship—patient reminiscing, and careful verbal reinforcement. The counselor was unsure about what the outcomes might be of contacting the offspring by telephone. This was a risky outreach strategy that happened to work in this case.

The focus was on Mrs. Wilson's life-long strengths and assets, not on her mistakes and guilts. She needed some reality-oriented attitude therapy in order to engage in her life to the fullest. It was important, however, to take her complaints seriously, and to understand that they were communicating messages of loneli-ness, frustration, and fear. By so doing, the counselor could help Mrs. Wilson to overcome her dependency on her symptoms and to risk developing new relation-ships and activities. There was no need to dwell on alcoholism issues and insight into past patterns. Time was too short.

This was a case in which no retirement planning had occurred and the client's identity had been totally wrapped up in the work role. It was as if no "insurance policy" for living beyond the work role had been considered. Thus, the client was unable to cope with this unanticipated life stage and she needed a great deal of patient support and reconstruction.

The reminiscing or life review strategy was fascinating in that it allowed the counselor to be genuinely admiring of the courage and strength exhibited by this quarrelsome old woman during her adult life.

CASE 4: THE TRENTON FAMILY

Presenting Problem

Mr. and Mrs. Trenton, in their early sixties, came to see the counselor at their physician's suggestion. Mrs. Trenton had just learned that she had acute myelogenous leukemia and was unlikely to live more than a few months. Their one son Eric, 38, lived in Europe and visited his parents once a year on annual leave. The problem was Mrs. Trenton's 88-year-old mother, who had been living with the Trentons for more than twenty years. Mrs. Trenton had not told her mother of her illness. She did not know what type of arrangements to make for her mother's care after her death. Mrs. Trenton did not feel Mr. Trenton should have to assume the care of her mother. Also, being a mother herself, she could not bear for Mrs. Kerman, her mother, to have to endure the death of her only child. Mrs. Trenton perceived Mrs. Kerman as totally dependent on her in every way. Rather than dealing with her own mortality and concomitant issues, Mrs. Trenton was preoccupied with her mother's welfare.

Description of Clients

Mrs. Trenton was thin, pale, and agitated. She was nicely groomed and had her grey hair tied in a bun. She was dressed conservatively and neatly. Mr. Trenton was balding, robust, and very outgoing. He was dressed in sport clothes and frequently patted his wife on the back, addressing her with familiar affection. He allowed her to do the talking and nodded his head in agreement. Her speech was low and worried. Sometimes it appeared as if he were not really listening or involved.

Individual Contexts

Mrs. Trenton appeared resigned to her fate. She had been in good health all her life and was surprised when she began to feel weak and faint a month earlier. At her husband's urging, she finally consulted her physician. The diagnosis was a shock, but she did not deny or resist it. She was deeply religious and believed that she could accept her impending death as "God's will." She was worried about lingering on, about being a burden to her husband, and about what would happen to her mother. She was not worried about how Mr. Trenton would manage after she was gone.

Mrs. Trenton described herself as being "dutiful" and "obedient." She looked up to authorities and performed all the functions typically expected of women of her generation. She said that she was "easygoing, hard working, thrifty, and solitary." She cared for her husband, enjoyed raising her only son, and welcomed her mother's company over the past twenty years. Prior to her father's death (at which time her mother moved in with her), she had visited her parents every week and had them to her home for holidays. Mrs. Trenton did not have close friends, although she did enjoy having coffee with her neighbors. She liked to cook, clean house, and sew. She made all her own slipcovers, drapes, and bedspreads. Her life had been satisfying, meeting her expectations.

Mr. Trenton was a salesman for a local manufacturing firm. He enjoyed socializing with colleagues and customers, played golf once or twice a week, went fishing in the summer, and believed that he and his wife had a "fine marriage" with no real trouble up until now. Mr. Trenton was the older of two sons from a rural family. He left home to enter the service in World War II and never returned to his hometown. He attended a technical school under the GI Bill and married shortly thereafter. He came from a traditional family system with stereotypical roles and he replicated the same type of family for himself. He saw himself as "hardworking, loyal, conscientious, and dependable." He and his wife shared few interests. She was a "homebody" and he a golfer and a fisherman. The time they did spend together was usually focused on fixing up the house, shopping, tending the garden, or taking Mrs. Kerman for outings.

The news of his wife's terminal illness was indeed a shock for Mr. Trenton, but he seemed to have insulated himself from it by the time counseling began, possibly because Mrs. Trenton had evidenced no noticeable symptoms beyond fatigue. The reality of the course of the illness had not yet seeped through to Mr. Trenton, and his response was to intellectualize and talk about the illness as if it were not real. He listened to his wife as she worried aloud about her mother and said nothing—he did not offer to assume responsibility for Mrs. Kerman or express any opinions as to the possibilities for her care.

When Mrs. Kerman began to attend the sessions, she turned out to be a delightful 88-year-old woman with all her faculties intact; she was healthy and full of vim and vigor. She lived in a basement apartment and did her own cooking and housework. She could not walk outdoors in the winter, so she used an exercycle to keep in shape. She was alert, active, and interested. She was careful not to intrude on her daughter more than necessary and she seemed to be genuinely fond of her daughter and son-in-law. She watched television, cooked, and played solitaire to keep occupied. She liked being alone. Usually once a day, she and her daughter would have tea together and visit. Most evenings she was content to remain in her apartment unless the Trentons specifically invited her over.

Family Context

Mr. and Mrs. Trenton were married in their early twenties. Mrs. Trenton had been a saleswoman in a notions store, a job she was holding down "until she met the right man." Her goal was to marry, have a family, and be a homemaker. Mr. Trenton's goal was to find a steady job and a steady wife. Both felt that they had succeeded in meeting their goals.

Mr. Trenton rarely saw his own family of origin. Both he and his wife chose to be close to Mrs. Trenton's parents. Their social life was limited, save for an extended family. Mr. Trenton socialized with his business friends alone, going to bars after work, and so on.

Mrs. Trenton had two miscarriages before the birth of their son Eric. They later had twins but both died shortly after birth. Mrs. Trenton had a hysterectomy at that time and, thus, Eric was an only child. Mrs. Trenton was devoted to her son but was not enmeshed. Mr. Trenton was a bit distant. He was puzzled because the boy was not athletic. Eric was artistic and sensitive and always seemed to "march to the tune of a different drummer." He went to the state university after high school, began working for a newspaper, and then suddenly sought a European assignment, which he had maintained for fifteen years. Eric's move to Europe was hard for his parents. They were hurt but they made no attempts to dissuade him. He had married five years before and had brought his European wife and daughter over twice for brief visits. Contact was mostly by letter, between Mrs. Trenton and Eric. Eric seemed to play a peripheral role in the family's current life, although Mrs. Trenton and Mrs. Kerman referred to him frequently.

The Trenton marriage was solid and stable. They did not argue much since Mrs. Trenton usually acquiesced to Mr. Trenton's moods and wishes. They were satisfied with their life together and both accepted the rule that his business life comes first. Whereas Mr. Trenton expressed affection to his wife, Mrs. Trenton expressed more affection to her mother than to her husband.

The family sessions indicated that Mrs. Trenton and Mrs. Kerman were more closely allied than Mr. and Mrs. Trenton. He was like a respected male visitor. However, this status gave him power. He wielded his power indirectly and there were no overt struggles. Another thing that became clearer through observation of this family's interactions was that Mrs. Kerman was more self-sufficient, independent, and stronger than Mrs. Trenton. While Mrs. Trenton seemed to need to believe that her mother was lonely and dependent upon her for care and companionship, Mrs. Kerman expressed the view that sometimes she felt she needed to keep her daughter company so her *daughter* would not be lonely. Each woman, then, believed she was caring for and taking responsibility for the other. This gave Mr. Trenton and Eric the freedom to pursue their own lives.

Career Context

Mr. Trenton was to retire in two years. He expected to remain in his home, travel, and continue his usual activities. The house was paid up and he did not anticipate financial distress. As he talked about retirement, it was clear that he was not yet considering the fact that he would probably be widowed by then. He belonged to a social club and he was looking forward to having more time for it after retirement.

Mr. Trenton felt that his company had been good to him and that he had been good to the company. He described himself as a "cog in the wheel" who would never set the world on fire but who was necessary to keep it going. He had worked all his life and was proud of the way he had been able to provide for his family. He had no regrets whatsoever about his career development. He did worry, however, about Eric's career, wondering how secure and stable journalism could be.

Assessment

This family was thrown into crisis by the sudden onset of a fatal disease. Mrs. Trenton had held the family together by mediating, acquiescing, caretaking, and maintaining contact among the members. Perhaps her preoccupation with her mother's care at this time was her way of denying her own illness, to avoid thinking about how she felt about herself and her life.

Mr. Trenton was used to being protected and spared by his wife and he allowed her to perpetuate this pattern. At the onset of therapy, he had not yet realized the full import of what was going to happen. By protecting her mother, Mrs. Trenton was also protecting her husband from having to prepare for a change in the family system. Mrs. Kerman was perceptive and more aware of what was going on than the Trentons realized, but she continued to play her role as the noninterfering bystander. In that way, she could protect her daughter.

Thus, this system was on the precipice of dramatic change and the members were focusing on their concern for the elderly member of the family to give them time to recalibrate and deal with their crisis issues.

Goals

The first goal was to establish a trusting relationship with this family so that they would feel safe to relate more directly to each other and deal with Mrs. Trenton's illness. The next goal was to help the family cope with the nature and course of the illness, to mobilize mutual support, and to consider alternative options for Mrs. Kerman's and Mr. Trenton's lifestyles. Mr. Trenton needed to revise his retirement planning and lifestyle for postretirement. Each member of this family was communicating reluctance to move quickly, a style that had to be respected.

Interventions

First the counselor conducted individual sessions with Mrs. Trenton. In addition to responsive listening skills, the counselor used life-review strategies to help her reminisce. The counselor encouraged Mrs. Trenton to bring in old photographs and memorabilia to enhance this reminiscing. This strategy enabled Mrs. Trenton to begin to discuss her feelings of loneliness, fear, and anger about being ill and dying. When she felt comfortable, family sessions were held and all family members were helped to discuss their feelings. Mrs. Trenton was coached to ask her husband, mother, and son for help—a new approach for her, since she had always been the helper. She role played to learn how to ask for help and to be a needier, more dependent daughter, wife, and mother.

During the family sessions, Mrs. Kerman revealed that she was aware that her daughter was ill. She exhibited tremendous compassion and sensitivity and quickly took a protective, nurturing parental role to both Mr. and Mrs. Trenton. Thus, Mrs. Trenton learned to share her caretaking role with her mother. When Mrs.

Trenton was undergoing treatment and feeling ill side-effects, Mrs. Kerman assumed the caretaking role. During the periods in which Mrs. Trenton felt well, she resumed her normal caretaking function. Both women continued to protect Mr. Trenton. The counselor suggested the family keep this pattern, since it contributed to smooth functioning. Mr. Trenton became more at ease with his wife's illness and began sharing some of the nursing functions with his mother-in-law.

As a family, the three discussed practical matters and decided that at least for the time being Mrs. Kerman and Mr. Trenton would plan on maintaining a home together. Mr. Trenton felt that he could afford the help of a paid companion to help both women with the housework and other chores. He said that he would like to continue living with his mother-in-law as long as possible, and this was a tremendous relief to both women.

Outcome

As Mrs. Trenton became weaker, Mr. Trenton assumed more responsibility for her care. This helped him to form an alliance with Mrs. Kerman, as the two shared the caretaking role. Actually, the three members became very close during Mrs. Trenton's final months. Mr. Trenton also began to develop a relationship with Eric, whom he wrote and phoned regularly with reports about his mother's health. As Mrs. Trenton saw these changes, she became more relaxed and was able to concentrate more on herself and her illness. She was surprised at her neighbors' attentiveness; she had not realized she had so many friends.

Mrs. Trenton lingered for sixteen months. During this time, the counselor visited her regularly, either in the hospital or at home. She needed an outlet to express her fears and concerns without upsetting the very people she was protecting. She chose to die in the hospital, so as not to burden her family. She felt that she was in control until her last hospitalization, and she was able to tell her mother, husband, and son how much she appreciated their caring attentiveness.

After Mrs. Trenton's death, Mrs. Kerman rallied quickly as she sought to care for Mr. Trenton and help him with his grieving. He suffered more than he had anticipated and he allowed his mother-in-law to care for him. He began to return her caring and to reach out to his son, and he was able to be much more responsive and nurturing to them than before. He said that Mrs. Trenton had taught him a great deal about caring relationships and that now was his time to show what he had learned.

Comments

In this situation, the crisis occurred with the onset of a fatal illness for the critical middle-generation member. Originally the focus of attention had been on the oldest generational member as the needy one. However, she turned out to be a mobilizer in the system, possessing strength and coping capacities. When the shift in roles and responsibilities occurred, this family system moved toward more cohesiveness, exhibiting more symmetry than it had during decades of functioning. Communications strategies, prescriptions of behavior, and role-play rehearsals were the major strategies used to effect change in this system. The counselor became the objective but caring facilitator for the family system, providing each member with an opportunity to vent and express feelings and fears both individually and in a group forum.

CASE 5: MR. STRATTON

Presenting Problem

Mr. Stratton was a 78-year-old widower who had been living with his son and daughter-in-law for ten years. A month earlier, he had suffered a mild stroke that resulted in some difficulty walking. He was staying at a small convalescent center and beginning to improve physically. He was approaching discharge at the time of referral and there was concern about whether or not he could return to his son's home on the second floor of a walk-up duplex. He would be confined and no longer able to take walks or go to his social club at the community center. His son and daughter-in-law were ambivalent. On the one hand, they felt obligated to care for him. On the other hand, since their children no longer lived at home and they both worked, they were worried about how they could manage physically.

Mr. Stratton was very depressed. He, too, was ambivalent about whether or not to return to his son's home. He was worried about finances and unsure what his options were. He was afraid of being lonely and dependent and of feeling worthless and useless. He had not been particularly happy living at his son's after the children had left. But since he was able to attend his social club each day, he was satisfied. Now that he could no longer do that, he was very distressed.

Individual Context

Mr. Stratton was certainly upset about his physical and social losses. He was used to being active, in control of his comings and goings, and taking responsibility for his own life. Even though he had lived with his son for ten years, he had felt independent, since he had joined clubs and groups and maintained an active existence. The onset of his stroke was sudden, and for the first time in his life he felt a lack of control and a great deal of anxiety about his prognosis. Despite his physician's reassurances, he was pessimistic and glum.

Mr. Stratton described himself as "strong," "independent," and "hard working." He had managed a department store until his retirement at age 65 and had enjoyed his socializing activities and taking his grandchildren to baseball games and other activities. Since his son and daughter-in-law had always worked, he never felt as if he were intruding in their home, and they were not around much to bother him. He kept to himself when they were home or watched television in the family room. As the children drifted away, he became more active in his club and began attending more of the evening dances and parties. As far as he was concerned, everything was just fine. He even had a "lady friend" at the club. He also kept in contact with his other children in different locations.

Family Context

Mr. Stratton was married when he was 21. He was married for forty-six years and described this marriage as "ordinary." He was the provider in the family, and his wife raised their three sons. He was closest to his youngest son, the one with whom he now lived. They were interested in the same sports and this son followed his father into the retail field, much to his father's delight and approval. They never had any family problems, although he and his wife were disappointed when their oldest son married someone of a different religion, but this couple lived so far away, it did not matter much any more. The middle son was a career military officer and lived on the West Coast. The three sons were not close to each other although they kept in touch, to confer about their father. It was always assumed that the youngest son would take primary responsibility for Mr. Stratton.

Mr. Stratton was widowed suddenly when he was 67. His wife died in her sleep from a heart attack. She had never complained of not being well and he did not know she had a heart condition. Although it was a shock, her death coincided with his retirement so that it became just another aspect of a major change. His son and daughter-in-law immediately urged him to move in with them. At that time, his grandchildren were in school and he was able to help out by babysitting after school. Thus, the arrangement was mutually advantageous. Mr. Stratton had his own room and shared the family's bathroom and meals.

Career Context

Mr. Stratton had been in retail all his life. He started out as a stock boy while still in high school and worked his way up to store manager, a job he considered prestigious. He was very involved in his work and loved working long hours. He used to like to take his sons down to the store with him and show them off to his sales staff. He had not been an actively participating father, but then "men didn't do those things."

He had been fairly well prepared for retirement. He and his wife had planned to move to Florida, and he had just sold his house to do so when his wife died. This is why his son offered to take him in so quickly. He considered going to Florida alone, but decided to wait a few months and see how things went.

Assessment

This elderly man was faced with sudden physical and social losses that threatened his lifestyle and way of existence. It also put him in a more dependent position vis-à-vis his son, and this caused him to feel depression and despair. The son's family was in the postparenthood stage of family development, and their needs and concerns differed sharply from those they had when Mr. Stratton had first come to live with them. Thus, Mr. Stratton had been feeling somewhat displaced and useless before his stroke, which exacerbated the current situation. The son and daughter-in-law were genuinely concerned about him and their responsibilities, and they wanted to do "the right thing" but they were afraid of taking on more than they could handle. Mr. Stratton did not know what to do or what was possible. All he knew was that he was dependent and no longer in control.

Goals

The first goal was to provide support to Mr. Stratton and his son and daughter-in-law so that no one felt guilty or exploited. Then it was necessary to ascertain just what curtailments would be necessary for Mr. Stratton and to help him to understand and accept the nature and implications of his difficulties. The next goal was to problem solve with Mr. Stratton and his three sons about a viable caretaking residence for Mr. Stratton—a place that would be financially feasible and provide satisfactory health care. This would probably involve renegotiating the relationships among the brothers, Mr. Stratton, and his youngest son.

Interventions

After the counselor established a trusting relationship with Mr. Stratton and his son and daughter-in-law, he suggested that a family conference be called. While this was being arranged, the counselor and Mr. Stratton's youngest son looked into community resources. The counselor served as the coordinator among the family, the community, and the convalescent home. Also, the counselor conducted a four-hour family meeting attended by Mr. Stratton and his three sons. At that time, all the data collected were presented, clarified, and discussed. As each member was encouraged to communicate directly with the others, the counselor was able to provide support and encouragement for collaborative problem solving.

Outcome

The youngest Stratton son found that his older brothers were willing to help out financially. This allowed the family to decide upon a church-related home that would provide adequate health care, liberal visiting hours, and programmed activities for Mr. Stratton to participate in as his health allowed. In addition, he would be able to return to his club when possible, since an affiliative relationship existed between the community center and this home. The sons took Mr. Stratton to see the home and he found that he knew some of the residents. The decision was agreeable to all parties, and the brothers felt that they had communicated with each other for the first time as adults.

Comments

Again, this case required some active outreach work on the part of the counselor. He had to research community resources and their facilities and to coordinate information among the health staff, convalescent home staff, and the family. The counselor's knowledge of group work enabled him to conduct an effective problem-solving session with the family, to clarify communication patterns, and to strengthen possible alliances and supportive relationships.

SUMMARY

In this chapter, we presented some cases involving senior citizens and the elderly. Most of the issues involved alternative living arrangements, health care, intergenerational power struggles, and postretirement lifestyles.

As noted throughout this chapter, counselors working with the elderly need to be familiar with community resources and possess skills to help decision making and problem solving. At the same time, they need to provide support by developing empathic relationships with their clients and their families. The counselor is in the position of a consultant, educating the client and his or her family about the needs and issues of late adulthood, educating the community about necessary resources, and recommending possible options for clients. The counselor is also a coordinator, balancing the needs and issues of client systems and the community.

The types of strategies that are helpful include: reframing problems in a positive, developmental framework; assigning homework tasks; prescribing the symptom to disrupt the homeostasis of the family system; promoting life review and reminiscence; and helping people to evaluate possible options and attempted solutions that may be reinforcing the problem. Active coaching can achieve expedient results in changing communication patterns.

Perhaps more important than strategies and interventions are the attitudes of the counselor toward the older generations, including attitudes toward illness, mortality, dependency, and aging. If counselors view the elderly as people with strengths and assets rather than deficits, it is likely that they can find solutions to problems that help elderly clients retain self-respect, feelings of worth, productivity, and responsibility.

CHAPTER FIFTEEN

OVERVIEW

Having explored individual, family, and career life cycles, we can recapitulate the common themes and directions of adult development. In addition, we can now clarify exceptions to our generalizations. And certain questions remain unanswered:

1. What conclusions can we draw from this book?
2. Do these theories contradict each other?
3. Do any of these theories apply to all individuals and families?
4. What areas of research need to be developed or expanded?
5. How can the study of individual, family, and career development help us as mental health practitioners?

This chapter addresses the above questions in three sections. The first summarizes the common, overlapping theoretical themes and the variables influencing the nature and course of adult development. The second section discusses the implications for mental health practitioners resulting from research and theory building. The final section suggests current issues of adulthood needing further research and exploration.

THEORETICAL CONCLUSIONS

The one underlying conclusion we can draw from the theories and examples presented in this text is that adulthood is a period of active, systematic change. These changes include both losses and gains and are manifested in changing roles and relationships, and changing priorities, commitments, beliefs, assumptions, and values resulting from altered self-concepts. These changes are interrelated, and their effects are broadened or limited by such variables as biological aging, gender, economics, geography, health, life accidents, prior commitments and decisions, personal abilities, and social policy. Other variables are psychological factors such as level of cognitive development, level of individuation or self-differentiation, and personality characteristics. Reassessment, decision making, and interpersonal skills are required in all areas of life at each stage.

The individual, family, and career development theories studied in this text fall into two major categories: (1) those postulating changes occurring as a result of intrapsychic, internal variables, such as personality, needs, and drives; and (2) those postulating changes occurring as a result of external variables, such as life-span events, social roles, and sociocultural expectations. The systems perspective suggests a cybernetic interaction of the internal, or organic, factors and the experiential, or environmental, factors affecting the nature, duration, and timing of developmental change, rather than a focus on one (organic or experiential) to the exclusion of the other. The systems perspective also posits that individual, career, and family development are interrelated and that one dimension of development cannot be considered separately, since each is a subsystem of development. Thus, development is viewed as multifaceted and interactional, and a continuous interplay of internal and external forces has its impact on total development.

From developmental theory, we learn that there are predictable periods (stages or phases) of adulthood and that each period contains identifiable tasks and issues. The changes required by these tasks and issues are cumulative and sequential, in that those associated with earlier periods are the building blocks for those that arise later. Although these developmental tasks and issues are predictable, there is great variability in the way one perceives, interprets, and experiences them.

From systems theory, we draw a homeostatic model of functioning, whereby a natural tendency exists on the part of the organism or system to preserve the status quo, to resist change. Thus, there is always a pull between the forces for change and the forces to retain the known and familiar. This pull may become more intense during the transitions between predictable, stable stages of development than during the actual stage or phase. It is during these transitions that the homeostatic balance is threatened by impending changes. People in transition are likely to be more vulnerable to stress and disruption than those in an actual stage. Thus, difficulties are more likely to arise during the transitional passage, when the organism or system is in a state of imbalance.

An overlay on the developmental cycles is the meaning one gives to life—that is, the way one thinks about oneself and one's world. One's meaning of life comprises a complicated web of ideas, relationships, understandings, and attachments. This meaning is translated into the ways one relates to people and the ways one expresses and acts upon one's self-concept and one's value system. In other words, the meaning of one's life is represented by what one does rather than by what one says one believes.

Obviously, different people have different levels of meaning. What we learn about development from clinical practice is that people seem to devote their energies to conserving and preserving the meaning they give to life. This goal seems to underlie their resistance to change. People are afraid of the unknown and, therefore, attempt to avoid actions that may threaten their meaning of life and disrupt the homeostatic balance. In other words, people attempt to protect the investments they have already made in their values, their self-concepts, and their relationships and other commitments. They try to protect what they have already learned, what they have always thought, and what skills and abilities they have already developed. If we can understand the resistance to change as a natural phenomenon of individuals and human systems, we can better develop strategies to help clients overcome their fears and reluctances, and thus help them to change and grow.

Variables Influencing Development

At this point, let us briefly summarize the major variables affecting one's meaning of life and the course of one's development. These variables allow for the individual differences in people's meaning and experience of development. These variables are physiological, sociocultural, and psychological.

Physiological Variables

Physiological variables include biological aging and health factors. Although they influence and are influenced by sociocultural and psychological variables, they have a unique, distinct influence on one's experience of adulthood.

Biological aging.   Sexual maturity and physiological changes affect individual development in terms of an individual's views of him- or herself and of interactions with others. These physiological changes are age related, although they are also affected by genetic and environmental factors. They are cumulative and begin to demonstrate an apparently stronger influence in middle adulthood and a more predominant influence in late adulthood. Biological aging is inevitable. While it impacts individuals at different ages in different ways, ultimately everyone is overtaken by aging effects.

Family development is influenced by the reproductive capacity of the couple in terms of fertility factors and by the woman's biological time clock, which is very specifically related to age. Some couples decide it is "time to have children" because of their increasing age, or that it is "time to get divorced" before it is too late to start over with someone else.

In the career-development dimension, physiological factors can influence one's range of occupational choices as well as one's ability to implement occupational choice. Some occupations have specific physiological requirements and others have specific age limitations. Consider the following example.

A 33-year-old female nurse practitioner attended a health fair to see what type of career opportunities were available. She was actively recruited by an armed forces representative to be a flight nurse. After an hour of wooing, she mentioned her age to the recruiter (she looks several years younger) only to be told that the age limit for flight nurses was 30 and she was too old to be considered.

Health.   For the purposes of this discussion, *health* refers to the presence or absence of illness or disease as opposed to age-correlated biological changes. Illness affects one's self-concept and one's lifestyle choices. Some illnesses, particularly chronic ones, require specific life adaptations such as where, how, and with whom one can live and what type of work one can do. In terms of individual development, as one becomes older, illness becomes more likely. We have seen that in late adulthood it is sometimes difficult to differentiate between aging and health variables. The occurrence and meaning of illness affect people differently. Some people incorporate illness into their identities and base their relationships and lifestyle choices on it. Others find illness an obstacle and refuse to allow it to become a part of their identity and relationship issues. Increasing evidence suggests that illness and stress management are interrelated, and that illness is more likely to occur when one's stress level is high and one's normal defenses for coping with stress low.

In some family systems, health issues become the homeostatic mechanisms used to keep the family members together and possibly stuck at a particular stage of development. For example, in a family with a sick child, the parents may remain together, preoccupied with the child rather than with their marital issues. As this child approaches the end of high school, the parents might try to keep him or her ill and dependent in order to keep the family intact. In some families, remaining ill is the way one receives nurturance, and the incidence of illness is likely to be higher than in those families where illness is seen as a distraction and disruption. For both individuals and families, the meaning of illness influences the way one perceives and experiences illness as well as the way one uses it to interact with others.

Certainly, health issues affect initial occupational choice as well as one's performance and level of attainment within a particular occupation. Health issues present barriers and limitations to some people and challenges to overcome to others. They color one's perceptions of self and life choices and often impede development.

For example, Martha had rheumatic fever as a child and has always perceived herself as frail and sickly. Thus, she chose a local secretarial school and studied bookkeeping because she felt it would be less physically demanding than nursing, which was the career she really desired.

Sociocultural Variables

These are the types of factors that are external to the individual. They are largely environmentally determined.

Certainly one's economic status affects one's experiences and choices in every aspect of life. First, the economic class into which one is born imposes certain limitations or opportunities from the very beginning in terms of socializing experiences. There is evidence that one's socioeconomic class determines educational opportunities, health care services, and opportunities to meet basic physiological and safety needs as well as interpersonal, family, occupational, and lifestyle opportunities. These variables, in turn, will affect one's ability or opportunities to fulfill identity, intimacy, and later generativity needs.

We cannot overestimate the influence of available economic resources on individual, family, and career development. Money opens up alternative opportunities and limits one's choices. Economic security allows one to pursue higher level needs and goals. In the area of individual development, sufficient money allows one to pursue the career of choice, the leisure activities of choice, and the relationships of choice—all aspects of lifestyle. In terms of family development, money influences when people marry, when they have children and how many they have, where and how they live, and whether or not both partners will work. In terms of career development, money influences not only occupational choice, but also job location, the possibility of changing fields, and so on.

Too often, therapists have ignored the impact of money on development, assuming idealistically that true happiness has nothing to do with money. The types of presenting problems of people with a great deal of money differ sharply from those of people with no money, and these problems parallel the hierarchy of needs postulated by Maslow.

Climate, physical surroundings, population density, and other geographical factors also influence one's feeling of well-being and one's opportunities. The socialization of children is also influenced, to some degree, by geographical factors, and regional speech, behavioral, and values characteristics all have their effects. These factors influence not only one's identity but also one's relationships and choices.

The influences of geography on individual and family development may be subtle. Certainly, educational, leisure, and relationship opportunities are influenced by location, and there is increasing evidence that health and economic viability are also so influenced. Career choices are more demonstrably influenced by geographical factors. A deep-sea fisherman cannot live in the middle of Iowa any more than a farmer can live in the middle of Manhattan. Limitations on occupational opportunities are currently requiring more people to travel to find jobs, regardless of location. For dual-career families, the need to relocate can present a real problem when a particular location does not offer opportunities for both couple members. Often, career satisfaction (which impinges upon individual and family satisfaction) is influenced by geographical factors. Career changes may require a change in locale, and one's commitment to living in a certain location may limit one's career choices. Thus, geographical influences are tied to economic issues and, often, to health issues.

A third sociocultural factor is ethnicity. This country, a melting pot, consists of many different cultural groups at different levels of assimilation. The ethnic values of these different groups can affect one's meaning of life and one's perceptions of self, family, and career, and these views, in turn, can influence personal development. Pearce, McGoldrick, and Giordano (1982) point out that cultural variability affects belief systems, interactive patterns, definitions of normality and pathology, attitudes toward problem solving, life-stage transitions, gender roles, and family roles.

Thus, we must understand that ethnicity influences the norms of development and healthy adjustment and the lifestyle choices and practices of people from different groups. For example, first-generation immigrant families have different meanings and values than families in later, more assimilated generations. A second-generation Italian-American family may not value the individuation of daughters as a developmental task, and the rule in such a family may be that the daughter lives at home in adulthood until she marries, turning over a part of her income to her parents and obeying their rules. We need to be careful not to mistake ethnicity for pathology or pathology for ethnicity. Ethnic variables may influence the way one achieves tasks and issues in different stages more than the nature of the tasks and issues themselves.

As more intermarriage takes place among ethnic groups, we will see ethnic differences and clashes as more frequent sources of marital and family conflict and, again, we can help to reframe problems in that context so that family members can absorb the value and enrichment of multiethnic influences.

Life accidents constitute another important variable. Many unpredictable crises impede or accelerate development. These are referred to as life accidents or nondevelopmental crises (Okun and Rappaport, 1980). How one perceives such events will influence how one experiences and responds to them. The impact on the family system (either family of origin or current family) will influence the individual and career developments of one or several members of the family. Consider this example.

John, a 48-year-old policeman with a wife and seven children, was forced to go on indefinite disability leave following a gunshot wound. Not only was the family's income level reduced, affecting their entire lifestyle, but, more importantly, with Dad at home during the day, the power structure within the family system was dramatically altered, resulting in increased tensions and acting out. Although this family was referred to family therapy following a suicide attempt by the 13-year-old daughter, the import and impact of this life accident became significant factors in understanding the family process. It had never occurred to the parents that this incident had affected the adolescent's development or the life course of the entire family system. They assumed it just affected Dad's employability and his grouchiness. In fact, the incident had served to unleash much pent-up anger and rebelliousness, which caused both parents to reassess their belief systems about families and parenting.

Included in the life-accident category are chance happenings or incidents of luck. Often a chance happening or incident of luck influences career development. Perhaps someone meets an old acquaintance unexpectedly and learns of an opportunity heretofore not considered. Or, an opportunity for a particular career path opens up owing to someone else's misfortune, such as illness or accident, which opens up a particular job. Certainly, many people can cite unexpected strokes of luck as leading to marriage or career developments. Obviously, one has to perceive the luck and be available to take advantage of it.

Prior commitments and decisions are variables that can be psychological as well as sociocultural. Mainly, they are relationship and occupational decisions previously made that can limit or expand later reassessments and decision making. If one was married and had children in one's twenties, for example, and during one's mid-life transition decided that one had missed out on opportunities for more exciting intimate relationships, one could not ignore one's prior commitments. One may limit those regrets to fantasy and remain obligated to an earlier commitment. Or, one may leave one's family to pursue another relationship. Regardless of the final decision, individuals are influenced by such events and by the outcomes of prior commitments and decisions.

A 31-year-old businessman entered therapy reporting symptoms of depression. His anxiety level was interfering with his work performance and he was constantly engaging in arguments with his wife. It turned out that he was disturbed by persistently recurring fantasies about an attractive female coworker. Having been married seven years, he could not understand or accept his attraction to and secret lusting after another woman (who was married and unaware of his feelings). He was feeling so guilty about his secret fantasies that he was afraid to go to sleep at night, lest he talk in his sleep and hurt his wife by letting her know of his "unfaithfulness." This man was willing to explore his values, his "shoulds," and his disappointments in his personal, family, and work lives and to consider what kinds of choices he might make to improve these areas of his life. He considered himself committed to his marriage and he did not think of divorce as a viable alternative.

Another client had invested considerable money, energy, and time in a particular business endeavor, only to discover several years later that it was not as satisfying or successful as she had anticipated. She found, too, that her range of choices was limited by a prior commitment, in that she did not have available money to reinvest in another business and had to maintain a certain income level in order to support her husband and family. While she was unable to implement her new dream of a particular kind of business, she was able to find a job that more evenly met her obligations to her family, that met her need for a steady income, and that provided her with a satisfactory work self-concept. In order to achieve the latter, however, she had to work through the belief that she had "failed to make it on her own," and she concluded that working for someone else was acceptable.

Social policy—that is, governmental policy—can have a strong impact on development. Governmental policy affects the types of occupations available, the types of occupations emerging and other types of occupational trends. It also affects the reward systems within particular occupational fields and the unemployment rate. In terms of individual development, social policy affects educational opportunities, economic status, health care, and the choices and opportunities concerning retirement and postretirement life for the elderly.

Family development is affected by social policy regarding abortion, preschool education, daycare, divorce, custody decisions, and visitation rights. These overlap into career issues, since a lack of daycare facilities may force some people to abandon their chosen occupations and seek work that allows more flexibility and opportunity for parenting.

Thus, social policy affects the development and delivery of human services programs in all areas, touching on employment, educational practices, services, and many other areas involving lifestyle choices for adults of all ages. We have seen that the elderly are, perhaps, most directly affected by such policies regarding living arrangements, health care, and social security.

Gender issues.   Throughout the text, we have referred to the effects of gender issues on the socialization and development of males and females. We can conclude that the development of males and females does indeed differ and that gender variables influence one's meaning of life and experience of the life course. Gender issues are social, biological, sociological, and psychological, and they influence the choices and opportunities available to adults throughout the life cycle.

Psychological Factors

Psychological factors are the internally determined variables that affect thinking, feeling, and doing. These factors certainly influence and are influenced by physiological and sociocultural factors, but they originate within the individual rather than in the environment.

Needs.   Psychological needs serve as motivating drives for satisfaction and gratification. These needs have been conceptualized in many ways—for example, Freud's needs for love and mastery; Maslow's needs for love, esteem, and self-actualization; McClelland's needs for achievement and affiliation; Glasser's needs for self-worth and love; and so forth. Whatever paradigm of psychological needs one adopts, these psychological needs will influence one's choices and one's life experiences. Psychological needs that remain unfulfilled cause a greater expenditure of drive energy toward that need satisfaction. Someone, for example, with low self-esteem will have high esteem needs and may seek a series of relationships and jobs in the continuous search for reassurance and high levels of praise.

The hierarchical-needs concept suggests that psychological needs are dependent on the satisfaction of lower level physiological and safety needs. Thus, someone who is fighting poverty and struggling to survive does not have the luxury to strive for affiliation, aesthetic fulfillment, or self-actualization. That person's energy is devoted, rather, to basic needs.

It may be, then, that people concerned with survival needs do not reach the same levels of development as those concerned with higher level psychological needs. As mentioned in Chapter 7, the mid-life transition may be a middle-class luxury only available to people whose basic physiological and safety needs are fulfilled. One's life's meaning will depend on one's level of needs. Reassessment of earlier decisions, renegotiation of relationships, and long-range planning may be impossible for people involved in moment-to-moment existence.

Levels of self-differentiation and individuation. Repeatedly throughout this text, we have referred to individuation as a process of becoming more self-sufficient, with a separate and special personality derived less from parents or significant others than from one's own thoughts, feelings, and values. This process has been presented as a necessary condition for successful identity formation and for the development and maintenance of intimate relationships in adulthood. We have noted that females often have more difficulty achieving this task than males, owing to the different socialization messages they receive.

There are varying levels of individuation, and these too may be influenced by one's level of psychological need. Individuals who achieve only low levels of individuation may find later developmental tasks difficult or impossible. This, in turn, would affect their self-concepts and their relationships.

Marjorie, a 39-year-old divorcee with one son, had recently achieved success in her chosen occupation. However, she was unhappy because she was not involved with a man. She believed that she had never been successful in sustaining an intimate relationship and that it was unfair that there were no desirable men available. She reported that she married at 29 to please her mother and to be able to leave home. She divorced four years later to find "the right man." Now, six years after her divorce, she was bitter and disappointed that her fantasies had not been realized and that life had not turned out the way she had anticipated. Her anger was affecting her relationships with friends and co-workers as well as her attitude toward her work. She was so jealous of her close women friends who were involved in relationships with men that she refused to call them. Although she recognized the absurdity of her behavior, she felt isolated and lonely as she sat home sulking and feeling sorry for herself. Marjorie believed that a woman had to be attached to a man to be happy. Her level of individuation was low. She clung to her mother's notion that a woman should be married and she believed she was a failure and doomed to a life of misery. Thus, her meaning of life, resulting from her low level of individuation, was impeding her development. It had the potential to seriously harm her level of career attainment and destroy her few friendships with other adults.

In terms of family development, low levels of individuation can result in enmeshed relationships that prevent families from passing through the adolescent and launching stages. Many marriages fail because one or both partners have low levels of individuation, and seek and demand that their spouses play the all-nurturing, powerful parental role. Many of the family cases presented in this book illustrate the effects of low levels of differentiation on family systems.

A person's occupational choices may represent the parents' choice more than his or her own, where one's individuation level is low. And people with low levels of individuation may never go beyond an entry level of attainment, owing to their inability to perform self-sufficiently, to take risks, and to work outside a clearcut structure.

Cognitive development.   We have learned from some of the theories present-ed in this text that there are different levels of cognitive development. Not all adults reach the same level of cognitive development and not all have the same cognitive styles. One's level of cognitive development is not necessarily consistent with one's level of intelligence. An orderly, sequential series of cognitive-develop-ment stages exists which affects how people perceive and construe themselves, their experiences, and their relationships. We have seen how one's level of cogni-tive development affects the decision-making process that one needs in making choices at the various turning points in life. Considerable research in counseling psychology suggests an interrelationship between cognitive processing and emo-tional arousal. This implies that what one thinks and believes about an event is more responsible for the feelings about an event than the actual event itself. Thus, one's level of cognitive development determines the level of meaning that one ascribes to one's life.

Levels of cognitive development range from, at one end of the spectrum, a simple, undifferentiated and unintegrated egocentric thought, a kind of dualistic (right versus wrong, good versus bad) thinking, to, at the other end, a more complex, differentiated, integrated, and allocentric type of thinking, a more multi-plistic (many aspects and possible ways to view a situation) style. The lower end of the continuum is characterized by the inability to differentiate oneself from the environment or from others and by self-centered thinking and a belief in the power and influence of the environment over the person. The higher end of the continu-um is characterized by the capability to differentiate and integrate subtle differ-ences among people, objects, and events in the environment. At this level, one sees oneself as having more power and influence over one's life. Each level of cognitive development is characterized by a particular way of perceiving, interpreting, and reacting to oneself and the people, objects, and events in the environment.

Personality and personal attributes.   Other personality factors affecting de-velopment are flexibility/rigidity factors, level of defense mechanisms, introver-sion/extroversion, and temperament styles. Obviously, one's personality is influ-enced by heredity as well as by the environment, and, while personality influences development, the life experiences of development also influence personality.

Common Themes

As we look at individual, family, and career development we see that change is the common, inevitable theme in all three areas and that changes occur as part of a process that is both internally and externally based. A continuous interplay goes on of multiple environmental, interpersonal, and intrapersonal factors, even though different theories emphasize different factors.

Meaning system.   One's meaning system about oneself, one's family, and one's career influences the interrelationship of these dimensions of development. Regardless of level of functioning, everyone has some type of meaning about his or her life. Some people, at lower levels of cognitive functioning, have simple, concrete, fatalistic meanings and do not perceive themselves as having choices and options. Others, at higher levels of cognitive functioning, formulate and act on more sophisticated, abstract philosophies of life. One's meaning system evolves over the life span.

Stages.   The various individual-development theories we have studied, while differing in terms of approaches, indicate that adult stages of growth occur in a fixed sequence and that transitional periods exist between these stages of growth. Even though the theories are contradictory in terms of internal or external influences, most outline developmental tasks based on three major theses: self-concept or identity, mastery or productivity, and intimate relationships. The process of development encompasses passages of calm stability interspersed with periods or transitions of restlessness, questioning, and reassessment. People may use these transition periods as opportunities to recommit themselves to previous decisions or to pursue new paths in new directions.

The stages, tasks, and issues presented are, at best, general guidelines for conceptualizing adulthood. They do not necessarily apply to everyone. Remember, most development theory is based on educated, white, middle-class male norms. While these theories cannot be assumed to apply to women or to other cultural or socioeconomic groups, one can make some reasonable extrapolations as to how they may apply to different groups. The population on which the research is based does constitute a large portion of our American population, and therefore cannot be dismissed as being too narrow or irrelevant. One must remember that the variables just discussed affect the development of any individual, providing for individual differences. Thus, the theory we have on individual adult development is an important first step in terms of understanding adult development as a process of change and growth with some general tasks and issues. Existing theory needs to be replicated with other populations and modified accordingly.

There is much less contradiction and controversy about the stages of family development. Expansion and contraction of family-system members require boundary renegotiations and adaptations across cultural groups. However, the family's meaning system is influenced by sociocultural variables and will affect how a family perceives and experiences these stages in the family life cycle. Also, the parents' stages of individual development are important factors, in that no particular stage of family development coincides with a particular individual-development stage. Adults begin the family life cycle at various ages. We can look at the four family "careers" suggested by Feldman and Feldman (1975) within this model: (1) sex; (2) marriage; (3) parent-child relationships; and (4) adult-offspring-parent relationships. These "careers" peak during difficult stages of the family life cycle and are influenced by career and individual development.

The stages of career development are also based primarily on white middle-class males and have not been thoroughly researched beyond early adulthood. The timing and process of these stages are likely to differ for women. Likewise, many people do not engage in a progressive pattern of career development, but, rather, attempt to maintain whatever jobs are possible in order to survive. Career development may, in fact, be a middle-class luxury. Nevertheless, some choices and opportunities exist for everyone, and the purpose of career-education programs developed in schools is to provide exposure to the widest range of choices and opportunities for everyone, regardless of cultural and socioeconomic status.

In all three areas, early adulthood is characterized by decision making and establishment, by entering new roles, relationships, and arenas of life, and by learning new rules and boundaries. Middle adulthood is characterized by reassessment from a different perspective, which may result either in a last attempt at fulfilling the aspirations of early adulthood or in a gradual acceptance of one's achievements based on a reordering of priorities or a gradual letting go. Late adulthood is characterized by gradual detachment and the changing of roles, relationships, priorities, and functions. External variables become more prominent in later adulthood.

IMPLICATIONS FOR TREATMENT

The practitioner's understanding of adulthood as a process of growth and change serves as a developmental context within which one can assess and formulate treatment objectives and interventions for interrelated and competing issues and problems. For example, a client may present him- or herself with mid-life career issues and, in fact, be covering up underlying relationship issues affecting all spheres of his or her life, including marriage and relationships with children, colleagues, and friends. Two major tasks, then, are (1) differentiating pathological problems from developmental problems, and (2) understanding the reciprocal influences of individual, family, and career issues. Without carefully assessing all of the contexts affecting a particular client, one cannot clearly define the problem, plan appropriate treatment objectives, or implement effective interventions and strategies.

Pathology versus Development

The developmental perspective suggests different norms and perspectives for different stages of adult life. What is considered healthy in one stage of life may, in fact, be unhealthy in another. A person in his or her twenties who chooses to live alone, to be independent and self-sufficient, is seen as achieving self-differentiation, as behaving appropriately. That same person in his or her eighties and suffering from an illness that requires caretaking from another person is certain to be viewed differently. The developmental perspective enables the practitioner to consider whether clients are truly sick or are merely stuck in some developmental transition. This conceptualization influences the practitioner's understanding of the client as well as the type of treatment.

The client is often unaware of developmental stages and concomitant tasks and issues and views him- or herself as abnormal or sick when the reality is one of arrested growth and development. We do not deny the existence of pathology, but it is important to note that much of what is commonly defined as pathology, under careful scrutiny, reveals itself to be developmental dysfunction. Just as we need to consider the norms of development, we also need to consider the norms of pathology. To do this, we must consider such factors as ethnicity, gender, and other sociocultural, psychological, and physiological variables.

It is well known that the diagnosis of mental health disorders varies and is to a large degree speculative and subjective. Since assessment and diagnosis are crucial to effective treatment, we must consider carefully all aspects and meanings of presenting symptoms. Consider these examples.

Vicki, aged 13, was referred for treatment after a suicide attempt that came dangerously close to succeeding. She was diagnosed as *borderline,* and the recommendation was for intensive, individual therapy. The therapist requested a family session and, thus, was able to consider Vicki's symptoms in the context of the family stage of development. This family was experiencing a great deal of stress in the launching stage. Each child (Vicki was the third of five children) had needed to become ill or run away in order to leave the family. Now it was Vicki's turn. One of the underlying family secrets turned out to be family abuse. Dad beat the oldest child every time he came home frustrated from a hard day at work. Rather than continuing with individual therapy, co-therapists met with the entire family for three months. During this time, Vicki visibly relaxed, returned to school, and showed no other borderline symptoms. The parents, frightened by having three children with serious problems, became committed to therapy and were, in fact, helped with their parenting and with launching their children more constructively. The couple system became the unit of treatment for the last six weeks of therapy, and, when the partners acknowledged and worked through their marital problems, the entire family functioning improved.

Another example involved 83-year-old Mrs. Gaynor, whose 54-year-old daughter, Jenny, brought her in for counseling. The single daughter, who had always lived with her mother and cared for her, was concerned about her mother's increasing forgetfulness and repetitiveness. She was convinced that her mother was sick. Assessment revealed the mother to be aging normally with no apparent disease. Jenny was the real client, for she was found to be grappling with her own identity and relationship issues. Neither mother nor daughter was sick—their relationship was merely stuck and the daughter was having difficulty accepting the aging and eventual loss of her mother.

Control.   As people learn more about the common tasks and issues of different developmental stages, they ascribe a different meaning to their difficulties. This, in turn, can lead to their gaining a greater sense of personal control, which can enhance their appreciation and understanding of their participation in the helping process. In addition, clients can gain social support and understanding from peers who may have experienced similar difficulties or from models in later adult stages who may be empathic and helpful in supplying information for coping with specific issues. In Vicki's case, the parents were referred to a parents' group, which provided a great deal of support and information to them relevant to their parenting difficulties. If people know that others have been through what they are now experiencing, they do not feel alone with a terrible problem and they are able to reframe their problems and cope with them more easily. The knowledge that they are not alone helps them to feel that they are not unworthy or bad inside. "Being able to define and give meaning to the issues with which they are dealing can provide a much needed sense of personal control and a clearer foundation for decision making for the adult client" (Wortley & Amatea, 1982, p. 479).

Gender.   Gender issues are important considerations in their implications for treatment. Not only do therapists need to consider the gender differences in the norms of development—taking care not to measure females against male norms—but they need to consider the subtle (and perhaps not so subtle) effects of same-sex and opposite-sex therapist-client dyads. Male therapists view male clients differently from female clients and define their problems differently, plan different treatment strategies, and expect different outcomes. Female therapists view male clients differently from female clients and conduct different types of therapy with them. Hare-Mustin (1983) points to the continuing need for sophisticated research to deal with sex bias in psychotherapy: "A theory of women's development over their long lifespan is needed, that integrates women's unique, developmental experiences and life stresses."

Family systems therapy seems to encourage these gender issues to surface more readily than individual therapy, perhaps due to the powerful socialization of people's family of origin systems with respect to sex-role expectations and attitudes (Okun, 1983). Therefore, the family-system treatment unit is more likely to trigger the therapist's own gender issues than the one-to-one therapy. It is difficult to work with families without touching on sex role functioning within family systems.

Integrated model.   *Integrated model* refers to a preventive/developmental/ systems integration of individual, family, and career functioning. Such a model stresses health rather than illness. Heath (1980) argues that practitioners need a comprehensive holistic model of healthy development in order to help people learn identifiable qualities that aid adaptation to the vicissitudes of living. His research, for example, suggests that psychological maturity is necessary for effective adaptation and that the psychological maturity of an adolescent can be measured to predict subsequent adult effectiveness in a number of areas. If this is so, we can develop preventive programs that enhance the psychological maturity of adolescents, such as educating families in how to facilitate individuation and attachment in both males and females.

An integrated model will be flexible enough to apply to both low-functioning clients and high-functioning clients. Even though the research in adult development is based on high-functioning adults, the tasks and issues can be modified and flexibly applied to a variety of populations.

Counselor roles.   Blocher (1980) lists these implications resulting from the research and theory building of social, developmental, and general psychology:

1. The view that counseling is a social-influence process and that the way a client perceives the counselor's expertise, trustworthiness, and power is a crucial variable influencing the counseling process;
2. Counseling centers on the client's cognitive functioning or activity, on how clients think about themselves, and how they think about the crucial events in their lives;
3. How clients process information—their levels of cognitive development—is important in structuring counseling;
4. Intervention programs to raise clients' cognitive levels can improve the counseling process.

From this list, we can infer that counselors' own developmental experiences and processes will influence both their assessments of clients and the clients' perceptions of and receptivity to the counselors. Thus, counselors need to be aware of the nature and impact of their influences on the client and of the aspects of their own development likely to influence the counseling process. Also, counselors can focus on improving clients' cognitive-processing skills by teaching differentiating skills, by using cognitive restructuring, and by teaching decision-making skills. This approach could alter the clients' life meanings and result in greater adaptability to the changes necessitated by adulthood.

Counselors can also expose themselves to all adult stages of development in order to sharpen their understanding of development and their ability to communicate empathetically to people at all stages. Counselors' attitudes and conceptualizations of development underlie their successful uses of strategies or techniques.

The Interrelatedness of Individual, Family, and Career Issues

A major theme of this text is the reciprocal, cybernetic relationships among individual, family, and career areas of life. A change in one area affects the other areas, and growth does not progress evenly or consistently in all areas. One may be more mature, then, in one area of life than in others and one may function most effectively in a particular area of life.

As stated, practitioners must understand the issues and tasks in each of these dimensions of life in order to understand their interrelatedness and to combine methods and techniques to meet needs in any or all areas.

One might select as the initial target of treatment the area of development with the greatest potential for change. This approach can encourage the client, since he or she will perceive changes in one area of life and also free up energy resources for attention to other problems and issues. As the practitioner assesses the effects of change in one area on other areas, he or she will be able to plan further treatment.

Many counselors and therapists fail to consider career development or family issues when working with individual clients. They seem to believe that work-related issues are secondary to individual issues. Years ago, a young graduate student came into the clinic where I was training and proceeded to discuss her marital and sexual difficulties. It turned out that she was in individual therapy (and had been for two years). Her therapist refused to allow her to discuss her marital or sexual difficulties with him, insisting on dealing only with her intrapsychic conflicts. He referred her to our clinic, which did provide marital therapy. This type of compartmentalization reinforces barriers that contribute to the problems. Often, clients get divorced because marital issues are not addressed, an action that does not necessarily improve individual functioning where it does not proceed from careful processing.

Counselors and therapists who feel inadequate in their knowledge and understanding of career or family development can study these areas in order to provide a holistic type of help to all clients, whether they are working with an individual, a couple, or a family. Regardless of the unit of treatment, counselors need to be able to understand problems from a systems perspective and to formulate strategies that acknowledge and promote cybernetic changes.

Treatment Strategies

If most existing developmental research is based on white middle-class males, it may be true that many treatment strategies originating in developmental or psychological theory may be relevant only to white middle-class males. This is an age-old problem in counseling psychology, one that is constantly discussed.

Obviously, no sets of treatment methods and techniques apply to all types of clients. The area of a client's distress will influence the selection of type of treatment, and the practitioner's training and interpretation of the meaning of therapy will also shape the choice. The client's life stage, too, may help the practitioner to select a suitable modality of treatment. For example, individual treatment may be a choice for working with late adolescents and young adults in helping them to separate emotionally from their parents and to develop a positive identity. Cognitive strategies dealing with the decision-making process often characterize treatment in this stage of life. Or one might find family-systems therapy helpful in middle adulthood where families need aid in adjusting to the comings and goings of family members during the adolescent and launching stages. We have seen in Part IV that peer counseling is particularly helpful for the elderly, providing them with important peer affiliations and support.

Whereas many variables influence the choice of treatment strategies for adults at any age (such as level of cognitive functioning, level of psychological needs, and nature of problem and treatment variables), if we look at adulthood from the developmental/systems perspective, we may be better able to select strategies likely to help people with developmental tasks or issues. The interaction of individual, family, and career development will provide a framework to help the therapist to select a target and strategy for access. It does not matter what part of the system the therapist enters, since the concept of systems equifinality assures that different entrance points exist as do different ways of altering the cybernetic feedback systems both in each area and among all areas.

CURRENT ISSUES

Certain areas relating to development have not been addressed or developed in this text, not because they are unimportant but because insufficient theory, research, or clinical experience exist in the literature to permit substantive conclusions. The most prevalent issues are mentioned here in association with areas requiring further research and study.

Research and Study Needs

Although much study has been devoted to adult development in the past twenty years, this field is still in its embryonic phase and has a long way to go before it can match child and adolescent study in breadth and scope.

Gender, ethnic, and biological concerns.   As frequently noted, in the areas of individual and career development, we need to replicate the existing studies with females and other sociocultural groups. This will require longitudinal studies over several decades. International longitudinal studies would also highlight the effects of nationality on development.

There is increasing study about hormonal and other biochemical influences on development, and these studies may alter our views of what is biological and what is psychological in the etiology of difficulties. Increasing attention is also being paid to the effects of nutrition, both in the development and the treatment of difficulties.

Another area requiring further study is the effects of alternative lifestyles on development. For example, how do single people who have never had families fare in late adulthood compared with people who have been married and had children?

Family patterns.   Certainly we need more data about the influence of ethnic and sociocultural variables on family development. We are just now beginning to identify common issues of remarried families in different stages of family development. We know that many of the roles and rules attributed to natural families do not apply to stepfamilies. The boundaries, alliances, histories, and meanings differ.

Further study is also necessary to help us understand dual-career families. How do the issues in such families affect the marriage, parenting, and the career development of both spouses? Does one spouse need to accommodate his or her career to the other? Can the occupational involvement of the spouses be serial or is it always simultaneous? What about families where the mother's career is more valued than the father's? Or, where the father stays home and the mother is the economic provider?

Alternative family styles requiring study include homosexual couples, unmarried systems, families with special-needs members, joint-custody families, single-father families, and adoptive families. Which of the common family developmental tasks and issues apply and how do they interface with the overlay of special tasks and issues imposed by the alternative lifestyle?

Economics.   Much more study is needed on families constantly struggling with poverty. In coming years, we will be seeing more downward mobility and less upward mobility. How will this influence individual, family, and career development? What about the issue of unemployment—at which stage of life is it the most harmful or devastating? What are the different types of economic stress and how do they affect individuals and families?

Careers.   Career-development theory, to date, is insufficient to explain life-span, multiple, and serial-career patterns. In fact, there has been little, if any, follow-up research about the adequacy of early career decision making and its effects on later decision making. We need to formulate theories of career development that are applicable to populations other than white middle-class males and that allow for flexibilities due to changing socioeconomic, governmental, and occupational trends.

Interrelationships.   All adult-development study must take into account the interrelationships of individual, family, and career development. And, of course, research is needed in terms of the implications of these theories for practice. Are particular counseling approaches most effective for adults at different stages of life with different types of problems? Are these approaches similar to each other or very different? What are the implications for training practitioners?

Research Issues

It would not be fair to call for all this research without referring to the methodological issues that are genuine stumbling blocks. These methodological issues include finding researchers and subjects who will cooperate in longitudinal studies, obtaining adequate sampling in order to infer fairly general population behavior from a representative sample, and developing adequate data-collection strategies and methods of analysis. We must also consider reliability, validity, and ethical issues with regard to research instruments and actual testing and experimentation.

How do we know that the data we collect are valid? Consider, for example, the Kohlberg and Gilligan studies on moral development. What discrepancies exist between subjects' reporting of their possible responses to simulated situations and their actual behavior in real-life situations? We all have our desired theories about what we would do in tough situations, but how often are we trapped by reality into behaving differently than we would like? Perhaps theories of cognitive dissonance should be integrated with developmental research.

Other research issues are influenced by social policy and government funding. Research costs money and funding limits the nature and types of research possible. The politics of research funding is an important issue influencing how extensive and even how valid serious study will be.

Many of the speculations and hypotheses suggested in these chapters raise more questions than they answer. Further research will no doubt raise questions not yet considered. There will always be a certain amount of ambiguity and contradiction in developmental research, owing to the multifaceted, fluid nature of development. Practitioners depend as much on their meanings, common sense, openness, and personhood as on their knowledge of theory and clinical training.

SUMMARY

In this chapter, we reviewed the common overlapping themes of individual, family, and career development, and the variables influencing the nature and course of adult development. We also discussed the implications for treatment resulting from research and theory building and suggested some current issues needing further exploration and study.

Many aspects of adult development appear to be based on influences outside one's personal control. Treatment strategies need to be selected based on the differentiation of what is within one's control and what is not. Therapists can pay attention to that which is open to change rather than continually confronting impediments and obstacles. The educational aspect of treatment—teaching clients about the course of development and helping them to reframe their difficulties in terms of growth and learning—is an important strategy for effective helping. The more we understand about development, the better we can help people to cope with changes and both unpredictable and predictable happenings.

Many areas need study, among them alternative individual and family lifestyles, varying populations, and varying career patterns. The internal variables of development are more likely to remain consistent over the years. Sociocultural variables change more easily. Sensitivity to the reciprocal influences of internal and environmental factors and to individual, family, and career variables will result in a conceptual framework for understanding adults as they progress through their life span.

The point is to focus more on healthy functioning and development and on what works rather than on what does not work. We can learn more about functioning families, happy marriages, healthy adolescents, and happy workers. We will then be able to identify traits and variables contributing to healthy growth and change and to help clients learn and acquire these traits and emphasize these variables.

REFERENCES

Blocher, D. H. Some implications of recent research in social and developmental psychology for counseling practice. *Personnel and Guidance Journal,* 1980, *58,* 334–338.

Feldman, H., & Feldman, M. The family life cycle: Some suggestions for recycling. *Journal of Marriage and the Family,* 1975, *37,* 277–284.

Freud, S. *An outline of psychoanalysis.* New York: W. W. Norton, 1949.

Glasser, W. *Reality therapy.* New York: Harper & Row, 1965.

Gilligan, C. *In a different voice.* Cambridge, Mass.: Harvard University Press, 1982.

Hare-Mustin, R. An appraisal of the relationship between women and psychotherapy: 80 years after the case of Dora. *American Psychologist,* 1983, *38,* 593–602.

Heath, D. H. Wanted: A comprehensive model of healthy development. *Personnel and Guidance Journal,* 1980, *58,* 391–399.

Kohlberg, L. Stage and sequence: The cognitive-developmental approach to socialization. In D. Gaslin (ed.), *Handbook of socialization theory and research.* New York: Rand McNally, 1969.

Maslow, A. *The farther reaches of human nature.* New York: Viking, 1971.

McClelland, D. *Power: The inner experience.* New York: W. W. Norton, 1949.

Okun, B. F. & Gladding, S. (eds.) Gender issues for family systems therapists. *ACES-CAPS Monograph on Marriage and Family Counseling.* Ann Arbor: ERIC, 1983.

Okun, B. F., & Rappaport, L. J. *Working with families: An introduction to family therapy.* No. Scituate, Mass.: Duxbury Press, 1980.

Pearce, J., McGoldrick, M., & Giordano, J. *Ethnicity and family therapy.* New York: Guilford, 1982.

Wortley, D. B., & Amatea, E. S. Mapping adult life change: A conceptual framework for organizing adult development theory. *Personnel and Guidance Journal,* 1982, *60,* 476–486.

NAME INDEX

SUBJECT INDEX

Children *(continued)*
  birth of second, 108
  decision to have, 98–99
  and divorce, 109
Client-centered theory, 6
Climacteric *(see also* Menopause):
  female, 198–199, 201–202
  male, 198–199, 201–202, 203–204
Cognitive development:
  in adulthood, 411
  changes in, with age, 314–315, 325
  as developmental variable, 419
Cognitive-development theory:
  of career development, 40
  gender issues in, 18
  maturity in, 7
College:
  career choice and, 126–127
  value of, 120–121
Commitments, 60
  prior, as developmental variable, 416
Communications, in systems theory, 35–36
Communication styles:
  in early adulthood, 96, 102, 106, 111
  in family unit, 87
  in late adulthood, 344–345, 354
  in middle adulthood, 222–224, 234, 240–241
Complementarity, 91–92
Conception, anxiety about, 215
Conflict, in systems theory, 31, 36
Conflict resolution:
  forms of, 96
  strategies for, 223
  styles of, 96, 98, 102–103, 106–107
Conformity, in career choice, 122
Continua:
  of adult-development theories, 22–23
  personality, 311–312
Contracts, motivational, 93–94
Control, personal, 117, 322, 333
  sense of, affecting treatment, 422–423
Coping strategies, 324
Cornell Study of Occupational Retirement, 365, 367
Counseling *(see also* Treatment):
  for the aged, 320, 382–383, 409
  leisure, 362, 374, 379
  in middle adulthood, 275
  modalities, 174
Counselors, 412, 421–425
  age of, 275–276, 304
  attributes of, for adults, 49
  of elderly, 382–383, 409
  roles for, 424
  of young adults, 146
Counterculture revolution and meaning of work, 119
Couple system, 340–341, 348
  communication style, 344
Courtship, 89–94
Creativity:

Creativity *(continued)*
  and artists in mid-life, 181
  in late adulthood, 315
  theories, 208
Credentialing, 261–262
Crises:
  definition of, 44
  developmental, 44, 337
  in development theory, 43, 47, 411, 420
  interventions with elderly, 382
  mid-life, 27, 30, 180–181, 185
  nondevelopmental, 44–45, 415
Cutoff, family, 231
Cycles, 12–13 *(see also* Stages)

Death, 325–327, 328
  awareness of, 80, 190
  during bereavement, 352–353
  causes of, 201
  of parent, 237, 357
  preparation for, 329–330
  and process of dying, 330
  of significant other, 241–242
  thoughts about, 175, 185, 186, 187, 325–327
Deceleration, in career, 267–268
Decision making:
  in career choice, 125
  process of, 136, 256–258, 263
  theories of, for retirement, 362
De-illusionment, 182
Dementia, 318–319
Dependency/independency, 355
  issues of, for senior citizens, 323, 324
Depression:
  in aged, 320
  and disease, 318, 325
  in late adolescence, 56
  and loss, 326
  in middle adulthood, 193, 202
Despair, versus integrity, 328
Development *(see also* Adult-development theory):
  interrelatedness of variables, 424–425
  physiological variables influencing, 412–413
  process, 10
  psychological variables influencing, 417–419
  sociocultural variables influencing, 414–417
  stages of intellectual, 59–60
Differentiation, 17 *(see also* Individuation):
  in communications, 223
  definition, 218
  in middle adulthood, 243
  process of, 221, 223
  of young adult at launching, 231
Discrimination:
  age, 268
  sex, 259–260
Diseases, 190
  and bereavement, 352–353
  cardiovascular, 318, 319
  cerebral, 318–319
  chronic versus acute, 317